PUBLIC COMPANIES AND EQUITY FINANCE

PUBLIC COMPANIES AND EQUITY FINANCE

Catherine Shephard MA (Cantab), Solicitor

CLP

Published by
College of Law Publishing,
Braboeuf Manor, Portsmouth Road, St Catherines, Guildford GU3 1HA

© The College of Law 2007

All rights reserved. No part of this publication may be reproduced, stored in a retrieval system, or transmitted in any way or by any means, including photocopying or recording, without the written permission of the copyright holder, application for which should be addressed to the publisher.

British Library Cataloguing-in-Publication Data
A catalogue record for this book is available from the British Library.

ISBN 978 1 905391 301

Typeset by Style Photosetting Ltd, Mayfield, East Sussex
Printed in Great Britain by Ashford Colour Press Ltd, Gosport, Hampshire

Preface

For the uninitiated, there exists an air of mystery about public company work. Public companies are subject to an extra set of rules, some of which are not contained in Acts of Parliament or case law, but in publications such as the Prospectus Rules, the Listing Rules, the Disclosure Rules and the City Code. As there are relatively few public companies, experienced and well respected company lawyers may know little about how these rules work in practice. Public company lawyers enjoy this exclusivity; it makes us look clever.

In fact, it is not true that the provisions of the Listing Rules or the City Code, or indeed any other rules which apply to public companies, are particularly difficult. They are simply unfamiliar to many lawyers. Expertise, of course, comes with experience, but a little guidance along the way is always helpful. There seem to be few books which are devoted to guiding lawyers through the rules which apply to public companies, and even fewer which are readily accessible to lawyers who lack prior experience of these rules.

I have written this book to explain the issues a lawyer may encounter when advising a public company. It is the book I would have liked to have had in practice. I have sought in particular to explain the principles behind the rules and to decipher the jargon which lawyers like to use in relation to those rules.

This book should be useful to law students and trainees in corporate seats, as an overview of public company work and as a guide to using the primary sources more effectively. I also intend it to be helpful to qualified corporate lawyers, as a first point of reference and as a reminder of the principles which underlie their work. I hope it may also be of interest to the other professionals who work alongside public company lawyers, such as lawyers who undertake corporate support work, accountants and stockbrokers, as an insight into just what public company lawyers do all day (and often all night).

To achieve an overview of public company issues, the best way to read this book is to start at Chapter 1 and read through to Chapter 24. This will guide you in a logical manner through the issues which face a public company, from registration, through flotation, to complying with continuing obligations, raising funds and entering into transactions. However, the book is also suitably cross-referenced to enable it to be used in practice as a reference book.

I am very grateful to the following for their help with this book: Helen Abbott, Ed Davies, Marilyn Davies, Paul Devitt, Frances George, Mark Gould, Alistair MacQueen, Di Mattu, Sally Orr, Sophie Scott, Frank Shephard, David Stott and Mike Yardley. The copyright press cuttings in this book are reproduced with the kind permission of the *Financial Times*, the *Guardian*, the *Independent*, the *Telegraph*, and *The Times* (© NI Syndication).

The views expressed (and any mistakes) in this book are mine. Please feel free to email any comments to me at catherine.shephard@lawcol.co.uk.

The law is stated as at 1 September 2006.

CATHERINE SHEPHARD
The College of Law

Addendum

The Companies Bill received Royal Assent on 8 November 2006.

	4.5	Restructuring the company	39
	4.6	What next?	41

Chapter 5	**FLOTATION: THE FLOTATION PROCESS**		43
	5.1	Introduction	43
	5.2	The flotation process	43
	5.3	The lawyers' perspective	43
	5.4	Key dates	54

Chapter 6	**FLOTATION: THE PROSPECTUS**		59
	6.1	Introduction	59
	6.2	Purpose	59
	6.3	Prospectus or listing particulars?	59
	6.4	The requirement for a prospectus	60
	6.5	Content	64
	6.6	Responsibility	73
	6.7	Liability	74
	6.8	Verification	77
	6.9	Types of prospectus	78
	6.10	Validity	79
	6.11	Passporting	79

PART II	**BEING A LISTED COMPANY**		**81**

Chapter 7	**CONTINUING OBLIGATIONS**		83
	7.1	Introduction	83
	7.2	Why have continuing obligations?	83
	7.3	The new regime	84
	7.4	The Disclosure Rules	84
	7.5	The Listing Rules	90
	7.6	The Model Code	95
	7.7	Communication with shareholders	100
	7.8	The Prospectus Rules	102
	7.9	The Admission and Disclosure Standards	104
	7.10	Sanctions	104
	7.11	Future developments	105

Chapter 8	**CORPORATE GOVERNANCE**		107
	8.1	What is corporate governance?	107
	8.2	The UK framework	107
	8.3	The Combined Code	107
	8.4	The Directors' Remuneration Report Regulations 2002	118
	8.5	Institutional investors	119
	8.6	Future developments	120

Chapter 9	**THE FINANCIAL SERVICES AND MARKETS ACT 2000**		123
	9.1	Background	123
	9.2	Objectives	123
	9.3	Relevance to practice	123
	9.4	The general prohibition on carrying on a regulated activity	124
	9.5	Misleading statements and market manipulation	125

Chapter 10	**MARKET ABUSE**		129
	10.1	Introduction	129
	10.2	What is market abuse?	130
	10.3	The main offence	130
	10.4	The secondary offence	133
	10.5	Behaviour which does not amount to market abuse	135

	10.6	Sanctions	135
	10.7	Defences	136
	10.8	Future developments	138
Chapter 11	**INSIDER DEALING**		139
	11.1	Introduction	139
	11.2	The offence	139
	11.3	Three ways the offence can be committed	141
	11.4	Territorial scope	142
	11.5	Sanctions	143
	11.6	Defences	143
	11.7	Scope of the offence	145
Chapter 12	**FINANCIAL PROMOTION**		147
	12.1	Introduction	147
	12.2	Section 21 of the FSMA 2000	147
	12.3	Consequences of breach	148
	12.4	What is a financial promotion?	148
	12.5	Relevance in practice	148
	12.6	Purpose	151
	12.7	The detail of s 21	151
	12.8	Territorial scope	152
	12.9	Exemptions	152
	12.10	Conclusion	155
PART III	**EQUITY FINANCE**		**157**
Chapter 13	**SHARES**		159
	13.1	Introduction	159
	13.2	What is a share?	159
	13.3	Some terms relating to share capital	159
	13.4	What use is a share?	161
	13.5	Classes of share	162
	13.6	Shares or debt?	166
	13.7	Varying class rights	167
	13.8	Registration of share rights	168
	13.9	Employee share schemes	169
	13.10	Future developments	170
Chapter 14	**ISSUING SHARES**		171
	14.1	Introduction	171
	14.2	Terminology	171
	14.3	Issuing shares: three vital questions	172
	14.4	Authorised share capital	172
	14.5	Authority to allot	175
	14.6	Pre-emption rights on allotment	180
	14.7	Issuing the shares	190
	14.8	Conclusion	191
	14.9	Future developments	192
Chapter 15	**DISCLOSURE OF INTERESTS IN SHARES**		193
	15.1	Introduction	193
	15.2	Nominee shareholders	193
	15.3	The register of members	193
	15.4	Rules requiring the disclosure of share interests	194
	15.5	Sections 324 to 328 of the CA 1985	194
	15.6	Sections 198 to 220 of the CA 1985	195
	15.7	Non-statutory requirements	203
	15.8	Summary	211
	15.9	Future developments	212

Chapter 16	FINANCIAL ASSISTANCE		213
	16.1	Introduction	213
	16.2	Rationale	213
	16.3	The financial assistance prohibition	214
	16.4	What is financial assistance?	215
	16.5	What is not financial assistance?	216
	16.6	Whitewash	218
	16.7	Sanctions	219
	16.8	Conclusion	219
	16.9	Future developments	219
Chapter 17	EQUITY FINANCE		221
	17.1	Background	221
	17.2	What is equity finance?	221
	17.3	Why a company needs equity finance	222
	17.4	Listed company rules and regulations	222
	17.5	Equity finance documentation	224
	17.6	Methods of raising equity finance	227
	17.7	Rights issue	228
	17.8	Open offer	237
	17.9	Placing	239
	17.10	Acquisition issue	240
	17.11	Vendor consideration placing	242
Chapter 18	EQUITY FINANCE OR DEBT FINANCE?		245
	18.1	Introduction	245
	18.2	Income	245
	18.3	Capital	246
	18.4	Capital growth	246
	18.5	Taxation	246
	18.6	Rights	247
	18.7	Investors	247
	18.8	The problem	247
	18.9	The solution	248
	18.10	Conclusion	248
PART IV	**LISTED COMPANY TRANSACTIONS**		**251**
Chapter 19	ACQUISITIONS AND DISPOSALS		253
	19.1	Introduction	253
	19.2	Basic considerations	253
	19.3	Listed company considerations	254
	19.4	The classification of transactions	255
	19.5	Related party transactions	262
	19.6	The circular	268
	19.7	The transaction timetable	270
	19.8	Conclusion	271
Chapter 20	TAKEOVERS: REGULATION		273
	20.1	Introduction	273
	20.2	The Panel	273
	20.3	The Takeovers Directive	275
	20.4	The Takeovers Regulations	276
	20.5	The City Code	277
	20.6	Other rules and regulations	283
	20.7	Regulatory bodies	284
	20.8	Future developments	284

Chapter 21	TAKEOVERS: PREPARATION		287
	21.1	Introduction	287
	21.2	Recommended or hostile?	287
	21.3	The need for secrecy	288
	21.4	An example	289
	21.5	Appointing a team of advisers	290
	21.6	Due diligence	292
	21.7	Financing the offer	295
	21.8	Stakebuilding	295
	21.9	Stakebuilding thresholds	303
	21.10	Irrevocable undertakings	304
	21.11	Non-binding indications of intention to accept	306
	21.12	General offer or scheme of arrangement?	306
	21.13	Deal protection	309
Chapter 22	THE TAKEOVER PROCESS		313
	22.1	Introduction	313
	22.2	Timetable	313
	22.3	Announcing the offer	313
	22.4	The offer	321
	22.5	Accepting the offer	334
	22.6	Success or failure?	337
	22.7	Buying out minority shareholders	339
	22.8	Future developments	345
Chapter 23	TAKEOVERS: MERGER CONTROL		347
	23.1	Introduction	347
	23.2	Merger control provisions in the City Code	347
	23.3	EC merger control	348
	23.4	UK merger control	351

PART V	**AIM**		**359**
Chapter 24	AIM		361
	24.1	Background to this chapter	361
	24.2	An introduction to AIM	361
	24.3	Why AIM?	362
	24.4	Eligibility criteria	362
	24.5	The marketing document	363
	24.6	Continuing obligations	365
	24.7	Corporate governance	367
	24.8	Future developments	367

APPENDICES 369

Appendix 1	The Admission and Disclosure Standards	371
Appendix 2	Resolutions	377
Appendix 3	Forms	379
Appendix 4	The Combined Code on Corporate Governance	383
Appendix 5	The ABI Guidelines	399
Appendix 6	Statement of Principles of the Pre-Emption Group	401
Appendix 7	Websites	405
Appendix 8	The Takeovers Directive (Interim Implementation) Regulations 2006	407

GLOSSARY	433
BIBLIOGRAPHY	439
INDEX	441

Table of Cases

A

Ambrose Lake Tin and Copper Co, Re (Clarke's Case) (1878) 8 Ch D 635, CA	172
Attorney-General's Reference (No 1 of 1988) [1989] 2 WLR 729	139

B

Belmont Finance Corp Ltd v Williams Furniture Ltd (No 2) [1980] 1 All ER 393	219
Brady v Brady [1989] AC 755	217, 219

C

Caparo Industries v Dickman [1990] 1 All ER 568	76
Carney v Herbert [1985] AC 301	219
Criterion Properties plc v Stratford Properties UK plc and Others [2004] UKHL 28	332

H

Hector Whaling Ltd, Re [1935] All ER 302	230
Hedley Byrne & Co Ltd v Heller & Partners Ltd [1964] AC 465	76

N

National Westminster Bank plc and Another v IRC and Barclays Bank plc [1994] 2 BCLC 30, CA	172

O

OFT v IBA Health Limited [2004] EWCA Civ 142	354

R

R v Panel on Takeovers and Mergers, ex p Datafin plc and Another (Norton Opax plc and Another intervening) [1987] 1 All ER 564	275
R v Panel on Takeovers and Mergers, ex p Guinness plc [1989] 1 All ER 509	275

S

South Yorkshire Transport Ltd and Another v Monopolies and Mergers Commission and Another [1993] 1 All ER 289	353

W

Walford v Miles [1992] 2 WLR 174	310
Winpar Holdings Ltd v Joseph Holt Group plc [2001] 2 BCLC 604	340

Table of Statutes

Companies Act 1985 3, 10, 13, 14, 24, 32, 47, 71, 102, 107, 119, 123, 167, 173, 181, 186, 192, 196, 197, 198, 201, 212, 222, 223, 232, 233, 234, 266, 267, 296, 297, 340, 343, 367, 401
Part VI 195
Part VII 118
Part XV 200
s 1(1) 7, 166
s 1(3) 3
s 1(3A) 7
s 3 10
s 11 10
s 13(7) 10
s 18(2) 174
s 24 7
s 25(1) 10, 11
s 43 11
s 43(1)–(2) 11
s 43(3) 12
s 43(3)(a)–(e) 12
s 43(3A) 12
s 44 11, 12
s 45 11, 12
s 45(2)(a)–(b) 6, 12
s 45(3)–(7) 12
ss 46–47 11, 12
s 48 11
s 53 218
s 80 32, 47, 168, 169, 172, 175, 176, 177, 178, 179, 180, 182, 183, 187, 192, 223, 232, 290, 326, 399
s 80(2) 175, 177
s 80(4)–(5) 177
s 80(9)–(10) 180
s 80A 178
s 81 4
s 89 6, 32, 92, 169, 172, 181, 182, 183, 184, 185, 186, 188, 190, 192, 223, 230, 231, 232, 233, 234, 235, 236, 238, 239, 240, 242, 243, 290, 326
s 89(1) 182, 183, 400
s 89(4) 182
s 90 92, 185, 186, 232, 233
s 90(2) 232
s 90(5) 185
s 90(6) 230, 232, 233, 235
s 91 6, 92, 185, 186
s 92 92, 185, 190
s 93 92, 185
s 94 92, 182, 185, 400
s 94(5) 182
s 95 6, 92, 185, 186, 187, 188, 191, 223, 399, 400
s 95(1) 187
s 95(2) 186, 187
s 95(5) 186
s 95(6) 187
s 99(2) 190
s 100 6, 41, 160, 191, 228

Companies Act 1985 – *continued*
s 101 6, 11, 169
s 102 6
s 102(1) 190
s 103 6, 12, 191, 223, 242, 243
s 103(3) 191
s 104 6
s 106 166
s 108 6
s 111A 76
s 117 11
s 117(2) 6, 11
s 118 6, 10, 11, 12
s 121 32, 172, 174, 223
s 123 174, 223, 379
s 123(4) 174
s 125 167
s 125(2) 167, 168
s 125(3)–(5) 168
ss 127–128 168
s 135 168
s 137 217
s 142 6
s 150 6
s 150(2) 6
s 151 6, 214, 218, 219, 311
s 151(1) 214, 215, 216, 217
s 151(2) 214, 215, 216
s 151(3) 219
s 152(1)(a) 215, 218
s 152(1)(b)–(c) 218
s 152(2) 215
s 152(3)(a)–(b) 215
s 153 6, 216
s 153(1)–(2) 216
s 153(3) 217
s 153(4) 218
ss 154–155 6, 218
ss 156–158 6
s 159 165
s 159A 165
s 160 7, 166
s 160(1)–(2) 165
s 163(2) 278
s 171 7, 166
s 198 7, 93, 194, 195, 197, 200, 202, 203, 206, 211, 254, 296, 303
ss 198–219 217
s 198(1)(a) 195
s 198(1)(b) 195, 198
s 198(2) 195
s 198(3) 195, 198
s 199 7, 93, 194, 195, 197, 203, 206, 211, 254, 303
s 199(2)(a)–(b) 196
s 199(2A) 196
s 199(4) 196
s 199(5)(a)–(b) 196

Companies Act 1985 – *continued*
  s 200 7, 93, 194, 195, 196, 197, 203, 206, 211, 254, 303
  ss 201–202 7, 93, 194, 195, 197, 203, 206, 211, 254, 303
  s 202(2) 197
  s 202(2)(b) 197
  s 203 7, 93, 194, 195, 198, 203, 206, 211, 254, 303
  s 203(2) 198
  s 203(3) 198
  s 203(3)(a) 197
  s 203(3)(b) 198
  s 204 7, 93, 194, 195, 199, 203, 206, 211, 254, 303, 338
  s 205 7, 93, 194, 195, 198, 199, 203, 206, 211, 254, 303, 338
  s 205(4) 199
  s 206 7, 93, 194, 195, 199, 200, 203, 206, 211, 254, 303, 338
  s 207 7, 93, 194, 195, 199, 203, 206, 211, 254, 303, 338
  s 208 7, 93, 194, 195, 196, 203, 206, 211, 254, 303
  s 208(5) 198
  s 209 7, 194, 195, 196, 202, 203, 206, 303
  s 210 7, 194, 195, 200, 203, 206, 303
  s 210(1) 198
  s 210(3) 200
  s 211 7, 194, 195, 203, 206, 303
  s 211(8)(b) 203
  s 212 7, 93, 194, 195, 200, 201, 202, 203, 206, 211, 303
  s 213 7, 194, 195, 203, 206, 303
  s 214 7, 194, 195, 201, 202, 203, 206, 303
  s 215 7, 194, 195, 202, 203, 206, 303
  s 216 7, 194, 195, 200, 203, 206, 303
  ss 217–220 7, 194, 195, 203, 206, 303
  s 220(2) 197, 199
  s 234 294
  s 234ZZA 294
  s 234ZZB 294
  s 241 119
  s 241A 119
  s 244(1)(a)–(b) 5
  s 246 5
  s 246A 5
  s 247A 5
  s 262 118
  s 282(1) 5
  s 282(3) 5
  s 286 6
  ss 292–293 5
  s 317 268
  s 320 268
  s 323 9, 96
  s 324 90, 96, 194, 203, 204, 205, 211, 217, 268
  s 324(3) 195, 204
  s 325 96, 194, 195, 203, 204, 217, 268
  ss 326–327 96, 194, 203, 204, 217, 268
  s 328 96, 194, 203, 204, 205, 217, 268
  s 330(2)–(4) 5
  s 331(6) 5
  s 346 97
  ss 348–351 13

Companies Act 1985 – *continued*
  s 352 194
  s 360 194
  s 368(1) 235
  s 372 7
  s 379A 5
  s 380(4)(d) 168
  s 381A 5, 174
  s 425 217, 306, 307, 308, 339
  s 425(1)–(3) 307
  s 426 307, 339
  s 427 339
  s 428 284, 304, 330, 338, 339
  s 428(1) 340
  s 428(5) 305, 340
  s 429 53, 284, 309, 314, 338, 339, 342
  s 429(3) 344
  s 430 284, 338, 339, 342
  s 430(4) 341
  s 430A 304, 342
  s 430A(3)–(4) 344
  s 430C 341
  s 430C(1) 344
  s 430C(5) 342
  s 430E(1) 341
  s 442 201, 203
  s 442(1) 203
  s 442(3) 203
  s 444 201, 203
  s 454 201
  s 652A 7
  s 738 172
  Sch 6
    Pt 1 118
  Sch 7A 119
  Sch 13
    Pt II 195, 204
Companies Act 1989 13
Companies Act 2006 13, 295, 333
Companies (Audit, Investigations and Community Enterprise) Act 2004 24
Companies Bill 13, 14, 110, 120, 170, 192, 212, 219, 276, 339
  cl 941 345
  Part 28 275, 284, 285, 294, 333, 345
Criminal Justice Act 1993 95, 129, 143
  Part V 9, 139
  s 52 139, 143
  s 52(1) 141, 142, 144
  s 52(2)(a) 141, 142
  s 52(2)(b) 142
  s 53 143
  ss 54–55 141
  s 56 139
  s 57(1) 139
  s 57(2) 140
  s 58 140
  s 59 141
  s 62(1) 142
  s 63(2) 142, 143
  Sch 1 143
  Sch 2 141
    para 2(2) 144

Enterprise Act 2002 283, 347, 351, 353, 354, 355, 357
  s 23 352
  s 24 352
  s 28(1) 352
  s 33(1) 354
  s 129(1) 352
European Communities Act 1972 276

Fair Trading Act 1973 353
Financial Services Act 1986 123
Financial Services and Markets Act 2000 18, 22, 24, 25, 49, 53, 59, 61, 64, 72, 73, 74, 77, 95, 102, 123, 129, 139, 143, 145, 146, 147, 148, 212, 222, 223, 226, 255, 282, 297, 336, 364
  Part IV 125
  Part VI 22, 51, 59, 123, 223
  Part VIII 9, 129, 130, 133
  s 2 123
  s 19 123, 124, 153
  s 21 78, 123, 147, 148, 149, 150, 151, 152, 153, 154, 155, 291, 305, 321
  s 21(1)–(2) 147
  s 21(3) 152
  s 21(4) 151
  s 21(8)–(9) 152
  s 21(13) 151
  s 22 124, 131
  s 23 124
  s 25 148
  s 26 124
  s 30 148
  s 31(1) 125
  s 38(1) 125
  s 39(1) 125
  s 72(1) 22
  s 73A 21, 22
  s 74 323
  s 74(1) 22
  s 75 22
  s 77 25
  s77 25
  s 79 59
  s 83 54
  s 84 59, 60
  s 85 33, 59, 60, 123, 224, 363
  s 85(1) 36, 60, 62, 64, 224, 225, 226, 309, 363, 364
  s 85(2) 60, 62, 64, 224, 225, 226, 309, 362, 364
  s 85(3) 25
  s 85(5) 61, 224, 364
  s 85(5)(a) 62
  s 85(6) 62, 224
  s 86 59, 61, 224, 364
  s 86(1)(a)–(b) 61
  s 86(1)(c)–(d) 62
  s 87 25, 51, 59, 123
  s 87A 72, 73, 75, 77, 223
  s 87A(1)–(4) 65
  s 87A(7) 79
  s 87A(Q)(1)–(4) 79
  s 87C 54
  s 87G 79
  s 87H 79

Financial Services and Markets Act 2000 – *continued*
  s 87I 79
  s 87L 25
  s 87M 25
  s 87Q 225, 336
  s 89 362
  s 90 75, 76, 123, 223
  s 90(11)–(12) 75
  s 91 25, 77, 100
  s 91(1)–(2) 26
  s 91(2) 97
  s 91(3) 25
  s 96B 97
  s 98 53
  s 102A 61
  s 102B(1)–(3) 61
  s 103 60
  s 118 123, 129, 133, 135, 136
  s 118(1) 130
  s 118(2)–(3) 131
  s 118(4) 131, 132, 133
  s 118(5)–(7) 131, 132
  s 118(8) 131, 133
  s 118A(3) 132
  s 118A(5) 135
  s 118A(5)(a)–(c) 135
  s 118B 131
  s 118C 85, 86, 97, 99, 139
  s 118C(5) 86
  s 118C(8) 86
  ss 119–122 129
  s 123 129, 135, 137
  s 123(1)(b) 133
  s 123(2) 136, 137
  ss 124–130 129
  s 130A(3) 131, 133
  s 131 129
  s 131A 129
  s 144(1) 145
  s 150 148
  s 285 18, 125
  s 285(2) 125
  s 286 18
  s 290 18
  s 380 148
  s 381 135
  s 382 148
  s 383 135
  s 397 76, 77, 89, 123, 126, 127
  s 397(1) 77, 125, 127
  s 397(2) 77, 125
  s 397(3) 77, 127
  s 397(5) 127
  s 397(8) 127
  s 397(9)–(10) 126
  s 417(1)(b) 263
  Sch 2 124
  Sch 10 76
  Sch 11 61
    para 3 61
  Sch 11A 61, 224
    Pt 1 62
    para 9 62

Human Rights Act 1998 274

Insolvency Act 1986
  s 110 217

Misrepresentation Act 1967 76

Theft Act 1968 77
  s 19 77

Table of Secondary Legislation

Statutory instruments

Companies (Table A to F) Regulations 1985
  Table A 11
  Table F 10

Directors' Remuneration Report Regulations 2002 (SI 2002/1986) 107, 112, 118, 119, 120, 389, 396

Financial Services and Markets Act 2000 (Financial Promotion) Order 2001 (SI 2001/1335) 147, 154
Financial Services and Markets Act 2000 (Financial Promotion) Order 2005 (SI 2005/1529) 147, 152, 153, 154
  art 4 152
  art 7 153
  art 7(5) 153
  art 8 153
  art 12 152
  art 19 154, 305
  art 43 153
  art 45 154
  art 48 155
  arts 48–50 154
  art 50A 154, 155
  arts 59–60 154
  art 62 154, 305, 321
  art 69 154
  arts 70–71 154
  Sch 1 152
Financial Services and Markets Act 2000 (Market Abuse) Regulations 2005 (SI 2005/381) 130
  reg 1.3 131
  reg 1.3.17C 297, 305
  reg 1.4 131
  reg 1.5 131, 135
  reg 1.6 132
  reg 1.7 132
  reg 1.10G(1) 135
  reg 1.10.2G 135
  reg 1.10.3G 135
  reg 1
    Annex 2G 132
  reg 2 135
Financial Services and Markets Act 2000 (Misleading Statements and Practices) Order 2001
  arts 3–4 126
Financial Services and Markets Act 2000 (Offers of Securities) Order 2001 (SI 2001/2958) 24
Financial Services and Markets Act 2000 (Official Listing of Securities) Regulations 2001 (SI 2001/2956) 73
  reg 10 73
Financial Services and Markets Act 2000 (Prescribed Markets and Qualifying Investments) Order 2001 (SI 2001/996) 131

Financial Services and Markets Act 2000 (Recognition Requirements for Investment Exchanges and Clearing Housings) Regulations 2001 (SI 2001/995) 18
Financial Services and Markets Act 2000 (Regulated Activities) Order 2001 124
  Chapters IV–XII 124
  Part II 124
  Part III 124

Insider Dealing (Securities and Regulated Markets) Order 1994 (SI 1994/187) 141

Prospectus Regulations 2005 (SI 2005/1433) 23, 24, 65, 75
  Sch 1
    para 4 54
    para 6 75
    para 9 53
    para 16 61
  Sch 3
    para 2 60
    para 3 73
Public Offers of Securities Regulations 1995 24, 60

Takeovers Directive (Interim Implementation) Regulations 2006 (SI 2006/1183) 14, 276, 277, 284, 309, 343, 345, 407–31
  Part 4 294
  reg 1 407
  reg 2(1)–(4) 407
  reg 2(5) 408
  regs 3–5 408
  reg 6(1)–(6) 408
  reg 6(7)–(10) 409
  reg 7 409
  reg 8(1)–(3) 409
  reg 8(4) 409–10
  reg 9 410
  reg 10 282
  reg 10(1)–(6) 410
  reg 10(7) 410–11
  reg 10(8) 411
  regs 11–15 411
  reg 16(1) 411
  reg 16(2) 411–12
  reg 16(3) 412
  regs 17–18 412
  reg 19(1) 412–13
  reg 19(2) 413
  reg 20 333, 413
  reg 21 333, 414
  reg 22 333
  reg 22(1)–(6) 414
  reg 22(7) 414–15
  regs 23–24 333, 415
  reg 25 415

xx   Public Companies and Equity Finance

Takeovers Directive (Interim Implementation)
    Regulations 2006 – *continued*
    reg 26(1)–(4) 416
    reg 26(5)–(6) 417
    regs 27–32 417
    Sch 1 417–22
    Sch 2 284, 304, 330, 338, 339, 345, 422–31
        para 1 314
        para 1(5) 344
        para 1(10) 305, 340
        para 2(2)(b) 341
        para 3(5) 341
        para 4 342
        para 4(7)–(8) 344
        para 6 342
        para 6(1) 344
        para 6(6) 341
        para 8(1) 341

Rules and standards

AIM Rules 361, 362
    r 7 363
    rr 11–13 365
    r 14 365, 366, 367
    r 15 365, 366
    r 17 365
    rr 18–19 367
    r 21 367
    rr 34–35 363
    r 39 363
    Sch 2 364
    Sch 3 365, 366, 367
    Sch 4 366, 367
    Sch 6 363
Disclosure Rules 8, 9, 21, 22, 23, 24, 25, 83, 84, 86, 88, 89, 91, 93, 95, 102, 104, 126, 130, 135, 139, 194, 203, 204, 212, 222, 269, 297, 365
    DR 1.2 88
    DR 1.2.2R 88
    DR 1.3.1R 89
    DR 1.3.3R 89
    DR 1.3.4R 90
    DR 1.3.5R 90
    DR 1.3.6R 94
    DR 1.4.3 25
    DR 1.5.3G 25
    DR 2.2.1R 85, 88, 99, 126, 254, 315
    DR 2.2.3G 85
    DR 2.2.4G 85
    DR 2.2.4G(1)–(2) 86
    DR 2.2.5G–2.2.7G 85, 86
    DR 2.2.8 87
    DR 2.2.8G 85, 86
    DR 2.2.9G(2) 89
    DR 2.2.9G(4) 89
    DR 2.3 85
    DR 2.5.1R 85, 87, 315
    DR 2.5.2G(1) 87
    DR 2.5.3G(1) 87, 99
    DR 2.5.3G(2) 87
    DR 2.5.6R 87, 95

Disclosure Rules – *continued*
    DR 2.5.7G 87, 88
    DR 2.5.9G 88
    DR 2.6.3G 89
    DR 2.8.1 97
    DR 2.8.1R 90
    DR 2.8.3 90
    DR 2.8.7G 90
    DR 3.1.2 96
    DR 3.1.2R 90, 204, 211, 212
    DR 3.1.3R 204
    DR 3.1.4 100
    DR 3.1.4R(1) 96, 205
    DR 3.1.4R(1)(a) 90, 204, 205, 212
    DR 3.1.4R(1)(b) 90, 204, 205, 211
    DR 3.1.4R(2) 204
    DR 3.1.5R 204
    DR 3.1.6R 204
Listing Rules 8, 9, 21, 22, 23, 24, 25, 27, 28, 31, 32, 34, 35, 49, 51, 55, 72, 74, 75, 77, 80, 83, 84, 90, 93, 101, 102, 104, 105, 107, 108, 110, 111, 118, 119, 130, 135, 154, 171, 185, 186, 188, 190, 191, 194, 206, 211, 212, 222, 223, 226, 227, 228, 230, 232, 233, 234, 235, 236, 238, 240, 263, 269, 271, 297, 323, 325, 330, 361, 383, 389, 390, 399
    Chapter 5 25
    Chapter 10 365
    Chapter 11 365
    LR 1.3.4R 94
    LR 2.1.3G 55
    LR 2.2.1R 32
    LR 2.2.2R 32
    LR 2.2.3R 32, 91
    LR 2.2.4R 32
    LR 2.2.7R 32
    LR 2.2.8R–2.2.11R 33
    LR 3.2.7G 56
    LR 3.3 268
    LR 3.3.2R 52
    LR 3.3.3R 52, 224, 254
    LR 3.3.5R 53
    LR 3.3.7R 53
    LR 3.5.7R 235
    LR 4 33
    LR 6.1.3R–6.1.4R 33
    LR 6.1.8R–6.1.12 32
    LR 6.1.13G–6.1.15G 33
    LR 6.1.16R 33
    LR 6.1.19R 33, 91
    LR 6.1.19R(4) 33
    LR 6.1.20G 33
    LR 6.1.23R 34
    LR 7.2.1R 24
    LR 8.2.1R 28
    LR 8.2.2R 260, 262
    LR 8.2.3R 267
    LR 8.3 28
    LR 8.3.4R 269
    LR 8.3.6R–8.3.7R 28
    LR 8.4.1R 28
    LR 8.4.2R 28, 269
    LR 8.4.3R–8.4.6R 28
    LR 8.4.12R–8.4.13R 269

Listing Rules – *continued*
LR 8.6 28
LR 8.6.1G 28
LR 8.8.3R 269
LR 9.2 91
LR 9.2.1R 91, 104
LR 9.2.5G 91
LR 9.2.6R 91
LR 9.2.7R 100
LR 9.2.8 91
LR 9.2.8R 100
LR 9.2.9G 95
LR 9.2.9R 100
LR 9.2.10R 100
LR 9.2.11R 91
LR 9.2.12G 91
LR 9.2.14 91
LR 9.2.16R 91
LR 9.3 91
LR 9.3.1R 92, 187, 227
LR 9.3.2G 227
LR 9.3.3R 92
LR 9.3.3R(3) 92, 100
LR 9.3.4R–9.3.8 92
LR 9.3.11R 92, 185, 223
LR 9.3.12R 92, 223
LR 9.3.12R(1) 187
LR 9.3.12R(2)–(4) 185
LR 9.4 92
LR 9.5 93
LR 9.5.1R–9.5.2R 227
LR 9.5.3G 230
LR 9.5.3R 227
LR 9.5.4R 227, 230
LR 9.5.5R 227, 236
LR 9.5.6R 227, 230, 233, 235
LR 9.5.7 238
LR 9.5.7R–9.5.9R 227
LR 9.5.10R 240
LR 9.5.10R(1) 238
LR 9.5.10R(3) 238
LR 9.5.10R(3)(a)–(b) 240, 242
LR 9.5.15R 229
LR 9.6 93
LR 9.6.1R 93, 175, 179, 188, 268
LR 9.6.2R 93, 175, 179, 188
LR 9.6.3R 93, 175, 179, 188
LR 9.6.3R(1) 268
LR 9.6.4R 93
LR 9.6.4R(1) 175
LR 9.6.5R 93
LR 9.6.6R 236
LR 9.6.7 254
LR 9.6.7R 93, 206, 211
LR 9.6.8R 93, 206, 211
LR 9.6.9G 206, 211
LR 9.6.11R 94
LR 9.6.13R 94
LR 9.6.13R(2)–(6) 94
LR 9.6.16R–9.6.17R 94
LR 9.6.19R–9.6.21R 94
LR 9.6.22G 94
LR 9.7 95

Listing Rules – *continued*
LR 9.8 95
LR 9.8.6 395
LR 9.8.6R(5)–(6) 111
LR 9.8.8R 112
LR 9.8.10R(2) 112
LR 9.9 95
LR 10
  Annex 1 256
    para 10G 257
LR 10.1.3R 255
LR 10.1.4G 255
LR 10.2.2R(1)–(2) 258
LR 10.2.2R(3) 259
LR 10.2.2R(4) 261
LR 10.2.3R–10.2.4R 260
LR 10.2.5G 260
LR 10.2.7R 260, 311
LR 10.2.8R 260
LR 10.2.10R 257
LR 10.2.11G 257
LR 10.3.1R 258
LR 10.3.1R(2) 258
LR 10.3.2R 258
LR 10.3.2R(2) 258
LR 10.4.1R(1) 258, 259
LR 10.4.1R(2) 258
LR 10.4.2R(1) 259
LR 10.5.1R 259
LR 10.6.1R 262
LR 10.6.2G 262
LR 10.8.1G–10.8.6G 259
LR 10.8.9G 260
LR 11
  Annex 1
    para 7 264
    para 10 264
  Annex 1R
    paras 1–8 266
    para 9 266, 267
    para 10 266
LR 11.1.4R–11.1.5R 263
LR 11.1.6R 266
LR 11.1.7R(1)–(2) 265
LR 11.1.7R(3)(a)–(b) 265
LR 11.1.7R(4) 266
LR 11.1.10R 267
LR 11.1.12G 264
LR 13 259
  Annex 1R 101, 268, 269
LR 13.1.3R 268
LR 13.2.1 102
LR 13.2.2R 102
LR 13.2.4–13.2.9 102
LR 13.3 101, 102, 227, 264, 268, 269, 270
LR 13.3.1R(3) 269
LR 13.3.1R(5) 269
LR 13.4 101, 268, 269
LR 13.4.1R 269
LR 13.4.1R(4) 269
LR 13.5 101, 268, 269
LR 13.6 101, 264, 268, 269
LR 13.6.1R(3)–(5) 270

Listing Rules – *continued*
  LR 13.6.1R(7) 270
  LR 13.7 101
  LR 13.8 102
  LR 13.8R 102
  LR 13.8.1R 101, 179
  LR 13.8.2R 101, 187
  LR 13.8.3R 101, 175
  LR 13.8.4R–13.8.9R 101
  LR 13.8.11R–13.8.16R 101
  Appendix 1 227, 260, 264
  Appendix 1.1 36, 61, 64, 226, 228, 237, 239
  Appendix 2R 52
Listing Rules (Old) 23, 24, 25, 31, 32, 51, 53, 59, 64, 84, 88, 104, 240, 325, 400
  Chapters 18–26 23
  para 3.8 32
  para 3.9 32
  para 3.12 32
  para 3.13 32
  para 4.2 35
  para 4.8 240
  para 4.26 237
  para 4.30 242
  para 5.9(b)–(r) 52
  para 6.A.3 67
  para 8.7 55
  para 8.13 78
  para 9.1 25, 85, 88
  para 9.2 25, 85, 88
  para 9.2(c) 88
  para 9.4 25, 87
  para 9.5 25
  paras 9.6–9.7 25
  para 9.8 25, 88
  paras 16.13–16.17 203
Prospectus Rules 8, 9, 21, 22, 23, 24, 25, 27, 34, 49, 51, 52, 59, 64, 65, 69, 70, 72, 73, 74, 75, 77, 83, 84, 104, 130, 154, 191, 222, 223, 234, 268, 363
  PR 1.2.1UK 60, 224
  PR 1.2.2R 61, 224
  PR 1.2.2R(1)–(5) 62
  PR 1.2.3R 62, 224
  PR 1.2.3R(1) 62
  PR 1.2.3R(2)–(8) 63
  PR 2.1.1UK 65
  PR 2.1.2UK 66
  PR 2.1.4EU 66
  PR 2.1.5G 67
  PR 2.1.7R 66
  PR 2.2.1R–2.2.2R 66
  PR 2.2.5 79
  PR 2.2.10EU 52, 66
  PR 2.3 65
  PR 2.3.1EU 23, 65, 67, 70, 225
  PR 2.3.2R 78
  PR 2.4.1R 72
  PR 2.4.3R–2.4.5R 72
  PR 2.4.6EU 72
    para 4 72
  PR 2.5.2R 72
  PR 2.5.2UK 72
  PR 2.5.3R 52, 72

Prospectus Rules – *continued*
  PR 3.1.1R 52
  PR 3.1.3R 51
  PR 3.1.4R 51, 73
  PR 3.1.6G 79
  PR 3.1.7UK 51
  PR 3.1.8G 51
  PR 3.1.10R 51
  PR 3.1.14R–3.1.15R 325
  PR 3.2 54
  PR 3.2.1R 54
  PR 3.2.2R 78
  PR 3.2.3R 54
  PR 3.2.6R 55
  PR 3.3 53, 78
  PR 5.1.1R 79
  PR 5.1.4 66
  PR 5.2 102, 103
  PR 5.3 79
  PR 5.5.3R(2) 73
  PR 5.5.3R(2)(a) 73
  PR 5.5.3R(2)(b)(i)–(ii) 73
  PR 5.5.3R(2)(c) 73
  PR 5.5.3R(2)(d) 73, 74
  PR 5.5.3R(2)(e)–(f) 74
  PR 5.5.7R 74
  PR 5.5.9R 74
  Annex I 364
    para 1.2 74
    para 14 73
    para 23 74
  Annex II 364
  Annex III 364
    para 1.2 74
    para 10 74
  Appendix 3 52, 65, 67, 70, 225, 269, 327
  annexes 23
Stock Exchange Admission and Disclosure Standards 19, 27, 53, 55, 83, 84, 104, 224, 371–5
  para 1 34
  para 1.1 34, 371
  paras 1.2–1.3 371
  para 1.4 55, 371
  paras 1.5–1.6 371
  para 1.7 371
  para 1.8 372
  para 2.1 56, 372
  paras 2.2–2.3 372
  para 2.4 54, 372
  para 2.5 372
  para 2.6 372
  para 2.6(b)–(c) 53
  para 2.7 54, 372–3
  para 2.8–2.10 373
  paras 3.1–3.3 373
  paras 3.1–3.6 373
  paras 3.4–3.6 104, 373
  paras 3.7–3.9 104, 374
  para 3.10 104, 374
  para 3.11 104, 238, 374
  para 3.12 374
  paras 3.13–3.15 104, 374
  paras 3.16–3.17 374

Stock Exchange Admission and Disclosure
  Standards – *continued*
    paras 3.18–3.20 375
    paras 3.21–3.23 105, 375
Substantial Acquisition Rules 135, 194, 208, 222, 254, 277, 283, 297

European secondary legislation

Directive 79/91/EEC (Company Law) 191, 219, 401
Directive 2003/6/EC (Market Abuse Directive) 21, 22, 25, 84, 130
  art 1(3) 131
Directive 2003/71/EC (Prospectus Directive) 21, 22, 23, 24, 79, 130, 154, 277, 364
Directive 2004/25/EC (Takeovers Directive) 273, 275, 276, 277, 279, 282, 294, 339
  art 2.1(a) 275
  art 10 294
  arts 11–12 333
Investment Services Directive 61, 62
  art 1.13 62
  Annex B 86
Transparency Directive 14, 21, 22, 105, 212
Regulation 4064/89 348
Regulation 1996 (Merger Regulation) 351
Regulation 139/2004/EC (Merger Regulation) 283, 331, 347, 348, 349, 351, 357, 358
  art 1 349
  art 3 348, 349
  art 4(5) 349
  art 6(1)(c) 348
  art 9 348, 350, 351
  art 10 350
  art 22 350
Regulation 802/2004/EC 350
PD Regulation 23, 24, 52, 65, 72, 225
  art 21 65
  art 27(3) 103
  Annex III
    para 1 70
    para 2 70-1
    paras 3–9 71
    para 10 71-2
  Annex 1 269
  Annex 3 269
  Annex I 65, 66, 67, 225
    para 13 68
    para 14 69
    para 20.8 69
    para 23 71
    para 24 70
  Annex II 65, 66, 70, 225
  Annex III 65, 66, 70, 225
  Annex XVIII 65

Codes of practice

City Code on Takeovers and Mergers 25, 135, 194, 206, 208, 209, 211, 222, 254, 273, 274, 275, 276, 277, 278, 279, 281, 283, 284, 287, 289, 290, 291, 297, 299, 302, 304, 305, 306, 313, 326, 329, 332, 336, 338, 349

City Code on Takeovers and Mergers – *continued*
Intro
  para 2(a) 276
  para 2(b)–(c) 279
  para 3(b) 307
  para 3(f) 278
  para 4 274
  para 4(b) 274
  para 4(d) 274
  para 5 274
  paras 7–8 274
  para 9(a) 281
  para 10(a)–(c) 281
  para 10(d)–(e) 282
  para 11 282
r 1 287, 315, 326
r 2.1 288, 289, 318
r 2.2 296, 314, 315, 316, 317, 318
r 2.3 314, 315, 316
r 2.4 288, 314, 316, 317, 318, 319, 321
r 2.5 288, 299, 300, 314, 316, 317, 318, 319, 321, 325, 328, 329
r 2.5(a) 292, 293, 294, 295, 316
r 2.6 314, 318
r 2.7 314, 317
r 2.8 314, 318, 319, 320
r 2.9 315, 318, 322, 324, 335
r 2.10 208, 212, 317, 318, 321
r 2.4 318
r 2.5 280, 311
r 2.6 317
r 2.6(b)(i)–(ii) 317
r 2.9 317
r 3 290, 324
r 4 297, 302
r 4.1 297
r 4.1(1)–(b) 297
r 5 298, 299, 302, 303, 305
r 5.1 297, 298
r 5.2 298
r 5.2(a)–(e) 298
r 5.3 298
r 5.4 298
r 6 281, 296, 299, 302, 303, 305
r 6.1 299, 300, 302
r 6.1(c) 299
r 6.2 300, 302
r 8 209, 212, 317, 318
r 8.1 209
r 8.1(a) 209, 210
r 8.1(b)(i) 209, 210
r 8.3 209, 303
r 8.4(a) 305, 306
r 9 281, 296, 298, 299, 300, 302, 303, 305, 306, 315, 316, 319, 337
r 9.1 298
r 9.5(1)–(b) 299
r 10 296, 304, 330
r 11 275, 281, 296, 299, 300, 301, 302, 305
r 11.1 300, 302, 303, 306
r 11.2 301, 302, 303
r 12 348
r 12.1 331, 347, 350

City Code on Takeovers and Mergers – *continued*
  r 12.1(c) 331
  r 12.2 313, 338, 348
  r 13 329
  r 13.1 330, 331
  r 13.3 330, 331
  rr 14–16 281
  r 17.1 314, 326, 334
  r 19
    note 8 291
  r 19.1 280, 326
  r 19.2 327
  r 19.3 328
    note 1 307, 308
  r 19.7 321
  r 20 328
  r 20.1 328
  r 20.2 294, 328, 329
  r 21 332
  r 21.1(b) 332
  r 21.2 311
  r 23 280, 329
  r 24 322, 326, 335
  r 25 322, 326, 335
  r 25.1 322, 324, 335
  r 26 335
  r 27 334, 335
  r 27.1 329
  r 28 291, 326
  r 30.1 314, 321, 322
  r 30.2 314, 322, 324
  r 30.3 322, 324, 335
  r 31.1 314, 334
  r 31.2 337
  r 31.3 334
  r 31.4 314, 337, 338
  r 31.6 313, 314, 336, 337
  r 31.7 314, 337
  r 31.8 315
  r 31.9 314, 336
  r 32.1 314, 335
  r 32.3 335
  r 32.6 335
  r 32.7 335
  r 34 314
  r 35 348
  r 35.1 319, 337, 338, 348
  r 35.3 281
  r 35.4 338
  Appendix 4 292
  Appendix 6 282, 329
Code of Market Conduct 25, 107, 129, 132, 297
Combined Code on Corporate Governance 107, 108, 110, 118, 119, 120, 367, 383–97
  s 1 110, 111
    para A 110
    para A.1 113, 115, 384
    paras A.1.1–A.1.2 384
    paras A.1.3–A.1.4 115, 384
    para A.1.5 385
    para A.2 114, 385
    para A.2.1 114, 385

Combined Code on Corporate Governance – *continued*
    para A.2.2 114, 115, 385
    para A.3 113, 385
    para A.3.1 113, 114, 115, 385–6, 388
    para A.3.2 113, 386
    para A.3.3 115, 386
    para A.4 113, 386
    para A.4.1 113, 386
    para A.4.2 386
    para A.4.3 386–7
    paras A.4.4–A.4.6 387
    para A.5 113, 387
    paras A.5.1–A.5.2 387
    para A.5.3 387–8
    para A.6 113, 388
    para A.6.1 388
    para A.7 113, 388
    para A.7.1 388
    para A.7.2 115, 118, 388
    para B 110
    para B.1 116, 388–9
    paras B.1.1–B.1.4 389
    paras B.1.5–B.1.6 116, 389
    para B.2 116, 389–90
    para B.2.1 110, 116, 390
    paras B.2.2–B.2.4 390
    para C 110
    para C.1 117, 390
    para C.1.1 112, 390
    para C.1.2 390
    para C.2 117, 391
    para C.2.1 391
    para C2.1 112
    para C.3 118, 391
    paras C.3.1–C.3.3 112, 118, 391
    para C.3.4 112, 391–2
    paras C.3.5–C.3.7 112, 392
    para D 110
    para D.1 392
    para D.1.1 114, 118, 392
    para D.1.2 392
    para D.2 118, 392–3
    paras D.2.1–D.2.2 110, 393
    paras D.2.3–D.2.4 393
  s 2 111, 112
    para E 111
    para E1 393
    para E2 393–4
    para E3 394
  Sch A 394
  Sch B 115, 395
  Sch C 110, 395–7
Model Code 25, 91, 95, 96, 97, 100, 105, 107, 143, 255
  para 1(c) 98
  paras 2–4 98
  para 4(a)–(e) 98
  paras 5–7 98
  para 8(a)–(b) 99
  paras 9–11 100
  paras 20–22 96, 97

Guidelines

ABI Guidelines 222, 223, 243, 399–400
Pre-Emption Group Statement of Principles 171, 174, 188, 223, 228, 238, 240, 401–4
   para 4 189
   para 5 188, 233

Pre-Emption Group Statement of Principles – *continued*
   paras 8–10 189
   para 11 189, 240
   para 15 189, 234
   paras 17–20 189
Pre-Emption Guidelines 188, 191, 222, 399

Table of Abbreviations

ABI	Association of British Insurers
AGM	annual general meeting
AIM	Alternative Investment Market
CA 1985	Companies Act 1985
CARD	Consolidated Admission and Reporting Directive 2001/34/EC
CBI	The Confederation of British Industry
City Code	City Code on Takeovers and Mergers
CJA 1993	Criminal Justice Act 1993
CoMC	Code of Market Conduct
DR	Disclosure Rule
DTI	Department of Trade and Industry
EA 2002	Enterprise Act 2002
EC Merger Regulation	Council Regulation 139/2004/EC
EEA	European Economic Area
EGM	extraordinary general meeting
FPO 2005	Financial Services and Markets Act 2000 (Financial Promotion) Order 2005 (SI 2005/1529)
FSA	Financial Services Authority
FSA Handbook	FSA Handbook of Rules and Guidance
FSAP	Financial Services Action Plan
FSMA 2000	Financial Services and Markets Act 2000
gap	general accounting practice
ICSA	Institute of Chartered Secretaries and Administrators
IMA	Investment Management Association
Investment Services Directive	Directive 1993/22/EC
IPCs	Investment Protection Committees (representative bodies of major institutional investors)
IPO	initial public offer
ISC	Institutional Shareholders' Committee
Listing Regulations 2001	Financial Services and Markets Act 2000 (Official Listing of Securities) Regulations 2001 (SI 2001/2956)
LR	Listing Rule
MAD	Market Abuse Directive 2003/6/EC
MAD Regulations 2005	Financial Services and Markets Act 2000 (Market Abuse) Regulations 2005 (SI 2005/381)
Misleading Statements Order 2001	Financial Services and Markets Act 2000 (Misleading Statements and Practices) Order 2001 (SI 2001/3645)
NAPF	National Association of Pension Funds
NASDAQ	National Association of Securities Dealers Automated Quotations (a major world stock market)

Official List	The list of all securities listed by the FSA
OFT	Office of Fair Trading
OLR	Old Listing Rule
PAL	provisional allotment letter
Panel	Panel on Takeovers and Mergers
PDMR	Person discharging managerial responsibilities
PD Regulation	Regulation 809/2004
PERG	Perimeter Guidance Manual
PIP	Primary Information Provider
PIRC	Pensions & Investment Research Consultants
PMQI Order 2001	Financial Services and Markets Act (Prescribed Markets and Qualifying Investments) Order 2001 (SI 2001/1996)
Prospectus Directive	Directive 2003/71/EC
PR	Prospectus Rule
Prospectus Regulations 2005	SI 2005/1433
QCA	Quoted Companies Alliance
Regulated Activities Order 2001	Financial Services and Markets Act 2000 (Regulated Activities) Order 2001 (SI 2001/544)
RIE	Recognised Investment Exchange (includes the Stock Exchange)
RIS	Regulatory Information Service (includes RNS)
RNS	Company news service of the Stock Exchange (an RIE)
SARs	Substantial Acquisition Rules
SEAQ	Stock Exchange Automated Quotations
Second Company Law Directive	Directive 77/91/EC
SETS	Stock Exchange Electronic Trading Service
SIP	Secondary Information Provider
SLC	substantial lessening of competition
Stock Exchange	The London Stock Exchange plc
Takeovers Directive	Directive 2004/25/EC
Takeovers Regulations	Takeovers Directive (Interim Implementation) Regulations 2006 (SI 2006/1183)
Transparency Directive	Directive 2004/109/EC
UK GAAP	Generally Accepted Accounting Principles in the UK
UKLA	UK Listing Authority

Part I
BECOMING A LISTED COMPANY

Chapter 1
Public Companies

1.1	Introduction	3
1.2	What is a public company?	3
1.3	What is a listed company?	3
1.4	The distinction between 'public' and 'listed'	4
1.5	Advantages of public company status	4
1.6	Potential disadvantages of public company status	4
1.7	Advantages of listing	7
1.8	Potential disadvantages of listing	8
1.9	Achieving public company status	10
1.10	Achieving listed company status	13
1.11	Future developments	13

1.1 Introduction

There are more than two million companies registered in England and Wales. Fewer than 15,000 are public companies. Of those public companies, approximately 1,500 have shares admitted to listing on the Official List and admitted to trading on the Stock Exchange.

This book is concerned with the small minority of companies which are public, and the even smaller minority of public companies which have their shares listed on the Official List and which trade on the Stock Exchange.

1.2 What is a public company?

A public company is defined by s 1(3) of the Companies Act 1985 (CA 1985). It is a company limited by shares or by guarantee and having a share capital, the memorandum of which states that it is a public company, and which has complied with the requirements of the CA 1985 to enable it to be registered or re-registered as such.

How a company can achieve public company status is explained at **1.9**.

1.3 What is a listed company?

There are several specific definitions of a listed company in company law legislation, some of which are explored in more depth elsewhere in this book. However, broadly, a listed company is a public company any of the shares in which are officially listed and trade on a public market.

The public market which is the focus of this book is the Stock Exchange's principal market for listed securities (the 'Main Market'). Other markets include the Stock Exchange's global market for growing companies (AIM) in the UK, the Deutsche Börse in Germany, and NASDAQ and the New York Stock Exchange in the USA. AIM is considered in more detail at **2.4**.

Obviously, when working with specific legislation, care must be taken to analyse the specific definition of 'listed'. For example, under some legislation a company which has its shares quoted on AIM will be a listed company, while under other legislation the same company will fall outside the definition of a listed company.

The words 'quoted' and 'listed' are usually used interchangeably. However, again, care should be taken to use appropriate terminology in relation to specific markets; the Stock Exchange, for example, prefers to define shares listed on AIM as quoted but unlisted.

If all this sounds rather confusing, the key is to not take for granted the meaning of the terms 'listed' and 'quoted', but to examine (if interpreting such terms) or explain (if using such terms) the context in which they are used.

For the purposes of this book, 'listed' is used to mean ordinary shares of an English company admitted to listing on the Official List and admitted to trading on the Main Market.

1.4 The distinction between 'public' and 'listed'

Just because a company is a *public* company, it does not automatically follow that it is a *listed* company. There is some correlation between public companies and listed companies, in that a company must be a public company to become a listed company (private companies cannot become listed companies). However, we already know that, at the time of writing this book, only 10% of public companies were listed.

'Public' and 'listed' are further examples of legal terms which should not be interpreted or used without being clear as to the context in which they are used.

The distinction between the terms is important, because a company's status will determine how that company is regulated. Public companies are more heavily regulated than private companies; listed public companies are more heavily regulated than unlisted public companies. Of course, the increased level of regulation is counterbalanced by the additional benefits afforded to public and to listed companies.

1.5 Advantages of public company status

1.5.1 Ability to offer shares to the public

It is an offence for a private company to offer its shares to the public under s 81 of the CA 1985. In the event of a breach of s 81, the company and any officer in default are liable to a fine. The main reason for registering or re-registering as a public company, therefore, is to enable a company to offer its shares to the public. The ability to offer shares to the public is an advantage as it provides a company with a new source of finance (the consideration received for the shares) and opens up new opportunities which otherwise may be unavailable to the company.

1.5.2 Prestige

A secondary reason for a company to register or re-register as a public company is to benefit from the prestige conferred by the letters 'plc' ('public limited company'). Some companies opt for public company status even if they have no immediate plans to offer shares to the public. Subsidiaries of public companies are often public companies too, for this reason.

1.6 Potential disadvantages of public company status

As noted at **1.5.1** and **1.5.2** above, public company status brings with it the financial advantage of being able to offer shares to the public, and a certain element of commercial respectability. However, these advantages mean (in theory at least) that any public company, even if unlisted, can be owned by members of the public who have little day to day involvement in the company's business, and who therefore require statutory protection. For this reason, public companies are much more strictly regulated than private companies. **Table 1.1** below summarises the main differences between the regulation of public companies and private companies.

Table 1.1: Public companies compared to private companies

	Public company	**Private company**
Accounts	Must file within 7 months of accounting reference period (s 244(1)(b)).	Must file within 10 months of accounting reference period (s 244(1)(a)).
	Must file full accounts (s 247A).	Requirements to file full accounts can be relaxed for small and medium sized companies (ss 246, 246A).
Administration	Cannot take advantage of the elective regime (s 379A).	Can vary certain regulatory requirements of the CA 1985 under the elective regime (s 379A) (eg can confer an indefinite authority on directors to allot shares, or dispense with holding AGMs).
	Cannot use the written resolution procedure (s 381A).	Can use the written resolution procedure (s 381A).
	Subject to the City Code (even if unlisted).	Typically not subject to the City Code (but see exceptions at **20.5.1.2**).
Directors	Minimum of 2 (s 282(1)).	Minimum of 1 (s 282(3)).
	Restrictions apply on voting for more than one director in just one resolution (s 292).	No equivalent restriction applies.
	Age limits apply (s 293).	Age limits apply only if the company is a subsidiary of a public company (s 293).
	Restrictions apply on the ability to make loans to directors (a public company is a 'relevant company') (s 330(2), (3) and (4)).	Fewer restrictions apply on the ability to make loans to directors (s 330(3) and (4) will not apply unless the private company has a relationship with a public company which falls within s 331(6)).

	Public company	Private company
Financial assistance	Prohibited (s 151), subject to ss 153 and 154. See **Chapter 16**.	Prohibited (s 151), subject to s 153, but can be 'whitewashed' under ss 155–158.
Secretary	Qualification requirements (s 286).	No qualification requirements.
Share capital	Authorised share capital must not be less than, and the company must have allotted shares at least up to the value of, the authorised minimum (currently £50,000 (s 118)) to register (s 117(2)) or re-register (s 45(2)(a)).	No restriction on nominal value of authorised or allotted share capital.
	Each share allotted must be paid up to at least one-quarter of its nominal value together with the whole of any premium on it (ss 45(2)(b) and 101).	No equivalent restriction applies. Can allot shares nil paid, partly paid or fully paid.
	Section 89 pre-emption rights on allotment can be disapplied under s 95 only (by special resolution or provision in the articles).	Section 89 pre-emption rights on allotment can be disapplied under s 95 (by special resolution or provision in the articles) or under s 91 (by provision in the articles or memorandum).
	Restrictions apply on consideration for allotment of shares (ss 100, 102 and 104)	Sections 102 and 104 do not apply.
	Valuer's report required to value non-cash consideration for the allotment of shares (ss 103, 108).	No equivalent requirement applies.
	EGM required in the event of a serious loss of capital (s 142).	No equivalent requirement applies.
	Charges on own shares are void, subject to certain exceptions (s 150).	Subject to certain requirements in s 150(2), charges on own shares are permitted.

	Public company	**Private company**
	Can redeem and purchase shares out of distributable profits or the proceeds of a fresh issue, but not out of capital (ss 160, 171).	Can redeem and purchase shares out of distributable profits, the proceeds of a fresh issue, or out of capital (ss 160, 171).
Shareholders	Minimum of 2 (otherwise can lose limited liability) (ss 1(1), 24).	Minimum of 1 (ss 1(3A), 24)
	Has disclosure obligations under ss 198–220 (see **Chapter 15**).	No equivalent restrictions apply.
	Proxy has no right to speak at a general or class meeting (s 372).	Proxy has same right as shareholder who appointed him to speak at a general or class meeting (s 372).
Strike-off	Cannot apply for voluntary strike-off under s 652A	Can apply for voluntary strike-off under s 652A

1.7 Advantages of listing

If obtaining public company status enables a company to offer shares to the public, what further advantage is there in listing?

1.7.1 Accessible market

A listing will provide an accessible market on which members of the public and financial institutions can buy and sell shares. As the shares can be bought (at a pre-agreed price) and sold relatively easily, they will be an attractive investment, particularly for members of the public who may not be familiar with the methods of buying and selling shares off-market. This market also enables the original owners or venture capitalist investors to sell their shares and exit from the company (although they may be restricted from exiting for a period of time immediately following the listing, to promote confidence in the company).

As we know from **1.5** above, those same members of the public and financial institutions can buy and sell shares in an unlisted public company if that company chooses to offer them its shares, but as those shares will not be listed or trading on a public market, the process of buying the shares, and subsequently finding people to sell them to, will not be as easy (the shares are not as 'liquid') and so members of the public, in particular, will be less inclined to invest in them.

1.7.2 Easier access to capital

A listing enables the company to raise finance through shares ('equity finance'), both on the initial listing and afterwards. See **4.4** and **Chapter 17**.

1.7.3 Access to acquisition opportunities

As a result of its access to the market and to capital, a listed company can use cash or shares as consideration, affording it the opportunity to expand through acquisition. Unlisted companies do not have the same access to capital, and unlisted company shares are not attractive consideration from a seller's perspective.

1.7.4 Prestige

The prestige attached to public company status (see **1.5.2**) can be enhanced further if the company lists successfully. In order to list, a company has to receive regulatory approval following considerable investigation into the company's suitability for listing. As listed companies have had their affairs scrutinised yet still obtained this approval, potential customers and suppliers can perceive listed companies to have higher financial standing than unlisted companies. This may help a listed company to negotiate better terms on which to conduct its business.

1.7.5 Profile

The press usually focuses its coverage on listed rather than unlisted companies, and listed companies will also be the subject of analysts' reports, so the profile of the company will be raised. This can help create and sustain demand for, and therefore liquidity in, its shares.

1.7.6 Employee incentives

Listed companies can offer share ownership schemes to employees. While share ownership schemes are available to private companies, and are commonly used to motivate senior staff, listed companies have the additional advantage of being able to offer employees shares which have an identifiable value (as they are listed on a public market). If employees own part of the company, their commitment to the business will often increase. The company should, therefore, benefit from being able to recruit and retain key employees.

1.7.7 Increased efficiency

Listed companies are strictly regulated (see **1.8.1** below). To comply with regulatory requirements, listed companies often have to improve their existing regulatory checks and controls. These improvements can, in turn, improve the operating efficiency of the company as a whole.

1.8 Potential disadvantages of listing

1.8.1 Increased regulatory regime

As **Table 1.1** above shows, even an unlisted public company's regulatory regime is much stricter than that of a private company. However, once a public company is listed, the strict regime set out in **Table 1.1** is supplemented further. Perhaps this is because, as noted in **1.7.1** above, the ready market in listed company shares means that, in practice, members of the public tend to invest in listed companies, rather than in unlisted public companies, and therefore it is the shareholders of listed companies who require the most protection. So how is the regulatory regime summarised in **Table 1.1** supplemented for a listed company?

1.8.1.1 Prospectus Rules, Listing Rules and Disclosure Rules

Until 1 July 2005, the Listing Rules set out not only the procedure for listing, but also continuing obligations to which the listed company and its directors were subject with effect from the date the company was listed. However, on 1 July 2005, the Listing Rules were replaced by three new sets of rules: the Prospectus Rules, the Listing Rules and the Disclosure Rules. These rules apply to any listed company.

Such companies must consider the Prospectus Rules and the Listing Rules on flotation and when raising equity finance, and the Prospectus Rules, the Listing Rules and the Disclosure Rules for their continuing obligations. **Chapters 5** and **6** consider flotation; **Chapter 17** examines equity finance. **Chapter 7** looks at continuing obligations in more detail.

1.8.1.2 Statutory provisions

Certain statutory provisions apply to listed companies only:

(a) *The CA 1985.* Pursuant to s 323, it is a criminal offence for a director of a listed company to deal in options to sell or buy shares in his company or other companies in the same group.

(b) *The FSMA 2000.* The market abuse provisions in Pt VIII of the Financial Services and Markets Act 2000 (FSMA 2000) apply to shares listed on various markets, including the Main Market. **Chapter 10** explores the market abuse provisions in more detail.

(c) *The CJA 1993.* Part V of the Criminal Justice Act 1993 (CJA 1993) provides that it is a criminal offence for a person who holds knowledge as an insider to deal, or encourage someone else to deal, in shares listed on a regulated market (which includes the Main Market). This is known as 'insider dealing'. **Chapter 11** considers insider dealing in more detail.

1.8.2 External forces

External forces beyond the control of a listed company, such as market conditions, rumour or developments in a certain market sector, can affect the company's value. Occasionally external forces can have a positive effect on share price, such as when an unfounded rumour drives up the price, but more often external forces work to depress the share price (consider, for example, the effect of the global terrorist threat on the share price of companies in the travel industry). The fact that the value of the company can be so affected by forces outside its control can be a source of frustration to management.

1.8.3 Increased shareholder power

While this is a benefit for shareholders, the inevitable consequence is a decrease in management's level of control over the company. Not only will any equity held by management have been diluted by the influx of public shareholders, but listed companies require shareholder approval of certain transactions and decisions which, in unlisted companies, would fall to management alone. The pressure to please shareholders can tempt management to focus on short-term rather than long-term performance. There is also the risk that shareholders will sell to unwelcome buyers seeking to take over the company.

1.8.4 Loss of privacy

The listing process under the Prospectus Rules and the Listing Rules, and the continuing obligations of the Prospectus Rules, the Listing Rules and the Disclosure Rules (referred to at **1.8.1.1** above), the higher profile of the company (referred to at **1.7.5** above), and the greater accountability to shareholders (referred to at **1.8.3** above) mean that decisions of management are no longer private affairs. If the company is underperforming, this loss of privacy can be very unwelcome.

1.8.5 Cost and time

The cost and time spent on the listing process, raising equity finance, complying with the continuing obligations of a listed company and maintaining investor relations can be onerous, and the company must decide before listing whether this time and money would be better directed towards running the business.

1.9 Achieving public company status

A company can achieve public company status in two ways:

(a) registering as a public company on original incorporation; or
(b) registering as a private company on original incorporation then re-registering as a public company.

Both procedures ensure that the resulting public company complies with the CA 1985 requirements relating to a public company's memorandum, articles, name and share capital.

1.9.1 Incorporation of a company

The following must be sent to the Registrar of Companies to incorporate any company, private or public:

(a) memorandum of association;
(b) articles of association;
(c) Form 10 (statement of first directors, secretary and registered office);
(d) Form 12 (statutory declaration of compliance with legal requirements of incorporation); and
(e) registration fee.

1.9.2 Registration as a public company on original incorporation

In addition to sending the documents referred to at **1.9.1** above to the Registrar, there are the following extra requirements to register as a public company on original incorporation:

(a) *Memorandum.* The memorandum must state that the company is a public limited company and must be in a form suitable for a public company (namely that specified in Table F of the Companies (Tables A to F) Regulations 1985, or as near to that form as circumstances permit) (CA 1985, s 3).
(b) *Articles.* The articles must be in a form suitable for a public company.
(c) *Name.* The company name must end with 'public limited company', or the Welsh equivalent (s 25(1)).
(d) *Authorised share capital.* The authorised share capital of the company must be not less than the 'authorised minimum' (s 11). Currently the authorised minimum is £50,000 (s 118).

1.9.2.1 Certificate of incorporation

If the company meets all the requirements set out at **1.9.1** and **1.9.2** above, then it will be able to obtain a certificate from the Registrar that the company has been registered as a public company on original incorporation. However, although this certificate of incorporation will prove that the public company exists (s 13(7)), and details of the company will now be recorded at Companies House, the public company needs to obtain one other certificate before it can commence business – a trading certificate.

1.9.2.2 Trading certificate

A company which has been registered as a public company on original incorporation must not begin business or exercise any borrowing powers until it has a trading certificate, issued under s 117 of the CA 1985, confirming that the company has met the *allotted* share capital requirements of the CA 1985 (the company must meet *authorised* share capital requirements as part of the incorporation process – see **1.9.2** above). The certificate is proof that the company can trade and borrow. To obtain this certificate a statutory declaration must be sworn and delivered to the Registrar under s 117 of the CA 1985.

The allotted share capital requirements are that the company must have allotted shares at least up to the value of the authorised minimum (s 117(2)), which, as stated in **1.9.2** above, is currently £50,000 (s 118). Each allotted share must be paid up to at least one-quarter of its nominal value together with the whole of any premium on it (s 101). What does this mean in practice? Well, if 50,000 shares with a nominal value of £1 each are allotted at nominal value with no premium, the minimum consideration which must be paid to the company is one-quarter of the nominal value of each share, that is 0.25p per share, making a total minimum payment of £12,500 for 50,000 shares. If, however, the shares are allotted for, say, £3 each, then each share has a premium (the amount by which the price exceeds the nominal value) of £2. This premium must be paid to the company together with a minimum of a quarter of the nominal value of each share, which is £2 plus 0.25p, that is £2.25 per share, making a total minimum payment of £112,500 for 50,000 shares.

1.9.3 Re-registration as a public company

A company which has registered as a private company on original incorporation (by complying with the requirements detailed at **1.9.1** above) can re-register as a public company pursuant to ss 43–48 of the CA 1985. The company must pass a special (or written) resolution and submit an application in a prescribed form to the Registrar (s 43(1)).

1.9.3.1 Resolution

Pursuant to s 43(2), the special (or written) resolution must:

(a) approve the re-registration of the company;

(b) alter the memorandum so that it states that the company is to be a public company and conforms with the other requirements of the CA 1985 relating to the constitution of a public company, including compliance with the requirements of s 25(1) as to the name of the company. These requirements are referred to at **1.9.2** above; and

(c) alter the articles so that they are in a form suitable for a public company. It is probable that the existing private company articles will require substantial amendment; it is often easier to adopt an entirely new set of articles rather than to amend the existing articles. If the company is re-registering as a public company as a preliminary step to listing in the immediate future, it may be appropriate to adopt a set of articles suitable not only for a public company but also for a public company which is listed. In this case the articles will probably disapply Table A in its entirety and will be bespoke. These are known as long form articles (as opposed to articles which apply Table A either in its entirety or with some amendment, which are referred to as short form articles).

1.9.3.2 Share capital requirements

The resolution deals with the requirements as to a public company's memorandum, articles and name. What about the share capital requirements of a public company? This is dealt with by s 45. *At the time the shareholders pass the special resolution* (see **1.9.3.1**) the company must have satisfied certain conditions as to its share capital, namely that the company must have allotted shares at least up to the value of the authorised minimum (s 45(2)(a)), which is currently £50,000 (s 118), and that each allotted share must be paid up to at least one-quarter of its nominal value together with the whole of any premium on it (s 45(2)(b)).

(These requirements reflect the requirements which must be satisfied when a company originally incorporated as a public company applies for a trading certificate, set out at **1.9.2.2** above. A trading certificate therefore is not required for a private company which re-registers as a public company; the certificate of incorporation is all the company requires.)

Note that s 45(3) and (4) provide some further requirements as to shares which have been allotted in consideration of an undertaking. Note also that some shares can be disregarded for the purposes of satisfying the share capital requirements (see s 45(5), (6) and (7)).

1.9.3.3 Application for re-registration

The special resolution must be delivered to the Registrar together with an application for re-registration on Form 43(3), which has been signed by a director or the company secretary. The application must be accompanied by the fee for re-registration (currently £20, together with £10 for any change of name; there is a same-day service available for an increased fee) and the following documents:

(a) the revised memorandum and articles (s 43(3)(a));

(b) a balance sheet prepared not more than seven months before the application, containing an unqualified report by the company's auditors (s 43(3)(c), s 46). If the company's accounting reference date is within this seven-month period, this requirement can be met by the end of year balance sheet; if not, then an interim balance sheet must be prepared and must be audited, which can prove time-consuming and expensive. The auditors must also provide a written statement regarding the level of the company's net assets (as revealed by the balance sheet) in comparison to the company's called-up share capital and undistributable reserves (s 43(3)(b));

(c) a valuation report on any shares which have been allotted for non-cash consideration between the date of the balance sheet (referred to at (b) above) and the date the special resolution was passed (s 43(3)(d), s 44). This ensures that a private company seeking to re-register is brought into line with the general requirement under s103 that public companies seeking to allot shares for non-cash consideration must have such consideration valued before allotting the shares; and

(d) a statutory declaration in the prescribed form 43(3)(e), or in a statement sent to the Registrar by electronic means (s 43(3)(e), s 43(3A)).

1.9.3.4 Certificate of re-registration on incorporation as a public company

If the Registrar is satisfied with the application, he will issue the company with a certificate of re-registration on incorporation as a public company (s 47). The private company becomes a public company, and the revised memorandum and articles will take effect on the issue of this certificate, which is proof of public company status.

1.9.3.5 Company identification

Sections 348 to 351 of the CA 1985 set out the requirements for a company to identify itself, both outside its place of business and on its stationery. Breach of these requirements can result in a fine for the company and any officer of the company who is in default. The company must prepare new signs and stationery, which will reflect its new identity, in advance of re-registration to ensure that it can meet these requirements with effect from the date the certificate of incorporation on re-registration is issued.

1.10 Achieving listed company status

When a company which does not have any shares listed decides to list shares for the first time, the listing process is known as flotation. There are different methods of flotation, the main methods for a company new to listing being by offer for sale and/or subscription, placing or simple admission. Deciding to float is a serious step for a public company; the process is much more complex (and expensive) than that required for a private company to achieve public company status. **Chapters 4, 5** and **6** examine the complexities of flotation in more detail.

1.11 Future developments

Major changes to UK company law are imminent. At the time of writing, the Companies Bill (formerly known as the Company Law Reform Bill) is due to be enacted as the Companies Act 2006 in October 2007.

1.11.1 Brief history

The Bill has taken some time to progress through Parliament. The Company Law Reform Bill was introduced into the House of Lords in November 2005, and was intended to exist alongside the Companies Act 1985 and the Companies Act 1989. In May 2006 the Lords passed the Bill on its third reading. In June 2006, the Government announced that, rather than adding to the other Companies Acts, the Bill would instead consolidate these Acts. As a result, the Bill is now called the Companies Bill and further draft clauses are under consultation. At the time of writing, the Bill has received its second reading in the House of Commons and is expected to receive Royal Assent in October 2006. It is intended that Part 28 of the Bill, relating to takeovers, will be enacted soon after the Bill receives Royal Assent, and that the remainder of the Bill will be enacted in October 2007.

A copy of the latest draft of the Bill is available from the 'Public Bills' section of the UK Parliament website.

1.11.2 Summary of changes

The Bill makes major changes to UK company law. The changes will affect all UK companies, but certain regulatory changes are restricted to private companies only. To give a flavour of the extent of the changes introduced by the Bill, some of the changes in the draft Bill dated 20 July 2006 which affect public companies (subject to change following public consultation) are summarised below:

(1) A company no longer requires an authorised share capital.
(2) The main constitutional document is the company's articles of association; the status of the memorandum of association is reduced.

(3) The Secretary of State has power to prescribe model articles. In June 2006 the DTI published draft model articles for public companies (available on the DTI website) for public consultation.

(4) A public company requires a minimum of just one shareholder.

(5) A company can change its name not only by special resolution but also by any procedure set out in its articles of association.

(6) A shareholder of a listed company can nominate another to exercise his rights as a shareholder.

(7) Directors have statutory duties which they owe to the company.

(8) Only a public company requires a company secretary.

(9) The company must hold its AGM within six months of the end of the financial year.

(10) Listed companies must publish on a website the result of any poll vote, and in certain circumstances can be required to obtain an independent report on any poll vote.

(11) The prohibition on a private company offering shares to the public remains, but breach is no longer a criminal offence. Instead, any private company breaching the prohibition must either re-register as a public company or be wound up.

(12) Only a public company is prohibited from giving financial assistance (see **16.9**).

(13) There are new arrangements for the public inspection of a company's register of members; this can no longer be done anonymously.

(14) Once a public company has obtained a trading certificate, it is free to redenominate its share capital in a currency other than sterling.

(15) The Panel on Takeovers and Mergers is placed on a statutory footing (this has already been effected to a certain extent by the Takeovers Regulations 2006 – see **20.4**).

(16) The Transparency Directive is implemented (see **15.9**).

Companies Bill 'thrown into chaos'

By Louisa Gault

FRESH MOVES by the Government to consult the public over changes to key parts of the beleaguered Companies Bill will cause legislative chaos, according to the Conservative party.

The Tories have hit out at the Government's decision to open up over 400 clauses of the Companies Bill to changes over the summer recess, a move that shadow ministers fear will further jeopardise the bill's progress through Parliament.

The changes relate to clauses already contained in the Companies Act 1985 that are to be incorporated into the new legislation.

Last week the Department of Trade & Industry posted a notice on its website notifying the public of the review of the new clauses over the summer and inviting views on the drafts by September 8.

Alan Duncan, the shadow trade secretary, said: "It is odd to have what seems to be a new consultation at this stage - it should have been done much sooner. The Government has left it until the eleventh hour to add over 400 clauses and start a new consultation process where important and significant changes can be made. We now have only three days at the report stage to debate and amend these clauses."

Although the Conservatives voted to consolidate the bill by adding the clauses, they argue that it was not revealed until last week that the additions would be open to such extensive public consultation.

The Companies Bill will be debated again in the Commons in October and then returns to the House of Lords, where the changes made in the Commons will be examined.

Carol Shutkever, a partner at Herbert Smith, the law firm, said the new phase of public consultation was important but came at a very late stage in the bill's progress.

She added: "I think it is true that there is a lot of confusion and a lot is still open. And now we only have a few days to deal with these very important issues. It means the overall complexion of the bill will be very different and it adds to the general chaos surrounding this important piece of legislation.

"The Companies Bill was sent to the Commons in May. It is predicted to receive royal assent after the summer recess and to come into force in one block in October 2007.

Source: *Daily Telegraph*, 30 July 2006

Chapter 2
The Stock Exchange

2.1	What is the Stock Exchange?	15
2.2	The market place	15
2.3	The Main Market	15
2.4	AIM	16
2.5	Trading on the markets	16
2.6	Investors in the markets	18
2.7	Regulation of the Stock Exchange	18
2.8	The role of the Stock Exchange in the flotation process	19
2.9	Admission and Disclosure Standards	19
2.10	Future developments	19

2.1 What is the Stock Exchange?

London Stock Exchange plc is a listed company. It has four core areas of business:

(a) a market place for trading in company securities;

(b) a provider of trading platforms on which brokers can buy and sell securities;

(c) a supplier of market information to the financial community, and

(d) a market place for trading in equity derivatives.

The focus of this book is on the Stock Exchange's role as a market place for trading in a specific type of company securities – shares.

The Stock Exchange is at the heart of the world's three main financial centres – London, New York and Tokyo – and is the most international equities market in the world. It also has one of the world's largest pools (and Europe's largest pool) of capital.

2.2 The market place

The Stock Exchange has two markets, the Main Market and AIM. Both markets serve two main functions. First, they enable companies to raise funds by issuing new shares to the public. This is referred to as the primary market for shares. Secondly, they allow those issued shares to be traded (bought and sold) by the public. This is referred to as the secondary market for shares. The Main Market has both a primary and secondary market, therefore, as does AIM.

2.3 The Main Market

The Main Market is the Stock Exchange's principal market for listed companies and is what the layman will think of as 'the stock market'. This is the market on which the shares of many household-name companies, such as Cadbury Schweppes, Rolls-Royce, Sainsbury and Unilever (as well as a host of lesser-known companies), are listed. Within the Main Market, there are specific groupings for certain sectors: techMARK for innovative technology companies; techMARK mediscience for healthcare companies and landMARK for UK regional companies. There are currently about 1,800 companies listed on the Main Market, which includes not only UK companies but also approximately 350 overseas companies (from some 54 different countries).

2.4 AIM

AIM is the Stock Exchange's alternative investment market. It is a global market for smaller and growing companies. AIM is a separate market from the Main Market and, while some companies may choose to move from AIM onto the Main Market at some point, there is no obligation to do so. In fact, lately, the trend has been for Main Market companies to move to AIM.

There are currently more than 1,000 companies listed on AIM, which includes over 200 overseas companies. AIM is a rapidly expanding market; in 2004 it accounted for 65% of all flotations in Western Europe.

As stated at **1.3** above, the focus of this book is on companies which are listed on the Main Market. However, **Chapter 24** provides a brief overview of the regulation of AIM companies, compares AIM with the Main Market, and considers the advantages and disadvantages of an AIM listing.

2.5 Trading on the markets

Trading is not an area in which a corporate lawyer typically will have much involvement. The focus of the lawyer's role is to help to bring a client company to market successfully, and then ensure that the company is advised of the regulatory regime it must follow in order to maintain its listing. However, the corporate lawyer's clients usually will have an in-depth knowledge of trading and the markets, and those clients may be unsettled if the lawyer helping to bring the company to market has no comprehension of how that market works. The following, therefore, is intended to provide some basic information on the mechanics of trading.

2.5.1 Member firms

Member firms carry out most of the trading on the Stock Exchange's markets. They are investment firms (banks, stockbrokers and fund managers) which trade either on behalf of clients, or on behalf of their firms. Examples of current member firms are Barclays Bank plc, Brewin Dolphin Securities Limited, Crédit Suisse First Boston and Deutsche Bank AG London Branch.

2.5.2 Mechanics of trading

The Stock Exchange has devised various systems for trading shares. For the large listed companies, including those on the FTSE 100 index, there is the Stock Exchange Electronic Trading Service (SETS), which is known as the order book. This electronic system matches 'buy' and 'sell' orders for the same shares and executes the trade automatically. For smaller companies (including the most liquid AIM companies) there is the Stock Exchange Automated Quotations system. With this system certain member firms act as competing 'market makers' in relation to certain shares. They will set the 'buy' and 'sell' prices for these shares, using current news about the company, the market sector and the strength of demand for shares as a guide. Member firms acting as 'brokers' will then buy and sell the shares when they think the price set by the market makers is right. A further system, SEATS Plus, supports the trading of shares in companies with turnover which is insufficient for the SEAQ system (such as the less liquid Main Market companies and most AIM companies).

2.5.3 Settlement

Once a share has been traded on the market, it needs to be transferred from the seller to the buyer, and the consideration monies need to be transferred from the buyer to the seller. This process is known as 'settlement'. There is a risk during the time between the trade being struck and settlement being made that the transaction will fail (for example, if one of the parties is declared bankrupt).

2.5.3.1 CREST

CREST was introduced in 1996 and is a paperless (that is, the shares are uncertificated) share settlement system through which trades on the Stock Exchange's markets can be settled. CRESTCo Limited operates this system. As the system is electronic and paperless, settlement can be made swiftly (within three business days of any trade), so the risk period between trade and settlement is reduced. There are various options for a shareholder wishing to hold shares through CREST.

CREST member

A CREST member must be linked up to CREST by computer network, so typically it is the member firms of the Stock Exchange who have this type of membership. CREST members hold shares as nominees for individual clients (institutional or private investors), so the name of the CREST member, rather than the client, will be entered into the company's register of members as legal owner. The client will be the beneficial owner of the shares.

Each CREST member has an identification number for itself ('participant ID') and at least one other identification number for specific accounts it holds, such as an account for shares beneficially held on behalf of a specific institution ('member account ID').

CREST personal member (or 'sponsored member')

This type of membership is designed to attract private investors (institutions and individuals). The benefit to the private investor is that its name will appear on the company's register of members (in contrast to the position if it holds shares through a CREST member, where the CREST member's name will feature on the register). However, one drawback is that the CREST personal member does not have a computer link-up to CREST. A CREST sponsor, who will be a CREST member, will provide this, and will charge for the service.

Nominee shareholder

With this type of membership, the shareholder holds shares through a nominee. This means that, as with the CREST member category, the shareholder will be the beneficial owner of their shares rather than the legal owner, and the name of the nominee will appear on the register.

The corporate lawyer and CREST

In practice, the impact of CREST for the corporate lawyer is not dramatic. For example it may involve ensuring that some standard wording is drafted into certain documents, such as how CREST shareholders can accept an offer and receive consideration (in a takeover) or take up shares (when raising equity finance), or being aware of CREST shareholders when considering the mechanics of an AGM. Some standard wording is available on the CREST website. The lawyer should be aware that Stamp Duty Reserve Tax is collected on paperless share transactions such as the transfer of shares within CREST. CREST itself, however, is responsible for collecting this tax.

2.6 Investors in the markets

2.6.1 Members of the public

Members of the public have significant involvement with the Stock Exchange. They can invest directly in shares listed on the Main Market or on AIM, either in the primary market (by subscribing for new shares issued by a company on flotation) or in the secondary market (by buying or selling shares which are already in issue). They can also invest indirectly (because, for example, their pensions, other savings schemes or employment incentive schemes are tied up in the Stock Exchange's markets). Obviously, the aim of the member of the public who invests is to realise a healthy profit on the sale of the investment.

2.6.2 Institutional investors

Institutional investors (also known as institutional shareholders), such as pension funds and investment funds, have sizeable funds available for investment. The amount they have available to invest means that institutional investors have considerable influence over the companies in which they invest. The main institutional investors have formed their own representative bodies called Investment Protection Committees (IPCs). Well known IPCs are the Association of British Insurers (ABI), the National Association of Pension Funds (NAPF) and Pensions & Investment Research Consultants (PIRC). The IPCs have also joined together to form one representative body, the Institutional Shareholders' Committee (ISC). The IPCs issue guidelines as to how members should exercise their shareholder vote. While these guidelines do not have the force of law, listed companies do treat them as binding, such is the influence of the institutional shareholders.

Chapter 14 looks at some of these guidelines in more detail. **Chapter 8** also considers the role of institutional investors in relation to corporate governance.

2.7 Regulation of the Stock Exchange

The FSMA 2000 prohibits any person from carrying on any regulated activity unless that person is either authorised or exempt. This is known as the general prohibition (see **9.4**). The Financial Services Authority (FSA) has granted a recognition order to the Stock Exchange under s 290 of the FSMA 2000. This means that the Stock Exchange is a 'recognised investment exchange', and therefore, under s 285 of the 2000 Act, is exempt from the general prohibition. To remain a recognised investment exchange, the Stock Exchange must continue to satisfy various requirements drafted pursuant to s 286 of the FSMA 2000, including the Financial Services and Markets Act 2000 (Recognition Requirements for Investment Exchanges and Clearing Houses) Regulations 2001 (SI 2001/995) and the FSA Handbook of Rules and Guidance. These requirements include that the Stock Exchange must:

(a) ensure that business conducted by means of its facilities is conducted in an orderly manner and so as to afford proper protection to investors;

(b) limit trading to securities in which there is a proper market;

(c) ensure that it has effective arrangements for monitoring and enforcing compliance with its rules; and

(d) be able to promote and maintain high standards of integrity and fair dealing in the carrying on of regulated activities by persons using facilities provided by the Stock Exchange.

2.8 The role of the Stock Exchange in the flotation process

The Stock Exchange used to have responsibility for the official listing of securities in the UK. This role was transferred to the FSA on 1 May 2000. **Chapter 3** considers this role more closely; however the effect of the transfer of this role is that while the Stock Exchange continues to have responsibility for admitting shares to trading on its markets, the FSA has responsibility for overseeing the listing process. Any company seeking to be a listed company (as defined in **1.3** above) must seek to have its shares:

(a) admitted to *listing* on the Official List (for which it must liaise with the FSA); and

(b) admitted to *trading* on the Main Market (for which it must liaise with the Stock Exchange).

Chapter 5 considers this process in more detail.

2.9 Admission and Disclosure Standards

The Stock Exchange has its own set of rules for companies joining the Main Market (they do not apply to companies joining AIM). These rules are called the Admission and Disclosure Standards and they set out the requirements for companies seeking admission to trading, as well as the continuing obligations for companies admitted to trading. The Admission and Disclosure Standards as at 1 July 2005 are reproduced in **Appendix 1**. The Standards are also available on the Stock Exchange website. At the time of writing, the Stock Exchange had announced its intention to issue, but had not yet issued, a new version of the Standards for 2006/07.

2.10 Future developments

2.10.1 The Stock Exchange

The Stock Exchange is a potential takeover target. It is very profitable and has an excellent reputation worldwide.

Several potential offerors attempted to take over the Stock Exchange in 2005. In January, Deutsche Börse AG made a pre-conditional offer for the Stock Exchange at a price of 530p per share. The Stock Exchange rejected this offer and it was subsequently withdrawn. In February, Euronext NV, owner of the Paris Stock Exchange and London's derivatives exchange Liffe, made an offer, although it did not specify a price. The OFT has since referred this offer to the Competition Commission. Finally, in December, the Macquarie Group, the Australian investment bank, made an offer of 580p per share. The Stock Exchange rejected this offer, which then lapsed in February 2006.

The issue of a takeover of the Stock Exchange remains topical. In April 2006, the Stock Exchange issued a statement that, despite press speculation to the contrary, it had not received an approach from the New York Stock Exchange about a possible offer.

The Stock Exchange itself maintains that it can remain an independent company, although it has stated that 'a combination, on the right terms, of the London

Stock Exchange with another major stock exchange could be in the best interests of shareholders and customers'. Watch this space!

2.10.2 Trading

The Institute of Chartered Secretaries and Administrators (ICSA) published a consultation paper on 10 April 2006. The paper, entitled 'The Dematerialisation of shares and share transfers', is available on the ICSA website. It proposes replacing paper share certificates and stock transfer forms with an electronic system, for all share transactions of listed UK companies (a process referred to as 'dematerialisation'). In 2004 the European Securities Forum also advocated compulsory dematerialisation of all UK securities. At the time of writing, dematerialisation was not expected to be implemented in the UK until at least 2008.

Chapter 3
The UK Listing Authority

3.1	Background	21
3.2	The competent authority for listing in the UK	22
3.3	What does the FSA (in its capacity as the UKLA) do?	22
3.4	Relationship between the FSA and the Stock Exchange	22
3.5	Prospectus, Listing and Disclosure Rules	23
3.6	The UKLA Guidance Manual	25
3.7	Sanctions for breach of the Prospectus Rules, the Listing Rules and the Disclosure Rules	25

3.1 Background

The regulatory framework for listing in the UK has EC law at its origin. The Consolidated Admission and Reporting Directive (CARD) provided the EU framework for the Old Listing Rules, which comprised the compulsory 'minimum requirements' of CARD together with a number of measures beyond the CARD requirements, known as 'super-equivalent' provisions.

In 1999, the European Commission adopted a Financial Services Action Plan (FSAP), with the aim of creating a single financial market in Europe by the end of 2005. Several directives came into effect to implement the FSAP. Three in particular, namely the Prospectus Directive, the Market Abuse Directive (MAD) and the draft Transparency Obligations Directive, required changes to be made to the UK's regulatory regime for listing, in order to create a streamlined approach to listing shares for issuers in each Member State of the European Union. Each Member State had to implement the provisions of these Directives into its own law.

When the role of listing authority for the UK transferred from the Stock Exchange to the FSA in 2000 (see **2.8** above and **3.2** below), the FSA made very few changes to the Listing Rules, precisely because it knew that the FSAP would require fundamental changes to the listing regime. Instead, the FSA began its own comprehensive review of the Listing Rules, with the aim of simplifying and modernising the UK's listing regime, while also accommodating the changes required by the FSAP.

The FSAP and the FSA's comprehensive review of the Listing Rules were implemented on 1 July 2005, culminating in substantial changes to the UK's listing regime. On this date, the UKLA Sourcebook (comprising the Old Listing Rules and the UKLA Guidance Manual, and which, being purple, was known as the 'Purple Book') was replaced by three new sourcebooks, namely the Prospectus Rules (implementing the Prospectus Directive), the Listing Rules (implementing the FSA's comprehensive review) and the Disclosure Rules (implementing the MAD). Together, the three new sourcebooks form a new part of the FSA Handbook, entitled 'Listing, Prospectus and Disclosure'. Section 73A of the FSMA 2000 refers to these new rules as the 'Part 6 rules'.

For those familiar with the Old Listing Rules, reference is made throughout this book to how the regime under the new rules (the 'new regime') differs from that under the old rules (the 'old regime').

3.2 The competent authority for listing in the UK

The Directives referred to at **3.1** required each Member State to nominate an authority which is competent (the 'competent authority') to undertake the tasks which are set out in the Directives. Section 72(1) of the FSMA 2000 nominates the FSA as the competent authority for listing in the UK. This is not the FSA's only role; in fact, it regulates the entire financial services industry in the UK. The FSA has created a separate division, therefore, to perform the specific role of competent authority for listing in the UK, and this is called the UK Listing Authority (UKLA).

The FSMA 2000 itself does not in fact refer to the term 'UK Listing Authority' or 'UKLA'; it refers to the FSA as the competent authority for listing. The Old Listing Rules did refer specifically to the UKLA (the FSA acting in its capacity as UK Listing Authority), but the new Listing Rules do not; like the FSMA 2000, they refer simply to the FSA. This book follows the new Listing Rules and the FSMA 2000 and refers to the FSA rather than specifically to the UKLA. Note, however, that in practice the FSA does still operate through its UKLA division in relation to all things to do with listing, and the FSA website has a separate section for UKLA matters.

As stated at **2.8** above, the Stock Exchange performed the role of listing authority for the UK until 1 May 2000, and the transfer of this role to the FSA has led to a fundamental change in the flotation process. Lawyers need to be aware of this historical role of the Stock Exchange in order to identify out-of-date provisions in precedents or draft agreements (such as any reference to the Stock Exchange having responsibility for any of the matters set out at **3.3** below).

3.3 What does the FSA (in its capacity as the UKLA) do?

The FSA (in its capacity as the UKLA) has responsibility for the official listing of securities under Pt VI of the FSMA 2000. This includes:

(a) maintaining the Official List (s 74(1));
(b) drafting the Prospectus Rules, the Listing Rules and the Disclosure Rules (s 73A);
(c) determining applications for admission to listing, which includes reviewing the documentation which a company must produce to have its shares listed (s 75);
(d) ensuring that listed companies comply with their continuing obligations under the Listing Rules, the Disclosure Rules and the Prospectus Rules, which includes approving documentation prepared by listed companies, such as circulars; and
(e) having the power to sanction any listed company which does not comply with the Prospectus Rules, the Listing Rules or the Disclosure Rules (or any director of such a company).

Chapter 5 looks at the listing process in more detail and considers how the FSA is involved in that process in practice.

3.4 Relationship between the FSA and the Stock Exchange

As stated at **2.8** above, the FSA and the Stock Exchange have different roles in the listing and trading of shares in London. The FSA oversees the admission of shares to *listing* and the Stock Exchange oversees the admission of shares to *trading*. A listed company needs to have its shares admitted both to listing and to trading. **Chapters 4, 5** and **6** consider how a company can do this.

3.5 Prospectus, Listing and Disclosure Rules

As referred to at **3.3**, the FSA has three sets of new rules, discussed at **3.5.1** to **3.5.3** below.

References to the Prospectus Rules, Listing Rules and Disclosure Rules are prefaced with 'PR', 'LR' or 'DR' respectively. The paragraph number is suffixed with 'R' to indicate if this is a rule, or 'G' to indicate if this is guidance

3.5.1 The Prospectus Rules

The Prospectus Rules (together with the PD Regulation and the Prospectus Regulations 2005 – see **3.5.1.1** and **3.5.1.2**), all effective as of 1 July 2005, implement the Prospectus Directive in the UK. They contain provisions about the content of, and approval process for, a marketing document called a prospectus.

These Rules apply to companies:

(a) seeking to *offer* unlisted shares (including shares seeking admission, or which are admitted, to AIM) or listed shares (including shares seeking admission, or which are admitted, to the Official List) *to the public* in *the UK*; and/or

(b) seeking to *admit* shares to *trading on a regulated market* (which includes the Main Market but not AIM) *in the UK* (even where there is no offer to the public referred to at (a) above).

The fact that the Prospectus Rules apply both to companies which trade on AIM and companies listed on the Official List is a break with the tradition of having separate regulatory regimes for AIM companies and Official List companies. The focus of this book, however, remains with listed companies as defined at **1.3** above.

The Prospectus Directive was drafted as a 'maximum harmonisation' measure, meaning that the UK was unable to set higher standards (known as 'super-equivalent' provisions) for the issues covered by the Directive. For this reason, the Prospectus Rules effectively replace parts of Chapter 4, Chapters 5 and 6, and parts of Chapters 18 to 26 of the Old Listing Rules.

While the Directive covers the requirements relating to the content of, and approval process for, a prospectus, it does not cover the issue of eligibility for listing. The UK therefore was at liberty to retain the super-equivalent eligibility criteria of the Old Listing Rules in this respect. Having consulted on this issue, the FSA has retained revised eligibility criteria in the new Listing Rules (see **3.5.2** below). **Chapters 5** and **6** consider the Prospectus Rules in more detail.

3.5.1.1 The Prospectus Directive Regulation (PD Regulation)

The Prospectus Directive took the form of a framework directive. Much of the detail required for implementation is contained in an EC Regulation, the PD Regulation. Its articles and annexes specify in detail the form and content requirements of a prospectus. Helpfully for the practitioner, the Prospectus Rules, which, as explained above, implement the Prospectus Directive in the UK, replicate the contents of the Regulation (the articles are set out at PR 2.3.1EU and the annexes at Appendix 3). This means that the lawyer needs to be aware of the existence of the PD Regulation (it is referred to in the Prospectus Rules), but will not need to carry that Regulation with him; all he requires are the Prospectus Rules.

3.5.1.2 The Prospectus Regulations 2005

The Prospectus Regulations are UK legislation which effected appropriate changes to existing UK legislation in order to implement the Prospectus Directive. In particular, they amended parts of the FSMA 2000, the CA 1985 and the Companies (Audit, Investigations and Community Enterprise) Act 2004, and revoked the Public Offers of Securities Regulations 1995 and the Financial Services and Markets Act 2000 (Offers of Securities) Order 2001 (SI 2001/2958).

3.5.2 The Listing Rules

The Listing Rules contain the following key provisions:

(a) six Listing Principles (new as at 1 July 2005 – see **3.5.2.1** below);

(b) eligibility criteria for listing (but, as explained at **3.5.1**, the rules about when a prospectus is required, and the content of that prospectus, which were in the Old Listing Rules, are now contained in the Prospectus Rules);

(c) listing application process;

(d) sponsor regime;

(e) cancellation and suspension of listing; and

(f) continuing obligations of a listed company (supplemented by some continuing obligations in the Disclosure Rules and one continuing obligation in the Prospectus Rules).

The Listing Rules apply to shares which trade on a regulated market, so they will apply to shares which trade on the Main Market but *not* to shares which trade on AIM.

The Listing Rules are divided into 19 chapters. Chapters 1 to 5 apply to all securities; Chapters 6 to 16 apply to equity securities; and Chapters 17 to 19 apply to debt securities, depositary receipts and derivatives respectively (and so are not referred to again in this book).

3.5.2.1 The Listing Principles

One of the fundamental changes implemented on 1 July 2005 was the introduction to the Listing Rules of six Listing Principles. The Principles, set out at 7.2.1R of the Listing Rules, are as follows:

Principle 1   A listed company must take reasonable steps to enable its directors to understand their responsibilities and obligations as directors.

Principle 2   A listed company must take reasonable steps to establish and maintain adequate procedures, systems and controls to enable it to comply with its obligations.

Principle 3   A listed company must act with integrity towards holders and potential holders of its listed equity securities.

Principle 4   A listed company must communicate information to holders and potential holders of its listed equity securities in such a way as to avoid the creation or continuation of a false market in such listed equity securities.

Principle 5   A listed company must ensure that it treats all holders of the same class of its listed equity securities that are in the same position equally in respect of the rights attaching to such listed equity securities.

Principle 6   A listed company must deal with the FSA in an open and co-operative manner.

The Principles are intended to ensure adherence to the spirit as well as the letter of the Listing Rules, and it is intended that they will work much like the general principles of the City Code (see **20.5.5** below). The Listing Rules must be interpreted in line with the Listing Principles. The FSA has provided guidance on the application of the Principles and has stated that it does not intend that they will apply any different standards to companies than are expected under the Listing Rules. The Principles are, however, enforceable like any other Listing Rule, and breach can lead to sanction by the FSA (see **3.7** below).

3.5.3 The Disclosure Rules

The Disclosure Rules (together with amendments made to the FSMA 2000), effective 1 July 2005, implement the Market Abuse Directive in the UK.

These Rules contain rules and guidance about a listed company's continuing obligation to:

(a) inform the market about new developments and its financial condition and performance (that is, to disclose 'inside information'); and

(b) disclose transactions in shares by directors and senior executives and persons connected to them.

These Rules replace paras 9.1 to 9.8 and parts of Chapter 16 of the Old Listing Rules and are examined in detail in **Chapter 7**. The Code of Market Conduct and the Model Code should also be considered in addition to the Disclosure Rules and the FSMA 2000.

As with the Listing Rules, the Disclosure Rules apply to shares which trade on a regulated market, so they will apply to shares which trade on Main Market but *not* to shares which trade on AIM.

3.6 The UKLA Guidance Manual

Those familiar with the old regime should note that the UKLA Guidance Manual is no longer published. The FSA now publishes guidance (marked 'G' in the margin) next to the Rule to which it relates (marked 'R' in the margin).

3.7 Sanctions for breach of the Prospectus Rules, the Listing Rules and the Disclosure Rules

Disclosure Rules 1.5.3G and 1.4.3R, Chapter 5 of the Listing Rules and ss 77, 87 and 91 of the FSMA 2000 set out the sanctions for breach of the rules. They include:

(a) private or public censure of the company (ss 87M, 91);
(b) private or public censure of a person discharging managerial responsibilities (PDMR) (see **7.6.2.1**) or connected person (ss 87M, 91(3));
(c) suspension of listing (although compliance with the Disclosure Rules and the Listing Rules must continue) (ss 77, 87L; Listing Rules, Chapter 5);
(d) cancellation of listing (s 77; Listing Rules, Chapter 5);

(e) fining the company (s 91(1) and (2)); and
(f) fining a director who was knowingly concerned in the breach (s 91(2)).

There are also specific sanctions for specific breaches (for example, imprisonment for offering transferable securities to the public without an approved prospectus, in breach of s 85(3)).

Chapter 4
Flotation: Preparation

4.1	What is flotation?	27
4.2	Appointing a team of advisers	27
4.3	Is the company ready to float?	31
4.4	Choosing how to float	35
4.5	Restructuring the company	39
4.6	What next?	41

4.1 What is flotation?

Flotation, also known as an initial public offering (IPO), is the process by which a company becomes a listed company (for our purposes as defined at **1.3** above). As **Chapters 2** and **3** established, any company seeking to become such a listed company must undergo a parallel admission procedure to have its shares:

(a) admitted to *listing* on the Official List (for which it must liaise with the FSA and comply with the Prospectus Rules and the Listing Rules); and

(b) admitted to *trading* on the Main Market (for which it must liaise with the Stock Exchange and comply with the Admission and Disclosure Standards).

While lawyers and other advisers need to be aware of the distinction between admission to listing and admission to trading, in practice the FSA and the Stock Exchange co-operate to ensure that the process is seamless. In fact, the layman would probably not be aware that, technically, flotation involves two admission procedures. **Chapter 5** considers the actual flotation process in more detail. This chapter looks at the preparatory steps a company should take in the year (or two) preceding flotation.

4.2 Appointing a team of advisers

The flotation process is complex and good corporate advisers are vital to a successful float. In the year before flotation the company must consider carefully who to appoint as its advisers for the float. Usually it will seek preliminary advice on this matter from its everyday advisers (typically its lawyers and accountants). These everyday advisers may not have the necessary expertise to advise in relation to the float itself, but they should be able to recommend suitable advisers who can provide guidance to the company regarding the composition of any flotation team. The company will sign engagement letters with each adviser to govern the terms and conditions of their appointment specifically in relation to the flotation.

Any company seeking to float requires professional advice in relation to a wide range of issues. Lawyers advising on the legal aspects of the flotation process form just part of a considerably larger team of advisers, who each take responsibility for various aspects of the float. Lawyers advising on a flotation cannot expect to work in isolation. They need excellent communication and project management skills. They also need a good understanding of the roles and responsibilities of the rest of the team. So who does what?

4.2.1 The company and the directors

As set out in **Chapter 6** below, the main marketing document for a float is the prospectus, and this must contain a substantial amount of information about the company. It is the directors who have primary responsibility for the accuracy of this information. While the directors cannot delegate this responsibility, practically they cannot supply all the information required in the time provided. Instead they enlist the help of the company secretary and key managers to locate, and provide to the advisers drafting the prospectus, accurate information about the company. Obviously this diverts many of the company's senior employees and directors from their usual role of day-to-day management and ensuring that the company is profitable. Companies need to be made aware of this hidden cost.

4.2.2 Sponsor

Listing Rule 8.2.1R provides that any company applying for a listing which requires the publication of a prospectus must have a sponsor who is independent (as defined in LR 8.3.6R and LR 8.3.7R) (see **4.3.1.1** below). Chapter 8 of the Listing Rules contains the rules relating to the sponsor, whose role is given much more emphasis under the new regime. Listing Rule 8.3 sets out the general role of a sponsor; LR 8.4.1R to LR 8.4.6R set out the specific duties of the sponsor in relation to a float. The sponsor owes duties to the FSA, and a firm must take up an appointment as sponsor only once it is satisfied of the company's suitability for listing. Of course, no sponsor likes to be associated with an unsuccessful float in any event.

The sponsor has a key role in guiding the company through the flotation process and advising the company on the interpretation of the Listing Rules. It will liaise with the FSA and, to a lesser extent, the Stock Exchange on behalf of the company, and will relay any comments back to the company. The sponsor also co-ordinates the team of advisers. The lawyers in particular will have day-to-day contact with the sponsor as the flotation process progresses.

Usually an investment bank, a stockbroker, a corporate finance house or an accountancy firm will adopt the role of sponsor, but it must be approved by the FSA. Listing Rule 8.6 sets out the criteria for sponsor approval. A list of approved sponsors is available from the FSA website (LR 8.6.1G).

4.2.3 Broker

The broker advises the company with a view to ensuring that there is sufficient demand for the company's shares once the company has floated. The broker will analyse market conditions, liaise with potential investors to market the shares and advise the company on the best method of flotation (see **4.4** below) and other tactical issues, such the price of the shares to be marketed and the timing of the flotation. If the firm appointed as sponsor (see **4.2.2**) has stockbroking capability then it may also take on the role of broker.

4.2.4 Financial adviser

The financial adviser will advise on a wide range of tactical issues, such as the timing of the float, how the offer should be structured (see **4.4** below) and the offer price. Again, this role is usually adopted by the firm acting as sponsor.

4.2.5 Reporting accountants

The reporting accountants review the company's finances. This is an important role, because whatever the company states in the prospectus about its financial situation will influence potential investors as to whether the company is an attractive investment. The company will want to present a rosy financial picture, but the reporting accountants must ensure that this picture is accurate.

The reporting accountants will produce three main reports. The lawyers will have little involvement in the production of these, but they do need to know what they are (there will be frequent references to them in meetings). The first report is the 'long form' report, which is not published but forms the basis of the financial information required to draft the prospectus. The second report is the 'short form' report. This is based on the long form report, but it is published; it forms part of the prospectus. The third report is the 'working capital' report. The reporting accountants prepare this so that the sponsor can ascertain the company's anticipated working capital position for a period following the float (see **4.3.1.1(j)**).

The reporting accountants may also provide 'comfort letters' to the directors, to enable the directors to make certain statements in the prospectus about the financial status of the company which are required by the Listing Rules (the directors cannot, however, delegate responsibility for such statements to the accountants). The reporting accountants may also advise on taxation issues.

Note that the role of reporting accountants is separate from the role of the company's existing auditors. Often the same accountancy firm does adopt both roles, but allocates a different team to each. The sponsor, however, may prefer that the role of reporting accountant is adopted by an entirely different firm, so that it is seen to be independent.

4.2.6 Lawyers

There are usually two teams of lawyers, from different firms, involved in a flotation. They will be specialists in corporate finance. One team advises the company and one team advises the sponsor. Both teams must work closely together to provide a seamless service. The requirement for two teams reflects the fact that, while both the sponsor and the company have the common aim of a successful float, there are issues on which their needs conflict. The sponsor owes certain duties to the FSA (see **4.2.2**) which the company does not owe. The sponsor will be highly sensitive about the risks of being involved with an unsuccessful float, or one which generates bad publicity, and the impact this will have on its ability to obtain work in the future. It may, therefore, wish to exercise a more cautious approach than the company in certain areas. The company and the sponsor are also likely to have conflicting interests regarding underwriting (see **4.2.7** below).

In addition to the company's lawyers and the sponsor's lawyers, there may also be other lawyers representing any selling shareholders, if there is a conflict of interest between the company and such shareholders. If there is no conflict, the company's lawyers may also act for any selling shareholders.

4.2.6.1 The company's lawyers

The company's lawyers draft all the documentation relating to the flotation. This includes not only the prospectus but also any ancillary documents, including any preparatory documentation required to restructure the company (see **4.5** below), such as changing the articles of association, drafting new service contracts and re-registering the company as a public company (see **1.9.3** above). The company's lawyers are also responsible for the verification process (see **5.3.5** and **6.8** below). The workload of the lawyers is examined in more detail at **5.3**.

4.2.6.2 The sponsor's lawyers

The sponsor's lawyers work with the company's lawyers to negotiate the agreements between the sponsor and the company and its shareholders (for example, the underwriting agreement). While the company's lawyers will have primary responsibility for processing the float documentation, the sponsor's lawyers will also contribute towards drafting. They will keep a close eye on the company lawyers' progress regarding the legal documentation and the verification exercise (see **5.3.5** and **6.8**) and advise the sponsor accordingly. Remember, the sponsor will not wish to be involved with a flop; if anything is not progressing as planned, the sponsor's lawyers must alert the sponsor.

4.2.7 Underwriters

The underwriters take up any shares left over after the float (in the event that the float is 'undersubscribed') in return for a negotiated fee, which is typically around 3 to 5% of the amount underwritten. If the float is 'fully subscribed' and there are no shares left over, the underwriter has no liability to take any shares. This arrangement is recorded in an underwriting agreement. The underwriter will usually allocate some or all of the risk of the offer being undersubscribed to sub-underwriters, by way of a sub-underwriting agreement (the company will not be party to any sub-underwriting agreement). Often the sponsor will adopt the role of underwriter. Occasionally the broker (if different to the sponsor) will be the underwriter. Usually the sub-underwriters will be other banks and brokers, and the large institutional investors.

4.2.8 Receiving bank

If the flotation is by way of an offer for sale and/or subscription (see **4.4.1.1** below), the receiving bank deals with the application forms (see **5.4.2.2**) and consideration for shares. Often the company's clearing bank fulfils this role.

4.2.9 Registrars

The registrars manage the company's share register. They send the share certificates to the successful applicants. This can be a considerable task if the offer is sizeable. Often the company's clearing bank takes this role in addition to the role of receiving bank.

4.2.10 Financial public relations consultants

It is important for a company to have a positive public profile before, during and after the flotation process. Financial public relations consultants liaise with the media and analysts to heighten the profile of the company. They also ensure that the company's communications are effective.

For reasons explained in **Chapter 6**, it is important from a legal perspective that the company's communications are not misleading and can be verified by the company (see **5.3.5** and **6.8** below). The lawyers, therefore, have a role in ensuring that the financial public relations consultants take into account these legal requirements. Unqualified statements, such as 'we are the biggest/the fastest/the best', while being excellent selling messages, rarely survive the lawyers' red pens during the flotation process.

Good financial public relations consultants will be aware of the legal limitations on the company's sales pitch from the outset, and can manage the company's expectations in this regard. It is not just pre-prepared communications which need to be handled cautiously, though. The consultants and the lawyers may also provide the directors with media training, so that when the directors are marketing the float they do not say anything ('we are the biggest/the fastest/the best') which might have adverse legal implications because it cannot be verified.

4.2.11 Printers

The flotation documentation will be created initially by word processor, but ultimately the final version will be professionally printed. Once each document is in substantially final draft form, it will be taken to print. Thereafter, each draft will be printed rather than take the form of a word-processed document. The printers need to turn around the documentation quickly, accurately and securely. Towards the end of the flotation process the lawyers will spend some time, often well into the night, at the printers, checking *in situ* the final amendments to the draft.

4.3 Is the company ready to float?

The company may consider that it is ready to float, but the advisers, and particularly the sponsor, will need to ensure that the company has taken account of all relevant factors in reaching this conclusion. There are two main considerations, namely:

(a) Will the company meet the regulatory requirements for flotation laid down by the FSA (in relation to listing) and the Stock Exchange (in relation to trading) (see **4.3.1** below)?

(b) Will investors perceive the company to be an attractive investment opportunity (see **4.3.2** below)?

4.3.1 Regulatory requirements

The company may not have considered any regulatory requirements at the time it appoints its advisers. However, as soon as the advisers are on board they will go through the regulatory requirements with the company and discuss the extent to which the company fulfils them. The company can then take action to remedy any problems.

4.3.1.1 Regulatory requirements for admission to listing

The FSA has the following requirements which a company must meet before its shares can be admitted to listing. The flotation team must be aware of these requirements and ensure that, by the time the FSA hears the listing application, the company is capable of meeting all of them.

Sponsor

Chapter 8 of the Listing Rules (which replaces Chapter 2 of the Old Listing Rules) provides that any company seeking a listing must appoint a sponsor. The sponsor's role is discussed in more detail at **4.2.2** above; however, the key role of the sponsor from the FSA's point of view is to ensure that the company is suitable for listing, to act as a link between the FSA and the company, and to advise the company in relation to the application for admission to listing and in relation to the Listing Rules.

Eligibility criteria (or 'conditions for listing')

Chapter 2 of the Listing Rules sets out the conditions which a company must satisfy before it can admit any type of security to the Official List. Chapter 6 of the Listing Rules sets out additional conditions which must be satisfied by companies wishing to list equity securities, such as shares. A company wishing to list shares on the Official List, therefore, must fulfil the conditions for listing in both Chapter 2 and Chapter 6 of the Listing Rules (which replace Chapter 3 of the Old Listing Rules). (Chapters 15 to 19, rather than Chapter 6, set out the additional conditions if the securities to be listed are other than equity securities. As the focus of this book is on equity securities, and in particular shares, these chapters are not considered further.)

As referred to at **3.5.1** above, the FSA consulted on the conditions for listing in the Old Listing Rules. The new conditions remain largely the same for new applicants seeking to float, but those familiar with the old regime should note the following differences:

- The condition requiring directors to have sufficient expertise and experience, and to be free from conflict (Old Listing Rules, paras 3.8 and 3.9), and the condition requiring independence from a controlling shareholder (Old Listing Rules, paras 3.12 and 3.13) have been deleted. These matters are now dealt with through disclosure in the prospectus.
- The specialist chapters in the Old Listing Rules for mineral companies and scientific research-based companies have been deleted; however, there are now separate conditions for listing for such companies (LR 6.1.8R to LR 6.1.12R).
- There are no specific exemptions for high growth or innovative companies.

The conditions in Chapters 2 and 6 are discussed below, although the Rules, and particularly the Guidance to the Rules, should be consulted for further detail:

(a) *Incorporation (LR 2.2.1R)*. The company must be duly incorporated and operate in conformity with its constitution. For UK companies this means being a public company (as referred to at **1.5.1**, a private company cannot offer shares to the public). The methods by which a company can achieve public company status are discussed at **1.9** above.

(b) *Validity of securities (LR 2.2.2R)*. The securities (for our purposes, shares) of the company must comply with all legal requirements and be authorised under the company's memorandum and articles. This means that the company must comply with all the provisions of the CA 1985 relating to the issue of shares, such as ss 80, 89 and 121 (see **14.3** and **Chapters 13** and **14** generally).

(c) *Admission to trading (LR 2.2.3R)*. Shares must be admitted to trading in order to be admitted to listing. As explained at **4.1**, companies seeking to float must not only apply to have their shares listed on the Official List, they must also apply to have their shares traded (for our purposes, on the Main Market). It is this condition to listing which links the two requirements and ensures a company cannot have shares which are admitted to listing but not to trading.

(d) *Transferability (LR 2.2.4R)*. In order to list successfully, shares must be marketable. Therefore they must be freely transferable. This means that rights attaching to shares which are common in private companies, such as rights of pre-emption on transfer and the right of directors to refuse to register share transfers, generally are not permitted in the articles of any company seeking to list. (Note, for the avoidance of confusion, that s 89 of the CA 1985 provides a right of pre-emption on the *allotment*, not *transfer*, of shares, and so does not affect this condition in any way.)

(e) *Market capitalisation (LR 2.2.7R)*. Market capitalisation refers to the number of issued shares in a company multiplied by the current market value of each share. It is a condition to listing that the expected aggregate market capitalisation of the shares to be listed should be at least £700,000. In practice, given the amount of time and costs a company must invest in the flotation process, it would be a disaster if the company raised only £700,000. The market capitalisation of shares to be issued on flotation is usually considerably in excess of this figure (for example, the Debenhams plc float in May 2006 raised £950 million). Nevertheless, the FSA has discretion to accept a lower threshold if it is satisfied that there will be an adequate market for the shares (LR 2.2.8G).

(f) *Whole class to be listed (LR 2.2.9R).* If a company has different classes of share (eg, ordinary shares and preference shares), it can choose to list one class and not another (eg, list only the ordinary shares), but it cannot choose to list only part of one class (eg, half of the ordinary shares); all shares of that class must be listed.

(g) *Prospectus (LR 2.2.10R).* A marketing document, known as a prospectus, must be approved by the FSA and published if s 85 of the FSMA 2000 applies to the listing (see **Chapter 6**). (Note that LR 2.2.11R refers to the need for listing particulars, rather than a prospectus, if LR 4 applies. This concerns the issue of specialist securities which are not the focus of this book.)

(h) *Accounts (LR 6.1.3R).* The company must have published or filed independently audited accounts for at least three years ending not more than six months before the date of the prospectus. The accounts must be consolidated for the company and all of its subsidiaries.

The FSA has discretion to accept accounts for a period of less than three years if satisfied that it is desirable in the interests of investors and that investors have the necessary information to make an informed judgement about the company and its listed shares (LR 6.1.13G).

(i) *Nature and duration of business activities (LR 6.1.4R).* The company must carry on an independent business as its main activity, and at least 75% of the company's business must be supported by a three-year trading record, during which the company must have controlled (and must still control, at the time of application for listing) the majority of its assets.

The FSA has discretion to accept a trading record shorter than three years on the basis outlined at (h) above (desirability and investors having necessary information), but it must be satisfied that there is an overriding reason for the company seeking a listing on the Official List as opposed to seeking admission to a market more suited to a company with a trading record of less than three years (LR 6.1.13G to LR 6.1.15G).

(j) *Working capital (LR 6.1.16R).* The company and its subsidiaries must have sufficient working capital for the group's requirements for at least 12 months from the date on which the prospectus is published.

(k) *Shares in public hands (LR 6.1.19R).* Following the flotation, at least 25% of the class of shares to be listed should be 'in public hands' across the European Economic Area (EEA). Listing Rule 6.1.19(4)R explains what are *not* considered to be 'public hands', including directors, anyone connected with a director (again, as defined by the Listing Rules) and anyone interested in shares which represent 5% or more of that class of share. The current EEA States are named in the definitions section of the Listing Rules.

The FSA has discretion to accept a percentage below 25% if it considers the market will nevertheless operate properly in view of the large number of shares of the same class and the extent of their distribution to the public (LR 6.1.20G).

(l) *Electronic settlement (LR 6.1.23R).* All shares listed must be capable of electronic settlement (see **2.5.3.1** above).

Application procedure

The Listing Rules set out a detailed application procedure, to which the company must adhere in order to have its shares admitted to listing. In particular, the company and its advisers must publish an important marketing document which gives potential investors information about the company so that they can make an informed decision about whether to invest. This document must comply with the requirements of the Prospectus Rules and be submitted to the FSA in accordance with the Listing Rules. Before the document can be published, the FSA must approve it. The marketing document required for a share issue is called a prospectus (where the issue is of specialist securities – encountered rarely in practice – it is called 'listing particulars'). **Chapter 6** examines the prospectus further.

4.3.1.2 Regulatory requirements for admission to trading

As noted at **4.3.1.1**, the Listing Rules provide that shares cannot be admitted to listing without also being admitted to trading. There is a parallel provision in para 1.1 of the Stock Exchange's Admission and Disclosure Standards (see **Appendix 1**), which provides that shares cannot be admitted to trading unless they are listed or proposed to be listed. As the two processes are tied together in this way, there is no need for the Stock Exchange to duplicate the onerous regulatory requirements for listing. Instead, the Stock Exchange can 'piggy-back' onto the requirements for listing, and can proceed safe in the knowledge that any company seeking to have its shares admitted to *trading* will have to fulfil the regulatory requirements for *listing* set out in the Listing Rules, and comply with the Prospectus Rules, before its application for admission to trading can succeed.

For this reason there are few formal regulatory requirements for admission to trading. Instead, the Stock Exchange's Admission and Disclosure Standards set out a very straightforward set of conditions (para 1), which state that the company must be in compliance with the Stock Exchange's requirements and that the Stock Exchange has discretion to refuse admission in certain circumstances (including the inability to comply with any bespoke condition the Stock Exchange imposes for admission). In effect, therefore, these conditions simply give the Stock Exchange the flexibility to supplement the requirements for listing should it wish. The Admission and Disclosure Standards also set out a basic admission procedure which is detailed at **5.3.7** and **5.4.3** below.

4.3.2 Commercial requirements

The regulatory requirements detailed in **4.3.1** above obviously exist to ensure that the company is in good shape for flotation. However, just because a company meets these criteria does not necessarily mean that investors will think the company is an attractive investment. As part of its preparation, the company needs to take an objective view of its business and consider whether, commercially, it is good enough to meet the expectations of potential investors. The sponsor and broker will be able to guide the company through the relevant considerations, but matters to consider include:

(a) Does the company have a good track record?
(b) Where is the company headed; does it have a viable business plan?
(c) Does the company have an effective board and management team?

(d) Is there anything about the company which could alienate investors? Is the company open to any criticism over corporate governance issues (see **Chapter 8**)? Is there an influential substantial shareholder? Have there been any accounting issues?

(e) Are the market conditions right for a float?

(f) Is this the right time in the company's development for a float, or would it be better to wait a couple of years?

4.4 Choosing how to float

The company must choose the most suitable method of flotation (also known as initial public offering, or IPO). There are four different ways in which a company seeking to float can list its shares, namely:

(a) offer for sale and/or subscription;

(b) a placing;

(c) an intermediaries offer; or

(d) simple admission.

Methods (a) to (c) above are defined in the Listing Rules, but there is no equivalent of OLR 4.2, which listed the specific methods by which a company could float. References to flotation by way of introduction have also been deleted, but it seems that it is still open to a company to float by simple admission (see **4.4.1.4**).

The Listing Rules no longer purport to deal exhaustively with methods of flotation; they concentrate on special features of certain methods, and new applicants should always discuss any other methods, not specifically referred to, with the FSA. (Other methods are available to list further shares once the company has floated; see **17.6**.)

The method chosen for flotation will depend on:

(a) the advantages and disadvantages of each method (see **4.4.1** below); and

(b) the type of offering, discussed at **4.4.2** below.

4.4.1 Methods of flotation

4.4.1.1 Offer for sale and/or subscription

With an offer for sale and/or subscription, the public are invited to take shares in the company. The offer might be to subscribe for shares not yet in issue (an 'offer to subscribe'), or to buy existing shares from the current shareholders in the company (an 'offer for sale'), or a combination of the two. Usually, the price for the shares is fixed at a level advised by the sponsor and the broker. It is crucial to set the price at the correct level: if it is too low the company will lose potential revenue and the offer will be oversubscribed, placing an administrative burden on the company (which will need to scale down the offer (eg, if X has applied for 200 shares he will be allotted only 100) or ballot to choose the successful applicants); if the price is too high the offer will be undersubscribed, the underwriters will take up the remaining shares and when dealing starts the share price will fall to reflect the lack of demand.

The advantages of an offer for sale and/or subscription are:

(a) This is the most appropriate method to raise large amounts of capital.

(b) Private investors can purchase shares. This means that the shareholder base will be broader (there will be more investors, holding fewer shares), which in turn facilitates the trading of the shares on the market (that is, the shares are more 'liquid').

The disadvantage is that this is the most expensive method of flotation.

4.4.1.2 Placing

A placing involves the marketing of shares (either by the allotment of new shares, or by the transfer of existing shares which are not yet listed, or by a combination of the two) to specified persons, or clients of the sponsor or other securities house assisting the placing. As such, LR Appendix 1.1 defines a placing as not involving an offer to the public (although note that this definition appears to be unconnected to s 85(1) of the FSMA 2000, where a placing may constitute an offer to the public unless it is structured (as it would be, in practice) to take advantage of an exemption – see **6.4.1.3**). Typically, the sponsor will place the shares for the company and the investors are relatively large investors and institutions which are clients of the sponsor. The agreement between the sponsor and the company will be recorded in a placing agreement.

The advantages of placing are:

(a) This is cheaper than an offer for sale and/or subscription (although still more expensive than a simple admission – see **4.4.1.4** below).

(b) The company has greater discretion to choose its shareholders.

(c) The company can raise capital (although typically not as much as it could raise through an offer for sale and/or subscription).

The disadvantage is that the shareholder base will be narrower (there will be fewer shareholders, holding more shares), which can impede trading in the company's shares (shares have less 'liquidity').

4.4.1.3 Intermediaries offer

An intermediaries offer is similar to a placing (see **4.4.1.2**). However, the shares can be marketed only to firms who comply with the definition of an intermediary in the FSA Handbook, which broadly means they are offered to stockbrokers independent of the sponsor and any securities house assisting with the float. On receipt of the shares, the stockbroker then acts as intermediary and sells them to clients in exchange for a commission.

The advantage of an intermediaries offer is that this method can achieve a wider spread of professional investors than a placing alone.

The disadvantage of an intermediaries offer is that it involves considerable administration and tends to be suitable only in very large floats. For this reason, intermediaries offers are quite rare.

4.4.1.4 Simple admission

Under the old regime, if a company had at least 25% of its shares owned by the public ('in public hands') and there was a reasonable number of shareholders, the company could float by way of an 'introduction' to the market. This involved simply admitting to listing and trading shares which were already in existence, without offering any further shares.

The theory behind this method of flotation was that, as the company's shares were already widely held and in public hands, the company had already demonstrated the marketability of its shares.

The advantages of an introduction were:

(a) this was the cheapest method of flotation;

(b) as it did not involve the issue or marketing of any shares, there was no need for underwriting (as underwriting covers the risk that shares offered are not taken up); and

(c) there was little need for advertising.

The disadvantages of an introduction were:

(a) it did not afford an opportunity to raise capital (as no shares are being issued, the company receives no consideration); and

(b) the method had a relatively low profile and did not afford the company the same opportunities for publicity as an offer for sale and/or subscription, placing or intermediaries offer. This could affect the marketability of the shares after flotation (although as the shares were widely held in public hands, and were therefore clearly marketable before flotation, often this would not be an issue).

Under the new regime, all references to an 'introduction' as a method of flotation have been deleted. However, it seems that it is still open to a company to float by the simple admission of its shares to listing and trading, without offering any further shares.

4.4.2 Type of offering

The four types of offering are summarised at **4.4.2.1** to **4.4.2.4** below. The different types of offering can be, and often are, combined, to ensure a distribution of investors. For example, the flotation of lastminute.com involved an institutional offering, a retail offering confined to registered users of the website, and a friends and family offering which gave preferential allocation to friends and business contacts of the directors.

4.4.2.1 Institutional offering

An institutional offering involves offering shares on flotation to sophisticated investors. Typically the offer is made by way of a placing, although it can also be made by way of intermediaries offer. The institutional offering can be made on a fixed price basis or a bookbuilt basis.

Fixed price

The investment bank uses its knowledge of the market to advise on a suitable fixed price per share which should be attractive to potential investors, but which is not too low. Typically the offering will be fully underwritten.

Bookbuilding

The investment bank sends potential investors an invitation to bid for shares before it sets the share price and the size of the offer. Usually the invitation to bid will set out a range of prices. The institutional investor will then bid, stating the number of shares it is willing to buy and at what price, or range of prices. The bids are revocable. The bank will keep a record ('book') of the bids it receives, which helps it to assess the appropriate share price and the likely level of demand for the shares. As the offering is not underwritten until all bids have been received, the underwriting risk is reduced to some extent, as the demand for the shares has already been tested among institutional investors, and the period of risk tends to be shorter. This means that usually the offering can be underwritten at a much lower commission rate than with a fixed price institutional offer.

4.4.2.2 Retail offering

A retail offering is when the shares are offered to members of the public. This can increase demand for the shares and can raise the profile of the company, because the media will market the float to the public. A retail offering is made by way of offer for sale and/or subscription.

As the public need more protection than institutional investors, a retail offering is more heavily regulated than an institutional offering. Usually a retail offering is made together with an institutional offering.

4.4.2.3 Employee offering

This is when the shares are offered to employees of the company (and often to employees of other group companies). The employees may be given preferential allocation rights. As referred to at **1.7.6** above, an employee offering allows the company to reward its employees. It also encourages employees to invest in the company, which then ensures they have a vested interest in the ongoing success of the company.

As with a retail offering, an employee offering can increase demand for the shares. The company will set eligibility criteria, such as age and length of service, to determine which employees can take up the offer. Usually an employee offering is made together with a retail offering, and will mirror its terms.

4.4.2.4 Friends and family offering

This is when the shares are offered to certain individuals. 'Friends and family' captures the essence of the nature of these individuals, but in practice other people, such as suppliers, customers and initial backers, can be offered shares as part of a friends and family offering. Usually an employee offering is made together with a retail offering, and will mirror its terms.

4.4.3 Summary

Table 4.1 below summarises the methods of flotation.

Table 4.1: Methods of flotation

	Offer for sale and/or subscription	Placing/intermediaries offer	Simple admission
Cost	Expensive	Cheaper	Cheapest
Raising capital	Considerable potential	Good potential	No potential
Liquidity of shares	High	Potentially low	No change: the number of shares in public hands remains the same
Type of offering	Retail	Institutional and retail	N/A: there is no offer

4.5 Restructuring the company

It is not always necessary to restructure a company before flotation. The company seeking to float may be in perfect shape. However, it is important that the company is in good order when it floats, and so in the year prior to the float the company must consider whether it needs to implement any changes. The following are some of the common areas of concern.

4.5.1 Group structure

In all likelihood the company seeking to float will form part of a wider group of companies. Before the company floats, the lawyers must make sure that this group has a rational structure. The most common structure is for the company seeking to float to be the holding company of the group. The other companies will then be subsidiaries, organised in a logical manner. A tour operator, for example, might group its travel agency companies together, its airline companies together and its foreign exchange companies together, as in **Figure 4.1** below.

Figure 4.1: Group structure

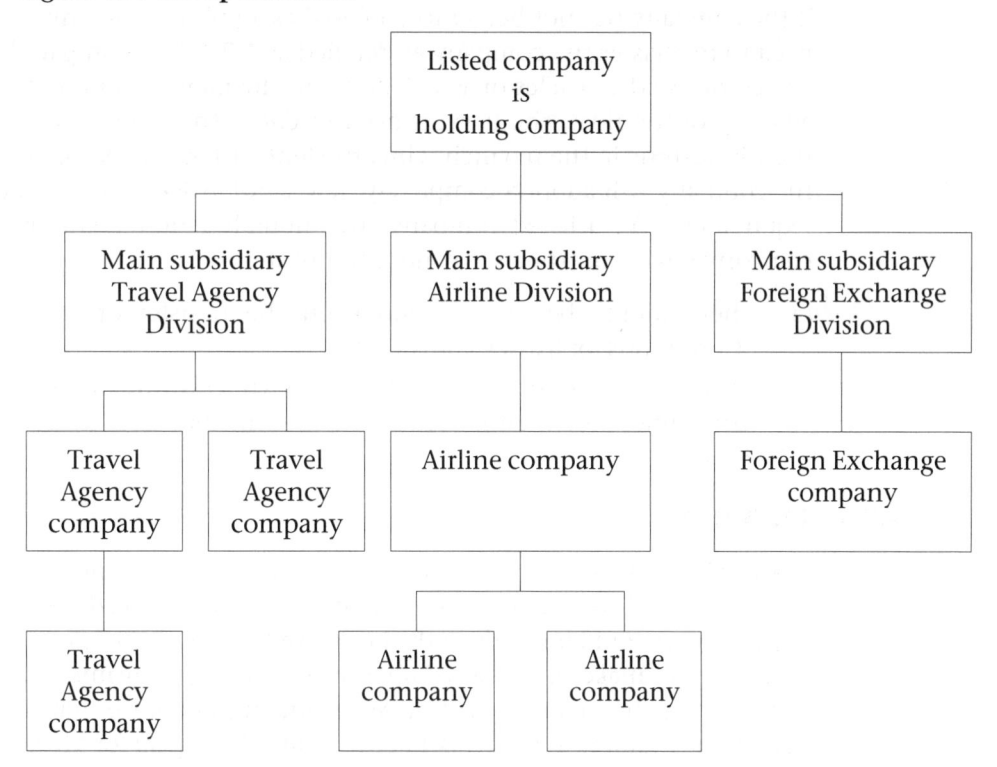

```
                    ┌──────────────────┐
                    │ Listed company   │
                    │       is         │
                    │ holding company  │
                    └────────┬─────────┘
        ┌────────────────────┼────────────────────┐
┌───────┴────────┐  ┌────────┴────────┐  ┌────────┴────────┐
│ Main subsidiary│  │ Main subsidiary │  │ Main subsidiary │
│ Travel Agency  │  │ Airline Division│  │ Foreign Exchange│
│   Division     │  │                 │  │    Division     │
└───────┬────────┘  └────────┬────────┘  └────────┬────────┘
   ┌────┴────┐               │                    │
┌──┴───┐ ┌───┴──┐       ┌────┴────┐         ┌─────┴─────┐
│Travel│ │Travel│       │ Airline │         │  Foreign  │
│Agency│ │Agency│       │ company │         │ Exchange  │
│  co. │ │  co. │       │         │         │  company  │
└──┬───┘ └──────┘       └────┬────┘         └───────────┘
   │                    ┌────┴────┐
┌──┴───┐           ┌────┴──┐ ┌────┴──┐
│Travel│           │Airline│ │Airline│
│Agency│           │company│ │company│
│  co. │           │       │ │       │
└──────┘           └───────┘ └───────┘
```

While this seems straightforward, in fact many businesses have grown in an unwieldy fashion, with little thought paid to group structure. The company wishing to float might be a subsidiary company. Subsidiaries may exist which are now dormant (for example, because all the assets were transferred out of a subsidiary by a previous business sale) and may need to be dissolved. It may be that the company is planning to acquire or dispose of a business or company. If this is the case, the transaction should be completed as soon as possible so that the company structure is stable in the run up to completion. The lawyers need to examine the group structure well in advance of the float and effect any necessary changes, possibly by way of share and/or asset transfers, company incorporation and/or dissolution, so that the company forms part of a logical group of companies.

4.5.2 Capital structure

As stated at **4.4.1.1** above, it is important that the offer price of the shares is fixed at the correct level. The share capital of the company may need to be altered to take account of this. For example, imagine that the advisers have stated that the offer price should be between £1.50 and £2.50 per share. However, the company has a current issued share capital of 25,000 shares of £1 each (nominal value) and is currently worth £500,000. This means that each share has a current value of £20. How could the shares be offered at the advised offer price without the company suffering a huge loss?

There are various solutions which the lawyers can effect. The simplest here would be to subdivide each share of £1 into 10 shares of 10p. This would mean that the company is still worth £500,000, but has an issued share capital of 250,000 shares of 10p each, so each share has a current value of £2.00, which is within the acceptable price range.

4.5.3 Company constitution

If the company has not been incorporated as a public company, the lawyers will need to re-register the company as detailed at **1.9.3**. The company's constitution will comprise the articles of association and the memorandum of association. In advance of the float, the lawyers need to check these documents to make sure there is nothing in them which is inconsistent with *listed* company status. Usually the company will adopt a completely new set of articles which comply with the requirements for a listed company. Two notable requirements with which the company's existing articles may not comply are:

(a) there should be no restrictions on the transfer of shares (see **4.3.1.1**, 'Conditions for listing' above); and

(b) each class of shares should have the same voting rights (often unlisted companies attach enhanced rights to some, but not all, shares in a certain class).

4.5.4 The board

As explained in **Chapter 8**, the board of a listed company needs to comply with various principles of corporate governance. The lawyers need to consider whether any changes should be made to the board well in advance of flotation, so that the company can make the required appointments and/or dismissals. In addition, it may be that the boards of subsidiary companies could be rationalised further (taking the example in **Figure 4.1** above, it may be logical for Mr X, a key manager in the Airline Division, to sit on the board of each of the companies in the Airline Division), or perhaps the records of board appointments at Companies House need to be updated.

4.5.5 Legal issues

As **Chapter 6** explores further, the flotation process involves considerable disclosure about the company. Any negative news may discourage potential investors. The lawyers will examine the company's history to identify any breaches of the law and, to the extent possible, remedy them (for example, ensure that all filings at Companies House are up to date). However, when the structure of the float is being planned, the lawyer also needs to be alert to any issues which may give rise to legal problems. Two potential problems lawyers need to bear in mind at this stage are:

(a) Might the flotation arrangements give rise to any financial assistance issues (see **Chapter 16**)?

(b) Section 100 of the CA 1985 provides that no share should be issued at a discount to its *nominal* value (see **13.3.1**).

4.6 What next?

This chapter has outlined the preliminary steps a company can take in advance of the flotation process. While it can take a year (or longer) for the company to prepare for flotation, the actual flotation process is much shorter (usually between three to six months). **Chapter 5** considers the flotation process.

Chapter 5

Flotation: The Flotation Process

5.1	Introduction	43
5.2	The flotation process	43
5.3	The lawyers' perspective	43
5.4	Key dates	54

5.1 Introduction

This chapter must be read in conjunction with **Chapter 4**, which explains what flotation is and the preliminary steps a company seeking to float must take, and **Chapter 6**, which examines the content of the vital float document. This chapter considers the flotation process itself, that is, the period of between 12 and 24 weeks before flotation when the company applies to the FSA for admission to listing and to the Stock Exchange for admission to trading. The preparation referred to in **Chapter 4**, which takes place in the year or two before the float, is generally referred to as 'pre-float preparation' rather than as part of the flotation process itself.

5.2 The flotation process

A simplified version of the flotation process (other than by way of a bookbuilt offer – see **4.4.2.1**) is set out in **Table 5.1** below. The timing of the process is by reference to impact day. This is the day when the flotation is announced to the market, the offer price is made known and the marketing document, the prospectus (see **Chapter 6**), is advertised. Impact day is not the day the company actually floats. The company floats when the FSA makes an Official List announcement (see **5.4.3.1** below) and the Stock Exchange publishes a London Stock Exchange Notice (see **5.4.3.2** below). Dealing in the company's shares can then begin. This day is known as admission day.

5.3 The lawyers' perspective

Table 5.1 provides a flavour of the flotation process. It shows the integration not only of the dual applications for listing and trading, but also of the advisers' roles. As mentioned previously, it is important that the lawyers appreciate not only who the company's other advisers are, but also what they do and when. Of course, there are some areas where the lawyers will have little or no involvement, and other areas where the lawyers' role will be vital. So where does the lawyers' work lie?

5.3.1 Agreeing the timetable and the list of documents

At the beginning of the flotation process the sponsors will draw up a draft timetable of the flotation process. Several factors drive the timetable. The FSA and the Stock Exchange have their own rules about timing, which cannot be changed. The company may have particular requirements as to timing, which may be inflexible (such as a desire to dovetail the float with a particular point in the company's financial year) or subject to change (for example, if the company's float is dependent on the occurrence of a certain event which has no fixed deadline). There are also practicalities to be taken into account, such as market movement and the fact that it is virtually impossible to reduce the flotation procedure to anything less than three months (even on the premise that the advisers require very little sleep). The lawyers will be asked to comment on the draft timetable and agree it. The sponsor will have the task of ensuring that the agreed timetable does not slip. The lawyers need to ensure that:

(a) there are no omissions in the timetable; and
(b) the timetable is viable.

The lawyers will also be involved early in the flotation process in commenting on the list of documents drawn up by the sponsor. Like the timetable, this will be used as a 'ready reckoner' by all advisers, and there are pitfalls in working to a documents list that has not been well considered and so is incomplete.

Table 5.1: The flotation process

24–52 weeks (6–12 months) before impact day	**Pre-float preparation.** Company chooses advisers, considers its suitability for flotation and the most appropriate method of flotation, and effects any necessary restructuring (see **Chapter 4**). Company takes decision to float.
12–24 weeks (3–6 months) before impact day	**The flotation process begins.** Company appoints advisers and meets sponsor. Sponsor drafts and advisers agree a timetable. Sponsor informs FSA about intended float. First marketing meetings with sponsor and broker. Initial planning meetings with advisers take place. Legal and financial due diligence begins (see **5.3.4**).
6–12 weeks (1.5–3 months) before impact day	**The process gathers momentum.** Key managers work full-time on float. Accountants produce long form and draft short form report (see **4.2.5**). Lawyers produce draft prospectus and begin the verification process (see **5.3.5** and **6.8**). Initial drafting meetings with advisers. Sponsor submits draft documentation relating to the approval of the prospectus (including 2 drafts of the prospectus) to the FSA (see **5.3.6.1** and **5.3.6.2**). Pay FSA fee for approval of the prospectus (see **5.3.6.2**). Sponsor and company have first meeting with the Stock Exchange. Initial pricing meetings with sponsor, broker, and any underwriters and sub-underwriters. Valuation of any assets. PR meetings with Financial PR consultants (sponsors, brokers and lawyers present).

2–6 weeks (the month before) impact day	**The process is intense.** Detailed drafting meetings, incorporating FSA's comments. Lawyers complete verification. Publish any pathfinder prospectus. Accountants and sponsors review cash-flow statements and any profit forecasts. Convene completion EGM. PR meetings. Ensure any ancillary documentation (re-registering the company, new memorandum and articles) is prepared. First meeting with registrars. Deadline for submitting draft prospectus to the FSA is 20 days before impact day (see **5.3.6.1**).
The week before impact day	**The preparation peaks.** Completion EGM. Directors' roadshows.
The day before impact day	**All documentation must be signed off:** (a) Verification meeting. (b) Completion board meeting. (c) Underwriting agreement signed and held in escrow. (d) Any other agreements (placing, offer for sale) signed and held in escrow. Submit final version of prospectus (and any ancillary documentation referred to in the prospectus) to the FSA. Pricing meeting to agree offer price.
Impact day	**Flotation announced.** Offer price is made public. FSA approves prospectus. Bulk print prospectus. Advertise prospectus. Release underwriting agreement from escrow.
The week after impact day	**Attend to formalities.** Continue to publish prospectus and advertise the flotation. Directors' roadshows. Submit '48 hour' documents to the FSA (see **5.3.6.4**) and 'Two day' documents to the Stock Exchange (see **5.3.7.2**) to apply for admission to listing and to trading. Pay FSA admission fee (see **5.3.6.4**). **Day of admissions hearings.** Submit 'on the day' documents to the FSA (see **5.3.6.5**). The FSA hears application for admission to listing. The Stock Exchange hears application for admission to trading. Open application lists and receive applications from investors (see **5.4.2.2**). Close application lists (see **5.4.2.2**).

2 weeks after impact day	**Admission week.** Announce basis of allotment. Despatch letters of acceptance/regret to investors. **Admission day.** The FSA makes an Official List announcement that shares have been admitted to listing (see **5.4.3.1**) and the Stock Exchange publishes a London Stock Exchange Notice that shares have been admitted to listing (see **5.4.3.2**). Dealing in shares commences. Stock Exchange invoice raised (see **5.3.7.3**).
3–5 weeks after impact day	**Formalities.** Receive letters of acceptance. Issue share certificates. Lodge information with the FSA (see **5.3.6.7**) and the Stock Exchange (see **5.3.7.4**). Pay Stock Exchange fee (see **5.3.7.3**).

Debenhams meets investors prior to float

Debenhams has begun testing the market for its flotation on the London Stock Exchange, which could see the department store valued at about £3bn, including debt.

The investment banks are now sounding out institutional investors and are expected to launch a formal roadshow in two weeks time.

The initial price range is expected to be set just after Easter, with final pricing at the beginning of May when the company launches on the LSE, paving the exit of the management, buy-out and private equity groups that bought into the group three years ago.

Debenhams will float on the back of half-year figures to the end of February. In the full year ended September, total sales rose 9.7 per cent to £2.09bn. The flotation is expected to be one of the biggest in the UK this year.

Debenhams appointed Citigroup and Merrill Lynch as joint global co-ordinators for the flotation in January and mandated Morgan Stanley and CSFB as bookrunners.

Since January, seven companies raising a total of £2.79bn have joined the UK's main market via initial public offerings - the highest level of activity since the first quarter of 2000 when eight companies floated, raising £524m, according to KPMG.

Debenhams - which is owned by Texas Pacific Group and CVC Capital, the buy-out groups, and the private equity wing of Merrill Lynch - is expected to use part of the proceeds from the float to pay down debt, which was £1.9bn at the end of August 2005.

Last summer, the group completed a £2bn re-financing, its second since it was acquired by the buy-out trio in 2003 for £1.9bn.

Since then, they have received capital repayments of about £1.3bn from Debenhams, more than twice their combined equity investment of £600m.

The management, led by Rob Templeman, the chief executive, owns up to 12 per cent of Debenhams' equity. TPG has 36 per cent, CVC just less than 26 per cent and Merrill Lynch 20 per cent.

The buy-out trio are expected to retain small shareholdings in Debenhams after the flotation.

Since the group was taken private, it has increased the number of stores from 120 to 200 and its market share has risen from 15.2 per cent to 18.6 per cent.

Source: *Financial Times*, 6 April 2006

5.3.2 Drafting documentation

The majority of the lawyers' time will be divided between drafting, meetings (see **5.3.3**) and due diligence (see **5.3.4**). The most important document the lawyers will draft is the main marketing document which is called the prospectus. This is a lengthy, detailed document and **Chapter 6** considers it in more detail.

There will also be ancillary documentation for the lawyers to draft. This could include documents to effect any restructuring (see **4.5** above). It will certainly include board minutes which record the board's progress through the flotation process, and the board's approval of the process and related documentation.

There will also be documentation relating to the method of flotation. If it is by way of an offer for sale and/or subscription (see **4.4.1**), an agreement (between the company, its directors, any selling shareholders and the sponsor) will be required. For a placing (see **4.4.1.2**), a placing agreement is needed (the parties are the same as for an offer for sale and/or subscription agreement).

The lawyers will also produce a sizeable document called a verification note (see **5.3.5** below).

5.3.3 Attending meetings

5.3.3.1 Drafting meetings

So many advisers, as well as the company, need to feed information into the prospectus that it becomes impossible for the adviser with responsibility for the document (the sponsor or the lawyers) to collate and rationalise comments on the draft by fax or telephone. Once the draft prospectus is reasonably progressed, there will be numerous drafting meetings, where all the parties can contribute and discuss their comments on the draft. If more than one party has comments on a certain point, those parties can agree revised wording. The meetings are productive, but can be very time-consuming.

5.3.3.2 Completion EGM

The completion EGM takes place a few days before impact day. The flotation itself does not require shareholder approval, but some matters which are vital to the preparation of the company for flotation often do require such approval. The completion EGM is the forum to obtain this consent. Usually, the lawyers will draft the notice to convene this meeting and ensure that it is sent out within the required time limits in the CA 1985 (14 clear days' notice if all resolutions are ordinary resolutions, 21 clear days' notice if there are any special resolutions). The lawyers will then draft the necessary resolutions and usually will attend the EGM to deal with any issues which may arise on the day; there is little scope for error.

The resolutions which may be necessary depend on the particular requirements of the company, but they may include:

(a) if the flotation involves an offer of shares by way of subscription (ie, it involves the company issuing shares):
  (i) increasing the authorised share capital,
  (ii) granting authority to allot under s 80 of the CA 1985,
  (iii) disapplying pre-emption rights on allotment (see **Chapter 14**);
(b) reorganising the share capital (see **4.5.2** above); and/or
(c) adopting new articles of association (see **4.5.3** above).

5.3.3.3 Verification meeting

The verification meeting takes place just before the completion board meeting. The board sign the verification note at this meeting (see **5.3.5** and **6.8** below).

5.3.3.4 Completion board meeting

The completion board meeting takes place the day before impact day. The directors will approve all the float documentation and the steps required to float the company. In particular, the board will resolve to:

(a) approve the terms of the prospectus;

(b) approve the terms of any ancillary documentation; and

(c) proceed with the flotation, and in particular the application for admission to listing and the application for admission to trading.

After the completion board meeting the prospectus is submitted to the FSA for final approval.

5.3.4 Due diligence

Due diligence, often referred to as 'DD' or 'due dil', is a time-consuming exercise that begins early on in the flotation process. The aim of due diligence is to investigate the company thoroughly and collate comprehensive information about it, which can then be used in the prospectus, the financial reports and other flotation documentation. The process also helps the advisers to identify the value of the company (and therefore fix the offer price) and any steps which are necessary to prepare the company for flotation, such as those outlined at **4.5** above.

Due diligence falls into three main categories:

(a) business due diligence;

(b) financial due diligence; and

(c) legal due diligence.

5.3.4.1 Business due diligence

This is an investigation into the commercial aspects of the company, such as its performance, competitors and strategy. The lawyers do not lead this due diligence, but they do need some of the results of it for the legal due diligence exercise (see **5.3.4.3**).

5.3.4.2 Financial due diligence

This is the investigation carried out by the reporting accountants so that they can produce the long form report, the short form report and the working capital report to which **4.2.5** above refers.

5.3.4.3 Legal due diligence

The lawyers have responsibility for the legal due diligence exercise. Trainees are heavily involved in this process. Basic information about the company will be obtained from public registries, such as Companies House, the Land Registry and Land Charges department, the Patent Office, the Trade Mark Registry and the Designs Registry, and the lawyers will also request copies of the company's statutory books. However, the scope of the legal due diligence exercise is very broad, and the lawyers really need access to the company's management to obtain the level of information required.

As should be clear from the timetable in **Table 5.1** above, the company's management are not time-rich during this stage of the flotation process, and so the lawyers need to make the most of the time that management makes available to them. The usual procedure is for the lawyers to draw up a document called a due diligence questionnaire, which has a heading for each area to be investigated and then lists questions requesting information and documentation relating to each area. The usual areas for investigation are:

(a) corporate – structure and constitution of the company;

(b) business and trading – including requests for all material agreements;

(c) assets;
(d) property;
(e) environmental;
(f) insurance;
(g) basic financial information – for example, requests for report and accounts, details of charges and insolvency events (the accountants will request more detailed information as part of the financial due diligence process referred to at **5.3.4.2**);
(h) intellectual property and information technology;
(i) employees;
(j) pensions;
(k) disputes;
(l) insurance; and
(m) any market-specific regulatory issues.

Each question will be given a number, as will each document requested, so that when the deluge of responses arrive, the lawyers can identify the question to which each response relates. It also means that the responses can be filed in an orderly and logical manner. The company can respond to the due diligence questionnaire in a variety of ways. Some responses can be faxed or posted; some need to be discussed face to face. In some circumstances the company may choose to set up a data room, where all the information provided in response to the questionnaire is kept. This has some advantages for the trainee responsible for due diligence; if there is no data room, often the trainee's office will become the storage place for all the due diligence files.

The lawyers must review all the responses very carefully. This involves disseminating the information to specialist teams of lawyers within the firm (for example, all the information will be received by the corporate lawyer who sent out the questionnaire, but when he or she receives a response relating to pensions, that response will be copied to the pensions department for their comment, and similarly information about employees will be copied to the employment department and so on). The corporate lawyer who co-ordinates the due diligence process must have excellent project management skills.

Once all the information has been reviewed by the appropriate specialists, the corporate lawyer must compile the product of the review into a due diligence report. The level of detail in the report can vary. Some reports focus solely on any problematic issues revealed by the due diligence process; others report in detail on all areas which were reviewed, even if they were problem-free. Either way, the most important part of the due diligence report from the company's point of view is what is known as the 'executive summary'. This is a chapter at the beginning of the report which states succinctly, and in layman's terms, the key issues revealed by due diligence and advises of any steps which are required before or after the float in relation to such issues. It is the executive summary which the directors will actually read and act upon. The detail in the rest of the report is still important, however, both for the lawyers (to record that the process was carried out thoroughly and diligently) and for the directors (to record the efforts they have made to ensure that the information in the prospectus complies with the requirements of the Prospectus Rules, the Listing Rules and the FSMA 2000 (see **Chapter 6**)).

5.3.5 Verification

While due diligence is undertaken early in the flotation process, to provide the information which goes into the prospectus, verification does not begin until the first draft of the prospectus is reasonably progressed. Verification is actually part of the due diligence process, but it has evolved into a discrete exercise. Again, trainees are heavily involved in verification. So what is it? Essentially it is a process which produces a written record (called a 'verification note') so that the company can support what it has said in the prospectus. The purpose of verification is to protect those who have responsibility for the prospectus (particularly the directors) (see **6.6** and **6.8** below).

Verification can involve a painstaking line-by line examination of the prospectus. In the verification note, each statement in the prospectus is phrased as a question, to test that it is true, accurate and not misleading. For example, if there is a line in the prospectus which states, 'We, X plc, are the largest chain of supermarkets in the world', the verification note would contain a question along the lines of, 'Please confirm that X plc is the largest chain of supermarkets in the world'. The answer to this question would then be recorded and copies of any supporting documentation would be annexed to the verification note. It may be, of course, that the answer to the question has already been provided as a response to the due diligence questionnaire. If so, management will not appreciate the lawyers asking the same question again. By the time the lawyers carry out verification, therefore, they must be familiar with the responses to the due diligence questionnaire. If the verification process raises questions not dealt with in the due diligence process (which is often not as detailed as the verification process) then the lawyer will send this new list of questions to the company, so management can collate the necessary information before meeting with the lawyers to provide the responses.

Alternatively, the verification process may be limited to ensuring the key selling messages in the prospectus are adequately supported and may ignore the more obvious statements.

The directors and anyone else who has formal responsibility for the prospectus (see **6.5**) cannot be available to all advisers at all times, so in practice they delegate responsibility for answering verification questions to key management (however, they cannot delegate ultimate responsibility for the prospectus).

The lawyers must be vigilant in ensuring that the responses the company provides to the due diligence or verification questionnaire really do answer the questions posed. For example, in the example above, a full answer would detail the basis of this pivotal statement: What is the measure of 'largest' – is the company referring to turnover, profits, number of outlets, number of employees?; What constitutes a 'chain' – two shops, or more?; How is 'supermarket' defined?; What is meant by 'world'?; and so on. The verifier must bear in mind all the elements of the statement and ensure he covers them adequately when drafting his response.

If the lawyers are not satisfied that the company can support the statement sufficiently, they will feed this information into the drafting meetings and the statement in the prospectus will be amended until the lawyers are satisfied that the statement can be supported. For example, the reference in the statement above to the 'largest' might be amended to 'one of the largest'.

As you might imagine, although this process is ultimately for the benefit of those responsible for the prospectus, including the directors, it is often a source of great frustration to those who have to provide the information, and each lawyer involved in the process (often a junior lawyer or a trainee) must have well developed social skills, a good sense of humour and a thick skin to survive the process. Each director, and any other person bearing responsibility for the prospectus (see **6.5**), will sign the verification note in the verification meeting (just before the completion board meeting), and it, together with the due diligence report, will provide reassurance to jittery directors as they accept responsibility for the prospectus in the completion board meeting itself.

5.3.6 Submission of documentation to the FSA

The sponsor will have the responsibility of ensuring that the documents listed below are submitted to the FSA, and that the documents listed at **5.3.7** below are submitted to the Stock Exchange, in a timely manner. However, each adviser, including the lawyers, needs to be aware of the deadlines.

The documents referred to at **5.3.6.1** (prospectus) and **5.3.6.2** (documents to be submitted with the prospectus) are required by Chapter 3 of the Prospectus Rules as part of the prospectus approval process. The documents referred to at **5.3.6.4** to **5.3.6.7** ('48 hour' documents, 'on the day' documents and information to be lodged after admission day) are required by Chapter 3 of the Listing Rules as part of the listing application procedure. (Under the old regime the prospectus approval process and the listing application procedure were both governed by the Old Listing Rules.)

5.3.6.1 Prospectus

The FSA must approve the prospectus, pursuant to the procedure set out in the Prospectus Rules, before it can be published (PR 3.1.10R). The company must submit two copies of the draft prospectus to the FSA, in hard copy or an agreed electronic format, at least 20 clear business days before impact day (PR 3.1.3R and PR 3.1.4R). The draft must be annotated in the margin to indicate compliance with all applicable requirements of Part VI of the FSMA 2000 and the Prospectus Rules (this is a common trainee task) (see **6.5.2.4**).

The FSA will provide its comments on the draft, and the document will be redrafted in the light of these comments. In practice, 20 days would not allow much time to deal with any comments the FSA might make. The earlier the draft is submitted the better, and the sponsor will aim to submit the draft some two to three months before impact day. On receipt of the FSA's comments, the document will be redrafted and resubmitted to the FSA. This process will continue until the FSA confirms it has no further comments. At this point, the prospectus can be printed and submitted in final form to the FSA for approval.

The FSA can approve the prospectus only when it is satisfied that it meets certain criteria set out in s 87 of the FSMA 2000, PR 3.1.7UK and PR 3.1.8G. In practice, the FSA will not give formal approval until impact day itself.

5.3.6.2 Documents to be submitted with the prospectus

As part of the process set out in the Prospectus Rules for approving the prospectus, the draft prospectus, referred to at **5.3.6.1** above, must be accompanied by the following (PR 3.1.3R):

(a) completed Form A (available from the UKLA section of the FSA website) in final form;

(b) the relevant fee; and

(c) drafts of the documents set out at PR 3.1.1R, namely:

    (i) a cross-referenced list identifying where each item in the PD Regulation (set out, for information, in Appendix 3 of the Prospectus Rules; see **3.5.1.1** and **6.5.2**) can be found in the prospectus (if the order of items in the prospectus does not coincide with the order set out in the PD Regulation – see PR 2.2.10EU, para 4),

    (ii) a letter identifying any items from the PD Regulation (set out in Appendix 3 of the Prospectus Rules) which are not applicable and so have not been included,

    (iii) a copy of any document incorporated into the prospectus by reference (annotated to indicate which item of the schedules and building blocks in the PD Regulation it relates to) (see **6.5.2.2**),

    (iv) information required by PR 2.5.3R (if requesting permission to omit information from the prospectus – see **6.5.2.3**),

    (v) an application form to buy or subscribe for shares,

    (vi) a copy of the board resolution allotting the shares (or confirmation that this will be submitted to the FSA within three working days of the date the prospectus is approved),

    (vii) contact details of individuals, sufficiently knowledgeable about the documents submitted, who can answer queries from the FSA between the hours of 7 am and 6 pm, and

    (viii) any other information the FSA specifically requires.

5.3.6.3 '10 day' documents

Those familiar with the old regime should note that the requirement under OLR 5.9(b)–(r) to submit certain draft documents at least 10 clear days before impact day has been deleted in the context of a flotation. (For a secondary issue, the documents referred to at **5.3.6.1** and **5.3.6.2** are '10 day' rather than '20 day' documents.).

5.3.6.4 '48 hour' documents

No later than midday, at least two business days before the FSA hears the company's application for the admission to listing, the company must submit to the FSA, in final form, the documents set out at LR 3.3.2R. These include:

(a) the application for admission to listing;

(b) the FSA-approved prospectus;

(c) any circular published in connection with the application;

(d) any FSA-approved supplementary prospectus; and

(e) a copy of the board resolution allotting the shares.

In addition, LR Appendix 2R provides that a fee becomes payable on the date the company makes its application for listing.

5.3.6.5 'On the day' documents

By 9 am on the day the FSA hears the company's application for admission to listing (see **5.4.3**), the company must lodge with the FSA the completed Shareholder Statement, signed by the sponsor (LR 3.3.3R). The form is available from the UKLA section of the FSA website.

5.3.6.6 Advertisements in connection with the listing application

Section 98 of the FSMA 2000 used to provide that advertisements and other information of a kind specified by the Old Listing Rules could not be issued in the UK until their contents had been approved by the FSA. However, on 1 July 2005, s 98 was repealed by para 9 of Sch 1 to the Prospectus Regulations 2005, so advertisements no longer need to be submitted to the FSA. Instead, the advertisements must conform to the requirements of PR 3.3, which include that a written advertisement should contain a bold, prominent statement that it is not a prospectus.

Advertisements may be subject to statutory control, however, under the financial promotion provisions of the FSMA 2000 (see **Chapter 12**).

5.3.6.7 Information to be lodged after admission day

The company must provide the following further information to the FSA as soon as practicable following the hearing of the application for admission to listing (LR 3.3.5R):

(a) the number of shares issued (and, where different, the total number of issued shares of that class);

(b) a completed Issuer's Declaration (available from the UKLA section of the FSA website) relating to compliance with legal requirements; and

(c) a copy of any CA 1985, s 429 notice (see **22.7** below).

The FSA also has discretion to request certain other documents relating to the company and its shares (LR 3.3.7R).

5.3.7 Submission of documents to the Stock Exchange

5.3.7.1 Application for admission to trading

New applicants (that is, all companies seeking to float) must complete the application form (appended to the Admission and Disclosure Standards as Form 1) and submit it to the Stock Exchange no later than 12.00 pm at least 10 business days before the requested date for the hearing of the company's application for admission to trading (para 2.5).

5.3.7.2 'Two day' documents

By 12.00 pm on the day which is at least two business days before the Stock Exchange hears the company's application for admission to trading, the company must submit to the Stock Exchange an electronic copy of the documents listed at para 2.6(b) and (c) of the Admission and Disclosure Standards (see **Appendix 1**), namely:

(a) the prospectus;

(b) any circular, announcement or other document relating to the issue;

(c) any notice of meeting referred to in any of the documents mentioned above; and

(d) any board resolution allotting the securities or authorising the issue (otherwise written confirmation that the shares have been allotted must be provided to the Stock Exchange by 7.30 am on the expected day of admission).

This deadline will correspond with that for the submission of the '48 hour' documents to the FSA (see **5.3.6.4**).

5.3.7.3 Fee payable on the day of the application hearing

The Stock Exchange will raise an invoice on admission, which the company must pay within 30 days (para 2.4).

5.3.7.4 Information to be lodged after admission day

The company must lodge a statement of the number of shares which were issued (and, where different, the total number of issued shares of that class) as soon as this information is available (para 2.7). This corresponds with the requirement of the FSA referred to at **5.3.6.7** above.

5.4 Key dates

5.4.1 Impact day

By the time of impact day all paperwork will have been finalised and the offer price will have been set (at the previous day's completion board meeting). The prospectus will have been submitted to the FSA at least 20 clear business days (probably more) before impact day (see **5.3.6.1** above). Section 87C of the FSMA 2000 provides that the FSA must notify the company whether it has decided to approve the prospectus before the end of the period of 20 working days beginning with the date the application is received. In practice, while the FSA will indicate that is has no further comments on the prospectus, actually it will formally approve the prospectus on impact day itself. Once it is approved, the prospectus must then be filed with the FSA under PR 3.2.1R.

(Those familiar with the old regime should note that there is no longer a requirement to file the prospectus at Companies House; s 83 of the FSMA 2000 was repealed by para 4 of Sch 1 to the Prospectus Regulations 2005.)

Other ancillary agreements, such as the offer for sale agreement, placing agreement and underwriting agreement, will be dated.

The float is 'live' with effect from impact day. Investors can apply to invest in the company. However, the company has not yet floated. Flotation is still conditional upon the FSA admitting the shares to listing and the Stock Exchange admitting the shares to trading, and this will not be done until admission day (see **5.4.3**). The shares in the company are not yet being traded.

5.4.2 Between impact day and admission day

5.4.2.1 Publishing the prospectus

Having been approved by and filed with the FSA, the prospectus can be published. The company must publish the prospectus at least six working days before the end of the offer (PR 3.2.3R). Prospectus Rule 3.2 governs the publication process.

There are four different ways to publish the prospectus:

(a) insert it into one or more newspapers circulated in the EEA State in which the offer is made (for our purposes, the UK);

(b) make it available to the public, in printed form, free of charge, at the offices of the market on which the shares are admitted to trading (for our purposes, at the Stock Exchange) or the company's registered office and at the office of any intermediary placing or selling the shares;

(c) make it available in electronic form on the company's website and on the website of any intermediary placing or selling the shares; or

(d) make it available in electronic form on the website of the regulated market where admission to trading is sought (for our purposes, the Stock Exchange website).

Note that the FSA made clear in issue 10 of its newsletter, *List!*, that there is no requirement for the prospectus to be published on the company's website, and that it is possible to publish in hard copy only. However, if the company chooses to publish in electronic form, pursuant to (c) or (d) above, it should be aware that, nevertheless, any investor is entitled to demand a free hard copy under PR 3.2.6R.

There is no longer a requirement for the company to advertise in a national newspaper the fact that the prospectus is available (OLR, para 8.7 has been deleted).

5.4.2.2 Applications for shares

Investors who have been impressed by the prospectus and wish to invest in the company will complete the application form attached to the prospectus and send it to the receiving bank (see **4.2.8**). The application form states the deadline by which the form must reach the receiving bank. This is usually 10.00 am on the day following the FSA's admission hearing. This deadline is known as the time the lists open.

If the offer is popular and over-subscribed, the lists will close at 10.01am. The board, advised by the sponsor, will then decide on the basis of allotment. If the offer is over-subscribed, clearly not all applicants will receive all the shares they applied for. The basis of allotment is a formula which decides the proportion of shares each applicant will receive. It varies according to the circumstances of the flotation, but it could be, for example, that each applicant receives, say, two-thirds of the number of shares applied for. On the other hand, it could be that the two-thirds ratio is applied only to those investors applying for significant numbers of shares, and those investors applying for small numbers of shares simply enter into a ballot system where they may be allotted their full quota, or none at all. Once the board has decided the basis of allotment, the company will make a formal announcement of the decision to investors.

If the offer is under-subscribed, the lists will remain open longer. The company will then inform the underwriters how many shares they need to take up.

The receiving bank will cash the applicants' cheques and account to the company, and any shareholders who sold existing shares, for the proceeds. The company will then send share certificates, or letters of acceptance (see **5.4.3.3** below), to the successful investors, and (in the event that the float is over-subscribed) will send letters of regret to the investors who applied but have not been successful in buying any or all of the shares for which they applied.

5.4.2.3 Admission hearings

The FSA will hear the application for admission to listing on the same day that the Stock Exchange hears the application for admission to trading. The Listing Rules provide that the FSA can refuse admission to listing in certain circumstances, such as if it considers that admission would be detrimental to investors' interests (LR 2.1.3G). The Admission and Disclosure Standards (see **Appendix 1**) also reserve the right for the Stock Exchange to refuse admission to trading if admission might be detrimental to the operation or reputation of the market (para 1.4). However, by the time the hearings take place, all the hard work on the float has been completed. The company and its advisers will have been in regular contact with

56   Public Companies and Equity Finance

the FSA and the Stock Exchange throughout the flotation process. It is very rare, therefore, for the FSA or the Stock Exchange to refuse admission at this stage.

5.4.3 Admission day

5.4.3.1 The Official List announcement

When the FSA is satisfied that it is prepared to admit the shares to listing, it must announce the admission through an RIS (LR 3.2.7G). In practice, the Official List issues an announcement, referred to as an Official List announcement or notice, to the Regulatory News Service (RNS) each day at 8am. This announcement refers to all companies who will list securities that day (both new applicants and companies which are already listed but which are listing further securities). The list does not distinguish the new applicants from the applicants which are already listed but which are listing further shares. Once the announcement is made (often referred to as 'going down the wire') the listing is effective, and dealing in the company's shares can begin. The company has floated.

An excerpt from the Official List announcement dated 9 May 2006 (the date Debenhams plc floated) is set out below:

NOTICE OF ADMISSION TO THE OFFICIAL LIST
09/05/2006 08:00 AM

The Financial Services Authority ("FSA") hereby admits the following securities to the Official List with effect from the time and date of this notice:-

AVIVA PLC
    9,538,374   Ordinary Shares of 25p each fully paid   (GB0002162385)

BALFOUR BEATTY PLC   After allotment
    526,315   Ordinary Shares of 50p each fully paid   (GB0000961622)

DEBENHAMS PLC
    858,974,359   Ordinary shares of 0.01p each fully paid   (GB00B126KH97)

If you have any queries relating to the above, please contact Listing Applications at the FSA on 020 7066 8333 Option 3.

Notes

– Dealing notices issued by the FSA in respect of admission of securities to the Official List must be read in conjunction with notices issued by the London Stock Exchange in respect of admission of securities to trading on its markets.

– SEDOL numbers which are allocated by the London Stock Exchange as a Stock Exchange identifier may be found on their dealing notice.

5.4.3.2 The London Stock Exchange Notice

Similarly, when the Stock Exchange is satisfied that it wishes to admit the shares to trading, it must announce the admission using its website (Admission and Disclosure Standards, para 2.1). In practice, this will go down the wire at the same time as the Official List announcement.

An excerpt from the London Stock Exchange Notice dated 9 May 2006 is set out below:

NOTICE OF ADMISSION TO TRADING ON THE LONDON STOCK EXCHANGE
09/05/2006 08:00

The following securities are admitted to trading on the LSE with effect from the time and date of this notice.

AVIVA PLC
9,538,374   Ordinary Shares of 25p each   (0-216-238)(GB0002162385)
             fully paid

BALFOUR BEATTY PLC   After Allotment
526,315   Ordinary Shares of 50p each   (0-096-162)(GB0000961622)
             fully paid

DEBENHAMS PLC

858,974,359 Ordinary Shares of 0.01p each (B126KH9)(GB00B126KH97)
             fully paid
             Classification Code 5373

If you have any queries relating to the above, please contact Issuer Implementation at the LSE on 020 7797 1614.

5.4.3.3 Dealings in shares

The company and its advisers will watch the market with bated breath on the first day of dealings. Ideally, the market price will rise a little above the offer price, meaning that the shares are trading at a small premium. This can suggest that the company pitched the offer price correctly. If the market price rises significantly, this may suggest that the offer price was something of a giveaway. If the market price drops below the offer price, the shares are trading at a discount, which may evidence a lack of demand for the shares. Sometimes, however, the first day of dealings can be distorted by market conditions altogether unrelated to the company.

5.4.3.4 Letters of acceptance

Sometimes the offer is structured so that initially successful applicants do not receive a share certificate, but a renounceable letter of acceptance. This is a bearer document, and the recipient can transfer title in the shares to someone else simply by handing them the letter (rather than by stock transfer form which is the usual method of transferring shares). Shares can be traded by way of renounceable letter for six weeks from admission day. The company's registrars will enter into the company's register of members whoever holds the letter at the end of that six-week period, and will send them a share certificate.

Letters of acceptance can be a useful method by which shares can be transferred easily at time when there tends to be substantial trading in shares. This also saves the registrars from issuing several new certificates in respect of the same shares.

5.4.4 After admission day

Admission day should not be seen as the end of a process but as the beginning of one. The company is now a listed company. The directors, key managers and the advisers will take the opportunity to celebrate the flotation together, and will then attempt to catch up on the many hours of sleep lost in the previous weeks. Then the company has to get back to business. The directors and management will return to their day-to-day business of running the company. However, life cannot simply return to how it was pre-float. There is now a whole new set of rules and regulations for the company to comply with. **Parts II, III and IV** of this book consider what life is like for a public company. Before we leave behind the flotation process, however, **Chapter 6** takes a detailed look at the main marketing document for any float: the prospectus.

Chapter 6
Flotation: the Prospectus

6.1	Introduction	59
6.2	Purpose	59
6.3	Prospectus or listing particulars?	59
6.4	The requirement for a prospectus	60
6.5	Content	64
6.6	Responsibility	73
6.7	Liability	74
6.8	Verification	77
6.9	Types of prospectus	78
6.10	Validity	79
6.11	Passporting	79

6.1 Introduction

The Prospectus Rules replace the Old Listing Rules relating to the preparation and content of a prospectus. The lawyer must refer to the Prospectus Rules and Pt VI of the FSMA 2000 in order to advise whether a prospectus is required and, if so, what information the document must contain.

6.2 Purpose

The prospectus is the main marketing document for the flotation process. Potential investors will read the document and (hopefully) the information it contains will encourage them to invest in the company. However, the company cannot be selective about what information to include in the document. The Prospectus Rules and the FSMA 2000 prescribe its contents. The lawyers must make sure that the document complies with all of the legal requirements as to content, but that it also retains the style of a marketing document which will attract investors. The prospectus is vital to the success of the float and, as is evident from **Chapter 5**, the drafting of this document takes up a large proportion of the flotation process.

6.3 Prospectus or listing particulars?

Until 1 July 2005, the main marketing document for a float involving the issue of shares might have been a prospectus or listing particulars. This depended on whether the float fell within the definition of s 84 of the FSMA 2000 (an offer of shares to the public in the UK for the first time before admission to the Official List). If the float fell within this definition then the marketing document was called a prospectus. If it fell outside of this definition then s 79 of the FSMA 2000 provided that the document was called a listing particulars.

In fact, in practice, the prospectus and listing particulars were the same in all but name, and the process of working out what the document should be called seemed pointless. Fortunately, the new regime implemented in 1 July 2005 recognised this, and made appropriate changes to the FSMA 2000, in particular substituting new ss 84 to 87.

The old distinction between a prospectus and listing particulars has now fallen away for transactions relating to shares. As of 1 July 2005, the marketing document required for any float involving the issue of shares will be a prospectus. Listing particulars are required only for the issue of certain specialist securities, which, typically, the lawyer will only encounter rarely in practice. As the focus of this book is on the listing of shares, it makes no further reference to listing particulars but focuses on the prospectus.

6.4 The requirement for a prospectus

Prospectus Rule 1.2.1UK and s 85 of the FSMA 2000 provide that a prospectus, approved by the FSA, is required if the company wishes to do either or both of the following events:

(a) *offer* transferable securities *to the public* in *the UK* (s 85(1)); or

(b) request *admission* of transferable securities to *trading* on a regulated market situated or operating *in the UK* (even if there is no offer to the public) (s 85(2)).

This book focuses on floats which involve the issue and/or sale of ordinary shares which will be listed on the Official List and admitted to trading on the Main Market. This type of float involves both (a) and (b) above; both s 85(1) and s 85(2) apply, and, subject to any exemptions, a prospectus will be required (one prospectus will suffice, as confirmed in issue 10 of *List!*). For the avoidance of confusion, note that even if the circumstances of a float meant that it involved only (a) or (b) above, then, subject to any exemptions, a prospectus would still be required.

The FSMA 2000 includes exemptions to s 85(1) and s 85(2). If these exemptions apply, a prospectus is not required, so the lawyer must be ready to advise how the float might be structured to avoid the need for this time-consuming and costly document.

It is important to recognise that the exemptions are drafted to apply specifically either to s 85(1) (offer to the public) or to s 85(2) (admission to trading). To take the example of our float, which involves both an offer to the public and admission to trading, even if it benefits from one of the 'offer to the public' exemptions, it will still require a prospectus unless one of the 'admission to trading' exemptions also applies.

Paragraphs **6.4.1** and **6.4.2** below examine the criteria of s 85(1) and s 85(2), and consider the different exemptions which apply to them.

6.4.1 Section 85(1): offering transferable securities to the public in the UK

Section 85(1) refers to all public offers of shares, including shares not listed on the Official List (such as shares admitted to the AIM). This is wider than the old s 84 of the FSMA 2000, which was restricted to the public offer of shares listed on the Official List. (Consequently, the Public Offers of Securities Regulations 1995, which, under the old regime, regulated public offers of shares not listed on the Official List, have been revoked by para 2 of Sch 3 to the Prospectus Regulations.)

Section 103 of the FSMA 2000 provides guidance on the interpretation of the s 85(1) criteria.

6.4.1.1 Offer

There will be an offer if there is a communication to any person which presents sufficient information, on the shares to be offered and the terms on which they are offered, to enable an investor to decide to buy or subscribe for those shares (s 102B(1)). The communication may be made in any form and by any means (s 102B(3)).

A flotation by way of an offer for sale and/or subscription, placing or intermediaries offer will fulfil this criterion.

6.4.1.2 Transferable securities

Section 102A defines 'transferable security' by reference to the Investment Services Directive. For our purposes it is enough to note that this term includes ordinary shares. Therefore our example of a flotation involving the issue or sale of ordinary shares will fulfil this criterion.

6.4.1.3 To the public

Under the old regime, Sch 11 to the FSMA 2000 defined 'to the public'. As of 1 July 2005, Sch 11 was repealed by para 16 of Sch 1 to the Prospectus Regulations 2005. Under the new regime, s 102B(2) of the FSMA 2000 provides that if the offer is made to 'a person in the United Kingdom' it is made to the public in the UK.

It is likely that an offer for sale or subscription will fulfil this criterion, but that a placing and intermediaries offer will be structured to fall within one of the exemptions, such as the 'qualified investors' or '100 persons' exemption, so that they do not fulfil this criterion. Note that LR Appendix 1.1 defines a placing as *not* constituting a public offer; however, this appears to be unconnected to the definition of a public offer under the FSMA 2000.

6.4.1.4 In the UK

As referred to at **6.4.1.3** above, s 102B(2) of the FSMA 2000 makes clear that this criterion is satisfied if any recipient of the offer is in the UK.

The list of recipients of any offer for sale and/or subscription, placing or intermediaries offer must be analysed to see if this criterion is fulfilled.

6.4.1.5 Exemptions

The public offer exemptions are set out in s 85(5) (which in turn refers to Sch 11A of the FSMA 2000 and PR 1.2.2R) and s 86 of the FSMA 2000. The principal exemptions are as follows:

(a) *Offers to qualified investors (FSMA 2000, s 86(1)(a))*. The FSA maintains a register of qualified investors (the 'QIR') which it makes available to companies and their agents exclusively for the purpose of making an offer of shares to qualified investors only. Certain individuals and small and medium-sized enterprises can self-certify that they are qualified investors. (Those familiar with the old regime will remember the old 'professional investor' exemption under para 3 of Sch 11 to the FSMA 2000. The new qualified investor exemption replaces that exemption.)

(b) *Offers to fewer than 100 persons (who are not qualified investors) in each EEA State (FSMA 2000, s 86(1)(b))*. The Treasury has confirmed that there is no need to include the clients of discretionary brokers in calculating the number of persons to whom the offer is made.

(c) *Offers involving significant investment by each investor (FSMA 2000, s 86(1)(c) and (d))*. This will apply where each investor invests a minimum total consideration of €50,000 or where the shares being offered are denominated in amounts of at least €50,000 (or equivalent).

(d) *Small offers*. There are two exemptions relating to small offers. First, s 86(1)(c) of the FSMA 2000 exempts offers where the total consideration for the *transferable securities* is less than €100,000. Secondly, s 85(5)(a) of and para 9 of Sch 11A to the FSMA 2000 exempt offers where the total consideration for the *offer* is less than €2,500,000. The second exemption was inserted into the Directive at a very late stage and there has been little commentary on the interaction between the two small offer exemptions.

(e) *Share swops (PR 1.2.2R(1))*. The issue of shares must not involve any increase in the company's issued share capital.

(f) *Offers in conjunction with takeovers (by way of share for share exchange) or mergers (PR 1.2.2R(2) and (3))*. However, a document must be available which contains information which the FSA regards as equivalent to that of a prospectus (referred to as an 'equivalent document').

(g) *Bonus issues and scrip dividends of a class of shares already listed (PR 1.2.2R(4))*. However, a document must be available which contains basic information about the number and type of shares offered, and the reasons for and the detail of the offer.

(h) *Offers by listed companies to employees and/or directors (PR 1.2.2R(5))*.

6.4.2 Section 85(2): admitting transferable securities to trading on a regulated market

6.4.2.1 Transferable securities

The definition of transferable securities is discussed at **6.4.1.2** above. Ordinary shares are transferable securities, so our float will fulfil this criterion.

6.4.2.2 Admit to trading

The type of flotation which is the focus of this book involves the admission of shares to trading (on the Main Market) and so fulfils this criterion.

6.4.2.3 Regulated market

This is defined as having the meaning given in Art 1.13 of the Investment Services Directive. This includes the Main Market but does not include AIM.

Our float will fulfil this criterion. (Note, however, that an AIM float will require a prospectus only if s 85(1) applies, ie that shares are being offered to the public and no exemptions apply.)

6.4.2.4 Exemptions

The admission to trading exemptions are set out in s 85(6) (which in turn refers to Pt 1 of Sch 11A to the FSMA 2000 and PR 1.2.3R). The principal exemptions are as follows:

(a) *Admission of shares representing less than 10% of shares of the same class already admitted to trading on the same market (PR 1.2.3R(1))*. Issue 10 of *List!* confirms that the 10% limit is applied over a rolling 12-month period (after 1 July 2005). This means that any shares admitted over the previous 12 months, which have not benefited from any *other* exemption, would count towards the 10%.

Example

Imagine a company has 200 shares in issue on 28 April 2005. It issues a further 10 shares on 2 June. On 5 July it issued 20 shares to employees under the admission to trading exemption referred to at (e) below. On 5 January 2007 it issues a further 15 shares which are placed with institutions, under the offer to the public exemption referred to at (a) in **6.4.1.5** above. The calculation to work out whether the 10% admission to trading exemption applies to this issue of 15 shares is as follows:

$$\frac{\text{Number shares to be issued (including shares admitted over last 12 mths (or after 1 July 2005) which have not benefited from any other exemption)}}{\text{Number of shares of the same class already admitted to trading on the same market}}$$

that is,

$$\frac{15 \text{ (other issues within the last 12 months either preceded 1 July 2005 or benefited from another exemption)}}{230}$$

that is, 6.5%. This issue of 15 shares would therefore be covered by the 10% exemption.

One month later, the company issues a further 6 shares. The calculation is now:

$$\frac{15 \text{ (this was covered by the 10\% exemption, not any other exemption, so counts)} + 6}{245}$$

that is, 6.1%, so this issue is covered by the 10% exemption.

One month later, the company issues a further 10 shares. The calculation is:

$$\frac{15 + 6 + 10}{251}$$

that is, 12.3%, so this issue is outside the 10% exemption and will require a prospectus.

(b) *Share swops (PR 1.2.3R(2))*. As **6.4.1.5(e)** above.

(c) *Offers in conjunction with takeovers (by way of share for share exchange) or mergers (PR 1.2.3R(3) and (4))*. As at **6.4.1.5(f)** an equivalent document must be available.

(d) *Bonus issues and scrip dividends of a class of shares already listed (PR 1.2.3R(5))*. As **6.4.1.5(g)** above.

(e) *Offers to employees and/or directors of a class already listed (PR 1.2.3R(6))*.

(f) *Shares of a class already listed resulting from the exercise of exchange or conversion rights (PR 1.2.3R(7))*.

(g) *Shares already admitted to trading on another regulated market (subject to conditions) (PR 1.2.3R(8))*.

6.4.3 Conclusion

Having analysed the criteria, we can conclude that:

(a) a float;

(b) involving the offer or sale of ordinary shares;

(c) which will be listed on the Official List and admitted to trading on the Main Market,

will require a prospectus, *unless* it benefits from *both*:

(d) an 'offer to the public' exemption; and

(e) an 'admission to trading' exemption.

In practice, as the table below shows, it is unlikely that a float can be structured to benefit from the required combination of exemptions.

Table 6.1

Method of flotation	Public offer under s 85(1)?	Admission to trading under s 85(2)?	Prospectus required?
Offer for subscription and/or sale	Yes. '100 persons' exemption possible but highly unlikely, given size of most retail offers.	Yes. '10%' exemption irrelevant in context of flotation, as no shares currently admitted to trading.	Yes.
Placing	Yes (note that LR Appendix 1.1 defines a placing as *not* constituting a public offer; however, this appears to be unconnected to the definition of a public offer under the FSMA 2000 (see 6.4.1.3)). Likely to benefit from 'qualified investor' or '100 persons' exemption.	Yes. '10%' exemption irrelevant in context of flotation, as no shares currently admitted to trading.	Yes.
Intermediaries offer	Yes. Likely to benefit from 'qualified investor' or '100 persons' exemption.	Yes. '10%' exemption irrelevant in context of flotation, as no shares currently admitted to trading.	Yes.
Simple admission with no offer	No. No offer involved.	Yes. '10%' exemption irrelevant in context of flotation, as no shares currently admitted to trading.	Yes.

6.5 Content

The FSMA 2000 and the Prospectus Rules prescribe the content of a prospectus. The new regime has not changed significantly the content requirements set out in the Old Listing Rules. There are, however, a handful of key changes introduced by the new regime and I have drawn attention to them when referred to below.

Reading about the content requirements of a prospectus is helpful, but there is no substitute for having a look at the real thing. I would recommend checking the websites of companies which have recently floated as, increasingly, companies are posting the prospectus and other documents, such as RNS announcements, on the area of their website aimed at shareholders (sometimes entitled 'investor relations'). At the time of writing, the Standard Life plc prospectus (comprising a prospectus summary, registration document and securities note) was available on the 'downloads section' of its shareholder website.

6.5.1 General content requirements

As set out in PR 2.1.1UK, s 87A(2), (3) and (4) of the FSMA 2000 provide for the general content requirements of a prospectus. These provisions, introduced in 1 July 2005 by the Prospectus Regulations 2005, require that any prospectus must:

(a) contain information necessary to enable investors to make an informed assessment of the assets and liabilities, financial position, profits and losses and prospects of the company, and the rights attaching to any securities (for our purposes, shares) (s 87A(2)); and

(b) present the information referred to at (a) above in a form which is comprehensible and easy to analyse (s 87A(3)).

The information must be prepared having regard to the particular nature of the shares and the company (one prospectus does not fit all) (s 87A(4)). The FSA must not approve a prospectus unless it is satisfied that such general content requirements have been met (s 87A(1)).

6.5.2 Specific content requirements

As explained at **3.5.1.1**, the requirements regarding the content of a prospectus (other than the summary – see **6.5.2.1** below) are set out in the articles and annexes of the PD Regulation. These requirements are duplicated in the Prospectus Rules (the articles are set out at PR 2.3.1EU and the annexes are replicated at Appendix 3 of the Prospectus Rules).

Prospectus Rule 2.3 sets out the minimum information to be included in a prospectus. This rule refers to the 'schedules' and 'building blocks' of the annexes of the PD Regulation (and therefore of Appendix 3 of the Prospectus Rules), which are defined as follows:

> *Schedule* a list of minimum information requirements adapted to the particular nature of the different types of issuers and/or the different securities involved.
>
> *Building block* a list of additional information requirements, not included in one of the schedules, to be added to one or more schedules, as the case may be, depending on the type of instrument and/or transaction for which a prospectus ... is drawn up.

In other words, the Prospectus Rules contain various minimum content requirements which may apply, depending on the type of company issuing shares and the nature of the shares. Not all of the information will be required in every prospectus. It is the lawyer's job to select which minimum content requirements are relevant for the particular transaction.

How can the lawyer find the content requirements required specifically for a float? In Annex XVIII of the PD Regulation (again, set out in Appendix 3 of the Prospectus Rules) there is a table which summarises which schedules and building blocks are required, depending on the circumstances of the issue (PR 2.3.1EU, citing PD Regulation, art 21).

For a straightforward float of ordinary shares the appropriate schedules will be the share schedules (Annexes I and III) and the pro forma financial information building block (Annex II). (The other annexes are relevant, for example, for the issue of debt securities, derivatives, depositary receipts or guarantees, or if the issuer falls within a certain category, for example it is a Member State.)

6.5.2.1 Format of the prospectus

Under the old regime, a prospectus comprised a single document. Under the new regime, the company has a choice to draw up the following three separate documents (PR 2.2.1R):

(a) a summary (PR 2.1.2UK);

(b) a registration document (PR 2.2.2R); and

(c) a securities note (PR 2.2.2R),

or to continue with the single document format used under the old regime, but which now must include a separate summary. Prospectus Rule 2.2.10EU sets out brief requirements as to the basic format of the prospectus.

It is intended that the option to draw up three separate documents will assist companies who are regular issuers of shares in circumstances which require a prospectus (see **6.4** above), as PR 5.1.4 provides that any approved registration document remains valid for up to 12 months (subject to the requirement to update). This means that once a registration document has been approved, any further issue of shares will require only a new summary and securities note. However, as explained at **6.10**, the new securities note must also update the registration document as to any material changes. This means that due diligence is still required each time the company wishes to use its registration document. As a result of this, and the fact that a bespoke prospectus tends to have advantages from a marketing perspective, to date companies have continued to use the single document format.

The summary, registration document and securities note are considered in more detail below. Note that even if the company chooses the single document format, the document must include a summary and the information required by the registration document and securities note.

The summary

Prospectus Rule 2.1.2UK provides that in the UK, whichever format of prospectus is selected, the prospectus must include a summary. This must set out, briefly and in non-technical language, the essential characteristics of, and any risks associated with, the company and the shares to which the prospectus relates. The requirement for a summary is one of the key changes introduced by the new regime, although, in practice, under the old regime it was customary to include a 'key information' section in the prospectus, which is a similar concept to the summary. While it was common for the 'key information' section to make cross-references to the prospectus, however, this will not be appropriate practice in the summary, which must be self-contained.

Prospectus Rules 2.1.4EU to 2.1.7R explain how the content of the summary will be determined. The following are the key requirements:

(a) It is for 'the issuer, the offeror or the person asking for admission to trading' (usually the company) to decide the content of the summary (PR 2.1.4EU).

(b) The summary should contain a warning that any prospective investor should read the full prospectus, not just the summary, before deciding to invest (PR 2.1.7R). (In practice, of course, many investors will choose not to heed this warning.)

(c) The summary generally should not exceed 2,500 words (PR 2.1.5G), which is a commonsense approach to prevent the summary from becoming unwieldy, but may be difficult to achieve in practice. In issue 10 of *List!*, the FSA commented that a summary could exceed this word limit when the particularly complex nature of the company or the securities would make it difficult to meet the content requirements of the summary within 2,500 words. Even in such circumstances, however, the summary should not exceed excessively the 2,500 word limit.

Note that the summary has particular importance under the passporting procedure (see **6.11** below) as it is the only part of the prospectus which another Member State can request to be translated.

The onerous task of deciding what to include in the summary is relieved somewhat by the knowledge that limited liability attaches to it (see **6.7.1.1**).

The registration document

The registration document must provide information about the company. Prospectus Rule 2.3.1EU provides that it should contain the information set out in Annex I of the PD Regulation (set out at Appendix 3 of the Prospectus Rules). The main content requirements of Annex I are summarised below, but this is intended to provide only a flavour of the content of the prospectus. For comprehensive details of the content requirements, reference must be made to the Prospectus Rules themselves. The numerical paragraph references below correspond to the paragraph numbers of Annex I.

1. *Persons responsible*. The document must identify all persons responsible for the information given in the registration document, and those persons must declare in the document that:

    having taken all reasonable care to ensure that such is the case, the information contained in the registration document is, to the best of their knowledge, in accordance with the facts and contains no omission likely to affect its import.

    This is referred to as the 'responsibility statement' and it is broadly similar as to the statement required under the old regime (OLR 6.A.3). (Paragraphs **6.6** and **6.7** below discuss further the issues of responsibility and liability for the document.)

2. *Statutory auditors*. The document must identify the company's auditors.

3. *Selected financial information*. Certain financial information must be provided.

4. *Risk factors*. A section headed 'risk factors' must include prominent disclosure of any and all risk factors which are specific to the company or its industry. This requirement is a key change introduced by the new regime.

5. *Information about the issuer*. The document must refer to the company's history and development, including information such as its date of incorporation, the address of its registered office and important events in the development of the company's business. The document must also contain a description of the company's principal investments, existing and future.

6. *Business overview.* The principal activities and markets of the business must be described.
7. *Organisational structure.* The document must detail if the issuer is part of a group, a brief description of the group and the company's position within that group. It must also identify the company's significant subsidiaries.
8. *Property, plant and equipment.* The company's existing and planned material tangible fixed assets, such as leased properties, and any encumbrances to which they are subject, must be listed. The document must also highlight any environmental issues which may affect the company's ability to use such assets.
9. *Operating and financial review.* The document must include a description of the company's financial condition and other information which has materially affected, or could materially affect, the issuer's operations. In each case information is required for each of the years covered by the audited financial statements. This requirement is a key change introduced by the new regime.
10. *Capital resources.* The document must detail the company's capital resources, including cash flow, borrowing requirements, any restrictions on the use of capital resources and information regarding the anticipated sources of funds for any future investments.
11. *Research and development, patents and licences.* Information must be provided about the company's research and development policy.
12. *Trend information.* Information is required about the most significant trends in production, sales and inventory, costs and selling prices, and any known trends or uncertainties which are reasonably likely to have a material effect on the company's prospects for the current financial year.
13. *Profit forecasts or estimates.* If an issuer chooses to include a profit forecast in the prospectus, then it must also provide the information set out in para 13 of Annex I, including a statement setting out the assumptions on which the forecast is based and a report by the company's auditors or independent accountants that the forecast has been properly compiled. Under the old regime the inclusion of profit forecasts was avoided because of similar content requirements unless absolutely necessary (eg, because previous profits were very weak or out of date), and undoubtedly this will continue to be the approach under the new regime; the company and its advisers have enough to do without adding this to their lists of tasks.
14. *Administrative, management and supervisory bodies and senior management.* The document must provide information about the company's management, particularly the directors, but also potentially any founders (if the company is less than five years' old) and senior managers who are relevant to establishing that the company has appropriate expertise and experience for the management of the company's business. Some of this information could be seen as rather 'personal', such as details of any unspent convictions in relation to fraudulent offences, details of any insolvency events and details of any public criticisms of any director by any statutory or regulatory bodies. Ideally there will be no skeletons hiding in the directors' (or, if relevant, founders' or senior managers') closets which need to be aired in the prospectus (and if there are not, an appropriate 'negative statement' must be made in the document). However, if there are, then the due diligence process should ensure that they come to light sooner rather than later, so that the financial PR consultants have time to consider how they can manage the issues in a way that will not stop potential investors from investing in the

company. Details of any conflict of interest between any of the people covered by para 14 must also be disclosed (and if there are none, an appropriate negative statement must be made).

15. *Remuneration and benefits.* Details of the remuneration (for the last full financial year) and benefits of the directors (and, if relevant, founders and senior managers) must be provided.

16. *Board practices.* Certain information about the running of the board, including periods of service, service contract information and corporate governance compliance (see **Chapter 8**), must be included.

17. *Employees.* The document must include information relating to employees, including the number of employees, information regarding their share or share option ownership, and a description of any arrangements for involving the employees in the company's capital.

18. *Major shareholders.* The document must identify any major shareholder of the company (that is, anyone other than a director who has an interest in the company's capital or voting rights which is notifiable under national law (3% in the UK – see **Chapter 15**), and provide other information as to such shareholders, such as whether or not they have different voting rights.

19. *Related party transactions.* Details of any related party transactions (see **19.5**) must be provided, together with the amount to which such transactions form part of the company's turnover. This is a key change introduced by the new regime.

20. *Financial information concerning the issuer's assets and liabilities, financial position and profits and losses.* The prospectus must contain a significant amount of financial information, prepared with the help of the reporting accounts. Paragraph **4.2.5** above refers to some of this information. In particular, the short form report, containing information relating to the profits and losses, assets and liabilities, financial record and position of the group for the period of three years before the float, must form part of the document. The document must also include a statement as to whether or not there has been any significant change in the financial or trading position of the group since the date to which the last accounts or interim statements were made up. This paragraph also refers to the inclusion of the 'building block' pro forma financial information required by Annex II.

Information is also required, by para 20.8, about any litigation or arbitration (including any pending or threatened) which might have, or has had, a significant effect on the group's financial position. This can be a very sensitive area for the company, which would not usually consider publicising litigation, or the threat of it. However, the Prospectus Rules are very clear that it must do so, subject to the 'significant effect' qualification. If the company does not consider it has anything to disclose in this regard, it must include a 'negative statement' to that effect.

Information about the company's dividend policy must also be included. Note that a key change introduced by the new regime is that unaudited financial information can now be included in a prospectus, subject to certain conditions.

21. *Additional information.* The document must include information about the company's share capital, such as the authorised and issued share capital, and certain details of the history of the company's share capital. In addition, various information about the company's memorandum and articles of association must be provided, including a description of the company's objects, a description of the rights attaching to each class of existing shares

and a description of certain issues in the articles, such as any change of control clause or any conditions governing changes in capital which are more stringent than those required by law.

22. *Material contracts.* The document should summarise the principal contents of certain contracts referred to as 'material contracts', namely those contracts which have been entered into other than in the ordinary course of business by the company or any member of the company's group:

    (i) in the two-year period preceding the publication of the document (if the contract is material); or

    (ii) at any time (if the contract provides the company or any member of the company's group with any entitlement or obligation which is still material to the company or the group as at the date the prospectus is published).

    The lawyers will help the company to identify which documents fall within the definition and draft the summaries of those contracts for inclusion in the document.

23. *Third party information and statement by experts and declarations of any interest.* If the document includes a statement or report attributed to a person as an expert, it must provide information about the expert. If the document contains any information sourced from a third party, the source of that information must be identified, and confirmation must be provided that the information has been reproduced accurately and that, as far as the issuer is aware, no facts have been omitted which would render the information inaccurate or misleading. This is another key change introduced by the new regime.

24. *Documents on display.* The document should include a statement that, for the life of the registration document, certain documents (set out in para 24) are available at a named location for inspection. These documents include the company's memorandum and articles of association and historical financial information. The lawyers will assist the company in creating and indexing the files of display documents.

25. *Information on holdings.* Information must be provided about any undertakings in which the company holds shares which are likely to have a significant effect on the assessment of the company's finances.

The securities note

The securities note must contain information about the securities (for our purposes, shares) to be offered or admitted. Prospectus Rule 2.3.1EU provides that the securities note should contain the information set out in Annex III of the PD Regulation (set out at Appendix 3 of the Prospectus Rules). The main content requirements of Annex III are summarised below. Again this is intended to provide only a flavour of the content of the prospectus, and for a comprehensive list of the content requirements, you should refer to the Prospectus Rules themselves. The numerical paragraph references below correspond to the paragraph numbers of Annex III.

1. *Persons responsible.* As with the registration document, a responsibility statement must be included; this time by all those responsible for the information given in the prospectus.

2. *Risk factors.* Again, there is a requirement similar to that which exists for the registration document, that the securities note must include prominent disclosure, under the section headed 'risk factors', of risk factors that are

material to the shares being offered and/or admitted. This is to enable investors to assess the market risk associated with the shares.

3. *Key information.* The document must include what is referred to as the 'working capital statement', namely a statement that, in the company's opinion, the working capital is sufficient for the issuer's present requirements or, if not, how it proposes to provide the additional working capital it requires. Of course, this ensures the directors address their minds to the ability of the company to thrive, or at least survive, after flotation, and address the likelihood of insolvency problems after the float. (When a company goes insolvent, it is colloquially referred to as having 'gone belly up'. The working capital statement is, in effect, a statement that the company is not going to 'go belly up' straight after flotation.) The document must also include a capitalisation and indebtedness statement, which is a key change introduced by the new regime. In addition, information must be provided in relation to anyone with any particular interest in the issue/offer of shares (including any conflicting interest), and in relation to the reasons for the offer and how it is intended any proceeds will be used.

4. *Information concerning the securities to be offered/admitted to trading.* Information must be provided about the shares which are to be offered or admitted, including a description of the type and class of shares, the legislation under which the securities were created (for our purposes, the CA 1985), the rights which attach to the shares (such as voting rights, rights to share in capital, dividend rights and pre-emption rights: see **Chapters 13 and 14**). In the case of new issues, the resolutions, authorisations and approvals by virtue of which the shares have been created and/or issued must also be stated (see **Chapter 14**).

5. *Terms and conditions of the offer.* The document must set out detailed terms and conditions of the offer, including the total amount of the offer, the period for which the offer will be open and the circumstances under which the offer can be revoked, and an indication of the offer price. Details of any underwriters and when the underwriting agreement was or will be reached are also required.

6. *Admission to trading and dealing arrangements.* As a prospectus is required for all public offers (unless an exemption applies), there is a requirement to include a statement as to whether the shares offered will be admitted to trading with a view to their distribution on a regulated market. For our purposes, in the context of a flotation the shares will be admitted to trading on the Main Market.

7. *Selling securities holders.* If the float involves an offer for sale of shares (see **4.4.1**) then specific details must be provided, including the name and address of the selling shareholders and the number and class of shares being sold by each shareholder.

8. *Expense of the issue/offer.* The securities note must detail the total net proceeds and an estimate of the total expenses of the issue/offer.

9. *Dilution.* The amount and percentage of immediate dilution (see **14.6.2**) resulting from the offer must be included in the document.

10. *Additional information.* There is a requirement, to mirror the requirement in para 23 of Annex I relating to the registration document, that if the securities note includes a statement or report attributed to a person as an expert, then it must provide information about the expert. If it contains any information sourced from a third party, the source of that information must be identified, and confirmation must be provided that the information has

been reproduced accurately and that, as far as the issuer is aware, no facts have been omitted which would render the information inaccurate or misleading. This is a key change introduced by the new regime. Other additional information which must be included is a statement of the capacity in which any advisers, referred to in the securities note, have acted, and to identify and reproduce, or summarise, audited information referred to in the document.

6.5.2.2 Incorporation by reference

Before 1 July 2005, a company could not incorporate any information into its prospectus by reference to other documents. One of the key changes introduced by the new regime, however, is that information can be incorporated by reference into the registration document or the securities note, in certain circumstances. To be incorporated, the information must:

(a) have been approved by, filed with, or notified to the FSA (PR 2.4.1R);
(b) be the latest available (PR 2.4.3R);
(c) be accessible using a cross-referenced list in the prospectus (PR 2.4.5R); and
(d) not endanger investor protection (PR 2.4.6EU, para 4).

In practice, the effect of these requirements may be to limit the usefulness of the ability to incorporate information by reference. For example, a company which has been listed only for a short time is unlikely to have filed many sets of accounts with the FSA under the continuing obligations of the Listing Rules (see **7.5.6**). It will have to include in the prospectus any unfiled accounts from the last three years, as it will not be able to incorporate them by reference.

Prospectus Rule 2.4.6EU sets out examples of information which can be incorporated by reference, such as information in the audited report and accounts of the company, or the company's memorandum and articles of association. As explained at **5.3.6.2** above, the company must submit to the FSA a copy of any document incorporated into the prospectus by reference (annotated to indicate to which item of the schedules and building blocks in the PD Regulation it relates). To date reference to information incorporated by reference seems to have been made in the rubric on the cover page of the prospectus.

Unlike the registration document and the securities note, the summary cannot incorporate information by reference (PR 2.4.4R).

6.5.2.3 Derogations

Prospectus Rule 2.5.2UK provides that the FSA has the discretion to authorise the omission of any information required by the Prospectus Rules or s 87A of the FSMA 2000 if:

(a) disclosure of the information would be contrary to the public interest; or
(b) disclosure of the information would be seriously detrimental to the company and the omission of the information is not likely to mislead investors in their assessment of the investment; or
(c) the information to be omitted is of minor importance for a specific offer or admission and is unlikely to influence the investors' ability to make an informed choice as to whether to invest.

As mentioned at **5.3.6.2** above, any request to omit information under PR 2.5.2R must comply with the requirements of PR 2.5.3R.

The lawyers must make the directors aware of this discretion of the FSA, but they must manage the message carefully. As we have seen, the Prospectus Rules and the FSMA 2000 require significant disclosure in the prospectus. The directors may not want certain information to be included in the prospectus, and will ask the lawyers how they can avoid disclosure of that information. The general message is that if the Prospectus Rules, or the general disclosure requirement in s 87A of the FSMA 2000, require such disclosure then the prospectus must contain that information. The FSA will exercise its discretion to omit information only in exceptional circumstances, and it will not thank lawyers for making spurious and ill-founded requests to omit information from the float document. Indeed, the very fact that directors wish to omit certain information may suggest that they think that such information would deter investors from investing in the company. This means that the information is likely to be highly relevant to investors, and so would not fall within the FSA's discretion in any event. Lawyers need to be firm with directors who try to conceal facts. Ultimately, if the lawyers think the directors are not disclosing information, they should cease to act.

6.5.2.4 Checking content

Chapter 5 describes how the prospectus is submitted to the FSA for approval. To help the FSA check that the document complies with its content requirements, PR 3.1.4R requires that the draft document must be annotated in the margin to indicate which Prospectus Rule requirement the text complies with. So, for example, the margin opposite the list of directors' names and addresses would be annotated with 'Annex I, para 14' to indicate that the list fulfils the content requirements of this paragraph.

6.6 Responsibility

6.6.1 Who is responsible?

Who has responsibility for the prospectus? Those familiar with the old regime will recall that the answer used to be provided by the Financial Services and Markets Act 2000 (Official Listing of Securities) Regulations 2001 (SI 2001/2956), which listed the persons responsible for listing particulars, and reg 10, which confirmed that the same people were responsible for a prospectus. However, on 1 July 2005, para 3 of Sch 3 to the Prospectus Regulations 2005 revoked reg 10, so under the new regime we must look elsewhere to find those responsible for the prospectus.

The answer now lies in the Prospectus Rules themselves. Where, as in our case, the prospectus relates to equity securities for which the UK is the home Member State, PR 5.5.3R(2) provides that the following people will be responsible for the prospectus:

(a) the issuing company (PR 5.5.3R(2)(a));
(b) the directors of the company (as at the date the document is published) (PR 5.5.3R(2)(b)(i));
(c) anyone who has agreed to be named, and is named, in the prospectus as a director, or as having agreed to become a director, either immediately or in the future (after flotation, for example) (PR 5.5.3R(2)(b)(ii));
(d) anyone who accepts, and is stated in the prospectus as accepting, responsibility for the prospectus (PR 5.5.3R(2)(c));
(e) anyone, other than the company, who is offering shares (and if this is another company, the directors of that company at the time the prospectus is published) (PR 5.5.3R(2)(d));

(f) the person requesting admission to trading of the shares (if not the company) (and if this is another company, the directors of that company at the time the prospectus is published) (PR 5.5.3R(2)(e)); and

(g) anyone else who authorises the contents of the prospectus (PR 5.5.3R(2)(f)).

In fact, this is very similar to the old responsibility regime.

As with the old regime, there is a broad caveat to the category of persons listed at (e) above. The most obvious people who could be caught by this category are any selling shareholders. They may well be individuals who would not be comfortable taking such responsibility. However, comfort is at hand. Prospectus Rule 5.5.7R provides that a person will not be responsible under PR 5.5.3R(2)(d) if the shareholder is making the offer in association with the issuer and it is primarily the issuer, or the issuing company's advisers, who draw up the prospectus. This is the case in the majority of floats, so usually the lawyer will be able to reassure any selling shareholders on the issue of responsibility.

One difference to the old regime, particularly relevant to advisers, is the fact that anyone responsible for the prospectus by virtue of (g) above (because they have authorised content of the prospectus) must set out a statement in the prospectus that they are responsible for such content (Annex 1, para 23 and Annex III, para 10 – see **6.5.2.1** above). This means, for example, that a prospectus must contain a statement from the accountants in respect of financial information prepared specifically for the prospectus. However, they will not be required to give such a statement in respect of financial information incorporated by reference which was not prepared specifically for the prospectus.

It appears that the FSA does not consider the sponsor to have authorised the prospectus for the purposes of the responsibility regime, as current practice is for sponsors not to provide such a statement.

Lawyers do not have a final say on the release of the prospectus and so their role is covered by the exemption in PR 5.5.9R; they do not have responsibility by reason only of giving advice about the content of the prospectus in a professional capacity.

6.6.2 What does responsibility mean?

The persons with responsibility for the document must ensure that the document complies with the general disclosure obligation imposed by the FSMA 2000 (see **6.5.1** above), the specific content requirements set out in the Prospectus Rules (see **6.5.2** above) and the requirements of the Listing Rules in relation to the listing application to the FSA (see **Chapter 5**). The consequences of this are discussed at **6.7** below.

6.6.3 Practicalities

6.6.3.1 Responsibility statement

The responsibility statement, which must be included in the prospectus pursuant to para 1.2 of both Annex I and Annex III of the Prospectus Rules, is referred to at **6.5.2.1** above.

6.7 Liability

As stated in **6.6.2** above, those with responsibility for the prospectus must ensure that it meets the content requirements of the Prospectus Rules and the FSMA

2000, and the rules relating to the application for listing under the Listing Rules. The document must not omit any information or contain information which is incorrect or misleading. The consequence of this is that the persons responsible for the document may incur civil and/or criminal liability in relation to any inaccuracies or misstatements in, or omissions from, the document.

6.7.1 Civil liability

6.7.1.1 Section 90 of the FSMA 2000

The effect of s 90 of the FSMA 2000 is that those responsible for *listing particulars* must pay compensation to anyone who has acquired shares which are the subject of the listing particulars, and has suffered loss as a result of any inaccurate or misleading statement in the document, or any omission of information which should have been disclosed under s 87A. Section 90(11) (added by para 6 of Sch 1 to the Prospectus Regulations 2005) provides that this applies equally in relation to a *prospectus*. While it includes specific reference to the general disclosure requirement under s 87A of the FSMA 2000, in practice s 90 is construed to apply not only to a failure of the prospectus to meet this requirement, but also to any failure to meet the content requirements of the Prospectus Rules.

Note that s 90(12) (again, added in July 2005 by the Prospectus Regulations 2005) provides that a person can be liable for the contents of the summary (see **6.5.2.1**) only if the summary is misleading, inaccurate or inconsistent when read together with the rest of the prospectus, ie the registration document and the securities note.

It may help to consider the issue of liability by way of an example.

> **Example**
>
> Imagine that an investor, Mr X, encouraged by the positive messages in the prospectus, invests in Company A. In fact, the prospectus failed to include information about a very real risk that a rival's new invention could significantly reduce Company A's sales. Imagine that, after the float, the rival's new invention goes terribly wrong; Company A continues to prosper and Mr X makes a good profit. Mr X has suffered no loss and the persons responsible for the inaccurate prospectus, through sheer luck, will incur no liability under s 90.
>
> Consider now what would happen if, in fact, the rival's new invention is a huge success, to the extent that Company A loses significant sales and ultimately goes belly up. Mr X loses his entire investment. He has suffered loss and wants compensation. Section 90 of the FSMA 2000 provides that he should obtain compensation from those persons responsible for the incorrect selling document (that is, mainly, the directors).

What is the scope of s 90? There are two particular phrases in the provision which have caused some debate:

(a) 'who has acquired' – s 90 concerns the loss suffered by a person 'who has acquired' securities. Is this restricted to the original investor, or does it include those who buy the shares from that original investor?

(b) 'as a result of' – for any investor to have a claim to compensation under s 90, he must prove that he suffered loss 'as a result of' the deficiencies in the document. Does this mean that the investor must have relied on the document? Must the investor have read the document?

These phrases leave open the possibility that any aggrieved original investor who had not even read the document, or any subsequent purchaser of the shares from the original investor, could try to run the argument that s 90 is wide enough to afford him a claim for compensation.

There are some exemptions from liability under s 90, which are set out in Sch 10 to the FSMA 2000. These exemptions include:

(a) if, at the time the prospectus was submitted to the FSA, the persons responsible (having made reasonable enquiries) believed the erroneous information was true and not misleading;

(b) where loss arises as a result of a statement by an expert;

(c) where a correction had been published before shares were acquired;

(d) where the erroneous information was reproduced from a public official document; and

(e) where the person seeking compensation knew the information was deficient.

6.7.1.2 Liability in tort

The persons responsible for the document may also incur tortious liability under the following heads:

(a) *Negligent misstatement.* Those with responsibility for the prospectus owe a duty of care to those investing at the time of flotation. The publication of a deficient document breaches this duty. If an investor relies on a deficient document and suffers loss because of that reliance then, on the basis of *Hedley Byrne & Co Ltd v Heller & Partners Ltd* [1964] AC 465, those responsible for the prospectus will be liable to that investor. Note that, applying *Caparo Industries v Dickman* [1990] 1 All ER 568, the persons responsible for the document would not owe any duty to any subsequent purchasers of the shares. This, and the fact that the investor must have *relied* on the erroneous information or omission, can be contrasted with the position under s 90 of the FSMA 2000 (see **6.7.1.1**).

(b) *Deceit.* If an investor can prove that any misstatement in the prospectus was made fraudulently, he may have a claim in damages for deceit.

(c) *Misrepresentation Act 1967.* If an investor chooses to invest in the company on the basis of an incorrect or misleading prospectus, he may be able to rescind the contract for the purchase of shares and/or claim damages from the other party to the contract (see also CA 1985, s 111A). Note that the other party will be the issuer of the shares, ie the company (in the case of an offer for subscription) or the selling shareholder (in the case of an offer for sale), rather than the directors.

6.7.1.3 Liability in contract

The prospectus will form part of any contract between an investor buying shares and either the company issuing shares to the investor, or any existing shareholder selling shares to the investor (the circumstances will vary from float to float). If the prospectus is deficient, the investor may be able to rescind the contract, or sue the other party to the contract (the company or the selling shareholder) for damages.

6.7.2 Criminal liability

6.7.2.1 Section 397 of the FSMA 2000

While a director may be comfortable with the threat of civil liability, no director likes the sound of criminal liability. Mentioning this sanction does tend to help any director, who is tiring of the legal due diligence or verification process, to refocus. A director risks criminal liability under the following provisions of the FSMA 2000:

(a) *Section 397(1) and (2) (misleading statements).* These provisions make it a criminal offence for any director knowingly or recklessly to make a materially misleading, false or deceptive statement, promise or forecast, or to conceal dishonestly any material facts, in order to induce an investor to buy shares.

(b) *Section 397(3) (market manipulation).* This provision catches anything the director does to create a false or misleading impression as to the market in, or price or value of the shares, if he does so deliberately to induce investors to buy shares.

Section 397 of the FSMA 2000 is considered in more detail at **9.5** below.

6.7.2.2 Theft Act 1968

Section 19 of the Theft Act 1968 imposes criminal penalties on any director who makes false or misleading statements with intent to deceive shareholders. Clearly this could apply to any director who is responsible for a deficient prospectus, if intent can be proved.

6.7.3 Fines

Section 91 of the FSMA 2000 provides that the FSA can fine the company for breach of the Listing Rules and, if it can prove that any director was knowingly concerned in the breach, can also fine that director.

6.7.4 Public censure

Section 91 of the FSMA 2000 provides that the FSA may choose to publish a statement censuring the company or a director, as an alternative to a fine.

6.8 Verification

As **6.7** above makes clear, it is not a good idea for the directors to make incorrect statements in the prospectus, or to omit material from it. During the flotation process great care is taken to ensure that the prospectus meets the requirements of the Prospectus Rules and the FSMA 2000. As **6.6.1** above explains, directors are not the only people with responsibility for the document; but they do have responsibility, and their responsibility is for the entire document. Accordingly, a process has emerged which aims to ensure that the directors make all reasonable enquiries to satisfy themselves that:

(a) each material statement of fact or opinion in the document is not only true, but also not misleading in the context in which it appears;

(b) the document as a whole gives a true and fair impression of the history, business and prospects of the company; and

(c) the document does not omit any information which makes it misleading or which contravenes the Prospectus Rules and/or s 87A of the FSMA 2000.

This process is called verification. It protects the directors by providing evidence that they have taken reasonable care to ensure the information required by s 87A of the FSMA 2000 has been included. It also helps to avoid breaching s 397 of the FSMA 2000 (see **9.5**) and the market abuse regime (see **Chapter 10**), and so provides comfort to the sponsor. The verification process is considered in more detail at **5.3.5** above.

6.9 Types of prospectus

6.9.1 Full

So far, this chapter has considered the document which will ultimately be submitted to the FSA as part of the company's application for admission to listing. This is known as the full prospectus. However, references to various other forms of the prospectus may be made during the float process. These references are explained below.

6.9.2 Mini

Under the old regime, the company had the option of publishing a mini-prospectus in addition to a full prospectus. The mini-prospectus would contain a summary of the key information in the full prospectus, together with an application form and certain information required by OLR 8.13. Under the new regime, the requirement for a summary (see **6.5.2.1**) means that there is no longer a need for a mini prospectus, and the old rules relating to them have been deleted.

6.9.3 Pathfinder (or red herring)

A pathfinder, or red herring, prospectus is basically a very advanced draft of the full prospectus, but does not include details of the final price per share. References to the price are usually left blank, although occasionally a price range will be indicated. The aim of the pathfinder is to raise interest in the float before the actual prospectus is ready.

There is a potential problem, however, in that this could breach s 21 of the FSMA 2000 (see **Chapter 12**). The effect of s 21 is that it is an offence for a company to send out a pathfinder to induce investors to buy shares. The company can avoid this problem by sending the pathfinder only to persons exempt from s 21 (usually institutional investors) (see **12.9**). Issue 12 of *List!* makes clear that a pathfinder must comply with the rules relating to advertisements set out in PR 3.3 (see **5.3.6.6**).

Under the new regime, it was anticipated that demand for a pathfinder prospectus might reduce, as a result of the FSA's ability to approve the full prospectus without the inclusion of the final offer price or the amount of securities to be offered (PR 2.3.2R). PR 3.2.3R provides that the prospectus must be made available to the public at least six working days before the end of the offer (see **5.4.2.1**). The six-day period runs from the day the final prospectus is approved, even if that prospectus does not contain the final offer price or the amount of securities. However, if the company issues a pathfinder, this will not trigger the start of the six-day period (which will be triggered only once the final prospectus is approved). Issues 10 and 11 of *List!* discuss this matter further. In particular, issue 12 states that the six-day rule will not apply to a pathfinder in relation to an institutional placing in any event. This has removed much of the uncertainty relating to the use of pathfinders under the new regime (traditionally, in an institutional bookbuilt placing the approved prospectus is published only three days before closing so, if the six-day rule had applied, companies would have been reluctant to use a pathfinder).

There is, however, a potential disadvantage of the company choosing to use a final prospectus without the final offer price and amount of securities (and therefore a potential advantage of using a pathfinder). Investors have the right to withdraw their acceptances within two working days of the date the company eventually provides this information to the FSA in writing under s 87A(7) of the FSMA 2000 (FSMA 2000, s 87(Q)(1) and (2)). However, if the prospectus details the method and conditions for determining the price and amount (or, in relation to the price, states a maximum offer price) then this right to withdraw will not arise (FSMA 2000, s 87Q(3)).

6.9.4 Supplementary

Section 87G of the FSMA 2000 and PR 3.4.1UK provide that if, in the period following the approval of the full prospectus but before dealings in shares commence, there arises or is noted any significant new factor, material mistake or inaccuracy relating to the information included in the approved prospectus, the company must produce a supplementary prospectus. This document must contain details of the new factor, mistake or inaccuracy, and must be approved by the FSA. Significantly, investors have the right to withdraw their acceptances of the offer during the two working days following publication of the supplementary prospectus (FSMA 2000, s 87Q(4)).

6.10 Validity

A prospectus is valid for 12 months after its publication, for any further offers or admissions to trading, provided that it is updated by a supplementary prospectus, approved by the FSA (see **6.9.4**) (PR 5.1.1R). As mentioned at **6.5.2.1** above, the registration document is valid for a period of up to 12 months after it has been filed, but this is also subject to updating, using a new securities note, which again requires the approval of the FSA (PR 2.2.5R and PR 5.1.4R).

Given the requirements for FSA approval of any update to either the prospectus or the registration note, any advantage of this extended validity period may be limited.

6.11 Passporting

Under the old regime, a mutual recognition procedure existed under which, in theory, a prospectus drawn up in one Member State could be valid in another Member State. In practice, the procedure was difficult (because the rules of each Member State governing the drawing up of a prospectus were so diverse) and so was seldom used.

Under the new regime, of course, the Prospectus Directive has ensured that each Member State has the same rules regarding the drawing up of a prospectus. This has enabled the introduction of a new 'passporting' procedure, whereby a company will not need to produce a prospectus for an offer of shares to the public, or an admission of shares to trading, in one Member State ('MS2') if another Member State ('MS1') has already approved and published a prospectus in the previous 12 months. Subject to updating (see **6.10** above), the company simply must translate the summary (not, interestingly, any other part of the prospectus) into a language acceptable to MS2 and obtain a 'certificate of approval' from the competent authority in MS1 (in the UK, the FSA) that the prospectus has been drawn up and approved in accordance with the Prospectus Directive. Prospectus Rule 3.1.6G suggests that any request for such a certificate should be included with the company's application for approval of the initial prospectus. Prospectus Rule 5.3 and ss 87H and 87I of the FSMA 2000 set out the rules relating to the certificate of approval.

While the passporting procedure will be easier to use than the old mutual recognition procedure, clearly a potentially lengthy due diligence exercise is still required to ensure any previous prospectus is up to date. In addition, the eligibility criteria for listing are not covered by the Prospectus Directive and so remain diverse in each of the Member States (remember that in the UK the conditions for listing are set out in the Listing Rules – see **4.3.1.1**). The company may have to meet further criteria in order to list shares in MS2 which it did not have to meet to list shares in MS1.

To date, a number of companies have taken advantage of the passporting procedure. However, certain jurisdictions have been requesting that the summary be translated on the basis that English is not an acceptable language.

Part II
BEING A LISTED COMPANY

Chapter 7
Continuing Obligations

7.1	Introduction	83
7.2	Why have continuing obligations?	83
7.3	The new regime	84
7.4	The Disclosure Rules	84
7.5	The Listing Rules	90
7.6	The Model Code	95
7.7	Communication with shareholders	100
7.8	The Prospectus Rules	102
7.9	The Admission and Disclosure Standards	104
7.10	Sanctions	104
7.11	Future developments	105

7.1 Introduction

Chapter 1 explained that, once a company is listed, it becomes subject to continuing obligations. Both the FSA (in the Disclosure Rules, the Prospectus Rules and the Listing Rules) and the Stock Exchange (in the Admission and Disclosure Standards) impose continuing obligations on listed companies. As with the flotation process, however, the FSA and the Stock Exchange have worked together to dovetail their requirements.

7.2 Why have continuing obligations?

The continuing obligations exist to protect both existing and potential investors; they ensure that there is an orderly market for investments and that all investors have access to information at the same time.

Put into context, it makes sense that listed companies should bear these obligations; remember that their shareholder base is diverse, and the vast majority of shareholders will not be involved in the management of the company.

At first glance, there may seem to be so many continuing obligations that you might wonder why any company would choose to float. Before embarking on the flotation process a company should of course consider, as part of its pre-float preparation, whether it is capable of meeting the continuing obligations that will be imposed on it after flotation. However, the obligations are certainly not meant to deter companies from listing. In practice, once companies have put in place the administrative processes to enable them to deal with the obligations, most find that meeting the continuing obligations simply becomes part of the day-to day running of the business.

The company will, of course require advice on the continuing obligations from its advisers from time to time. If the company was impressed by the work of its advisers on the float, it may well retain those advisers on a permanent basis after flotation. Due to the day-to-day nature of the continuing obligations, the in-house legal department of the listed company will often take responsibility for ensuring that the company meets those obligations. However, where a second opinion is required, or where the in-house solicitors are not available, the company will often call on its external lawyers, who will be expected to know what the continuing obligations are and how to meet them. As is explained below, due to the need to meet the obligations in a timely manner, the company will often require advice on an urgent basis, and possibly out of hours.

7.3 The new regime

Those familiar with the old regime will know that the continuing obligations of listed companies, including both the general obligation of disclosure and more specific disclosure obligations, used to be contained in Chapter 9 of the Old Listing Rules. This has changed under the new regime. Chapter 9 of the Listing Rules continues to include most of the continuing obligations (including the specific disclosure, or 'notification', obligations), but the general disclosure obligation has been rewritten (to comply with the Market Abuse Directive) and is now contained in the Disclosure Rules. The Prospectus Rules also contain a new continuing obligation: to prepare an annual information update. As before, there are a few additional continuing obligations in the Admission and Disclosure Standards.

The PSI Guide and Continuing Obligations Guide, published by the FSA under the old regime, are no longer in effect. Instead, some guidance is contained in the Rules themselves (with the suffix 'G'), and the FSA intends to provide further, informal, non-binding advice in its newsletter, *List!*.

While the new regime has introduced some new continuing obligations, broadly the obligations under the new regime are similar to those under the old regime, albeit rewritten and reordered.

The continuing obligations under the Disclosure Rules are considered at **7.4**, the continuing obligations (including specific disclosure obligations) under the Listing Rules are considered at **7.5** to **7.7**, the obligation under the Prospectus Rules to prepare an annual information update is considered at **7.8**, and the continuing obligations under the Admission and Disclosure Standards are considered at **7.9**.

7.4 The Disclosure Rules

As outlined at **3.5.3**, the Disclosure Rules implement the Market Abuse Directive (MAD) in the UK, and also contain the general obligation of disclosure previously found in Chapter 9 of the Old Listing Rules. This is because the MAD makes clear that, by ensuring the market operates on the basis of prompt and fair disclosure of information to the public, the disclosure regime plays an important part in preventing market abuse. It seemed logical, therefore, to keep the rules relating to market abuse and the rules relating to disclosure in the same sourcebook.

As explained at **3.5.3**, the Disclosure Rules apply to any company which has requested admission of, or has admitted, its securities to trading on a regulated market in the UK. As such, all listed companies (as defined at **1.3**) must comply with the Disclosure Rules.

The main continuing obligation under the Disclosure Rules is the general obligation of disclosure, considered at **7.4.1** to **7.4.3** below. However, there are also some other continuing obligations relating to disclosure, which are considered at **7.4.4** to **7.4.8** below.

7.4.1 The general obligation of disclosure

The general obligation of disclosure reflects Listing Principle 5 and ensures that the company gives information to the market as a whole (rather than just to a few select investors) and in a timely manner. It replaces the general obligation of disclosure under OLRs 9.1 and 9.2.

The obligation is set out at DR 2.2.1 R and requires that, subject to DR 2.5.1R (see **7.4.2.8**), the company:

(a) must notify an RIS;
(b) as soon as possible;
(c) of any inside information (see **7.4.2.3**) which directly concerns the company.

Where an issuer has a website, the company must also disclose the information on its website in accordance with DR 2.3.

7.4.2 Fulfilling the obligation

While this obligation is simple enough to understand, to comply with the obligation an understanding of the following issues is required.

7.4.2.1 What is a Regulatory Information Service (RIS)?

An RIS is a Primary Information Provider (PIP) service, which has been approved by the FSA and is on the list of Regulatory Information Services maintained by the FSA. Basically, companies use an RIS to discharge their continuing obligations to make announcements to the public. The best known RIS (for historical reasons; it used to have a monopoly) is the Stock Exchange's own RNS service. As at the time of writing, the other RISs are Business Wire Regulatory Disclosure (provided by Business Wire), PR Newswire Disclose (provided by PR Newswire), Firstsight (provided by Romeike), Hugin Announce (provided by Hugin ASA) and News Release Express (provided by CCN Matthews UK Limited).

The PIP service criteria, published on the UKLA section of the FSA website, set out headline categories which the RIS must use when releasing information. For example, the release of information about the admission of shares to listing must be headed 'Official List Notice' and information about an acquisition must be headed (imaginatively) 'Acquisition'. Lawyers will need to learn to use their firms' databases to access copies of company announcements made through an RIS. Announcements made through RNS can be accessed from the Stock Exchange website.

7.4.2.2 What is a Primary Information Provider (PIP)?

A PIP is an organisation which ensures that information from listed companies (such as regulatory announcements and company news) is disseminated to secondary news sources (Secondary Information Providers, or SIPs), such as Reuters or Bloomberg, at the same time. Due to the electronic nature of these communications, when the information is disseminated by the PIP it is often referred to as being 'sent down the wire'. The SIPs then pass on the information to the public.

7.4.2.3 What is inside information?

Disclosure Rules 2.2.3G to 2.2.8G contain guidance as to how to identify inside information. Disclosure Rule 2.2.3G refers to the definition of inside information in s 118C of the FSMA 2000. It is information:

(a) of a *precise nature* (see **7.4.2.4**):
(b) which is not *generally available* (see **7.4.2.5**);

(c) which relates, directly or indirectly, to an issuer of a *financial instrument* (see **7.4.2.6**) or to the *financial instrument* itself; and

(d) if generally available, would be likely to have a *significant effect* (see **7.4.2.7**) on the price of the *financial instrument* or the price of related investments.

The FSA believes that the company and its advisers are best placed to make an initial assessment of whether information is 'inside information' which therefore must be disclosed (DR 2.2.7G). The board must continuously monitor any changes in the company's circumstances which may mean an announcement is required (DR 2.2.8G). The criteria referred to in the above definition of 'inside information', which the board must understand in order to decide whether to disclose information, are set out at **7.4.2.4** to **7.4.2.7**.

7.4.2.4 What is information of a 'precise nature'?

Section 118C (5) of the FSMA 2000 provides that information is of a precise nature if it:

(a) indicates circumstances that:
    (i) exist; or
    (ii) may reasonably be expected to come into existence; OR

(b) indicates an event that:
    (i) has occurred; or
    (ii) may reasonably be expected to occur; AND

(c) is specific enough to enable a conclusion to be drawn as to the possible effect, on the price of the financial instrument, of those circumstances or that event.

7.4.2.5 When is information 'generally available'?

Information which can be obtained by research or analysis conducted by, or on behalf of, users of a market is regarded as being generally available (FSMA 2000, s 118C(8)).

7.4.2.6 What is a financial instrument?

The s 118C definition of inside information uses the term 'qualifying investments'. However, when considering the definition of 'inside information' for the purpose of the general obligation of disclosure under the Disclosure Rules, the term 'financial instrument' is substituted. This is defined in Annex B of the Investment Services Directive. Most importantly for our purposes it includes shares (transferable securities), but it also includes other investments such as options to acquire shares, and interest rate, currency and equity swaps.

7.4.2.7 What is a 'significant effect' on a price?

As with the old regime, the inside information test hinges on this criterion, namely price sensitivity. Basically, if the information is price sensitive, it must be disclosed.

There is no specific figure which can be set which constitutes a 'significant effect' on the price (DR 2.2.4G(2)). The test will be satisfied if a reasonable investor would be likely to use the information as part of the basis of his investment decision (DR 2.2.4G(1)). This is referred to as the 'reasonable investor test'.

Further guidance on how to apply this test is set out at DR 2.2.5G and DR 2.2.6G. In particular, DR 2.2.6G provides that information about the following matters is likely to fulfil the reasonable investor test (and therefore likely to have a 'significant effect' on price):

(a) the company's assets and liabilities
(b) the performance, or the expectation of the performance, of the company's business;
(c) the company's financial condition;
(d) the course of the company's business;
(e) major new developments in the company's business; or
(f) information previously disclosed to the market.

Disclosure must be made even if the information would only have a significant effect on shares listed outside the UK.

7.4.2.8 What if dissemination of the information will have adverse consequences for the company?

Often this is precisely the reason for the FSA requirement that the information is announced, and the FSA will not permit breaches of the disclosure obligation just because the obligation may result in a fall in the company's share price. However, there are two points to be aware of:

(a) *Delaying disclosure*. Disclosure Rule 2.5.1R provides that the company can delay disclosure, in order to avoid prejudicing its legitimate interests, if:

  (i) it would not mislead the public;
  (ii) anyone who does receive the information owes a duty of confidentiality to the company; and
  (iii) the company can ensure the confidentiality of that information.

  If the company does choose to delay disclosure, it should continue to monitor the situation and be ready to disclose as soon as circumstances change which means that the proviso in DR 2.5.1R no longer applies (DR 2.5.2G(1)). This reinforces the guidance in DR 2.2.8 that the board must carefully and continuously monitor any changes in the company's circumstances (see **7.4.2.3**).

  The Disclosure Rules provide two specific examples of circumstances when the company is likely to be able to make use of the delay permitted by DR 2.5.1R. The second, under DR 2.5.3G(2), relates to companies with dual board structure, and so is of little use in the UK, (where companies have unitary board structure). The first, however, in DR 2.5.3G(1), is likely to be very useful. It reflects OLR 9.4 under the old regime. It provides that disclosure of matters in the course of negotiation, or related matters, may be delayed where the outcome, or normal pattern, of negotiations would be affected by the disclosure. In particular, disclosure of information may be delayed where the financial viability of the company is in grave and imminent danger, and disclosure would undermine the conclusion of specific negotiations designed to ensure the company's long-term financial recovery.

  The company can, however, disseminate such information to those who owe it a duty of confidentiality in the normal exercise of employment, profession or duties (including its advisers and the people with whom it is negotiating) pursuant to DR 2.5.7G. This is an exception from the general rule, under DR 2.5.6R, that inside information should not be given to anyone (including advisers) until it has been given to an RIS. It is only if there is a breach of confidence during these negotiations that the information must be given to the RIS (see **7.4.1**). The company can, therefore, talk to its lawyers about an impending deal without having to make the information public through an RIS.

The lawyers who receive such information should note two things. First, it would not be very professional to be responsible for any leak of information which would force the company to make an announcement. This means that the lawyers need to make sure that they limit the number of people in their team who have access to such information, and that everyone in their team is aware of the confidential nature of the information (there is an urban myth about the unfortunate trainee who, chatting to a fellow trainee in the pub about what he had done that day, arrived in the office the next day to find the information splashed all over the papers; you never know who else is in the pub). Disclosure Rule 2.5.9G highlights the fact that the wider the group of people to whom information is provided, the greater the risk that there will be a leak, leading to the triggering of the full disclosure obligation. Secondly, the lawyers themselves (and other advisers who receive information pursuant to DR 2.5.7G) cannot deal in the company's shares until the information has been made public.

(b) *Dispensation*. The FSA has the discretion to grant a dispensation in relation to any of the Disclosure Rules, including the disclosure requirements under DR 2.2.1R. Disclosure Rule 1.2 provides that the company must apply to the FSA in writing, usually at least five business days before the proposed modification or dispensation is required. The application must contain the information required by DR 1.2.2R. Like the dispensation permitted under OLR 9.8 under the old regime, the FSA is likely to grant this dispensation only in limited circumstances (for example, when an announcement at a particular time might jeopardise the company's ability to continue to trade).

7.4.2.9 What does 'as soon as possible' mean?

The Disclosure Rules require general disclosure to be made 'as soon as possible'. Under the old regime, OLRs 9.1 and 9.2 required disclosure to be made 'without delay'. The FSA has said that it does not consider that the Disclosure Rules allow a longer period of time to make disclosures than was allowed under the Old Listing Rules. The following statement, released by the FSA in relation to the breach by Marconi plc of its general obligation of disclosure under the Old Listing Rules, is still useful guidance from the FSA, therefore, regarding the meaning of 'as soon as possible':

> On 2 July 2001 Marconi changed its expectation as to its performance for the half year ending 30 September 2001 and the full year ending 31 March 2002. That change, if made public, was likely to lead to a substantial movement in the price of its listed securities and gave rise to the obligation to notify the [RIS] without delay. The notification should have been made by, at the latest, the evening of 3 July 2001. By not making that notification until 18:41 on 4 July 2001 Marconi contravened Rule 9.2(c) of the Listing Rules ...
>
> By reason of his absence overseas and the decision not to involve him between 26 June 2001 and 3 July 2001, the Deputy Chief Executive's concurrence was not required for the change in Marconi's expectation to take place. Fulfilment of this obligation involved reporting the matter to the Board without delay to enable the Board to make a formal decision to issue the necessary trading statement. It was not necessary to await the return of the Deputy Chief Executive before accelerating steps to do so ...
>
> The period of time which it is reasonable for a listed company to take in making an announcement under the Listing Rules regarding a change in its expectations will

depend upon all the circumstances relevant to the particular situation in which the change occurs. However, save in exceptional circumstances, a listed company must prioritise its disclosure obligations under the Listing Rules. (FSA Final Notice: Marconi plc, 11 April 2003)

Companies which envisage that they will not be able to comply with the 'as soon as possible' requirement should discuss with the FSA whether they can waive this obligation (DR 2.2.9G(4)). Alternatively, it may be possible that the company is in a position to make an announcement 'as soon as possible', but it would prefer to include more detail than is strictly required, and collating this information would delay the announcement. In this case, the company should publish what is known as a 'holding announcement', which discharges its formal obligations under the Disclosure Rules, but which informs the market that further information will be announced in due course. Disclosure Rule 2.2.9G(2) sets out further information about the content of a holding announcement.

The ability of the company to delay an announcement is discussed at **7.4.2.8** above. Again, if the company is delaying a disclosure in accordance with the Disclosure Rules, it must prepare a holding announcement which can be released quickly in the event of a breach of confidentiality (DR 2.6.3G).

7.4.3 Consequences of breaching the general obligation of disclosure

7.4.3.1 Breach of the Disclosure Rules

Any breach of the general obligation of disclosure could lead to the FSA imposing any of the sanctions set out at **7.10** below.

7.4.3.2 Criminal offence

Any breach of the general obligation of disclosure may also constitute a criminal offence under s 397 of the FSMA 2000, which contains provisions relating to misleading statements and market manipulation. This section is considered in more detail at **9.5**.

7.4.3.3 Civil offence

Failure to comply with the general obligation of disclosure may well constitute the civil offence of market abuse (see **Chapter 10**).

7.4.4 Information gathering and publication

Disclosure Rule 1.3.1R provides that the company, person discharging managerial responsibility (PDMR) (see **7.6.2.1**), or connected person must provide to the FSA as soon as possible following a request:

(a) any information which the FSA considers appropriate to protect investors or ensure the smooth operation of the market; and

(b) any other information or explanation that the FSA may reasonable require to verify whether the Disclosure Rules are being and have been complied with.

The FSA can require the company to publish information disclosed under DR 1.3.1R (or, after giving the company an opportunity to make representations as to why it should not be published, the FSA itself may publish the information) (DR 1.3.3R).

7.4.5 Misleading information

The company must take all reasonable care to ensure that the information it provides to an RIS (see **7.4.2.1**) is not misleading, false or deceptive and does not omit anything likely to affect the import of the information (DR 1.3.4R). The company must not combine any marketing of its activities with an RIS announcement if this is likely to be misleading (DR 1.3.5R).

7.4.6 Insider lists

Disclosure Rule 2.8.1R provides that the company must compile a list of those persons who work for it who have access (on a regular or occasional basis) to insider information relating directly or indirectly to the company.

'Persons who work for it' is not restricted to employees. The list should include the company's own employees who have access to inside information, but it should also include principal contacts at any other firm or company acting on its behalf, or on its account, with whom it has had direct contact and who have access to inside information about it (DR 2.8.7G).

In addition, and of particular interest to the lawyer, the company must ensure that persons acting on its behalf, or for its account, such as advisers, compile such lists.

'Access to inside information' is not defined, and the FSA has provided little guidance in the Disclosure Rules as to the contents of the list (see DR 2.8.3). However, it has provided informal guidance in a newsletter (see *FSA Market Watch Newsletter*, issue 12). It remains to be seen whether the FSA develops this idea by encouraging firms of advisers to restrict as far as possible those employees (including secretaries) who have access to inside information on a transaction.

7.4.7 Transactions by persons discharging managerial responsibilities

DR 3.1.2R requires PDMRs (see **7.6.2.1**) and their connected persons (see **7.6.2.3**) to disclose to the company certain transactions, including their dealings in the company's shares. This is considered further at **15.7.1.2**.

7.4.8 Notification of transactions to an RIS

A listed company must pass on to the market, through an RIS, the information it receives under:

(a)   DR 3.1.2R (see **7.4.7**) (DR 3.1.4R(1)(a)); and
(b)   s 324 of the CA 1985 (see **15.5**) (DR 3.1.4R(1)(b)).

This obligation is considered further at **15.7.1.1** and **15.7.1.2** below.

7.5 The Listing Rules

Chapter 9 of the Listing Rules is entitled 'Continuing Obligations' and sets out most of the general continuing obligations of listed companies. More specific continuing obligations are contained in chapters 10 (significant transactions), 11 (related party transactions), 12 (dealing in own securities and treasury shares), 13 (contents of circulars) and 14 to 19 (secondary listings of certain securities and companies). The main continuing obligations are discussed below.

7.5.1 Requirements with continuing application

Listing Rule 9.2 sets out some of the eligibility requirements (see **Chapter 4**) which continue to apply to the company, once listed, as continuing obligations. Those most commonly encountered by the lawyer are set out below.

7.5.1.1 Admission to trading

You will recall that a condition for listing is that the shares are admitted to trading (LR 2.2.3R) (see **4.3.1.1**). Listing Rule 9.2.1R provides that it is a continuing obligation that the company's shares are admitted to trading at all times.

7.5.1.2 Compliance with the Disclosure Rules

There is a new continuing obligation, under LR 9.2.5G and LR 9.2.6R, that a listed company must comply with chapter 2 of the Disclosure Rules (that is, the general obligation of disclosure discussed at **7.4.1** above).

7.5.1.3 Compliance with the Model Code

Listing Rule 9.2.8 provides that a listed company must require persons discharging managerial responsibilities and certain employees to comply with a code relating to how they deal in shares, called the Model Code. The Model Code is annexed to chapter 9 of the Listing Rules.

Further detail on the Model Code is provided at **7.6** below.

7.5.1.4 Contact details

Another new continuing obligation introduced on 1 July 2005 is that the company must provide to the FSA contact details of at least one person which it nominates to be the first point of contact with the FSA in relation to matters of the company's compliance with the Listing Rules and the Disclosure Rules (LR 9.2.11R and LR 9.2.12G). The chosen person must be knowledgeable about the company, the Listing Rules and the Disclosure Rules, and, best of all, they must be contactable on business days between 7 am and 7 pm. It remains to be seen who companies will tend to choose for this role; probably the company secretary.

7.5.1.5 Amendments to constitution

Listing Rule 9.2.14 provides that the company must provide the FSA with two copies of any proposed amendment to its constitution (no later than when it sends out the notice of EGM to shareholders to vote on the proposal).

7.5.1.6 Shares in public hands

One of the conditions for listing is that at least 25% of the company's shares are in public hands (LR 6.1.19R) (see **4.3.1.1**). Listing Rule 9.2.16R provides that the company must give written notice to the FSA without delay if the proportion of listed securities in public hands falls below 25%.

7.5.2 Shareholders (and other security holders)

One of the underlying principles of the continuing obligations is equal treatment of shareholders. This reflects Listing Principle 5 (see **3.5.2.1** and **Appendix 2**). This principle is reflected strongly in LR 9.3, which deals with various obligations relating to shareholders, including the following.

7.5.2.1 Equality of treatment

The effect of LR 9.3.1R is that information should not be given to one shareholder unless it is also given, at the same time, to all other shareholders who hold shares of the same class. The obligation does not change the fact that different rights can attach to different classes of shares.

7.5.2.2 Prescribed information to shareholders

The company must keep its shareholders informed of all information necessary for them to exercise their rights. Listing Rules 9.3.3R to 9.3.8R set out this continuing obligation, but other chapters set out the detail of the requirements:

(a) chapter 10 details the requirements in connection with the company entering into a Class 1 transaction;

(b) chapter 11 contains the requirements in connection with related party transactions; and

(c) chapter 13 deals specifically with the method by which a company tends to circulate information to its shareholders – the circular.

Listing Rule 9.3.3R(3) lists certain information which the company must communicate to its shareholders. It includes:

(a) the allocation and payment of dividends and interest;

(b) the issue of new securities; and

(c) redemption and repayment of securities.

For further detail as to how the company communicates with its shareholders, see **7.7** below.

7.5.2.3 Pre-emption rights

Listing Rule 9.3.11R provides that if the company issues equity shares for cash, the company must first offer those shares to the existing equity shareholders pro rata (that is, in proportion to their existing holdings). This right reflects the statutory rights of shareholders under ss 89 to 95 of the CA 1985. However, the shareholders of a listed company can agree to dispense with their pre-emption rights, and LR 9.3.12R makes it clear that any general disapplication by the shareholders of their statutory pre-emption rights will also disapply the pre-emption rights under LR 9.3.11R.

So what happens in practice? Well, most listed companies have listed with a view to raising cash by issuing shares at some point. This is an advantage of being listed (see **1.5.1**). Pre-emption rights would, of course, impede this process, as the shares would first have to be offered to the existing shareholders. Therefore, most public companies effect a general dispapplication of the statutory pre-emption rights (but, typically, agree to comply with the Listing Rules pre-emption rights) at each annual general meeting (AGM). Resolution 2 of the ABI Guidelines on directors' power to allot share capital and disapply shareholders' pre-emption rights is an example of a typical disapplication. It is reproduced in **Appendix 5**.

For further information on pre-emption rights, see **Chapter 14**.

7.5.3 Documents requiring prior approval

Listing Rule 9.4 provides that certain documents, including employees' share schemes and long term incentive plans (see **13.9**) and discounted option arrangements, require the prior approval, by ordinary resolution, of shareholders.

7.5.4 Transactions

Listing Rule 9.5 sets out the continuing obligations relating to transactions. **Chapter 19** of this book considers in detail the Listing Rules relating to transactions.

7.5.5 Notifications

In addition to the general disclosure obligation under the Disclosure Rules, the Listing Rules set out various specific disclosures, or 'notifications', that a listed company must make. The rules relating to notifications are set out in LR 9.6.

7.5.5.1 Copies of documents

Listing Rules 9.6.1R to 9.6.3R provide that the company must file two copies of the following documents with the FSA:

(a) all circulars, notices, reports (at the same time they are issued); and
(b) resolutions, other than resolutions concerning ordinary business at an AGM (as soon as possible after the relevant meeting).

The FSA will then publish these documents through its document viewing facility. The company must also notify an RIS that it has filed such documents with the FSA, and set out where copies of the document can be obtained. Alternatively, the company can provide the full text of such documents to the RIS, but this is likely to be impractical with more weighty documents.

7.5.5.2 Notification relating to capital

Listing Rules 9.6.4R and 9.6.5R set out a specific obligation to disclose various developments relating to the company's capital, such as:

(a) proposed changes to capital structure;
(b) any change in the rights which attach to any class of listed securities; and
(c) the results of any fresh issue or offer of listed securities.

The company must notify the information to an RIS as soon as possible. There are also specific rules relating to notifications about offers to the public for cash, open offers and underwriting.

7.5.5.3 Notification of major interests in shares

Chapter 15 considers ss 198 to 208 of the CA 1985, which require every major shareholder to notify the company if his, her or its shareholding:

(a) has fallen from above 3% to below 3%;
(b) has risen from below 3% to above 3%; or
(c) is over 3% and rises or falls to a different percentage level.

It also sets out the right of the company, pursuant to s 212 of the CA 1985, to request certain information from shareholders.

Listing Rules 9.6.7R and 9.6.8R oblige the company to disclose to the public the information it acquires under ss 198–208, or which it should have acquired under those sections but actually acquired under s 212. The company must make this disclosure in the usual way, that is, by notifying the information to an RIS as soon as possible. See further at **15.7.2.1**.

7.5.5.4 Notifications of board charges and directors' details

The company must notify an RIS when a new director is appointed, an existing director resigns, retires or is removed, or there is a change to any important function or executive responsibility of a director (LR 9.6.11R).

Listing Rule 9.6.13R provides that the company must notify an RIS of certain information about new directors, including details of certain current and past directorships, unspent convictions, bankruptcies and any public criticism by a regulatory or statutory body. An example of this type of notification is set out below:

> **Merrill Lynch World Mining Trust plc – New Director**
> On 16 June 2005 the Board of Merrill Lynch World Mining Trust plc announced the appointment of Anthony Lea as a non-executive director of the Company with effect from 29 July 2005.
> Mr Lea is a director of Anglo American Finance (UK) PLC, Anglo American plc and Anglo American Capital plc.
> Mr Lea does not have any interest in the Company's shares at the date of this appointment.
> There are no details in respect of Mr Lea that require disclosure under paragraph 9.6.13R(2) to (6) of the Listing Rules.

7.5.5.5 Notification of lock-up arrangements

Listing Rules 9.6.16R and 9.6.17R provide that the company must notify an RIS of any lock-up arrangements that have not already been disclosed, or of any changes to any lock-up arrangements previously disclosed. A lock-up arrangement is also known as an irrevocable undertaking (see **21.10**).

7.5.5.6 Notification of shareholder resolutions

The company must notify an RIS as soon as possible after a general meeting of all resolutions passed (other than resolutions concerning ordinary business passed at an AGM). See also the obligation at **7.5.5.1** above.

7.5.5.7 Change of name

If the listed company changes its name, LR 9.6.19R provides that it must, as soon as possible:

(a) notify an RIS (stating the date on which the change has effect);
(b) inform the FSA in writing; and
(c) send the FSA a copy of the revised certificate of incorporation.

7.5.5.8 Change of accounting date

The company must notify an RIS as soon as possible of any change in its accounting reference date. If the change extends the accounting period to more than 14 months, the company must produce a second interim report (LR 9.6.20R to LR 9.6.22G).

7.5.5.9 Notification when the RIS is not open for business

It should now be clear that the method prescribed by the Disclosure Rules and the Listing Rules for making disclosures to the public is through the company's chosen RIS. What happens when the company suddenly discovers it needs to make an announcement, to comply with the 'as soon as possible' requirement, and the RIS is closed? The answer lies in DR 1.3.6R and LR 1.3.4R, which provide that the company must ensure that it distributes the information to at least two national newspapers in the UK and to two newswire services operating in the UK. This is an exception from the general rule, under DR 2.5.6R, that price-sensitive information should not be given to anyone before it has been notified to an RIS. The information should be notified to an RIS as soon as it re-opens. This is a useful paragraph to know about, as the client may well call its lawyers late at night (when its RIS has closed), needing to know very quickly how to effect the disclosure that same night. Some corporate finance specialists have two copies of the Part 6 rules – one in the office and one by the bed.

7.5.6 Financial information

Listing Rules 9.7 to 9.9 set out the requirements for a listed company to publish financial information on an ongoing basis. The company's accountants will advise in relation to these specific disclosure requirements; however, they contain three publications of which lawyers must be aware:

(a) *Preliminary statement of annual results and dividends (LR 9.7)*. The company must approve and publish a preliminary statement of annual results within 120 days of the end of the period to which it relates. The statement must be notified to an RIS as soon as possible after the board has approved it.

(b) *Annual report and accounts (LR 9.8)*. The company must publish an annual report and accounts as soon as possible after the accounts have been approved, and no later than six months after the end of the financial period to which they relate. So, if a company's year end is September, the accounts must be published at the latest by the end of March. While the lawyers will not usually be involved in the financial content of the annual report and accounts, they will often be involved in checking that the report contains the information required by the Listing Rules (for example, the information on corporate governance, considered in **8.3.4.1** and **8.3.4.3** below). The annual report and accounts are also used by the company as a marketing tool. They are a useful source of information to any corporate lawyer seeking further information on clients, potential clients or companies involved in transactions on which they are advising.

(c) *Half yearly reports (known as 'interims') (LR 9.9)*. The company must publish interims within 90 days of the end of the six-month period to which they relate.

If the company fails to publish either the annual report and accounts, or the interims within the prescribed time limits, the listing of its shares will be suspended (but the company must continue to comply with the Listing Rules and the Disclosure Rules).

7.6 The Model Code

As stated at **7.5.1.3**, the company must ensure that its persons discharging managerial responsibilities (PDMRs) (see **7.6.2.1**) and certain employees comply with the Model Code, which is set out at Annex 1R to chapter 9 of the Listing Rules. The company can, however, impose more rigorous obligations than those required by the Model Code (LR 9.2.9G). The Model Code restricts how PDMRs and employees can deal in the company's shares. It is in addition to the other rules which apply to dealing by such persons, such as:

(a) the market abuse provisions of the FSMA 2000 (see **Chapter 10**);
(b) the insider dealing regime of the CJA 1993 (see **Chapter 11**);

(c) the notification obligations under ss 324 to 328 of the CA 1985 and DR 3.1.2 and the obligation on the company to pass on to the market the information it receives under those rules (DR 3.1.4R(1)) (see **Chapter 15**);

(d) the prohibition on directors dealing in share options (CA 1985, s323); and

(e) the fiduciary duties of directors.

The task of making sure the directors comply with the Model Code is usually dealt with in-house, by the company secretary or an in-house lawyer, because the day-to-day nature of compliance means that it would be administratively difficult (and expensive) for external lawyers to police. For example, the Model Code contains detailed provisions relating to share schemes, trusts and options, which require a detailed knowledge of the company's affairs before they can be applied. However, external lawyers will be expected to advise on aspects of the Model Code on occasion, for example if the company secretary or in-house lawyer is unavailable, or if they want a second opinion. As always, recourse should be made to the detail of the Model Code itself; however,the following provides a flavour of those parts of the Model Code with which the external lawyer will need to be familiar.

7.6.1 Purpose of the Model Code

Why is so much attention paid to the dealings of PDMRs and certain employees, over and above the dealings of any other shareholder? Well, PDMRs, including directors, manage the day-to-day business of the company. They, together with certain employees (who, because of their office, possess price-sensitive information), are best placed to know when they can trade in shares to make a personal profit. For example, say the directors receive an approach from a bidder with a lucrative offer to take over the company. Imagine at this point that the company's shares are worth £1 each and the offer is that bidder will pay £2 for each share. The shareholders do not know it yet, but they are about to double their money. The PDMRs, and certain key employees, however, will know it, so what is to stop them from using their advantage over the other shareholders by suddenly investing huge amounts in the company before the offer becomes public knowledge? Answer: the Model Code (or its equivalent). The integrity of the market requires that directors do not abuse their position in this way. The Model Code, therefore, restricts the ability of PDMRs and certain employees to deal in the company's shares.

7.6.2 Applicability of the Model Code

Under the old regime, the Model Code used to apply to directors and certain employees. Under the new regime, the Model Code applies to a wider set of people, namely PDMRs and 'employee insiders' (together referred to in the Model Code as 'restricted persons').

In addition, the PDMRs must also comply with the following rules in relation to 'connected persons' (Model Code, paras 20 to 22):

(a) take reasonable steps to prevent dealings in the company's securities, by, or on behalf of, his connected persons, on considerations of a short-term nature (see **7.6.4.3**) (para 20); and

(b) seek to prohibit dealings in the company's securities, by, or on behalf of his connected persons (or by an investment manager on his behalf) during a close period (see **7.6.4.3**) (para 21).

In order to fulfil the obligation set out in paras 20 and 21, the director must comply with para 22 and advise the connected persons and invetsment managers of:

(a) the listed company's name;

(b) the close periods during which they cannot deal; and

(c) the fact that they must advise the company immediately after they have dealt in the company's securities.

Note that the Model Code will not apply to PDMRs or employees once they leave the company. They will, however, still be caught by the market abuse and insider dealing regimes (see **Chapter 10** and **Chapter 11**). The FSA can also impose a financial penalty on any former director who, while a director, was knowingly concerned in a breach of the Listing Rules (FSMA 2000, s 91(2)).

(Those familiar with the old regime will note that a similar rule applied; however, the requirement for a director to seek to prohibit other persons from dealing, because that director was in possession of price-sensitive information, has, thankfully, disappeared. It was difficult for a director to comply with that obligation without breaching his duty of confidentiality to the company.)

7.6.2.1 Persons discharging managerial responsibilities

A PDMR is defined in s 96B of the FSMA 2000 as:

(a) a director; or

(b) a senior executive of a company who:

    (i) has regular access to inside information relating, directly or indirectly, to the company; and

    (ii) has power to make managerial decisions affecting the future development and business prospects of the company.

Practically, this will include directors and a few other managers of sufficient seniority to be classified as PDMRs.

7.6.2.2 Employee insiders

An employee insider is an employee of the company, or any group company, whose name is required to be placed on an insider list in accordance with DR 2.8.1 (see **7.4.5**). In practice this is an employee who has access to inside information on a regular or occasional basis. 'Inside information' is as defined by s 118C of the FSMA (see **7.4.2.3**, substituting 'qualifying investments' for 'financial instruments').

7.6.2.3 Connected person

This is defined by s 96B of the FSMA 2000. It includes a 'connected person' as defined by s 346 of the CA 1985, as if s 346 applied to PDMRs, that is:

(a) the spouse, child or step child of a PDMR;

(b) a body corporate with which the PDMR is associated (that is, the PDMR and connected persons control, or can exercise, more than 20% of its voting power in general meeting, or are interested in at least 20% of its equity shares);

(c) the trustee of a certain trust of which the beneficiary or potential beneficiary includes the PDMR, his spouse, children or step-children under 18, or an associated body corporate;

(d) any partner of the PDMR, or any connected person's partner,

as well as the additional categories of person:

(e) a relative of a PDMR with whom, as at the date of the transaction, the PDMR has shared a house for at least 12 months; and

(f) a body corporate in which a PDMR, or any connected person as defined at (a) to (e) above, is a director or senior executive with the power to make managerial decisions affecting the future development and business prospects of that body corporate.

7.6.3 Prohibited dealings

The key provision of the Model Code is para 3: a restricted person (that is, a PDMR or employee insider) must not deal in any of the company's securities unless he obtains advance clearance to deal.

Dealing is defined by para 1(c) of the Model Code. At its simplest, it includes buying and selling shares, or agreeing to buy and sell shares. Paragraph 2 of the Model Code sets out dealings which are not subject to the Model Code.

7.6.4 Clearance to deal

This is dealt with in paras 4 to 7 of the Model Code.

7.6.4.1 Who can give clearance to deal?

Under the old regime, any director could be designated as the person from whom clearance could be sought. This has been changed under the new regime, as follows:

Person seeking clearance	Person able to give clearance
Director (other than Chairman or Chief Executive)	Chairman, or other director designated by the board (para 4(a))
Company Secretary	As above
Chairman	Chief Executive (para 4(b))
Chief Executive	Chairman (para 4(c))
Combined Chairman and Chief Executive	Board (para 4(d))
PDMR (other than a director)	Company secretary, or designated director (para 4(e)).
Employee insider	As above

7.6.4.2 The clearance procedure

The company must:

(a) keep a written record of the requests for clearance it receives, and of any clearance given (para 6);

(b) respond within five business days of the request for clearance (para 5); and

(c) provide a copy of the response and any clearance to the restricted person concerned (para 7).

Once clearance has been given, the restricted person must deal as soon as possible, and in any event within two business days of clearance being received.

7.6.4.3 Refusal of clearance to deal

Clearance to deal must not be given in the following circumstances.

During a prohibited period (Model Code, para 8(a))

A prohibited period means:

(a) any close period (see below); and

(b) any period during which inside information exists in relation to the company.

Broadly, a 'close period' is the 60-day period prior to publication of the preliminary announcement of the company's annual results (see **7.5.6**) and, if the company reports on a half-yearly basis, the half-yearly report. (If the company reports on a quarterly basis, the close period is the 30-day period before the announcement of the quarterly results.) See the definition at para 1(a) of the Model Code for further information.

'Inside information' is as defined by s 118C of the FSMA (see **7.4.2.3**, substituting 'qualifying investments' for 'financial instruments'). Remember that, usually, if inside information does exist about the company, it should be disclosed to an RIS under the general obligation of disclosure provided by DR 2.2.1R (see **7.4.1** above), and so would no longer be inside information. The prohibition on giving clearance while such inside information exists assumes that an exception to the obligation to disclose must exist, for example because the matter is still under negotiation (DR 2.5.3G(1) – see **7.4.2.8(a)**). The fact that any request for clearance would have to be refused, however, may well flag up, to a restricted person otherwise unaware of it, that there is some inside information – perhaps an acquisition or disposal in the course of negotiation – in existence. (In addition, it is possible that the restricted person might then consult the company's insider list (see **7.4.5**) to see who might well have access to that information, and so who might be interesting to take to lunch to pump for gossip.) For this reason, the lawyer will advise the company to train its restricted persons in relation to the requirements of the Model Code and the Disclosure Rules, and the importance of avoiding any breach.

On considerations of a short-term nature (Model Code, para 8(b))

Unlike under the old regime, there is now guidance as to what this means. An investment with a maturity of one year or less will always be considered to be of a short-term nature.

Why will clearance to deal not be given in such circumstances? Most shareholders can buy and sell shares as quickly as they like. For example, if you or I invest £100 in Company X tomorrow, and the next day our investment has grown to £1,000, we might well choose to realise our investment that day and treat ourselves to a week in the sun. We have made what is known as a 'fast buck'. PDMRs and certain employees subject to the Model Code cannot do this. Why? Directors' shareholdings are seen as a barometer of the company's fortunes. If a director buys shares, it sends a certain message to the market (usually positive). Similarly, if a director sells shares, it can send a negative message to the market. If a director was buying or selling shares left, right and centre, the market might well lose confidence in the company and the share price might become unstable. The

Model Code's aim is to protect investors and maintain the integrity of the market; hence it prohibits such short-term trading.

7.6.4.4 Exception for severe financial difficulty and other exceptional circumstances

Despite the rules set out at **7.6.4.3** above, paras 9, 10 and 11 provide that clearance to sell (but not buy) shares may be given where the restricted person:

(a) is not in possession of inside information; and

(b) either:

    (i) is in severe financial difficulty (eg, he has a pressing financial commitment which cannot be satisfied otherwise than by selling the shares, but this would not include a liability to tax unless the person had no other means of satisfying the liability); or

    (ii) is in other exceptional circumstances (eg, there is a court order, or other overriding legal requirement, for the transferor sale).

Ultimately, the person with responsibility for giving clearance to deal must decide whether the exception applies, but FSA guidance can be (and, in the case of exceptional circumstances, should be) sought.

If the 'exceptional circumstances' exception is used, when the company notifies an RIS of the information under DR 3.1.4 (see **Chapter 15**), it must include the nature of the exceptional circumstances.

A similar exception existed under the old regime, and in practice was rarely used. If the basis of the exception is severe financial difficulty, then the restricted person would have to show he could not wait a maximum of 60 days for the close period to expire, which will happen rarely.

7.6.5 Sanctions for breach of the Model Code

The Model Code forms part of the continuing obligations of the Listing Rules, and is enforceable against the company itself, if it has breached the requirements of LR 9.2.7R to 9.2.10R. If the company is in breach, then the FSA may impose the sanctions referred to at **7.10.1** below.

However, it may be that the company has complied with its obligations, but nevertheless a PDMR has breached the Model Code. If so, the FSA may impose a financial penalty under s 91 of the FSMA 2000, but only if the PDMR is a director or former director who was knowingly concerned in a breach of the Listing Rules.

7.7 Communication with shareholders

The Listing Rules set out many different circumstances when the company must communicate information to its shareholders.

7.7.1 The circular

As suggested by LR 9.3.3R(3) (see **7.5.2.2**), the usual way of communicating with shareholders is by way of a document known as a circular. The Listing Rules define a circular as:

> Any document issued to holders of listed securities including notices of meetings but excluding prospectuses, listing particulars, annual reports and accounts, interim reports, proxy cards and dividend or interest vouchers.

Chapter 13 of the Listing Rules, entitled 'Contents of Circulars', prescribes general content requirements of any circular (LR 13.3) (see **7.7.3**) and specific content requirements for particular types of circular (see **7.7.2**).

7.7.2 When is a circular required?

The Listing Rules set out the circumstances when a circular is required. The following are the most commonly encountered by the lawyer. The Chapter 13 Listing Rule governing the specific content requirements of the required circular is provided in brackets.

- Class 1 transactions (LR 13.4, LR 13.5 and LR 13, Annex 1R) (see **19.6.1**)
- Related party transactions (LR 13.6) (see **19.6.2**)
- Circulars regarding the purchase of own securities ('buyback') (LR 13.7)
- Authority to allot shares (LR 13.8.1R) (see **14.5.6**)
- Disapplying pre-emption (LR 13.8.2R) (see **14.6.15**)
- Increase in authorised share capital (LR 13.8.3R) (see **14.4.4**)
- Reduction of capital (LR 13.8.4R)
- Capitalisation or bonus issue (LR 13.8.5R)
- Scrip dividend alternative (LR 13.8.6R)
- Scrip dividend mandate schemes/dividend reinvestment plan (LR 13.8.7R)
- Notices of meetings (including business other than ordinary business at an AGM) (LR 13.8.8R)
- Amendments to constitution (LR 13.8.9R)
- Employees' share scheme arrangements (LR 13.8.11R to LR 13.8.14R)
- Discounted option arrangements (LR 13.8.15R)
- Reminders of conversion rights (LR 13.8.16R)

7.7.3 General content requirements

The basic content requirements of all circulars are prescribed by LR 13.3. To provide a flavour of what is in a circular, a sample of the requirements include:

(a) a clear and adequate explanation of the subject matter;
(b) a statement why the shareholder is being asked to vote, or otherwise why the circular is being sent;
(c) if voting or other action is required:
   (i) all information necessary to allow the shareholder to make a properly informed decision; and
   (ii) a heading drawing attention to the importance of the document and advising the shareholder to consult an independent adviser if he is unsure what action to take;
(d) if voting is required, a recommendation from the board as to how shareholders should vote, indicating whether the proposal is, in its opinion, in the shareholders' best interests.

7.7.4 FSA approval

Under the old regime, circulars which required FSA approval were called 'non-routine circulars', and those which did not require approval were called 'routine circulars'. This terminology is not used by the new regime, but the basic premise remains that some circulars require the prior approval by the FSA before the company can circulate them to shareholders, and others do not. The lawyer will need to be able to advise on whether a circular requires prior approval.

Once published, any circular, approved or otherwise, must be sent to FSA for publication on its document viewing facility (see **7.5.5.1**).

7.7.4.1 Circulars which do not require approval

Listing Rule 13.2.2R provides that circulars which do not require prior approval (formerly known as routine circulars) are those which:

(a)   are listed in LR 13.8R (or relate only to a proposed change of name);

(b)   comply with LR 13.3 and any requirements of LR 13.8; and

(c)   have no unusual features.

As can be seen from the list at **7.7.2** above, there are many circulars listed in LR 13.8. They include circulars relating to share capital changes, such as an increase in authorised share capital, the grant of an authority to allot and the disapplication of pre-emption rights.

7.7.4.2 Circulars which require approval

Conversely, all other circulars require approval (LR 13.2.1). By definition, these will be circulars which:

(a)   are not listed in LR 13.8R; and

(b)   have unusual features.

The approval process is detailed in LR 13.2.4 to 13.2.9. The company must submit the draft circular to the FSA at least 10 clear business days before the intended publication date.

7.8 The Prospectus Rules

As outlined above, most continuing obligations are contained in the Listing Rules, and a few, including the general obligation of disclosure, are contained in the Disclosure Rules. However, the Prospectus Rules contain one new continuing obligation, the obligation under PR 5.2 to produce an Annual Information Update.

7.8.1 The Annual Information Update

A listed company must file an annual information update with the FSA every 12 months. This update must refer to or contain all information the company has published or made available to the public in compliance with securities laws in the UK or elsewhere. In the UK, this includes information published or made available under the CA 1985, the FSMA 2000, the Disclosure Rules and the Listing Rules.

The update is filed with the FSA by way of notification to an RIS. The notification must be made within 20 working days of the date on which the company files its annual accounts with the FSA. All the information referred to must be available to investors, and the update should state where investors can obtain the information.

Practically, the lawyer must make sure the company is aware of this new obligation, so that the company can maintain a composite list of all such information. There is no prescribed form for the update, and as at the date of writing, various formats were being used. An excerpt of a typical example of an update is set out below:

HMV Group plc

Annual Information Update – 12 months to 8 August 2005.

In accordance with Prospectus Rule 5.2 the following information has been published or made available to the public in the previous 12 months.

Date	Via	Item	Brief Description
9/8/04	Companies House	Form 88 (2)	Return of allotment of shares on exercise of share options
16/8/04	RNS	Director Shareholding	Directors' share purchase via Company SIP
19/8/04	RNS	Holding(s) in Company	Notification of major interests in shares
23/8/04	Companies House	Form 363s	Annual return
26/8/04	Companies House	Form 88(2)	Return of allotment of shares on exercise of share options
2/9/04	Companies House	Form 88(2)	Return of allotment of shares on exercise of share options
7/9/04	Companies House	Form 88(2)	Return of allotment of shares on exercise of share options
10/9/04	RNS	Notice of Results	Notice of date of release of 2004/05 Interim results and Christmas trading update
15/9/04	RNS	Director Shareholding	Directors' share purchase via Company SIP
17/9/04	Companies House	Form 88(2)	Return of allotment of shares on exercise of share options
22/9/04	RNS	Holding(s) in Company	Notification of major interests in shares
22/9/04	Companies House	Form 88(2)	Return of allotment of shares on exercise of share options

The information referred to above as having been filed with the Registrar of Companies can be obtained from Companies House, Crown Way, Cardiff, CF14 3UZ. That referred to as published via the RNS may be obtained from the Regulatory News Service provided by the London Stock Exchange and any related documents are available at the UKLA's Document Viewing Facility, Financial Services Authority, 25 The North Colonnade, Canary Wharf, London, E14 5HS, or from the Company's website at www.hmvgroup.com.

Copies of all documents referred to are also available for inspection at the Company's registered office at Shelley House, 2-4 York Road, Maidenhead, Berkshire, SL6 1SR during normal business hours on weekdays.

In accordance with Article 27(3) of the Prospectus Directive Regulation, it is acknowledged that whilst the information referred to above was up to date at the time of publication, such disclosures may, at any time, become out of date due to changing circumstances.

7.9 The Admission and Disclosure Standards

As stated at **7.1** above, the Admission and Disclosure Standards contain continuing obligations which are additional to those set out in the Listing Rules. These obligations are set out at para 3 (see **Appendix 1**), and they include that the company must comply with the Listing Rules. The other continuing obligations are very brief, compared with the requirements of the Listing Rules. They include:

(a) requirements relating to the timetable for what are referred to as 'corporate actions', that is, open offers, rights issues, dividends and the like (paras 3.4 to 3.11);

(b) that the Stock Exchange will suspend the admission to trading of any shares which are suspended from admission to listing (paras 3.14 and 3.15) (this is a mirror image of LR 9.2.1R – see **7.5.1.1** above); and

(c) that the company must pay an annual fee to the Stock Exchange (para 3.13).

7.10 Sanctions

7.10.1 Sanctions for breach of the Disclosure Rules, the Prospectus Rules or the Listing Rules

Sanctions for breach of the Disclosure Rules, the Prospectus Rules or the Listing Rules are set out at **3.7** above. As the articles below show, the FSA has used its powers to censure or fine companies or directors who breached the Old Listing Rules.

Car salvage firm fined for Listing Rules breach

Richard Miles

A MOTOR vehicle disposal business was yesterday fined £90,000 by financial regulators because its former chief executive had failed to inform the market of a major contract loss early enough.

Universal Salvage is only the second company to receive a penalty from the Financial Services Authority (FSA) for a serious breach of the Listing Rules, which govern the disclosure of price-sensitive information to markets.

The FSA said that although Universal Salvage had known about the imminent loss of a substantial contract with Direct Line, the insurance group, on April 16, 2002, it had failed to make a public announcement until April 23.

Martin Hynes, chief executive at the time, was deemed by the watchdog to bear the brunt of the blame. Mr Hynes, who stepped down as a non executive director of Universal Salvage yesterday, was also fined £10,000.

Andrew Procter, director of enforcement at the FSA, said companies and their directors had to be aware of their obligations to inform the market "without delay" of any changes to their business because this was a "fundamental protection for shareholders".

He added: "That this is the second director of a listed company that we have fined in as many months demonstrates how seriously we expect firms to take these responsibilities."

At the end of March the FSA censured Sportsworld Media Group and fined its chief executive, Geoffrey Brown, £45,000 over a breach of the listing rules. The FSA is expected to take action against other firms as investigations begun in 2002 bear fruit.

Universal Salvage said it had been given credit for its co-operation with the investigation.

Source: *The Times*, 20 May 2004

SFI spared penalty despite censure from regulator

SFI Group, the troubled operator of the Slug and Lettuce and Litten Tree pub chains, has been censured by the Financial Services Authority for misleading the market, but has escaped a financial penalty.

The company, which in November last year revealed a £20 million accounting black hole, is the first to be censured by the FSA for contravention of stock market listing rules since the City regulator began operating in December 2001.

In a statement on findings of its investigation into SFI, the FSA said that the pub company "failed to take reasonable care" that its full-year results announcement in July 2002 "was not false or misleading".

It said that the results had presented "an overstated and over-optimistic view of SFI's financial results and its future prospects" not only for that financial year, but also for the previous two years.

In its conclusion, the regulator said that the seriousness of the breaches was sufficient to merit a "significant financial penalty". But it had stepped back from imposing such a penalty because of SFI's parlous financial position and because the company had alerted the regulator to the accounting discrepancies as soon as they had come to light.

The FSA also said that it had found "no evidence to suggest that SFI contravened the listing rules deliberately or that it knowingly failed at any time to have proper regard to its obligations under the listing rules".

In a statement, SFI acknowledged "with concern" the conclusions of the FSA's report, which it said had highlighted "the lack of adequate financial controls in place at the time to cope with SFI's aggressive expansion and growth".

Stuart Lawson, the group's recently appointed executive chairman, said: "Since then, SFI has taken a number of significant steps to respond comprehensively to the underlying causes and more recently has started to implement a three-year recovery plan."

The FSA's damning assessment said that SFI's accounting systems and controls had been unreliable and insufficiently robust to determine the group's financial position and support internal forecasts and projections.

In particular, there had been "serious failures in its management of cashflow and capital expenditure" because of inaccurate forecasting and monitoring.

The FSA conceded that the pressure put on the group's finance department by the chain's rapid growth – it expanded from 24 pubs to 186 between 1996 and 2002 – had been exacerbated by the lack of a finance director between the departure of James Kowszun in April 2002 and the arrival of Tim Andrews in July of that year.

The FSA highlighted the absence of other key staff from the department because of illness and pointed to a reliance on an accounting system based on spreadsheets.

Another problem had been the "operations-driven management culture" that had reduced the company's finance department to a secondary role.

The publication of the FSA's report, which appears to rule out the possibility of action against individuals, comes after the revelation by *The Times* last week that SFI had breached its banking covenants twice in 2001, well before its financial plight first came to light more than a year later.

SFI, which was delisted in April, admitted in October that the investments of ordinary shareholders had been wiped out.

The company has total debts of more than £150 million and analysts believe that, with an asset writedown of about £60 million believed to be imminent, the pubs would be lucky to fetch £75 million.

Despite Mr Lawson's three-year turnaround plan, analysts believe that he has an almost impossible task and that SFI's banking consortium, which is led by Barclays, may yet be forced to call in receivers.

Breaches of The Listing Rules
Announced 2002 pre-tax profits of £19.5m instead of £13.4m
Stated net assets to be £85.5m instead of £62.4m
Materially mis-stated headline figures in profit & loss account/balance sheet
Made statements based on inadequate/unreliable accounting systems
Erroneously stated it was in a strong position to maintain earnings growth

Source: *The Times*, 13 December 2003

7.10.2 Sanctions for breach of the Admission and Disclosure Standards

The sanctions are set out at paras 3.21 to 3.23 of the Admission and Disclosure Standards. In the event of breach of any continuing obligation, the Stock Exchange may publicly censure a company, or alternatively cancel the company's admission to trading.

7.11 Future developments

The Transparency Directive was adopted on 15 December 2004 and must be implemented in Member States by 20 January 2007. The Directive is likely to change the continuing obligations of the Listing Rules relating to financial reporting and communication with shareholders.

On 6 October 2006 the FSA published Consultation Paper 06/17 which proposes changes to the scope of the Model Code. The changes include the deletion of all references to employee insiders (see **7.6.2.2**).

Chapter 8
Corporate Governance

8.1	What is corporate governance?	107
8.2	The UK framework	107
8.3	The Combined Code	107
8.4	The Directors' Remuneration Report Regulations 2002	118
8.5	Institutional investors	119
8.6	Future developments	120

8.1 What is corporate governance?

Corporate governance refers to how a company is run. This includes not only how a company is directed and controlled, but also how a company is performing, how that performance can be enhanced, and how a company should account to interested parties such as shareholders and employees.

Corporate governance is relevant to all companies, but once a company is listed, those who control the company (directors and controlling shareholders) are not the same as, and therefore may have conflicting interests to, those who own the company (shareholders). This means that corporate governance is a particularly important issue for listed companies.

8.2 The UK framework

Common law, the CA 1985, the Listing Rules (in particular, the continuing obligations, Model Code and listing principles), the Combined Code on Corporate Governance (the 'Combined Code'), the Directors' Remuneration Report Regulations 2002, the FSA's Code of Market Conduct and various non-legal guidelines produced by institutional shareholders (such as the ABI, the NAPF and PIRC) and the accountancy profession all contain provisions which address corporate governance issues. The Combined Code and the 2002 Regulations are discussed further below.

8.3 The Combined Code

8.3.1 Nature

The Combined Code is the most prominent part of the UK corporate governance framework. It is a codification of best practice in corporate governance. The Combined Code does not have the force of law. Rather, as **8.3.4** below explains in more detail, companies are required to comply with the Combined Code, or to explain their non-compliance. The original combined code was annexed to, but did not form part of, the Listing Rules. Since 2003 the Combined Code is no longer annexed to the Listing Rules but instead is available on the Financial Reporting Council (FRC) website.

8.3.2 Background

To date there have been three editions of the combined code: the original of 1995, a revised version published in 2003, and a recently updated version published in 2006.

For the reasons explained at **8.3.2.3** below, at the time of writing, the 2006 code was still in an interim period regarding compliance. For this reason, the FRC currently has both the 2003 and 2006 version of the code on its website. However, to avoid confusion, only the 2006 version of the code is appended at **Appendix 4**, and references in this book to the Combined Code are to the updated code of 2006, unless otherwise indicated. If, for the reasons explained at **8.3.2.2**, recourse is required to the 2003 version of the combined code, please access it on the FRC website.

8.3.2.1 Background to the original combined code of 1995

The provisions of the original combined code were based on the findings of three reports, namely the Cadbury, Greenbury and Hampel Reports, which were commissioned in the 1990s to consider corporate governance in detail. The Hampel Committee 'combined' the recommendations of all three reports to produce the original combined code. This combined code was annexed to the Listing Rules in 1995 and the Listing Rules were amended to refer to compliance with it. In 1999 a further report (the Turnbull Report) was commissioned, to provide guidance to listed companies regarding implementation of the requirements in the original Combined Code relating to internal control.

8.3.2.2 Background to the combined code of 2003

In 2002, financial scandals involving Enron (see the article below) and WorldCom put corporate governance in the spotlight again. In the UK, two further reports were commissioned immediately. The Financial Reporting Council commissioned the Smith Report (concerning audit issues) and the DTI commissioned the Higgs Report (concerning non-executive directors and remuneration). Those responsible for compiling these reports worked closely together to propose a consolidated revised code. Some of the proposals proved controversial, however, so the Financial Reporting Council set up a working group to revise the code further. The final text of this revised code was published in July 2003 and took effect for reporting periods beginning on or after 1 November 2003.

Enron: The Countdown to Court
Leader of boys' club culture
The Chief Executive

Before he became the most prominent alleged white collar criminal of his era, Jeffrey Skilling was the quintessential Enron executive.

Perhaps no one at the Houston-based energy company so embodied its combustible corporate culture of brains and arrogance as Mr Skilling, a Harvard Business School graduate and McKinsey & Company alumnus.

Like Kenneth Lay, his Enron boss, Mr Skilling rose from humble roots to become one of the most celebrated - and later reviled - American executives. The son of a salesman, he worked his way through university despite earning a scholarship.

Academia came easy to Mr Skilling, and he demonstrated a brash self-confidence well before he had scaled the heights of the business world.

When asked during his Harvard interview if he was smart, Mr Skilling famously replied: "I'm f***ing smart," according to The Smartest Guys in the Room, a book about Enron by Bethany McLean and Peter Elkind.

After graduation, Mr Skilling moved on to become one of the youngest partners in the history of McKinsey. It was a remarkable achievement at a consulting firm known for its over-achievers.

It was at McKinsey, leading the energy practice, that Mr Skilling encountered Enron, a relatively unexciting pipeline company that had been strung together by a series of mergers.

After years of advising its then chief executive, Mr Lay, he finally moved over full time in 1990. Mr Skilling's phenomenal success at Enron was something known as the Gas Bank, which was an attempt to apply emerging financial techniques to a stubborn patch of the traditional energy business.

His plan was to insert Enron between natural gas buyers and sellers to smooth out the notoriously unpredictable prices for the commodity that were embedded in rigid, long-term contracts, or a wild spot market.

Enron then went on to create a secondary market to trade natural gas contracts in the same way as other commodities to give buyers and sellers even more flexibility. To spur the venture, Mr Skilling convinced the Securities and Exchange Commission in 1992 to allow the gas contracts to be marked-to-market, an accounting treatment that would allow their entire projected value, sometimes over 20 years or more, to be recognised upfront. A decade later, this would prove to be a fateful accomplishment as Enron routinely abused mark-to-market accounting to record billions of dollars of dubious profits that were never likely to materialise.

In the meantime, however, the Gas Bank was an enormous success. It created a robust trading market that boosted the natural gas industry as a whole.

And Enron was at the centre of it all.

Not only did the company reap trading commissions, its own traders were able consistently to bet on the right side of the market.

Part of Mr Skilling's downfall was a stubborn insistence that the Gas Bank's success could be replicated. Under his leadership, Enron shed dependable assets such as its pipelines and instead made markets in everything from paper pulp to broadband internet access.

The results were disastrous. One problem, among many, was that Enron simply did not understand these commodities in the same way it did natural gas, with which it had an intimate history.

As the debacles mounted, Enron executives resorted to ever more aggressive accounting techniques to satisfy Mr Skilling's obsession with hitting Wall Street earnings targets and boosting the share price.

In keeping with many other big companies, this focus on share price and short-term earnings, often to the exclusion of all other business measures, would be a hallmark of the 1990s stock market bubble and its ensuing corporate scandals.

For all his intellectual brilliance, Mr Skilling did not prove to be much of a manager. He favoured raw intelligence over experience in his recruits, and presided over a ruthless compensation system in which top performers were lavishly rewarded while others were tossed out. A boys' club culture prevailed at the company, where a cadre of loyalists such as Andrew Fastow, the former chief financial officer; Lou Pai, the former head of Enron Energy Services; and Ken Rice, the former head of Enron Broadband; joined Mr Skilling on exotic company-paid vacations where they raced off-road vehicles across Mexico.

Meanwhile, internal controls were practically non-existent, and inter-office affairs became de rigeur.

Even as Enron's fortunes, and his own, have collapsed, Mr Skilling has not abandoned his trademark arrogance. At a Congressional hearing two years ago, the former executive declined to exercise his Fifth Amendment right as so many embattled executives had done, including Mr Lay, and remain quiet. Instead, he proceeded to lecture enraged legislators on the intricacies of accounting rules.

It was an audacious performance, and one that Mr Skilling will now have the opportunity to replay with federal prosecutors at an upcoming criminal trial.

Source: *Financial Times*, 20 February 2004

In May 2006 Jeffrey Skilling was convicted on 19 counts of conspiracy and fraud in a joint trial with Kenneth Lay, the former Enron chairman. Skilling was found not guilty of nine counts of insider trading. On 23 October 2006 Skilling was sentenced to 24 years and 4 months in prison, a penalty which is the second most severe ever for white-collar fraud in America (the former chief executive of MCI WorldCom, Bernard Ebbers, who defrauded employees and shareholders of some $11 billion, received a 25-year sentence in 2005).

Kenneth Lay was also convicted of 10 counts of fraud and other related charges, but died of a heart attack in July 2006, prior to sentencing. The guilty verdict against him has now been overturned on the basis that Mr Lay did not have the opportunity to appeal against his conviction before his death.

Enron's former chief financial officer, Andrew Fastow, pleaded guilty to conspiracy to commit wire fraud and securities fraud and turned supergrass against Skilling and Lay in return for a more modest sentence of six years in prison.

8.3.2.3 Background to the 2006 Combined Code

In July 2005, the FRC announced a review of the implementation of the 2003 version of the combined code. As a result of this review, a small number of changes were incorporated into an updated version of the code, referred to in this book as the Combined Code, published in June 2006. The main changes are as follows:

(a) if the Chairman is considered independent at the time of appointment, he can now serve on (but should not chair) the remuneration committee (B.2.1);

(b) shareholders can indicate 'vote withheld' on a proxy appointment form, if they have reservations on a resolution but do not wish to vote against the resolution (D.2.1);

(c) the Code recommends that a company publishes on its website details of proxy votes lodged at a general meeting where votes are taken on a show of hands (D.2.2); and

(d) Schedule C has been added, to collate the various disclosure requirements in the Combined Code (see **8.3.4.3**).

Changes have also been made to make the wording of the Combined Code consistent with that of the Companies Bill (see **1.11**).

It is important to note that, at the time of writing, listed companies cannot be required to disclose how they have applied the 2006 version of the Code as they can with the 2003 version of the Code (see **8.3.5.1**). This is because the FSA must carry out a separate consultation before it can amend the Listing Rules to require this. The FSA intends to begin this consultation in September 2006 with the hope that the Listing Rules will apply to the 2006 version of the Code with effect from Spring 2007. In the meantime, given the limited nature of the changes made, the FRC is encouraging companies and investors to comply voluntarily with the 2006 Code for reporting years beginning on or after 1 November 2006.

8.3.3 Structure

The Combined Code consists of 17 main principles of good governance. Each principle is supplemented by a set of supporting principles and code provisions. The supporting principles were drafted with the intention of affording companies an element of flexibility regarding the implementation of the main principles.

The Combined Code is divided into two main sections. Section 1 sets out the main principles relating to:

(a) directors (para A – seven principles);
(b) remuneration (para B – two principles);
(c) accountability and audit (para C – three principles); and
(d) relations with shareholders (para D – two principles).

Section 2 sets out three main principles relating to institutional shareholders (para E).

In recognition that smaller listed companies can find it difficult to achieve full compliance with the Combined Code, certain provisions have been relaxed for companies below the FTSE 350.

8.3.4 Associated guidance

The following guidance on the Combined Code is also available from the FRC website.

8.3.4.1 The Turnbull Guidance

The Turnbull Guidance was published originally in 1999, to set out best practice on the internal control of companies. Following a review by the FRC, the guidance was updated in October 2005. It applies to listed companies for financial year beginning on or after 1 January 2006.

8.3.4.2 Good Practice Suggestions from the Higgs Report

Companies are not obliged to follow this guide to best practice in relation to non-executive directors (see **8.3.6.1**), but they may find it helpful. The suggestions, published in June 2006, provide guidance on the role of the Chairman and the non-executive director, a summary of the principal duties of the remuneration and nomination committees, a due diligence checklist for new board members, a sample letter of appointment of a non-executive director, an induction checklist and a performance evaluation guidance.

8.3.4.3 The Smith Guidance on Audit Committees

This guide to best practice in relation to audit committees was published in 2003. It includes guidance on how to establish a committee, the relationship of the committee with the board, the role and responsibilities of the committee, and how it should communicate with shareholders. As with the Higgs Report suggestions, companies are not obliged to follow the Smith Guidance.

8.3.5 Compliance

8.3.5.1 Section 1

While any company can choose to follow the provisions of section 1 of the Combined Code, the Listing Rules provide that, strictly, section 1 applies only to listed companies incorporated in the UK. Even these companies are not subject to any requirement to comply with section 1. Instead, the requirement is that any such company must include in its annual report a statement, known as a 'disclosure statement', which details:

(a) how it has applied the *principles* (main and supporting) set out in section 1 (in a way which shareholders will understand) (LR 9.8.6R(5)); and

(b) whether it has complied throughout the accounting period with the code *provisions* set out in section 1 and, if it has not, which provisions it has not complied with, the period of non-compliance, and why it has not complied (LR 9.8.6R(6)).

The disclosure requirements are often referred to as the 'comply or explain' approach. This approach encourages compliance even though strictly it does not require it, because the requirement to disclose any failure to comply carries with it a risk of adverse publicity. The institutional investors have made it clear, however, that they do expect compliance and, in practice, companies which do not comply with section 1 are often subject to significant pressure from institutional investors such as the ABI, the NAPF and PIRC.

There is no prescribed form of disclosure statement, which, as with other aspects of the corporate governance regime, is intended to afford companies a degree of flexibility.

Listing Rule 9.8.10R(2) provides that, before it publishes its annual report, the company must ensure that its auditors review the disclosure statement in relation to nine provisions of the Combined Code which deal with audit and accountability, and which are objectively verifiable (namely C1.1, C2.1 and C3.1 to C3.7).

Listing Rule 9.8.7R sets out the obligations of any overseas company listed on the Official List, in relation to the matters referred to above. Such companies are not required to 'comply or explain', but they must state their compliance with their domestic corporate governance code or law and explain how their actual practices differ from the Combined Code.

In Summer 2006 the FRC met with the Chairmen of various FTSE 100 companies. A summary of their discussions, published on the FRC website, confirms that the 'comply or explain' approach is generally well received.

Note that, for the reasons explained at **8.3.2.3** above, until the Listing Rules are amended to refer to the 2006 version of the Combined Code (expected Spring 2007), references in this paragraph to the Combined Code are to the 2003 version of the code. Companies are, however, encouraged (but cannot be compelled) to 'comply and explain' in relation to the 2006 version of the Code instead.

8.3.5.2 Section 2

Section 2 of the Combined Code applies to institutional shareholders rather than companies. Companies do not, therefore, need to comply with, or make a disclosure statement in relation to, section 2.

8.3.5.3 Disclosure of corporate governance arrangements

In addition to the disclosure statement referred to at **8.3.4.1** above, several of the Combined Code provisions require further disclosure, including in the company's annual report, of other information relating to corporate governance. These provisions are highlighted in schedule C to the Combined Code. It is expected that changes will be made to the Listing Rules so that they refer to the requirement for such disclosure.

8.3.5.4 Directors' remuneration

Listing Rule 9.8.8R sets out the information on directors' remuneration which must be included in a report to shareholders in the company's annual report. There is, at present, some duplication of, and in some places difference between, requirements relating to remuneration in the Listing Rules and those in the Directors' Remuneration Regulations 2002. The FSA is discussing with the DTI how to address this.

8.3.6 Key features

As explained at **8.3.3** above, section 1 provides guidance for good corporate governance in relation to directors, remuneration, accountability and audit, and relations with shareholders. The key features of the provisions relating to each area are discussed below, to provide a flavour of the issues the Combined Code addresses.

The Combined Code does, of course, go into some detail in relation to each of these, and other, issues; therefore any in-depth analysis must involve recourse to the Combined Code itself (reproduced at **Appendix 4**).

Numerous practical guides are also available. The Stock Exchange publishes 'Corporate Governance; a Practical Guide' on its website. The website of the Institute of Chartered Secretaries and Administrators (ICSA) features guidance notes on how to implement the requirements of the Code, which are useful to lawyers seeking to draft corporate governance documentation. The Institute of Directors has also collated some useful corporate governance information on its website, which is updated regularly.

8.3.6.1 Directors

The board

The Combined Code highlights the important role of the board of directors in taking the company forward. It sets out provisions about the appointment, composition and ability of the board. Guidance on the role of the nomination committee is set out in 'Good Practice Suggestions from the Higgs Report' (see **8.3.4.2**). The ICSA has also published specimen terms of reference for the nomination committee, together with a guidance note on induction training for directors. The DTI has published on its website a guide to best practice in recruitment and performance in the boardroom, entitled 'Building Better Boards'.

The following is a selection of some of the main provisions in the Combined Code regarding the board:

(a) All companies should be headed by an effective board, which has collective responsibility for the success of the company and which meets regularly (A.1).

(b) The board should consist of a balance of executive and non-executive directors (in particular *independent* non-executive directors). At least half of the board should comprise independent non-executive directors, unless the company is below the FTSE 350, in which case there should be at least two independent non-executive directors (see 'Non-executive directors' below) (A.3, A.3.1, A.3.2).

(c) The procedure for appointment of directors should be formal, rigorous and transparent (that is, the 'old school tie' approach to appointing directors is inappropriate). A nomination committee, a majority of which are independent non-executive directors, should lead the appointment process (A.4, A.4.1).

(d) The company secretary must ensure that the directors receive adequate induction training, and must assist with the directors' ongoing professional development (A.5).

(e) Directors' performance should be evaluated (A.6).

(f) All directors should be submitted for re-election at regular intervals (A.7).

Compliance with these requirements of the Combined Code is the reason that companies tend to announce new NED appointments prior to flotation. As the press announcement below shows, Debenhams appointed five non-executive directors to its board in April 2006, prior to its flotation in May. As a result, on flotation the Debenhams board met the requirement of the Combined Code that at least half the board comprise independent NEDs.

Debenhams positions for float
City figures recruited for expanded board
£700m raised by offer will pay down debt

Debenhams' attempts to attract investors to one of this year's biggest stock market floats will gather pace next week when the retailer unveils an expanded board rich with City figures.

Adam Crozier of the Royal Mail; Richard Gillingwater, a former Credit Suisse banker and head of the government's Shareholder Executive; and Paul Pindar, chief executive of support services group Capita, all agreed this month to join the department store group as non-executive directors.

Peter Long, chief executive of First Choice Holidays, and Dennis Millard, former finance director of Cookson, the electronics manufacturer, have also signed up, according to Debenhams' draft prospectus, a copy of which has been obtained by the Financial Times.

The document, titled "Project Delilah", also shows that Debenhams shares are scheduled to be priced and begin conditional dealings on May 4.

The offer will raise £700m that will be used to pay down debt.

Net debt was £1.74bn at the end of the half-year on March 4 and should fall to about £1.1bn by the time of the float. Analysts believe Debenhams could command a market value, excluding debt, of about £1.8bn-£1.9bn.

Details of the indicative price range and the amount of capital to be raised by Debenhams' trio of private equity backers - Texas Pacific Group, CVC Capital and Merrill Lynch's buy-out wing - are expected after Easter when the formal investor roadshow kicks off.

The new non-executives will sit alongside Debenhams' retail executives - John Lovering, chairman, Rob Templeman, chief executive, and Chris Woodhouse, finance director. The three have been involved in a string of lucrative retail buy-out deals, including Homebase, the DIY group, and Halfords, the cycles and car parts retailer.

Potential investors will want to know how long the trio intend to stay at Debenhams and will take a hard look at the group's figures for the first half of its current financial year. These show total sales up more than 9 per cent to £ 1.22bn in the period to March 4, with like-for-like sales up 0.6 per cent. "The directors believe this exceeded almost all other retailers' performances," the draft prospectus says.

Interim operating profits rose from £144.5m to £153.1m. Debenhams generated more than £200m of cash from operating activities during the half, only £60m below the figure of £264m generated in the 12-month period ended September 2003, Debenhams' last full-year financial period when it was quoted on the London Stock Exchange.

Of the £700m raised by the company, an estimated £20m will go to cover underwriting commissions and other fees.

Source: *Financial Times*, 15 April 2006

Roles of the Chairman and the Chief Executive

The Chairman and the Chief Executive are both responsible for the leadership of the company, but in different ways. While the Chief Executive is responsible for running the business, the Chairman must ensure that the board runs effectively. Guidance on the role of the Chairman is set out in 'Good Practice Suggestions from the Higgs Report' (see **8.3.4.2**). The ICSA has also published a guidance note on the roles of the Chairman and the Chief Executive.

Some key provisions in the Combined Code relating to these roles are as follows:

(a) The Chairman's responsibilities (as proposed by the Higgs Report) are incorporated into the Combined Code as a supporting principle (A.2). The part of the Combined Code containing related guidance and good practice suggestions provides further guidance on the Chairman's role (based on the Higgs Report). The emphasis is on the role of the Chairman both as a leader of the non-executive directors and as a conduit between the shareholders and the board (D.1.1).

(b) The role of Chairman and Chief Executive should be separate (A.2.1).

(c) When appointed, the Chairman should be independent, measured against criteria set out at A.3.1 of the Combined Code (A.2.2).

(d) The Chief Executive should not become the Chairman. This was introduced by the Higgs Report and was controversial, as many companies have a tradition of 'sending the Chief Executive upstairs', to be Chairman. This was one of the draft provisions which the Financial Reporting Council reviewed (see **8.3.2.2**), and it introduced a concession – that this provision can be waived in exceptional circumstances if the board consults with major shareholders first and discloses the reasons behind the decision in the annual report and accounts (A.2.2).

Non-executive directors

Guidance on the role of the non-executive director (commonly referred to as a NED), and a sample letter of appointment, is set out in 'Good Practice Suggestions from the Higgs Report' (see **8.3.4.2**). These guidelines provide the following useful description of the role of the NED:

> In addition to these requirements for all directors, the role of the non-executive director has the following key elements:
>
> *Strategy.* Non-executive directors should constructively challenge and help develop proposals on strategy.
>
> *Performance.* Non-executive directors should scrutinise the performance of management in meeting agreed goals and objectives and monitor the reporting of performance.
>
> *Risk.* Non-executive directors should satisfy themselves on the integrity of financial information and that financial controls and systems of risk management are robust and defensible.
>
> *People.* Non-executive directors are responsible for determining appropriate levels of remuneration of executive directors, and have a prime role in appointing, and where necessary removing, executive directors and in succession planning.

Some of the main provisions in the Code itself relating to NEDs are as follows:

(a) Schedule B to the Combined Code provides guidance on the liability of NEDs.

(b) The NEDs must scrutinise the performance of the executive directors (A.1.3, A.1.4).

(c) To be effective, NEDs ideally should be 'independent'. The board should identify, in the annual report, each NED it considers to be independent. Guidance as to the meaning of 'independent' is provided in para A.3.1.

(d) The term of appointment of any NED requires careful consideration (A.7.2).

(e) The role of the NED is set out at supporting principle A.1.

(f) The Chairman should hold some meetings with the NEDs alone, where the executive directors are not present (A.1.3).

(g) The board should appoint one of the NEDs to be the Senior Independent Director (A.3.3).

The ICSA has produced a guidance note on the role of the Senior Independent Director.

As the article below shows, the role of the NED is not a particularly easy one in today's climate. Companies need to take care to select a suitable NED who will take the role seriously. The website of the Institute of Chartered Accountants maintains a register of independent directors.

Finance: Changing roles: Responsibility without power for those in the hot seats

The experience of Integrated Dental Holdings' non-executive Graham Smith will do little to swell the ranks of experienced businessmen willing to become non-executive directors. A few years ago, their role was seen as little more than a lucrative mutual appreciation society made up of ageing executives who graced each other's boards. It was not an onerous task, rather a sinecure that conferred status and some useful extra cash in return for doing little more than turning up at board meetings.

Some organisations, such as supermarket group Wm Morrison, simply didn't see the point. Sir Ken Morrison said he would rather have a couple of extra checkout operators than a non-exec in his boardroom. BBC chairman Michael Grade - who has had a string of non-exec roles - once likened them to bidets: "You're not sure what they're for, but they add a touch of class."

In recent years, though, the role of the non-executive has changed. The process started after the Maxwell pensions scandal in the early 1990s, but it is since the collapse of Enron in the US that with non-executive office has come what some directors believe are frightening levels of responsibility. In large corporations the job is now said to be viewed as too onerous for the reward owing to the risk that non-execs will be held to account when disaster strikes. This was shown at Equitable Life when the new board launched a claim for more than £1bn against former directors for negligence over its near-collapse, although this case was later dropped.

In smaller companies, especially those with a dominant shareholder - such as IDH - non-executives complain that they have responsibility but no power. Under the corporate governance guidelines outlined in the Combined Code, which sets out best boardroom practice, at least 50% of directors in any boardroom should be independent. There are rules on what constitutes independence - so that non-executives who serve more than nine years are no longer regarded as independent.

One in five FTSE 100 companies do not meet the 50% rule. Firms say there is not enough available talent to meet demand but seem reluctant to cast their nets wider to find candidates other than from the ranks of the "pale, male and middle aged", as Derek Higgs, author of the most recent governance guidelines, had urged. The proportion of non-execs on FTSE 350 boards who are female, for instance, is still less than 10%.

Last year a report from Deloitte forecast a looming shortage of independent directors. Head of remuneration Carol Arrowsmith said: "We expect it will become more difficult to recruit non-executive directors ... as the responsibilities and time commitment prevents individuals taking up positions."

The increased demand for, and responsibilities of, non-execs, has been blamed for their pay increasing. According to the Deloitte survey the average fees paid to non-execs rose 10% last year - against a rise of less than 6% a year earlier. The average fee for a non-executive in a FTSE 100 company is £41,000, or £31,000 in a FTSE 250 business, and that buys 12-15 days' work. Chairmen can command up to £500,000.

There have been suggestions, however, that that is not nearly enough. David Jones, the deputy chairman at Morrisons who took it upon himself to force chairman Sir Ken to hire non-execs, has said fees need to double.

However, evidence from the sharp end contradicts the doom-sayers. Peter Waine, founder of Hanson Green, the leading non-exec headhunting business, says talk of talent shortages is simply wide of the mark. "Logically, it should be becoming more difficult because the downside has been highlighted by the Equitable legal action ... and the responsibilities are increasing. It certainly doesn't sound attractive. But there is no shortage whatsoever." Hanson Green, he says, has 20-30 would-be non-execs sending in their CVs every day. The lack of supply problems, he says, is down to chief executives actively wanting their co-directors to get experience of other companies in non-exec roles. "They come away having learned something."

Source: *Guardian*, 5 April 2006

On 15 February 2005 the Commission published a non-binding Recommendation which promotes the role of independent NEDs. The Recommendation is available from the Commission website.

8.3.6.2 Remuneration

(a) While directors need to be paid an amount which will motivate them to perform, their pay should also be related to their performance. The company should avoid paying more than is necessary to attract, retain and motivate directors (B.1).

(b) Notice periods under service contracts should not exceed one year. The remuneration committee should avoid rewarding poor performance in the event of an early termination of a director's service contract (B.1.5, B.1.6).

(c) Policy on directors' remuneration should be formal and transparent. A remuneration committee, of at least three (two in the case of a company below the FTSE 350) independent non-executive directors, should determine the remuneration of directors (B.2, B.2.1).

Remuneration, and indeed the remuneration committee, are increasingly in the public eye. 'Good Practice Suggestions from the Higgs Report' (see **8.3.4.2**) sets out guidance on the role of the remuneration committee. The ICSA has produced specimen terms of reference for the remuneration committee.

Investors 'letting the fat cats in again'
Soaring salaries to spark summer of pay rows

Sophie Brodie

SHAREHOLDER groups are warning that backroom deals between investors and companies are allowing the "fat cat" culture to thrive despite attempts to improve corporate governance.

Top executives have long tried to push the boundaries on pay packets. In 2002, GlaxoSmithKline boss Jean-Pierre Garnier asked for an 80pc pay rise from £6.3m to around £11.5m.

The proposals triggered outrage from shareholders whose investment had fallen by 30pc that year. Eventually the board backed down. A year later, it was defeated again over Garnier's proposed £20m incentive package.

The Government held back from legislation despite outcry at the time. Instead, directors were told to publish their pay packages, and shareholders were given the right to vote on executive deals at annual meetings. Now, four years on, the days of the bloated pay packets are back.

Shareholder groups PIRC, Manifest and Rrev, which is backed by the National Association of Pension Funds, have raised concerns about fund manager Amvescap ahead of Thursday's annual meeting.

The company had proposed paying outgoing chairman Charles Brady a $9m (£5m) bonus to reward his success in fighting off a bid from Canadian rival CI Fund Management, rebuilding Amvescap's reputation after a US funds scandal and finding a new chief executive.

Many investors see this as part of Mr Brady's job description. Four out of six major shareholders are expected to vote against the company's remuneration report at the AGM.

The report includes a £6.7m award to incoming chief executive Martin Flanagan and an initial four-year contract.

The City's corporate governance code recommends contracts that last just 12 months.

Marc Jobling, of corporate governance group PIRC, warned yesterday: "Investors talk about pay for performance but not enough of them are willing to confront management. It's shocking that some investors still don't think this is a problem."

Meanwhile, BP and Vodafone remuneration packages have raised concerns too. Vodafone shareholders, who have already had to face boardroom rows and profit warnings, have objected to plans to give directors easier bonus targets.

Executives would only have to deliver 5pc to 10pc earnings growth rather than the current 8pc to 16pc to scoop their bonuses.

The remuneration committee, headed by ex-Marks & Spencer chief Luc Vandevelde, disagreed on the issue before finally voting in favour.

One City source predicted: "Vodafone will be a litmus test of investor willingness to hold management to account. Asking Luc Vandevelde to be in charge of the remuneration committee is like putting Sweeney Todd in charge of a bakery." BP, meanwhile, faced questions from one of its biggest shareholders, Standard Life Investments, although it was overwhelmingly backed by other shareholders. The fund manager, which holds 1.2pc of BP's shares, was one of the investors that voted against the oil major's remuneration report at BP's annual meeting late last week.

The Edinburgh-based fund manager raised similar concerns last year, when it withheld support for BP's remuneration report.

Standard Life declined to comment. However, in a note on its website it explained the decision not to support the remuneration report last year was because BP's "remuneration policies have the potential to reward executives for achieving unchallenging performance conditions".

Other recent pay windfalls include those at online betting group Party Gaming. Executives revealed last week in the annual report that they hit the jackpot in 2005 with $36m (£20m) shared among 10 directors - one of the largest for a FTSE 100 board.

This summer is set to be marked by more rows between shareholders and the executives who run their companies, with Vodafone leading the way. Let battle commence.

Source: *The Daily Telegraph*, 24 April 2006

8.3.6.3 Accountability and audit

As explained at **8.3.4.3** above, it is useful to consult the Smith Guidance on Audit Committees when considering what the Code has to say on this issue. Some of the key provisions in the Combined Code relating to accountability and audit are as follows:

(a) The board should present a balanced and understandable view of the company's prospects (C.1).

(b) The board should ensure there are internal controls in place to safeguard shareholders' investments and the company's assets (C.2).

(c) There should be an audit committee with at least three members (unless the company is below the FTSE 350, in which case there should be at least two members) who are independent non-executive directors. At least one member should have recent and relevant financial experience (C.3, C.3.1, A.3.1).

(d) The main role and responsibilities of the audit committee should be set out in written terms of reference, which are available both on the company website and on request (C.3.2, C.3.3). The lawyer may be required to draft the terms of reference for the audit committee. The ICSA has published standard form terms of reference for audit committees.

(e) The role of the audit committee is set out at C.3.2.

8.3.6.4 Relations with shareholders

(a) The Chairman should ensure that the views of shareholders are communicated to the board (D.1.1).

(b) The board should use the AGM to communicate with shareholders (D.2).

8.4 The Directors' Remuneration Report Regulations 2002

8.4.1 Background

There are rules governing the remuneration of listed company directors in both the Listing Rules (see **8.3.4.4**) and the Combined Code (see **8.3.5.2**). Listed company directors must also comply with the rules set out at Pt 1 of Sch 6 to the CA 1985 (which apply to directors of unlisted companies as well as listed companies).

Despite these requirements, however, in the last few years an increasing number of column inches have been dedicated to tales of 'fat cat' directors, who are criticised for being overpaid while their companies underperform.

The Directors' Remuneration Report Regulations 2002 (SI 2002/1986) have now supplemented the regime regulating the remuneration of directors of listed companies.

On 14 December 2004 the Commission published a Recommendation on fostering an appropriate regime for the remuneration of directors of listed companies. Member States were invited to implement necessary measures to comply with the Recommendation by 30 June 2006. The Regulations are very similar to the Recommendation.

8.4.2 Nature

The Regulations came into force on 1 August 2002 to apply in respect of financial years ending on or after 31 December 2002.

The Regulations apply to 'quoted companies', which are defined by s 262 of the CA 1985 as including not only companies admitted to the Official List and the Main Market (referred to as 'listed companies' in this book; see **1.3** above), but also companies listed on certain other markets in Europe and the USA. The scope of the Regulations is therefore wider than the scope of the Listing Rules and the Combined Code (see **8.3.4.1** above). The Regulations do not, however, apply to companies listed on AIM.

The Regulations have amended Pt VII of the CA 1985.

8.4.3 Key features

The Regulations have two key requirements, set out below. Any director of a company which fails to comply with these requirements will be guilty of an offence under the CA 1985 and liable to a fine.

8.4.3.1 Remuneration report

The company must produce an annual remuneration report which contains the information required by Sch 7A to the CA 1985, in the form prescribed by that schedule. The information which the report must disclose (including the company policy on directors' remuneration, details of the directors' service contracts and a company performance graph) is considerable, and goes beyond the disclosure requirements of the Listing Rules and the Combined Code. The report forms part of the annual report and accounts and must be filed at Companies House.

8.4.3.2 Shareholder approval

The company must table the remuneration report at general meeting (s 241 of the CA 1985) and obtain approval of the report (by ordinary resolution) of the shareholders (s 241A of the CA 1985). Several listed companies had already adopted this procedure as best practice even before the Regulations came into force. Note that this requirement does not mean that any specific director's service contract is conditional upon shareholder approval. If shareholders do not approve the remuneration report the effect is advisory only (in other words, this and the accompanying adverse publicity sends a public message to the board that it will be unable to ignore). As the article below shows, shareholders have shown that they are willing to exercise their rights to refuse to approve the remuneration report tabled.

Shareholders Veto Aegis Boss's Fat-cat Pay Deal
City and Business Edited by **Stephen Kahn**

DISGRUNTLED shareholders yesterday struck out at media group Aegis by voting down its boss's lucrative two year contract, writes Megan Davies.

Aegis pledged to "discuss the appropriate steps" with investors after its remuneration report was slammed by 50.8 per cent of votes at its annual meeting in London.

Shareholders objected to chief executive Doug Flynn's two-year rolling contract. He was paid GBP 1.2 million last year in salary and bonus.

Investors were also unhappy with the contracts of two other directors – Adrian Chedore and Jeremy Hicks. The pair had one-year notice periods but these increased to 24 months under a change-of-control provision.

It is the first time shareholders have voted down a remuneration report since drugs group GlaxoSmithKline's high profile defeat last year and it shows investors remain unafraid to show their teeth when unhappy with corporate practices.

Powerful shareholder lobby group the NAPF had recommended shareholders vote against the report – a step up from its "abstain" recommendation last year.

A spokesman said: "This shows the concerns shareholders have. The company would do well to listen to them."

Source: *Express*, 27 May 2004, 'City Section', p 62

8.5 Institutional investors

As explained at **8.3.5.1** above, it is really the institutional investors (see **2.6.2**) who enforce the Combined Code by making life difficult for those companies who do not comply. Certain institutional investors publish their corporate governance expectations and circulate them to shareholders and listed companies. Recent examples include:

(a) 'The Responsibilities of Institutional Shareholders and Agents – Statement of Principles', published by the Institutional Shareholders' Committee on 30

September 2005 and available from the Institutional Voting Information Service website.

(b) 'Corporate Governance Principles', published in March 2006 by Hermes, the independent fund manager, on its website.

(c) 'Shareholder Voting Guidelines', published in February 2006 by PIRC (these guidelines must be ordered from the PIRC website).

Investors bite back: The shareholder power movement is gathering strength

First they wanted a say in executive pay. Then they started dictating changes in boardroom structure. Now they have just toppled the chairman of one of Britain's largest media groups. Shareholders these days seem to think they own the companies they invest in!

For years, institutional investors worked behind the scenes to change boards and improve corporate governance. But they have become increasingly willing to go public if backroom pressure is failing to produce results. This week, City institutions launched a pre-emptive strike by demanding that Michael Green stand down as chairman-elect of ITV, the new company to be formed by merging Carlton and Granada, by midday on Tuesday. Their success will embolden other shareholders and alarm the boardrooms of lacklustre companies.

One reason for the gathering insurgency is the collapse of the internet bubble. The rising tide of the stock market boom lifted most boats, well run or mismanaged. When the waters receded, investors nursing big losses looked for explanations. In some cases, greedy executives had looted their companies through stock options; in others, managers had frittered away shareholder value on megalomaniac mergers or fashionable investments. In both cases, directors had failed to rein in executives on behalf of shareholders.

But there is a longer-term trend towards improved corporate governance that pre-dates the excesses of the late 1990s. Shareholders increasingly feel that cashing a dividend cheque and voting with the board at the annual meeting too often leave them with disappointing returns. Meanwhile, concentration of share ownership in large investment institutions creates voting blocks powerful enough to demand changes when things are going badly.

This trend has gone furthest in the UK, with codes of practice on corporate governance and new best practice guidelines on the role of non-executive directors. The government has backed such moves in response to public concern over corporate greed and mismanagement by pressing institutional shareholders to be more active.

In the US, the corporate governance reform process is only just starting after the collapse of companies such as Enron and WorldCom. It is not yet clear that private sector funds either are willing to use their voting power to make changes, or have the capacity to do so. It is the public pension funds such as Calpers and TIAA-Cref that mostly do the heavy lifting.

Yet the response of investors to recent revelations about mutual funds suggests individual shareholders will no longer stand by when they feel wronged. Four mutual fund groups investigated for allowing hedge funds to profit from improper trading at the expense of small investors suffered outflows of almost $8bn (£4.8bn) last month. Shareholder activism may lose impetus when the stock market recovery looks firmer, but the days of the passive investor are disappearing.

Source: *Financial Times*, 25 October 2003

8.6 Future developments

The recently revised Combined Code and the Directors' Remuneration Report Regulations 2002 are both indications of just how important corporate governance issues are considered in the UK.

Looking forward, all indications are that corporate governance will remain a topical issue for some time. In the UK the Companies Bill (see **1.11**) will include provisions to codify the duties of directors.

There are developments in Europe too. On 21 May 2003 the European Commission released for consultation an Action Plan on company law and corporate governance (*Modernising Company Law and Enhancing Corporate Governance in the EU*). The Action Plan is available on the website of the European Commission (or by link from the DTI website). The Action Plan contains 24 measures. Some of the measures have already been adopted. It is intended that most measures will be adopted by Member States before 2009.

On 20 July 2005 the DTI published *The UK Approach to EU Company Law and Corporate Governance*, available on the DTI website, which encourages UK businesses to become involved in shaping the EU agenda on corporate governance. Appendix 1 of the document summarises how the Action Plan has been implemented so far. The following implementation measures will be of particular relevance over the next few years:

(a) *Annual corporate governance statement.* The Commission published a draft directive in October 2004 to give effect to the proposal that every listed EU company should provide a corporate governance statement in its annual report or on its website. Member States must implement the directive within two years of it entering into force.

(b) *Shareholders' rights.* On 5 January 2006, the Commission published a directive in relation to the enhancement of shareholders' rights. The directive includes provisions to protect shareholders, such as increasing the number of days' notice for general meetings to 30 days. Member States must implement the directive by 31 December 2007.

It seems, therefore, that corporate governance will be an increasingly important issue for listed companies, and therefore for their lawyers, for some time to come.

Chapter 9

The Financial Services and Markets Act 2000

9.1	Background	123
9.2	Objectives	123
9.3	Relevance to practice	123
9.4	The general prohibition on carrying on a regulated activity	124
9.5	Misleading statements and market manipulation	125

9.1 Background

The Financial Services and Markets Act 2000 (FSMA 2000) received Royal Assent on 14 June 2000. The majority of the Act, and some of the secondary legislation and rules made pursuant to it, came into force on 1 December 2001. This date is often referred to as 'N2'.

At N2 the FSA became the single regulator for the financial services industry. The FSMA 2000 replaced the Financial Services Act 1986.

9.2 Objectives

Some of the provisions of the FSMA 2000 are complex. They are easier to understand if you consider them in the context of the objectives of the Act. The principal objectives of the FSMA 2000 are set out in s 2. They are:

(a) *market confidence* – maintaining confidence in the financial system;

(b) *public awareness* – raising public understanding of the financial system;

(c) *the protection of consumers* – securing the appropriate degree of protection for consumers; and

(d) *the reduction of financial crime* – reducing the extent to which it is possible for a business to be used for a purpose connected with financial crime.

9.3 Relevance to practice

No corporate finance lawyer can avoid the FSMA 2000. Together with the CA 1985, the 2000 Act will be the most thumbed statute on the lawyer's desk. It affects all professional firms which carry on regulated activities, and also affects how companies, particularly listed companies, conduct their day-to-day corporate and trading activities. The lawyer will have most involvement with the following provisions of the FSMA 2000:

(a) the general prohibition on carrying on a regulated activity in the United Kingdom (s 19);

(b) the financial promotion regulatory framework (s 21);

(c) the rules relating to the official listing of securities (Pt VI and in particular ss 85, 87 and 90);

(d) the market abuse regime (s 118); and

(e) the provisions relating to misleading statements and market manipulation (s 397).

The remainder of this chapter considers (a) and (e) above. **Chapter 12** considers financial promotion; **Chapter 6** explores the rules of the FSMA 2000 relating to the listing of securities; and **Chapter 10** considers market abuse.

9.4 The general prohibition on carrying on a regulated activity

Lawyers must be aware of the general prohibition in s 19 of the FSMA 2000 not only so that they can advise their clients accordingly, but also so that they can ensure that neither they nor their law firm breaches that section.

9.4.1 The general prohibition

Section 19 of the FSMA 2000 prohibits any person from carrying on a regulated activity in the United Kingdom unless he is:

(a) an authorised person; or
(b) an exempt person.

This is known as the 'general prohibition'. Contravention of the general prohibition is a criminal offence (s 23). Any agreement which results from a breach of s 19 will be unenforceable (s 26).

9.4.2 Regulated activities

The general prohibition relates to the carrying on of a 'regulated activity'. What is a regulated activity? The actual definition is provided by s 22 of the FSMA 2000. It is:

> an activity of a specified kind which is carried on by way of business and:
> (a) relates to an investment of a specified kind; or
> (b) in the case of an activity of a kind which is also specified for the purposes of this paragraph, is carried on in relation to property of any kind.

This is not particularly helpful. Schedule 2 to the Act, together with a number of statutory instruments including the Financial Services and Markets Act 2000 (Regulated Activities) Order 2001 (SI 2001/544) ('Regulated Activities Order 2001'), seeks to clarify the definition. Schedule 2 to the FSMA 2000 provides examples of regulated activities, and the Regulated Activities Order 2001 details the meaning of specified activities (Pt II) and specified investments (Pt III). In practice, recourse should be made to these sources. However, for our purposes it is more useful to consider a few of the more common examples of 'regulated activities' which a corporate finance lawyer might encounter, namely those relating to investments (such as shares). The regulated activities include:

(a) dealing in investments (Regulated Activities Order 2001, Chapters IV and V) – this includes dealing as principal or agent;

(b) arranging deals in investments (Regulated Activities Order 2001, Chapter VI) – this includes making arrangements with a view to another person buying or selling shares;

(c) managing investments (Regulated Activities Order 2001, Chapter VII) – this includes managing someone else's shares;

(d) advising on investments (Regulated Activities Order 2001, Chapter XII) – this includes giving advice to someone buying or selling shares. It will not include general advice in relation to an investment, or merely explaining the implications of exercising rights. So, for example, explaining the meaning of technical jargon, or advising how to complete an application form will not amount to advising on investments. (It could, however, still amount to arranging deals in investments – see (b) above.)

The definition of 'regulated activities' is wide. The prohibition prevents any person carrying on a regulated activity, unless that person is an authorised person or an exempt person. So who are these persons?

9.4.3 Authorised person

Section 31(1) of the FSMA 2000 defines an 'authorised person'. The most common example of an authorised person is someone who has obtained permission from the FSA to carry on regulated activities (under Pt IV of the Act), such as an accountant or financial adviser seeking to act as a sponsor or broker (see **Chapter 4**). Part IV of the Act contains the detail of how such permission is obtained. From the lawyer's point of view, however, the important issue is that, unless a client is an authorised person or an exempt person, it will be prohibited from carrying out any regulated activity, and the lawyer must advise the client to instruct an authorised person (or, more rarely, an exempt person) to carry out the activity instead.

9.4.4 Exempt person

A person is exempt if he has been granted an exemption order under s 38(1) of the FSMA 2000, or is exempt as an 'appointed representative' under s 39(1) of the Act. In practice, exempt persons are encountered rarely. However, the most common 'exempt person' with which lawyers will be familiar is any recognised investment exchange or recognised clearing house pursuant to s 285 of the FSMA 2000. For example, in certain circumstances (see s 285(2)) the Stock Exchange will be exempt from the general prohibition.

9.5 Misleading statements and market manipulation

As stated at **9.3** above, this is another area covered by the FSMA 2000 in relation to which the lawyer must be able to advise.

9.5.1 Misleading statements

9.5.1.1 The criminal offence

As outlined at **6.7.2.1** above, s 397(1) and (2) of the FSMA 2000 provides that it is a criminal offence for a person to:

(a) make a statement, promise or forecast which he *knows is* materially misleading, false or deceptive;

(b) dishonestly conceal any material facts; or

(c) *recklessly* make (dishonestly or otherwise) a statement, promise or forecast which *is* materially misleading, false or deceptive,

in order to induce (or be reckless as to whether it may induce) another person to:

(i) enter into, or offer to enter into, or refrain from entering or offering to enter into a *relevant agreement*, or

(ii) exercise, or refrain from exercising, any rights conferred by a *relevant investment*.

Note that the person who is induced does not have to be the recipient of the statement, promise or forecast. This offence is generally referred to as the restriction on making misleading statements (but clearly it applies equally to promises and forecasts).

9.5.1.2 'Relevant agreement'

A relevant agreement is defined by s 397(9) of the FSMA 2000. The definition refers to 'specified kinds of activity', which are contained in art 3 of the Financial Services and Markets Act 2000 (Misleading Statements and Practices) Order 2001 (SI 2001/3645) ('Misleading Statements Order 2001'). An example of a relevant agreement is an agreement to sell (or not sell) shares.

9.5.1.3 'Relevant investment'

A relevant investment is defined by s 397(10) of the FSMA 2000. Reference is made to 'specified kinds of investment', which are contained in art 4 of the Misleading Statements Order 2001. Shares and bonds are examples of relevant investments.

9.5.1.4 'Reckless'

'Reckless' includes not only someone not giving any thought to the accuracy of a statement, but also someone making a statement when he is aware that he should first make some enquiries as to the accuracy of the statement yet fails to make such enquiries (provided those enquires would have revealed that the statement was false or misleading).

9.5.1.5 The Disclosure Rules

Failure to comply with the Disclosure Rules, and in particular the general obligation of disclosure set out at DR 2.2.1R (see **7.4.1**), may constitute the dishonest concealment of material facts for the purpose of s 397 (see **9.5.1.1(b)**).

9.5.1.6 Example

The most common s 397 scenario which a corporate finance lawyer will encounter is where a client makes a misleading statement so that shareholders continue to buy, or do not sell, shares, when if the statement was actually truthful, those shareholders might be tempted not to buy, or to sell, their shares. The article below provides a real-life example of this.

FSA takes directors to court over 'misleading' statement
By Dominic White

THREE former directors of Henley-based software group AIT appeared in court yesterday accused of misleading the financial markets in the first criminal prosecution of its kind brought by the Financial Services Authority.

Carl Rigby, Alistair Rowley and Gareth Bailey were charged with four counts under the Financial Services and Markets Act 2000 when they appeared before City of London magistrates.

Mr Rigby, former chief executive, Mr Rowley, ex-sales director, and Mr Bailey, former finance director, are alleged to have issued a statement about the company's turnover and profits on the Regulatory News Service, knowing it to be "misleading, false or deceptive".

The statement on May 2, 2002, said turnover and profits were expected to be in line with market expectations. But four weeks later, the company issued a shock profits warning that caused the shares to plunge 80% in a single day.

Soon after the once well-regarded group was forced into a £20.5m rescue refinancing that almost wiped out the existing shareholders.

The men face two similar charges relating to making a statement to the financial markets and two further similar charges of conspiracy.

Mr Rigby, 41, Mr Rowley, 41, and Mr Bailey, 35, all dressed in dark suits, were remanded on unconditional bail to appear before Southwark Crown Court for a preliminary hearing on March 2.

The FSA said it was the first prosecution it had brought using its criminal powers.

Separately, a company secretary who sold shares ahead of a sales warning by his company was yesterday fined £15,000 in the first case of its kind by the City watchdog.

Robert Middlemiss avoided a loss of £6,825 by selling 70,000 shares in publishing and communications company Profile Media Group, according to the FSA.

Source: *Daily Telegraph*, 11 February 2004

On 18 August 2005 the FSA announced that it had secured criminal convictions against the former chief executive and former finance director; these are the first criminal convictions under s 397 of the FSMA 2000.

9.5.2 Market manipulation

9.5.2.1 The criminal offence

This is a separate offence from that of making a misleading statement, although it is also contained within s 397 of the FSMA 2000. Section 397(3) provides that it is a criminal offence to:

(a) do any act, or engage in any course of conduct;
(b) which creates a false or misleading impression;
(c) as to the market in, or the price or value of, any relevant investment (see **9.5.1.3**);
(d) in order to:
  (i) create that impression, and
  (ii) induce another person to deal or not deal in those investments.

This offence is referred to as the restriction on market manipulation.

> **Example**
>
> Bidder plc plans to make a takeover offer for Target plc. It therefore seeks to undertake a stakebuilding exercise (see **Chapter 21**). Target plc suspects that Bidder plc is going to make a bid for it, and is not pleased. It arranges for its associate companies to buy shares in Target plc, so that the share price of Target plc rises, which makes Bidder's stake-building exercise more costly. Bidder will have to pay more for its stake. This contravenes s 397(3), because Target plc has deliberately manipulated the market to discourage Bidder plc from dealing in the shares of Target plc.

9.5.2.2 Defence

Section 397(5) provides a defence for a person charged under s 397(3) if he can show that he reasonably believed the act or conduct would not create a false or misleading impression.

9.5.3 Relationship between s 397(1) and s 397(3)

The sections are not mutually exclusive. One act can give rise to charges under both sections.

9.5.4 Sanctions

Section 397(8) of the FSMA 2000 provides that the offences of making a misleading statement or manipulating the market are punishable by imprisonment and/or a fine. On summary conviction, the maximum sentence is six months, and on conviction on indictment the maximum sentence is seven years.

The risk of directors breaching s 397 by making a misleading statement in a prospectus was examined at **6.7.2.1** above. As noted in that paragraph, the verification process is used to try to ensure that s 397 is not breached during the marketing of a flotation, and the threat of a prison sentence is usually enough to focus the directors' attention on this process.

Chapter 10

Market Abuse

10.1	Introduction	129
10.2	What is market abuse?	130
10.3	The main offence	130
10.4	The secondary offence	133
10.5	Behaviour which does not amount to market abuse	135
10.6	Sanctions	135
10.7	Defences	136
10.8	Future developments	138

10.1 Introduction

As discussed in **Chapter 9**, the market abuse regime is one of the key features of the FSMA 2000. Part VIII (ss 118 to 131A) of the Act sets out that regime. Market abuse is a civil offence which was created by the FSMA 2000. It supplements the criminal offences of:

(a) misleading statements and market manipulation under the FSMA 2000 (see **9.5** above); and

(b) insider dealing under the CJA 1993 (see **Chapter 11**),

which target the same kind of behaviour covered by the market abuse regime.

10.1.1 The civil offence

The new civil offence of market abuse was introduced so that the FSA could catch abusers of the market who might otherwise have escaped punishment for the criminal offences referred to at (a) and (b) above. It has the following advantages over the criminal regime:

(a) it is wider in scope;

(b) it is easier to prove. The standard of proof in criminal cases is 'beyond all reasonable doubt'. This high standard means that it is very difficult to convict anyone of insider dealing, or of making misleading statements and/or manipulating the market. To date there have been very few convictions for these offences. Market abuse, however, as a civil offence, has a lower standard of proof, namely 'on the balance of probabilities';

(c) it assesses behaviour according to its effect rather than the intention behind it (although there is an element of intention lurking in the detail of the regime); and

(d) it can be committed by anyone – an individual or a company (contrast **11.7** below).

10.1.2 The Code of Market Conduct

Section 119 of the FSMA 2000 requires the FSA to provide guidance to market users as to what behaviour amounts to market abuse. The FSA has obliged with the Code of Market Conduct (CoMC). The CoMC confirms that the scope of market abuse is wide, and the FSA has significant power to tackle market abusers. It is not binding but it does have evidential weight. The CoMC forms chapter 1 of the FSA Market

Conduct Sourcebook (known as 'MAR'), which is part of the FSA Handbook and can be downloaded from the FSA website. To follow market practice, references below to 'MAR 1' are to paragraphs of the CoMC.

10.1.3 The Market Abuse Directive

The market abuse regime has recently been revised, through the implementation of the Market Abuse Directive (MAD). Although the MAD should have been implemented in 2004, the UK delayed implementation so that it corresponded with the implementation of the Prospectus Directive (through the Prospectus Rules) and the publication of the revised Listing Rules on 1 July 2005.

The MAD has been implemented through:

(a) the new Disclosure Rules;
(b) amendments to Part VIII of the FSMA 2000 (made by the MAD Regulations 2005); and
(c) a new version of the CoMC.

Those familiar with the old regime may appreciate the following broad outline of the changes under the new regime:

(a) Two of the original three types of abusive behaviour under the old regime, misuse of information and distortion, remain under the new regime. These tests continue to be subject to the regular user test.
(b) The new regime has added five new types of abusive behaviour (see **10.3** below), which are not subject to the regular user test.
(c) Abusive behaviour relates not only to investments which are trading, but also to those in respect of which an application for admission to trading has been made.
(d) The territorial scope is wider.
(e) There are far fewer safe harbours.

The new market abuse regime has the potential to secure more convictions than was possible under the old regime.

10.2 What is market abuse?

Market abuse, in layman's terms, is certain behaviour (see **10.3.4** below), relating to certain investments which trade, or are seeking admission to trade, on certain markets, which is deemed improper. The offence punishes those who seek to manipulate the market for their own benefit.

10.3 The main offence

Section 118(1) of the FSMA 2000 sets out the test which must be satisfied for behaviour to constitute market abuse. The behaviour of the market abuser must:

(a) occur in the UK;
(b) occur in relation to:
  (i) a *qualifying investment* admitted to trading on a *prescribed market*, or
  (ii) a *qualifying investment* in respect of which a request for admission to trading on a prescribed market has been made, or
  (iii) (in the case of 'insider dealing' or 'improper disclosure' offences – see **10.3.4** below) an investment *related* to such a qualifying investment; and

(c) fall within any one or more of the types of behaviour set out at **10.3.4**.

10.3.1 Qualifying investment

This term is defined by the Financial Services and Markets Act 2000 (Prescribed Markets and Qualifying Investments) Order 2001 (SI 2001/996) ('PMQI Order 2001'), which refers to s 22 of the FSMA 2000, which in turn refers to the definition of 'financial instrument' under art 1(3) of the MAD. For our purposes, note that qualifying investments include shares and bonds.

10.3.2 Prescribed market

The PMQI Order 2001 specifies the prescribed markets for the purposes of the market abuse regime. For our purposes, note that both of the Stock Exchange's markets (ie, the Main Market and the AIM), as well as other markets, such as OFEX, are prescribed markets.

10.3.3 Related investments

This term is defined by s 130A(3) of the FSMA 2000 as an investment whose price or value depends on the price or value of the qualifying investment. This would include, for example, an equity swap on a share traded on the Main Market.

10.3.4 The seven types of behaviour

Section 118(2) to (8) provide that the following types of behaviour will constitute market abuse:

Type 1: Insider dealing (s 118(2))

This is behaviour where an insider (as defined by the FSMA 2000, s 118B) deals, or attempts to deal, in a qualifying investment (see **10.3.1**) or related investment (see **10.3.3**), on the basis of inside information (see **7.4.2.3**, substituting 'qualifying investment' for 'financial instrument') relating to that investment. Further guidance is provided in MAR 1.3.

(Remember this is a type of behaviour under the civil offence of market abuse and is quite separate from the criminal offence of insider dealing referred to in **Chapter 11**.)

Type 2: Improper disclosure (s 118(3))

This is behaviour where an insider (as defined by the FSMA 2000, s 118B) discloses inside information (see **7.4.2.3**, substituting 'qualifying investment' for 'financial instrument') to another person other than in the proper course of his employment, profession or duties. Further guidance is provided in MAR 1.4.

Type 3: Misuse of information (s 118(4))

This is a type of behaviour carried forward from the old regime. It is behaviour based on information *not generally available* to those using the market, but which, if available to a regular user of the market, would be, or would be likely to be, regarded by him as *relevant* when deciding the terms on which transactions in investments of the kind in question should be effected. The behaviour must fail the regular user test (see **10.3.5** below). Further guidance is provided in MAR 1.5. This type of behaviour may also amount to the criminal offence of insider dealing (see **Chapter 11**).

Note that if behaviour falls within type 1 or type 2 behaviour, as well as type 3 behaviour, it should be dealt with as type 1 or type 2, rather than type 3, behaviour (s 118(4)).

'Relevant information'

The CoMC (see **10.1.2**) sets out the factors to be taken into account to determine whether information is relevant. The information must relate to matters which regular users would reasonably expect to be disclosed to market users. The CoMC also gives examples of relevant information. Of particular interest to the corporate lawyer is the example of information concerning business affairs or prospects (such as entering into a significant contract with a supplier).

'Not generally available'

The CoMC states that information *is* generally available if it can be obtained by research or analysis conducted by, or on behalf of, users of the market. Information notified to an RIS, or sent to a public registry such as Companies House, would be classed as generally available information.

Type 4: Manipulating transactions (s 118(5))

This is behaviour which effects a transaction (other than for legitimate reasons, in conformity with accepted market practices – as defined by s 130A(3) and MAR 1, Annex 2G) which either:

(a) gives, or is likely to give, a false or misleading impression as to the supply of, or demand for, or as to the price of, a qualifying investment (see **10.3.1**); or

(b) secures the prices of such an investment at an abnormal or artificial level.

This offence is most likely to be committed by a market professional, such as a trader. Further guidance is provided in MAR 1.6. It includes two specific situations:

(a) *An abusive squeeze.* This is perhaps less interesting than it sounds. It describes a situation where a person corners the market and uses that position to distort the market.

(b) *Price positioning.* This consists of entering into a transaction, or series of transactions, to position the price at a distorted level (that is, materially different to that which reflects the operation of usual market forces).

Type 5: Manipulating devices (s 118(6))

This is behaviour which effects transactions which employ fictitious devices or any other form of deception or contrivance. Again, this is most likely to be committed by a market professional, such as a trader. Further guidance is provided in MAR 1.7. An example of this type of behaviour is a trader who buys shares, then spreads misleading positive information about the shares to increase their price, before selling the shares at a profit (known as a 'pump and dump').

Type 6: Dissemination (s 118(7))

This is behaviour which disseminates information which gives, or is likely to give, a false or misleading impression as to a qualifying investment (see **10.3.1**), by a person who knew, or could reasonably be expected to have known, that the information was false or misleading.

Type 7: Distortion (s 118(8))

This is a type of behaviour carried forward from the old regime. It is behaviour which is:

(a) likely to give a regular user of the market a false or misleading impression as to the supply of, or demand for, or price or value of, a qualifying investment (see **10.3.1**); or

(b) would be, or would be likely to be, regarded by a regular user of the market as behaviour that would distort, or would be likely to distort, the market in such an investment.

The behaviour must fail the regular user test (see **10.3.5** below).

Note that if behaviour falls within type 4, 5, or 6 behaviour, as well as type 7 behaviour, it should be dealt with as type 4, 5 or 6, rather than type 7, behaviour (s 118(4)).

10.3.5 The regular market user test

10.3.5.1 Application

The test now applies only to the abusive behaviour carried forward from the old regime, that is type 3 and type 7 behaviour.

10.3.5.2 The test

The test is whether a regular user of the market would regard the behaviour of the person (let us call him X) as failing to observe the standard of behaviour reasonably expected of a person in X's position. If so, X has failed the regular market user test.

10.3.5.3 The regular market user

The regular market user is 'a reasonable person who regularly deals on that market in investments of the kind in question' (s 130A(3)). There are difficulties in applying this test. It is not easy to identify a hypothetical regular market user, or to identify the standards of behaviour which that user would expect of someone else.

10.3.6 Summary

The main offence under s 118 of the FSMA 2000 is summarised in Figure 10.1 below.

10.4 The secondary offence

The main offence under Pt VIII of the FSMA 2000 is that of market abuse (under s 118), which is considered at **10.3** above. However, there is also a secondary offence under Pt VIII; that of 'requiring or encouraging'. Section 123(1)(b) of the FSMA 2000 provides that penalties can be imposed on a person (let us call him A) if, by taking or refraining from taking any action, he 'requires or encourages' another person, X, to engage in behaviour which, if engaged in by A, would amount to market abuse. This secondary offence is designed to catch those people who might otherwise circumvent the market abuse offence by asking someone else to carry out their instructions.

134　Public Companies and Equity Finance

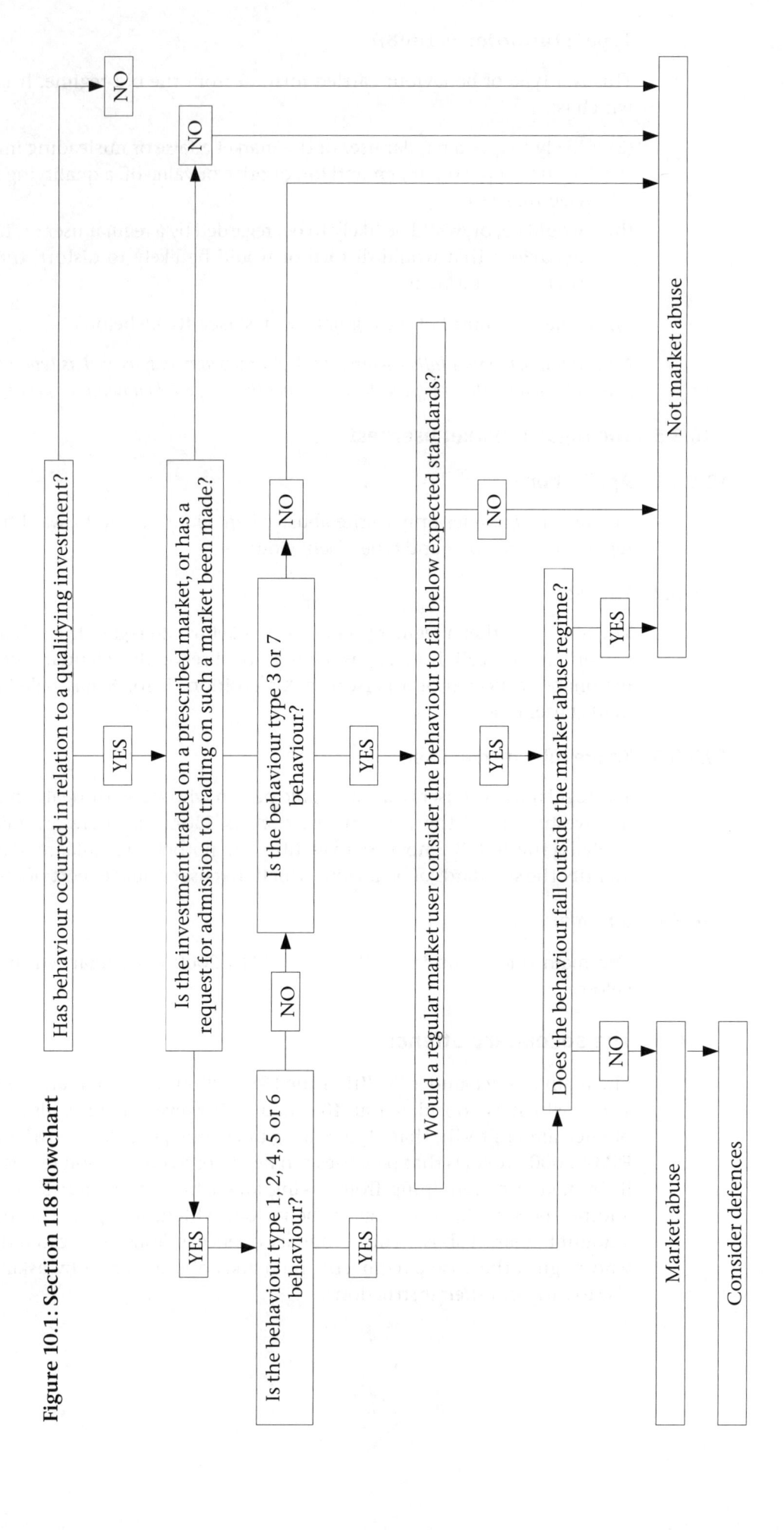

Figure 10.1: Section 118 flowchart

Further guidance is provided in MAR 1.5. Examples include a director, in possession of relevant and disclosable information which is not generally available, who instructs an employee to deal in qualifying investments in respect of which the information is relevant information. If the director did the dealing, it would constitute market abuse and would be an offence under s 118. Section 123 ensures that the director will still be caught, albeit under the s 123 offence of requiring or encouraging, rather than the s 118 offence of market abuse.

10.5 Behaviour which does not amount to market abuse

10.5.1 Safe harbours under the MAD

A safe harbour is a type of behaviour which will not constitute market abuse, even if it satisfies the test in s 118 of the FSMA 2000.

Under the new regime, many of the safe harbours under the old regime have been deleted. Some of the old safe harbours are now simply matters that the FSA may take into account in determining whether behaviour amounts to market abuse.

The MAD itself provided only two safe harbours, one relating to share buyback (now in s 118A(5)(b) and MAR 1.10.1G(1)) and the other relating to price stabilisation activities (now in s 118A(5)(b) and MAR 2).

10.5.2 Section 118A(5)

Section 118A(5) of the FSMA 2000 stipulates specific behaviour which will not amount to market abuse. It includes not only the two safe harbours referred to at **10.5.1**, but also behaviour which conforms to a rule which includes a provision to the effect that behaviour conforming with that rule does not amount to market abuse (s 118A(5)(a)). This includes the parts of the Listing Rules and the Disclosure Rules which relate to a disclosure, announcement, communication or release of information. In addition, MAR 1.10.2G and MAR 1.10.3G specify that there are no FSA rules or rules in the Takeover Code or SARs which permit or require a person to behave in a way which amounts to market abuse.

In practice, behaviour falling within s 118A(5) will also be referred to colloquially as falling within a 'safe harbour'.

Behaviour which is done by a person acting on behalf of a public authority in pursuit of monetary policies, policies in respect of exchange rates, the management of public debt or foreign exchange reserves will also not amount to market abuse (s 118A(5)(c)).

10.6 Sanctions

If the FSA suspects that market abuse may have occurred, it can use its statutory powers to investigate the issue. Once market abuse has been proved, the FSA can:

(a) impose a fine (FSMA 2000, s 123). The second article reproduced overleaf shows the matters which the FSA took into account in imposing a fine on Michael Davies of Berkeley Morgan Group plc;

(b) make a public statement that the person has engaged in market abuse (s 123);

(c) apply to the court for an injunction (s 381);

(d) require the person to pay back profits made, or losses avoided (s 383); or

(e) require the person to compensate any victims (s 383).

Business roundup: Regulation: Insider dealer is fined

Richard Wray

THE FORMER head of communications at Whitehead Mann, who made just under £3,000 short-selling shares in the recruitment consultant on insider information, was fined £15,000 yesterday by the Financial Services Authority.

Peter Bracken, who left Whitehead Mann in January 2003, is only the second person to be fined by the regulator under its new civil powers aimed at combating market abuse.

Earlier this year Robert Middlemiss, former company secretary at Profile Media Group, was fined an identical amount for dumping shares in his AIM-listed employer just before it warned on profits.

The FSA said Mr Bracken had dealt on inside information in September and November 2002, amassing a total of £2,823. On the first occasion he learned that the company was going to issue a profits warning and sold shares in it, while his second bout of short-selling was on information that the group's chief executive was stepping down.

Andrew Procter, director of enforcement at the regulator, said: "We view the misuse of unpublished confidential information in this case as being particularly serious given the privileged position Mr Bracken occupied."

A spokesman for Whitehead Mann said: "It's a private issue between Peter Bracken and the FSA."

The fine is a much-needed success for the FSA which has been criticised recently for its handling of an appeal by businessman Paul "The Plumber" Davidson against his £750,000 fine for market abuse. The entire FSA tribunal hearing the appeal resigned last month after details emerged of a midnight meeting between tribunal member Terence Mowschenson QC and senior FSA official Christopher FitzGerald.

Source: *Guardian*, 8 July 2004

FSA Imposes First OFEX Trading Fine

David Hellier

THE FINANCIAL Services Authority, the City's regulator, announced yesterday that it had fined an individual for the misuse of price-sensitive information relating for the first time to a company listed on the lightly regulated Ofex market.

The FSA said it had fined Michael Davies £1,000 for trading in shares in the Ofex-listed Berkeley Morgan Group (BMG) while in possession of information concerning the Blackburn-based financial services group's interim results.

Mr Davies had helped to prepare the results, which were better than expected, and had been given a draft copy of the chairman's statement in early December last year.

On 5 January, the day before the public announcement of the group's results, Mr Davies bought 4,000 BMG shares. He sold the shares the day after the results announcement, netting a profit of £420 after the group's share price rose 29 per cent.

The FSA originally considered levying a harsher fine of £4,000 but decided to reduce this on account of Mr Davies' full disclosure of his actions.

Mr Davies, who no longer works for Berkeley Morgan, is the third individual to be fined for market abuse this year, but it is the first for dealings in an Ofex-listed company.

The FSA is investigating allegations of "insider" trading in Marks & Spencer shares ahead of the now-aborted bid by Philip Green. It has already cleared Stuart Rose, M&S's chief executive, of wrongdoing.

Andrew Procter, the director of enforcement at the FSA, said: "This is the first time that we have fined someone for market abuse on Ofex, reminding investors that the FSA can and will take action against market abuse on any of the UK's prescribed markets.

"The FSA has fined three individuals this year using its market abuse powers so the message for senior management is clear: positions of trust should not be abused for personal gain."

Source: *Independent*, 3 August 2004

10.7 Defences

If behaviour falls outside the market abuse regime (see **10.5** above) then it is not market abuse. However, even if behaviour falls within the regime, and is market abuse, the perpetrator may still be able to avoid any penalty, by raising a defence under s 123(2).

10.7.1 Defences to the s 118 offence of market abuse

If the market abuser, X:

(a) believed, on reasonable grounds, that his behaviour did not amount to market abuse; or

(b) had taken all reasonable precautions and exercised all due diligence to avoid engaging in market abuse, then the FSA cannot impose a penalty on X (s 123(2)).

10.7.2 Defences to the s 123 offence of requiring or encouraging

If A, the person requiring or encouraging X to abuse the market:

(a) believed on reasonable grounds that his behaviour did not require or encourage X to engage in behaviour which, if engaged in by A, would have amounted to market abuse; or

(b) had taken all reasonable precautions and exercised all due diligence to avoid requiring or encouraging X to engage in behaviour which, if engaged in by A, would have amounted to market abuse,

then, under s 123(2) of the FSMA 2000, the FSA cannot impose a penalty on X.

Jabre's scalp uncovers sharp practice among hedge funds

Chris Hughes examines how finding GLG Partners' managing partner guilty of market abuse sheds light on the special treatment that investment banks are prepared to allow and the potential for that trust to be misused.

When the bear market was at its worst, many struggling companies had no choice but to turn to hedge funds to raise capital and bail them out.

Few would have imagined that a star hedge-fund manager who participated in these rescue refinancings would later become the Financial Services Authority's first scalp in its mission to stamp out sharp practice in the hedge fund industry.

The UK regulator yesterday formally found Philippe Jabre, former managing partner of GLG Partners, guilty of market abuse after trading on inside information relating to a fundraising more than three years ago.

While the ruling only rubber stamps an earlier judgment that Mr Jabre appealed unsuccessfully, the accompanying reasoning sheds light on the special treatment that hedge funds receive from investment banks - and the potential for abuse.

In February 2003, Goldman Sachs was appointed to raise up to $3bn for Sumitomo Mitsui Financial Group, the Japanese bank. Before launching the issue - codenamed "Project Shoot" - Goldman called potential investors.

Mr Jabre was on the list. GLG is among a handful of hedge fund experts in trading convertible bonds, the instrument that SMFG planned to issue. Convertibles were then a popular financing tool for companies. They pay a coupon like ordinary bonds, but can later be converted into equity.

It was - and remains - common for investment banks to tell potential investors about forthcoming securities issues. That helps the pricing. The proviso is that the investor must agree to keep the sensitive information secret - and not trade on it. For their trouble, investors sometimes receive a chunky allocation.

Goldman telephoned Mr Jabre one evening six days before the issue was made public. The firm had a script for such calls, that involved asking the investor to agree to the necessary confidentiality and trading restrictions before proceeding with questions about the issue.

In his dealings with the regulator, Mr Jabre disputed he was read the script in its entirety. But he had agreed to be "wall-crossed" - jargon for being made an insider - and to restrictions on trading. He was then told certain key details of the forthcoming SMFG bond issue. Later, Mr Jabre asked the salesman, understood to be John Rustum, a Goldman managing director, if participating in the earlier call restricted his existing trading strategies relating to SMFG. The Goldman salesman took this request to his compliance department via e-mail.

The compliance department replied that Mr Jabre could not "put out any new orders or trade the name at all". What followed is unclear. The salesman told compliance he had spoken to Mr Jabre, "and he understands". But Mr Jabre disputes he was told he could not put out new orders or trade. He says he was told he could "maintain his existing trading pattern".

Mr Jabre then short-sold nearly 5,000 SMFG shares, worth $16m, in eight successive trades. Short-selling involves selling borrowed shares so as to profit from any fall in a share price.

When the issue was launched, Mr Jabre shorted a further 11,000 shares. This made a small profit of $500,000 in the short-term. Come the pricing three days later, SMFG had dropped 22 per cent as other hedge funds sold the stock.

However, his trade lost as much as $30m, when the price of the $205m of convertibles that Mr Jabre subsequently received in the issue collapsed. It was months before his trade recovered those losses - and more - according to a person familiar with the situation.

Mr Jabre argued that his trading was legitimate because he had not been told that any issue was definitely coming. Moreover, he was told he could maintain his "existing trading pattern". This included one short trade on SMFG and a large borrowed position of Japanese bank stocks that he could have potentially sold short.

The FSA rejected these defences. It said Mr Jabre's trading in SMFG between the Goldman call and the issue's launch was based on what "a regular market user" would have recognised as inside information.

Source: *Financial Times*, 2 August 2006

10.8 Future developments

On 17 March 2006 the FSA published an occasional paper called 'Measuring Market cleanliness'. The paper sought to assess the level of market cleanliness by analysing share price movement ahead of regulatory announcements. It concluded that there had been potential market abuse in relation to almost a third of takeovers in 2004. Not surprisingly, the press seized the opportunity to criticise the FSA once more for failing to deal effectively with market abusers. It is predicted that both the negative findings and the negative press comment will motivate the FSA to enforce the market abuse regime more aggressively in the future.

Chapter 11
Insider Dealing

11.1	Introduction	139
11.2	The offence	139
11.3	Three ways the offence can be committed	141
11.4	Territorial scope	142
11.5	Sanctions	143
11.6	Defences	143
11.7	Scope of the offence	145

11.1 Introduction

Part V of the Criminal Justice Act 1993 (CJA 1993) contains the insider dealing provisions. These provisions existed before the FSMA 2000 came into force. As explained at **10.1** above, the criminal offence of insider dealing overlaps considerably with the civil offence of market abuse. The new market abuse regime, however, does not affect the insider dealing regime

Lord Lane explained the reason for the insider dealing regime very effectively in layman's terms as follows: '... the clear intention to prevent, so far as possible, what amounts to cheating when those with inside knowledge use that knowledge to make a profit in their dealing with others' (*Attorney-General's Reference (No 1 of 1988)* [1989] 2 WLR 729).

11.2 The offence

Section 52 of the CJA 1993 provides that the offence of insider dealing can be committed in three ways, namely, if an *insider*:

(a) *deals* in price-affected securities, when in possession of *inside information*;

(b) *encourages another* to deal in price-affected securities, when in possession of *inside information*, or

(c) *discloses inside information* other than in the proper performance of his employment, office or profession.

Whichever way the offence is committed, there are two common requirements, namely, an 'insider' and 'inside information'.

11.2.1 Insider

An insider is defined by s 57(1) of the CJA 1993. A person is an insider if:

(a) he has information which is *inside information*;
(b) he has received that information *from an inside source*; and
(c) he *knows* (a) and (b).

11.2.2 Inside information

Unlike the market abuse regime and the Disclosure Rules, which use the definition under s 118C of the FSMA 2000, the insider dealing regime uses the definition of 'inside information' under s 56 of the CJA 1993. This is information which:

(a) relates to particular, rather than general, securities or companies;
(b) is specific or precise;
(c) has not been made public; and
(d) is price-sensitive (that is, would be likely to have a significant effect on the price of securities, such as shares, if it were made public).

This definition has been criticised because there is not much guidance about the meaning of the terms used. Until these words are defined, or their meaning falls to be decided by the courts, they must be given their ordinary dictionary meaning. It is not clear, for example, whether a rumour which turns out to be false would be 'specific or precise' (although common sense would suggest it would not).

11.2.2.1 Particular not general

This includes information which may affect a company's prospects (which may be about the sector in which the company operates rather than about the company itself).

11.2.2.2 Specific or precise

There is no definition of these terms. Until these words are defined, or their meaning falls to be decided by the courts, they must be given their ordinary dictionary meaning. It is not clear, for example, whether a rumour which turns out to be false would be 'specific or precise' (although common sense would suggest it would not).

11.2.2.3 Not made public

If information has been made public it is not inside information. Think back to Lord Lane's comments at **11.1** above; how can someone cheat if he is using freely available information? Section 58 provides some guidance as to when information has been made public. Information which a company provides to an RIS has been made public and therefore will not be inside information. Where s 58 falls down, however, is that it provides that information made available only to a section of the public can still be treated as having been made public. It is difficult to see the logic in this. Surely it is unfair if, in order to make a profit, you use information I am unable to access? There is no guidance as to what constitutes a 'section' of the public.

11.2.2.4 Price-sensitive

It is unclear what amounts to a 'significant effect' on price.

11.2.3 From an inside source

Section 57(2) provides that a person has information from an inside source if he:

(a) is an inside source (that is, a director, employee or shareholder) of 'an issuer of securities' (for our purposes, a company (but not necessarily the company whose securities are the subject of insider dealing)); or
(b) has access to the information because of his employment, office or profession; or
(c) obtained the information from someone who obtained it by way of (a) or (b) above.

Persons falling within (a) and (b) are known as 'primary insiders'. Persons falling within (c) are known as 'secondary insiders', or 'tippees'. An example of a tippee, if a little clichéd, is a director's relative, who overhears talk about an impending takeover bid and then invests in the target company.

11.3 Three ways the offence can be committed

As explained at **11.2**, the offence can be committed in three different ways.

11.3.1 The dealing offence (s 52(1))

It is an offence to *deal* in price-affected *securities* on a *regulated market*, or by or through a *professional intermediary*.

11.3.1.1 Dealing

Section 55 of the CJA 1993 explains the meaning of 'dealing'. It includes:

(a) the acquisition, or disposal, of securities;
(b) any agreement to acquire securities (for example, entering into a share option agreement);
(c) any agreement to create securities (for example, subscribing for shares), whether as principal or agent; and
(d) procuring an acquisition or disposal of securities by any other person.

11.3.1.2 Securities

Securities are defined by s 54 of and Sch 2 to the CJA 1993. The definition is wide and includes shares, bonds, warrants and options.

11.3.1.3 Regulated market

This has been defined by the Insider Dealing (Securities and Regulated Markets) Order 1994 (SI 1994/187) as including both the Main Market and the AIM, as well as OFEX. Dealing on a regulated market is referred to as an 'on-market' transaction. If you or I decide to buy shares in Marks and Spencer Group plc through the Stock Exchange, that is an on-market transaction. The dealing offence is concerned with on-market transactions.

11.3.1.4 Professional intermediary

A professional intermediary is a person who carries on a business of acquiring or disposing of securities, or who otherwise acts as a professional intermediary between persons taking part in any dealing in securities (s 59). A stockbroker acting in the normal course of business will be a professional intermediary, but lawyers and accountants acting in their normal course of business will not.

Example

Imagine that B plc is considering making a takeover bid for X plc, a listed company. B's merchant bank acquires some shares in X plc on B's behalf, as a preliminary stake-building exercise. The shares are purchased privately, directly from a shareholder in X plc. This is known as an 'off-market' transaction. Although this acquisition has not taken place on a regulated market, B plc made the deal through a professional intermediary, the merchant bank, and therefore the deal has the potential to be within the scope of the dealing offence.

11.3.2 The offence of encouraging another to deal (s 52(2)(a))

It is not necessary for the person who is encouraged to deal either:

(a) actually to deal; or
(b) to realise the securities are price-affected.

A simple statement such as 'I cannot tell you why, but now is a good time to buy shares in X plc' could be caught by s 52(2)(a).

11.3.3 The disclosing offence (s 52(2)(b))

This prohibits any individual from disclosing inside information to another person other than in the proper performance of the functions of his employment, office or profession.

Example

Imagine that X plc, a listed company, is a weapons manufacturer. X plc is about to sign a lucrative deal with the MoD. D, a director of X plc, knows about the transaction. L is the company's lawyer. B is L's brother. Over a family dinner at which much wine is consumed, L mentions to B that this transaction is pending. B, D and L all buy shares in X plc on the Stock Exchange before details of the transaction have been made public. Who is guilty of an offence (subject to any defences)?

(a) D is guilty of insider dealing under s 52(1) (see **11.3.1**). He is an insider. He has inside information (he knows about the proposed takeover, which is specific information relating to X plc which has not been made public and is likely to have a significant effect on X plc's share price). D, presumably, knows that he is an insider with inside information. He received the information from an inside source (he has the information as a director of X plc). He has dealt in price-affected securities (the shares) on a regulated market (the Main Market).

(b) L is also guilty of insider dealing under s 52(1). He is in a similar position to D, although L is an insider because he has information through having access to it by virtue of his profession.

L is also guilty of an offence under s 52(2)(b) (see **11.3.3**) as he has disclosed the information to his brother, which is not in the proper performance of his profession.

If L encouraged his brother to buy shares in X plc, L is also be guilty of an offence under s 52(2)(a) (see **11.3.2**).

L is also guilty of serious professional misconduct; he has made a secret profit and is in breach of his duty of confidentiality.

(c) B may also be guilty of the dealing offence under s 52(1) (see **11.3.1**). Is he an insider? He is a tippee (see **11.2.3**). The source of the information is a primary insider (his brother, a lawyer) and B knows this. B has inside information. Does B know this? If B does, he will be guilty of the dealing offence.

11.4 Territorial scope

11.4.1 Dealing

Section 62(1) of the CJA 1993 provides that a person is not guilty of the dealing offence unless:

(a) he was within the UK at the time of dealing;
(b) the market is a UK regulated market (such as the Main Market, or the AIM); or
(c) the professional intermediary was within the UK at the time he is alleged to have committed the offence.

11.4.2 Encouraging or disclosing

Section 62(2) of the CJA 1993 provides that a person is not guilty of the encouraging or disclosing offence unless:

(a) he was within the UK at the time of the encouragement or disclosure; or
(b) the recipient of the encouragement or information was within the UK when he received that encouragement or information.

11.5 Sanctions

The offence of insider dealing is punishable in the same way as the criminal offence of making a misleading statement or manipulating the market (under the FSMA 2000 – see **9.5** above), namely by imprisonment and/or a fine. On summary conviction, the maximum sentence is six months, and on conviction on indictment the maximum sentence in seven years.

Note that s 63(2) provides that no contract shall be void or unenforceable solely because an offence has been committed under s 52.

Insider dealing may also amount to a breach of the Model Code (see **7.6** above).

The FSA has responsibility for enforcing the insider dealing provisions of the CJA 1993.

11.6 Defences

11.6.1 General defences

Section 53 of the CJA 1993 provides defences to each of the three ways of committing the offence.

11.6.1.1 Dealing or encouraging

No offence will be committed if the defendant can prove that:

(a) he did not expect to gain an advantage. This is a difficult defence to run. The prosecution will have proved already that he was an insider and knew he had insider information;

(b) he believed the information had been (in the case of the dealing offence) or would be (in the case of the encouraging offence) disclosed widely enough to ensure no-one would be prejudiced; or

(c) he would have traded anyway, even if he did not have inside information. This could be used, for example, if he had to meet urgent financial commitments.

11.6.1.2 Disclosing

No offence will be committed if the defendant can prove that:

(a) he did not expect dealing to occur; or

(b) he did not expect profit to result.

Again, the defence set out at (b) is a difficult defence to run once the prosecution has proved the defendant was an insider who knew he had inside information.

11.6.2 Special defences

Schedule 1 to the CJA 1993 includes some special defences relating to market-makers, market information and price stabilisation.

11.6.2.1 Market-makers

A market-maker (see **2.5.2**) has a special defence to the dealing and encouraging offences (but not the disclosing offence) if he acts in good faith in the course of his business as, or employment by, a market-maker.

11.6.2.2 Market information

There are special defences available to those who have inside information which qualifies as 'market information'. Market information is information consisting of any of the following facts:

(a) that securities of a particular kind have been, or are to be, acquired or disposed of, or that their acquisition is under consideration or the subject of negotiation;

(b) the number or price (or range of prices) of those securities;

(c) the identity of those involved, or likely to be involved, in any capacity in an acquisition or disposal; or

(d) the fact that securities of a particular kind have not been, or are not to be, acquired or disposed of.

There are two separate defences available. In each case, the defences are only available to an individual charged with dealing and/or encouraging. They are not available in relation to the disclosing offence. The defences are:

(a) The information which the individual had as an insider was *market information* and it was *reasonable* for a person in his position to have acted as he did, despite having that information as an insider at the time. Paragraph 2(2) of Sch 2 sets out a non-exhaustive list of factors to be taken into account in determining reasonableness (the content of information, the circumstances and the capacity in which the individual first had the information and the capacity in which he now acts).

(b) The individual acted in connection with an acquisition or a disposal which was under consideration or the subject of negotiation (or in the course of a series of such acquisitions or disposals), and with a view to *facilitating the accomplishment* of the relevant transaction(s). The individual must also show that the information he had was *market information* arising directly out of his involvement in the transaction(s) in question. This is referred to as the 'facilitation defence'. Note that there is no reasonableness element for this defence.

It may help to consider an example of the 'market information' defence.

Example

Imagine that X plc is considering making a takeover bid for Y plc, a listed company. The directors of X plc decide that, as a preliminary to the bid, X plc should purchase shares in Y plc on the Stock Exchange. X plc's directors instruct the company's stockbrokers to buy shares in Y plc. Are the directors guilty of insider dealing?

At the time of dealing the directors are insiders. They have inside information (namely, that X plc is about to make a bid for Y plc). The directors have that information from an inside source (in their capacity as directors). They will know that they have inside information from an inside source. The directors are dealing in price-affected securities (remember that the definition of dealing includes the situation where a person procures an acquisition of securities by another, here X plc (see **11.3.1.1**)) on a regulated market (the Main Market). It would seem that they are guilty of insider dealing under s 52(1).

Nonetheless, in these circumstances, the directors may be able to rely on the market information defence if they can show they acted to facilitate the accomplishment of the takeover of Y plc, and the information they had was solely market information arising directly out of their involvement in the takeover, and not any other confidential price-sensitive information.

11.6.2.3 Price stabilisation

There is a special defence for individuals engaged in price stabilisation operations within any price stabilisation rules made under s 144(1) of the FSMA 2000. Price stabilisation is market activity undertaken to support the price of shares offered on an IPO (see **Chapter 4**) and some secondary issues (see **Chapter 17**). The defence is available as the practice is justified on policy grounds (that it encourages equity finance).

11.7 Scope of the offence

The offence of insider dealing is narrower in scope than the offence of market abuse. Unlike market abuse, only an individual can commit the offence of insider dealing; a company cannot (although an individual can commit the offence by requiring a company to deal). A company can, however, be convicted of aiding and abetting the offence. Anything done by an individual acting on behalf of a public sector body in pursuit of monetary policies, or policies with respect to exchange rates, the management of public debt or foreign reserves, cannot be the subject of an insider dealing offence.

As the offence is so narrow, it is notoriously difficult to convict anyone of it, and there have been very few insider dealing cases (and no convictions since the FSMA came into force). This was one of the reasons, of course, for the introduction of the market abuse regime (see **Chapter 10**).

Paul 'The Plumber' Davidson: his case has brought bad PR for the FSA—PA

One Player at the centre of the Marks & Spencer share-trading brouhaha seems to hold all the cards. But it is not Philip Green, the billionaire yearning for control of the high-street retailer, or Stuart Rose, M&S's chief executive. It is the Financial Services Authority.

The City watchdog thrust itself into the spotlight last week when it took the unusual step of confirming it was investigating share dealing at M&S. Unusual, because the FSA normally only reveals that it has been probing so-called "market abuse" suspicions once a conviction has been secured.

Says a spokeswoman: "It is exceptional that the FSA would make this kind of announcement and would only do so in regards to a firm or company, rather than an individual. But it is such a high-profile case and people rightly expected us to be looking at it." Mr Green and Mr Rose both announced that they would be interviewed by the watchdog; the information did not come from the FSA.

For most observers, the affair is just another twist in the bitter battle for M&S. For the FSA, however, it could prove crucial to shoring up the regulator's lacklustre reputation.

Insider trading is notoriously hard to prove and this is one of the unofficial reasons why the Financial Services and Markets Act 2000, which came into force in December 2001, was introduced. The Act gave the FSA far-reaching powers to investigate and penalise "market abuse", which is a civil rather than criminal offence but also a broader term than "insider trading" and, crucially, easier to prove. People can be sued for creating a false or misleading impression, distorting markets or misusing information – such as buying shares in a company that they privately know will be the subject of a takeover bid.

Yet ask the FSA for a list of people convicted under the Act and you will be disappointed. There have been a handful of market abuse prosecutions but not one successful insider trading case. And the pressure is on the watchdog to get a big scalp.

"The FSA is keen not to pursue only smaller cases, so a lot of pressure is on it to get a high-profile case," says one former FSA director.

Insider trading, on various scales, is generally thought to be fairly widespread. But how do you prove it? Jonathan Herbst, a partner at law firm Norton Rose and another former FSA employee, says: "You can prove that a trade took place, that's easy. What's hard to prove is whether there was passing of information or whether it was just legitimate market rumour.

"There are always rumours flying about – that's part of the way markets work. But it's hard to disentangle how much of that is legitimate pub talk and how much is information."

Hard evidence is also scarce. As the former director at the regulator says: "The FSA has to prove possession of information and then use of that information. People don't tend to write things down if they are going to do insider trading." He believes the Financial Services and Markets Act is just "playing with the edges".

"Unless you are going to assume that whenever someone who's close to a company trades, it's insider trading, it's going to be difficult to prove.

"As soon as we see individuals trading in a timely fashion, that does raise question marks. But it only raises them. If you establish that a close friend of a company director had a meeting two days before, that might look suspicious. But if they are such close friends that they meet every couple of days ...? It's tough."

The FSA spent most of last week interviewing interested parties about M&S; the watchdog can compel people to attend, though few refuse. Along with Mr Green and Mr Rose, the regulator interviewed Michael Spencer, the chief executive of City broker Icap, who bought two million M&S contracts for differences – a form of financial instrument – the day after a meeting with Mr Rose. Further meetings are likely to be carried out this week with other people.

When its investigations are complete, the FSA will piece together all the circumstantial evidence – phone logs, emails, share trades, when trading accounts were opened and so on – and decide whether to launch a case. And while the pressure may be on to claim a big scalp, it is going to have to be sure of its evidence before proceeding.

As Mr Herbst says: "You really have got to have your ducks in a row to launch a prosecution for insider trading. It would be surprising, when they do bring a case, if they don't feel they have a pretty clearcut one, especially as it will be funded by the financial institutions."

So any reticence would be understandable: as the City provides the FSA's financial backing, it will not take kindly to seeing its money wasted on collapsing cases. Indeed, mutterings have already been heard about the trial of Paul Davidson. Better known as "The Plumber", Mr Davidson was fined £750,000 for market abuse but his appeal tribunal ran into trouble recently when it emerged that an FSA enforcement officer, Christopher Fitzgerald, had been discussing the case with his neighbour, a tribunal member. Mr FitzGerald resigned and the tribunal dismissed itself.

That is the problem that the FSA, and indeed any watchdog, faces. Not only do they have to police their field, they have to be seen to be policing it efficiently. Any failures will raise questions about how the City's money is spent.

Most commentators argue that, from a legal standpoint, three years is not that long a period when it comes to bedding down new legislation. They also point out that London has some of the world's most-respected and best-regulated markets.

Some also believe that proving insider trading should be tough. As the ex-FSA director says: "I'm not sure anything needs to be changed. Prosecutors are far too quick to say there's a problem with the underlying legislation. Insider trading may be hard to prove, but as you can go to prison for seven years, that's probably how it should be."

And most believe that, eventually, the FSA will get its man in an insider-trading case. Whether that will be a member of the City's upper echelons is, at this point, anyone's guess.

Source: *Independent on Sunday*, 4 July 2004

Chapter 12

Financial Promotion

12.1	Introduction	147
12.2	Section 21 of the FSMA 2000	147
12.3	Consequences of breach	148
12.4	What is a financial promotion?	148
12.5	Relevance in practice	148
12.6	Purpose	151
12.7	The detail of s 21	151
12.8	Territorial scope	152
12.9	Exemptions	152
12.10	Conclusion	155

12.1 Introduction

As **Chapter 9** stated, the regulation of financial promotion is one of the key features of the FSMA 2000. The main restriction on financial promotion is in s 21 of the Act, but there are two other important sources which provide further detail about the financial promotion regime. Both are new, having been introduced with the new regime on 1 July 2005.

The first is the Financial Services and Markets Act 2000 (Financial Promotion) Order 2005 (SI 2005/1529) ('FPO 2005'), which revokes, re-enacts and amends the previous Financial Promotion Order (the Financial Services and Markets Act 2000 (Financial Promotion) Order 2001 (SI 2001/1335)).

The second is chapter 8 of a new regulatory guide, the Perimeter Guidance manual ('PERG'), which replaces guidance formerly contained in Appendix 1 of the Authorisation Manual. However, as at the time of writing, PERG had not been fully updated to take account of the FPO 2005.

The FSA Conduct of Business sourcebook, in particular Chapter 3, is also relevant, as it contains the rules for authorised persons on financial promotion.

The financial promotion regime is not confined to listed companies. The majority of the provisions referred to in this chapter are equally applicable to unlisted companies, other than the exemptions referred to in **12.9.2**, some of which apply to listed companies only.

12.2 Section 21 of the FSMA 2000

Section 21(1) provides that a person must not, in the course of business, communicate an invitation or inducement to engage in investment activity. This is referred to as the 's 21 restriction'; the criteria are explored in more detail at **12.7** below. Section 21(2) provides that s 21(1) does not apply if:

(a) the person making the communication *is* an authorised person; or

(b) the content of the communication *has been approved by* an authorised person.

Section 21(1) will also not apply if the communication is covered by an *exemption* (see **12.9**).

12.3 Consequences of breach

The consequences of a breach of s 21 of the FSMA 2000 are as follows:

(a) it is a criminal offence punishable by a fine and/or imprisonment (a maximum of six months on summary conviction; two years on conviction on indictment) (s 25);

(b) any agreement which results from a communication made in breach of s 21 may be unenforceable (s 30);

(c) any third party to the unenforceable agreement can sue for any loss incurred (s 30);

(d) there may be an order for an injunction or for restitution (ss 380, 382); and

(e) there may be an action for damages (s 150).

12.4 What is a financial promotion?

Before we proceed, it would be helpful to identify what a financial promotion actually is. The term 'financial promotion' can be confusing. It is the name of an entire regime, yet the term is not actually referred to in the FSMA 2000, other than in the heading and side note to s 21. There is certainly no definition of the term. It does not mean much to the layman, or indeed to the lawyer who has not encountered it before. So what is a 'financial promotion'? Well, consider it as a generic term to refer to a communication covered by s 21. In very basic layman's terms, it is a communication that contains information which might entice someone to invest in a company, or do certain other activities in relation to investments in that company.

A financial promotion is not like an elephant; you may well not recognise one when you see one. Of course, some financial promotions set off alarm bells immediately. Take, for example, the company secretary who calls to inform you that the company is about to place a newspaper advertisement, 'Need extra cash? Invest in us – we are doing really well'. Even the most inexperienced lawyer would consider that this might fall foul of s 21. However, consider a company which is planning to run a television advertising campaign to raise its profile. You happen to know that the company is preparing to float within the next month. The TV advertising campaign does not mention this at all. Would s 21 spring to mind? Would the company even consider bringing the existence of the campaign to the notice of its lawyers? Perhaps not, but it should, as in the context of the impending float, the advertisements might well fall within s 21.

12.5 Relevance in practice

In practice, the rules relating to financial promotion mean that, if a client company is proposing to make a communication, the lawyer must check whether that communication will fall within s 21 of the FSMA 2000. If it does then this is not good, for the reasons set out at **12.3** above. The lawyer must advise the client that it needs to ensure that the communication falls outside s 21. The easiest way to do this is to instruct an authorised person (see **9.4.3**) to approve the communication before it is made (see **12.2** above). Sometimes it is not possible for an authorised person to approve the communication (see **12.9.1.1** below), and in such circumstances the lawyer must advise the client not to make the communication at all, or to change it to a form which can be approved. This approach is summarised by the flowchart in **Figure 12.1** below.

To put this into context, it is important for a lawyer advising a listed company to be alert to the types of communication that company might make, and to analyse whether these communications might fall within s 21. For example, if a company is raising funds, as considered in **Chapter 17**, then the company will publish a prospectus, perhaps a pathfinder document (although this may not be as popular under the new regime as under the old regime – see **6.9.3**), and a press announcement. If the company is effecting a takeover, as considered in **Chapters 20, 21** and **22**, then the company may seek irrevocable undertakings and will make a r 2.5 announcement, circulate an offer document and announce levels of acceptance. The lawyers must advise as to whether these communications fall within the s 21 restriction or not, and the consequences of this. This advice will depend on the individual circumstances of the communication (which may affect, for example, whether an exemption applies).

An example of an approved document (albeit under the old regime) is set out at **12.5.1** below.

Figure 12.1: Financial promotion flowchart

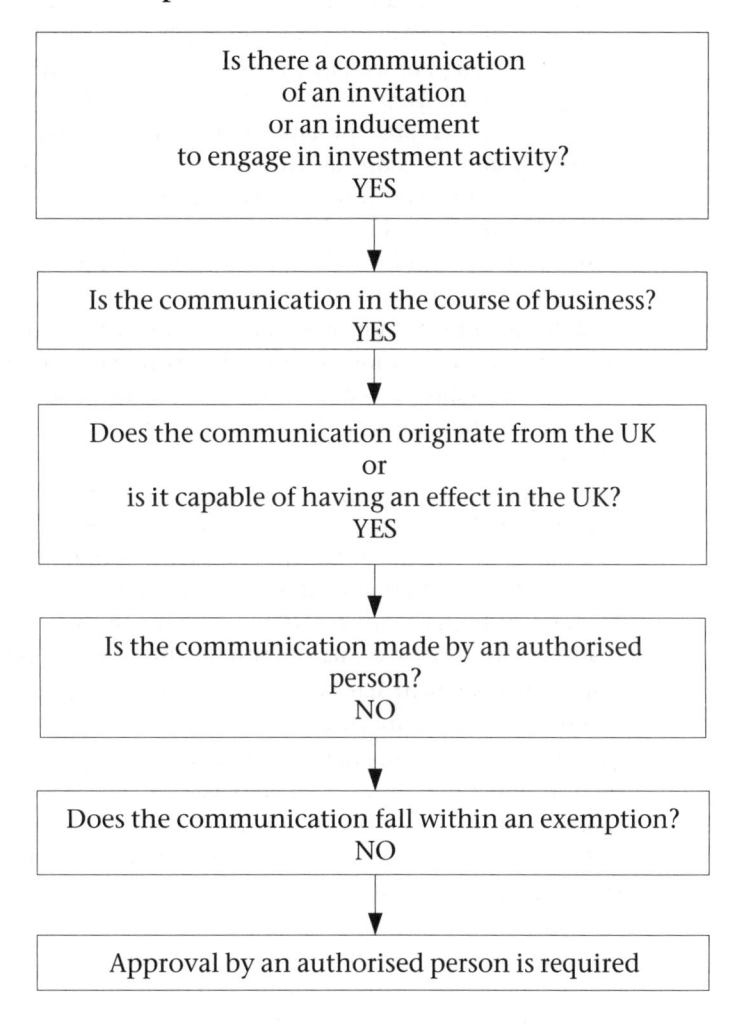

```
┌─────────────────────────────────────────┐
│      Is there a communication           │
│          of an invitation               │
│          or an inducement               │
│    to engage in investment activity?    │
│                YES                      │
└─────────────────────────────────────────┘
                    │
                    ▼
┌─────────────────────────────────────────┐
│ Is the communication in the course of   │
│ business?                               │
│                YES                      │
└─────────────────────────────────────────┘
                    │
                    ▼
┌─────────────────────────────────────────┐
│ Does the communication originate from   │
│ the UK or                               │
│ is it capable of having an effect in    │
│ the UK?                                 │
│                YES                      │
└─────────────────────────────────────────┘
                    │
                    ▼
┌─────────────────────────────────────────┐
│ Is the communication made by an         │
│ authorised person?                      │
│                NO                       │
└─────────────────────────────────────────┘
                    │
                    ▼
┌─────────────────────────────────────────┐
│ Does the communication fall within an   │
│ exemption?                              │
│                NO                       │
└─────────────────────────────────────────┘
                    │
                    ▼
┌─────────────────────────────────────────┐
│ Approval by an authorised person is     │
│ required                                │
└─────────────────────────────────────────┘
```

12.5.1 Sample approved pathfinder prospectus

IMPORTANT NOTICE

X PLC

THIS DOCUMENT AND ITS CONTENTS ARE CONFIDENTIAL AND SHOULD NOT BE DISTRIBUTED, PUBLISHED OR REPRODUCED IN WHOLE OR IN PART OR DISCLOSED BY RECIPIENTS TO ANY OTHER PERSON.

This document, comprising a draft prospectus, is issued by Financial Adviser Limited ('Financial Adviser') which is regulated by the Financial Services Authority, as financial adviser to X Limited (planned to become X PLC) (the "Company") in connection with, *inter alia*, the proposed placing of ordinary shares in the capital of the Company and the proposed admission of the issued and to be issued ordinary shares of the Company to trading on the Main Market of London Stock Exchange plc ('Admission').

The information in this document, which is in draft form and is incomplete, is subject to updating, completion, revision, further verification and amendment. In particular, this document refers to certain events as having occurred which have not yet occurred but are expected to occur prior to publication of the final prospectus relating to the Company. No assurance is given by the Company or Financial Adviser that any ordinary shares in the Company will be issued or sold.

No representation or warranty is made by Financial Adviser or the Company or any of their advisers, agents, officers, directors or employees, as to, and no responsibility or liability is accepted by any of them for any errors or mis-statements in, or omissions from, this document nor for any direct or consequential loss howsoever arising from any use of, or reliance on, this document or otherwise in connection with it. In particular, but without limitation, no representation or warranty is given as to the prospects of the Company and nothing in this document should be relied on as a promise or representation as to the future.

This document does not constitute or form part of any offer or invitation to sell or issue, or any solicitation of any offer to purchase or subscribe for, or otherwise acquire, any ordinary shares in the Company nor shall it, or any part of it, or the fact of its distribution, form the basis of, or be relied on in connection with, any contract therefore.

Recipients of this document who intend to subscribe for ordinary shares in the Company following the issue of the prospectus in its final form (should such issue take place) are reminded that any such subscription may only be made solely on the basis of the information contained in the prospectus in its final form, which may be different from the information contained in this document. No reliance may be made for any purpose whatsoever on the information contained in this document.

This draft document has been approved by Financial Adviser for the purposes of section 21 of the Financial Services and Markets Act 2000.

This document should not be distributed by recipients and, in particular, should not be distributed to persons with addresses in the United States of America, Canada, Japan, Australia, the Republic of Ireland or South Africa, or in any other country outside the United Kingdom where such distribution may lead to a breach of any law or regulatory requirement.

The information in this document is confidential and must not be copied, reproduced or distributed to others at any time except for the purposes of analysis by certain employees of the recipient who have agreed to be bound by the restrictions contained herein. Financial Adviser is acting as financial adviser to the Company and will not regard any person (whether or not a recipient of this document or other information) other than the Company as its customer in relation to the proposals contemplated by this document. Any prospective investor interested in investing in the Company is recommended to seek independent financial advice.

.... 200*

12.6 Purpose

The s 21 restriction on making financial promotions, like so many other statutory provisions in the field of corporate finance, is to protect investors. A financial promotion is basically a business communication which could encourage the recipient to take some action in relation to an investment. Section 21 controls how those communications are made and what they say, so that advantage is not taken of investors and potential investors.

FSA in Crackdown on Misleading Ads

JAMES DALEY

THE FSA, the City watchdog, yesterday announced a crackdown on misleading advertising by financial services companies, launching a whistle-blowing hotline and creating a 30-strong department to police financial marketing material.

The move comes after a year that has seen a record number of complaints concerning financial adverts, with almost 600 cases relating to more than 350 firms. Several of the complaints have already led to the Financial Services Authority asking for adverts to be withdrawn or amended, whilst Chase de Vere was fined £165,000 last December for misleading marketing literature concerning "precipice" bonds.

Anna Bradley, the FSA's director of retail themes, who will head up the new division, said: "We hope that firms will make use of the new hotline, as well as consumers. Consumers can pay a heavy price when they buy a financial product as a result of a misleading advert. But the industry also pays a heavy price when their reputation is damaged."

The FSA also revealed yesterday that it had written to the chief executives of companies that sell investments for children, warning them to be especially careful of how they promote the products. It said firms should be very careful to warn of the risks if savings products are linked to the stock market, and should not refer to products as "safe" or "secure" if there was any risk to capital.

It said: "Many consumers may not see the difference between the savings plans' referred to in these promotions, which include an equity-linked element, and safer methods of saving such as regular deposit accounts ... Financial promotions should provide adequate information, which the target audience is able to understand."

The FSA's hotline number is 08457 300168.

Source: *Independent*, 7 July 2004

12.7 The detail of s 21

The following paragraphs consider some of the detail of the s 21 restriction and the exemptions from it. The FSA has provided over 60 pages of guidance on the interpretation of the restriction and the main exemptions in PERG. PERG does not bind the courts, but it may be influential.

12.7.1 Person

'Person' includes a corporate entity such as a company.

12.7.2 Course of business

Section 21(4) of the FSMA 2000 gives the Treasury the power to define this term, but to date it has not done so. This requirement excludes from the ambit of s 21 communications of a personal nature. So, if tonight in the pub I mention that I am going to buy a few shares in company X, and suggest that my friends do the same, my suggestion will not be caught by the s 21 restriction; the communication would not have a commercial nature. Further guidance is provided by PERG 8.5.

12.7.3 Communication

'Communication' means all communication, through whatever medium, so it includes oral and written communication as well as electronic communication (for example, a website announcement). 'Communicate' includes causing a communication to be made (FSMA 2000, s 21(13)). This means that if a company makes an announcement through, for example, financial PRs, and the announcement is in breach of s 21, then, subject to any exemptions which apply, not only the company but also the financial PRs would be responsible for the communication, and therefore caught by the s 21 restriction. PERG 8.6.3 sets out categories of persons whom the FSA does not consider will communicate or cause a communication to be made.

12.7.4 Invitation or inducement

Neither term is defined by the FSMA 2000. 'Invitation' will catch direct invitations to engage in investment activity, such as an invitation to buy shares. It can range from a polite request to an encouragement. A prospectus, together with an application form (see **Chapter 6**) would constitute an invitation to buy shares. 'Inducement' is thought to be wider. The Treasury stated that the term is intended to catch any communication which contains a degree of incitement to engage in an investment activity and that a communication of purely factual information would not amount to an inducement. It is unclear how wide this could be: what if a company embarks on a marketing campaign to raise its profile? It is possible that this could amount to an inducement if it contains any incitement to invest in that company. If the campaign involves putting the company's name onto a few umbrellas, then it would probably not amount to an inducement. PERG 8.4 provides further guidance.

12.7.5 Engaging in investment activity

Section 21(8) and (9) of the FSMA 2000, together with art 4 of and Sch 1 to the FPO 2005, define 'engaging in investment activity' as:

(a) entering into an agreement which constitutes a 'controlled activity' (such as buying, selling and underwriting shares; see Sch 1 to the FPO 2005); and

(b) exercising any rights conferred by a 'controlled investment' (such as shares and bonds; see Sch 1 to the FPO 2005) to buy, sell, underwrite or convert that investment.

This definition could affect how a company chooses to structure transactions. For example, while share sales constitute 'investment activity', asset sales do not.

12.8 Territorial scope

The s 21 restriction will apply to any communication which is:

(a) made from the UK; or

(b) made from overseas, but is capable of having an effect in the UK (s 21(3)).

(However there are exemptions, under art 12 of the FPO 2005, for certain communications which are made to a recipient who receives the communication outside the UK, or which is directed only at persons outside the UK.)

12.9 Exemptions

It was made clear at **12.7** above that the s 21 restriction is wide. However, to counterbalance this, the FPO 2005 contains over 75 exemptions from the restriction. Remember that while approval by an authorised person brings the communication outside the scope of s 21, it is not an exemption. If an exemption applies, there is no requirement for the communication to be approved by an authorised person.

The exemptions do contain some new terminology, however. The application of certain exemptions depends on the nature of the communication, in particular whether it is 'real time' or 'non real time' and, if real time, whether it is 'solicited' or 'unsolicited'. The meaning of these terms is explained at **12.9.1** below.

The s 21 restriction applies to both listed and unlisted companies. Nevertheless, there are some very useful exemptions which apply to listed companies only. The exemptions are detailed in, and in practice recourse must be made to, the relevant article of the FPO 2005 and PERG. However, the exemptions of particular use to listed companies are summarised at **12.9.2** below.

12.9.1 Terminology

In **12.9.1.1** and **12.9.1.2** below, references to 'art' are references to articles of the FPO 2005.

12.9.1.1 Real time and non real time communications (art 7)

A real time communication is any communication made in the course of a personal visit, telephone conversation or other interactive dialogue. A non real time communication is any communication which is not a real time communication. Examples include letters, e-mails and newspaper announcements. Article 7(5) contains a list of indicators that the communication is 'non real time'.

The reason that the exemptions distinguish real time communications from non real time communications is that the FSA considers that investors require more protection from real time communications (because people can get carried away in interactive dialogue and there is less opportunity for a cooling-off period). The exemptions which apply to real time communications therefore are narrower in scope than those exemptions which apply to non real time communications. In fact, it is not possible for even an authorised person to approve real time communications, so care must be taken to ensure that any real time communication does fall within the scope of an exemption.

PERG 8.10 provides further guidance on this issue.

12.9.1.2 Solicited and unsolicited real time communications (art 8)

A solicited real time communication is a real time communication which has been initiated by the recipient, or which has been made in response to a request from the recipient. An unsolicited real time communication is a real time communication which is not a solicited communication.

12.9.2 Exemptions useful to listed companies

In **12.9.2.1** to **12.9.2.9** below, references to 'art' are references to articles of the FPO 2005.

12.9.2.1 Communications to shareholders and creditors (art 43)

The s 21 restriction does not apply to non real time or solicited real time communications made by, or on behalf of, a company to, or directed at, its shareholders, provided that the communication does not relate to an investment (for example, shares) issued, or to be issued, outside the company's group. (However, any individual who sends such a communication, for example the chairman, may be at risk of breaching s 19 of the FSMA 2000; see **9.4**.)

12.9.2.2 Group companies (art 45)

The s 21 restriction will not apply to any communication between a company and any of its group companies.

12.9.2.3 Annual report and accounts (art 59)

The s 21 restriction will not apply to the distribution by a company of its annual report and accounts, provided it meets certain criteria, such as not including any invitation or advice to persons to buy, sell, underwrite or subscribe for any investments.

12.9.2.4 Employee share schemes (art 60)

The s 21 restriction will not apply to any communications by the company, or its group companies or trustees, which are for the purpose of any employee share scheme (see **13.9**).

12.9.2.5 Sale of body corporate (art 62)

This is subject to certain conditions. The intention of this exemption seems to be to enable controlling shareholders of small companies to buy and sell those companies without being caught by the s 21 restriction. However, as drafted, the scope of this exemption is not clear. If read literally, this exemption would apply to takeovers of public companies, which many consider cannot have been intended. The Treasury recognised this issue and, during 2004, drafted proposals to narrow the exemption. It was expected that the exemption would be amended when the FPO 2005 replaced the previous Financial Promotion Order. However, surprisingly, no changes were made, and the Treasury has not yet clarified why it has not implemented its proposals.

12.9.2.6 Other communications by listed companies (art 69)

The s 21 restriction will not apply to some communications made by listed companies, provided that certain criteria are met.

12.9.2.7 Promotions included in listing particulars, etc (art 70)

The s 21 restriction will not apply to any non real time communication in a prospectus or supplementary prospectus which has been approved in accordance with the Prospectus Rules, or to any other document required or permitted to be published by the Listing Rules or the Prospectus Rules (except an advertisement within the meaning of the Prospectus Directive). This is because it is presumed that the FSA will provide sufficient protection to investors in these rules, so protection under the financial promotion regime is unnecessary.

The FSA considers that 'permitted' means something which is expressly permitted rather than simply not expressly prohibited (PERG 8.21.14G).

12.9.2.8 Material relating to prospectus for public offer of unlisted securities (art 71)

The s 21 restriction will not apply to any non real time communication relating to a prospectus or supplementary prospectus, in the circumstances set out in art 71.

12.9.2.9 Investment professionals (art 19), certified high net worth individuals (art 48), high net worth companies (art 49) and certified and self-certified sophisticated investors (arts 50 and 50A)

Section 21 will not apply to communications made to the above-mentioned recipients. This can be useful to a company seeking to raise funds; by targeting these recipients only, the communication will be exempt from the s 21 restriction. There is the problem, of course, of how a company would know that the high net worth individuals and sophisticated investors it targets are certified.

Note that arts 48 and 50A apply only to communications relating to investments in *unlisted* companies.

12.10 Conclusion

Section 21 of the FSMA 2000 is very wide. It covers most of the communications a listed company would make in its day-to-day corporate and trading activities. The exemptions, and the ability of authorised persons to approve non real time communications, narrow the scope of the s 21 restriction. The exemptions are drafted with the rationale of s 21 in mind (see **12.6** above). The more inexperienced the recipient, the more likely it is that the exemptions will not apply, and that s 21 will either prohibit the communication, or ensure that the communication is approved by an authorised person, in order to protect that recipient.

Part III
EQUITY FINANCE

Chapter 13
Shares

13.1	Introduction	159
13.2	What is a share?	159
13.3	Some terms relating to share capital	159
13.4	What use is a share?	161
13.5	Classes of share	162
13.6	Shares or debt?	166
13.7	Varying class rights	167
13.8	Registration of share rights	168
13.9	Employee share schemes	169
13.10	Future developments	170

13.1 Introduction

Shares are not unique to listed companies, or even to public companies. Most companies have limited liability. Most companies with limited liability have a share capital, and are limited by shares rather than by guarantee. So why dedicate a whole chapter of this book to shares? Well, any corporate finance lawyer needs to have a sound understanding of the basic law relating to share capital. **Chapter 1** established that the principal reason most companies choose to float is to take advantage of the opportunities afforded by the market to raise funds, both on flotation (considered in **Chapters 4, 5** and **6**) and once listed (considered in **Chapter 17**). **Chapter 1** also set out the requirements that a company's share capital has to meet before the company can re-register as a public company. **Chapter 4** explained that the company's share capital has to meet further requirements before the company can float. **Part IV** of this book also explains that listed companies often use their share capital as consideration when entering into various transactions, such as acquisitions or takeovers.

So listed companies are always playing with their share capital. It is the lawyer's job to make sure they do so in a way permitted by law. **Chapters 13** to **16** explore the law relating to the share capital of a company, with particular focus on the law relating to listed companies.

13.2 What is a share?

A share represents ownership of a company. A person who owns a share owns a stake in the company. This person is referred to as a 'member', or 'shareholder', of that company. This book uses the term 'shareholder', but 'member' means exactly the same thing. The term 'investor' may be used to describe someone who has invested cash in return for shares in a company, but it could also be used to describe someone who has provided a loan to the company. In the former scenario, the investor will be a shareholder; in the latter, he will not.

13.3 Some terms relating to share capital

13.3.1 Nominal value (also known as par value)

Shares are created with a fixed nominal value. A company can have shares with a nominal value of 1p ('1p shares'), 10p ('10p shares') £1 ('£1 shares') – in fact, shares of any nominal value, although the nominal value should not be too high, as, under s 100 of the CA 1985, a company cannot issue a share at a discount to (that is, for any less than) its nominal value. This means, for example, that a company could not issue a £1 share for 80p. If it wanted to issue the share for 80p, the nominal value of that share would have to be equal to or less than 80p.

As stated at **13.3.3** below, the company's memorandum of association must state the nominal value of the company's authorised share value. Note that the nominal value will usually bear no correlation to the current market value of the share (see **13.3.5**). Most shares will be sold at a premium (see **13.3.2**). A share with a nominal value of £1 (a £1 share) could be worth, say, £5 when sold on the market.

13.3.2 Premium

A premium is the difference between the nominal value of the share and the price paid for that share. For example, if I pay £5 for a share which has a nominal value of £1, I have paid £1 nominal value and a premium of £4.

13.3.3 Authorised share capital

The authorised share capital is the total nominal value of the shares that a company has been authorised to issue by its shareholders. The company's memorandum of association must state this amount, together with the number of shares and the nominal value of each share. For example, the articles of X plc may state that X plc has an authorised share capital of £1m, divided into 1 million shares of £1 each.

Remember that there is a minimum authorised share capital requirement for a public company of at least £50,000 (see **1.9.2** and **1.9.3.2** above).

13.3.4 Issued share capital

This is the total nominal value of the shares a company has in issue. It may be equal to the authorised share capital (if all authorised shares are in issue), or less than the authorised share capital (if not all authorised shares are in issue), but it cannot be more than the authorised share capital. Take the example of X plc at **13.3.3** above. If X plc has 75,000 shareholders, who each hold 10 shares of £1 each, then the issued share capital of X plc is £750,000. This means that there are 250,000 shares of £1 each which are authorised but unissued. It may help to think of authorised share capital as a pool of shares from which the company may issue shares. When all the shares in this pool have been issued, the pool must be replenished before the company can issue any further shares. **Chapter 14** considers this process further.

Remember that there is a minimum issued share capital requirement of £50,000 for a public company which is trading (see **1.9.2.2** and **1.9.3.2** above).

13.3.5 Market value

The market value is the price that investors are willing to pay for a share on the market. It usually bears no correlation to the nominal value of the share (see **13.3.1**). Market-makers (see **2.5.2**) will set a price at which they are willing to buy shares and a price at which they are willing to sell shares. The market value of shares which are quoted in the newspaper is, in fact, a middle price between these two prices.

13.3.6 Market capitalisation

Market capitalisation is one method of valuing a company. It represents the market value of the company's issued share capital. It is calculated as follows:

number of issued shares × current market value of each share

13.3.7 Fully, nil or part paid

A share is 'fully paid' when the shareholder has paid the company the nominal value of the share together with any premium payable on it. If the shareholder has paid nothing in this regard, the share is 'nil paid'. If the shareholder has made a payment towards this, but has not paid the full amount, the share is 'part paid'.

Remember that there are specific requirements as to the amount which must be paid up on any share if the company is a public company. Each share (other than a share allotted pursuant to an employee share scheme – see **13.9**) must be paid up at least as to one-quarter of its nominal value together with the whole of any premium paid on it (see **1.9.2.2** and **1.9.3.2** above).

13.4 What use is a share?

The share has certain endearing qualities.

13.4.1 Limited liability

Any shareholder is liable to pay the company the amount due on the share. Once the share is fully paid, the shareholder (together with any person to whom the shareholder transfers that share) will have no further liability to the company. Even if the share is nil paid or part paid (see **13.3.7** above), the shareholder will have liability only up to the balance due on the share.

Why is this relevant? Well, imagine that Marks and Spencer Group plc goes bust tomorrow. I have 100 shares of 25p (nominal value) in the company, for which I paid £270 but which are now worth about £350. I am a lecturer living on the breadline. Should I be worried? Might I have to stand behind the company's debt and help to satisfy all those unpaid suppliers of socks? No, because my shares limit my liability to the company and to any liquidator of the company. In paying the amount due on the shares, I discharged my liability in full. The only issues that may concern me are that I might have lost the £270 paid up on my shares (see **13.5.2.3**), I have lost the opportunity to sell the shares and realise the capital growth of £80, and I have lost the potential for further capital growth.

13.4.2 Rights

A share will convey various rights on the shareholder. The rights may be set out in the company's memorandum of association (but this is rare), or in a special resolution, but usually they are set out in the company's articles of association, under the following headings (or similar):

(a) *Income rights.* This is the right to share in the profits of the company, through the right to a dividend.

(b) *The right to receive notice of, attend and vote at meetings.* The right which gives the shareholder the most power is the right to vote.

(c) *Capital rights.* This is the right to share in the capital of a company, on a winding up, after payment of the company's debts. This may be a right to be repaid the capital paid up on the shares (that is, the nominal value and any premium paid for the shares), or an additional right to share in any surplus assets once the amount paid up on all classes of shares has been repaid.

13.4.3 Capital growth

Many investors are attracted to shares because of the opportunity they afford for capital growth. A shareholder will buy shares on the Main Market at a certain price. The price of those shares is likely to change throughout the period the shareholder owns the shares. The shareholder's original investment will rise or fall in value. The shareholder therefore takes the risk of capital gains or losses. Investors hope, of course, that they will be able to weather any storms and sell when their investment has increased in value. This is looking at the market through rose-tinted spectacles, though. Everyone will remember the dotcom 'boom and bust', when shareholders who bought shares in dotcom businesses early enough became millionaires overnight. Some of these shareholders had the good sense to sell some shares and deposit the profit in the bank for a rainy day, but others lost considerable amounts when the dotcom bubble burst.

13.5 Classes of share

Often the company will want to create different types of share, with different rights attaching to each type. The company may, for example, be pre-float, and want to attract a venture capital company to invest, in return for shares. Usually, the venture capital company will be in a position to demand enhanced rights over the other ordinary shareholders. Alternatively, perhaps the company wants to reward its loyal employees, or the original owners who built up the company, with some shares to provide for them in old age, but does not want to give them the power to vote, which ordinary shares would convey. The company will create a separate class of shares to issue to the venture capital company, or to its employees. Again, the company's articles will detail the rights attached to each class of share, using the headings set out at **13.4.2** above. The lawyer may well have to draft these rights, and they can be quite complex.

The common classes of shares are discussed below. Note, however, that it is impossible to list all the classes you are ever likely to encounter. That is another advantage of the share; there is an infinite number of permutations. Take care, however, not to presume anything from the name of the class of share; always check the articles for the specific rights, and any restrictions, which attach to a share.

13.5.1 Ordinary shares

Ordinary shares are the most common class of share. Usually listed companies will list their ordinary shares. They may, however, choose not to list other classes of share. Remember that if a company chooses to list a class of shares, it must list all the shares in that class (see **4.3.1.1** above). It is Marks and Spencer Group plc's ordinary shares of 25p that you or I are able to buy on the Main Market.

Typical rights attaching to ordinary shares are examined at **13.5.1.1** to **13.5.1.3** below.

13.5.1.1 Income rights

The holders of other classes of shares might be entitled to a preferential dividend payment before the ordinary shareholders (see **13.5.2.1** below), but usually any profits to be paid out over and above that preferential dividend will be paid entirely to the ordinary shareholders. Shares which carry this unlimited right to income are referred to as equity shares (to draw an analogy with a law firm, equity shareholders are like equity partners; they have an unlimited, but proportionate, right to share in profits). Note, however, that the company is not obliged to declare a dividend. It may not declare one if it has not had a profitable year and there are insufficient profits available for distribution (see **18.2.1**).

13.5.1.2 The right to receive notice of, attend and vote at meetings

The ordinary shareholders are usually entitled to receive notice of, attend and vote at company meetings. Occasionally, however, non-voting ordinary shares are created, for example to raise capital without diluting control of the company. Usually, other classes of share will not afford the right to vote.

13.5.1.3 Capital rights

On a winding up of the company, the company's assets are used, first, in paying off the company's liabilities, then in repaying the capital (that is, the amount paid up) on all the classes of shares other than ordinary shares. Only then will the ordinary shareholders be repaid the amount paid up on their shares. However, if there are any surplus assets once all these payments have been made, they will usually be distributed between the ordinary shareholders.

13.5.2 Preference shares

A preference share is any share which has preferential rights over other classes of share, particular ordinary shares. A company may have more than one class of preference shares, for example it may have 'A' preference shares, with one set of rights, and 'B' preference shares, with another set of rights. Again, the company's articles will list the rights which attach to the shares.

Often, as stated in **13.5** above, preference shares are tailor-made for a particular scenario and with particular preference shareholders in mind. The bargaining position of these shareholders might dictate the rights which attach to the shares. If preference shares are being created as a 'freebie' reward, the company will have a free hand in drafting the rights. However, if the company is keen to bring on board a venture capital company, that venture capital company might well be demanding as to the share rights it obtains in return for its cash injection into the company.

Typical rights which may attach to preference shares are examined at **13.5.2.1** to **13.5.2.3** below.

13.5.2.1 Income rights

Preferential dividend

The holders of preference shares might be entitled to a fixed preferential dividend payment from distributable profits before the ordinary shareholders are entitled to their dividend (see **3.5.1.1** above). This is often expressed as a percentage of the nominal value of the share. For example, a '5% preference share' will entitle a preference shareholder, on the declaration of a dividend, to a fixed payment of 5% of the nominal value of his shareholding before any dividend is paid to ordinary shareholders. To continue the analogy with a law firm from **13.5.1.1** above, preference shareholders are like salaried partners; they have a limited right to share in profits.

If the company does not declare a dividend then, subject to any cumulative rights (see below), the shareholders are not entitled to a dividend payment.

Cumulative right to a dividend

Unless the articles expressly state to the contrary, all preference shares will be 'cumulative'. Usually the articles state expressly that preference shares are cumulative. This means that if the company does not declare a dividend, or if it declares a dividend so small that the preference shareholders do not receive their full dividend, then the dividend (or the shortfall, as the case may be) will be carried forward to the next year automatically; and if there is no dividend that year, it will be carried forward to the following year, and so on.

Example

Imagine that X plc has an issued share capital of £100m, divided into 90 million ordinary shares of £1 each and 10 million cumulative 5% preference shares of £1 each. This means that in any year in which a dividend is declared, the first £500,000 (5% of £10 million, the nominal value of the shares) is payable to the preference shareholders. Any excess is payable to the ordinary shareholders. The table below shows the dividend payments over a five-year period.

Year	Total dividend	Preference dividend	Ordinary dividend	Preference entitlement carried forward
1	£900,000	£500,000	£400,000	Nil
2	£400,000	£400,000	Nil	£100,000
3	£550,000	£550,000	Nil	£50,000
4	Nil	Nil	Nil	£550,000
5	£1,200,000	£1,050,000	£150,000	Nil

In year 3, although a total dividend of £550,000 is declared, the ordinary shareholders do not receive £50,000. Instead, that is also paid to the preference shareholders, to make up some (but not all) of the £100,000 arrears carried forward from year 2. The rest of the shortfall (£50,000) is not paid to the preference shareholders in year 4; no dividend at all was declared then. Instead, it, together with the arrears of £500,000 from year 4, is made up in year 5, and there is even some left for the ordinary shareholders this year.

Dividend on a winding up

When preference shares are cumulative, the articles should make clear whether any arrears of the preference dividend are payable to the preference shareholders on a winding up of the company. For example, in the example used above, if X plc was wound up in year 4, the articles should clarify whether the £550,000 arrears would be payable to the preference shareholders.

Participating preference shares

Participating preference shares have further rights to a dividend, not just a preferential right to a fixed amount before the ordinary shareholders. Participating preference shares can be cumulative, but they do not have to be. Take again the example above. You can see that once the preference shareholders have taken their 5% dividend, the remainder goes to the ordinary shareholders in their entirety. Take year 5. The remaining £150,000 is paid to the ordinary shareholders. If the preference shares had been participating preference shares, the preference shareholders would have had some right to part of this amount. The articles will provide what that right is, but it could be, for example, that the ordinary shareholders also take a fixed percentage, then the balance is divided equally between the preference shareholders and the ordinary shareholders. Participating preference shares may also have further rights to capital (see **13.5.2.3** below).

13.5.2.2 The right to receive notice of, attend and vote at meetings

Usually, preference shares will give preference shareholders the right to receive notice of general meetings and to attend meetings. However, they will seldom give preference shareholders the right to vote, other than in relation to certain limited matters, such as on a resolution to wind up the company, or to vary the rights which attach to the preference shares.

13.5.2.3 Capital rights

Just because a preference shareholder has a preferential right to a dividend does not necessarily mean that he will have a preferential right on a return of capital, and vice versa. Often in practice, however, preference shareholders do have preferential rights as to capital. It may be that once the company has repaid its debts, the preference shareholders are repaid their capital before the ordinary shareholders. If there are any surplus assets remaining after even the ordinary shareholders have been repaid, then the preference shareholders may have some rights over the surplus, for example to divide it between themselves and the ordinary shareholders. In this case the preference shares would be participating preference shares. Unless there is an express provision to the contrary, however, this surplus will belong to the ordinary shareholders alone.

13.5.3 Redeemable shares

13.5.3.1 Creation

Under s 159 of the CA 1985, a company can issue shares which will, or may, be redeemed at the option of the company or the shareholder, if:

(a) the company is authorised to do this by its articles of association; and

(b) the company has in issue other shares which are not redeemable.

A company may find it useful to issue redeemable shares if, for example, a venture capital company wishes to invest in the company for a fixed period of time. Any lawyer drafting redeemable share rights should pay particular attention to s 159A of the CA 1985, which provides some guidelines as to the terms and manner of redemption which must be dealt with on creation of the shares.

13.5.3.2 Redemption

The general rule under s 160(1) of the CA 1985 is that redeemable shares can be redeemed only out of either:

(a) distributable profits of the company; or

(b) the proceeds of a fresh issue of shares made for the purpose of the redemption.

Any premium payable to redeemable shareholders on redemption must be paid out of distributable profits rather than capital (but see s 160(2) of the CA 1985, which provides that any premium payable in relation to redeemable shares which were issued at a premium may be made out of the proceeds of a fresh issue of shares, up to a certain amount). There is, however, an exception for private companies, which can redeem out of capital, provided the articles of association permit redemption out of capital and the company adopts a certain procedure to effect the redemption (s 171). ***Business Law and Practice*** considers further the law relating to the redemption of redeemable shares.

13.5.3.3 The effect of redemption

Pursuant to s 160 of the CA 1985, the effect of redemption is that the shares are treated as cancelled. This means that the issued share capital of the company will be reduced by the nominal value of the shares redeemed. The authorised share capital, however, is not reduced.

13.5.4 Convertible shares

A company may issue convertible shares, which, as their name suggests, can be converted into ordinary shares. The conversion may be at a specified time, or may be triggered by the happening of some event (eg, flotation). The attractions to a convertible shareholder of converting to ordinary shares may be the acquisition of voting rights, or the fact that the market value of the ordinary shares has risen above the conversion price of the convertible shares.

13.5.5 Bonus shares (also known as 'scrip' or 'scrip issues')

If its articles permit, a company can transfer profits to a fund called its 'capital redemption reserve' and use it to issue 'bonus' shares to the shareholders in proportion to their existing shareholdings. Since the issue may reduce the amount of money available for paying dividends, the term 'bonus' is not really appropriate. The correct term is 'capitalisation of reserves' (or 'capitalisation issue'), but the terms 'scrip', or 'scrip issues' are also used to describe such shares.

13.5.6 Subscriber shares

The memorandum will show the names of the people who agreed to own shares when the company was first registered. These people are called the subscribers, and the shares which were allotted to them on the company's registration are referred to as subscriber shares (see CA 1985, s 1(1)). Section 106 of the CA 1985 provides that in a public company the subscriber shares must be paid up in cash.

13.5.7 Summary

You will now appreciate that, usually, ordinary shares bear the greatest financial risk, because, unlike preference shares, typically they do not afford any prior right to a dividend or return of capital. It is because ordinary shareholders bear this risk that, generally, they also are afforded full voting rights. However, ordinary shares also carry the greatest potential for financial gain, because the rights they do afford in relation to income and capital tend to be unlimited, unlike preference shares, which often afford fixed rights to income and capital.

13.6 Shares or debt?

This book is concerned with equity finance. There is another book in the series which deals with debt finance (see ***Banking and Capital Markets***). **Chapter 18** provides an overview of the difference between equity and debt finance.

Some classes of share, which are equity finance, can be confused with debt finance. Take, for example, a 5% cumulative redeemable preference share. It will yield a return (the 5% fixed dividend), like interest on a loan, and it is redeemable, so repayable, like a loan. However, a closer inspection reveals that preference shares are in fact equity finance, not debt finance, for the following reasons:

(a) The 5% return is a dividend, not interest. It will therefore have different tax consequences. It will not be a deductible expense in the calculation of the taxable profits of the company.

(b) There is no guaranteed right to a dividend. The company will pay a dividend only to the extent that distributable profits are available for that purpose. The cumulative nature of preference shares does not alter this fact, as it is a benefit only if there are distributable profits in the future which are sufficient to cover the arrears of the preference dividend (or if the preference shareholder is afforded a right to arrears on a winding up). Conversely, an investor would expect the company to guarantee interest payments on a loan.

(c) The fact that the shares are redeemable is not a guarantee that the shareholder will be repaid. The company can redeem the shares only out of distributable profits or a fresh issue of shares (unless it is a private company; see **13.5.3.2** above). If it cannot redeem the shares this way, the shareholder will not be repaid.

13.7 Varying class rights

13.7.1 Introduction

Section 125 of the CA 1985 provides that rights attaching to a class of shares, 'class rights', can be varied. This is good news for a company, as it provides a degree of flexibility, for example to reduce the amount of a preference dividend, or to create a new class of preference shares which rank ahead of an existing class of preference shares.

In both of these examples, however, there will be a class of shareholders who are worse off as a result of the variation of the rights of the existing preference shares, namely, the existing preference shareholders. As you might expect, the CA 1985 provides some protection for these shareholders in the procedures it prescribes for the variation of class rights. The Act provides different procedures, and the procedure the company must follow is dictated, first, by where the class rights are defined and, secondly, by whether the articles of association provide a variation procedure.

13.7.2 Class rights defined in the articles of association or in a special resolution

13.7.2.1 If the articles do not contain a variation procedure

If the articles do not contain a procedure for variation, s 125(2) provides that class rights can be varied if:

(a) the holders of 75% in nominal value of the issued shares of the class of shares to be varied consent in writing to the variation; *or*

(b) an extraordinary resolution, passed at a separate general meeting of the class in question (known as a 'class meeting'), sanctions the variation (this means that 75% of those who attend the class meeting and vote in person or by proxy must vote in favour of the resolution).

While this affords protection to the holders of the shares whose rights are to be varied, in that a majority of them must agree to the variation, it does mean that the rights attached to the 25% minority of shares can be changed without their owners' consent.

Section 127 of the CA 1985 addresses this. It provides a procedure by which those shareholders who hold, in aggregate, not less than 15% of the issued shares of the class can (provided they did not consent to, or vote for, the variation) apply to the court within 21 days of the consent to, or vote for, the variation to have it cancelled. The court can then choose either to disallow, or to confirm the variation. If a s 127 application is made, the variation has no effect until the court confirms it.

13.7.2.2 If the articles contain a variation procedure

If the articles contain a procedure for varying class rights, s 125(4) states that it is this procedure which should be followed, not the procedure under s 125(2). The rationale behind this is that the class of shareholders need no extra statutory protection; they had notice of the articles when they became shareholders, and also have power to change the articles.

The rule in s 125(4) is subject to an exception. If the variation related to an authority to allot shares under s 80 of the CA 1985, or a reduction in the company's share capital under s 135 of the CA 1985, then s 125(3) requires the procedure set out at **13.7.2.1** above to be followed, together with any more stringent requirements of the variation procedure set out in the articles.

Note that if the articles contain a variation procedure which requires consent to the variation to be obtained from a specified proportion of the shareholders of the class, or the sanction of a resolution passed at a class meeting (that is, the requirements are along the lines of those in s 125(2)), then the s 127 objection procedure will apply (see **13.7.2.1** above).

13.7.3 Class rights defined in the memorandum of association

It is rare for class rights to be defined in the memorandum of association. However, if they are, it may be difficult to vary those rights. Any lawyer asked to draft class rights needs to be aware of this drawback; in any event, it would be unusual to draft these rights into the memorandum rather than the articles.

13.7.3.1 If the articles and memorandum do not contain a variation procedure

If the articles (and, in this case, the memorandum) do not contain a procedure for variation then s 125(5) provides that the unanimous consent to the variation of all the shareholders (of all classes) of the company is required.

Contrast this to the position set out at **13.7.2.1** above; it gives much more protection to the shareholders. This reflects the fact that rights in the memorandum are deemed to be more entrenched than rights in the articles.

13.7.3.2 If the articles or memorandum contain a variation procedure

If the articles or memorandum contain a procedure for variation and, if the provision is in the articles, that provision was included in the articles at the time the company was incorporated, then the procedure in s 125(4) applies, as set out in **13.7.2.2** above.

13.8 Registration of share rights

A company must send details of share rights it has created or varied to the Registrar of Companies (that is, to Companies House). This obligation arises under various sections of the CA 1985, such as ss 128 and 380(4)(d).

13.9 Employee share schemes

It was explained at **1.7.6** above that one of the benefits of listing is that companies can issue shares with an identifiable value to their employees to incentivise and reward them. Companies do this through schemes known as employee share schemes, which, if structured correctly, have the following tax benefits:

(a) for the company – the cost to the company is a deductible expense for corporation tax purposes;

(b) for the employee – the benefit is not normally subject to income tax or national insurance contributions (if all the criteria of the individual plan are met). The shares do have some tax consequences, however; capital gains tax will be charged when the employee disposes of the shares.

Note that share schemes do not usually create a separate class of share; in fact, this is specifically avoided, as it can mean that the scheme does not attract the beneficial tax treatment outlined above.

The law relating to share schemes is particularly specialised, and firms will often have a discrete team dedicated to advising solely in relation to such schemes. The corporate lawyer will, however, need to know about the existence of any share schemes, because they will be referred to in documents he drafts, such as a prospectus (see **Chapter 6**) or an offer document (see **22.4.1**). A 'bluffer's guide' to the four share schemes which are currently approved by the Inland Revenue is provided at **13.9.1** to **13.9.4** below, so that the corporate lawyer does not look completely clueless when talk turns to this subject.

The corporate lawyer should also appreciate the following points about employee share schemes:

(i) they are exempt from the application of s 80 of the CA 1985 (see **14.5.2**);

(ii) they do not trigger pre-emption rights under s 89 of the CA 1985, although they do entitle their holders to pre-emption rights (see **14.6.8.2**);

(iii) there is an exception for employee share scheme shares from the prohibition on financial assistance (see **16.5.3**);

(iv) shares allotted in pursuance of an employee share scheme are also excluded from the requirement, under s 101 of the CA 1985, that shares must be paid up to at least one quarter of their nominal value, together with the whole of any premium (see **13.3.7**); and

(v) generally a prospectus is not required where shares are offered by a listed company to existing or former directors or employees. Instead, a short document giving details of the company, the offer and the shares will suffice (see **6.4.1.5(h)** and **6.4.2.4(e)**). (However, at the time of writing there is concern that this exemption has been drafted too narrowly, and that a prospectus may still be required in certain circumstances, such as if shares are offered to the employees of an unlisted subsidiary.)

13.9.1 Approved savings-related share option scheme

This scheme must be open to all employees. The company grants options to purchase shares in the company. At the time the option is granted, the price of the shares is fixed and the employees start to make regular monthly contributions to savings accounts. When an employee's account matures, the employee can use the proceeds to fund the exercise of the option.

13.9.2 Share incentive plan

This scheme must also be open to all employees. There is a number of possible features. The company may:

(a) issue up to £3,000 worth of shares each year to an individual employee;
(b) allow an individual to purchase shares each year up to a value of the lower of £1,500, or 10% of salary; or
(c) issue up to two shares for each share purchased by an individual employee.

13.9.3 Approved company share option plan

This scheme can be made available to selected employees, and so is often used to reward senior executives. The company grants options to purchase shares in the company. As with the approved savings-related share option scheme (see **13.9.1** above), at the time of the option is created, the price for the shares is fixed. However, with this scheme there is no associated savings account; the employee must provide his own funds to exercise the option.

13.9.4 Enterprise management incentives

This scheme can also be made available to selected employees, and, like the approved company share option plan (see **13.9.3** above), it is often used to reward key employees. The company grants options to purchase shares in the company. Again, at the time the option is created, the price for the shares is fixed. There is no associated savings account. A number of significant conditions attach to this scheme (for example, the scheme is only available to companies with gross assets not exceeding £30m).

13.10 Future developments

The Companies Bill (see **1.11**) will make significant changes to the law affecting shares. For example, under the draft Bill dated 20 July 2006, the requirement for an authorised share capital is abolished and the procedure for the variation of class rights is changed.

Chapter 14
Issuing Shares

14.1	Introduction	171
14.2	Terminology	171
14.3	Issuing shares: three vital questions	172
14.4	Authorised share capital	172
14.5	Authority to allot	175
14.6	Pre-emption rights on allotment	180
14.7	Issuing the shares	190
14.8	Conclusion	191
14.9	Future developments	192

14.1 Introduction

Chapter 13 explored the concept of the share and the classes of share which may comprise a company's share capital. Once a listed company has created a class of share, it will want to use those shares to raise capital. This will involve issuing shares to shareholders, in return for consideration.

The legislation relating to the issue of shares is relatively easy to apply when the issuing company is a private company. However, the application of those rules to the issue of shares by a public company can be more complex, not because the legislation is fundamentally different (it is not), but because usually public companies have more complex share structures, so it is necessary to delve a little further into the detail of the legislation. In the case of the issue of shares by listed companies, there are other considerations in addition to the legislation to take into account, namely guidelines issued by the ABI, the Statement of Principles issued by the Pre-Emption Group and the requirements of the Listing Rules. This chapter considers share issues by a listed company.

14.2 Terminology

Some terminology, which has the potential to be confusing, is explained below.

14.2.1 Issuing shares or transferring shares?

'Issuing' relates to the issue of a share from the company to a shareholder. It is different to 'transferring' or 'selling' a share, which is when a shareholder transfers a share to another person. On a share issue, the company is party to the transaction. On a share transfer, the parties will be the shareholder selling the share and the shareholder buying the share, not the company. This chapter considers only the issue of shares. **Chapter 19** considers the transfer of shares.

14.2.2 Allotted shares or issued shares?

When considering the subject of issuing shares, the terms 'allotted' and 'issued' arise frequently. Let us be clear from the outset what they mean and the distinction between them. In practice the terms are used interchangeably and, usually, it is entirely appropriate to do this. However, it is always helpful to be aware of the specific meaning of terminology you use when advising a client; if an inquisitive client asks for clarification of the distinction of these two terms, it will not look very good if the lawyer cannot provide it.

14.2.2.1 Allotted

Pursuant to s 738 of the CA 1985, shares are allotted when a person acquires the *unconditional right to be included* in the company's register of members in respect of those shares.

14.2.2.2 Issued

Although there is no statutory definition of the meaning of 'issued', case law suggests that shares are issued when the allottee's name *is registered* in the company's register of members in respect of those shares (*Ambrose Lake Tin and Copper Co, Re (Clarke's Case)* (1878) 8 Ch D 635, CA and *National Westminster Bank plc and Another v IRC and Barclays Bank plc* [1994] 2 BCLC 30, CA).

14.2.2.3 The distinction

The above explanations reveal the minute difference between the two terms. The distinction lies in whether the shareholder's name has been included in the register of members. Of course, the majority of companies ensure that the register of members is kept up to date. This will remove any distinction between the two terms, as one will equate to the other; as soon as a person has an unconditional right to be entered into the register of members in respect of certain shares, his name will be entered into the register of members in respect of those shares. At that stage, the shares will be both allotted and issued.

14.3 Issuing shares: three vital questions

Now that the terminology is clear, let us turn to the topic of issuing shares. There are three important questions which the lawyer must consider in relation to any issue of shares, namely (and in this order):

(a) Authorised share capital – does the company have sufficient unissued authorised share capital from which to issue the shares, or does it need to increase its authorised share capital pursuit to s 121 of the CA 1985?

(b) Authority to allot – do the directors have sufficient authority to allot the shares under s 80 of the CA 1985?

(c) Pre-emption rights – do the pre-emption rights under s 89 of the CA 1985 apply to the issue and, if so, does the company need to disapply them?

The detail of, and the potential action required by, these questions is considered at **14.4** to **14.6** below.

14.4 Authorised share capital

Chapter 13 suggested that you consider the company's authorised share capital as a pool from which the company can issue shares (see **13.3.3** and **13.3.4**). When there are no more authorised but unissued shares in this pool, the company must increase the authorised share capital so that the pool is replenished with authorised but unissued shares which the company can issue. The first question the lawyer must consider, then, on a share issue, is whether the existing authorised share capital is sufficient, or whether it must be increased.

14.4.1 Checking the existing authorised and issued share capital

14.4.1.1 Locating the filings at Companies House

The lawyer must check back through the records the company has filed at Companies House, to identify the existing authorised and issued share capital. The easiest way to find the current figures is to take the figures provided in the latest filed annual return, then to check all the filings made since that annual return to see if any of them alter either the authorised share capital, or the issued share capital. The lawyer should then check that the figure on record at Companies House corresponds with the company secretary's records (see **14.4.1.2** below).

Once the lawyer has identified the current figures, and knows how many shares the company is proposing to issue, it should be easy to calculate whether the company needs to increase its authorised share capital.

> Examples
>
> X plc, a listed company, wants to issue 50,000 shares in return for cash consideration. It has an authorised share capital of £1m divided into 1 million ordinary shares of £1 each. Let us take a few scenarios and analyse whether X plc needs to increase its authorised share capital.
>
> (a) *Issued share capital is £1m*
>
> It is easy to see that in this case, X plc must increase its authorised share capital by £50,000 to £1.05 million, by creating another 50,000 ordinary shares of £1 each.
>
> (b) *Issued share capital is £500,000*
>
> In this case, X plc has 500,000 authorised shares which are unissued; it does not need to increase its authorised share capital.
>
> (c) *Issued share capital is £975,000*
>
> X plc needs to increase its authorised share capital, but only by £25,000 to £1.025 million; it already has 25,000 authorised but unissued shares.

14.4.1.2 Ensuring filings are up to date

The lawyer should always check that the authorised and issued share capital figures on record at Companies House correspond with the company secretary's records. This is to make sure the company is up to date with its filings. If it is not, it will need to make late filings, otherwise this will lead to problems later on in the share issue.

> Example
>
> Imagine that X plc has filed its annual return for the year ended June 2004. It states that the authorised share capital of X plc is £1m, divided into 1 million shares of £1 each, and that all authorised shares are issued. In August 2004, as a preliminary step to a share issue, the company increased its authorised share capital to £1.05m, by the creation of 50,000 shares of £1 each. However, the company secretary forgot to file this resolution at Companies House (in breach of the CA 1985 (see **14.4.3.2** below)).
>
> In October 2004, X plc issues the 50,000 shares. The company sends the appropriate filing (Form 88(2)) to the Registrar at Companies House. The Registrar rejects the filing relating to the issue of the 50,000 shares, because, according to the records at Companies House, X plc does not have sufficient authorised share capital from which to issue 50,000 shares.

The lawyer should have spotted this discrepancy between the company's records and the records at Companies House, and removed the discrepancy *before* the company issued the 50,000 shares. The company could have made a late filing of the resolution from August together with Form 123 (risking a fine (see **14.4.3.2**) for failing to file the August resolution on time), before issuing the shares.

14.4.2 Checking the guidelines

If the company is a listed company, the guidelines issued by the ABI and the Statement of Principles issued by the Pre-Emption Group have a bearing on the extent to which the company can issue new shares. It is preferable to check these guidelines and principles at this stage, to identify from the outset whether they will affect the proposed share issue. If they will, the company may decide not to proceed with the issue, and any preliminary steps, such as increasing the authorised share capital, will be pointless. The provisions of the guidelines and principles are considered at **14.5.7** and **14.6.16** below.

14.4.3 Increasing the authorised share capital

Let us assume that X plc wishes to issue 50,000 shares of £1 each. The records at Companies House reveal the following:

(a) Authorised share capital is £1m, divided into 1 million shares of £1 each.
(b) All shares are issued.

The company secretary has confirmed that the records at Companies House accord with his records and are up to date. The lawyer has checked, and the issue will be within the guidelines issued by the ABI and the Pre-emption Group (see **14.5.7** and **14.6.16** below).

X plc instructs its lawyer to draft the documentation to increase its authorised share capital by £50,000 to £1.05m, by the creation of 50,000 shares of £1 each. So what now?

14.4.3.1 Ordinary resolution

Section 121 of the CA 1985 provides that the company can increase its share capital by an ordinary resolution of the shareholders, provided the company's articles so permit. The first thing the lawyer must do, therefore, is to check the articles of association. It would be rare for articles to prohibit any increase; however, occasionally articles may require a special or an extraordinary resolution to effect the increase.

The articles of association of X plc permit an increase of the authorised share capital by ordinary resolution. The lawyer must now draft the ordinary resolution. An example of a suitable resolution is set out at **Appendix 2** (Resolution 1). The shareholders must pass this resolution by way of an ordinary resolution in general meeting; the written resolution procedure under s 381A of the CA 1985 is not available to a public company.

14.4.3.2 Notifying Companies House

The lawyer must ensure that the Registrar is notified of the increase, to comply with s 123 of the CA 1985. This is achieved by filing Form 123, together with a copy of the resolution and the amended memorandum, at Companies House within 15 days of the date of the resolution (s 18(2)). A specimen Form 123 is set out at **Appendix 3**. Failure to comply with s 123 renders the company, and every officer who is in default, liable to a fine (s 123(4)).

14.4.4 The Listing Rules

The lawyer must also ensure that if the issuing company is a listed company, like X plc, it complies with the continuing obligations of the FSA in relation to communicating with its shareholders about the increase in share capital. These requirements are explained at **7.7** above. In particular, the company must publish a circular giving information on the issue of new securities, including the arrangements for the allotment. Listing Rule 13.8.3R provides that this circular must include the following information:

(a) a statement of the proposed percentage increase in the authorised share capital of the relevant class; and

(b) a statement as to the reason for the increase.

The company must lodge two copies of the resolution and circular with the FSA, and notify an RIS that it has done so (LR 9.6.1R, LR 9.6.2R and LR 9.6.3R) (see **7.5.5.1**). Any proposed alteration of the company's capital structure must be notified to an RIS as soon as possible (LR 9.6.4R(1)).

14.5 Authority to allot

Once the company has sufficient authorised capital from which it can issue the shares, the second question the lawyer must consider is whether the directors have authority to allot the shares.

14.5.1 Section 80 of the CA 1985

Section 80 of the CA 1985 prohibits directors from allotting 'relevant securities' unless they are authorised to do so by:

(a) ordinary resolution of the shareholders; or

(b) the company's articles of association.

14.5.2 'Relevant securities'

Section 80(2) defines 'relevant securities'. Basically:

(a) any type of share *other than*:
   (i) the subscriber shares, and
   (ii) shares allotted under an employee share scheme (see **13.9**) (limb 1); and
(b) any right to subscribe for, or convert to, any type of share *other than* under an employee share scheme (limb 2),

is a 'relevant security' for the purposes of s 80.

The exceptions are clear; no s 80 authority is needed to issue the initial subscriber shares in a company (see **13.5.6**), or to issue employee share scheme shares. Clearly, most shares fall outside the exceptions referred to at (a)(i) and (ii) above and so are caught by limb 1 of the test; s 80 authority is needed before those shares can be allotted.

What is not so obvious, however, is the effect of limb 2 of the test. Basically, limb 2 brings more than just shares within the ambit of s 80. A few typical examples, which often are the source of some confusion as to *when* s 80 authority is required in respect of them, are considered below.

14.5.2.1 Convertible loan stock

Convertible loan stock is a class of debt security which carries the right to convert into shares.

Is it a 'relevant security'?

Yes, provided:

(a) the stock does not convert to employee share scheme shares; and
(b) the right is unconditional.

A conditional right (for example, a right to convert which requires authorisation by the shareholders at the time of conversion) is not a relevant security. Once the right becomes unconditional, the stock will become a relevant security.

When is s 80 authority needed?

There are three possibilities. Is it:

(a) when the debt securities are allotted; or
(b) when the debt securities are converted into shares; or
(c) both (a) and (b)?

The answer is (a). This is important; *at the time the debt securities are allotted* there must be sufficient s 80 authority to cover the ordinary shares into which the debt securities will convert.

Where the right to convert is conditional (see above), s 80 authority will be needed prior to the allotment of the shares when conversion takes place, or at the time when the right to convert becomes unconditional (if earlier).

14.5.2.2 Options

Is an option a 'relevant security'?

The grant of an option to subscribe for shares (other than employee share scheme shares) will be a relevant security.

When is s 80 authority needed?

Section 80 authority is required *at the time of the grant*, not at the time of the exercise, of the option.

14.5.2.3 Convertible preference shares

A convertible preference share is a share which carries the right to convert into ordinary shares.

Is it a 'relevant security'?

Yes. In fact, both limbs of the 'relevant security' test (see above) catch the shares. Limb 1 of the test catches the intial allotment of preference shares. However, the preference shares also carry a right to convert into ordinary shares, and this right is caught by the second limb of the test, assuming the right to convert is unconditional (see **14.5.2.1** above).

When is s 80 authority needed?

Again, the question is whether s 80 authority is required:

(a) when the convertible preference shares are allotted; or

(b) when the shares are converted into ordinary shares; or
(c) both (a) and (b)?

The answer is (a). Note, however, that, on the basis of the analysis set out above, the s 80 authority will need to cover *both* of the relevant securities comprised in the shares, namely, the convertible preference shares and the ordinary shares they will convert into. For example, if the company is issuing 50 preference shares (relevant security 1), which carry the right to convert into 50 ordinary shares (relevant security 2), *at the time the convertible preference shares are allotted* the directors require authority to allot both relevant security 1 and relevant security 2, so two separate s 80 authorities are required.

14.5.3 Checking the existing s 80 authority

We now know that it is necessary to examine carefully the nature of the securities to be issued, to determine whether s 80 authority is required. However, our example of X plc wishing to issue 50,000 ordinary shares (see **14.4.3** above) is relatively straightforward. The shares are relevant securities within limb 1 of the s 80(2) test. Section 80 authority is required. So now what? First the lawyer will need to check the existing s 80 authority, to see whether the directors already have authority to allot the 50,000 shares, or whether a new s 80 authority is required.

As explained at **14.5.1**, any s 80 authority will either be in the articles of association, or in an ordinary resolution. The lawyer must check the articles and the records at Companies House to identify the most recent s 80 authority. The lawyer must then check this authority to identify two key features, namely:

(a) the date on which it expires; and
(b) the maximum amount of relevant securities which can be allotted under it.

If the expiry date has passed then the answer is obvious; a new s 80 authority is required for the new issue in its entirety.

If the expiry date has not passed, so the s 80 authority is still current, then the lawyer must identify how many shares have been issued pursuant to that authority. If the maximum amount of shares has been issued, or if the proposed issue would exceed that amount, then a new s 80 authority is required. If not, then the existing s 80 authority will suffice.

14.5.4 Obtaining a new s 80 authority

Section 80(5) provides that whether the original authority was given in the articles of association, or by ordinary resolution, it can be renewed by ordinary resolution. The lawyer will need to draft this resolution.

14.5.5 The resolution

The authority can be restricted to a specific allotment, or it can be drafted as a general power to allot. It may be made subject to conditions, or it can be unconditional. An example of a resolution granting a general, unconditional s 80 authority is set out in resolution 1 of the ABI Guidelines on directors' powers to allot share capital and disapply shareholders' pre-emption right (see **Appendix 5**).

As **14.5.3** explained, s 80(4) provides that the authority must include two key pieces of information:

(a) the date on which it expires; and
(b) the maximum amount of relevant securities which can be allotted under it.

The lawyer must bear this in mind, not only when checking any existing s 80 authority, but also when drafting a new s 80 authority. The two key pieces of information are considered at **14.5.5.1** and **14.5.5.2** below.

14.5.5.1 The expiry date

The expiry date must not be more than five years from either:

(a) the date on which the company was incorporated (if the authority is contained in the articles of association); or

(b) the date of the resolution giving the authority.

Clearly (a) is relevant only in relation to drafting the original s 80 authority, and therefore it is (b) which applies in relation to drafting the majority of s 80 authorities. The authority can be for up to a fixed period of five years. To err on the side of caution, this is usually expressed in the resolution as being the fifth anniversary of the resolution, less one day.

Note that s 80A of the CA 1985 provides the opportunity for private companies to opt out of this time restriction, by elective resolution. However, it is important to note that the companies which are the subject of this book, namely public companies and particularly listed companies, cannot opt out in this way. In fact, in practice, listed companies usually grant the directors a new s 80 authority each year, at the AGM, as a safeguard against inadvertently allowing an authority to expire. Another safeguard in relation to the expiry date which can be drafted into a s 80 authority is to allow the directors to allot relevant securities, even if the s 80 authority has expired, if they do so pursuant to an offer or agreement made by the company before the authority expired (see para 2 of the specimen resolution in **Appendix 3**).

14.5.5.2 Maximum amount of relevant securities

The s 80 authority must state the maximum amount of relevant securities which can be allotted under it. The amount is usually stated in terms of the maximum nominal amount (for example, £50,000), rather than the number of shares (for example, 50,000 shares of £1 each), so that if the company consolidates or subdivides its shares (for example, into shares of £2 or 10p), it will not need to amend the s 80 authority.

In relation to limb 2 of the 'relevant securities' test (see **14.5.2** above), the maximum amount relates to the shares which will be issued on exercise of the right. If the issue were of 10 debt securities, for example, which will be converted to a maximum of 100 ordinary shares of £1 each, then the maximum amount would be £100.

When determining this maximum amount, if the company is a listed company, regard must be had to the ABI guidelines, which impose a limit on the amount. The provisions of the guidelines are considered at **14.5.7** below.

14.5.5.3 Notifying Companies House

The lawyer must ensure that any ordinary resolution giving, varying, revoking or renewing an authority to allot shares is delivered to Companies House within 15 days of being passed.

14.5.6 The Listing Rules

Again, if the company issuing the shares is a listed company then it must comply with the continuing obligations of the Listing Rules regarding communications with shareholders (see **7.7** above). In particular, LR 13.8.1R provides that a listed company must send out an explanatory circular to its shareholders when it sends out the s 80 resolution. This circular must include the following information:

(a) a statement of:
  (i) the maximum amount of relevant securities which the directors will have authority to allot, and
  (ii) the percentage which that amount represents of the total issued ordinary share capital as at the latest practicable date before publication of the circular;
(b) a statement by the directors as to whether they have any present intention of exercising the authority, and if so for what purpose; and
(c) a statement as to whether the authority will lapse.

The circular must also include information relating to any treasury shares held by the company.

The company must lodge two copies of the resolution and circular with the FSA, and notify an RIS that it has done so (LR 9.6.1R, LR 9.6.2R and LR 9.6.3R) (see **7.5.5.1**).

14.5.7 The ABI Guidelines

The ABI has issued guidelines (see **Appendix 5**) which restrict the amount of share capital which can be included in a s 80 authority. The ABI Guidelines provide that the 'maximum amount' of relevant securities for which authority can be given is the lesser of:

(a) the authorised but unissued ordinary share capital; and
(b) one-third of the issued ordinary share capital.

Examples

Let us use X plc as an example. X plc now has an authorised share capital of £1.05m and an issued share capital of £1m.

(a) X plc wants to issue 50,000 shares of £1 each.
  (i) The authorised but unissued ordinary share capital is £50,000.
  (ii) The sum equal to one-third of the issued ordinary share capital is £333,333.
  (iii) £50,000 is the lesser figure, so it is fine to give the directors the s 80 authority over £50,000.
(b) Imagine instead that X plc wants to issue 500,000 rather than 50,000 shares. X plc has already increased its share capital to £1.5m. The issued share capital is still £1m.
  (i) The authorised but unissued ordinary share capital is £500,000.
  (ii) The sum equal to one-third of the issued ordinary share capital is £333,333.
  (iii) £333,333 is the lesser figure, so the ABI Guidelines would prevent the company giving s 80 authority over the entire amount of shares the company wants to issue, namely £500,000. It could issue only 333,333 shares.

This is why, as stated in **14.4.2** above, it is important to analyse the ABI guidelines upfront. Fortunately, X plc's lawyer checked this issue, and was aware from the outset that the Guidelines did not cause a problem. Imagine if he had not; would X plc agree to pay the lawyer's fees for the work done so far?

The ABI Guidelines are non-statutory and, if the company considers that it has good reason to exceed the limit set out in the Guidelines, it can discuss this with the ABI in advance of any allotment.

14.5.8 Sanctions for breach of s 80

Breach of s 80 does not actually invalidate the share allotment (CA 1985, s 80(10)). However, s 80(9) provides that any director who knowingly and wilfully contravenes, or permits or authorises a contravention of, s 80 is liable to a fine.

A flowchart summarising the application of s 80 is set out at **Figure 14.1** below.

Figure 14.1: Section 80 flowchart

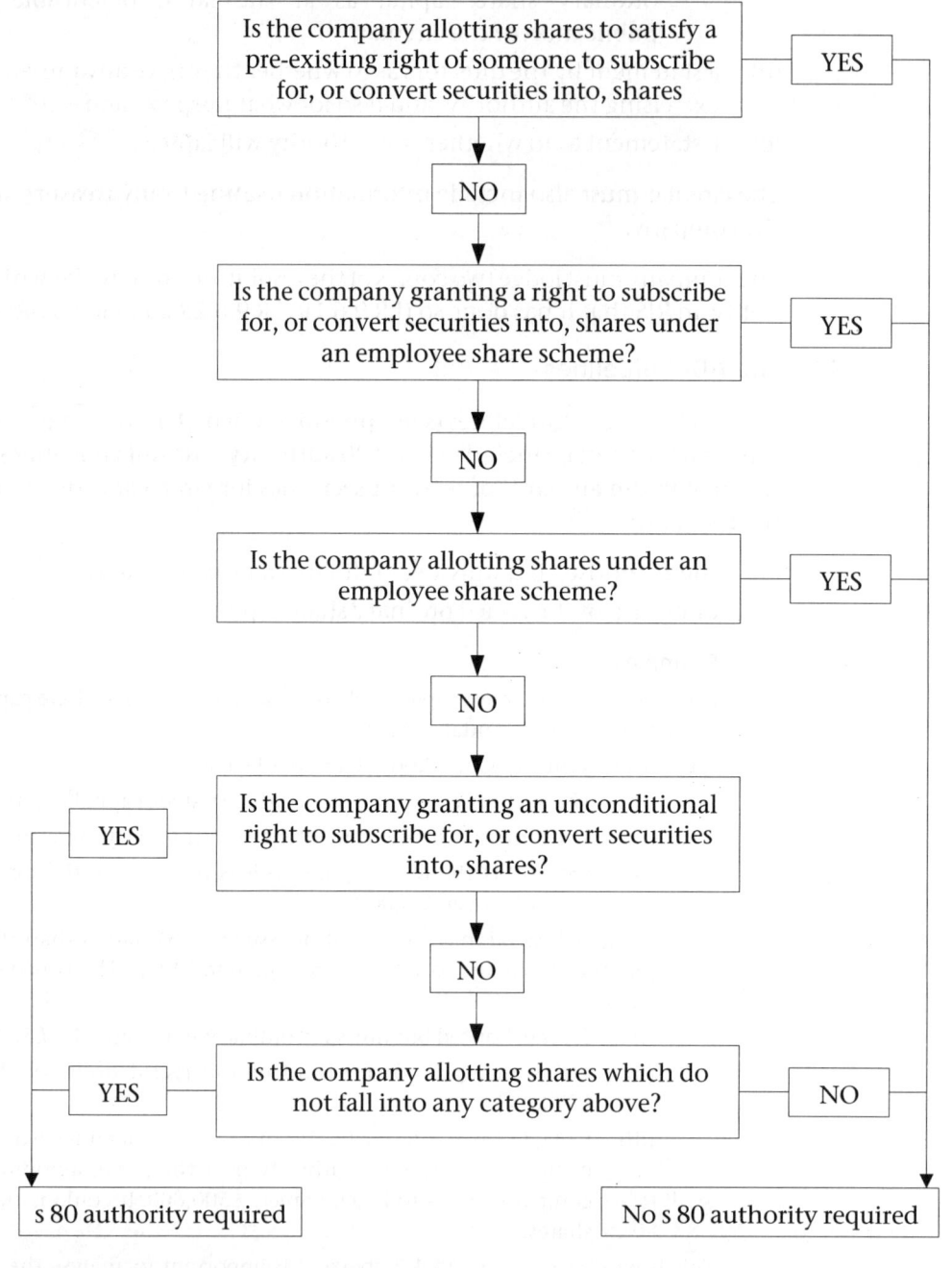

```
                    ┌─────────────────────────────────┐
                    │ Is the company allotting shares │
                    │ to satisfy a pre-existing right │──YES──┐
                    │ of someone to subscribe for, or │       │
                    │ convert securities into, shares │       │
                    └────────────────┬────────────────┘       │
                                    NO                        │
                                     ▼                        │
                    ┌─────────────────────────────────┐       │
                    │ Is the company granting a right │       │
                    │ to subscribe for, or convert    │──YES──┤
                    │ securities into, shares under   │       │
                    │ an employee share scheme?       │       │
                    └────────────────┬────────────────┘       │
                                    NO                        │
                                     ▼                        │
                    ┌─────────────────────────────────┐       │
                    │ Is the company allotting shares │──YES──┤
                    │ under an employee share scheme? │       │
                    └────────────────┬────────────────┘       │
                                    NO                        │
                                     ▼                        │
                    ┌─────────────────────────────────┐       │
         ┌──YES─────│ Is the company granting an      │       │
         │          │ unconditional right to subscribe│       │
         │          │ for, or convert securities into,│       │
         │          │ shares?                         │       │
         │          └────────────────┬────────────────┘       │
         │                          NO                        │
         │                           ▼                        │
         │          ┌─────────────────────────────────┐       │
         │  ┌─YES───│ Is the company allotting shares │──NO───┤
         │  │       │ which do not fall into any      │       │
         │  │       │ category above?                 │       │
         │  │       └─────────────────────────────────┘       │
         ▼  ▼                                                 ▼
   ┌──────────────────────┐                     ┌──────────────────────────┐
   │ s 80 authority       │                     │ No s 80 authority        │
   │ required             │                     │ required                 │
   └──────────────────────┘                     └──────────────────────────┘
```

14.6 Pre-emption rights on allotment

Now that X plc has sufficient authorised share capital from which to issue the 50,000 shares, and the directors have authority to allot the 50,000 shares, what is preventing the company from allotting the shares? Well, there is one final question to consider: do the pre-emption rights under s 89 of the CA 1985 apply to the allotment and, if so, does the company need to disapply them?

(Remember not to confuse pre-emption rights on allotment with pre-emption rights on transfer. This chapter is considering the issue, not transfer of shares, and therefore is concerned only with pre-emption rights on allotment.)

14.6.1 What is a pre-emption right on allotment?

A pre-emption right on allotment is a right of first refusal for existing shareholders on an issue of shares by a company. This means that when a company wants to issue shares, it must first offer those shares to the existing shareholders in proportion to their existing shareholdings.

14.6.2 Rationale

The right of pre-emption protects the shareholders against the dilution of their shareholdings. If each shareholder takes up the shares offered to him under the right of pre-emption, although the number of shares held by him will increase, his percentage shareholding will be preserved. Of course, the right helps the existing shareholder to preserve his percentage shareholding only if he can afford to buy the shares offered to him.

14.6.3 Where are pre-emption rights on allotment?

The main provisions relating to pre-emption on allotment are in the CA 1985 and the Listing Rules. A company's articles of association may also contain specific provisions relating to pre-emption on allotment. If a listed company has issued any convertible securities, or warrants and options etc, the deeds or agreements setting out the terms of issue may also contain specific pre-emption provisions on allotment.

14.6.4 Obstruction

We are about to consider the complex provisions relating to pre-emption rights. Bear in mind, while you are reading, that from the company's perspective pre-emption rights are not good. They obstruct the company from issuing shares to those to whom it would prefer to issue and compel the company to offer those shares to existing shareholders. We will come back to this at **14.6.13** below.

14.6.5 Section 89 of the CA 1985

Section 89 of the CA 1985 provides statutory pre-exemption rights on allotment. A company proposing to issue *equity securities* in return for *cash* must first offer the shares to holders of *relevant shares* or *relevant employee shares* in proportion to the nominal value of their existing shareholdings.

Let us be very clear: this means that there are two types of securities we need to analyse:

(a) equity securities – that is, the shares the company is proposing to issue which might *trigger* pre-emption rights, so that those equity securities must be offered first to those people who have pre-emption rights; and

(b) relevant shares or relevant employee shares – that is, the shares which *entitle* their owners to pre-emption rights, so that their owners are offered first refusal over an issue of equity securities.

These two types of securities are considered further at **14.6.6** and **14.6.8** below.

(Note that s 89 is concerned solely with pre-emption rights on allotment; it does not imply any pre-emption rights on transfer (this is a common misconception among trainees). Any pre-emption rights on transfer will be drafted into the company's articles of association or, if the company has issued any convertible securities, or warrants and options etc, the deeds or agreements setting out the terms of issue may also contain specific pre-emption rights on transfer.)

14.6.6 Equity securities

This term relates to the shares the company is proposing to issue; if the company is proposing to issue an equity security, it will trigger pre-emption rights under s 89. Section 94 of the CA 1985 defines 'equity securities'. Rather confusingly, it does so by reference to the term 'relevant shares'. (Even more confusingly, 'relevant shares' are different to, but can be confused with, 'relevant securities' under the s 80 provisions (see **14.5.2** above).)

Basically, equity securities are:

(a) any 'relevant shares' (see **14.6.8** below) *other than*:
    (i) a subscriber share (see **13.5.6**), and
    (ii) a bonus share (limb 1); and

(b) any right to subscribe for, or convert securities into, relevant shares (limb 2).

14.6.7 For cash

Section 89(4) provides that the pre-emption rights under s 89(1) will apply only if the issue of shares is wholly in return for cash. If the consideration for the issue is anything other than cash (for example, shares or land), the s 89 pre-emption rights on allotment will not apply.

14.6.8 Relevant shares

This term relates to the shares that entitle their owners to benefit from pre-emption rights in the event that the company issues equity securities. Section 94(5) defines 'relevant shares' as any shares *other than*:

(a) a share which, in relation to both dividends and capital, carries a right to participate only up to a specified amount (such as a non-participating preference share – see **13.5.2.1**); and

(b) an employee share scheme share.

If you compare the definition of 'equity securities' (see **14.6.6**) with the definition of 'relevant shares', you will notice several important distinctions between the two.

14.6.8.1 The right to subscribe for, or convert into, relevant shares.

This falls within the definition of equity securities (limb 2), but outside the definition of 'relevant shares'. This means that while the issue of a right to subscribe for, or convert securities into, relevant shares will *trigger* the pre-emption rights (see (a) and (b) below for more detail), those rights to subscribe or convert will not *entitle* their owners to pre-emption rights. Let us delve a little further into this by exploring the position regarding two different types of convertible security and whether they *trigger* pre-emption rights:

(a) *Convertible loan stock.* It is significant (just as it was for our s 80 analysis: see **14.5.2.1** above) whether the loan stock grants an unconditional right to convert. If it does, then the loan stock will fall within limb 2 of the definition of 'equity securities' and the issue of convertible loan stock for cash will *trigger* s 89 pre-emption rights. If, however, the right to convert is conditional, it will not be caught by limb 2 and the issue of the stock for cash will *not trigger* pre-emption rights.

(b) *Convertible preference shares.* The significant issue here is whether the convertible preference shares are participating or non-participating shares. If they are participating, they will be caught by the definition of 'equity securities' (limb 1: they are relevant shares) and will *trigger* s 89 pre-emption rights, assuming they are issued for cash. If they are non-participating, they will fall outside limb 1 (they are not relevant shares); however, they might still be caught by limb 2. This will depend on whether the right to convert is conditional or unconditional. If unconditional, the issue of those shares will *trigger* the pre-emption rights, assuming they are issued wholly for cash. If conditional, the shares will fall out outside limb 2 and the issue will not trigger pre-emption rights.

14.6.8.2 Employee share scheme shares

In effect, the exclusion of employee share scheme shares from the definition of 'relevant shares' is negated for the purposes of determining whether the shares will entitle their holders to pre-emption rights, as s 89(1) expressly states that the holders of relevant employee shares *will* benefit from pre-emption rights (see **14.6.5** above). The exclusion of employee share scheme shares is, however, relevant for the purposes of the definition of 'equity securities' referred to at **14.6.6** above. This means that employee share scheme shares will *not trigger* the s 89 pre-emption provisions when they are issued, but, once issued, they will *entitle* their owners to pre-emption rights in the event that the company issues equity securities. (This is the reverse of the position relating to rights to subscribe and convert, described at **14.6.8.1** above.)

Employee share schemes are explored in more detail at **13.9**.

14.6.8.3 Bonus/subscriber shares

Bonus/subscriber shares are not equity securities, so they will *not trigger* pre-emption rights if they are issued, but holders of bonus and subscriber shares will be *entitled* to pre-emption rights provided they are relevant shares and are not excluded because they carry only a limited right to participate in income and share capital.

14.6.9 Technique

When analysing whether s 89 will apply to a share issue, you first need to separate your analysis of the securities the company is proposing to issue, which might *trigger* pre-emption rights, from your analysis of the securities which might *entitle* their holders to a pre-emption right on an issue of equity securities. Secondly, appreciate that the definitions used overlap (and can be confused with s 80 definitions) to a certain extent.

Now, two pieces of good news. The first is that the summary at **14.6.10** below, and the examples at **14.6.11** below, should simplify the application of s 89. The second is that, if the company decides to disapply the pre-emption rights, you will not need to apply s 89 at all (see **14.6.15** below) (although unfortunately you do need

184 Public Companies and Equity Finance

to be capable of applying s 89 to find out whether you need to disapply it in the first place; good corporate lawyers take a dim view of colleagues who disapply statutory pre-emption rights 'just to be on the safe side').

14.6.10 Summary of statutory pre-emption rights on allotment

(a) Equity securities which *can trigger* pre-emption rights when they are issued:
   (i) ordinary shares;
   (ii) participating preference shares; and
   (iii) unconditional rights to subscribe for, or convert into, ordinary or participating preference shares.

(b) Securities which are not equity securities and *cannot trigger* pre-emption rights when they are issued:
   (i) non-participating preference shares;
   (ii) employee share scheme shares;
   (iii) any share issued for non-cash consideration;
   (iv) bonus shares; and
   (v) subscriber shares.

(c) Relevant shares and relevant employee shares which *entitle* their owners pre-emption rights on an issue of equity securities:
   (i) ordinary shares;
   (ii) participating preference shares; and
   (iii) employee share scheme shares.

(d) Shares which are not relevant shares or relevant employee shares and which *do not entitle* their owners to pre-emption rights on an issue of equity securities:
   (i) non-participating preference shares;
   (ii) rights to subscribe for, or to convert into, ordinary or participating preference shares.

14.6.11 Examples

The following examples assume that there is not already in place a disapplication of the statutory pre-emption rights on allotment and that, unless otherwise stated, the consideration for the proposed issue is wholly cash.

Example 1

A plc is proposing to issue ordinary shares. The company's existing share capital comprises ordinary and participating preference shares. The shares to be issued are equity securities and the proposed issue is for cash consideration. Therefore, unless a s 89 disapplication is obtained, the directors must offer the shares first to the holders of the ordinary and the preference shares (both are relevant shares) pro rata to their respective holdings.

Example 2

B plc is seeking to acquire the entire issued share capital of Z plc and is offering Z's shareholders two B plc shares for each of their Z shares. Section 89 does not apply to the issue of B shares because the consideration for them is not cash. The consideration comprises the shares in Z.

Example 3

C plc intends to issue ordinary shares. The existing capital structure comprises ordinary shares and convertible loan stock. This is an issue of equity securities but the new shares will be offered only to the holders of the ordinary shares. Convertible loan stock does not fall within the definition of relevant shares and so does not entitle its owners to pre-emption rights.

Example 4

D plc intends to issue convertible loan stock. The existing capital structure comprises ordinary shares and non-participating preference shares. The issue of convertible loan stock does amount to an issue of equity securities if the stockholders are being given an unconditional right to convert. On this assumption, s 89 applies. Unless the section is disapplied the directors must offer the convertible loan stock first to the ordinary shareholders. The holders of the non-participating preference shares do not have statutory pre-emption rights as they are not the holders of relevant shares.

14.6.12 Pre-emption rights on allotment under the Listing Rules

As explained at **7.5.2.3** above, LR 9.3.11R provides pre-emption rights on allotment. On an issue of *equity shares for cash*, there is a continuing obligation on a listed company to offer those shares first to the *existing equity shareholders* (of shares of that class, or of another class who are entitled to be offered them) in proportion to their existing holdings.

Any issue by a listed company pursuant to the pre-emption rights set out in LR 9.3.11R is known as a 'rights issue'. **Chapter 17** considers rights issues in more detail.

These rights of pre-emption on allotment under the Listing Rules reflect the statutory rights of shareholders of any company, listed or not, under ss 89 to 95 of the CA 1985, but the pre-emption rights on allotment under the Listing Rules are more flexible. For example:

(a) The definition of equity securities is different. Under the Listing Rules, equity securities are:
   (i) ordinary shares;
   (ii) participating preference shares; and
   (iii) shares which convert into (i) or (ii).

(b) Listing Rule 9.3.12R(2) provides that a company does not need to comply with the pre-emption rights in LR 9.3.11R in relation to equity shares which:
   (i) represent fractional entitlements; or
   (ii) the directors think it is necessary or expedient to exclude from any offer due to legal problems under the laws of any territory or due to any regulatory body.

In addition, LR 9.3.12R(3) and LR 9.3.12R(4) provide that the pre-emption rights under the Listing Rules will not apply if the company is selling treasury shares for cash to an employee share scheme, or if the company is an overseas company with a primary listing.

Section 89 makes no provision for fractional entitlements (so, in practice, entitlements are rounded down), and in order to comply with s 89 without making an offer in jurisdictions with onerous requirements, companies must follow the procedure under s 90(5) of the CA 1985, known as the 'Gazette route'.

Note, however, that the pre-emption rights in the Listing Rules under the new regime no longer provide that shares convertible into equity shares will entitle their holders to pre-emption rights if their terms say they will; in this case, the pre-emption rights under the Listing Rules, like the pre-emption rights under s 89, must be disapplied.

These differences are easier to understand in the context of an offer. Their practical effect is considered at **17.7.6** below. Pre-emption rights under the CA 1985 can cause problems on a rights issue in a way that the pre-emption rights under the Listing Rules do not.

Note that there are no pre-emption rights on *transfer* in the Listing Rules. (Indeed, this would be contrary to the requirement that the shares of listed companies should be freely transferable – see **4.3.1.1**.)

14.6.13 What is the problem with pre-emption rights?

By now (perhaps with the help of a cold towel) you should be able to work out whether the proposed issue will trigger pre-emption rights either under the CA 1985, or under the Listing Rules. Let us consider the example of X plc again. X plc is proposing to issue 50,000 ordinary shares. These fall within limb 1 of the 'equity securities' test. The shares are to be issued wholly for cash. They will therefore *trigger* pre-emption rights; they must first be offered to holders of relevant shares and relevant employee shares who are entitled to pre-emption rights.

Does this suit the company's purposes? Well no, not really. If pre-emption rights apply, the company must follow the detailed procedure set out in s 90 of the CA 1985, regarding the form the offer must take and the length of time for which it must remain open (21 clear days from the date the offer is made). Only once this period has expired, or the company has received a reply from each shareholder who benefits from the pre-emption rights, can it allot any shares which have not been taken up through pre-emption.

This does not suit the company at all, so it instructs its lawyer to disapply the pre-emption rights.

14.6.14 Disapplication of pre-emption rights under the CA 1985

The CA 1985 provides two ways in which a company can disapply s 89 when allotting equity securities for cash. The first, under s 91, is available only to private companies. It allows a private company to disapply s 89 in its memorandum or articles. We are not concerned with private companies, and so will not consider this any further.

The second way, which is relevant to public companies, is under s 95 of the CA 1985. Section 95 provides that the company can disapply the s 89 pre-emption rights:

(a) specifically (see **14.6.14.1**); or
(b) generally (see **14.6.14.2**).

14.6.14.1 Specific disapplication (s 95(2))

A disapplication of pre-emption rights in relation to a specific allotment must be effected by a special resolution. However, this is not a popular method because of the requirements of s 95(5). This section provides that before the resolution is proposed, the directors must recommend that the resolution be passed and circulate a written statement setting out:

(a) their reasons for making the recommendation;
(b) the amount of consideration for the shares; and
(c) the justification of that amount.

The directors risk imprisonment or a fine if the statement contains anything which is materially misleading, false or deceptive (s 95(6)).

14.6.14.2 General disapplication (s 95(1))

This is the most common method of disapplying pre-emption rights, and can be used where there is in place a general authorisation for the purposes of s 80 of the CA 1985. The disapplication can be effected either by special resolution, which is most common, or by a provision in the articles. Unlike under s 95(2), the directors are not required to make any recommendation in relation to the resolution (see **14.6.14.1**).

14.6.14.3 Duration

Whether the disapplication is specific or general, it will be effective only until the s 80 authority to which it relates expires. This means that the disapplication cannot last more than five years. Whenever a new s 80 authority is obtained, a new s 95 disapplication should also be obtained. (The s 95 disapplication is inextricably linked to the s 80 authority by the use of the words 'where the directors of a company are generally authorised for the purposes of section 80' (s 95(1)).)

14.6.14.4 Example

An example of a s 95 disapplication, which shows how it relates to the s 80 authority, is set out in resolution 2 of the ABI Guidelines on directors' powers to allot share capital and disapply shareholders' pre-emption right (see **Appendix 5**).

14.6.14.5 Notifying Companies House

The company must file a copy of the resolution at Companies House within 15 days of it being passed.

14.6.15 Disapplication of pre-emption rights under the Listing Rules

As explained at **7.5.2.3** above, the shareholders of a listed company can also agree to dispense with their pre-emption rights under the Listing Rules. Listing Rule 9.3.12R(1) makes clear that a general disapplication by the shareholders of their statutory pre-emption rights in accordance with s 95 of the CA 1985 will also disapply the pre-emption rights under LR 9.3.1R. In practice, most public companies effect a general disapplication of the statutory pre-emption rights at each AGM, at the same time that they take any s 80 authority. Although in theory this also disapplies the pre-emption rights under the Listing Rules in their entirety, listed companies prefer to state in the resolution that they will nevertheless comply with the pre-emption rights under the Listing Rules. The s 95 disapplication, set out in resolution 2 of the ABI Guidelines on directors' powers to allot share capital and disapply shareholders' pre-emption right (see **Appendix 5**), is a typical example. This allows directors to make small, non pre-emptive issues and rights issues or open offers that follow the pre-emption provisions in the Listing Rules. The rationale for the provision that rights issues and open offers should follow the pre-emption rights under the Listing Rules but not the pre-emption rights under the CA 1985, is explained at **14.6.12** and **17.7.6**.

Again, if the company is listed, it will need to observe the continuing obligations of the Listing Rules relating to communications with shareholders. These obligations are considered at **7.7** above. Listing Rule 13.8.2R provides that a circular should accompany the s 95 disapplication containing the following information:

(a) a statement of the maximum amount of equity securities that the disapplication will cover; and

(b) (in the case of a general disapplication in respect of equity securities for cash made otherwise than to existing shareholders in proportion to their existing shareholdings) the percentage which the amount generally disapplied represents of the total ordinary share capital in issue as at the latest practicable date before publication of the circular.

The company must lodge two copies of the resolution and circular with the FSA, and notify an RIS that it has done so (LR 9.6.1R, LR 9.6.2R and LR 9.6.3R) (see **7.5.5.1**).

14.6.16 The Pre-Emption Group

The institutional investors do not support issues of shares other than by way of rights, because of the diluting effect this has on a shareholder's shareholding. The original Pre-Emption Group was established in 1987 under the auspices of the Stock Exchange and consists of representatives of listed companies, institutional investors and corporate finance practitioners. The Group issued Pre-Emption Guidelines advising shareholders not to vote in favour of any annual disapplication of pre-emption rights unless certain conditions were met.

Following concerns that the Guidelines were out of date, the DTI sponsored an investigation by Paul Myners at the end of 2004 on the impact of pre-emption rights on a public company's ability to raise new capital. The report was published on 10 February 2005 and concluded that pre-emption rights were valauble to shareholders and should remain a cornerstone of UK company law. The report advocated, among other things, a revival of the Pre-Emption Group and the publication of updated, more flexible Pre-Emption Guidelines (see **17.12**). Copies of the report are available from the DTI website.

As a result of the Myners Report, a new Pre-Emption Group was established in 2005. The Group's members represent listed companies, investors and intermediaries. In May 2006, the Group produced a 'Statement of Principles' to provide guidance to shareholders and companies on the disapplication of pre-emption rights. The Principles, supported by the ABI, the NAPF and the IMA, replace the Pre-Emption Guidelines. They are set out in full at **Appendix 6**.

The Principles do not have the force of law, but are stated to be a basis for discussion between companies and their investors. In practice, they reflect the position that the powerful institutional shareholders will take in relation to any s 95 disapplication. Paragraph 5 of the Statement makes clear that the Principles apply to equity issues for cash by UK companies which are listed on the Main Market. AIM companies are encouraged to comply too, although it is recognised that they may require a greater degree of flexibility (para 5). Paragraph 5 also makes clear that the Principles do *not* apply to issues of equity securities for cash if the issue is on a pre-emptive basis. This means that if a company is disapplying s 89 statutory pre-emption rights, but complying with the slightly more flexible pre-emption rights in the Listing Rules (see **14.6.12** and **17.7.6**), the Principles will not apply. (The Guidelines were stated not to apply to issues on a pro rata rights issue basis.)

The Pre-Emption Group has stated that it will monitor the application of the Principles.

14.6.16.1 Routine disapplications

The Statement recognises that shareholders will consider some requests to disapply pre-emption rights as non-controversial, or 'routine'. While the company needs to explain why the disapplication is required, and notify shareholders of the need for it in good time, shareholders are likely to agree in principle with such requests and will require less in-depth discussion about them. Typically, a routine disapplication can be made by way of an appropriate resolution at an AGM (para 17).

The Statement sets out the following guidance as to what constitutes a 'routine disapplication':

(a) A request is more likely to be 'routine' when the company is seeking authority to issue non-pre-emptively 5% or less of ordinary share capital in any one year (regardless of how the issue is structured) (paras 8 and 9);

(b) a company should not issue more than 7.5% of its ordinary share capital for cash, other than to existing shareholders, in any rolling three year period, unless:
   (i) it has consulted suitably in advance; or
   (ii) the matter was specifically highlighted when the disapplication request was made (para 10); and

(c) the price at which the shares are proposed to be issued is relevant; a discount of greater than 5% is not likely to be regarded as routine (paras 11, 18 and 19).

Those familiar with the old Pre-Emption Group will recognise that these thresholds reflect those in the Pre-Emption Guidelines. However, the Principles are intended to be more flexible in their approach to disapplication requests above these thresholds – non-routine disapplications – than the Guidelines were.

14.6.16.2 Non-routine disapplications

As recommended by the Myners Report, the Principles recognise that some requests to disapply pre-emption rights might be non-routine, but nevertheless in the interests of the company and its shareholders. Unlike the Guidelines, the Principles emphasise that the limits set out above are intended to ease the granting of authority to routine requests to disapply pre-emption rights, not prohibit the granting of non-routine disapplications. Rather, any request for a non-routine disapplication should be considered by shareholders on a case by case basis.

The Principles set out examples of issues which are likely to be critical to shareholders in terms of voting on any non-routine disapplication, such as the size and stage of development of the company in the sector in which it operates and the extent to which the issue would dilute the value and voting control of existing shareholdings (para 15). Any non-routine disapplication should be made at a specially convened EGM, unless the company is in a position to provide all the necessary information to shareholders at its AGM, in which case the request can be made at the AGM (para 17).

14.6.16.3 The disapplication procedure

For both routine and non-routine disapplications, the company must communicate with shareholders as soon as possible (para 4). Following the granting of any disapplication, the company should publish in its annual report certain information about the non-pre-emptive issue, such as the level of discount, the amount raised and how it was used (para 20).

Example

Let us apply the Statement of Principles to our example of X plc. The issued ordinary share capital at the date of the last published accounts was £1m. 5% of £1m is £50,000, so the disapplication required relating to the issue of 50,000 shares of £1 is 'routine', provided X plc has not made any other issues in the last three years which would exceed the 7.5% cumulative total referred to at **14.6.16.1(b)**. The lawyer needs to check that the consideration complies within the requirement set out at **14.6.16.1(c)**, then, finally, X plc will be in a position to issue shares.

14.6.17 Sanctions for breach of s 89

A breach of s 89 will not invalidate or cancel an allotment. However, s 92 of the CA 1985 provides that the company and any director who knowingly permitted the breach are jointly and severally liable to compensate any person to whom the shares should have been offered under the pre-emption rights.

14.6.18 Sanctions for breach of the Listing Rules

The sanctions for breach of the Listing Rules are as set out at **3.7** above.

14.7 Issuing the shares

Once the three questions listed at **14.3** above have been considered and the appropriate action taken, the company is in a position to issue the shares. However, the lawyer must check that the circumstances of the issue do not trigger any other legal problems. The areas to check are as follows.

14.7.1 Directors' fiduciary duties

The directors must issue the shares in accordance with their common law obligations. In particular, they must:

(a) issue the shares bona fide in the interests of the company; and
(b) exercise their powers for the purpose for which they were given.

14.7.2 Financial assistance

There is a general prohibition on a company providing financial help to anyone acquiring its shares. This can cause problems on a share issue, and the lawyer must analyse the terms of the issue carefully to identify any potential problems relating to financial assistance. **Chapter 16** considers this topic in detail.

14.7.3 Consideration

'Consideration' means the price paid for the shares. Generally, this does not have to be cash; a subscriber may pay cash, but may also pay in money's worth, such as with other shares (if the subscriber is a company) or other assets. However, where the issuer of shares is a public company, s 99(2) of the CA 1985 provides that it cannot accept consideration in the form of an undertaking:

(a) to do work; or
(b) to perform services.

In addition, a public company cannot allot shares as fully or partly paid up otherwise than in cash, if the consideration is or includes an undertaking which will, or may, be performed more than five years after the date of the allotment (s 102(1)). This is referred to as a 'long-term undertaking'.

14.7.4 Issuing shares at a discount

As explained at **13.3.1** above, s 100 of the CA 1985 provides that no company, public or private, listed or unlisted, can issue a share at a discount to its nominal value. The company can, of course, issue a share which is partly paid, but, as discussed at **13.3.7** above, in the case of a public company, each share (other than a share allotted pursuant to an employee share scheme – see **13.9**) must be paid up at least as to one-quarter of its nominal value together with the whole of any premium paid on it.

Finally, as **14.6.16** above explained, the Pre-emption Guidelines provide that a listed company should not issue any share under a s 95 disapplication (on a non pre-emptive basis) at a discount of more than 5% of its market value. This restriction does not apply, however, if the pre-emption requirements of the Listing Rules are followed.

14.7.5 Valuation of non-cash consideration

Section 103 of the CA 1985 provides that if the consideration for the allotment is not cash ('non-cash consideration'), the consideration must be independently valued, and a report of the valuation must be given to the company and the subscriber. There are some exceptions to this rule, however, and one important exception relates to a 'share-for-share exchange', that is, when the consideration for the issue of shares by one company is shares in another company. In this case no valuation is required (s 103(3)). Note that the European Commission's proposed directive to amend the second Company Law Directive suggests limiting this requirement (see **16.8**).

14.7.6 Class rights

The procedure required to vary rights which attach to a certain class of shares was examined at **13.7** above. The lawyer must examine the rights attaching to the shares the company proposes to issue, to check that the issue will not, in fact, vary any existing class rights (for example, if the shares to be issued are a new class which will rank above an existing class in terms of dividend rights). If they will vary class rights, the procedures detailed in **13.7** above will need to be followed.

14.7.7 The Prospectus Rules

The lawyer must analyse the terms of the share issue to check whether a prospectus is required. **Chapter 17** considers this in relation to listed companies which are seeking to issue shares.

14.7.8 Filing details of the issue

The company must notify the Registrar of any allotment of shares within one month of the allotment, by completing and delivering Form 88(2) to Companies House. A specimen Form 88(2) is set out at **Appendix 3**. Note that the form must include a brief description of the consideration for which the shares were allotted. If the consideration was other than for cash, a simple description of the asset which comprises the consideration will suffice, such as '100 ordinary shares of £1 in Z Limited' if the consideration for the issue is shares.

14.8 Conclusion

This chapter has shown that, while it is common for a company to issue shares, it can cause a few headaches for the lawyer. However, a methodical approach will ensure that all the required checks are made, and appropriate action taken. Do not forget, either, that while the lawyer should consider the three vital questions outlined at **14.3** above in relation to all issues of shares, not all issues will require action to be taken in relation to all three questions. For example, it may be that the company already has enough authorised but unissued share capital from which to make the issue, the directors already have authority to allot those shares, and the pre-emption rights have already been disapplied.

Also, the introduction to this chapter stated that it is not that the legislation which applies to listed companies is any more onerous than that applying to privates companies, it is simply that the share capital of listed companies tends to be more complex. We have considered some of the more complex classes of securities that a listed company may have, such as convertible debt securities and convertible preference shares, in the context of whether an issue of such securities would require a s 80 authority, or trigger, or entitle recipients to, s 89 pre-emption rights on allotment. However, often listed companies will be issuing ordinary shares, like our example of X plc, where the process is much more straightforward because it is easier to determine whether the shares fall within the definitions in the CA 1985.

Considering the three vital questions is bread-and-butter work for a junior corporate lawyer, and once you have done it, it will not seem quite so daunting the next time.

14.9 Future developments

The Companies Bill (see **1.11**) will make significant changes to the process by which a company issues shares. The draft bill of 20 July 2006 proposes to:

(a) abolish the requirement for authorised share capital;
(b) make minor changes to the process of allotting shares (the term 'relevant shares' is not used); and
(c) enable the Secretary of State to reduce the period for exercise of pre-emption rights from 21 days to 14 days.

The European Commission is also proposing extensive reform through its *Action Plan on Company Law and Corporate Governance*, referred to at **16.9** below. However, legislation is unlikely until at least 2009.

Chapter 15
Disclosure of Interests in Shares

15.1	Introduction	193
15.2	Nominee shareholders	193
15.3	The register of members	193
15.4	Rules requiring the disclosure of share interests	194
15.5	Sections 324 to 328 of the CA 1985	194
15.6	Sections 198 to 220 of the CA 1985	195
15.7	Non-statutory requirements	203
15.8	Summary	211
15.9	Future developments	212

15.1 Introduction

People become shareholders of a company, public or private, in one of two ways. They either subscribe for shares which the company issues (see **Chapter 14**), or they buy shares from existing shareholders (see **Chapter 19**). In both cases, the new shareholder will identify himself (or itself) to the company, so that the company can record the shareholder's details in its register of members and send out a share certificate.

This chapter considers the rules which require certain shareholders of public companies to disclose their interests in shares to the company, and why, despite the seemingly adequate process outlined above, a public company requires this extra protection.

15.2 Nominee shareholders

A 'nominee' shareholder is the registered owner of a share, but he holds that share on trust for the benefit of another person, the 'beneficial owner'. The nominee will hold the legal title to the share, but will have no beneficial interest in that share. Usually the beneficial owner (if he has any sense) will require the nominee to execute a declaration of trust in respect of the share, in which the nominee will give various undertakings to the beneficial owner, such as:

(a) to account to the beneficial owner for dividends and other income received in respect of the share;

(b) to exercise rights attaching to the share, such as voting rights, as the beneficial owner directs; and

(c) to transfer the share as the beneficial owner directs.

In its consultation document of 1988, *Disclosure of Interests in Shares*, the DTI stated that nominee shareholders were essential if investment managers were to be able to manage the accounts of small shareholders efficiently.

15.3 The register of members

All companies must maintain a register of members, pursuant to s 352 of the CA 1985. However, s 360 of the CA 1985 prohibits a company from recording notice of any trust in the register of members. This means that the register will record details of the holder of the legal title only. It will not record any details of the holder of the beneficial title. In some cases, of course, this is one and the same person. If I buy a share in Marks and Spencer Group plc tomorrow, I will own both legal and beneficial title to it. However, anyone who buys shares through a nominee will remain off the register; it is the nominee's details which the register will record.

15.3.1 Advantages of s 360

The purpose of s 360 is to make the company's administration easier, because the company does not have to concern itself with matters of beneficial entitlement to shares. The company has no obligation to identify the beneficial owner, or to involve itself in the detail of what a nominee shareholder can or cannot do in relation to the shares. As far as the company is concerned, no one has an interest in the share other than the person entered in the register of members. This is so helpful to a company that it will often reiterate this provision in its articles of association.

15.3.2 Disadvantages of s 360

Section 360 does have its disadvantages. It means that the company is not aware of who has beneficial ownership of its shares. Why is this a problem? For private companies it does not tend to be problematic. Often in private companies the shareholders are a relatively small group of people who know each other.

However, with public companies, particularly listed companies, this is not the case. There are many shareholders. Nominee shareholders can be useful to market abusers or insider dealers seeking to hide their true identities (see **Chapter 10** and **11**). The value of public, and particularly listed, companies means that they are often targets for a takeover offer (see **Chapters 20** to **23**). If the company is not aware of the beneficial ownership of its shares, what is to stop a potential bidder secretly building up a large shareholding in the target company by buying shares through a nominee? These shares would come in very useful when it comes to securing acceptance of the offer from target company shareholders.

For these reasons, there are rules which require the disclosure to the company of certain interests in shares. Some of them should be familiar, as we encountered them briefly in **Chapter 7** when we examined the continuing obligations of listed companies; others are introduced in **15.7** below.

15.4 Rules requiring the disclosure of share interests

Sections 324 to 328 of the CA 1985, which apply to all companies, private and public, listed and unlisted, are outlined at **15.5** below.

Sections 198 to 220 of the 1985 Act, which apply to public companies but not private companies, are considered at **15.6**.

Certain non-statutory provisions, such as the Disclosure Rules, the Listing Rules, the City Code and the Substantial Acquisition Rules, also require the disclosure of beneficial ownership of public company shares, in particular circumstances. These requirements are discussed at **15.7**.

15.5 Sections 324 to 328 of the CA 1985

The effect of ss 324 to 328 of the CA 1985 is that a *director* of any company, listed or unlisted, must notify the company of his dealings, and of the dealings of any person connected with him, in the company's shares. He must do so within five business days following the day he becomes aware of the interest (s 324(3) and Pt II of Sch 13 to the CA 1985). Section 325 of the CA 1985 provides that the company must keep this information in a register called the register of directors' interests.

15.6 Sections 198 to 220 of the CA 1985

Sections 198 to 220 apply to public companies (listed and unlisted) only. For the reasons given at **15.3.2** above, the extent of the protection given to private companies in relation to the disclosure of share interests is not as wide as that offered to public companies. Sections 198 to 220 (Pt VI of the CA 1985) requires a *shareholder* to disclose his interests to the company in certain circumstances. It is fair to say that the legislation relating to the disclosure of share interests is not set out in a way which is particularly easy to follow. The obligation itself is quite straightforward, however (see also **7.5.5.3**).

15.6.1 Purpose

The purpose of ss 198 to 220 is to enable public companies to discover the identity of the beneficial owners of their shares. As explained in **15.3.2** above, this is particularly helpful in terms of assisting the company to expose insider dealing or market abuse and to defend an unwanted takeover bid.

15.6.2 Pre-conditions

The obligation to disclose interests in shares will not apply to any person until one of the following has happened:

(a) The person (Z) knowingly *acquires* an interest, or knowingly *ceases* to be interested in *shares comprised in the company's relevant share capital* (ie, Z buys or sells shares) (s 198(1)(a)).

(b) Z *becomes aware* that he has acquired an interest in *shares comprised in the company's relevant share capital*, or *becomes aware* of ceasing to be so interested (eg, Z becomes aware that a person with whom he is acting in concert has bought or sold shares) (s 198(1)(b)).

(c) Z *becomes aware* of anything, other than those circumstances set out in (a) and (b) above, which results in him having a *notifiable interest* which he did not have before (eg, because the company has re-registered as a public company, or has reduced its share capital thereby increasing the proportion of shares Z holds) (s 198(3)).

Basically, the effect of these long-winded provisions is that the obligation to disclose share interests does not arise only on a purchase or disposal of shares (where obviously the shareholder is likely to be aware of the notifiable interest); it can be triggered by something a third party does. Z cannot, however, be obliged to disclose anything of which he is not aware. Knowledge is an important pre-condition of the disclosure of interests obligation. There are also certain rules to reduce the opportunity Z has to claim that he did not have the requisite knowledge. These are examined at **15.6.6** below.

'Shares comprised in the company's relevant share capital' are defined by s 198(2) as issued shares (excluding treasury shares) which carry the right to vote in all circumstances at general meetings of a public company. As explained at **13.5.1.2** above, it is usually only ordinary shares which carry these full voting rights, so typically the disclosure of interests obligation is confined to interests in ordinary shares.

15.6.3 When the obligation arises

15.6.3.1 Notifiable interest

The obligation is triggered, subject to the pre-conditions, once a person has a 'notifiable interest', in other words, when he becomes interested in 3% or more of the nominal value of a public company's voting shares (s 199(2)(a)). This, in effect, catches those whom the CA 1985 perceives to be major shareholders. It is unlikely, for example, that I will own 3% of the voting shares in Marks and Spencer Group plc at any point in the near future (but never say never).

Note that s 199(2)(b) provides a 10% rather than a 3% threshold if the interests in shares are not material. Section 199(2A) defines interests in shares which are not material. The definition includes, for example, the interests of professional investors in securities, such as unit trust managers.

15.6.3.2 Interest in shares

Section 208 defines what an interest is, and s 209 lists a number of interests which should be disregarded for the purposes of the disclosure obligation. The circumstances in which a person will have an interest include:

(a) when shares are held on trust for him (but interests in reversion, discretionary interests and interests for life must be disregarded);

(b) if he agrees to buy shares;

(c) if he has a 'put' or 'call' option over shares (a put option is the right to 'put' your shares onto someone else, that is, you can force that person to buy your shares; a call option is the right to 'call' someone else's shares, that is, you can force that person to sell his shares to you); or

(d) if he is entitled to control the exercise of rights attached to shares (the classic example of this is a beneficial owner, who has the right to exercise the rights attached to shares owned by a nominee).

Note, however, that a person will not be interested in shares just because he has been appointed as a proxy or representative in relation to those shares.

15.6.4 The interests which must be disclosed

The shareholder must notify the company if his shareholding:

(a) has fallen from 3% or more to below 3% (that is, he has ceased to be a major shareholder) (s 199(5)(a));

(b) has risen from below 3% to 3% or more (that is, he has become a major shareholder) (s 199(4)); or

(c) is 3% or more and rises or falls to a different *percentage level* (s 199(5)(b)).

15.6.4.1 Percentage level

Section 200 provides that 'percentage level' is the aggregate nominal value of the shareholder's shareholding, expressed as a percentage of the nominal amount of the whole of the company's voting share capital. If there are different classes of share, the percentage level is calculated separately, by reference to each class. In all cases, however, the percentage level figure must be rounded down to the next whole number, which can be significant.

For example, if Z has an interest in 5% of the voting share capital of X plc (a listed company) and he knowingly acquires an interest in a further 1.1%, he must notify X plc. He has an interest of 6.1%, rounded down to 6%, which is a different percentage level to his previous holding of 5%. However, if Z had acquired an interest in 0.9%, the obligation to disclose would not have arisen, because he would have an interest in 5.9%, which, rounded down, is not a different percentage level to his previous holding of 5%.

15.6.4.2 Increase of share capital

The application of the percentage level test on an increase of share capital is, perhaps, not what you might expect. Take, for example, an increase of share capital which relates to a rights or bonus issue. If Z, the shareholder, takes up his full entitlement under the issue, his actual percentage shareholding will remain the same. For example, imagine that X plc has an issued share capital of £100,000, divided into 100,000 shares of £1 each. A holds 5,000 shares, that is, 5%. This is above the notifiable percentage, so A will already have had to disclose information on his interest to X plc. X plc then makes a 'one for one' rights issue, so that 200,000 shares of £1 each are now in issue. If Z takes up his rights, he will hold 10,000 shares. This still represents a 5% shareholding (5% of 200,000). However the effect of s 200(3) is that, for the purposes of the disclosure obligation under s 198, the percentage level *both before and after* the increase is calculated with reference to the *increased* share capital. In our example, then, Z is deemed to have held 5,000 of 200,000 shares immediately before the rights issue (that is, 2.5%), and 10,000 of 200,000 shares immediately after the rights issue (that is, 5%). There is deemed to have been a percentage change from below to above the notifiable percentage as a result of the rights issue, so Z must disclose his interest to the company.

15.6.5 Content of the notification

We now know what the disclosure obligation is, and when it arises, but how does the shareholder fulfil this obligation? He must send a notification to the company containing information prescribed by the CA 1985. This is why the disclosure obligation under s 198 is commonly referred to as the 'notification obligation'.

Section 202 and s 220(2) provide that the notification must:

(a) be in writing; and
(b) be made within two business days following the day on which the notification obligation arose.

If the obligation to notify has arisen because the shareholder's percentage level held has dropped below 3%, the notice must simply state that the shareholder no longer has a notifiable interest (s 202(2)(b)).

However, for those notifications which state that the shareholder does have an interest, the notification must:

(a) specify the shares to which the notice relates (s 202(2));
(b) state the number of shares in which there is a notifiable interest (s 202(2));
(c) identify (to the extent that this is known) each registered holder (this includes any nominee shareholder) of shares to which the notification relates, and the number of shares held by each of them (s 203(3)(a));
(d) identify the notifier and give his address (and where the notifier is a director, state that the notice is given in fulfilment of the obligation under ss 198 to 202 of the CA 1985); and

(e) state the number of shares in which the person notifying has an interest which is a right or an obligation to acquire shares within s 208(5) of the CA 1985 ('put and call' options – see **15.6.3.2**) (s 203(3)(b)).

It is, of course, the requirement at (c) above which is at the heart of the legislation; beneficial owners who have major shareholdings, and are obliged to make a disclosure to the company, must reveal the nominees who hold shares on their behalf. The nominee arrangement is revealed.

15.6.6 Closing the loophole

It was highlighted at **15.6.2** above that the shareholder's knowledge that he has a notifiable interest is fundamental to the obligation to disclose. This leaves open the possibility that the shareholder can defend any non-disclosure by claiming he did not have the knowledge required by s 198(1)(b) or s 198(3), either because he used an agent to buy or sell shares, and the agent did not inform him of the acquisition or disposal, or because he uses someone else to buy or sell the shares so he can plead ignorance about any acquisition or disposal. The CA 1985 contains various anti-avoidance provisions to close this loophole.

15.6.6.1 Acquisitions and disposals by an agent

Section 210(1) of the CA 1985 relates to acquisitions or disposals of shares made through an agent. The section imposes an obligation on any principal to ensure that the agent notifies him immediately of any acquisitions or disposals which will, or may, give rise to an obligation of disclosure. If the principal does not fulfil this obligation, he is guilty of an offence and liable to imprisonment, or a fine or both. Perhaps not surprisingly, this section seems to discourage principals from avoiding the disclosure obligation by asserting that the agent did not provide the appropriate information.

15.6.6.2 Attributed interests

To prevent a shareholder (Z) circumventing s 198 by using someone close to him to buy shares, the CA 1985 deems that the interests of that other person will also be attributed to Z.

Z is deemed to have an interest in any shares:

(a) in which Z's spouse, infant child or step-child is interested (s 203);

(b) in which a company is interested, if he has considerable influence either:

  (i) at board level, ie the company or its directors are accustomed to act in accordance with Z's instructions, or

  (ii) at shareholder level, ie Z is entitled to exercise, or control the exercise of, at least one-third of the voting power at general meetings (note that if Z has this power and the company has the controlling vote in another company, then Z will also be deemed to be interested in the shares of that other company, as he has effective voting control over it) (s 203(2) and (3)); and

(c) in which anyone *acting in concert* with him is interested (s 205).

Note that the other person does not have to be the registered owner of the shares; he simply needs to be interested in the shares. This is enough for Z to be fixed with an interest too.

15.6.6.3 Concert parties

Sections 204 to 207 provide the rules relating to concert parties. They apply to prevent people clubbing together to acquire interests in a particular company, which do not need to be disclosed because no individual would have a disclosable interest. The provisions assist companies to defend takeover bids; thus, a company cannot be 'hijacked' by finding not only that it is the subject of a bid from Z plc, but also that Z plc and all its group companies, its financial advisers (acting on behalf of Z plc), its owner, Z, all Z's friends and the companies they own (all concert parties) have already bought a substantial number of shares in the company which they will use to vote in favour of the bid. Instead, ss 204 to 207 of the CA 1985 provide that each concert party is deemed to be interested in all the shares in which the other concert parties are interested. This means that as soon as the concert parties acquired a 3% shareholding between them, they would have been obliged to disclose this to the company, which would then have been alerted to their predatory behaviour.

Concert party agreement

Section 204 of the CA 1985 provides that, for the concert party provisions to apply, there must be:

(a) a concert party agreement, which is:
  (i) an agreement,
  (ii) between two or more persons,
  (iii) which provides that at least one of those persons will acquire interests in voting shares in a public company, and
  (iv) which imposes obligations or restrictions on at least one of the parties in relation to how they use, retain or dispose of those interests; and
(b) an acquisition of shares pursuant to the concert party agreement.

Any existing shareholdings of the concert parties will not be caught just because of the existence of the concert party agreement. It is the acquisition referred to in (b) above which will actually trigger the application of ss 204 to 207.

Once this acquisition is made, any existing shareholdings of the concert parties will then be relevant and will be attributed to each other concert party.

Content of the notification

The concert party must include in its notification all the information referred to at **15.6.5** above, and in addition must include the following information pursuant to s 205(4):

(a) a statement that he is party to a concert party agreement;
(b) the names and (if known) the addresses of all the other concert parties; and
(c) the number of shares in which he is deemed to be interested by virtue of the concert party provisions.

Section 206

As the disclosure obligation is based on knowledge (see **15.6.2** above), s 206 prohibits a concert party from using the defence that he was not aware of the interests of the other concert parties. The section provides that each concert party must provide written details of his interests in the company to each of the other concert parties, within two business days (s 220(2)) of that interest arising. The details should include the number of shares in which he is interested and (if known) details of the registered owner of the shares. This obligation will arise on the acquisition referred to at (b) under 'Concert party agreement' above. Following this, each concert party must notify the company if he knowingly acquires an interest, or becomes aware that he has acquired an interest, whether pursuant to the concert party agreement or not, or indeed if he ceases to be interested in any shares.

Example

Day 1

A, B and C are shareholders in X plc.

A owns 5% and has already notified the company of this major shareholding.

B owns 2.5%.

C owns 2%.

Neither A, nor B nor C has any other interest in the voting shares of X plc.

Day 2

A, B and C enter into a concert party agreement relating to X plc. Although they all own shares in X plc, no disclosure obligation arises at this point, because no party has yet acquired any shares pursuant to the concert party agreement.

Day 3

C acquires an interest in another 3% of the shares of X plc, pursuant to the concert party agreement. C must notify A and B of the acquisition, under s 206 of the CA 1985.

A is now interested in 12.5% of the shares (A's 5%, B's 2.5% and C's 5%).

B is now interested in 12.5 % of the shares (A's 5%, B's 2.5% and C's 5%).

C is now interested in 12.5% of the shares (A's 5%, B's 2.5% and C's 5%).

Each of A, B and C must notify X plc of their holding. The company secretary of X plc will probably be a little perturbed when he receives these notifications. Is the company about to be the target of a hostile takeover bid?

15.6.7 Sanctions

The sanctions for breach of the disclosure obligations are severe.

15.6.7.1 Criminal penalties

Section 210(3) provides that the following are all criminal offences, punishable by imprisonment, or a fine (or both):

(a) failing to disclose information to the company within the two business day limit;

(b) knowingly or recklessly making a false statement when disclosing;

(c) failing to give notice to another person under the concert party provisions within the two business day limit; and

(d) failing to secure notification from an agent under s 210.

15.6.7.2 Imposing restrictions on shares

Restrictions may be placed on shares when the beneficial ownership of those shares is being kept secret in breach of the s 198 disclosure obligations, such as when:

(a) a person has not replied to a s 212 notice (see **15.6.8**) (s 216);

(b) a person has been convicted of any of the offences listed at **15.6.7.1** above (s 210); or

(c) the Secretary of State is investigating the ownership of those shares under ss 442 or 444 (see **15.6.9**) (s 445).

These restrictions are often referred to as 'Part XV restrictions'. If the company's articles allow the company to impose restrictions on shares, the company itself will be able to impose the restrictions on the shares. If the company is listed, however, it must ensure that its articles permit restrictions only to the extent allowed by the FSA. If the company's articles do not permit the company to impose restrictions, then, in the case of (a) above, the company must apply to the court for an order to subject shares to restrictions and, in the case of (b) and (c) above, the Secretary of State can impose the restrictions. Clearly, it is an advantage for the company to have articles which allow the company to impose these restrictions; it can be effective in deterring shareholders from breaching the disclosure obligations.

Section 454 of the CA 1985 provides that while the shares are subject to restrictions:

(a) any transfer of the shares is void;
(b) no voting rights are exercisable in respect of the shares;
(c) the shareholder cannot benefit from any rights given by his shares to receive new shares in the company (such as a bonus or rights issue); and
(d) except on liquidation, no payment can be made of any sums due from the company on the shares, such as a dividend.

These restrictions are onerous, and are intended to prevent the person in breach of the disclosure obligations from taking advantage of the breach, such as by launching a surprise takeover bid (the shares acquired could not be used to vote in favour of the bid) or by profiting from insider dealing or market abuse (the transfer is void). If the person who imposed the restrictions, namely the company, the court or the Secretary of State, is satisfied that the relevant facts about the shares have been disclosed to the company and that no unfair advantage has accrued to anyone as a result of the breach of the disclosure obligation, they can order that the restrictions should be removed.

15.6.8 The company's power to investigate beneficial ownership: ss 212 and 214

We have now established that major beneficial owners of shares must disclose their interests to the company. We have also established that such shareholders cannot avoid this obligation by hiding behind a nominee or agent, or pool their resources with certain family members or concert parties. However, the legislation also provides that in certain circumstances the company can be proactive and investigate the beneficial ownership of its shares either:

(a) on its own initiative, pursuant to s 212 of the CA 1985; or
(b) because a shareholder has asked it to, under s 214 of the CA 1985.

This power reflects just how important it is considered to be that the company is able to identify shareholders who may have predatory intentions; the CA 1985 does not render the company wholly reliant on these predators complying with their disclosure obligations.

15.6.8.1 Section 212 notice

If the company knows, or has reasonable cause to believe, that a person:

(a) is interested; or

(b)   has been interested, at any time within the last three years,

in the company's shares, the company can serve a s 212 notice on that person, requesting details of those interests and certain other relevant information. Section 212 details the specific information which the company can request, but it includes, for example, details of any concert party arrangements (see **15.6.6.3** above). In fact, the company can request information which is not covered by the disclosure obligation; for example, even if the recipient's interests are less than 3%, the recipient can be requested to disclose his interests. In addition, the interests to be disregarded under s 209 for the purposes of the disclosure obligation (see **15.6.3.2**) are not disregarded for the purposes of the s 212 notice, and the company can require the recipient to disclose them.

The s 212 notice must specify a reasonable time within which the recipient must respond. This is not defined. In practice, this seems to be interpreted as two days in an emergency situation (such as when the company suspects it is the target of an impending takeover bid), and five days in all other circumstances.

Of course, s 212 is particularly welcome when a company suspects it is about to be the target of an unwanted takeover bid. Imagine that the share price of X plc has been falling dramatically and that the press has speculated that now would be a good time for one of X plc's competitors to launch a takeover bid. The company secretary of X plc will send out s 212 notices in order to expose any prospective bidder. In the event that the bidder then makes the bid, the company secretary will continue to send out s 212 notices, to monitor the level of acceptances. Of course, the bidder should also comply with the s 198 disclosure obligations and notify the company whenever its shareholding increases by a percentage level.

In practice, while the company secretary will often draft the notice (as it is the company secretary who will have daily contact with the company's registrars), he will often consult the company's lawyers about the interpretation of aspects of the legislation, for example what the current practice is as to the minimum 'reasonable time' within which the company can demand a reply.

The CA 1985 does not specify a format for a s 212 notice. The DTI, however, has produced a model s 212 notice which is available on its website.

15.6.8.2   Shareholders' s 214 requisition

Section 214 provides that shareholders who hold at least one-tenth of the company's paid-up voting share capital can requisition the company to use its powers under s 212. The requisition must:

(a)   specify how the shareholders want the company to exercise its powers under s 212;

(b)   give reasonable grounds for requiring the company to exercise its powers in that way;

(c)   be signed; and

(d)   be deposited at the company's registered office.

Section 215 provides that the company must respond by carrying out the requested investigation and compiling a report of its findings, which it must make available at the company's registered office.

The company must act on the request within certain time limits set out in s 215. If it fails to do so, the company and any of the company's officers who are in default will be liable to a fine

15.6.9 The DTI's power to investigate beneficial ownership: ss 442 and 444

Usually the company's powers of investigation under s 212 are adequate to expose beneficial shareholdings in the company. However, the Secretary of State has a residual power to appoint inspectors to investigate the company ownership under s 442 of the CA 1985, either:

(a) on his own initiative (s 442(1)); or
(b) following an application by:
  (i) at least 200 shareholders of the company, or
  (ii) shareholders holding at least one-tenth of the company's issued share capital (s 442(3)).

Also, if the Secretary of State considers that there is good reason to investigate share ownership, s 444 grants him power in his own capacity (that is, without appointing inspectors) to obtain information about the ownership of shares in the company.

15.6.10 The register of share interests

Section 211 of the CA 1985 provides that the company must keep a separate register which records interests disclosed to it under ss 198 to 202. Section 213 also provides that the company must record, in a separate part of this register, any interests revealed by s 212 investigations. The company must keep the register together with the register of directors' interests referred to at **15.5** above, and the public have the right to inspect this register under ss 211(8)(b) and 219 of the CA 1985.

Section 217 provides protection for anyone who has been entered into the register who does not consider they should be in that register. If, in the process of fulfilling the disclosure obligation, a shareholder identifies another person as being interested in shares, the company must notify that other person that he has been entered into the register. Section 217 then provides a process whereby that person can insist on being removed from the register, provided the information which has been supplied is incorrect.

15.7 Non-statutory requirements

The provisions of the CA 1985 relating to the disclosure of interests in shares apply to all companies (in relation to ss 324 to 328) and to public companies (in relation to ss 198 to 220) at all times. However, there are also certain non-statutory provisions which cover the disclosure of interests in shares, which may apply, depending on the nature of the company and the time the shareholder acquires the interest.

15.7.1 The Disclosure Rules

The provisions of the Disclosure Rules apply to listed companies only. The provisions relating to ss 324 to 328 of the CA 1985 are considered at **15.7.1.1** below. In addition, **15.7.1.2** below considers the overlapping requirement under the new regime, for persons discharging managerial responsibilities (PDMRs) (see **7.6.2.1**) and their connected persons to disclose certain dealings to the company. (Together, these provisions replace OLRs 16.13 to 16.17.)

15.7.1.1 Disclosure Rules relating to ss 324 to 328 of the CA 1985

It was explained at **7.4.8** above that the continuing obligations contained in DR 3.1.4R(1)(b) provide that a listed company must pass on to the market the information it receives under ss 324 to 328 of the CA 1985. To comply with this requirement, the company must notify an RIS of the information it receives under ss 324 to 328, together with the information required by DR 3.1.3R (including details of the person notifying, and details of the acquisition or disposal (DR 3.1.5R)). They must do this as soon as possible (and in any event by the end of the business day following the day the company receives the information) (DR 3.1.4R(2)). A proforma entitled *'Notification of Transactions of Directors, Persons Discharging Managerial Responsibility or Connected Persons'*, available from the UKLA section of the FSA website, can be used to make the notification to the RIS.

15.7.1.2 Disclosure Rules relating to transactions by PDMRs and their connected persons

As mentioned at **7.4.7** above, DR 3.1.2R requires PDMRs and their connected persons to disclose to the company all transactions conducted on their own account in the shares of the company (or derivatives or any other financial instruments relating to those shares) within four business days of the day on which the transaction occurred. The PDMR must include in the disclosure the information required by DR 3.1.3R.

The disclosure the PDMR must make under DR 3.1.2R is in addition to the requirement of directors to notify the company of their dealings under ss 324 to 328 of the CA 1985, referred to at **15.5** above. Clearly there is some overlap of the two requirements, but they do remain distinct (for example, there are differences between the timing obligations; under s 324(3) and Pt II of Sch 13 to the CA 1985, a director must notify the company no later than the fifth business day after he becomes aware of his interest, while under DR 3.1.2R the PDMR must notify the company within four business days of the day on which the transaction occurred).

Listed companies must then notify an RIS of the information it receives under DR 3.1.2R (DR 3.1.4R(1)(a)). As with the ss 324 to 328 disclosure referred to at **15.7.1.1** above, the company must comply with DR 3.1.4R(2), include the information required by DR 3.1.3R, and provide the information to the RIS as soon as possible, and in any event no later than the end of the business day following the receipt of the information.

Clearly, in practice, there is scope for confusion in the market as to whether the two notifications relate to the same transaction. Disclosure Rule 3.1.6R provides that the company must make clear in its notification that the disclosures relate to a single transaction, and in fact the proforma *'Notification of Transactions of Directors, Persons Discharging Managerial Responsibility or Connected Persons'* allows one notification to be used to satisfy the requirement under DR 3.1.4R(1)(a) (to pass on the information provided to it under DR 3.1.2R) and the requirement under DR 3.1.4R(1)(b) (to pass on the information provided to it under ss 324 to 328 of the CA 1985). An example of a joint notification, made on this proforma, is set out below. Such notifications can be accessed from the RNS section of the Stock Exchange's website, under the heading 'Director/ PDMR shareholding'.

NOTIFICATION OF TRANSACTIONS OF DIRECTORS, PERSONS DISCHARGING MANAGERIAL RESPONSIBILITY OR CONNECTED PERSONS

This form is intended for use by an issuer to make a RIS notification required by DR 3.1.4R(1).

(1) An *issuer* making a notification in respect of a transaction relating to the *shares* or debentures of the *issuer* should complete boxes 1 to 16, 23 and 24.

(2) An *issuer* making a notification in respect of a derivative relating to the *shares* of the *issuer* should complete boxes 1 to 4, 6, 8, 13, 14, 16, 23 and 24.

(3) An *issuer* making a notification in respect of options granted to a *director/person discharging managerial responsibilities* should complete boxes 1 to 3 and 17 to 24.

(4) An *issuer* making a notification in respect of a *financial instrument* relating to the *shares* of the *issuer* (other than a debenture) should complete boxes 1 to 4, 6, 8, 9, 11, 13, 14, 16, 23 and 24.

Please complete all relevant boxes in block capital letters.

1. Name of the *issuer*
   ITV plc

2. State whether the notification relates to
   (i) a transaction notified in accordance with DR 3.1.4R(1)(a); or
   (ii) DR 3.1.4(R)(1)(b) a disclosure made in accordance with section 324 (as extended by section 328) of the Companies Act 1985; or
   (iii) both (i) and (ii)
   (iii) both (i) and (ii)

3. Name of person *discharging managerial responsibilities/director*
   Charles Allen – executive director of ITV plc

4. State whether notification relates to a person connected with a *person discharging managerial responsibilities/director* named in 3 and identify the *connected person*
   No

5. Indicate whether the notification is in respect of a holding of the *person* referred to in 3 or 4 above or in respect of a non-beneficial interest
   Beneficial holding

6. Description of *shares* (including *class*), debentures or derivatives or financial instruments relating to *shares*
   Ordinary shares of 10p each

7. Name of registered shareholders(s) and, if more than one, the number of *shares* held by each of them
   Charles Allen

8. State the nature of the transaction
   Dividend reinvestment in ISA

9. Number of *shares*, debentures or financial instruments relating to *shares* acquired
   29.00

10. Percentage of issued class acquired (*treasury shares* of that *class* should not be taken into account when calculating percentage)
    Less than 0.1%

11. Number of *shares*, debentures or financial instruments relating to *shares* disposed
    n/a

12. Percentage of issued *class* disposed (*treasury shares* of that *class* should not be taken into account when calculating percentage)
    n/a

13. Price per *share* or value of transaction
    115.94p per share

14. Date and place of transaction
    15 August 2005, London
15. Total holding following notification and total percentage holding following notification (any *treasury shares* should not be taken into account when calculating percentage)
    3,639,774 (less than 0.1%)
16. Date issuer informed of transaction
    23 August 2005

If a person *discharging managerial responsibilities* has been granted options by the issuer complete the following boxes

17. Date of grant
    n/a
18. Period during which or date on which it can be exercised
    n/a
19. Total amount paid (if any) for grant of the option
    n/a
20. Description of shares or debentures involved (class and number)
    n/a
21. Exercise price (if fixed at time of grant) or indication that price is to be fixed at the time of exercise
    n/a
22. Total number of *shares* or debentures over which options held following notification
    n/a
23. Any additional information
24. Name of contact and telephone number for queries

Name and signature of duly authorised officer of *issuer* responsible for making notification
Deputy Company Secretary
Date of notification
23 August 2005

15.7.2 The Listing Rules

The provisions of the Listing Rules apply to listed companies only.

15.7.2.1 Listing Rules relating to ss 198 to 220 of the CA 1985

Listing Rules 9.6.7R and 9.6.8R require a listed company to disclose to the public the information it acquires from shareholders under ss 198 to 208 (or which it should have acquired under ss 198 to 208, but actually acquired under s 212) (see **7.5.5.3**). The company must make this disclosure in the usual way, that is, by notifying the information to an RIS as soon as possible and in any event by the end of the business day following receipt of the information. The notification should include the date on which the information was disclosed to the company and the date on which the transaction was effected, if known. The notification can be made using the proforma '*Notification of Major Interests in Shares*', which is available from the UKLA section of the FSA website.

Note that LR 9.6.9G provides that if a shareholder has notified an RIS of his shareholding pursuant to the requirements of the City Code, that notification is deemed to satisfy the requirements of LR 9.6.7 and LR 9.6.8R (see **15.7.3.5** and **15.7.4.5** below).

Lawyers will need to know how to obtain a copy of any disclosures that listed companies make through an RIS. Note that disclosures of this type will often be headed 'Holding in company'. Examples of information provided by listed companies to the RNS (which can be accessed through the Stock Exchange's website) are set out below.

NOTIFICATION OF MAJOR INTERESTS IN SHARES

1. Name of company

   HMV Group plc

2. Name of shareholder having a major interest

   Aviva plc and its subsidiary Morley Fund Management Ltd

3. Please state whether notification indicates that it is in respect of holding of the shareholder named in 2 above or in respect of a non-beneficial interest or in the case of an individual holder if it is a holding of that person's spouse or children under the age of 18

   As 2 above

4. Name of the registered holder(s) and, if more than one holder, the number of shares held by each of them

BNY Norwich Union Nominees Ltd	5,255,871
Chase GA Group Nominees Ltd	14,621,058
Chase Nominees Ltd	662,546
CUIM Nominee Ltd	3,640,793

5. Number of shares / amount of stock acquired

   178,526

6. Percentage of issued class

   0.04%

7. Number of shares / amount of stock disposed

   N/a

8. Percentage of issued class

   N/a

9. Class of security

   Ordinary shares of 1p

10. Date of transaction

    15 August 2005

11. Date company informed

    16 August 2005

12. Total holding following this notification

    24,180,268 ordinary shares

13. Total percentage holding of issued class following this notification

    6.03%

14. Any additional information

15. Name of contact and telephone number for queries

16. Name and signature of authorised company official responsible for making this notification

Company Secretary

Date of notification

17 August 2005

Holding(s) in Company

Pursuant to Section 198 of the Companies Act 1985, British American Tobacco p.l.c. ("the Company") has been informed by a letter from Franklin Resources, Inc and its affiliates ("Franklin") dated 19 August 2005 that, as of that date, Franklin no longer has a notifiable interest in the issued ordinary share capital of the Company.

23 August 2005

15.7.3 The Substantial Acquisition Rules (SARs)

The SARs used to impose an obligation of disclosure on anyone who acquired voting shares, or rights over voting shares, which represented 15% or more of the company's voting rights, or who increased a shareholding of 15% or more beyond a whole percentage figure. As part of the Code Committee's recent review of the City Code, however, the SARs have been abolished with effect from 20 May 2006.

15.7.4 The City Code

15.7.4.1 Application of the City Code

Chapter 20 explores this in more detail, but, broadly speaking, the City Code applies during an offer period (see **22.3.4**). If the City Code does apply, it applies to everyone participating in the transaction, such as the offeror (the bidder) and the offeree (the target company), and their directors and any advisers.

15.7.4.2 Nature of the City Code

The City Code is non-statutory and exists to ensure that the general principles (see **20.5.5**) are observed during a takeover offer (see **20.3**).

15.7.4.3 The obligation

Disclosure of issued shares (r 2.10)

The main disclosure obligation is under r 8 of the City Code and relates to dealings in shares during the offer period. However, as a precursor to that disclosure obligation, those companies whose securities will be subject to that disclosure obligation must notify the market, via an RIS, of the exact number of relevant securities which are in issue during the offer period.

Rule 2.10 of the City Code provides that:

(a) as soon as possible after the commencement of the offer period (and in any event by 9.00 am on the next business day) the offeree company; and

(b) by 9.00 am on the business day after any announcement of a firm intention to make an offer (unless it has already stated that its offer will be, or is likely to be, solely in cash) the bidder, or a potential named bidder,

must each announce details, through an RIS, of all classes of relevant securities it has in issue, together with the numbers of such securities in issue.

Relevant securities are defined as:

(a) voting shares in the offeree company;
(b) any other shares in the offeree company which are the subject of the offer;
(c) equity share capital in the offeree company;
(d) any securities in the offeree company which are convertible into, or carry subscription rights over, any of the shares referred to at (a) to (c) above; and
(e) options in relation to and derivatives referenced to any of the shares referred to at (a) to (c) above.

If the consideration for the offer is shares in the offeror (this is known as an 'acquisition issue', a 'securities exchange offer' or a 'share-for-share' offer: see **17.10** below), 'relevant securities' will also include the following offeror securities:

(a) equity share capital of the offeror;
(b) the securities which the offeror is offering as consideration; and

(c) securities which are convertible into, or carry subscription rights over, the shares referred to at (a) and (b) above; and

(d) options in respect of and derivatives referenced to any of the shares referred to (a) and (b) above.

Disclosure of dealings (r 8)

Rule 8 of the City Code provides that, once the offer period has commenced:

(a) the offeror;

(b) the offeree company; and

(c) any associates of the offeror or offeree company,

must disclose any dealings (as defined by the City Code) in relevant securities (see above) to an RIS and the Panel no later than 12 noon on the business day following the date of the transaction.

There is no definition of 'associate', because the City Code considers that it is not possible to cover all the possible permutations, which depend on the structure of the offer. However, the term is clearly intended to cover those who have an interest in the outcome of the offer. The Code gives the following expamples of persons who typically will be associates:

(a) the offeree group companies and the offeror group companies (and their associated companies, namely companies in which they have a shareholding of 20% or more);

(b) connected advisers of the offeree company and the offeror (and any members of the connected adviser's groups);

(c) directors (and their close family and related trusts) of the offeree group companies and the offeror group companies;

(d) pension funds of the offeree or the offeror group companies;

(e) any investment company, unit trust or other person whose investments are managed by an associate on a discretionary basis;

(f) employee benefit trusts of any of the companies referred to at (a) above; and

(g) companies which have material trading agreements with the offeree company or the offeror.

1% shareholders (r 8.3)

Rule 8.3 of the City Code provides that if a person is interested or, as the result of any transaction, will be interested (directly or indirectly), in 1% or more of any class of relevant securities of an offeror or offeree, then he must disclose his dealings in any relevant securities of that company, as well as the dealings of any other person through whom he derives his interest. The disclosure must be made by 3.30 pm on the business day following the date of the transaction (Note 3).

If disclosure is required under r 8.1(a) or (b)(i), then the same information does not also need to be disclosed under r 8.3 (Note 5).

15.7.4.4 Content of the notification

The 'Disclosure Forms' section of the Takeover Panel website contains a specimen disclosure form which sets out the format a r 8 notification should follow. An example of a r 8.1 notification is set out below.

8.1

DEALINGS BY OFFERORS, OFFEREE COMPANIES OR THEIR ASSOCIATES FOR THEMSELVES OR FOR DISCRETIONARY CLIENTS

(Rules 8.1(a) and (b)(i) of The City Code on Takeovers and Mergers)

Name of purchaser	Red Football Limited
Company dealt in	Manchester United PLC
Relevant security dealt in	Ordinary Shares
Name of offeree/offeror with which associated	Red Football Limited
Specify category and nature of associate status #	1 - Offeror
Date of dealing	17 May 2005

DEALINGS †

Amount bought	Price per unit (currency must be stated)
1,202,178	300 Pence
Amount sold	Price per unit (currency must be stated)
N/A	N/A

Resultant total amount and percentage of the same relevant security owned or controlled	200,623,211 (76.16%)

IS A SUPPLEMENTAL FORM 8 (DERIVATIVE)/FORM 8 (OPTION) ATTACHED?
NO

Date of disclosure	17 May 2005
Contact name	–
Telephone number	–

*   Specify the owner or controller in addition to the person dealing. The naming of nominees or vehicle companies is insufficient. In the case of disclosure of dealings by fund managers on behalf of discretionary clients, the clients need not be named.
\#   See the definition of 'associate' in the Definitions Section of the Code.
†   If disclosing dealings/holdings in derivatives or options, please attach Supplemental Form 8 (Derivative) or Supplemental Form 8 (Option), as appropriate.

For details of the Code's dealing disclosure requirements, see Rule 8 and its Notes which can be viewed at www.thetakeoverpanel.org.uk.

15.7.4.5 Relationship with the disclosure of interest obligation under the Listing Rules

Listing Rule 9.6.9G provides that the obligations of a company under LR 9.6.7R and LR 9.6.8R (to disclose information provided to it, or obtained by it, under ss 198 to 208 of the CA 1985) will be deemed to have been discharged if an RIS has already been notified of that information pursuant to the disclosure provisions of the City Code.

15.8 Summary

The table below summarises the notification obligations, relating to the disclosure of interests in shares, covered by this chapter. The table is intended to be a useful overview only, and recourse should be made to the text for the specific detail of the rules.

Rule	Notifier	Notifiee	Interest	Deadline
s 198 CA 1985	Shareholder of public company	Company	Broadly, acquires over 3% (or further increase beyond whole percentage point), or falls below 3% (see **15.6.4** for detail)	2 business days after they become aware of interest
LR 9.6.7R and LR 9.6.8R (but no need if shareholder has notified RIS under the City Code – LR 9.6.9G)	Listed company	RIS	Information received under s 198 CA 1985 (or s 212 CA 1985)	ASAP, and in any event by end of business day following the day the company receives the information
s 324 CA 1985	Director of any company	Company	Dealings in the company's shares by them and any person connected with them	5 business days following the day they become aware of interest
DR 3.1.4R (1)(b)	Listed company	RIS	Information received under s 324 CA 1985	ASAP, and in any event by end of business day following the day the company receives the information
DR 3.1.2R	PDMRs of listed company (and their connected persons)	Company	All transactions conducted on their own account in the company's shares (or derivatives or any other financial instruments relating to those shares)	4 business days of day on which transaction occurred

Rule	Notifier	Notifiee	Interest	Deadline
DR 3.1.4R (1)(a)	Listed company	RIS	Information received under DR 3.1.2 R	ASAP, and in any event by end of day following the day the company receives the information
City Code Rule 2.10	Offeror, offeree company and associates	RIS	Number of relevant securities in issue	ASAP after start of offer period, and in any event by 9am next business day (offeree) By 9am on business day after announcement of firm intention to make offer (offeror)
City Code Rule 8	Offeror, offeree company and associates	RIS and Panel	Any dealings in relevant securities	12 noon on business day following date of transaction

15.9 Future developments

The Transparency Directive, an important part of the Financial Services Action Plan, was adopted on 15 December 2004. It must be implemented in Member States by 20 January 2007. The Directive deals with the disclosure requirements of companies whose securities are admitted to trading on a regulated market. Parts of the Directive relate to the disclosure of major shareholdings, currently addressed by the CA 1985 (see **15.6**), the implementation of which requires primary legislation.

In order to implement the Transparency Directive, ss 198 to 211 of the CA 1985 are to be repealed and replaced by regulations made under the FSMA 2000. This has the advantage of bringing all the Transparency Directive obligations under one competent authority: the FSA.

On 30 March 2006 the FSA published a consultation paper setting out its proposed changes to the Listing Rules and Disclosure Rules to implement the Transparency Directive. The paper reveals the FSA's intention to implement the minimum requirements of the Transparency Directive in new Transparency Rules, which it will publish in the Disclosure Rules Sourcebook. The Sourcebook will then be renamed the Disclosure and Transparency Sourcebook. The FSA will set out in the Listing Rules any rules with which it chooses to supplement the minimum requirements of the Transparency Directive. The progress of the consultation process can be tracked on the FSA website.

The draft Companies Bill dated 20 July 2006 (see **1.11**):

(a) restates much of ss 212 to 219 of the CA 1985 (although unfortunately the Bill has not taken the opportunity to clarify what constitutes a 'reasonable time' to respond to a s 212 notice);

(b) gives the Secretary of State increased powers to investigate a company; and

(c) repeals ss 198 to 211 and ss 324 to 328 of the CA 1985.

Chapter 16
Financial Assistance

16.1	Introduction	213
16.2	Rationale	213
16.3	The financial assistance prohibition	214
16.4	What is financial assistance?	215
16.5	What is not financial assistance?	216
16.6	Whitewash	218
16.7	Sanctions	219
16.8	Conclusion	219
16.9	Future developments	219

16.1 Introduction

So far, **Part III** of this book has considered the concept of shares: what they are; the different classes of share; the law relating to share issues; and how a company can find out who owns its shares. This chapter, let us be clear, is still very much about shares. It considers a potential problem which can arise on the *acquisition* of shares; the problem that, subject to certain exceptions, a company cannot give 'financial assistance' for the purchase of its shares.

In its simplest form this means that if I want to buy shares in X plc, X plc cannot give me any financial help to buy those shares.

The rule itself is straightforward enough. So why is it described as a problem? In practice, financial assistance can arise in ways which are not easy to spot. In addition, the lawyer is often removed from the detail of the funding arrangements and is concentrating, instead, on the negotiation of the transaction. These two factors can conspire to make financial assistance an area that can inject an element of last-minute panic into a share acquisition that is otherwise running quite smoothly.

16.2 Rationale

To achieve a good understanding of the financial assistance rules, it can help to consider the rationale behind those rules. Why is financial assistance prohibited?

Let us consider a practical example of financial assistance. I am a financier and I want to buy a company. I lack significant funds. I find a company, X plc, which has substantial cash reserves and easily realisable assets (that is, they can be sold for cash readily). I agree to buy X plc for cash consideration. I am the buyer, and the shareholders of X plc are the sellers. I structure the transaction so that X plc uses its cash reserves, and cash realised from selling some of its assets, to advance me the cash I need to pay consideration to the shareholders of X plc. I then buy the company, but in effect X plc has funded the transaction.

Can you spot who has lost out in this transaction? Think of X plc's creditors. Their security is that X plc is cash-rich. This cash is now lining the pockets of the shareholders who sold shares in the company. It is no longer in X plc. X plc has misused its assets.

The prohibition on financial assistance would not permit the transaction described above. The reason? To protect creditors.

16.3 The financial assistance prohibition

Section 151 of the CA 1985 contains the prohibition on financial assistance. In fact, it actually contains two prohibitions, s 151(1) and (2), both of which relate to financial assistance. The difference between them is:

(a) s 151(1) applies to financial assistance given *before or at the same time as* the acquisition of shares; and

(b) s 151(2) applies to financial assistance given *after* the acquisition of shares.

16.3.1 Financial assistance given before or at the same time as the acquisition of shares

Section 151(1) provides that:

(a) where a person is acquiring or *proposing to acquire* shares in a company;
(b) it is not lawful for the company;
(c) or any of the company's *subsidiaries*;
(d) directly or indirectly;
(e) to give financial assistance;
(f) *for the purpose* of that acquisition;
(g) before or at the time the acquisition takes place.

The following points are of interest here:

(i) 'Proposing to acquire' means that there does not actually have to be an acquisition of shares for s 151(1) to apply; it is the fact that the person *intends* to acquire shares which is important.

(ii) The person giving the financial assistance (Assistor) does not necessarily have to be the company whose shares are being acquired (Target); if the Assistor is a subsidiary of Target, s 151(1) will apply.

(iii) 'For the purpose' (see (f) above) means that this is a purpose-based, not a results-based, test. It is not sufficient simply that financial assistance results in the acquisition, or is somehow connected with the acquisition. The Assistor must have *intended* to facilitate the transaction by giving the assistance. It is vital, therefore, to identify why the Assistor has provided the assistance.

16.3.2 Financial assistance given after the acquisition of shares

Section 151(2) provides that:

(a) where a person has acquired shares in a company;
(b) and any *liability has been incurred* (by that, *or any other*, person) for the purpose of that acquisition;
(c) it is not lawful for the company;
(d) or any of the company's *subsidiaries*;
(e) directly or indirectly;
(f) to give financial assistance;
(g) *for the purpose* of *reducing or discharging the liability incurred*.

Again, note the following points:

(i) Section 152(3)(a) provides that 'incurring a liability' includes a change in financial position (there is no indication that this change must be for the worse). The obvious example of this (and one which may be particularly familiar to anyone who has ever been a student) is someone borrowing money to fund an acquisition.

(ii) The liability does not have to have been incurred by the person acquiring the shares.

(iii) As with s 151(1), the Assistor does not have to be Target; if the Assistor is a subsidiary of Target, s 151(2) will apply.

(iv) As with s 151(1), the words 'for the purpose' feature in s 151(2) too. This means that the financial assistance does not actually have to reduce or discharge the liability incurred, as long as it was *intended* to reduce or discharge that liability. As with s 151(1), it is vital to identify why the Assistor has provided the assistance.

(v) Section 152(3)(b) provides that 'reducing or discharging the liability incurred' includes wholly or partly restoring a person's financial position to what it was before the acquisition.

16.4 What is financial assistance?

Section 152(1)(a) of the CA 1985 defines 'financial assistance' as:

(a) financial assistance given by way of:
  (i) gift (that is, where the Assistor transfers an asset of value for nil consideration),
  (ii) guarantee, security, indemnity (subject to a limited exception), or by way of release or waiver, or
  (iii) loan (or certain other types of agreement such as credit); and
(b) any other financial assistance given by a company:
  (i) the net assets (defined by s 152(2) as the actual value of assets less liabilities) of which are thereby reduced to a material extent (this is not defined, but appears to be a de-minimis level), or
  (ii) which has no net assets.

You will note that the 'definition' of financial assistance actually uses the words 'financial assistance'. Section 152(1)(a) therefore does not really define what financial assistance is, rather it gives examples of financial assistance.

Nethertheless, this definition makes clear that financial assistance is not limited to the more obvious situations, such as where the Assistor makes a gift or loan to the buyer to fund the acquisition of shares. Assistance of an indirect nature, such as when a bank gives a loan to the buyer to fund the acquisition, but the Assistor guarantees that loan or gives any type of security for it, will also constitute financial assistance. As mentioned in the introduction to this chapter at **16.1** above, these less obvious examples of financial assistance can cause problems for the corporate lawyer.

Example

Imagine a typical day in practice. X plc calls you, its lawyer, to instruct you in relation to a share disposal. X plc is selling the entire issued share capital of its wholly-owned subsidiary, Target plc, to Buyer plc. As seems to be the rule in practice, the acquisition must be completed urgently. X plc needs the cash consideration from the sale by the end of the month (three days' time) or it will go bust.

After cancelling all your plans for the weekend (again), you download your firm's precedent agreement and launch yourself into a series of meetings, first with your client, X plc, to find out the detail of the transaction, then with Buyer plc and its lawyers, to thrash out a deal.

Can you imagine how easy it is, in that first meeting with your client, for the client to say to you, 'We are selling all the shares in our subsidiary, Target plc. The buyer, Buyer plc, is paying a good price; it has secured a loan on really good terms from the bank', for you to make a note of this, then move on to more pressing areas of detail, such as the structure of the deal and the warranties X plc is prepared to give?

The next thing you know, you have worked 48 hours without sleep and have an agreement ready to sign. At that point, you receive a call from a colleague in your firm's banking department, who says he has just received a call from the assistant company secretary of Target plc, asking him to review the form of guarantee Target plc is giving to Buyer plc's bank.

Suddenly you have a problem. Target plc cannot give Buyer's bank a guarantee, as this would be financial assistance and prohibited under s 151(1). The bank will not provide the loan to Buyer plc unless it receives the guarantee from Target plc it was promised. Without the bank loan, Buyer plc cannot purchase the shares in Target plc. Without the consideration, X plc will go bust. You have to explain this problem to X plc.

How could this situation have been avoided? Well if, at that first meeting, you had probed a little more into the funding arrangements with Buyer plc's bank, you might have prompted the client to mention the bank guarantee. This is clear with hindsight, but can be very easy to miss in the rush to make a start on the acquisition agreement.

16.5 What is not financial assistance?

Section 153 of the CA 1985 provides exceptions to the financial assistance prohibition. These exceptions are considered below.

16.5.1 Sections 153(1) and 153(2): the purpose exceptions

It was explained at **16.3.1** and **16.3.2** above that purpose and intention are important when considering the prohibition on financial assistance. It should come as no surprise, then, to find that one of the exceptions to the financial assistance prohibition is concerned with purpose.

Section 153(1) provides that s 151(1) (that is, pre-acquisition financial assistance) does not prohibit the Assistor from giving financial assistance if:

(a) either:
  (i) the Assistor's *principal purpose* is not to give the financial assistance for the purpose of the acquisition (principal purpose exception), *or*
  (ii) the giving of the financial assistance for the purpose of the acquisition was only an incidental part of some *larger purpose* of the Assistor (larger purpose exception); *and*
(b) the Assistor gives the financial assistance in good faith in the interests of the Assistor.

Section 153(2) provides principal purpose and larger purpose exceptions for financial assistance under s 151(2) too (that is, post-acquisition financial assistance), but the words 'the acquisition' (see (a)(i) and (ii) above) are replaced with 'reducing or discharging the liability which has been incurred'.

The 'principal purpose' and 'larger purpose' exceptions are somewhat vague, and it is difficult for the lawyer to be able to state definitively that they will apply. The decision in *Brady v Brady* [1989] AC 755 has made the application of the purpose exceptions even less clear.

16.5.1.1 *Brady v Brady*

In this case, an arrangement was made in good faith to divide a family company's assets into two new companies, so that the two brothers who ran the family company could go their separate ways. The arrangement involved the family company giving financial assistance, as Assistor. At first instance, it was held that while the arrangement was prohibited by s 151(1), it was saved by the larger purpose exception; the Assistor's giving of the assistance for the purpose of the acquisition was only an incidental part of the Assistor's *larger purpose*. The House of Lords, however, did not agree that the exception applied.

16.5.1.2 The principal purpose exception

In *Brady v Brady*, Lord Oliver explained that, for this exception to apply, there must be a principal and a secondary purpose behind the giving of the financial assistance. For example, if the principal purpose of the Assistor is to obtain an asset that it really wants, but the secondary purpose is to put the person who is willing to sell the asset in a position to acquire shares in the company, then, as long as the Assistor genuinely enters into the transaction in the belief that it is in the Assistor's best interests, the transaction will fall within the exception. There may be difficulties, however, in proving that the secondary purpose was not, in fact, the primary purpose.

16.5.1.3 The larger purpose exception

This exception covers transactions where the financial assistance is intended but it is incidental to the Assistor's 'larger purpose'. As outlined at **16.5.1.1** above, the House of Lords has interpreted this exception very narrowly and, as such, it is largely ignored by practising lawyers.

16.5.2 Section 153(3): specific 'common sense' exceptions

Section 153(3) permits the following (which all involve stripping value out of the company) on the basis that they are not anything against which creditors require protection:

(a) a dividend lawfully made – this would allow, for example, the Assistor to pay a pre-sale dividend to its shareholders before its shares are sold (this may have tax benefits, as it allows shareholders to take some of the value of the company as income not capital);

(b) a distribution in a winding up;

(c) the allotment of bonus shares;

(d) a reduction of capital confirmed by a s 137 court order;

(e) a lawful redemption or purchase of own shares;

(f) schemes of arrangement made pursuant to a s 425 court order;

(g) anything done pursuant to an arrangement under s 110 of the Insolvency Act 1986 (this will cover a liquidator accepting shares as consideration for property sold in a winding up); and

(h) anything done pursuant to a voluntary arrangement made between the company and its creditors.

16.5.3 Section 153(4): money lending and employee exceptions

Section 153(4) provides the following exceptions:

(a) the lending of money by money lending companies in the ordinary course of their business;

(b) where the financial assistance is given in good faith to fund an employee share scheme; and

(c) loans to bona fide employees (not directors) to allow them to buy shares in the company, or its holding company (no share scheme is required for the exception to apply).

The s 154 proviso

Section 154 adds a proviso to the application of the s 153(4) exemptions where the Assistor is a public company. If the Assistor is a public company, it can rely on the s 153(4) exemptions only if the company has *net assets*:

(a) which are not thereby reduced; or

(b) to the extent those assets are thereby reduced, the assistance is provided out of distributable profits.

Note that net assets are defined as the *book value* of assets less liabilities (that is, their value for accounting purposes). This is different to the definition of net assets for the purposes of s 152(1)(a) (see **16.4** above), where the definition is the *actual value* of net assets less liabilities. (Liabilities are defined by s 152(1)(b) and distributable profits by s 152(1)(c).)

16.6 Whitewash

It has already been highlighted at **16.5.3** above that the financial assistance rules are more relaxed for private companies, in that a private company is not subject to the s 154 proviso. There is, however, another major difference in the way the financial assistance rules apply to private companies compared with public companies, namely the whitewash procedure under s 155 of the CA 1985. If this procedure is followed, any financial assistance is 'whitewashed'. This means that there has been financial assistance, but it is not prohibited by s 151 of the CA 1985. The procedure is only available, however, if:

(a) Target is not a plc; and

(b) (if the Assistor is not Target but a subsidiary of Target) there is no plc between the Assistor and Target in the company structure.

As the focus of this book is on public companies, and in particular on listed companies, there is no need to consider the whitewash procedure in any detail here. However, be aware that, in dire straits, there is always the option of re-registering a public company as a private company, under s 53 of the CA 1985, so that the company is a private company at the time the financial assistance is given, and that financial assistance can then be whitewashed. This is, of course, a little extreme, and certainly would not be appropriate in the case of a listed company. Another book in the series (see *Business Law and Practice*) considers the whitewash procedure in detail.

16.7 Sanctions

16.7.1 Criminal sanctions

Section 151(3) provides that breach of the prohibition on financial assistance is a criminal offence. The company is liable to a fine, and any officer in default is liable to a fine and/or imprisonment.

16.7.2 Consequences for the share acquisition

The acquisition will be void and unenforceable (*Brady v Brady*) unless the offending term can be severed from any acquisition agreement (*Carney v Herbert* [1985] AC 301). The directors who were parties to the breach are liable to compensate their company for any loss it has incurred. Any third party who received the financial assistance may be required to account for any cash or assets received in breach of s 151 (*Belmont Finance Corp Ltd v Williams Furniture Ltd (No 2)* [1980] 1 All ER 393).

16.8 Conclusion

The prohibition on financial assistance has the potential to cause serious problems with share acquisitions. It is particularly problematic in relation to public companies, where the financial assistance cannot be whitewashed.

The key is to consider the issue of financial assistance as soon as possible in any share acquisition transaction. This will involve asking questions about how the transaction is funded. Finally, if financial assistance is an issue, the purpose exceptions should be applied with caution, in the light of *Brady v Brady*.

16.9 Future developments

The law relating to financial assistance is not easy to understand, and leads to uncertainty. As a result, companies are forced to spend considerable time and effort obtaining legal advice on the meaning of the current law. As such the area is ripe for reform.

On 29 October 2004 the European Commission announced a proposal for a directive to amend the Second Company Law Directive (79/91/EEC). The proposal is part of the Commission's *Action Plan on Company Law and Corporate Governance* and aims to reduce some procedural restrictions which apply to public companies. The full text of the proposal is available at www.europa.eu.int. One of the proposed amendments is a (partial) relaxation of the prohibition on public companies providing financial assistance if the level of assistance does not exceed distributable reserves (and the transaction meets various other requirements aimed at protecting shareholders and creditors).

The Companies Bill (see **1.11**) addresses some of the problems posed by the current financial assistance provisions, as it abolishes the prohibition on financial assistance in relation to private companies. Public companies, unfortunately, must continue to struggle with the financial assistance regime, and the Bill does nothing to resolve many of the issues which cause concern. Even the definition of 'financial assistance' remains vague.

Chapter 17

Equity Finance

17.1	Background	221
17.2	What is equity finance?	221
17.3	Why a company needs equity finance	222
17.4	Listed company rules and regulations	222
17.5	Equity finance documentation	224
17.6	Methods of raising equity finance	227
17.7	Rights issue	228
17.8	Open offer	237
17.9	Placing	239
17.10	Acquisition issue	240
17.11	Vendor consideration placing	242

17.1 Background

Part I of this book considered the flotation process, that is (for the purposes of this book) how a company can admit its shares to listing on the Official List and to trading on the Main Market.

A company seeking to float can obtain a listing in four different ways:

(a) an offer for sale and/or subscription;

(b) a placing;

(c) an intermediaries offer; or

(d) a simple admission.

These methods were considered in some detail in **Chapter 4**.

Chapter 1 explained that one of the advantages of flotation is that, after flotation, a listed company can raise further finance through shares ('equity finance') in a way that an unlisted company cannot. This chapter explores the various methods by which a listed company can seek a listing for further share capital, in order to raise equity finance.

17.2 What is equity finance?

Equity finance involves a company using its equity, namely securities (and more specifically for our purposes, shares), in order to raise finance. An example of a company raising equity finance is when it issues shares in return for cash, or in exchange for an asset.

As you will realise on reading this chapter, equity finance involves both:

(a) the issue of shares; and

(b) the listing of those shares.

It is the listing of those shares which gives them their value. The issue and listing of shares in a listed company in this way is often referred to as a 'secondary issue'. The 'primary issue' is when the company floats and its issued shares are listed for the first time. Subsequent issues of shares, and the listing of those shares, are therefore 'secondary issues'. (Be aware that this terminology can be confusing, as sometimes the term 'primary issue' is used to describe any issue of shares by the company, and the term 'secondary issue' is used to refer to a sale (transfer) by a shareholder of existing shares. However, for the purposes of this book, the terminology is given the meanings outlined above: a 'primary issue' is an issue of shares by the company on flotation; and a 'secondary issue' is any subsequent issue of shares by the company.)

When a company raises equity finance, then, the lawyer must be aware of, and be able to apply, not only the law which relates specifically to the raising of equity finance, but also the wider set of rules and regulations which apply to listed companies:

(a) generally;
(b) on the issue of shares; and
(c) on the admission of those shares to listing and trading.

This chapter looks at the law which relates specifically to the raising of equity finance. However, at **17.4** below there below is a brief reminder of the other rules and regulations which relate to (a), (b) and (c) above, and an indication of where you can read about them in this book.

17.3 Why a company needs equity finance

There are numerous reasons why a company might want to raise equity finance. Just like us, it may want to pay off debt, buy something, or just make its bank balance look a little healthier. Unlike us, it may be concerned about gearing (its ratio of debt to equity). By increasing the amount of share capital in issue, the company will improve its gearing ratio without having to repay any debt. This may enhance the company's ability to borrow in the future. The company will also have the option to use the cash proceeds from the rights issue to pay off debt, which will improve the company's gearing even more. **Chapter 18** considers the concept of gearing. It also considers briefly the concept of debt finance, and examines the issues a company will take into account in deciding whether to raise equity or debt finance.

17.4 Listed company rules and regulations

17.4.1 General rules

The general rules relating to listed companies are set out in **Part II** of this book. The general obligation of disclosure under the Disclosure Rules (see **7.4.1**) and the continuing obligations of the Listing Rules, relating to the disclosure of new issues (see **7.5.5** above) and communicating with shareholders in relation to new issues (see **7.7** above), are particularly relevant to any company seeking to raise equity finance. The lawyer must also be alert to any suggestion that the issue might fall foul of the rules relating to corporate governance (see **Chapter 8**), misleading statements and market manipulation (see **Chapter 9**), market abuse (see **Chapter 10**) or insider dealing (see **Chapter 11**). Finally, the lawyer must ensure that the issue is not marketed in a way which would breach the financial promotion rules of the FSMA 2000 (see **Chapter 12**).

17.4.2 Issuing shares

Part III of this book considers the rules of the CA 1985, the Prospectus Rules, the Listing Rules, the City Code, the SARs and the ABI Guidelines and the Pre-Emption Guidelines which relate to the issue of shares. The following are particularly important, from the company's perspective, when raising equity finance.

17.4.2.1 The Companies Act 1985

Sections 80, 89, 95, 103, 121 and 123 of the CA 1985 are all relevant to the issue of shares (see **Chapter 14**). The 1985 Act also sets out the procedure which companies must follow if a share issue will vary the class rights of any existing shares. Again, this may be relevant in an equity finance transaction (see **13.7** above). Finally, the issue must be structured in a way which does not cause the company to fall foul of the prohibition on financial assistance (see **Chapter 16**).

17.4.2.2 The Listing Rules

Listing Rules 9.3.11R and 9.3.12R set out the pre-emption rights provisions which are relevant on an issue of shares (see **14.6.12** above).

17.4.2.3 Guidelines and principles

Institutional investors such as the ABI impose their own requirements relating to the issue of shares. These requirements do not have the force of law, but they are significant because listed companies do not want to get on the wrong side of their largest shareholders. **Chapter 14** considers the ABI Guidelines (see **14.5.7**) and the Statement of Principles of the Pre-Emption Group (see **14.6.16**) which are relevant on an issue of shares.

17.4.3 Admitting new shares to listing and trading

Part I of this book considered the listing of shares on a flotation. Many of the issues addressed by **Part I** are also relevant to the listing of shares on a secondary issue.

It was explained at **4.3.1.1** above that a company cannot choose to list only part of a class of shares. It must list all of the shares in a class. So, if a listed company proposes to issue more shares *of a class which is already listed*, it must seek admission to listing on the Official List and admission to trading on the Main Market in respect of those shares. As mentioned above, this is not only a requirement of the Listing Rules, it also makes the issues commercially attractive, as listing gives the shares value.

In relation to the listing aspects of a secondary issue, the lawyer must be aware of the following rules and regulations:

(a) *The FSMA 2000.* Part VI of the FSMA 2000 sets out the rules relating to the listing of shares. Sections 87A (general duty of disclosure) and 90 (compensation for loss) are particularly important. See **Chapter 6**.

(b) *The Prospectus Rules.* The requirement for a prospectus under the Prospectus Rules is discussed at **17.5.1** below. The requirement for a prospectus on flotation was considered in **Chapter 6**. The prospectus and accompanying documents must be submitted to the FSA as required by the Prospectus Rules (see **5.3.6.1** and **5.3.6.2** above; but note that the submission date for a secondary issue is 10 business days before the prospectus is due to be published (impact day), rather than the 20 working days required for a float).

(c) *The Listing Rules.* A formal application for admission of the shares to the Official List must be made to the FSA under the Listing Rules. This involves a process very similar to that set out at **5.3.6.4** to **5.3.6.7** above, in the context of a float, namely the submission of:

(i) '48 hour' documents;

(ii) 'on the day' documents (note the documents differ on a secondary issue to those required for a float; a pricing statement, rather than a shareholder statement signed by the sponsor, is required – see LR 3.3.3R); and

(iii) certain information following admission.

Where the requirements are the same as those for a float, see **5.3.6** for further detail. Any raising of equity finance will be made conditional upon admission to listing (for our purposes, on the Official List). Admission will be effective when the FSA makes it Official List announcement (see **5.4.3.1**).

(d) *The Admission and Disclosure Standards*. A formal application for admission of the shares to the Main Market must be made to the Stock Exchange under the Admission and Disclosure Standards. Again, the process involved practically mirrors that required for the application for admission to trading set out in **5.3.7** in relation to a float, namely the submission of:

(i) an application for admission to trading (note that for a secondary issue this is submitted with the other two-day documents, rather than 10 days in advance, as on a float);

(ii) various two-day documents;

(iii) an invoice; and

(iv) certain information following admission.

Where the requirements are the same as those for a float, see **5.3.6** for further detail. Any raising of equity finance will be made conditional upon admission to trading (for our purposes, on the Main Market). Again, admission will be effective when the Stock Exchange makes an announcement on its website (see **5.4.3.1**).

Note that, in the context of a rights issue, once the shares have been admitted to listing and trading nil paid, no further application is required to admit the shares fully paid.

17.5 Equity finance documentation

The lawyer spends much of his time drafting, and therefore any lawyer will need to know what documentation is required on a secondary issue. Specific documentation required for each method of raising equity finance considered by this chapter is detailed at **17.7** to **17.11** below. However, the reason these documents are required is explained below.

17.5.1 Prospectus

As referred to at **6.4**, the effect of PR 1.2.1UK and s 85 of the FSMA 2000 is that, if the company wishes to do either or both of the following:

(a) *offer* transferable securities *to the public* in *the UK* (s 85(1)); or

(b) request *admission* of transferable securities *to trading* on a regulated market situated or operating *in the UK* (even if there is no offer to the public) (s 85(2)),

an FSA-approved prospectus is required.

Section 85(5) of the FSMA 2000 (which in turn refers to Sch 11A to the FSMA and PR 1.2.2R) and s 86 of the FSMA 2000 set out various circumstances when an *offer to the public* will not require a prospectus. Section 85(6) (which in turn refers to Sch 11A to the FSMA and PR 1.2.3R) sets out the circumstances when an *admission to trading* will not require a prospectus.

These rules apply equally to a secondary issue as they do to a flotation (see **6.4** above). Under the old regime, the content requirement for any prospectus relating to a secondary issue was significantly less than that required for a flotation prospectus. This is no longer the case. As set out at **6.5.2** above, the content requirements are prescribed by the articles and annexes of the PD Regulation (which are set out at PR 2.3.1EU and PR Appendix 3). For a secondary issue of ordinary shares the appropriate schedules will be the share schedules (Annexes I and III) and the pro forma financial information building block (Annex II), so the level of disclosure required in any prospectus relating to a secondary issue of ordinary shares is exactly the same as for a prospectus relating to a flotation of ordinary shares. An approved supplementary prospectus (see **6.9.4**) will also be required if, during the rights issue period, there arises or is noted any significant new factor, material mistake or inaccuracy relating to the information included in the approved prospectus. This supplementary prospectus will trigger statutory withdrawal rights under s 87Q of the FSMA 2000 (see **6.9.4**). Issue 11 of *List!* confirms that the right to withdraw will cease when shareholders pay up their subscription in full.

The only difference is that the exemptions, unlikely to be relevant in the context of a flotation (see **6.4.3**), may apply on a secondary issue, depending on its circumstances, with the effect that a prospectus is not required. Clearly, if the lawyer can structure a secondary issue so that no prospectus is required, this will save the company considerable time and expense. The table at **Figure 17.1** below analyses whether the exemptions are likely to apply to a rights issue, open offer, placing, acquisition issue or vendor consideration placing. As you can see, it is likely that only a placing, acquisition issue or vendor consideration placing can be structured in a way which avoids the need to prepare a prospectus. Those familiar with the old regime will note that the fact that most rights issues and open offers will now require a full prospectus is a significant change, and will add considerably to the task of advising on a secondary issue, which in turn will render these methods much more expensive for the company.

Table 17.1

Method of equity finance	Public offer under s 85(1)?	Admission to trading under s 85(2)?	Prospectus required?
Rights issue	Yes. Unlikely to benefit from any exemption. (As a pre-emptive offer made to all shareholders, is unlikely to benefit from the '100 persons' or 'qualified investors' exemptions).	Yes, however small rights issues may be structured so that '10%' exemption applies.	Yes.
Open offer	As for rights issue.	As for rights issue.	As for rights issue.

Method of equity finance	Public offer under s 85(1)?	Admission to trading under s 85(2)?	Prospectus required?
Placing	Yes (note that LR Appendix 1.1 defines a placing as *not* constituting a public offer; however, this appears to be unconnected to the definition of a public offer under the FSMA 2000 (see **6.4.1.3**). Likely to benefit from 'qualified investor' or '100 persons' exemption.	Yes, however small placings may be structured so that '10%' exemption applies.	Yes, unless structured so that is exempt from the requirement for a prospectus.
Acquisition issue	May benefit from 'qualified investor' or '100 persons' exemption, depending on target shareholder profile.	Yes, however small rights issues may be structured so that '10%' exemption applies.	Yes, unless structured so that is exempt from the requirement for a prospectus. (Where shares are issued in the context of a takeover, the publication of a document the FSA deems to be 'equivalent to' a prospectus will suffice – see **22.4.4.2**.)
Vendor consideration placing	As for acquisition issue.	As for acquisition issue.	As for acquisition issue.

17.5.2 Press announcement

The press announcement will announce the issue to the market. It will contain all material information about the issue, and any related acquisition.

17.5.3 RIS notification

Any new issue of listed securities must be notified to an RIS under the specific disclosure requirements of the Listing Rules (see **7.5.5.2** above).

17.5.4 Circular

The Listing Rules require the company to communicate to its shareholders by way of circular on a new issue (see **7.5.2.2** above). This may take the form of a notice of EGM, and incorporate by reference information in any prospectus. The circular must conform with the requirements of LR 13.3 (see **7.7.3**).

In practice, often the requirement for the circular is met by the propspectus, which will contain all the information required to be in the circular. However, the prospectus also contains an offer of securities, which can cause problems with regard to draconian securities law in certain overseas jurisdictions. Often, the solution is not to send the prospectus to such jurisdictions. A circular, however, must be sent to overseas shareholders (LR 9.3.1R and 9.3.2G). If there are overseas shareholders therefore, the company is likely to prepare both a prospectus and a separate circular.

17.5.5 Sale and purchase agreement

If the company is issuing shares as consideration for the acquisition of a non-cash asset, such as shares in another company, then a sale and purchase agreement (also referred to as an acquisition agreement, an S&P or an SPA) will be required for the transfer of that asset.

17.5.6 Underwriting agreement

The concept of underwriting in the context of a float was introduced at **4.2.7** above. It is also relevant on a secondary issue. In return for a fee, the underwriters will agree to take up any shares which are not subscribed for. The underwriting agreement will record the agreement between the company and the underwriter.

17.5.7 Placing agreement

If the chosen method of raising equity finance involves a placing of shares, a placing agreement will also be necessary (see **4.4.1.2** above).

17.6 Methods of raising equity finance

As **17.1** above explained, a company issuing shares on flotation is restricted to four methods of issue. However, once listed, a company can bring securities to listing using a wider variety of methods.

The main methods by which a company can raise equity finance once it is listed are:

(a) a rights issue (LR 9.5.1R to LR 9.5.6R);
(b) an open offer (LR 9.5.7 to LR 9.5.8R);
(c) a placing (Appendix 1 of the Listing Rules);
(d) an acquisition issue ; and
(e) a vendor consideration placing (LR 9.5.9).

These methods are considered in detail at **17.7** to **17.11** below, and we examine why a company might choose one method rather than another. Specific documentation required for each method is also set out.

Note that some of the less common methods of raising equity finance are not discussed in detail in this chapter. Two of these, an offer (for sale and/or subscription) and an intermediaries offer, are considered in **Chapters 4** and **6**, albeit in the context of a flotation rather than a secondary issue.

Chapter 9 of the Listing Rules contains the rules relating to the methods by which secondary issues can be listed.

17.7 Rights issue

17.7.1 What is a rights issue?

A rights issue was referred to at **14.6.12** above, when considering pre-emption rights. Appendix 1.1 of the Listing Rules defines a rights issue. Basically, it is:

(a) an offer to issue new shares or transfer existing shares (or other securities);
(b) to existing shareholders (or security holders) in proportion to their existing holdings;
(c) made by way of the issue of a renounceable letter;
(d) which may be traded 'nil paid' for a period before payment for the shares (or other securities) is due.

For example, a company could offer to issue two shares to each shareholder for every one share that shareholder already holds.

17.7.2 Price

The shares are usually allotted for cash, at a discount to the market price of the existing shares. Why is that? Well, if the company is going to raise finance, it requires shareholders to take up their rights under the rights issue and pay the cash consideration for the shares to the company. This means that the price for the shares must be better (that is, cheaper) than the price of buying shares on the open market. If it is not, the shareholders might choose to buy shares on the market instead, in which case they will pay the selling shareholder, not the company, for the shares.

Occasionally a company will make what is known as a 'deep-discount rights issue', when it issues shares at a substantial discount to market value. It may do this so that it does not have to pay for the issue to be underwritten (because no shareholder is likely to refuse to take up the rights) (see **17.7.5**), although it is becoming increasingly common for even deeply discounted rights issues to be underwritten where certainty of funds is important (eg, the Royal Sun Alliance rights issue in 2003). Issuing shares at a deep discount will make the issue more attractive to shareholders, so it can increase the chances of success of the rights issue in a weak market (which, in turn, can help to reduce any underwriting costs, as the company may be able to negotiate lower fees with the underwriter to reflect the reduced risk that shareholders will not take up the shares).

Note that, as long as the price exceeds the nominal value of the share (s 100 of the CA 1985), there is no legal limit to the discount at which the company can sell the shares. As explained at **14.6.16**, the Pre-Emption Group's Statement of Principles does not apply if the company observes the pre-emption requirements of the Listing Rules. In practice, the rule of thumb is that companies can discount by up to 50%, a typical discount being 15–20%, and a deep discount being 45–50%.

One disadvantage of the discount applied to shares is that it tends to cause a drop in the market value of the shares for a period following the rights issue.

17.7.3 Structure

17.7.3.1 The PAL

The offer is made by way of a renounceable letter, known as a provisional allotment letter (PAL). This does exactly what its name suggests: it provisionally allots to the shareholder his pro rata entitlement of shares. The PAL will provide details of the rights issue, including the number of shares to which the shareholder is entitled and the price of those shares. As a temporary document of title, the PAL must comply with the requirements of LR 9.5.15R.

On receiving the PAL, the shareholder can:

(a) renounce the rights and sell them on to a third party, nil paid;
(b) take up the rights, by subscribing for the shares;
(c) combine (a) and (b), by taking up some rights and renouncing the rest; or
(d) do nothing.

17.7.3.2 Renouncing the rights to subscribe

Rationale

If the shareholder takes up the rights, he ensures that his existing percentage shareholding is not diluted. However, if the shareholder renounces the rights, he risks the dilution of his shareholding. So why would a shareholder renounce the right to subscribe for shares? Usually the motivation is financial.

> **Example**
>
> Imagine that shares in X plc have a current market value of £2 each. X plc gives its shareholders the right to subscribe for more shares, in proportion to their existing shareholdings, for £1.60 per share (that is, at a discount of 20%). The right to subscribe has a value, therefore, of 40p per share. However, the fact that the market value in the shares is likely to drop (see 17.7.2 above) must be taken into account. Imagine that the market value drops to £1.95. If the shareholder renounces his rights and sells them for 35p each, he will have made a profit of 35p per share (less any dealing costs). If the shareholder has, say, 1,000 shares, he can make £350 with no capital outlay. He might consider that this makes diluting his shareholding worthwhile.
>
> (Note, however, that the shareholder may incur an immediate capital gains tax charge if he sells his rights. If he exercised the rights, however, capital gains tax would arise only on a subsequent disposal of the shares.)

The shareholder wishing to renounce and sell rights should not find it too difficult to find a buyer for those rights, as the buyer will be able to buy shares from the shareholder at the market value, here £1.95. The buyer will pay £1.60 per share to the company under the rights issue, plus 35p per share to the shareholder for the right to subscribe. Of course, the risk to the buyer is that the market price drops further.

> **Example**
>
> Imagine the market price of shares in X plc drops not to £1.95, but to £1.50. The buyer has already paid 35p per share to the selling shareholder for the right to subscribe and must pay an additional £1.60 to the company for shares he can buy in the market for £1.50. In this case, the buyer will probably cut his losses; while he cannot claim back the price he has paid to the selling shareholder for the right to subscribe, he can avoid paying the remaining £1.60 to the company simply by not exercising the right, and letting it lapse.

Nil paid dealings

So how does the shareholder renounce and trade his rights to subscribe? The PAL is negotiable, which means that it can be transferred by delivery. As **17.7.4** below explains, the offer must be open for at least 21 days. 'Nil paid dealings' can take place during this 21-day period. This means that a shareholder can trade the rights to subscribe simply by signing the PAL and passing it on to someone else. These dealings are referred to as 'nil paid dealings' because trading takes place before any subscription monies have been paid. The third party can then exercise the right to subscribe in the manner described at **17.7.3.3** below. It is on the admission of the shares to trading in nil paid form that the FSA will grant admission of the shares to the Official List (LR 9.5.3G). (Once the shares are paid up, and the allotment becomes unconditional, there is no need for a further listing application).

17.7.3.3 Taking up the rights to subscribe

Before the end of the offer period, those people who hold rights to subscribe, and wish to exercise them, must submit the consideration and the PAL to the company's receiving agents, if they have not already done so. At the end of the offer period, the right will lapse.

17.7.3.4 Taking up some rights and renouncing the rest

As mentioned at **17.7.3.1**, the shareholder may choose to take up some rights (using the procedure outlined at **17.7.3.3**) and renounce the remainder (using the process outlined at **17.7.3.2**). The proceeds received from trading some of the rights may help to finance the purchase of the balance of these rights (known as 'tail swallowing').

17.7.3.5 Doing nothing

Even lazy shareholders can benefit from a rights issue, because arrangements are made for the sale of any shares not taken up. Even if a shareholder does not take up the shares and does not trade the PAL, he may still receive a cash payment to the extent that the shares which were provisionally allotted to him are sold in the market for more than their subscription price (LR 9.5.4R).

17.7.4 Timing

The FSA does not allow listed shares to be allotted provisionally on a conditional basis. This means that if any shareholder approvals are required in relation to the issue (such as to increase the share capital, or give the directors authority to allot – see **Chapter 14**), the PALs can be posted only after all necessary shareholder approvals have been obtained at the EGM. Once the PALs are posted, LR 9.5.6R provides that the offer must remain open for at least 21 days (if s 89 of the CA 1985 has not been disapplied (see **17.7.6**) then the effect of s 90(6) of the Act is that the offer must be open for 21 clear days – see *Re Hector Whaling Ltd* [1935] All ER 302).

The combination of the time required for the EGM notice, added to the subsequent minimum offer period of 21 days (under the Listing Rules) or 21 clear days (under s 89), means that a rights issue is a relatively lengthy method of raising equity finance. This, of course, delays the receipt by the company of its consideration for the issue, and increases underwriting costs (see **17.7.5** below).

17.7.5 Underwriting

The role of underwriters on a flotation was explored at **4.2.7** above. The process of underwriting is equally relevant to a secondary issue. The underwriters (usually a merchant bank or broker) basically guarantee that the company will receive the equity finance it seeks, by agreeing to take up, at no less than the subscription price under the rights issue, any shares which are not taken up by shareholders and which cannot be sold in the market (including fractional entitlements if s 89 has been disapplied – see **17.7.6.1**). These shares are referred to as 'the rump'. As explained at **17.7.3.5**, any premium received over the subscription price must be given to the person to whom the shares were provisionally allotted.

The underwriters must buy any of the rump which is left (that is, which they have been unable to sell). These shares are referred to as 'the stick'. The stick represents the underwriter's risk, and the underwriter will try to predict what the stick, and therefore the risk, will be, in calculating his commission (see **17.7.5.1** at (a) below). As with a flotation, it is common for a secondary issue to be sub-underwritten either in part, or in its entirety.

17.7.5.1 The underwriting agreement

The underwriting arrangements will be recorded in an underwriting agreement, which typically includes the following:

(a) *Details about the commission payable.* Underwriting costs increase with the length of time for which the underwriter is 'on risk' to take up shares, because the longer the period, the less certain the underwriter can be about how the market in those shares will move. The higher the risk for the underwriter, the more the underwriter will charge for his services. With a rights issue, the underwriter is 'on risk' for a considerable period of time (see **17.7.4** above); therefore the underwriting costs can be high. A typical underwriting agreement might provide, for example, that the underwriter's fees will be 2% of the amount underwritten for the first 30 days of the rights issue, and a further commission of 0.125% of the aggregate amount raised in respect of any further period.

(b) *Conditions.* These will include the passing of any necessary resolutions at an EGM and the admission of the shares to the Official List and the Main Market, nil paid (known as the 'admission condition').

(c) *Representations and warranties from the company.* Breach of these may give rise to the right to terminate the agreement, in addition to damages.

(d) *Material adverse change (MAC) clause and force majeure clause.* These clauses will allow the underwriter to terminate the agreement in certain circumstances.

As stated at **17.7.4**, the FSA does not allow listed shares to be allotted provisionally on a conditional basis. This means that underwriters should not have any right to terminate their underwriting obligation once the nil paid rights have been admitted. Issue 12 of *List!* states that the FSA has been asking companies to confirm that their underwriting arrangements do not allow the underwriters to invoke withdrawal rights (see **6.9.4** and **17.5.1**) under any circumstances.

17.7.6 Pre-emption rights

A rights issue is a pre-emptive offer, that is, it is in accordance with the statutory pre-emption rights on allotment under s 89 of the CA 85; the company is issuing *equity securities* (for our purposes, ordinary shares) to holders of *relevant shares* (the ordinary shareholders), in proportion to the nominal value of their existing shareholdings, in return for cash consideration (see **14.6.5**).

As the issue is in accordance with s 89, there is no requirement to disapply s 89; however, the company must comply with s 90 of the CA 1985, which sets out how to make the offer. In particular, the offer:

(a) must be in writing (s 90(2));

(b) must be made either personally, or by post to the shareholder's registered address in the UK (s 90(2));

(c) if made by post, will be deemed to be made at the time at which the letter would be *delivered* in the ordinary course of post (s 90(2)); and

(d) must state a period of not less than 21 days clear during which it can be accepted (s 90(6)) (see **17.7.4**).

However, having said that there is no *legal requirement* to disapply s 89 for a rights issue, *in practice* typically s 89 is disapplied, for the reasons set out at **17.7.6.1** to **17.7.6.5** below. As explained at **14.6.15**, for this reason typically listed companies effect a general disapplication of the statutory pre-emption rights (that is, s 89) at each AGM, in a way which allows directors to make small rights issues provided they follow the pre-emption rights in the Listing Rules (see **17.7.6.5**). Remember, however, that any existing s 89 disapplication will relate to an existing s 80 authority (see **14.6.14.3**). If the rights issue requires a new s 80 authority (because the existing s 80 authority has expired in terms of time or number of shares) then the existing s 89 disapplication will be of no use. If this is the case, the company will balance the benefit of obtaining a new s 89 disapplication, specifically for the issue, as considered at **17.7.6.1** to **17.7.6.6** below, against the burden of a delay in the timetable (disapplication of s 89 requires a special resolution, while the other consents which may be required to increase the authorised share capital and obtain a new s 80 authority require only an ordinary resolution) and the extra underwriting costs.

The differences outlined below should be familiar to you from **14.6.12**.

17.7.6.1 Fractional entitlements

If the company offered shareholders their exact proportional entitlements under a rights issue, the calculation may entitle some shareholders to fractions of shares. The CA 1985 is unclear as to how a company should deal with fractional entitlements, so, in practice, the company rounds down each shareholder's entitlement to the nearest whole share. The fractional entitlements which have not been offered have the potential to raise further finance, if the company can aggregate them and sell the aggregate. Unfortunately, the CA 1985 is not clear as to whether fractional entitlements are covered by s 89. Selling the aggregate might infringe the existing shareholders' pre-emption rights. However, if those pre-emption rights are disapplied, the company can sell the aggregate fractional entitlements. The company will take the subscription price, but will account to the shareholders for any premium over the subscription price which it receives.

Example

The company has 500,000 shareholders. One of them, X, holds 302 shares. The company announces a '1 for 3' rights issue, that is 1 new share is offered for every 3 shares held. Strictly X is entitled to 100 shares plus two-thirds of a share (302 divided by 3).

However, as the CA 1985 is unclear as to whether fractional entitlements can be allocated, the company rounds down X's entitlement to 100 shares. This leaves two-thirds of a share unissued. A similar situation has arisen for most of the other 499,999 shareholders, so that, together with X's two-thirds of a share, there is an aggregate of, say, 200,000 shares unissued.

If s 89 applies to the issue, it is thought that selling these 200,000 shares to a third party may infringe the pre-emptive right of X (to his two-thirds of a share) and of each of the other existing shareholders (to their respective fractional entitlements), so the company cannot do anything with these shares.

However, if s 89 is disapplied, these shares can be sold to one or more third parties, raising further finance for the company. The company will take the subscription price for the 200,000 shares. Any premium received for the shares will be shared out equally among the 1,000 original shareholders.

17.7.6.2 Overseas shareholders

Certain jurisdictions, such as Japan, Canada and the USA, have draconian security laws. These laws mean that it is so expensive to make an offer of securities in those jurisdictions, companies prefer not to make an offer there. If the pre-emption rights have not been disapplied and the company has shareholders in those jurisdictions, the company has a problem. Section 90 of the CA 1985 does provide for this situation; it allows companies to make an offer to those overseas shareholders by way of a notice in the *Gazette*. However, companies often prefer instead to disapply the pre-emption rights, and arrange for the entitlements of those shareholders to be aggregated and sold in the market, nil-paid. Any premium the company receives over the subscription price will then be given to those overseas shareholders.

17.7.6.3 Convertible securities

If a company has issued shares and the terms of those shares state that they will entitle the shareholder to pre-emption rights, but under the CA 1985 the holder is not entitled to pre-emption rights (because the shares do not fall within the definition of 'relevant shares': see **14.6.8** above), the company must disapply s 89. This will ensure that the company will be able to make the rights issue to those shareholders, in accordance with the terms of the shares.

Example

The company has in issue convertible loan stock. The terms of the loan stock state that the holders of the stock are entitled to pre-emption rights on any rights issue. However, under s 89, convertible loan stock does not fall within the definition of relevant shares (it is not a share), and so, under s 89 the loan stock does not entitle its holders to pre-emption rights. There is a conflict. It would be very difficult to change the terms of the stock, so instead s 89 is disapplied to resolve the conflict; and the rights issue is offered to the holders of the convertible loan stock.

17.7.6.4 Offer period

If s 89 of the CA 1985 is not disapplied, s 90 will govern the terms of the rights issue. Section 90(6) provides that the offer period must be 21 clear days (see **17.7.4**). If s 89 of the CA is disapplied then the offer period is provided for by LR 9.5.6R, which is the shorter period of 21 days; there is no requirement for 'clear' days.

17.7.6.5 Pre-emption rights under the Listing Rules

If the statutory pre-emption rights are disapplied, does this mean that the Pre-emption Group will no longer support the issue? No. As explained at **14.6.16** above, para 5 of the Pre-Emption Group's Statement of Principles makes clear that the Principles do not apply to issues of equity securities on a pre-emptive basis, provided the rights issue complies with the pre-emption requirements of the Listing Rules. As **14.6.12** explained, the pre-emption rights under the Listing Rules are slightly more flexible than the pre-emption rights under the CA 1985, and they do not raise the problems listed at **17.7.6.1** and **17.7.6.2** above (although, under the new regime, they do raise similar problems relating to convertible securities).

It is possible, therefore, to have a rights issue which complies with the pre-emption rights of the Listing Rules but which does not comply with the pre-emption rights of the CA 1985, and in practice this is usually what happens. The company disapplies s 89 and, while technically this also disapplies the pre-emption rights under the Listing Rules (see **14.6.15**), the company will nevertheless comply with the Listing Rules pre-emption rights. This removes the practical problems of the statutory pre-emption rights in relation to fractional entitlements and overseas shareholders, but keeps the IPCs happy (as stated at **14.6.16** above, the Pre-emption Guideline limits do not apply if the company issues shares in accordance with the pre-emption requirements of the Listing Rules). Note also that, as stated at **17.7.6.4** above, the offer period under the Listing Rules is slightly shorter than that required to comply with the statutory pre-emption rights.

17.7.6.6 The IPCs

Under the old regime, a rights issue was the preferred method of the IPCs for raising equity finance. No statement or guidelines have been published commenting on the new regime, although para 15 of the Pre-Emption Group's Statement of Principles (see **14.6.16**) evidences the IPC's preference for pre-emptive issues; it states that the choice of financing options (that is, the method of raising equity finance) is one of the critical considerations relating to a request for a non-routine disapplication (see **14.6.16.2**). The Group notes that a wide variety of financing options are now available to companies, and if a non-pre-emptive issue of shares is the most appropriate means of raising capital, companies should explain why that is, and why other financing methods have been rejected.

17.7.7 Timetable

Table 17.2 below is an example of a basic rights issue timetable, assuming that an EGM is required.

Table 17.2

Date	Event
1.5 to 3 months (deadline is 10 business days) before D day.	Submit draft prospectus and related draft documentation to FSA for approval under the Prospectus Rules.
At least 2 business days before impact day	FSA must have approved prospectus and related documentation under the Prospectus Rules, and prospectus must be filed with FSA.
Day before impact day	Board meeting to approve rights issue. Underwriting agreement signed and held in escrow.
Impact day	Press announcement released. Underwriting agreement released from escrow. Prospectus published, containing notice of EGM. (PALs cannot be sent out until after EGM.)

Date	Event
2 business days before D day (LR 3.5.7R)	Apply for admission of shares, nil paid, to the Official List and Main Market (by submitting '48 hour' documents to FSA under the Listing Rules, and 'two-day' documents to the Stock Exchange under the Admission and Disclosure Standards).
14 or 21 clear days after impact day (depending on whether special resolution required) (s 368(1) CA 1985)	EGM to pass shareholder resolutions (e.g. increase authorised share capital, grant directors authority to allot, disapply s 89, create a new class of shares, alter articles of association, and/or approve any related acquisition). PALS sent out immediately after EGM.
One business day after EGM ('**D day**')	Submit 'on the day' documents to the FSA under the Listing Rules (LR 3.3.3R). Shares admitted to Official List and Main Market, nil paid. Statement made by FSA to an RIS and statement published by the Stock Exchange on its website. 'Admission condition' in underwriting agreement is satisfied. Nil paid dealings in shares begin. Sale of overseas shareholders' shares and fractional entitlements (if s 89 pre-emption rights disapplied).
21 clear days (if complying with s 89 pre-emption rights) (s 90(6)) or 21 days (if s 89 pre-emption rights disapplied) (LR 9.5.6R) after D day ('Close of offer')	End of nil paid dealing period. Deadline for acceptance and payment in full.
1 business day after close of offer	Dealings in shares commence, fully paid. Notify underwriters of acceptances. Underwriters try to sell rump.
2 business days after close of offer	Identify stick. Final confirmation of acceptances announced. Announce result of rights issue to RIS.
Week after close of offer	Underwriters pay company consideration for the stick. Company receives net proceeds of the issue and despatches share certificates to shareholders.

17.7.8 Advantages of a rights issue

A rights issue has the following advantages:

(a) *Price*. If the issue is in accordance with the pre-emption requirements of the Listing Rules, there is no limit on the level of discount at which the company can issue the share.

(b) *The IPCs*. The IPCs are more likely to support this pre-emptive method of raising equity finance (see **17.7.6.6**).

17.7.9 Disadvantages of a rights issue

A rights issue has the following disadvantages:

(a) *Cost*. The costs of underwriting can be high.

(b) *Market value*. The shares issued under a rights issue are usually issued at a discount. This can cause the market value of the shares to fall.

(c) *Timing*. The offer period is 21 days (21 clear days if s 89 has not been disapplied), which cannot run concurrently with the EGM notice.

(d) *Pre-emption*. Even though the offer is on a pre-emptive basis, a s 89 disapplication is usually required (see **17.7.6** above).

17.7.10 Is a rights issue appropriate?

When considering whether a rights issue is the most appropriate method to raise equity finance, the following questions may provide a useful 'ready reckoner':

(a) Is the company concerned about underwriting costs? If so, a rights issue may not be the best method.

(b) Does the company need to raise finance quickly? If so, a rights issue may not be the best method.

(c) Does the company need flexibility in the amount by which it can discount shares? If so, a rights issue has some advantage over the other methods of equity finance in this regard.

17.7.11 Documentation

The following documentation may be required for a rights issue:

(a) press announcement;
(b) underwriting agreement;
(c) PAL;
(d) notice of EGM;
(e) prospectus;
(f) perhaps, a separate circular (see **17.5.4**);
(g) documents required for admitting shares to listing and to trading (see **17.4.3**); and
(h) RIS notification (LR 9.5.5R and LR 9.6.6R).

It's time to stand up for your rights issue

United Utilities is looking for the nod from its shareholders to issue new stock

BY ALISON STEED

ABOUT 140,000 shareholders in United Utilities, the water and electricity group, should each receive an 80-page tome this weekend concerning the company's £1 billion deeply discounted rights issue.

Tempting though it may be to put this to one side until you next suffer insomnia, you should at least leaf through it to decide whether you want to vote for the issue to go ahead.

A rights issue is simply a way for a company to raise money, so named because the company gives existing shareholders the "right" to buy shares in proportion to their existing holdings.

The company announced its intention to raise the money ahead of an expected £5.5 billion upgrade of its water network over the next six years, as required by the water regulator Ofwat.

United is offering shareholders the chance to buy five new shares for every nine they have at August 20 at 330p each, compared with a market price of around 548p this week, with the new shares being issued and paid for in two instalments.

United is looking to raise £510m this year from subscribers who will pay 165p per new share, with a second instalment of £510m at the same price in June 2005.

But if you do not take up the first offer, you cannot take up the second. Anyone who is not a shareholder now but wants to get in on the rights issue can do so if they buy United Utilities shares before August 20. Although the rates appear favourable, you should remember that the company is not out to lose money. Hilary Cook of Barclays Private Clients said: "The issue has to be priced lower than the current share price to ensure it is taken up and the company gets the money."

One advantage of obtaining extra shares this way is that you avoid paying stamp duty and dealing charges.

The rights offer is conditional on shareholders voting in favour of the special resolution at the company's extraordinary general meeting on August 26, which will be held at the Bridgwater Hall on Lower Mosley Street in Manchester at 11am.

Institutional investors will, as usual, heavily influence the result but individual holders have nothing to lose by making their voice heard.

Evelyn Brodie of United Utilities said: "You don't have to do anything if you don't want to, but all you can do is cast your vote or turn up at the egm.

"If you want to vote, you need to send the form of proxy, showing your approval or disapproval of the proposal, to the registrars before August 24, unless you want to attend the egm." It does not matter how many votes are cast but 75% of those voting must vote in favour for the rights issue to proceed.

United will adjust the dividends paid on the ordinary shares to take account of the bonus elements of the rights issue. In other words, if you do not take up the offer the dividend income you receive will decrease because of what is known as "dilution". With the same number of shares, you will own a smaller percentage of the company.

However, if you take up the rights in full you should receive the same dividend income. But you do not need to consider this until August when allotment letters will be sent out if the issue goes ahead. Your Money will return to this issue then.

The company says it is committed to maintaining the dividend in real terms – to preserve its purchasing power by keeping pace with inflation – until at least March, 2005. Ms Cook said: "Your total payout will remain about the same if you sell enough of your rights to take up the remaining rights without investing in any further cash."

This keeps your investment in the company in pound terms the same, and the company said it is maintaining the percentage yield, which is currently more than 8%.

There is a United Utilities shareholder helpline available on 0870 600 3971 from 8.30am to 5.30pm Monday to Friday and 9am to 1pm on Saturday. It cannot give investment advice.

Source: *The Daily Telegraph (London)*, 2 August 2003.

17.8 Open offer

17.8.1 What is an open offer?

Appendix 1.1 of the Listing Rules defines an open offer. Like a rights issue (see **17.7** above), an open offer is:

(a) an offer to issue new shares, or transfer existing shares (or other securities);

(b) to existing shareholders (or security holders) in proportion to their existing holdings.

Again, the offer is usually for cash. However, unlike a rights issue, the offer is not made by means of a PAL (see **17.7.3.1** above), but by an application form. The structure of the offer is considered at **17.8.3** below.

17.8.2 Price

The shares are offered at a discount, but the discount tends to be less than that for a rights issue (see **17.7.2** above). Under the old regime, an open offer could not be priced at a discount of more than 10% of market value, unless the FSA agreed otherwise, which it would do so only in exceptional circumstances (OLR 4.26).

This is no longer the case under the new regime. While the default position remains that an open offer cannot be priced at a discount of more than 10% of market value (LR 9.5.10R(1)), LR 9.5.10R(3) provides that this rule does not apply if:

(a) the company's shareholders have specifically approved the terms of the open offer at a discount of more than 10%; or

(b) the shares are being issued for cash consideration under a pre-existing general authority to disapply s 89 of the CA 1985.

It is now possible, therefore, for shares to be issued a discount of more than 10% by way of an open offer.

One curious effect of LR 9.5.10R(1) is that an open offer made wholly in accordance with s 89 of the CA 1985 would still be subject to the 10% limit, while an open offer not in accordance with s 89, but which benefits from the exception outlined at (b) above, would not be subject to this limit.

Note that any shares issued under the exception at (b) above will render the disapplication 'non-routine' under the Pre-Emption Group's Statement of Principles, which advocate limiting any discount to 5%, unless the issue is in accordance with the pre-emption requirements of the Listing Rules (see **14.6.16**).

17.8.3 Structure

The company sends a personal application form to each shareholder. Unlike the PAL used in a rights issue, this form simply offers shares; it does not provisionally allot them. The shareholder can either take up the offer, or do nothing. No shareholder can assign or sell the benefit of the offer. In addition, no arrangements are made for the sale of shares which shareholders do not take up. This is bad news for the 'lazy shareholder'; in contrast to a rights issue (see **17.7.3.5** above), if a shareholder does nothing in relation to the offer, he will receive nothing under the offer.

The structure of an open offer gives shareholders less flexibility than on a rights issue (the shareholder cannot trade the rights nil paid, and the lazy shareholder receives nothing) and open offers tend to be cheaper for companies than rights issues. The IPCs have stated that if an issue represents more than 15–18% of a company's issued share capital, or if the discount is greater than 7.5%, this may cause them concern (if the issue does not otherwise protect shareholders adequately). In such circumstances, the IPCs prefer a rights issue to an open offer. (Note that the IPCs have not issued formal guidance on this.)

17.8.4 Timing

Listing Rule 9.5.7 provides that the offer period for an open offer must be approved by the RIE on which the shares are traded. For the Stock Exchange, the approved period is 15 business days from the date of posting the application forms (Admission and Disclosure Standards, para 3.11 - see **Appendix 1**). The offer period is usually slightly shorter, therefore, than the 21 days required for a rights issue (although 15 business days can be longer than 21 days in the few periods of the year when there are many public holidays, such as Christmas).

In addition, and of more significance to timing, is the fact that, unlike with a rights issue, the application forms do not provisionally allot shares. This means that the problem with provisionally allotting shares on a conditional basis does not arise. Therefore, if an EGM is required in order to obtain the consent of the shareholders in connection with the share issue (to increase the company's share capital and such like – see **Chapter 14**), the offer period can run concurrently with the EGM notice. This means that, compared to a rights issue, the underwriting commission is less and the company will receive its cash sooner.

17.8.5 Advantages of an open offer

An open offer has the following advantages for the company:

(a) *Timing.* The offer period is 15 business days, which can run concurrently with the EGM notice.

(b) *Cost.* The default position is that shares cannot be offered at a discount of more than 10%. Unless the offer is structured to fall within one of the exceptions to this, the open offer will be cheaper for the company (but see **17.8.6(b)** below).

17.8.6 Disadvantages of an open offer

An open offer has the following disadvantages for the company:

(a) *Pre-emption.* Even though the offer is on a pre-emptive basis, a s 89 disapplication is usually required, because the statutory pre-emption rights have the potential to cause problems (as they do on a rights issue; see **17.7.6**).

(b) *Flexibility.* The default position is that shares cannot be offered at a discount of more than 10%. Unless the offer is structured to fall within one of the exceptions to this, an open offer might be less attractive to shareholders than a rights issue.

(c) *The IPCs.* The IPCs prefer rights issues to open offers in certain circumstances (see **17.8.3**).

17.8.7 Documentation

The following documentation may be required for an open offer:

(a) press announcement;
(b) underwriting agreement;
(c) notice of EGM;
(d) prospectus;
(e) perhaps, a separate circular (see **17.5.4**); and
(f) other documents required for admitting shares to listing and to trading (see **17.4.3**).

17.9 Placing

A placing is one of the methods by which a company can float (see **4.4.2** above). It is also a method which can be used for a secondary issue.

17.9.1 What is a placing?

The formal definition of a placing is in Appendix 1.1 of the Listing Rules. Basically, a placing is:

(a) an offer by the company to issue new shares, or transfer existing unlisted shares (or other securities);
(b) to specified persons or clients of any financial adviser assisting in the placing;
(c) which does not involve an offer to the public or to existing holders of the company's securities.

Again, a placing is usually for cash.

17.9.2 Price

Paragraph 11 of the Pre-Emption Group's Statement of Principles (set out at **Appendix 6**) provides that a request for a discount of more than 5% of market value is not likely to be regarded as 'routine' (see **14.6.16**).

Listing Rule 9.5.10R also provides that a placing, as with an open offer, cannot be priced at a discount of more than 10% of market value unless it is structured to fall within either of the exceptions set out at LR 9.5.10R(3)(a) or (b) (see **17.8.2**). (Those familiar with the old regime will note that LR 9.5.10R provides more flexibility, in terms of permitting a discount of more than 10% of market value, than the old regime, where OLR 4.8 provided that such a discount was permitted only with the consent of the FSA, which would be given only in exceptional circumstances.)

17.9.3 Advantages of a placing

The advantage of a placing is its cost. The limitations on the discount that can be applied (see **17.9.2**) mean that a placing can be cheaper for the company than a rights issue.

17.9.4 Disadvantages of a placing

A placing is not a pre-emptive offer, so:

(a) a s 89 disapplication is required; and
(b) the Pre-Emption Group's Statement of Principles will restrict the number of shares which can be issued (see **14.6.16** above) (and the discount which can be applied – see **17.9.2**). So a placing may struggle to attract investors.

17.9.5 Documentation

The following documentation may be required for a placing:

(a) press announcement;
(b) placing agreement;
(c) underwriting agreement;
(d) prospectus, unless the placing is exempt (see **17.5.1**);
(e) if the placing is exempt, or there are overseas shareholders, a separate circular (see **17.5.4**); and
(f) other documents required for admitting shares to listing and to trading (see **17.4.3**).

17.10 Acquisition issue

17.10.1 What is an acquisition issue?

Unlike under the Old Listing Rules, the current Listing Rules no longer specifically refer to an acquisition issue. It is expected, however, to remain a useful method of raising equity finance to fund an acquisition. (The Listing Rules no longer purport to deal exhaustively with all methods of raising equity finance; they concentrate on special features of certain methods.)

An acquisition issue is also known as a 'share-for-share exchange', or a 'securities exchange offer'. It is:

(a) an issue of new shares by the company;
(b) to the seller(s) of an asset or assets (which includes shares);

(c) in consideration for the acquisition by the company of that asset or assets.

17.10.2 Structure

An acquisition issue does not involve marketing shares, as in the case of a rights issue, an open offer or a placing. Instead, it consists of the offer of shares as consideration for an acquisition.

Example

Imagine that X plc wants to buy the entire issued share capital of another company, Y Ltd. The buyer is X plc. The sellers are all the shareholders of Y Ltd. The sellers will transfer the shares they hold in Y Ltd to X plc. X plc will then issue shares in itself to the shareholders of Y Ltd, as consideration. See **Figure 17.1** below.

Figure 17.1: Acquisition issue

Before the acquisition

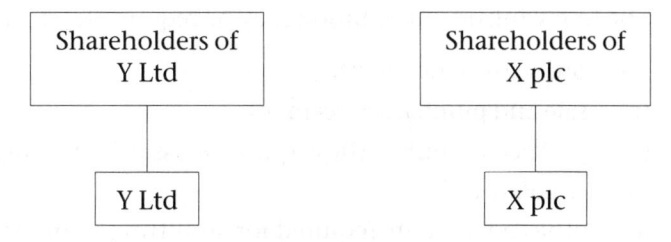

```
┌─────────────────┐        ┌─────────────────┐
│ Shareholders of │        │ Shareholders of │
│      Y Ltd      │        │      X plc      │
└────────┬────────┘        └────────┬────────┘
         │                          │
      ┌──┴──┐                    ┌──┴──┐
      │Y Ltd│                    │X plc│
      └─────┘                    └─────┘
```

The acquisition

1. Shareholders in Y Ltd *transfer* all the shares in Y Ltd to X plc, so X plc becomes the sole shareholder of Y Ltd.

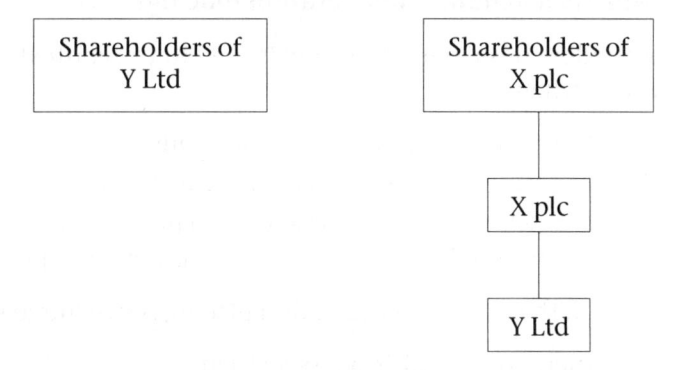

```
┌─────────────────┐        ┌─────────────────┐
│ Shareholders of │        │ Shareholders of │
│      Y Ltd      │        │      X plc      │
└─────────────────┘        └────────┬────────┘
                                    │
                                 ┌──┴──┐
                                 │X plc│
                                 └──┬──┘
                                    │
                                 ┌──┴──┐
                                 │Y Ltd│
                                 └─────┘
```

2. X plc *issues* shares in itself to the shareholders of Y Ltd, as consideration for the transfer, so the former shareholders of Y become additional shareholders of X plc.

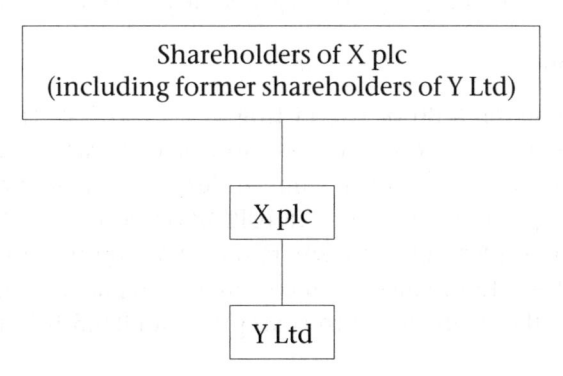

```
┌──────────────────────────────────────────┐
│         Shareholders of X plc            │
│ (including former shareholders of Y Ltd) │
└────────────────────┬─────────────────────┘
                     │
                  ┌──┴──┐
                  │X plc│
                  └──┬──┘
                     │
                  ┌──┴──┐
                  │Y Ltd│
                  └─────┘
```

17.10.3 Advantages of an acquisition issue

An acquisition issue has the following advantages:

(a) *Timing.* There are no significant timetabling issues.

(b) *Cost.* An acquisition issue is inexpensive.

(c) *Pre-emption.* The issue is not for cash, so s 89 pre-emption rights are not triggered.

17.10.4 Disadvantages of an acquisition issue

An acquisition issue has the disadvantage that a valuation may be required under s 103 of the CA 1985 (see **14.7.5** above), if the asset to be acquired is anything other than shares.

17.10.5 Documentation

The following documentation may be required for an acquisition issue:

(a) press announcement;

(b) sale and purchase agreement;

(c) prospectus, unless the acquisition issue is exempt;

(d) circular; and

(e) other documents required for admitting shares to listing and to trading (see **17.4.3**).

17.11 Vendor consideration placing

17.11.1 What is a vendor consideration placing?

A vendor consideration placing is used in the context of an acquisition only. It is useful when:

(a) the company wants to make an acquisition; but

(b) the company does not have any cash; and

(c) the seller is not willing to accept non-cash consideration (so that an acquisition issue (see **17.10** above) is not appropriate).

Instead, the vendor consideration placing is structured so that:

(a) there is an acquisition issue; then

(b) the company arranges for its bank to place the shares it has issued to the seller as consideration; then

(c) the company's bank gives the proceeds of the placing, in cash, to the seller.

17.11.2 Price

Paragraph 4.30 of the Listing Rules provides that, as with an open offer and a placing, a vendor consideration placing cannot be priced at a discount of more than 10% of market value unless it is structured to fall within either of the exception set out at LR 9.5.10R(3)(a) (see **17.8.2**). Again, this is a more flexible rule than under OLR 4.30, where such a discount was permitted only with the consent of the UKLA. The vendor consideration placing is not an issue of shares for cash, so it will not fall within the exception at LR 9.5.10R(3)(b).

17.11.3 Advantages of a vendor consideration placing

(a) *Cost.* The limitation on the discount that can be applied (see **17.11.2**) means that a vendor consideration placing can have cost advantages for the company.

(b) *Pre-emption.* A vendor consideration placing is not an issue for cash. The company issues the shares for non-cash consideration (it exchanges them for shares). The pre-emption rules do not apply, therefore, so no s 89 disapplication is required. However, the ABI has issued guidelines which provide that vendor consideration placings:

  (i) of over 10% of the company's issued equity share capital; or

  (ii) at more than 5% discount,

must be placed on a basis which gives existing shareholders the right to claw back their pro rata share of the issue. The claw-back is usually offered by way of an open offer (vendor consideration placing with open offer), but it can also be made by way of rights issue (vendor consideration rights issue). The ABI Guidelines relating to claw-back are set out at Pt B of **Appendix 5**.

17.11.4 Disadvantages of a vendor consideration placing

A valuation may be required under s 103 of the CA 1985 (see **14.7.5** above), if the asset to be acquired is anything other than shares.

17.11.5 Documentation

The following documentation may be required for a vendor consideration placing:

(a) press announcement;
(b) sale and purchase agreement;
(c) placing agreement;
(d) underwriting agreement;
(e) prospectus, unless the vendor consideration placing is exempt;
(f) circular; and
(g) other documents required for admitting shares to listing and to trading (see **17.4.3**).

Chapter 18
Equity Finance or Debt Finance?

18.1	Introduction	245
18.2	Income	245
18.3	Capital	246
18.4	Capital growth	246
18.5	Taxation	246
18.6	Rights	247
18.7	Investors	247
18.8	The problem	247
18.9	The solution	248
18.10	Conclusion	248

18.1 Introduction

Chapter 17 considers that, when a company needs finance to provide working capital, reduce borrowings, fund a specific acquisition, or, indeed, for any other reason, it may decide to raise equity finance. This involves the company issuing shares in return for cash or assets. Another book in the series, *Banking and Capital Markets*, discusses another way in which a company may raise finance – debt finance. This involves the company using debt to obtain the cash or assets it requires.

The remainder of this chapter provides a brief overview as to why a company might choose to raise equity finance rather than debt finance, and vice versa. It then examines why most companies, regardless of their size, are financed by a combination of both debt and equity, and considers the key to the right combination.

18.2 Income

18.2.1 Equity finance

A company does not have to declare a dividend. If it does not, the shareholders will not receive any income from their investment. The company does not have to pay any interest to the shareholders. The shareholders do not have a *right* to income.

However, in the real world, any listed company will be aware that if it does not declare a dividend, it risks both losing the support of its shareholders and damaging its reputation as a good investment. It is not a good idea, therefore, for a company to perceive a dividend as something which it can withhold without good reason.

To the extent a company does declare a dividend, the shareholders will share in the profits of the company. For equity shareholders, this right is infinite (see **13.5.1.1**).

18.2.2 Debt finance

Lenders will negotiate a rate of interest with the company. The cost of debt to the company depends on the interest rate which a lender charges. The company will have to pay interest regardless of profits (unlike a dividend). Interest provides lenders with income from their investment (unlike a dividend, this income is finite).

The term 'leverage' is often used in this regard. Leverage is the opportunity to create profit by financing a business through debt which is entitled to a finite return. Imagine that you and nine of your friends own a company; you are its shareholders. You have no more cash to invest. If you finance the business solely through equity, you need to bring on board other shareholders who are willing and able to inject cash into the company in return for shares. All the profits of the company will now be shared not just between you and your nine friends, but between all the other shareholders too. Now imagine that you decided to finance the company solely through debt. Any profits which are surplus, once the interest on the debt has been paid, will be shared just between you and your nine friends. Perhaps now you see the attraction of debt finance (but see **18.9.1** below).

18.3 Capital

18.3.1 Equity finance

On a winding up of the company, the company repays its debts first, then it pays to the shareholders the nominal value of their shares, together with any premium they paid on those shares. The shareholders do not have a *right* to capital. This risk, that shareholders will lose their capital, is balanced by the opportunity, described at **18.2.1** above, to share in the profits of the company without limit, and the potential, described at **18.4** below, for capital growth.

18.3.2 Debt finance

Ultimately, the company must repay the capital to the lender. The holders of debt securities will be paid in priority to shareholders on a winding up.

18.4 Capital growth

18.4.1 Equity finance

There is scope for capital growth. The share value will reflect the success of the company. This can help a successful company to market shares.

18.4.2 Debt finance

There is no scope for capital growth. The lender has a right to be repaid only the capital sum, plus interest, no matter how well the company is performing.

18.5 Taxation

18.5.1 Equity finance

Dividends are not a deductible expense in calculating the company's corporation taxation liability.

18.5.2 Debt finance

Interest payable on a loan is tax deductible.

18.6 Rights

18.6.1 Equity finance

When a company issues shares, unless it issues such shares in proportion to the existing shareholders' shareholdings, the issue will dilute those shareholdings.

If the issue is of voting shares, the balance of power within the company could change. This may be a high price to pay for raising finance.

18.6.2 Debt finance

Debt finance will not affect the power structure of the company, nor afford the lender any right to vote in the company.

18.7 Investors

The differences between debt and equity considered above mean that investors have different priorities, depending on how they intend to invest in a company.

The extent to which a potential investor will investigate a company before choosing to invest will differ, depending on whether the investor is seeking to invest by way of equity or debt.

18.7.1 Equity investors

Substantial equity investors include pension funds and other similar financial institutions. Potential equity investors will analyse not only the company's current financial position, but also how the company is placed in the long term, by considering the business sector in which the company operates, the company's expenditure on research and development for new products (R&D), and the company's future earning potential. This reflects the fact that once equity investors invest in a company, they pass the point of no return. They have no right to recover their cash, unless they can sell the shares. They risk losing all their capital.

18.7.2 Debt investors

Substantial debt investors include banks and finance houses. Potential lenders tend to confine their analysis to whether the company can service a loan (and any other loans taken out by the company which would rank ahead of, or equal with, the investor's loan) from current earnings.

This reflects the fact that lenders are entitled to be repaid their capital, and also that it is common for the lender to negotiate the right to monitor the financial position of the company through a series of tests known as 'financial covenants' (which relate to issues such as the net worth, cash flow and gearing (see **18.9.1** below) of the company).

18.8 The problem

It should now be clear that equity finance and debt finance both bring advantages and disadvantages for a company.

With equity finance, there comes the significant risk for shareholders that they will lose capital. This risk usually means that it is impossible for a company to find enough shareholders with sufficient funds to enable it to finance itself solely through equity. Even if it could, a company would still be likely to use debt finance in order to achieve some leverage.

Why not finance the company entirely through debt, to achieve complete leverage, as in the example at **18.2.2** above? The company must repay debt on a regular basis, regardless of the profits the company has made. Imagine what happens if there is a downturn in business. Perhaps the company's major customer goes bust and cannot repay its debts to the company, or perhaps interest rates rise dramatically, or there is a world event which adversely impacts on trading (consider, for example, the impact on the travel industry of the terrorist attacks of recent years). If a business is financed through too much debt, any of these events might mean that the company cannot generate enough cash to enable it to pay its debts as they fall due. (With equity, of course, the company would not have to declare a dividend.)

18.9 The solution

The solution is for a company to achieve a proper balance between debt and equity finance. What is a 'proper balance'? The company needs:

(a) sufficient equity to provide a cushion against any unexpected problems with the business and/or cash flow; and

(b) sufficient debt to achieve appropriate leverage and an appropriate return to the equity shareholders.

18.9.1 Gearing

The ratio of a company's debt to equity is referred to as 'gearing'. The higher the proportion of debt, the higher the gearing will be.

Prospective investors in the company will be interested in the company's gearing. In particular, lenders will consider the company's gearing before they negotiate the terms of a loan. If the gearing is high, then, as considered above, there is a greater risk that unexpected problems with the business and/or cash flow will render the company unable to service its debt. This means that there is a higher risk of the company going bust. A lender will demand a higher interest rate, therefore, for a loan to a company which is highly geared.

18.9.2 Articles of association

A company seeking to raise equity finance must involve its shareholders in the decision at some point in the process (for example, to authorise the directors to allot shares). However, the decision whether a company should enter into a loan is usually reserved to the board.

A company's articles of association can protect shareholders in this regard. The articles can provide that, while the ratio of debt to equity is at a certain level, the company can borrow without having to seek permission from the shareholders, but that, once gearing reaches a certain level, the company will require the authorisation of the shareholders in order to borrow.

18.10 Conclusion

A public company must think carefully about whether it should use debt or equity to raise the finance it needs. The company needs to monitor its gearing carefully. Not only will a highly geared company bear a greater risk of going bust, but prospective investors will also scrutinise a company's gearing before deciding whether to invest in the company. It is important, therefore, that the company gets it right.

Jittery funds back bonds in 'dash for debt'

GARY DUNCAN, ECONOMICS CORRESPONDENT

BRITAIN'S financial institutions continued to pump money into the bond markets during the first quarter of the year in a remorseless "dash for debt", official figures released yesterday show.

Jitters over war and the world economy led risk-averse institutions to favour gilts and corporate bonds, but demand was also buoyed by pension schemes cutting their exposure to shares in favour of fixed-income securities.

Overall net investment fell to £7.6 billion in the first quarter, a dramatic reduction from £22.4 billion in the final quarter of 2003.

The gilt-edged market took the bulk of the reduced flow of funds, with net investment in UK government stocks of £6.7 billion. While this was down from £8.6 billion in the final quarter of 2003, it was sharply up from the £700 million for the same period last year, when the bulk of cash was still going into equities.

In contrast, net investment in equities in the first quarter was just £2 billion, down from £3.7 billion in the previous quarter and £5.7 billion a year earlier.

"The trend towards fixed income by UK institutions seems intact and we expect it to continue," Ciaran Barr, of Deutsche Bank, said.

The further flow of funds into the gilt-edged market was partly financed by institutions running down their holdings of short-term assets, such as cash balances and cash-based instruments, to the tune of £4.4 billion in the first quarter.

Similar trends towards government and corporate bonds and away from equities were shown in the official data by breakdowns of investment by different sectors.

Pension funds bought some £2.7 billion of fixed-income securities while they sold £2 billion of equities, Deutsche Bank noted.

Insurance groups bought nearly £8 billion of fixed-income securities, both government and corporate bonds, with their purchases of shares virtually flat.

Investors also pulled funds out of property for the third quarter in a row, the data revealed. Net investment in UK property in the first quarter was negative to the tune of £396 million.

This withdrawal of funds came after some £2 billion was pulled out of the sector in the previous six months.

Low and falling yields in commercial property are acting as a deterrent to investors, according to Ed Stansfield of Capital Economics. But he predicted that these trends could prove short lived, with some funds looking to increase their property stakes.

Source: *The Times (London)*: 30 June 2004.

Part IV
LISTED COMPANY TRANSACTIONS

Chapter 19
Acquisitions and Disposals

19.1	Introduction	253
19.2	Basic considerations	253
19.3	Listed company considerations	254
19.4	The classification of transactions	255
19.5	Related party transactions	262
19.6	The circular	268
19.7	The transaction timetable	270
19.8	Conclusion	271

19.1 Introduction

The main rules relating to listed company transactions are in chapters 10 and 11 of the Listing Rules. These chapters have been reorganised and rewritten under the new regime, but broadly they remain very similar to chapters 10 and 11 under the old regime. 'Transaction' is now defined, but still refers principally to acquisitions and disposals (see **19.4.1**). **Chapters 20** to **23** discuss the specific rules relating to takeovers and mergers. This chapter considers the main issues which arise when a listed company enters into an acquisition or a disposal.

19.2 Basic considerations

The basic issues which a listed company must consider when it is proposing to enter into a transaction are no different to those an unlisted company would consider. They are:

(a) Structure – assets or shares?

(b) Consideration – cash or non-cash?

(c) Finance – existing cash, equity or debt?

(d) Due diligence – how much?

(e) Contractual protection – warranties and indemnities?

The LPC Guide, *Acquisitions* explores these basic issues.

However, if a listed company is involved in the transaction, the approach of the company to these issues may differ in the following ways:

(a) *Consideration*. As **Chapter 17** explained, if the buyer is a listed company, it has the option of using its shares as consideration.

(b) *Finance*. Even if the seller does not want shares in the buyer as consideration, if the buyer is a listed company it can choose from a variety of methods (not available to an unlisted company) to raise equity finance (see **Chapter 17**).

(c) *Due diligence*. If the target company is a listed company, there will be information about it in the public domain, which will assist the due diligence process.

(d) *Contractual protection*. If the target company is a listed company and its shares are widely held by members of the public or institutions, they, as sellers, will not provide much (if any) contractual protection to any buyer. (Would you be willing to vouch for anything Marks and Spencer Group plc might warrant about its business in a sale and purchase agreement, just because you own a few ordinary shares?)

As well as having a different approach to the basic issues of a transaction, a listed company will also have some additional considerations. These are examined at **19.3** below.

19.3 Listed company considerations

Most of the additional considerations for listed companies should be familiar to you already, as they have been explained in the preceding chapters of this book. A summary of the main issues follows.

19.3.1 Consideration

If the company is:

(a) issuing shares as consideration; or

(b) using equity finance to raise cash to use as consideration

for the acquisition, then the rules and regulations considered in **Chapter 17** will be relevant.

19.3.2 The continuing obligation of disclosure

The general obligation of a listed company, under DR 2.2.1R, to disclose major new developments in its sphere of activity if the information is not already public knowledge and may lead to substantial movement in its share price, is discussed in **Chapter 7**. This obligation will require companies to disclose significant acquisitions and disposals. An exception to this rule – that a company does not need to disclose information about matters in the course of negotiation, unless there is a breach of confidence during those negotiations – is examined at **7.4.2.8** above. These rules are relevant during an acquisition or disposal, to make sure the company discloses the transaction, through an RIS, in a timely manner as soon as the Disclosure Rules require.

19.3.3 The disclosure of interests in shares

Chapter 15 considers the obligation:

(a) of a listed company, under LR 9.6.7, to disclose to the public the information it acquires under ss 198 to 208 of the CA 1985 (see **15.7.2**); and

(b) of a shareholder under the SARs, or the company (and others) under the City Code, to disclose his or its interest in shares to the public once his or its shareholdings exceed a certain level (see **15.7.2** and **15.7.3**).

These requirements can be particularly relevant in the context of acquisitions or disposals of shares.

19.3.4 Misleading statements, market manipulation, market abuse and insider dealing

Chapters 9, 10 and **11** consider the civil offence of market abuse and the criminal offences of making misleading statements, manipulating the market and insider dealing. These offences can be relevant on an acquisition or a disposal. The acquisition or disposal of shares by a listed company has the potential to increase that company's value. There is scope for the company's directors, and others, to abuse their inside knowledge that the transaction will take place, by investing in shares which will increase in value once the transaction becomes public knowledge.

19.3.5 Financial regulation

As **Chapter 9** explains, anyone who carries out regulated activities in the process of the transaction must be either authorised, or (less likely) exempt.

19.3.6 Financial promotion

Any communication which persuades someone to do something in relation to an investment must comply with the rules of the FSMA 2000 relating to financial promotion. This is discussed in more detail in **Chapter 12**.

19.3.7 Financial assistance

Chapter 16 explains that the lawyer must always check the structure of any share acquisition, to make sure that it does not give rise to financial assistance problems. There may be further scope for such problems if the consideration also involves shares (that is, the consideration is the issue of shares, or the consideration has been raised through equity finance).

19.3.8 The Model Code

Chapter 7 considers the Model Code. As explained at **7.6.4.3**, directors will not obtain clearance to deal in the company's shares if an acquisition or a disposal has not been made public and the announcement of the transaction would be likely to lead to a significant movement in the company's share price.

19.3.9 The classification of transactions

The remainder of this chapter examines:

(a) how acquisitions and disposals by listed companies are classified under the Listing Rules; and

(b) the consequences for the listed company of that classification.

19.4 The classification of transactions

19.4.1 What is a 'transaction' under the Listing Rules?

Listing Rule 10.1.3R defines 'transaction'. It includes all agreements entered into by a listed company or any of its subsidiaries, other than:

(a) a transaction of a revenue nature entered into in the ordinary course of business (eg, a foreign exchange company buying more currency, or a travel agency selling a holiday);

(b) an issue of shares, or a transaction to raise finance, which does not involve the acquisition or disposal of any fixed asset of the listed company or subsidiary (eg, a rights issue or open offer);

(c) a transaction between a listed company and its wholly-owned subsidiary, or between its wholly-owned subsidiaries (that is, certain intra-group transactions).

It also includes the grant of certain options.

Listing Rule 10.1.4G provides general guidance as to the FSA's intention regarding the chapter 10 regime. It states that it is intended to cover transactions that are outside the ordinary course of a company's business and may change a shareholder's (or other security holder's) economic interest in the company's assets or liabilities (whether or not any change is registered in the balance sheet). This clarifies that the regime is focused on the impact of the transaction on the company, not just on the size of the transaction. (The class tests, however, continue to relate to the size of the transaction (see **19.4.3**).)

Broadly, 'transaction' means acquisitions and disposals of assets or shares.

19.4.2 The classification regime

Chapters 10 and 11 of the Listing Rules contain rules relating to the classification of transactions. The rules in chapter 10 divide transactions into four different classes, according to the size of the transaction compared with the size of the listed company. This comparison is made using four calculations referred to as the 'class tests', set out at LR 10, Annex 1 (see **19.4.1**). Each calculation results in a figure which is expressed as a percentage and referred to as a 'percentage ratio'. The percentage ratios determine how the transaction is classified (see **19.4.3.1**, **19.4.4.1**, **19.4.5.1** and **19.4.6.1**).

Why is this classification necessary? The answer will not surprise you: it is to protect shareholders. The purpose of classifying a transaction is so that the Listing Rules can determine the extent to which the transaction needs to be regulated, in order to protect the interests of shareholders. If a transaction is of a significant size, it is classified in a way which means that the company must follow strict procedural requirements before it can complete the transaction (for example, the company must seek shareholder approval of the transaction). On the other hand, if a transaction is not so significant, it is classified in a way which means that the company does not have to follow such strict procedural requirements.

19.4.3 The class tests

If the thought of taking figures and applying percentage ratio tests to them fills you with horror, then do not worry. The company's financial advisers and its reporting accountants will actually apply the tests to the relevant figures. However, the lawyer must be aware of and understand the need for, and the principles behind, the class tests. In particular, the lawyer must make sure that the company considers these class tests at an early stage in the transaction.

The class tests, set out in LR 10, Annex 1, are as follows:

(a) Gross assets

$$\frac{\text{Gross assets which are the subject of the transaction}}{\text{Gross assets of the listed company}} \times 100\%$$

(b) Profits

$$\frac{\text{Profits attributable to the assets which are the subject of the transaction}}{\text{Profits of the listed company}} \times 100\%$$

(c) Consideration

$$\frac{\text{Consideration for the transaction}}{\text{Aggregate market value of the listed company's ordinary shares}} \times 100\%$$

(d) Gross capital

$$\frac{\text{Gross capital of the company or business being acquired}}{\text{Gross capital of the listed company}} \times 100\%$$

Those familiar with the old regime will note that there is no longer a fifth turnover test. This test was deleted on 1 July 2005 as its results often led to anomalies under the old regime and, in practice, it was commonly disapplied.

The 'listed company' referred to in the class tests is the listed company who is party to the transaction and whom you are advising. If both parties to the transaction, that is, buyer and seller, are listed companies, then the transaction will need to be classified twice, once from the buyer's perspective, where the buyer's details will be the 'listed company' referred to above (which will establish the formalities the buyer needs to comply with to make the acquisition), and once from the seller's perspective, where the seller will be the 'listed company' referred to above (this will establish the formalities the seller needs to comply with to make the disposal).

It is possible that one transaction can fall within two different classes, depending on from whose perspective the transaction is classified. For example, a disposal by small listed company A of a third of its assets is likely to be a really significant transaction for company A, probably Class 1. However, for the buyer, huge listed company B, the acquisition is less significant, say Class 2.

Note that in share sales the sellers are the shareholders rather than the company itself, so, even if the target is a listed company, the transaction will need to be classified from one perspective (the listed company buyer's) only.

Listing Rule 10, Annex 1, para 10G provides that the FSA can modify the class tests, to substitute other relevant indicators of size, in the event that they produce an anomalous result, or if the calculation is inappropriate to the activities of the listed company.

Listing Rule 10.2.10R provides that, for the purposes of the calculations, the transaction must be aggregated with certain other transactions (broadly those involving the same parties, the acquisition or disposal of shares in the same company, or which, taken together, result in a substantial involvement in a new business activity) which took place in the preceding twelve months. The FSA also has discretion to aggregate in other circumstances (LR 10.2.11G).

In practice, typically the consideration test proves to be the key test.

19.4.4 The classification of transactions

The percentage ratios resulting from the class tests at **19.4.3** above determine the class of the transaction, but what classes are there? There are four classes of transaction under chapter 10 of the Listing Rules, namely:

(a) Class 1 transaction;
(b) Class 2 transaction;
(c) Class 3 transaction; and
(d) reverse takeover.

In addition, there is a further class of transaction (a 'related parties transaction') which is dealt with separately under chapter 11 of the Listing Rules.

As mentioned at **19.4.2** above, the purpose of classifying a transaction is to determine the level of procedural safeguards which the Listing Rules will impose to protect the shareholders. Let us now consider:

(a) the percentage ratios required for the class to apply; and

(b) the requirements of chapter 10 of the Listing Rules in relation to transactions of that class.

19.4.5 Class 3

19.4.5.1 Percentage ratios

If *all* of the percentage ratios are less than 5%, the transaction will be a Class 3 transaction (LR 10.2.2R(1)). Class 3 transactions are the smallest, least significant transactions.

19.4.5.2 Chapter 10 requirements

Listing Rules 10.3.1R and 10.3.2R provide as follows:

(a) If the transaction involves an acquisition and the consideration includes the issue of shares which the company is seeking to list, the company must notify an RIS, as soon as possible after the terms of the acquisition have been agreed, of the information set out in LR 10.3.1R(2).

(b) If the transaction is any other Class 3 transaction and the company releases details of the transaction to the public, the company must notify an RIS of the information set out in LR 10.3.2R(2).

(c) If the transaction is a Class 3 transaction which does not fall within (a) or (b) above, chapter 10 does not impose any procedural requirements on the company at all.

These limited requirements reflect the small size of Class 3 transactions.

19.4.6 Class 2

19.4.6.1 Percentage ratios

If *any* of the percentage ratios is 5% or more, but *each* percentage ratio is less than 25%, the transaction will be classified as a Class 2 transaction (LR 10.2.2R(2)). Class 2 transactions are, therefore, more significant transactions than Class 3 transactions.

19.4.6.2 Chapter 10 requirements

Listing Rule 10.4.1R(1) provides that the company must notify an RIS as soon as possible after the terms of any Class 2 transaction are agreed. The announcement (referred to as a 'Class 2 announcement') must contain the information prescribed by LR 10.4.1R(2), which is more detailed than the information required in an announcement relating to a Class 3 transaction.

If the company later becomes aware that:

(a) there has been a significant change which affects any matter in the Class 2 announcement; or

(b) a significant new matter has arisen which the company would have been required to mention in the Class 2 announcement if it had arisen at the time it was preparing that announcement, the company must make a supplementary announcement through an RIS without delay (LR 10.4.2R(1).

19.4.7 Class 1

19.4.7.1 Percentage ratios

If *any* of the percentage ratios is 25% or more, the transaction will be classified as a Class 1 transaction (LR 10.2.2R(3)). For example, imagine that X plc, a listed company, is acquiring Y Ltd. The profits of X plc are £100m. The profits of Y Ltd are £30m. The percentage ratio resulting from the profits class test is 30% (30/100 × 100%). The transaction is a Class 1 transaction.

19.4.7.2 Chapter 10 requirements

Listing Rule 10.5.1R provides that the company must:

(a) comply with the Class 2 requirements, that is, make an announcement through an RIS which complies with LR 10.4.1R(1) (note that, in practice, this is still referred to as a Class 2 announcement, even when it relates to a Class 1 transaction), and make a supplementary announcement, if required;

(b) send an explanatory circular, approved by the FSA, to shareholders in the form prescribed by LR 13 (Class 1 circular: see **19.6.1** below);

(c) obtain the shareholders' approval of the transaction (by ordinary resolution in general meeting) before completing the transaction (the notice of meeting will be sent out with the circular referred to at (b) above); and

(d) ensure that, if the agreement is to be entered into before shareholder approval is obtained, completion of the transaction is conditional on shareholder approval being obtained.

19.4.7.3 Waiver of the requirements to prepare a circular and obtain shareholder approval

If the company is making a Class 1 disposal (not acquisition) because it is in severe financial difficulty, then LR 10.8.1G provides that the FSA may waive the requirement for a circular and shareholder approval referred to at **19.4.7.2(b)** and **(c)** above. If the company wants to make use of this waiver, it must demonstrate to the FFSA that it is in severe financial difficulty and must satisfy the conditions in LR 10.8.2G to LR 10.8.6G. The conditions are onerous, and include:

(a) the company demonstrating to the FSA that it could not reasonably have entered into negotiations earlier (thereby allowing time to seek shareholder approval);

(b) the sponsor confirming that the company is in severe financial difficulty and will not be in a position to meet its obligations as they fall due unless the disposal takes place according to the proposed timetable;

(c) the company's finance providers confirming that further finance or facilities will not be made available and, unless the disposal is effected immediately, current facilities will be withdrawn; and

(d) the company making a full announcement to an RIS, no later than the terms of the disposal are agreed, containing the information set out in LR 10.8.4G and LR 10.8.5G.

19.4.7.4 The sponsor's role

As **4.2.2** explained, the FSA has increased the role of the sponsor under the new regime. It is now a requirement that a listed company must obtain guidance from a sponsor as to the application of chapter 10 if the transaction could be a Class 1 transaction (or a reverse takeover) (LR 8.2.2R). In fact, this reflects common practice under the old regime.

19.4.7.5 Specific transactions

The new regime sets out rules which can result in the following specific types of transactions being classified as Class 1 transactions:

(a) *Joint ventures.* The new regime provides guidance that, on entering a joint venture, a company should consider the exit provisions of the venture, to determine whether they result in the transaction being classified as a Class 1 transaction (see LR 10.8.9G).

(b) *Reverse takeovers.* Listing Rule 10.2.3R provides that a reverse takeover will be treated as a Class 1 transaction if it meets the conditions set out in that rule.

(c) *Indemnities.* It is common, in a sale and purchase agreement, for a buyer to seek an indemnity from the seller, to cover specific areas of risk. An indemnity is an undertaking by the seller to meet a specific potential legal liability of the buyer. The indemnity will entitle the buyer to a payment from the seller if the event giving rise to the indemnity takes place. Unlike a claim for breach of warranty, there is no need for the buyer to establish that he has suffered loss.

Listing Rule 10.2.4R provides that certain exceptional indemnities, where the maximum liability is unlimited, or equal to or more than 25% of the average of the company's profits for the last three financial years, will be treated as Class 1 transactions. (The FSA has discretion to substitute other indicators of the size of the indemnity, in the event that this calculation gives an anomalous result.) Listing Rule 10.2.5G sets out the types of indemnity which are not exceptional (including indemnities customarily given in connection with sale and purchase agreements).

(d) *Break fees.* A break fee is a fee payable by a company if certain specified events occur which cause the transaction to fail, or which materially impede a transaction (see LR, Appendix 1).

Listing Rule 10.2.7R provides that any break fee payable in respect of a transaction will itself be treated as a Class 1 transaction if the total value of break fees in aggregate exceeds 1% of the value of the company, calculated by reference to the offer price (where the company is being acquired) or 1% of the company's market capitalisation (in all other circumstances).

(e) *Issues by major subsidiary undertakings.* Listing Rule 10.2.8R provides that if a major *unlisted* subsidiary of a listed company issues shares:

  (i) for cash;
  (ii) in exchange for other securities, or
  (iii) to reduce indebtedness,

which will cause a dilution with an economic effect equivalent to the sale of 25% or more of the group, then the share issue will be classified as a Class 1 transaction.

19.4.8 Reverse takeover

19.4.8.1 Percentage ratios

If:

(a) a listed company acquires:

(i) a business,
(ii) an unlisted company, or
(iii) assets; *and*

(b) either:
(i) *any* percentage ratio is 100% or more, *or*
(ii) the transaction will result in:
– a fundamental change in the business, or
– a change in the board, or in voting control of the listed company,

then the transaction will be a reverse takeover (LR 10.2.2R(4)). What this means, in layman's terms, is that the listed company is acquiring a company which is either bigger than it is (on the basis of the class tests), or will, in any event, cause fundamental changes to the listed company's business, or, the balance of power at either board or shareholder level. In other words, it is a really significant transaction.

In practice, reverse takeovers can be a useful way for an unlisted company to list shares when it might otherwise not meet the criteria of the Listing Rules considered in **Chapters 4, 5** and **6**. In effect, the unlisted company 'reverses into' a listed company.

Example

Imagine that X plc, our listed company, has fallen on hard times. A large private company, Z Ltd, is doing very well. The shareholders of Z Ltd negotiate a deal, whereby they will sell Z Ltd to X plc in return for an issue of shares in X plc. The shareholders in Z Ltd will become shareholders in X plc, a listed company. The original shareholders of X plc hope that the acquisition by X plc of the successful company, Z Ltd, might help X plc back on its feet.

Figure 19.1 below shows the reverse takeover process in simplified form, using the details in the example above.

Figure 19.1: Reverse takeover

Before the reverse

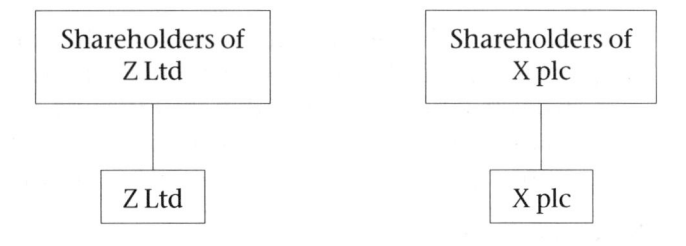

```
┌──────────────────┐         ┌──────────────────┐
│ Shareholders of  │         │ Shareholders of  │
│      Z Ltd       │         │      X plc       │
└────────┬─────────┘         └────────┬─────────┘
         │                            │
┌────────┴─────────┐         ┌────────┴─────────┐
│      Z Ltd       │         │      X plc       │
└──────────────────┘         └──────────────────┘
```

The reverse

1. Shareholders in Z Ltd *transfer* shares in Z Ltd to X plc

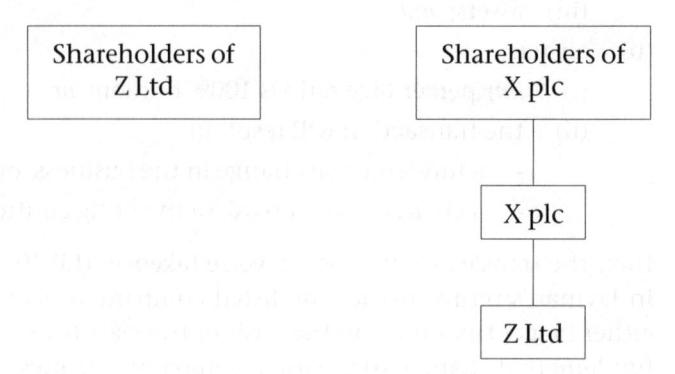

```
  Shareholders of         Shareholders of
      Z Ltd                    X plc
                                 |
                               X plc
                                 |
                               Z Ltd
```

2. X plc *issues* shares in itself to the shareholders of Z Ltd, as consideration for the transfer.

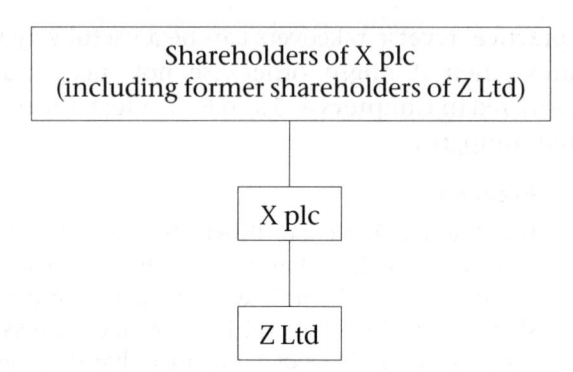

```
        Shareholders of X plc
  (including former shareholders of Z Ltd)
                  |
                X plc
                  |
                Z Ltd
```

19.4.8.2 Chapter 10 requirements

Listing Rule 10.6.1R provides that the company must comply with the Class 1 requirements. In addition, LR 10.6.2G provides that generally the FSA will cancel the listing of the company's shares. The company must then reapply for the listing of those shares and satisfy the relevant conditions for listing (other than one requirement relating to the company's accounts).

Those familiar with the old regime will note that the previous requirement for listing to be suspended automatically on the announcement of a reverse takeover has been deleted. However, given that the FSA will always consider suspension if it considers there is insufficient information in the market, in practice it may well continue to suspend the listing of some companies who announce a reverse.

19.4.8.3 The sponsor's role

A listed company must obtain guidance from a sponsor as to the application of chapter 10 if the transaction *could* be a reverse takeover (LR 8.2.2R).

19.5 Related party transactions

As **19.4.4** explained, while chapter 10 of the Listing Rules sets out the rules relating to the classification of transactions considered above, chapter 11 is dedicated solely to related party transactions. Class 1, Class 2 and Class 3 transactions and reverse takeovers are classified by reference to the size of the transaction compared to the size of the listed company. However, related party transactions are classified by the nature of the relationship between the parties to the transaction.

The rationale behind the related party classification is the same as that behind the chapter 10 classifications: the protection of investors. Related party transactions are subject to certain safeguards which are designed to prevent those who have considerable power over a listed company from taking advantage of their position.

19.5.1 What is a related party transaction?

A related party transaction is defined by LR 11.1.5R as:

(a) a transaction (other than a revenue transaction in the ordinary course of business) between a listed company (or any of its subsidiary undertakings) and a related party;

(b) any arrangements pursuant to which a listed company (or any of its subsidiary undertakings) and a related party each invests in, or provides finance to, another undertaking or asset; or

(c) a transaction (other than a revenue transaction in the ordinary course of business) between a listed company (or any of its subsidiary undertakings) and any person, the purpose and effect of which is to benefit a related party.

If the transaction falls within any of the above definitions, it will be a related party transaction, regardless of the size of the transaction and the classification system under chapter 10 of the Listing Rules. However, the transaction does still need to be classified by size, using the chapter 10 classification system. This is because one of the consequences of a transaction being a related party transaction is that the company must publish a circular, and some of the content requirements of that circular depend on whether the related party transaction is a Class 1 transaction or not (see **19.6.2** below). The size of the transaction can also affect whether the transaction is exempt from, or subject to more relaxed requirements than, the related party rules (see **19.5.4** below).

19.5.2 Who is a related party?

A 'related party' means a substantial shareholder, director or shadow director, a 50/50 joint venture partner, a person exercising significant influence and any of their associates (LR 11.1.4R).

19.5.2.1 Substantial shareholder

This refers to anyone who is (or, at any time in the 12 months before the transaction, was) entitled to exercise, or control the exercise of, 10% or more of the votes at a general meeting of either the listed company, *or any other company in the listed company's group* (but see **19.5.4.1** below in relation to insignificant subsidiaries).

The definition extends to those who were substantial shareholders at any time in the 12 months before the transaction, in order to prevent a shareholder circumventing the procedural requirements of the Listing Rules by reducing his shareholding to just below 10% the day before the transaction.

19.5.2.2 Director or shadow director

This refers to anyone who is (or, at any time in the 12 months before the transaction, was) a director or shadow director of the listed company, or of *any other company in the listed company's group* (but see **19.5.4.1** below in relation to insignificant subsidiaries). The Listing Rules define 'shadow director' as anyone who falls within the definition of a director in s 417(1)(b) of the FSMA 2000. This covers anyone in accordance with whose directions or instructions the directors of the company are accustomed to act. There is, however, some protection for the likes of lawyers; a person will not be a shadow director just because the directors act in accordance with advice he provides in a professional capacity.

19.5.2.3 50/50 joint venture partner

A 50/50 joint venture partner refers to a party to a 50/50 joint venture (namely a joint venture where the two parties have a deadlocked interest in the venture).

19.5.2.4 Person exercising significant influence

This is a person (other than a 50/50 joint venture partner) who exercises significant influence over the company. Listing Rule 11.1.12G and LR 11, Annex 1, paras 7 and 10 provide guidance as to the applicability of chapter 11 to 50/50 joint venture arrangements.

19.5.2.5 Associate

This means anyone who, at the time of the transaction, was an associate of the substantial shareholder, director, shadow director, 50/50 joint venture partner or person exercising significant influence, referred to at **19.5.2.1** to **19.5.2.4** above. 'Associate' is defined in LR Appendix 1.1 (amended as set out in para 11.3 of Issue 12 of *List!*) as follows:

- In relation to a director, substantial shareholder, 50/50 joint venture partner or person exercising significant influence, who is an individual:
  (1) that individual's spouse, civil partner or child (together 'the individual's family');
  (2) the trustees (acting as such) of any trust of which the individual or any of the individual's family is a beneficiary or discretionary object (other than a trust which is either an occupational pension scheme or an employees' share scheme which does not, in either case, have the effect of conferring benefits on persons all or most of whom are related parties);
  (3) any company in whose equity securities the individual or any member or members (taken together) of the individual's family or the individual and any such member or members (taken together) are directly or indirectly interested (or have a conditional or contingent entitlement to become interested) so that they are (or would on the fulfilment of the condition or the occurrence of the contingency be) able:
      (a) to exercise or control the exercise of 30% or more of the votes able to be cast at general meetings on all, or substantially all, matters; or
      (b) to appoint or remove directors holding a majority of voting rights at board meetings on all, or substantially all, matters.

  For the purpose of paragraph (3), if more than one director of the listed company, its parent undertaking or any of its subsidiary undertakings is interested in the equity securities of another company, then the interests of those directors and their associates will be aggregated when determining whether that company is an associate of the director.

- In relation to a substantial shareholder, 50/50 joint venture partner or person exercising significant influence, which is a company:

(1) any other company which is its subsidiary undertaking or parent undertaking or fellow subsidiary undertaking of the parent undertaking;

(2) any company whose directors are accustomed to act in accordance with the substantial shareholder's, 50/50 joint venture partner's or person exercising significant influence's directions or instructions;

(3) any company in the capital of which the substantial shareholder, 50/50 joint venture partner or person exercising significant influence and any other company under (1) or (2) taken together, is (or would on the fulfillment of a condition or the occurrence of a contingency be) interested in the manner described in (3) above.

As you can see, the definition is not succinct. It may help to consider an example of who is an associate:

Example

Mr A is a non-executive director (NED) of X plc, a fashion retailer. He also owns 30% of Y Ltd, a marketing company. X plc decides to acquire the entire issued share capital of Y Ltd, to provide an in-house marketing facility for its business.

Y Ltd is an associate of Mr A. This is because Mr A is a director of X plc, and an individual. Y Ltd is caught by para (3) of the appropriate part of the definition; it is a company in whose equity securities Mr A is directly interested and in which he can exercise 30% of the votes.

As a result of Y Ltd being an associate of a director of X plc, Y Ltd is also a related party of X plc. The acquisition by X plc of the entire share capital of Y Ltd is not a revenue transaction in the ordinary course of business (retailers do not buy marketing businesses on a day-to-day basis). The acquisition is a related party transaction. There is a risk that Mr A could abuse his position as a director of X plc, and so the shareholders of X plc will be afforded extra protection under Chapter 11 of the Listing Rules.

19.5.3 Chapter 11 requirements

Subject to the exceptions referred to at **19.5.4** below, the following 'related party rules' apply. The company must:

(a) make a Class 2 announcement (see **19.4.6.2** above), which must also contain the name of the related party and details of the nature and extent of the related party's interest, and make a supplementary announcement, if required (again, do not be confused by the fact that the announcement is still referred to as a Class 2 announcement even though it is being made in relation to a related parties transaction) (LR 11.1.7R(1));

(b) send an explanatory circular, approved by the FSA, and containing the information prescribed by LR 13.3 and LR 13.6, to shareholders (see **19.6.2** below) (LR 11.1.7R(2));

(c) obtain the shareholders' approval of the transaction (by ordinary resolution in general meeting before completing the transaction – see (d) below) (LR 11.1.7R(3)(a));

(d) if the agreement is to be entered into before shareholder approval is obtained, ensure that completion of the transaction is conditional on shareholder approval being obtained (LR 11.1.7R(3)(b)) (the notice of meeting will be sent out together with the circular referred to at (b) above); and

(e) ensure that the related party does not (and takes all reasonable steps to ensure that its associates do not) vote on any resolution to approve the transaction (LR 11.1.7R(4)).

19.5.4 Exceptions

There are two categories where the related party rules referred to at **19.5.3** above will not apply. The first is a full exception, where none of the related party rules will apply. The second is a limited exception, where the rules which apply are substantially more relaxed than the full related party rules.

19.5.4.1 When the related party rules will not apply

Listing Rule 11.1.6R provides that the related party rules will not apply if the transaction or arrangement is:

(a) a small transaction (defined by LR 11, Annex 1R, para 1 as any transaction where each of the chapter 10 class tests (see **19.4.3** above) results in percentage ratios which are equal to or less than 0.25%) (if this does not apply, consider **19.5.4.2** below); or

(b) a transaction of a kind referred to in LR 11, Annex 1R, paras 2 to 10, provided it does not have any unusual features.

This includes the following transactions:

New issues (LR 11, Annex 1R, para 2)

The rules will not apply to any issue of new securities to a related party:

(a) pursuant to a pre-emptive offering; or
(b) pursuant to the exercise of conversion or subscription rights attaching to listed securities; or
(c) previously approved by an ordinary resolution of the shareholders.

The rationale behind this exception is that the shareholders have been protected by other means.

Employees' share schemes (LR 11, Annex 1R, para 3)

The rules will not apply to various awards made pursuant to an employees' share scheme.

Directors' indemnities (LR 11, Annex 1R, para 5)

The rules will not apply to the grant of an indemnity to a director of a listed company or any of its subsidiaries, if the terms of the indemnity are in accordance with those specifically permitted under the CA 1985.

Underwriting (LR 11, Annex 1R, para 6)

The rules will not apply to the underwriting by a related party of certain share issues by the listed company or any of its subsidiaries, provided the consideration to be paid to the underwriter:

(a) is no more than the usual commercial underwriting consideration; and
(b) is the same as will be paid to any other underwriters.

50/50 Joint ventures (LR 11, Annex 1R, paras 7 and 10)

The rules will not apply to transactions with 50/50 joint venture partners if:

(a) the transaction is unrelated to the joint venture; or
(b) the joint venture has been in existence for at least one year and it is insignificant to the company, namely:

(i) its assets and profits are less than 10% of those of the company; and

(ii) consideration for the 50% stake is less than 10% of the company's market capitalisation.

Insignificant subsidiaries (LR 11, Annex 1R, para 9)

The rules will not apply if the related party is a related party only through being a substantial shareholder, director or shadow director of an insignificant subsidiary of the listed company (or the associate of any such person). An insignificant subsidiary is a subsidiary which has:

(a) contributed less than 10% of the profits, and

(b) represented less than 10% of the assets of,

the listed company for each of the three financial years preceding the date of the transaction for which accounts have been published (or for each financial year for which accounts have been published, if the insignificant subsidiary has been part of the group for less than three years).

Note that this exception will not apply in certain circumstances, such as if the insignificant subsidiary has been part of the group for less than one year, or if the insignificant subsidiary itself is party to the transaction and the ratio of consideration to market capitalisation is more than 10%.

19.5.4.2 When the related party rules will be relaxed

The rules will be relaxed in relation to any transaction where each of the chapter 10 class tests (see **19.4.3** above) results in percentage ratios which are less than 5%, but where one or more exceeds 0.25%. In other words, the related party transaction is small, but not small enough to benefit from the full exception referred to at **19.5.4.1** above. How are the rules relaxed? The following rules apply instead of the rules referred to at **19.5.3** above (LR 11.1.10R). The company must:

(a) inform the FSA in writing of the details of the proposed transaction;

(b) provide the FSA with written confirmation, from an independent adviser acceptable to the FSA, that the terms of the proposed related party transaction are fair and reasonable so far as the shareholders of the company are concerned; and

(c) undertake in writing to the FSA to include details of the transaction in the company's next published annual accounts.

Compared to the time and effort required to comply with the usual related party rules by making a Class 2 announcement, publishing a Class 1 circular, and seeking shareholder approval, these rules are much less demanding of the company.

19.5.5 The sponsor's role

As **4.2.2** explained, the FSA has increased the role of the sponsor under the new regime. It is now a requirement that a listed company must obtain guidance from a sponsor as to the application of Chapter 11 if the transaction *could be* a related party transaction (LR 8.2.3R). In fact, this reflects common practice under the old regime.

19.5.6 The Companies Act 1985

The Listing Rules operate alongside the statutory provisions of the CA 1985. In the event of a related party transaction, the following sections of the CA 1985 may also be relevant.

19.5.6.1 Section 317

This section requires directors to declare their interests in a transaction.

19.5.6.2 Section 320

This section requires shareholder approval of substantial property transactions between directors (but not substantial shareholders) and the company.

19.5.6.3 Sections 324 to 328

These sections require directors to notify the company of dealings in securities (see **15.5**).

19.5.7 The memorandum and articles

The company's memorandum and articles may also contain provisions about transactions between the company and its directors.

19.6 The circular

As explained in **Chapter 7**, the circular is a means by which a company communicates with its shareholders, particularly where the company requires the shareholders to approve a transaction. The circular should provide enough information to shareholders to allow them to make an informed decision whether to vote for or against the transaction. The circular will also contain the notice of EGM, convening the meeting at which the shareholders will vote on the transaction.

Chapter 13 of the Listing Rules prescribes the content of a circular. Listing Rule 13.3 sets out the content requirements for circulars generally; specific content requirements for specific types of circular are then prescribed by other chapter 13 Listing Rules. For example, LR 13.4, LR 13.5 and LR 13, Annex 1R set out the specific requirements, over and above the general LR 3.3 requirements, for a Class 1 circular, and LR 13.6 sets out the specific content requirements for a related party circular.

Just as the Prospectus Rules allow information to be incorporated by reference into a prospectus (see **6.5.2.2** above), so LR 13.1.3R allows information in a prospectus, or other published document filed with the FSA, to be incorporated into a circular.

It was explained at **7.7.4** above that the FSA categorises circulars either as requiring prior approval (referred to as 'non-routine' under the old regime), or not requiring prior approval (referred to as 'routine' under the old regime). The Class 1 circular and related party circular both require FSA approval.

Once a circular has been finalised and approved, LR 9.6.1R provides that the company must lodge two copies with the FSA, at the same time it sends the circular to shareholders and it must announce that it has done so through an RIS (LR 9.6.3R(1)). The FSA will then publish the circular through its document viewing facility.

Note that the preparation of the circular can be very time-consuming and costly, and may also delay the timing of the transaction to which it relates (see **19.7** below). In particular, a Class 1 related party transaction involves a great deal of work for both the company and its advisers.

19.6.1 The Class 1 circular

19.6.1.1 Content

As explained at **19.6**, LR 13.3 sets out the general requirements, and LR 13.4, LR 13.5 and LR 13, Annex 1R the specific requirements for a Class 1 circular. Listing Rule 13, Annex 1R cross-refers to Annex 1 and Annex 3 of the PD Regulation (replicated at Appendix III of the Prospectus Rules). This aligns the content requirements of a circular with some of the content requirement for a prospectus (see **6.5.2**). Some of the information in LR 13, Annex 1R must be provided not only for the listed company buyer or seller, but also for the target company. The requirements of the rules referred to above include the following:

(a) *General disclosure* (LR 13.3.1R(3)). All information necessary for shareholders to be able to make a properly informed decision on the proposal.

(b) *Recommendation* (LR 13.3.1R(5)). A recommendation to shareholders from the directors as to how they should exercise their votes for each resolution, and a statement from the directors as to whether they consider the proposal to be in the shareholders' best interests.

(c) *The directors' responsibility statement* (LR 13.4.1R(4)). A statement by the directors, in the form set out at LR 13.4.1R(4), that they take personal responsibility for the circular.

(d) *Major interests in shares* (LR 13, Annex 1R). The names of the shareholders holding 3% or more of the company's shares (or an appropriate negative statement if there are none).

(e) *Material contracts* (LR 13, Annex 1R). See **6.5.2.1** above.

(f) *Litigation* (LR 13, Annex 1R). See **6.5.2.1** above.

(g) *Significant changes* (LR 13, Annex 1R). A statement about any significant change since the last published accounts, in respect of the listed company, any other company in the listed company's group and the target company.

19.6.1.2 The sponsor's role

As explained at **19.4.7.4** above, the company must obtain the guidance of a sponsor before it enters into a Class 1 transaction. The sponsor has various obligations under the Listing Rules relating to the Class 1 circular, including the following:

(a) The sponsor owes a general duty of skill and care and taking reasonable steps to ensure that the company understands its obligations under the Listing Rules and the Disclosure Rules (LR 8.8.3R, LR 8.3.4R and LR 8.4.2R).

(b) Listing Rule 8.4.12R provides that, before the sponsor submits the Class 1 circular to the FSA for approval, it must be of the opinion, having made due and careful enquiry, that:

  (i) the company has satisfied all requirements of the Listing Rules relevant to the production of a Class 1 circular;

  (ii) the transaction will not have an adverse impact on the company's ability to comply with the Listing Rules or the Disclosure Rules; and

  (iii) the directors have a reasonable basis on which to make the working capital statement required by LR 13.4.1R.

The requirement at (ii) above is particularly onerous from the sponsor's point of view.

(c) Listing Rule 8.4.13R sets out further tasks for the sponsor, including:

(i) submitting to the FSA a Sponsor's Declaration for the Production of a Circular (on the day the circular is to be approved, but before such approval has been given); and

(ii) ensuring that all matters known to it, which, in its reasonable opinion, should be taken into account by the FSA in considering the transaction, have been disclosed with sufficient prominence in the documentation or otherwise in writing to the FSA.

The proforma Sponsor's Declaration for the Production of a Circular is available from the UKLA section of the FSA website.

19.6.2 The related party circular

Listing Rule 13.3 lists the general content requirements, and LR 13.6 the specific content requirements, of a related party circular. These requirements include:

(a) *Full particulars* (LR 13.6.1R(3)). Full particulars of the transaction, including the name of the related party and the nature and extent of that party's interest in the transaction.

(b) *The fair and reasonable statement* (LR 13.6.1R(5)). A statement by the board that the transaction is fair and reasonable so far as the shareholders of the company are concerned, and that they have been so advised by an independent adviser acceptable to the FSA.

If the transaction is also a Class 1 transaction, LR 13.6.1R(7) provides that the circular must also contain all the information which must be included in a Class 1 circular (see **19.6.1** above), and, if the acquisition or disposal is of an asset for which appropriate financial information is not available, an independent valuation of that asset is also required (LR 13.6.1R(4)).

On receipt of the circular, the shareholders will have all the information to hand to enable them to make an informed decision as to whether or not to approve the transaction (as required by the related party rule referred to at **19.5.3** at (c) above).

19.6.3 Verification

The verification process in the context of a flotation is explained at **5.3.5** and **6.8** above. Verification is also required in relation to other documents published by listed companies, such as circulars, to protect directors against claims from shareholders on the basis set out at **6.7** above.

19.7 The transaction timetable

The requirements of chapter 10 and chapter 11 of the Listing Rules can have a significant effect on the transaction timetable. The detail of an acquisition or disposal timetable for any company, listed or unlisted, is considered in another book in the series (see LPC Guide, *Acquisitions*).

The skeleton timetable below should provide a basic understanding of how the requirements for listed companies impact on an acquisition timetable. The listed company requirements are italicised. Remember, however, that not every listed company will need to follow these requirements; whether it does depends on the classification of the transaction.

(a) Sign heads of agreement.
This document will include legally binding provisions. It will contain important provisions about confidentiality and exclusivity.

(b) Sign the (*conditional*) agreement.

If the transaction is a Class 1, reverse takeover or related party transaction, the agreement must be conditional upon shareholder approval.

(c) *Make a Class 2 announcement.*

If the transaction is a Class 2, Class 1, reverse takeover or related party transaction, the company must make a Class 2 announcement through an RIS. In certain circumstances the company must also announce a Class 3 transaction.

(d) *Post the circular and the EGM notice.*

If the transaction is a Class 1, reverse takeover or related party transaction, a circular is required.

(e) *Hold an EGM.*

If the transaction is a Class 1, reverse takeover or related party transaction, shareholder approval is required.

(f) Completion.

Note that there are several steps in between steps (b) and (f) for a listed company. Usually an unlisted company can sign and complete a sale and purchase agreement simultaneously.

19.8 Conclusion

The Listing Rules regulate the process by which a listed company can make acquisitions and disposals. Depending on the size of the transaction and the relationship between the parties to the transaction, the Listing Rules can require a company to notify an RIS of the transaction and, for more significant transactions, circulate an explanatory circular and obtain shareholder approval of the transaction. These requirements can impact significantly on the timing and cost of the transaction.

Chapter 20

Takeovers: Regulation

20.1	Introduction	273
20.2	The Panel	273
20.3	The Takeovers Directive	275
20.4	The Takeovers Regulations	276
20.5	The City Code	277
20.6	Other rules and regulations	283
20.7	Regulatory bodies	284
20.8	Future developments	284

20.1 Introduction

Chapters 21 and **22** consider the detail of a takeover offer (also known as a 'takeover bid'). The purpose of this chapter is to introduce the regulation which will be relevant to any lawyer who advises on such an offer.

Those already familiar with the regulation of takeovers will note that the area has undergone some changes as a result of:

(a) the recent implementation in the UK of the Directive on Takeover Bids (Directive 2004/25/EC) (the 'Takeovers Directive'); and

(b) changes made as part of the ongoing review of the City Code (see **20.5**).

Further information on the Takeovers Directive and its implementation is set out at **20.3** and **20.4** below. While there have been some changes to the nature of the Panel, and changes to the nature, and some of the rules, of the City Code, in fact the Directive was based largely on the UK model of takeover regulation and so it has not changed the UK takeover regime in a fundamental way.

20.2 The Panel

The Panel on Takeovers and Mergers (the 'Panel') was established in 1968 with the support of the Bank of England. Since then it has supervised the regulatory aspects of takeovers. On 20 May 2006 it was designated as the supervisory authority to carry out certain regulatory functions in relation to takeovers pursuant to the Takeovers Directive (see **20.3**).

20.2.1 What does the Panel do?

The Panel is an independent body with two roles:

(a) *Rule-making*. The Panel issues and administers the City Code, the rulebook relating to takeovers (see **20.5** below).

(a) *Judicial*. The Panel supervises and regulates takeovers and other matters dealt with in the City Code.

20.2.2 Who is on the Panel?

The Panel comprises a maximum of 34 members. It self-appoints a Chairman, up to two Deputy Chairmen and a maximum of 20 other members. Certain financial institutions and professional bodies such as the ABI, the CBI and the NAPF appoint the remaining members.

20.2.3 The Panel Executive

The Panel itself meets rarely. Instead the Panel Executive carries out the day-to-day work of the Panel, monitoring dealings and interpreting, consulting on and giving rulings on the City Code. The Panel Executive is headed by the Director General, typically an investment banker seconded to the Panel, and is staffed not only by employees, but also by secondees, including accountants, brokers, investment bankers and, significantly, corporate lawyers. In practice, the term 'Panel Executive' is rarely used; if a lawyer is consulting the Panel Executive, he will invariably refer to this as 'consulting the Panel'. Further information about the Panel Executive is contained in para 5 of the Introduction to the City Code and is available on the Panel's website.

Tempus takeover

THE Clifford Chance partner Jeremy Sandelson has been advising the Takeover Panel over its decision on the recent appeal by WPP plc – the company wanted to challenge the executive's refusal to allow it to invoke a "material adverse change" condition so as to lapse its bid for Tempus. Unusually, the panel and executive were each legally advised: for the latter was Anthony McCaulay of Herbert Smith. Both Sandelson and McCaulay had been seconded to work on the executive panel in the early 1990s. One banker commented: "Blimey – there are more lawyers here than bankers – no doubt as a result of the Human Rights Act."

Source: *The Times*: 13 November 2001.

20.2.4 The Panel Committees

The Panel operates through the following committees.

20.2.4.1 The Code Committee

The Code Committee carries out the rule-making role of the Panel (see **20.2.1**). This Committee is responsible for reviewing and amending the City Code. Typically, the Committee will announce a period of public consultation before amending the Code. The Public Consultation Papers ('PCPs') are published on the Panel's website. Paragraph 4(b) of the Introduction to the City Code provides further detail on the Code Committee.

20.2.4.2 The Hearings Committee

The Hearings Committee carries out the judicial role of the Panel (see **20.2.1**). The Committee reviews the Panel Executive's rulings, and also hears any disciplinary proceedings (which the Panel Executive instigates – see **20.5.7.4**), relating to breaches of the City Code. Usually the secretary to the Hearings Committee is a partner in a law firm. Paragraphs 4 and 7 of the Introduction to the City Code provide further detail on the Hearings Committee.

There is a right to appeal to the Takeover Appeal Board in relation to a decision of the Hearings Committee (Introduction to the City Code, para 8).

Paragraph 4(d) of the Introduction to the City Code ensures that membership of the Committees are kept separate: a member of the Code Committee (see **20.2.4.1**) cannot be or become a member of the Hearings Committee or the Takeover Appeal Board.

20.2.4.3 The Nomination Committee

The Nomination Committee monitors the size, composition and balance of the Panel.

20.2.5 The nature of the Panel

Until recently, the Panel was a non-statutory body. In cases such as *R v Panel on Takeovers and Mergers, ex p Datafin plc and Another (Norton Opax plc and Another intervening)* [1987] 1 All ER 564 and *R v Panel on Takeovers and Mergers, ex p Guinness plc* [1989] 1 All ER 509, the courts marvelled at the unique nature of the Panel, which in practice had enormous power as a regulator of some of the largest, most expensive transactions in the financial industry, despite its lack of actual statutory powers. For example, when Guinness breached r 11 of the City Code during its offer for Distillers, the Panel had the power to force Guinness to pay a considerable sum to the former Distillers shareholders, despite its non-statutory footing at the time (see the article in **Chapter 21**).

However, on 20 May 2006, the implementation of the Takeovers Directive in the UK (see **20.4**) placed the Panel on a statutory footing in relation to takeover offers to which the Takeovers Directive applies (see **20.3**).

20.3 The Takeovers Directive

The Directive on Takeover Bids (Directive 2004/25/EC) (the 'Takeovers Directive') came into force on 20 May 2004. It aims to impose adequate takeover regulation across the Member States. Each Member State had to implement the Directive into its own law by 20 May 2006.

20.3.1 Application

The Directive applies to takeover *offers* of companies whose shares are admitted to a *regulated market*.

20.3.1.1 Offers

Article 2.1(a) of the Directive states that the Directive applies only to public offers to acquire control of a company. Therefore the Directive does not apply to takeovers effected by way of scheme of arrangement (see **21.12**) (although the City Code does – see **20.4.2**).

20.3.1.2 Regulated market

The reference to a regulated market is to a market within the meaning of art 1(13) of the Investment Services Directive. A list of regulated markets within the EEA is maintained on the website of the European Commission. UK regulated markets are listed on the websites of the Takeover Panel and the Financial Services Authority. For the purposes of this book it is important to note that the Main Market is a regulated market, but AIM is not.

To summarise, the Directive applies to takeovers of companies listed on the Main Market (the focus of this book), but not to takeovers of unlisted public companies or companies quoted on AIM (which are not regulated markets), or takeovers made by way of a scheme of arrangement (which does not involve an offer).

20.3.2 Implementation

In the UK, the original intention was to implement the Takeovers Directive through Pt 28 of the Companies Bill (see **1.11**). Part 28 seeks to implement broader changes to the takeover regime in addition to those required by the Takeovers Directive.

However, the Companies Bill addresses considerably more issues than takeovers alone, and has progressed through Parliament very slowly. Part 28 was not ready to enact in time to meet the Directive's implementation date of 20 May. As an interim measure, the Takeovers Directive (Interim Implementation) Regulations 2006 (see **20.4** below) were drawn up specifically to implement the Takeovers Directive in the UK, to remain in force until Pt 28 of the Companies Bill is enacted.

20.4 The Takeovers Regulations

On 20 May 2006 the Takeovers Directive was implemented in the UK by the Takeovers Directive (Interim Implementation) Regulations 2006 (SI 2006/1183) (the 'Takeovers Regulations'). The Takeovers Regulations are reproduced in full at **Appendix 8**.

20.4.1 Application

The Takeovers Regulations were drawn up using powers in the European Communities Act 1972, and apply only to transactions to which the Takeovers Directive applies (so they will apply to the takeover of a company listed on the Main Market, but not to the takeover of an unlisted public company, or a company quoted on AIM - see **20.3.1**).

The Regulations will be repealed as soon as Pt 28 of the Companies Bill is enacted. The DTI announced in August 2006 that this was expected to be in Autumn 2006, soon after the Bill receives Royal Assent. Until the Bill comes into force, the Panel has no power to change the City Code in relation to matters covered by the Directive (the European Communities Act 1972 does not permit the Panel to make and amend rules which have statutory effect).

20.4.2 The dual regime

Until Pt 28 of the Companies Bill comes into force, there will be dual regime for the Panel and the City Code. Where a transaction is outside the scope of the Directive, and therefore of the Regulations (for example, a takeover offer for an unlisted public company or AIM company, or a takeover by way of a scheme of arrangement), the Code and the Panel will continue to operate as they did prior to 20 May 2006, that is, on a non-statutory footing. Where a transaction is within the scope of the Directive, and therefore of the Regulations (for example, as is the focus of this book, a takeover of a company with its shares admitted to listing on the Official List and admitted to trading on the Main Market), the Code and the Panel will operate on a statutory footing. This is confirmed in the final sentence of para 2(a) of the Introduction the City Code.

This distinction is useful to know about from an academic perspective. In practice, however, the City Code will be mandatory regardless of whether it is operating on a statutory footing or otherwise. As explained at **20.2.5**, even before the implementation of the Takeovers Directive, the Code and the Panel had formidable non-statutory regulatory power, and this power will remain in relation to those takeovers not covered by the Takeovers Directive.

20.5 The City Code

The main source of regulation of takeovers is called the City Code on Takeovers and Mergers. This is often referred to as the 'Takeover Code', or the 'City Code'. This book refers to it as the City Code.

A new, eighth, edition of the City Code was published on and took effect from 20 May 2006. This new edition reflects the changes required by the Takeovers Regulations (see **20.4**), as well as other changes required as part of the Panel's ongoing review process (see **20.2.1(a)**), namely the abolition of the SARs (see **21.8.10**), the extension of several rules to include dealing in 'interests in shares', such as derivatives and options, rather than just actual shares (see **21.8.11.3** and **28.11.4**), and other miscellaneous amendments relating largely to the implementation of the Prospectus Directive (see **3.5.1**) and the new listing regime which came into force on 1 July 2005 (see **3.1**).

20.5.1 When does the City Code apply?

The introduction to the City Code explains that it applies to transactions where:

(a) one company (the 'offeror' or 'bidder');
(b) acquires control of;
(c) another company (the 'offeree company' or 'target').

Note that both takeovers and mergers can fall within this definition. In practice, it can be difficult to identify whether a transaction actually constitutes a takeover or a merger, but, in any event, it is really of no legal significance. If this definition is met, the City Code will regulate the transaction, whether the accurate description of the transaction is a takeover or a merger.

The City Code will apply regardless of how the takeover is effected (for example, it applies to a takeover effected by way of a general offer or by way of a scheme of arrangement – see **21.12**). Here, the City Code is broader than the Takeovers Directive, which does not apply to schemes of arrangement (see **20.3.1**).

The Code even applies to transactions which are in contemplation but not yet announced.

20.5.1.1 The offeror

The offeror may be any company, listed or unlisted, public or private, which makes an offer or intends to make an offer. It is the status of the *offeree company* which is important. In practice, the offeror may also be referred to as the 'bidder'.

20.5.1.2 The offeree company

The City Code will apply if the offeree company is:

(a) a public company, or Societas Europaea, registered in the UK, the Channel Islands or the Isle of Man, whose securities are admitted to trading on a *regulated market* in the UK or on any stock exchange in the Channel Islands or the Isle of Man (such as the Main Market, which is the focus of this book); or

(b) an unlisted public company, or Societas Europaea, or, in limited circumstances, a private company (namely a private company which during the last ten years has had its securities admitted to the Official List, or advertised dealings for a six-month continuous period, or been required to file a prospectus, or had securities subject to a CA 1985, s 163(2) marketing arrangement) which:

(i) is registered in the UK, the Channel Islands or the Isle of Man, and

(ii) in the Panel's opinion, has its place of central management and control in the UK, the Channel Islands or the Isle of Man.

Where the company is registered in the UK but its shares are admitted to trading elsewhere in the EEA (or vice versa) there is provision for shared jurisdiction.

The City Code uses the word 'offeree company' to describe the target company (or potential target company) whose shares are the subject of the offer (or potential offer). However, as lawyers, you will appreciate that in fact the offeror will make the offer not to the target company, but to that company's shareholders. In practice, the offeree company may also be referred to as the 'target'.

Regulated market

The meaning of 'regulated market' is discussed at **20.3.1.2** above. For our purposes it is important to note that the Main Market is a regulated market, but AIM is not.

In summary, then, it is the offeree company's status as a *public* company which is important for the purposes of the City Code, regardless of whether the offeree company happens to be listed or unlisted.

20.5.1.3 Control

'Control' is defined as:

(a) an interest, or interests, in shares;

(b) carrying 30% or more of the voting rights of a company;

(c) regardless of whether the interest or interests give actual control.

There is, in fact, no persuasive argument why 30% should be chosen as the interest which represents control of a company. A shareholder who has an interest in less than 30% may, in practice, have control of the company if that shareholder has an interest in the largest percentage shareholding in the company, or has the balance of power. Nevertheless, the City Code would not consider that person to have 'control'.

Note also that it is with the acquisition of interests in *voting shares* that the City Code is concerned. This means that acquisitions of assets are not covered by the City Code.

20.5.2 To whom does the City Code apply?

Paragraph 3(f) of the Introduction to the City Code confirms that the Code applies to everyone who is involved in a transaction to which it applies. This includes not only the offeror and the offeree company, but also the directors of the offeror and the offeree company, and their respective professional advisers. The lawyers advising on the transaction, therefore, will be subject to the City Code.

20.5.3 The purpose of the City Code

The introduction to the City Code explains that its purpose is to:

(a) ensure fair and equal treatment of all shareholders in relation to takeovers;

(b) provide an orderly framework within which takeovers are conducted; and

(c) promote the integrity of the financial markets.

The City Code is not concerned with the commercial advantages or disadvantages of a takeover (these are matters for the company and its shareholders), nor with other regulatory issues, such as competition policy (see **Chapter 23**).

20.5.4 The nature of the City Code

The City Code comprises six general principles (see **20.5.5**) and 38 rules which are based on, and develop, these principles. The rules must be read in conjunction not only with the general principles but also with the notes appended to them, which give practical guidance on the applicability of the rules.

The six general principles are taken directly from the Takeovers Directive. The previous edition of the City Code was also based on general principles, albeit 10 of them, so the six new general principles do not represent a fundamental change in the nature of the Code.

The City Code is an interesting creature from the lawyer's perspective, as it is the *spirit*, and not just the letter, of both the general principles and the rules which is paramount. This means that the Panel Executive may be willing to modify or relax the wording of the rules, on a case-by-case basis, if this is consistent with the underlying purpose of the rules. This, of course, is of significant interest to the lawyer, and affects how the lawyer must advise in relation to the Code in practice (see **20.5.6** below).

The interesting nature of the City Code is historic. Before 20 May 2006, the City Code was a non-statutory set of rules. As explained at **20.2.5** above, however, the Takeovers Directive gave the Panel a statutory basis in relation to takeover offers to which the Directive applies, and the City Code, as the Panel's rulebook, now has the force of law in relation to a transaction or rule which is subject to the Directive. However, despite this new statutory footing, the introduction to the new edition states that the spirit of the Code remains paramount (Introduction to the City Code, para 2(b)). This is not inconsistent with the statutory footing, so long as the modification is consistent with the general principles, which are taken from the Directive (Introduction to the City Code, para 2(c)). In practice, even before the Takeovers Directive was implemented, the Panel Executive used to justify derogations from the letter of the City Code on grounds of consistency with the previous 10 General Principles, so the new statutory footing should not change the flexible approach of the Panel Executive in any material way.

20.5.5 The general principles

The general principles are the key to understanding the spirit of the City Code. They are the cornerstone of the Code, and they may apply in situations which the rules of the City Code do not cover expressly. The six general principles are set out below, together with (the author's) summary to help reinforce the essence of each principle:

1. All holders of the securities of an offeree company of the same class must be afforded equivalent treatment; moreover, if a person acquires control of a company, the other holders of securities must be protected.
   Summary: shareholders should be treated equally.
2. The holders of the securities of an offeree company must have sufficient time and information to enable them to reach a properly informed decision on the bid; where it advises the holders of securities, the board of the offeree company must give its views on the effects of implementation of the bid on employment, conditions of employment and the locations of the company's

places of business.
Summary: sufficient information should be made available to shareholders in a timely fashion.

3. The board of an offeree company must act in the interests of the company as a whole and must not deny the holders of securities the opportunity to decide on the merits of the bid.
Summary: Directors have duties in relation to takeovers.

4. False markets must not be created in the securities of the offeree company, of the offeror company or of any other company concerned by the bid in such a way that the rise or fall of the prices of the securities becomes artificial and the normal functioning of the markets is distorted.
Summary: Parties should not create a false market.

5. An offeror must announce a bid only after ensuring that he/she can fulfil in full any cash consideration, if such is offered, and after taking all reasonable measures to secure the implementation of any other type of consideration.
Summary: The bidder should be in a position to implement its offer.

6. An offeree company must not be hindered in the conduct of its affairs for longer than is reasonable by a bid for its securities.
Summary: The offer timetable should be reasonable.

As stated at **20.5.4** above, the six general principles replaced the former 10 general principles on 20 May 2006. However, those familiar with the pre-20 May 2006 regime should note that all of the old general principles in fact have been incorporated in the new City Code, either enshrined in the six new principles, or in the rules themselves (amendments were made to rules 2.5, 19.1 and 23 to incorporate parts of old general principles 3, 4 and 5 which are covered only partially by the new general principles).

The practical effect of these general principles is considered in **Chapters 21** and **22**.

20.5.6 The City Code in practice

If there is any doubt as to how the City Code might apply in a certain situation, the parties and their advisers should consult the Panel Executive, who will provide a ruling on the issue. In fact, the introduction to the City Code states expressly that legal advice is not an appropriate alternative to obtaining a ruling from the Panel Executive. Does this mean that the lawyer does not need to know anything about the City Code? Far from it. In fact, the lawyer plays a pivotal part in the interpretation of the Code.

First, the lawyer will be involved in trying to identify a 'third way', in circumstances where the company will struggle to comply with the letter of the City Code, but there is a possibility of an alternative approach which would not compromise the spirit of the City Code. The Panel Executive is likely to be much more receptive to a company which approaches it in the hope of modifying the interpretation of a rule if the company has a well thought-out suggestion for such modification. Obviously the lawyer's knowledge and experience, of previous occasions when the Panel Executive has been willing to modify the interpretation of rules of the City Code, will assist in this role.

The second role of the lawyer in relation to the City Code is that, together with certain of the company's other advisers, he will have regular contact with the Panel Executive during the takeover process.

20.5.6.1 Practice Statements

The Panel Executive publishes Practice Statements, which it posts, in date order, on its website. These statements provide informal guidance on how the Panel Executive interprets and applies the City Code in certain circumstances. The Practice Statements do not form part of the City Code, and so are not binding, and no substitute for consulting the Panel Executive. That said, the lawyer would be most unwise to consult the Panel about an issue without having checked whether there are any Practice Statements which address that issue, and being familiar with the content of that Statement. An example of a Practice Statement (on schemes of arrangement) is set out in **Chapter 21**.

20.5.7 Enforcement of the City Code

The City Code has the force of law in relation to those takeovers which are subject to the Takeovers Directive. As noted at **20.4.2**, however, in practice the City Code remains mandatory for all transactions to which it applies. The following powers are available to the Panel to deal effectively with non-compliance.

20.5.7.1 Monitoring powers

Where the takeover is one to which the Takeovers Directive applies (see **20.3**), the Panel has new statutory powers to monitor the progress of the transaction. Those dealing with the Panel must do so in an open and cooperative way, and disclose all relevant information (subject to legal professional privilege) (Introduction to the City Code, para 9(a)). The Panel also has the power to require documents and information from persons dealing with the Panel (Introduction to the City Code, para 9(b)). These monitoring powers are a significant enhancement of the Panel's powers: prior to the eighth edition of the City Code, the Panel had very little power to investigate breaches of the Code. The Panel still lacks monitoring powers in relation to those takeovers to which the Directive does not apply.

20.5.7.2 Enforcement powers of the Panel

Anyone reporting a breach to the Panel must do so promptly, otherwise the Panel may exercise its discretion to disregard the complaint (Introduction to the City Code, para 10(a)).

Once it is certain that the Code has been breached, the Panel has several powers of enforcement, set out below.

Compliance rulings

The Panel has the power to make a compliance ruling, either to prevent a breach of the Code (if there is a reasonable likelihood of a breach of the City Code or a Panel ruling) or, if the breach has already occurred, to ensure the breach is remedied (Introduction to the City Code, para 10(b)).

Compensation rulings

The Panel has a limited power to make a compensation ruling to order a party to compensate any offeree company shareholders who have suffered financially as a result of a breach of the Code (Introduction to the City Code, para 10(c)). The Panel can exercise this power only in relation to breaches of those rules which deal with the offer consideration (namely rules 6, 9, 11, 14, 15, 16 and 35.3). The effect of a compensation ruling is to put the shareholders into the position they would have been had the breach not occurred. The Panel can also order that simple or compound interest be paid to the shareholders.

Enforcement by the courts

In relation to takeovers which are covered by the Takeovers Directive, the Panel can ask the courts to enforce the City Code (Introduction to the City Code, para 10(d)). The Panel has stated that it will exercise this power only as a last resort, or in urgent cases (PCP 2005/5, para 10.8.2).

Bid documentation rules

Again, in relation to takeovers which are covered by the Takeovers Directive, the Panel has further statutory powers. Since 20 May 2006, the failure to comply with bid documentation rules, set out in Appendix 6 of the City Code, constitutes a criminal offence (Takeovers Regulations, reg 10).

The bid documentation rules relate to the content requirements of the main takeover document, known as the offer document (see **22.4.1**) (the 'offer document rules'), and any defence documents (see **22.4.2**) (the 'response document rules'). In the event that the documents do not comply with the rules, a criminal offence is committed (in the case of a breach of the offer document rules) not only by the offeror but also by any director, officer or member of the offeror who caused the document to be published, and (in the case of a breach of the response document rules) by any director or officer of the offeree company if they knew, or were reckless as to whether, the document did not comply with the Code, and failed to take all reasonable steps to ensure compliance (Introduction to the City Code, para 10(e) and Appendix 6). The offence is punishable by a fine. The offence applies only to those takeover offers which are subject to the Takeovers Directive (so not to schemes of arrangement or to offers for unlisted companies, or companies listed on AIM).

In certain circumstances, disciplinary action may be appropriate (see **20.5.7.4**).

20.5.7.3 Enforcement powers of the FSA

The Panel can request the FSA to take enforcement action against any person authorised by the FSMA 2000 who contravenes the City Code or a ruling of the Panel. The definition of 'authorised person' is considered at **9.4.3**. In practice, this will cover the stockbroker (see **21.5.3**) and the financial adviser (see **21.5.1**) acting for the company in relation to the takeover. The stockbroker and financial adviser will not advise unless the takeover complies with the City Code, as otherwise they risk the sanctions listed below. Note that the FSA can also take enforcement action against an 'approved person', for example a director of an authorised firm.

The FSA can take the following enforcement action in the event of a breach of the City Code:

(a) public censure;
(b) fine;
(c) the removal of authorisation under the FSMA 2000;
(d) injunction; and
(e) order for restitution.

Note also the requirement, referred to at **20.5.7.4(e)** below, that the rules of the FSA prohibit a person authorised by the FSMA 2000 from acting for any offender.

20.5.7.4 Disciplinary powers

Paragraph 11 of the introduction to the Code outlines the power of the Panel Executive to institute disciplinary proceedings before the Hearings Committee (see **20.2.4.2**). If the Committee finds that there has been a breach of the City Code, it can impose the following sanctions:

(a) private reprimand;

(b) public censure;

(c) suspension or withdrawal of, or the imposition of conditions on, any exemption, approval or other special status the Panel has granted;

(d) reporting the offender's conduct to another regulatory body such as the DTI, the Stock Exchange or the FSA; or

(e) publishing a Panel Statement indicating that the offender is unlikely to comply with the City Code. This can trigger other requirements of the FSA and certain professional bodies which oblige their members, in certain circumstances, not to act for the offender in a transaction to which the City Code applies.

The Panel Executive has set out, in the 'compliance' section of its website, the issues it will take into account when considering whether to take disciplinary action.

20.6 Other rules and regulations

Chapter 17, which considers the methods of raising equity finance, and **Chapter 19**, which considers listed company acquisitions and disposals, explain that the specific subject matter of those chapters cannot be considered in a vacuum; most of the rules and regulations examined in this book are relevant to the specific areas of law those chapters consider. The same can be said of takeovers. In addition to the City Code, takeovers are subject to other rules and regulations, all of which are considered in this book. They are summarised below.

20.6.1 Consideration

If the company is:

(a) issuing shares as consideration, or

(b) using equity finance to raise cash to use as consideration,

for the acquisition, then the rules and regulations considered in **17.4** above will be relevant.

20.6.2 Acquiring shares

A takeover is, after all, just an acquisition of shares. This means that all the rules and regulations summarised at **19.3** above are relevant.

20.6.3 The Substantial Acquisition Rules

Until recently, the SARs were relevant in the period before a takeover was announced. These rules limited the speed and secrecy with which a person could build a significant stake in a company. However, the SARs were abolished with effect from 20 May 2006, following consultation by the Code Committee of the Panel (see **20.2.4.1**), as part of their ongoing review of the City Code.

20.6.4 Merger control

The takeover of a UK company can give rise to merger control issues in the UK under the EA 2002, or in the EC under the EC Merger Regulation. **Chapter 23** considers this issue further.

20.6.5 Sector-specific regulatory controls

Certain sectors have their own specific regulatory provisions. Examples include defence, travel and broadcasting. The lawyer may need to take advice from his client as to the sector-specific regulations which may apply to any takeover transaction.

20.6.6 Compulsory acquisition of minority shareholdings

The provisions of ss 428 to 430 of the CA 1985, and Sch 2 to the Takeovers Regulations, which are important in the context of a takeover, are discussed at **22.7** below.

20.7 Regulatory bodies

The rules and regulations which may apply to a takeover, and which are considered in this chapter, mean that the following regulatory bodies may become embroiled in a takeover bid:

(a) The Panel, which administers the City Code (see **20.2** above).

(b) The FSA, which has powers of enforcement in relation to the City Code (see **20.3.7.3** above)

(c) The FSA acting in its capacity as UK listing Authority. If the offeror is listed and is issuing new shares as consideration, or to raise cash consideration, those shares must be admitted to listing by the FSA. Also, if the acquisition is Class 1, the FSA will need to approve the Class 1 circular (see **19.6** above).

(d) The Stock Exchange. If the offeror is listed and is issuing new shares as consideration, or to raise cash consideration, those shares must be admitted to trading by the Stock Exchange.

(e) The OFT, the Competition Commission and the European Commission. If the takeover raises competition issues, these bodies may become involved (see **Chapter 23**).

(f) Sector-specific regulatory bodies. This will depend on the sector in which the parties to the takeover specialise. For example, the Civil Aviation Authority is likely to be involved in the takeover of an airline company, to check the company holds an ATOL licence.

20.8 Future developments

As explained at **20.4.1** above, the Takeovers Regulations and the dual regime are merely interim arrangements pending the enactment of Pt 28 of the Companies Bill (see **1.11**). On 14 August 2006 the DTI announced its intention that Part 28 would be enacted soon after the Bill receives Royal Assent. At the time of writing Royal Assent was expected in October 2006. It is possible, therefore (but not necessarily probable, given the Bill's painfully slow progress to date), that in the time between writing this book and publishing it, Pt 28 will be enacted and the Takeovers Regulations will be repealed.

Once Pt 28 is in force, note that (subject to any changes to the draft Bill) the Panel and the City Code will operate on a statutory footing in relation to all transactions which are the subject of the City Code (see **20.5.1.2**), not just in relation to companies whose shares are admitted to a regulated market, as is the case with the Takeovers Regulations. There will also be a universal compulsory acquisition procedure (see **22.8**).

Be aware, however, that some of the rules enacted by Pt 28 will apply only to companies whose shares are admitted to a regulated market, such as those relating to directors' reports (see **21.6.5.1**) and breakthrough provisions (see **22.4.9.1**).

Chapter 21

Takeovers: Preparation

21.1	Introduction	287
21.2	Recommended or hostile?	287
21.3	The need for secrecy	288
21.4	An example	289
21.5	Appointing a team of advisers	290
21.6	Due diligence	292
21.7	Financing the offer	295
21.8	Stakebuilding	295
21.9	Stakebuilding thresholds	303
21.10	Irrevocable undertakings	304
21.11	Non-binding indications of intention to accept	306
21.12	General offer or scheme of arrangement?	306
21.13	Deal protection	309

21.1 Introduction

Chapter 20 introduces the concept of a takeover and considers the rules and regulations which the lawyer will need to apply in relation to a takeover. In particular, it explains that the City Code contains the key rules relating to takeovers, and that the unique nature of the Code means that the lawyer will need to consult the Panel Executive (referred to in this chapter as 'the Panel') to determine how the City Code might apply in the circumstances of a particular takeover.

It is very exciting to be instructed in relation to a takeover. Of all the listed company issues considered in this book, it is the takeover which arrests the attention not only of your client, but also, once announced, of shareholders, your colleagues, the press and the general public.

Chapter 22 considers the takeover process once the bid has been announced. However, the lawyer's work begins long before that. This chapter considers the work which the lawyer undertakes prior to the announcement of a takeover bid.

Note that, as explained in **Chapter 20**, in practice the terms 'offer' and 'bid' are used interchangeably, as are the terms 'offeror' and 'bidder', and 'offeree' and 'target'. The City Code uses the terms 'offer', 'offeror' and 'offeree'.

21.2 Recommended or hostile?

The most significant factor which will determine the nature of the offeror's preparation is whether the takeover is intended to be recommended or hostile.

21.2.1 The recommended offer

Rule 1 of the City Code provides that the offeror must make the offer first to the directors (or advisers) of the offeree company. If the directors consider that the offer is in the best interests of the company's shareholders, employees and (if the company's solvency is in issue) creditors, they must recommend the offeree's shareholders to accept the offer. The offer is described as 'recommended'.

Bear in mind that a takeover often results in a change in management. The directors of the offeree company risk losing their jobs, or being relocated, if the takeover goes ahead. The culture of the business may change. However, the directors of the offeree company must not allow personal considerations to influence the exercise of their duties to the company when considering whether to recommend the offer.

With a recommended offer, both the offeror and the offeree company have a common aim in ensuring the takeover goes ahead. A recommended offer to acquire all the securities in a company is the most straightforward form of takeover. It has the best chance of success, and it can be completed in the shortest period of time.

21.2.2 The hostile offer

If the board of the offeree company advises its shareholders not to accept the offer, it is described as a 'hostile' offer. The offeror and the offeree company have conflicting aims. The offeror wants the takeover to be successful, while the offeree company will do everything in its power to ensure the offer fails. For both sides there is much at stake. For the offeror, the takeover could be central to the company's strategy of expansion. The shareholders of the offeree company, who ultimately decide whether to accept the offer, need to balance the fact that their board is advising them to reject the offer against the claims of the offeror about how attractive the offer is, in terms of the consideration they will receive in exchange for their shares in the offeree company.

21.2.3 The effect on preparation

If the offeror has an existing relationship with the offeree company, it may know in advance whether the offeree company will recommend the offer or not. If so, the offeror can prepare accordingly. However, if the offeror does not have an existing relationship with the offeree company, it has a choice: it can either approach the offeree company with a view to negotiating a recommended offer (and consider whether it is prepared to 'go hostile' in the event the offeree company decides not to recommend an offer), or it can launch a surprise hostile offer for the offeree company without discussing this first with the offeree company.

Whether the offer is intended to be recommended or hostile, the offeror must also plan for the possibility that another offeror may make a rival offer for the offeree company.

21.3 The need for secrecy

Rule 2.1 of the City Code provides that it is vital that the existence of the offer is kept secret until the offer is announced to the public under r 2.4 or r 2.5 (see **22.3**). In practice, this means that the lawyer must advise his client company, together with all advisers who are instructed to work on the transaction, of the importance of secrecy and security (Note 1 to r 2.1). The number of people to whom confidential information is given should be kept to a minimum. Anyone who receives confidential information can pass it on only if it is necessary to do so, and they must ensure that they inform the recipient of any information of the need for secrecy in relation to that information. For the lawyer, this translates into ensuring that:

(a) the team working on the transaction is no larger than it needs to be;

(b) each member of the team is aware of the secrecy obligation;

(c) due diligence (see **21.6**) is carried out discreetly;

(d) documents relating to the takeover are kept confidential (for example, not left lying around on the printer); and

(e) the transaction and each of the parties to the transaction are referred to by way of code name rather than their actual names. The code names should not be too obvious. The client may already have code names which it used while carrying out its initial research into the offeree company as a potential target. To take a facile example (although in real life the code names do tend to be facile), imagine a takeover of a company which has an American chairman. The transaction might be code-named 'Project Baseball', the offeror code-named 'Bat' and the offeree company code-named 'Ball'. This means that, in all conversations, meetings, telephone calls, documentation and such like, the code names will be used rather than the real names. The documentation will then be amended, to replace the code names with the real names, just before it is published.

To the layman (and, indeed, to a trainee who has not come across the concept before) this can all seem a little dramatic. It can also result in rather awkward situations for the lawyers. There will be a distinct buzz of activity around the offices of the team of lawyers who are working on a takeover. This can draw inquisitive comments from colleagues, regarding what the team is working on. The effect of r 2.1 is that those colleagues must be rebuffed politely. This can be particularly difficult for any trainee working on the takeover, who will not be able to discuss the transaction even with more senior lawyers who enquire what the trainee is doing. These measures, however, are vital. A leak can have disastrous consequences for the bid (see **22.3.3.2** and **22.3.3.3** below). While the secrecy obligation can lead to awkward moments for the lawyer, consider just how much more embarrassing it would be if a leak was traced back to him.

21.4 An example

Obviously, the work involved for a lawyer advising on a takeover depends on whether he is advising the offeror or the offeree company. This book examines the takeover from the point of view of the offeror. To make sense of what **Chapter 20** and **Chapter 21** have covered so far, let us consider an example.

21.4.1 The facts

Imagine that we advise X plc, a listed company, which is seeking to make an offer for the entire issued ordinary share capital of Y plc, also a listed company. The share price of X plc is looking healthy. Y plc, however, has had some bad press lately. It has been underperforming compared to its main rivals (which include X plc) and its share price is at an all-time low. The press have been speculating about whether Y plc is ripe for a takeover.

21.4.2 The analysis

The transaction is a takeover which is subject to the provisions of the City Code. X plc is seeking to acquire shares *carrying 30% or more of the voting rights* of a *listed company*, Y plc. X plc is the offeror. Y plc is the offeree company.

Note that the fact that X plc is a listed company is, in fact, irrelevant in terms of the application of the City Code, where it is the identity of the offeree company which is important. It is, however, relevant in terms of applying the class tests and in terms of the ability of X plc to offer shares as consideration, or raise cash consideration through the issue of shares.

For the purposes of the application of the City Code, it is irrelevant that Y plc is listed; it is enough that it is a public company.

21.4.3 Code names

The company secretary of X plc, after an uninspiring day, has decided that the code name for the transaction is Project Example. The code name of X plc is Bidder. The code name of Y plc is Target.

21.4.4 The parties

The main parties involved in Project Example will be as follows:

(a) The offeror, Bidder.

(b) The offeree company, Target.

(c) The board of Bidder.

(d) The board of Target.

(e) The shareholders of Bidder. The shareholders of Bidder may need to be involved for two reasons:

  (i) if the transaction is a Class 1 acquisition or a reverse takeover, Bidder will require shareholder approval before it can complete the acquisition (see **Chapter 19**); and

  (ii) if Bidder decides to issue Bidder shares to Target's shareholders as consideration, the shareholders may need to increase Bidder's authorised share capital and/or give the directors authority to allot the consideration shares under s 80 of the CA 1985. Bidder shareholders would not need to disapply s 89 of the CA 1985 in these circumstances, as the shares are to be issued for non-cash consideration (see **14.6.7**).

(f) The shareholders of Target. The shareholders of Target own the shares which Bidder wants to acquire. The fate of the takeover rests on whether they decide to accept the offer or not.

(g) The advisers. See **21.5** below.

21.5 Appointing a team of advisers

As with a flotation, a takeover involves not only lawyers, but a wider team of advisers, who must all work together seamlessly to advise the offeror on all aspects of the transaction.

21.5.1 Financial advisers

Rule 3 of the City Code provides that the offeree must have an independent financial adviser. In practice, the offeror will also have an independent financial adviser. An investment bank will usually adopt the role of financial adviser. In relation to advising the offeror, it will use its experience of other transactions, and its knowledge of the regulatory environment and the City Code, to:

(a) plan and coordinate the takeover (although increasingly the lawyers are leading coordination of the documentation);

(b) advise the board in relation to tactics, such as:

  (i) when to make the offer,

(ii) the level of consideration to be offered (including when to raise the level in the event that the offer is not well received),

(iii) the type of consideration to be offered (if equity finance is required to raise cash consideration, the financial advisers will advise on the method of equity finance to be used);

(c) be the offeror's principal point of contact with the Panel, to discuss any provisions of the City Code which are causing concern;

(d) issue and approve the offer documentation under s 21 of the FSMA 2000 (unless an exemption applies);

(e) underwrite any cash offer or cash alternative;

(f) report on profit forecasts (r 28) and merger benefits statements (r 19.1, note 8); and

(g) advise in relation to any information released during the offer (r 19.1) (see **22.4.5.1**).

21.5.2 Lawyers

The offeror will require lawyers as, of course, will the offeree. However, the financial adviser of the offeror may also be advised, separately from the offeror, by a further team of lawyers.

The lawyers will advise in relation to the rules and regulations considered in **Chapter 20**. They will also be involved in speaking to the Panel in relation to the interpretation of the City Code, and in drafting and, increasingly, coordinating the documentation for the takeover.

21.5.3 Stockbrokers

The investment bank acting as financial adviser will often take on the role of stockbroker. The stockbrokers play an important part in deciding tactics. They are able to do this because of the unique relationship they have with shareholders. Stockbrokers have day-to-day contact with key representatives of institutional shareholders. Remember that institutional shareholders have large stakes in public companies. Usually, therefore, the stockbrokers will have the 'inside track' on the appetite of the offeree company shareholders, and the market, for the offer. This is particularly important in a hostile bid, where the offeror will have to convince offeree company shareholders to accept the offer even though the offeree company board has advised them not to.

The stockbrokers will use this knowledge to:

(a) monitor market purchases and rumour;

(b) advise the offeror on the likely reaction of:

(i) its shareholders (see **21.4.4**) to the proposed acquisition, and

(ii) the offeree company's shareholders to the nature and amount of consideration to be offered; and

(c) arrange meetings with the offeree company's principal shareholders, before the offer is announced, to explain the basic terms of the offer and to see if those shareholders will commit irrevocably to accept the offer once it is made (see **21.10** below).

21.5.4 Accountants

The accountants will gather the financial information which must be included in the takeover documentation. They will also give comfort to the board in relation to financial information in the takeover documentation, and report on any profit forecast or merger benefits statement (or working capital or indebtedness statement in any prospectus or equivalent document).

21.5.5 Financial public relations consultants

The role of the public relations adviser is to liaise with the press to secure good coverage of the offer, and to ensure that the key messages in connection with the bid are published accurately. For example, the 'Lex' column of the *Financial Times* will comment on high-profile takeovers. The offeror, particularly on a hostile takeover, will hope that the column comments favourably on the offer, so that it might persuade offeree company shareholders to accept the offer.

21.5.6 Registrars or receiving bankers

The registrars or receiving bankers (often the same institution) will receive the forms of acceptance from the shareholders of the offeree company who want to accept the takeover offer. They will monitor the level of acceptances to determine whether the critical level necessary to allow the offer to be declared unconditional as to acceptances has been reached (see **22.4.7.1** below). If a meeting of the shareholders of the offeror is required (see **21.4.4** above), the registrars or receiving bankers will also receive and monitor the return of proxies for that meeting. Appendix 4 of the City Code sets out a code of practice for receiving agents.

21.5.7 Printers

The role of the printers on a takeover is not unlike that on a flotation (see **4.2.11**). The takeover documentation will be created by word processor at the outset of the transaction, but ultimately the final version will be professionally printed. Once each document is substantially in final draft form, therefore, it will be taken to print, and thereafter each draft will be printed (referred to as 'proof printing'). The printers need to process the documentation quickly, accurately and securely.

21.6 Due diligence

21.6.1 The requirement for due diligence

The effect of General Principle 5 (see **20.3.5** above) and r 2.5(a) of the City Code is that an offeror should announce a takeover offer only after the most careful and responsible consideration, when it has every reason to believe that it can and will implement the offer. This means that the offeror must undertake some careful planning and investigation before it announces an offer.

21.6.2 What is 'due diligence'?

The concept of due diligence in the context of a flotation was explained at **5.3.4** above. The concept is not so different on a takeover. While due diligence on a flotation involves investigating the company seeking to float, and collating comprehensive information about the company which can then be used in the prospectus, due diligence on a takeover seeks to investigate the offeree company (and, in certain circumstances, such as if shares in the offeror are to be issued as consideration, the offeror) so that this information can be used in the offer document. However, the effect of the secrecy obligation outlined at **21.3** above, means that the due diligence exercise is more limited on a takeover than on a flotation.

21.6.3 The purpose of due diligence

Due diligence is used to discharge the offeror's obligations under General Principle 5 and r 2.5(a) of the City Code (see **22.3.3.1**). For example, the Panel will not look too kindly on an offeror who announces an offer, only to discover that it does not have enough cash to fund it.

The information the offeror will require includes the following:

(a) Is the offeree company really an attractive acquisition?
  (i) How has it been performing lately?
  (ii) What are its main assets and liabilities?
  (iii) Where is it located?
  (iv) What do its latest report and accounts reveal?
(b) Can the offeror successfully integrate the offeree company into its business? What costs savings could be made after the takeover?
(c) How should the offer be structured?
  (i) Might the offeree company be willing to recommend the offer?
  (ii) If not, is the offeror willing to proceed on a hostile basis?
  (iii) Should the offeror offer cash or shares as consideration?
  (iv) If offering shares, does the offeror have sufficient unissued authorised share capital, and do the directors have sufficient authority to allot those shares?
  (v) If not, will the offeror's shareholders be willing to pass the necessary resolution(s)?
  (vi) Will the offer constitute a Class 1 acquisition, or a reverse takeover? If so, will the offeror's shareholders be willing to approve it?
  (vii) Are there any issues which might affect the timing of the offer; for example, should the offeror company wait until the offeree company's next annual report or accounts are published?
(d) What are the chances of success?
  (i) Who are the main shareholders of the offeree company, whom the offeror would need to persuade to accept the offer?
  (ii) How many offeree company shareholders might be willing to provide irrevocable undertakings? (See **21.10** below.)
  (iii) How many shares does the offeror hold which it can vote in favour of the bid? (See **21.8** below.)
  (iv) Is anyone else interested in the offeree company: might there be a more attractive competing bid?
  (v) Are there any competition or regulatory issues which could jeopardise the bid? (See **Chapter 23**.)

21.6.4 The due diligence process

21.6.4.1 If the offer is recommended

The offeror will undertake some initial due diligence itself, using publicly available information, before it approaches the offeree company. If the offeree company is receptive to the offer, it will then assist the offeror with its due diligence exercise and provide the information the offeror requires.

21.6.4.2 If the offer is hostile

If the offer is hostile, the offeror will not receive the help from the offeree company which is outlined above. However, if the offeree company has provided information to any competing bidder or potential competing bidder, then r 20.2 of the City Code provides that the offeree company must provide the same information on request to all other offerors or potential offerors. In practice, however, it is probable that a hostile offeror will want to launch a 'surprise' offer on the offeree company, so it will not avail itself of its rights under r 20.2 until its hostile offer has been announced, by which time it should already have completed its due diligence exercise, in order to comply with General Principle 5 and r 2.5(a) of the City Code (see **22.4.5.4**).

21.6.5 Publicly available information

The following information about the offeree company should already be in the public domain:

(a) memorandum and articles of association (Companies House);
(b) details of directors (Companies House, annual report and accounts, RIS disclosures, the offeree's register of directors);
(c) details of shareholders and share capital (Companies House, annual report and accounts, RIS disclosures, the offeree's register of members and register of directors' interests);
(d) financial information (annual report and accounts);
(e) any published prospectus (Companies House); and
(f) any analyst research (available from investment banks).

21.6.5.1 Directors' reports

The Takeovers Directive (see **20.3**) has ensured that information of particular importance to an offeror is now the public domain. Section 234 of the CA 1985 provides that a company must prepare a directors' report as part of its annual report and accounts, which contains the information set out in ss 234ZZA and 234ZZB of the CA 1985. The report should constitute a fair review of the development of the business of the company during the financial year and must state the amount of any dividend which the directors recommend be paid.

Article 10 of the Takeovers Directive requires companies whose voting shares are admitted to trading on a regulated market (see **20.3.1**; this includes the Main Market, but not AIM) to make additional disclosure in its directors' reports.

The additional requirements take effect in respect of financial years beginning on or after 20 May 2006, and supplement the requirements set out in s 234ZZA of the CA 1985 (see **8.4.3.1**). Why is the Takeovers Directive (which the Regulations implement on an interim basis) concerned with such issues? Well, the effect of the additional disclosure is to ensure that more information on the share structure of the company, including any share transfer or voting restrictions which might be triggered on a takeover, becomes public information. The aim of the requirements is to increase transparency in the market. The requirements are not limited, therefore, to companies which are the subject of a takeover offer.

The UK has implemented art 10 on an interim basis in Pt 4 of the Takeovers Regulations (see **20.4**). When Pt 28 of the Companies Bill is enacted (at the time of writing this was intended to be in Autumn 2006), it is intended that the

Takeoverfs Regulations will be repealed and these additional disclosure requirements will become part of the new Companies Act 2006.

21.7 Financing the offer

The offeror must know, before announcing a takeover offer, how it will finance that offer. This is not only a practical consideration; it is a requirement of General Principle 5 and r 2.5(a) of the City Code.

The choices available to the offeror are as follows.

21.7.1 Cash consideration

21.7.1.1 Debt finance

The offeror could obtain a loan to fund the takeover. However, as **Chapter 18** explained, this will affect the company's gearing and so may not be desirable.

21.7.1.2 Equity finance

The offeror could obtain the funds from its existing shareholders, using one of the methods described at **17.7** to **17.9** above. This depends on the existing shareholders being willing to subscribe to a fresh issue of shares.

21.7.2 Paper consideration

The company can offer shares (often referred to as 'paper') as consideration rather than cash. This is discussed at **17.10** above.

21.7.3 The option to take cash or shares

It is relatively common for an offeror to offer the offeree company's shareholders the option to take either cash or shares in the offeror in return for their shares in the offeree company. This sounds complicated, but in fact the method by which a company does this should be familiar to you already. This is achieved through a vendor consideration placing, described at **17.11** above. The offeror will actually issue only shares as consideration, but the issue will be on the basis that, for those shareholders in the offeree company who want to take up the cash alternative, the offeror will have those shares placed, and the shareholders will receive the cash proceeds of that placing.

21.8 Stakebuilding

21.8.1 What is stakebuilding?

Stakebuilding is the strategic purchase of shares in the offeree company by the offeror, in the period before the announcement of an offer, and during the offer period (see **22.3.4**).

21.8.2 The purpose of stakebuilding

The key to the success of the offer depends on whether the offeree company shareholders decide to accept the offeror's offer. Once the offeror owns offeree company shares, clearly it can be sure that it, as the holder of those shares, will accept the takeover offer.

21.8.3 Advantages of stakebuilding

The advantages of stakebuilding are as follows:

296   Public Companies and Equity Finance

(a) Rule 10 of the City Code provides that the offer can be declared unconditional as to acceptances once the offeror holds over 50% of the voting rights in the offeree company. Imagine, then, that an offeror already has a stake of 25% in the offeree company. The offeror would only need to persuade just over 25% of the offeree company shareholders to accept the offer in order to be able to declare the offer unconditional as to acceptances.

(b) The offeror can acquire shares at the market price before the offer is announced (once the offer is announced, the offeror would have to purchase shares at the offer price, which is usually at a premium).

(c) The offeror does not need to alert the offeree to the acquisition if it acquires the shares before it announces the offer and it acquires fewer than 3% of the shares (remember that the disclosure of interest obligations under the CA 1985 would require disclosure of the offeror's interest once that interest reached 3% (see **Chapter 15**)) – but see **21.8.4(e)** below.

(d) If the offeror has a substantial shareholding by the time it announces the offer, other shareholders may be more inclined to accept the offer.

21.8.4 Disadvantages of stakebuilding

The disadvantages of stakebuilding are as follows:

(a) The offeror will own the shares even if the offer fails.

(b) If anyone finds out about the strategic purchase (and this is likely given the requirement for the company to pass on information it receives under s 198 – see **Chapter 15**), market rumour may raise the market price of the offeree company's shares. As the consideration for a takeover offer is usually at a premium to the market price, this means that the offeror must offer more consideration.

(c) The increase in price and/or rumour referred to at (b) above may trigger an announcement under r 2.2 (see **22.3**).

(d) Purchases prior to the posting of the offer document do not count towards the 90% compulsory acquisition threshold (see **22.7.2** below).

(e) The purchase may dictate the level or nature of the consideration the offeror must pay pursuant to the offer, under r 6 and r 11 (see **21.8.11.4**), or trigger a mandatory offer under r 9 (see **21.8.11.3**).

21.8.5 Rules and regulations relating to stakebuilding

Some of the rules relating to stakebuilding are considered at **21.8.6** to **21.8.11** below. **Table 21.1**, at **21.9** below, summarises the various stakebuilding thresholds.

The lawyer must be familiar with these rules in order to advise an offeror client whether there are any reasons why it cannot build a stake in the offeree company, or whether it is restricted in building its stake in any particular way. (Note also that the provisions of any standstill letter (see **21.13.4**) will also affect the offeror's ability to build a stake in the offeree company.)

21.8.6 Insider dealing

The fact that the offeror is buying shares in the offeree company at a time when the takeover bid is not public knowledge might suggest that the directors of the offeror are guilty of insider dealing (by requiring the offeror to buy shares; remember that the offeror, as a company, cannot commit the offence – see **11.7**). However, as **11.6.2.2** above explains, in fact the directors may be able to make use of the 'market information' defence.

21.8.7 Market abuse

Again, you could be forgiven for thinking that the offeror's stakebuilding exercise might fall foul of the market abuse regime under the FSMA 2000 (see **Chapter 10**). However, the Code of Market Conduct provides protection which is similar to the defence that exists for insider dealing. MAR 1.3.17C provides that an offeror should not be prevented by the market abuse regime from acquiring shares in a potential target with a view to pursuing a takeover offer, simply because the offeror knew that it would be making an offer.

21.8.8 The Listing Rules

If the offeror seeks to acquire a large stake, consideration must be given to how the acquisition of the stake would be classified under the Listing Rules, and to related requirements of the Listing Rules (see **Chapter 19**).

21.8.9 Disclosure requirements

Stakebuilding can trigger the disclosure requirements under the CA 1985, the Disclosure Rules and (during the offer period – see **22.3.4**) the City Code, as set out in **Chapter 15**.

21.8.10 The Substantial Acquisition Rules

Prior to 20 May 2006, the SARs imposed timing restrictions on an offeror seeking to build a stake in the offeree company. However, as part of the ongoing review of the City Code, the SARs have now been abolished.

21.8.11 The City Code

The following rules of the City Code may affect any attempt to acquire a stake in an offeree company.

21.8.11.1 Rule 4.1: prohibited dealings

Rule 4.1(a) prevents anyone other than the offeror from building a stake in the offeree where they have confidential price-sensitive information about an intended offer, until the offer, or approach, is announced. Note 1 to r 4 also prohibits the offeror, and those acting in concert with the offeror, from dealing before an announcement if the offeree company has given the offeror confidential price-sensitive information in the course of offer negotiations.

To prevent a would-be stake builder avoiding this rule simply by asking someone else to buy the stake on his behalf, r 4.1(b) prohibits anyone who has confidential price-sensitive information about an intended offer from recommending to another person to buy offeree company shares.

21.8.11.2 Rule 5.1: acquiring 30% or more

Subject to exceptions, this rule prevents the offeror (or any concert party – see **22.6.1.2**) acquiring any interest in offeree company shares (see **21.8.11.5**), which, when aggregated with the offeree company shares in which he is already interested, would carry 30% or more of the voting rights in the offeree company. Paragraph 5 of the definition of 'interests in shares' and the preamble to r 5 confirm that irrevocable undertakings count towards the 30% threshold for the purpose of r 5.1 (see **21.10**).

As explained at **20.5.1.3** above, the City Code considers that a 30% shareholding represents 'control' of a company. The aim of r 5.1 is to prevent a person gaining control of an offeree company without making a full takeover bid for that company, governed by the City Code.

Rule 5.2 sets out the exceptions to r 5.1 referred to above. This rule provides that r 5.1 does not apply to an acquisition of an interest in shares:

(a) from a single shareholder, when it is the only acquisition within a 7-day period (r 5.2(a)). (Note that the offeror cannot then make any further acquisitions, other than pursuant to the exceptions below (r 5.3), and details of the acquisition must be disclosed (r 5.4));

(b) immediately before (and conditional upon) the r 2.5 announcement (see **22.3.3.1**) of a firm intention to make a *recommended* offer (r 5.2(b));

(c) after a r 2.5 announcement (see **22.3.3.1**) of a firm intention to make a bid (not subject to a pre-condition), and:
   (i) the offeree company board has agreed to the acquisition,
   (ii) the offeree company board has recommended the offer, or a competing offer,
   (iii) the first closing date of the offer, or a competing offer, has passed (at least 21 days after posting the offer document; see **22.5.2**) and the offer, or competing offer, has been cleared on competition grounds (see **Chapter 23**), or
   (iv) the offer is unconditional in all respects (see **22.4.7**) (r 5.2(c));

(d) by way of acceptance of the bid (r 5.2(d)); or

(e) which is permitted by Note 11 to r 9.1 or Note 5 to the Dispensations from r 9 (r 5.2(e)).

In the context of a *hostile* offer (see **21.2.2**) these exceptions tend to prevent the offeror from building a stake of more than 29.9% until after the first closing date (see **22.5.2**).

21.8.11.3 Rule 9: mandatory offer

Rule 5.1 of the City Code provides that a person can acquire an interest in shares carrying between 30% and 50% of the voting rights in the offeree company only if the acquisition falls within an exception to that rule. What happens if one of the exceptions to r 5.1 applies and the potential offeror does acquire such an interest? The answer is that r 9 will apply, and for the offeror the consequences of this can be serious.

Rule 9 provides that if:

(a) a person acquires an interest in shares (see **21.8.11.5**) in a company which results in that person holding 30% or more of the voting rights of that company; or

(b) a person already interested in shares carrying between 30% and 50% of the voting rights in a company for someone in concert with that person acquires an interest in any other voting shares of that company;

that person must make an offer to acquire all the equity share capital and all other transferable voting capital of that company on the terms set out in r 9.

If r 9 applies, therefore, not only is the potential offeror forced to make a takeover offer, but he cannot even choose the terms of that offer. The terms imposed by r 9 are not favourable to the offeror. Consideration must be cash, or there must be at least a cash alternative. The consideration must be at a level which is equal to the highest price paid by the offeror (or any person acting in concert with the offeror –

see **22.6.1.2**) for any interest in shares of that class in the 12 months preceding the announcement of the offer (r 9.5(a)). If the offeror acquires shares above the offer price during the course of the r 9 offer, then it must increase its offer to the highest price it has paid for the shares (r 9.5(b)). The only conditions which can be attached to the offer are that over 50% of the offeree company shareholders must vote in favour of the offer, and that the offer will lapse if referred on competition grounds. It is explained at **22.4.7** why these conditions are not ideal.

The reason for r 9 is that same as that for r 5; if r 9 is triggered, the offeror has acquired 'control', that is 30%, of the offeree company, and so must make a full takeover offer for the company, governed by the City Code.

Note that, in contrast to r 5; irrevocable undertakings do not count towards the 30% threshold for the purposes of r 9 (see **21.10** below).

21.8.11.4 Rule 6 and rule 11: consideration

The offeror cannot consider stakebuilding in isolation from the takeover offer itself. The acquisition of a stake may dictate the level (in the case of r 6), or the nature (in the case of r 11) of the consideration the offeror must pay for shares in the offeree company pursuant to the takeover offer. The rationale for these rules is General Principle 1, which provides that shareholders should be treated similarly.

> **Example**
>
> Imagine that A plc, seeking to make a takeover bid for Y plc, acquires a stake in Y plc from Shareholder 1 on Monday at £2.00 per share. A plc then announces a takeover offer on Tuesday for the entire issued ordinary share capital of Y plc at a price of £1.95 per share. Can you see that Shareholder 1 has been treated differently to the other shareholders? What if A plc had announced a takeover offer on Tuesday for the entire issued ordinary share capital of Y plc where the consideration was shares in A plc? Again, Shareholder 1 has received special treatment. The effect of r 6 and r 11 is to prevent an offeror breaching General Principle 1.

Rule 6: minimum consideration

Rule 6.1

Rule 6.1 provides that, unless the Panel otherwise consents, if:

(a) an offeror (or a person acting in concert with the offeror) (see **22.6.1.2** for the meaning of 'in concert');

(b) has acquired an interest in the offeree company shares (see **21.8.11.5**);

(c) within three months before the beginning of an offer period (see **22.3.4** for the meaning of 'offer period');

(d) or during the period (if any) between the commencement of the offer period and a r 2.5 announcement (see **22.3.4** below),

then the offer to shareholders of the same class must be on the same, or better, terms.

Let us consider the example of A plc bidding for Y plc, referred to above. The effect of r 6 is that A plc will not be able to fix the offer price at £1.95 per share. Instead, A plc must offer the Y plc shareholders at least £2.00 per share under the takeover offer.

Note that the Panel has discretion to extend the three-month period if it considers it is necessary to give effect to General Principle 1 (r 6.1(c)).

Rule 6.2

While r 6.1 covers acquisitions the offeror makes *before* the offer period, r 6.2 covers acquisitions the offeror makes *during* the offer period. Rule 6.2 provides that, if:

(a) an offeror (or a person acting in concert with the offeror);

(b) has acquired an interest in the offeree company shares (see **21.8.11.5**) above the offer price;

(c) after a r 2.5 announcement (see **22.3.3.1**) has been made but before the offer closes for acceptance,

then the offeror must increase its offer to equal the highest price it has paid for the interest in those shares, and, immediately after the purchase, it must announce that the revised offer will be made.

Note that while the example below involves cash consideration, neither r 6.1 nor r 6.2 requires the offer to be in cash. However, any paper consideration offered must, as at the date the offer is announced, have a value equal to the highest price the offeror has paid for the relevant prior purchase of offeree shares. (Note, however, that if r 9 or r 11 also apply, the offer does have to be in cash (or accompanied by a cash alternative); see **21.8.11.3** and below.)

Example

Imagine that A plc, having been advised that the offer price must be £2.00, pursuant to r 6.1, announces an offer for Y plc at a price of £2.00 per share on Tuesday. On Wednesday, A acquires some Y shares from Shareholder 2 at a price of £2.00 per share. On Thursday, A acquires some Y shares from Shareholder 3 at £2.05 per share. Can you see that, in breach of General Principle 1, Shareholders 1 and 2 have been treated differently to Shareholder 3? A plc has still got it wrong, and must make an announcement, immediately after it acquires the shares from Shareholder 3, that a revised offer will be made in accordance with r 6.2. Shareholders 1 and 2 will be pleased. They will receive the higher, revised price of £2.05 per share, not just £2.00 which they had originally expected.

Rule 11

Rule 11.1: cash consideration

The consideration the offeror might offer to the offeree's shareholders is examined at **21.7** above. However, r 11.1 provides that in certain circumstances the offeror must offer cash consideration.

If:

(a) the offeror (or any concert party) purchased interests in shares in the offeree company, of a class which is now under offer, during the offer period or within 12 months prior to the start of the offer period, and:

(i) the purchase was *for cash*, and

(ii) the shares carry 10% or more of the voting rights currently exercisable at a meeting of that class; or

(b) the offeror (or any concert party) purchased interests in voting or non-voting shares in the offeree company, of a class which is now under offer, during the offer period, and the purchase was *for cash*; or

(c) the Panel considers that cash consideration is required in order to give effect to General Principle 1, then, unless the Panel otherwise agrees, the offer for that class of shares must be in cash, or accompanied by a cash alternative (see **21.7.3**), at not less than the highest price paid by the offeror (or any concert party) for those shares.

Note that the words 'for cash' are very widely defined. Note 5 to r 11 provides that they actually include the situation where the offeror acquired interests in shares in exchange for *securities*, provided the seller of the offeree shares (or the other party to the transaction giving rise to the interest, if the interest is not the sale of the share itself) is not subject to selling restrictions, such as being required to hold the securities received in exchange for the interest in the offeree shares until the offer has lapsed, or the offer consideration has been posted to accepting shareholders. If the offer falls within this meaning of 'for cash' then, unless the offeror or its associates arranged the immediate placing of those shares, it must also comply with the provisions of r 11.2 (see below).

> Example
>
> Imagine that A plc intends to make an offer for the entire issued ordinary share capital of Y plc, offering two A plc shares as consideration for each Y plc share. A plc's lawyers will advise that A plc needs to consider whether it has purchased Y plc shares in the past. A plc provides information about its previous purchases of Y plc shares. It acquired a 4% stake at £3 per share 11 months ago, and a 6% stake at £4 per share 8 months ago. The lawyer must advise A plc that the consideration under the offer cannot be two A plc shares as consideration for each Y plc share, as A plc intended. It must be £4.00 per share, in cash, or at least include a cash alternative.

Guinness Told to Pay £85m to Former Distillers Shareholders

Philip Coggan

The Takeover Panel has ordered Guinness to make compensation payments totalling £85m to former shareholders of Distillers, which the brewing and spirits group acquired in 1986.

Mr Anthony Tennant, chairman of Guinness, said "the settlement of this matter on these terms is in the best interests of the company and its shareholders."

Guinness has accepted the decision and appointed Deloitte Haskins & Sells, the accountancy firm, as claims administrator. Advertisements will be placed in national newspapers on July 24 inviting claims.

Argyll - the supermarkets group from which Guinness wrested control of Distillers - and its advisers, which owned shares in the course of the bid, will be entitled under the ruling to payments of £7M and £35M respectively.

Guinness argued that it should not make those payments in view of the pending legal action between itself and Argyll.

The latter is claiming compensation for its failure to win control of Distillers.

Instead, Guinness suggested that payments should be made into an escrow account, but the Panel decided that Argyll should be treated as any other shareholder. Argyll said it "was pleased that the matter has been brought to a satisfactory conclusion."

The compensation payments arise from a breach of Rule 11, which the Panel has decided occurred in the course of the Distillers bid. Rule 11 requires bidders who buy more than 15 per cent of their target to make a general cash offer to all shareholders at the highest price they paid in the market.

On April 17 1986, at a time when Guinness and its bankers owned 14.9 per cent of Distillers, a Swiss company called Pipetec acquired 3 per cent of Distillers at 731p. The Panel ruled that this purchase was associated with Guinness and thus under Rule 11, Guinness should have made a cash offer of 731p per share.

However, the cash alternative to the Guinness share offer was only 630.3p per share. The Panel has ruled that those who accepted the Guinness cash alternative at the time should be compensated for the difference between the offer and the price paid by Pipetec - that is, 100.7p per share.

Guinness' share offer did not reach a value equivalent to 731p per share until August 21 1986. The Panel ruled that those Distillers shareholders who accepted the share offer and then sold their shares before August 21 1986 will be entitled to the difference between the sale price and 731p.

Those Distillers shareholders who sold their shares in the market between April 15 and August 21 will be entitled to the difference between their sale price and 731p. All those being compensated will also receive interest at the rate of 10 per cent per annum.

Seven men are awaiting trial accused of criminal offences in connection with the takeover, including Mr Ernest Saunders, the former Guinness chairman.

Source: *Financial Times*, 15 July 1989

Rule 11.2: paper consideration

Rule 11.2 provides that if:

(a) the offeror (or any concert party) purchased interests in shares in the offeree company, of a class which is now under offer, during the offer period or within three months prior to the start of the offer period; and

(b) the purchase was *in exchange for securities*; and

(c) the shares carry 10% or more of the voting rights currently exercisable at a meeting of that class,

then those securities must be offered to all other holders of shares of that class. As detailed above, an obligation will also arise, under r 11.1, to make an offer in cash, or to provide a cash alternative, unless the exchange falls outside the wide definition of 'for cash' in Note 5 to r 11.1 (because there are some selling restrictions on the seller of the offeree company shares, or, in the case of an interest in offeree company shares, the other party to the transaction giving rise to the interest).

Overlap between rules 6 and 11

Note that there is clearly the potential for overlap between r 6 and r 11, as both may apply where the offeror has purchased offeree shares *for cash*. Rules 6.1 and 6.2 provide that, in such a case, usually compliance with r 11 will be regarded as sufficient to satisfy the requirements of r 6.

21.8.11.5 Derivatives and options

As part of the ongoing review of the City Code, the Panel decided that, in relation to disclosure and stake building, the Code should apply to dealings in derivatives referenced to shares and options over shares, as well as actual shares. These terms are explained below. The effect of this is that, since 20 May 2006, the acquisition of 'interests in shares', and not just actual shares, are taken into account for the purposes of rr 5, 6, 9 and 11. In relation to r 4, the definition of 'dealing' includes the taking, granting, acquisition and disposal of an option over securities and a derivative referenced to securities, so if the rule applies, no interests in shares can be acquired.

Derivative

This term is defined in the City Code. Broadly, it is a financial product whose value depends on the performance of an underlying security. An example of a derivative is a contract for differences ('CFD') under which the holder of the CFD benefits from a change in the price of a company's securities from the reference price agreed at the time the CFD is entered into.

Option

An option is the right to buy or sell a share at a fixed price within a particular timeframe.

Interests in shares

This term is defined in the City Code. It includes:

(a) ownership of shares (para 1, definition of 'interests in shares');

(b) the right to exercise or direct, or having general control of, the voting rights attached to shares (para 2, definition of 'interests in shares');

(c) the right, option, or obligation to acquire shares (para 3, definition of 'interests in shares');

(d) being party to certain derivatives in relation to shares (para 4, definition of 'interests in shares'); and

(e) for the purposes of r 5 only (see **21.8.11.2**), irrevocable commitments (see **21.10**) in relation to shares (para 5, definition of 'interests in shares').

21.9 Stakebuilding thresholds

As the rules relating to stakebuilding are complex, **Table 21.1** below sets out the significant thresholds, and the consequences for the stakebuilder of acquiring certain stakes.

Table 21.1: Stakebuilding thresholds and consequences

Voting rights in target	Consequences for the stakebuilder
Any amount	Must disclose if issued with a s 212 notice (see **15.6.8.1**).
	If within three months prior to, or during, the offer period, any offer must not be on less favourable terms (r 6) (see **21.8.11.4**).
	If in exchange for cash, during the offer period, and these shares are now under offer, offer must be in cash, or accompanied by a cash alternative (r 11.1) (see **21.8.11.4**).
1%	Disclose dealings during an offer period (r 8.3) (see **15.7.4.3**).
3%	Disclose interests to the offeree company (CA 1985, ss 198 to 220 – see **15.6**) and disclose subsequent movements through another percentage point level, or if the interest falls below 3%.
10% or more in exchange for cash in the 12 months prior to an offer period and during the offer period	If shares are voting shares, offer must be in cash, or accompanied by a cash alternative (r 11.1) (see **21.8.11.4**).
10% or more, in exchange for securities, in the 3 months prior to an offer period and during the offer period	Must offer those securities (r 11.2). May also need to make a cash offer, or provide a cash alternative under r 11.1 (see **21.8.11.4**).
25% + 1	Power to block special resolutions.
30%	May be prohibited from dealing (r 5) (see **21.8.11.7**).
	May have to make mandatory bid for the offeree (r 9) (see **21.8.11.3**).
50%	Power to block ordinary resolutions.

Voting rights in target	Consequences for the stakebuilder
More than 50%	Power to pass ordinary resolutions. Offer capable of becoming unconditional as to acceptances (r 10) (see **22.4.7.1**). City Code generally no longer applicable.
75%	Power to pass special resolutions.
90% (applies to each class separately)	May be forced to buy the shares of offeree minority shareholders under s 430A of the CA 1985 or Sch 2 to the Takeovers Regulations (see **22.7.3**).
90% of shares subject to the offer (applies to each class separately)	Power to purchase minority shareholdings under s 428 of the CA 1985 or Sch 2 to the Takeovers Regulations (see **22.7.2**)

21.10 Irrevocable undertakings

How a potential offeror can acquire interests in shares in order to secure some votes in favour of the takeover offer is considered at **21.8** above. As you will appreciate, the restrictions set out at **21.8.6** to **21.8.11** above mean that it is not easy for the potential offeror to do this. In practice, stakebuilding is usually restricted to an acquisition from a single shareholder, or made immediately before the announcement of a recommended offer (see **21.8.11.2**), so that it falls within the exceptions in the City Code.

A more widely used technique, which also enables the potential offeror to improve the chances of success of the takeover offer, is the irrevocable undertaking (also known as an 'irrevocable commitment' or 'lock-up'). This is where the potential offeror obtains undertakings from certain offeree company shareholders (often major shareholders and directors who hold shares), in advance of the announcement of the offer and with the consent of the Panel (r 4.3), that they will accept the offer if it is made (and, sometimes also that they will vote in favour of any resolution that the offeree company may require to progress the offer).

While with stakebuilding the potential offeror knows that certain shares will vote in favour of the offer (because he owns interests in those shares), with irrevocable undertakings the potential offeror knows that certain shares will vote in favour of the offer because he has irrevocable undertakings from the shareholders which confirm that they will vote in favour.

Irrevocable undertakings fall into two categories:

(a) Hard irrevocables, which remain binding even if a higher offer is made for the offeree.

(b) Soft irrevocables, which will fall away to allow the shareholder to accept a higher offer which is made (typically one which is at least 110% of the value of the offer to which the irrevocable relates).

The consideration for providing an irrevocable is the promise of the potential offeror to make the offer. As a safeguard against the irrevocable being held void for lack of consideration, the lawyer should ensure that any irrevocable is entered into by way of deed (see **21.10.4**).

If the offeror (or any associate of the offeror – as defined by the City Code) obtains an irrevocable undertaking during an offer period (see **22.3.4**), it must disclose this through an RIS. The details it must disclose are set out in r 8.4(a) of the City Code.

The effect of irrevocables on certain other public company issues is considered below.

21.10.1 Stakebuilding

Paragraph 5 of the definition of 'interests in shares' and the preamble to r 5 confirm that, while irrevocable undertakings will not count towards the 30% shareholding threshold for the purposes of r 9 (see **21.8.11.3** above), they will count towards the 30% threshold for r 5 (see **21.8.11.2** above). Rule 5, therefore, acts as a cap on the level of undertakings the offeror can obtain. If one of the exceptions to r 5 applies, an offeror can obtain irrevocable undertakings over 30% or more of the offeree shares without triggering the r 9 mandatory bid provisions.

Is an irrevocable undertaking an 'interest in shares' for the purposes of rr 5, 6, 9 and 11? The effect of para 9(b) of Note 9 to the definition of 'interests in shares' is that the receipt of an undertaking falls outside the para 3 'right to acquire' category of interests (see **21.8.11.5(c)**). However, if the undertaking allows the offeror general control of the voting rights attached to the shares, the offeror will be treated as interested in those shares under para 2 of the definition of 'interests in securities' (see **21.8.11.5(b)**).

21.10.2 Financial promotion

Seeking an irrevocable undertaking may be capable of comprising an inducement or invitation to enter into investment activity. This means that any communication the company makes in order to persuade someone to provide such an undertaking will constitute a financial promotion under s 21 of the FSMA 2000 (see **Chapter 12**). Therefore the company must ensure that the communication either falls within an exemption (for example, because it is made to a professional investor under art 19 of the FPO 2005, or is a communication in relation to the sale of a body corporate under art 62 of the FPO 2005 – if takeovers do fall within this exemption), or that the communication is made by or authorised by an authorised person.

21.10.3 Insider dealing and market abuse

Giving an irrevocable undertaking may also amount to insider dealing (see **Chapter 11**); however, usually the market information defence (see **11.6.2.2**) will apply, unless the person providing the undertaking has confidential price-sensitive information other than simply knowledge that a takeover is proposed. Similarly, the provision of an irrevocable undertaking can amount to market abuse, but is likely to fall outside the regime under MAR 1.3.17C.

21.10.4 Squeeze out provisions

Shares which are the subject of irrevocable undertakings are not considered to be shares already held by the bidder. Therefore they are 'shares to which the offer relates' and count towards the 90% threshold (see **22.7**) provided as they are entered into by way of deed, or for no consideration other than the promise of the potential offeror to make the offer (CA 1985, s 428(5) or Takeovers Regulations, Sch 2, para 1.10).

21.10.5 Acting in concert

A person who provides an irrevocable undertaking usually is not treated as acting in concert with the offeror or offeree company (Note 9 to the definition of 'acting in concert'). However, if the undertaking allows the offeror or the offeree company to exercise voting rights, or allows the person providing the undertaking to acquire shares, then the Panel should be consulted before the undertaking is given.

21.11 Non-binding indications of intention to accept

Some shareholders, as a matter of policy, will not provide irrevocable undertakings. Sometimes, however, those shareholders will provide non-binding indications of their intention to accept the offer (also known as 'letters of intent'). While these indications are not legally binding, they can provide further reassurance to the potential offeror that the offer will be successful.

If the offeror (or any associate of the offeror – as defined by the City Code) obtains a letter of intent during the offer period (see **22.3.4**) then, as with an irrevocable undertaking (see **21.10**), it must disclose this through an RIS under r 8.4(a) of the City Code.

21.12 General offer or scheme of arrangement?

The bidder must decide how to structure the takeover. A takeover can be effected by:

(a) a general offer; or
(b) a scheme of arrangement under s 425 of the CA 1985.

21.12.1 General offer

The vast majority of takeovers are effected by way of a general offer. This involves the investment bank making an offer, on behalf of the offeror (for historical reasons), to acquire shares in the offeree for consideration. As set out at **21.7**, the consideration can take several forms, such as cash, loan notes, shares or other securities. Sometimes the offer gives the offeree shareholders a choice of consideration, such as cash or shares (and under r 9 and, in certain circumstances, r 11.1, the offeror must provide a cash alternative – see **21.8.11** above). The shareholder accepts the offer by returning a form of acceptance (see **22.4.2**).

This structure is suitable for use with both recommended and hostile offers. This book, and in particular **Chapter 22**, focuses on this structure.

21.12.2 Scheme of arrangement

An alternative way of structuring a takeover is by a scheme of arrangement pursuant to s 425 of the CA 1985.

21.12.2.1 What is a scheme of arrangement?

A scheme of arrangement is a court-sanctioned arrangement between a company and its shareholders or creditors. It is a statutory procedure governed by s 425 of the CA 1985. Section 425 of the CA 1985 does not limit the subject matter of the arrangement (although it must obtain the court's approval). There is, therefore, considerable scope for using a scheme (for example, to effect a reorganisation or return or capital). While the section was not drafted with the takeover in mind, it has also come to be used as a way of effecting a takeover.

There are two forms of scheme, namely a reduction scheme and a transfer scheme. A reduction scheme involves the cancellation of the existing offeree shares and the issue of new offeree shares to the offeror in exchange for the payment of consideration by the offeror to the offeree shareholders. A transfer scheme involves the transfer of the existing offeree shares to the offeror, in exchange for the payment of consideration by the offeror to the offeree shareholders.

In theory, the consideration offered by the offeror to the offeree shareholders under a scheme can take any form, as with a general offer. However, given the longer overall timetable of a scheme, underwritten cash offers can prove too expensive.

As the scheme is arranged by, and so requires the cooperation of, the offeree, a scheme is suitable only for a recommended takeover.

Section 425 of the CA 1985 sets out the following three main requirements for a scheme:

(a) *Members' meeting (s 425(1) and (2))*. The court must convene a meeting of the offeree shareholders (or the offeree company shareholders of the relevant class, as appropriate). At this meeting, the scheme must be approved by:

(i) a majority in number;

(ii) representing 75% in value of the offeree company shareholders, or class of offeree company shareholders, voting at the meeting (in person or by proxy).

The resolution to approve the scheme must be by way of a poll in order to calculate whether the test referred to at (ii) above has been satisfied. Neither the offeror, nor any shareholder connected with the offeror, can vote. This means the offeror cannot increase its chances of success by stakebuilding and/or obtaining irrevocable undertakings.

(b) *Explanatory statement (s 426)*. The offeree company must send an explanatory statement to its shareholders together with the notice of meeting. The statement should explain the effect of the scheme, and set out any material interests of directors and the effect of the scheme on those interests. The statement must be fair and, as far as possible, give all information reasonably necessary to enable the offeree shareholders to make an informed decision how to vote.

(c) *Court approval (s 425(3))*. The scheme must obtain not only the approval of the offeree company shareholders, referred to at (a) above, but also the approval of the court. A copy of the court order must be filed at Companies House before the scheme can take effect. The scheme will then bind the offeree company, its shareholders and the offeror (who will have agreed to be bound by it).

21.12.2.2 The City Code

Paragraph 3(b) of the Introduction to the City Code confirms that the City Code governs a scheme of arrangement (although currently on a non-statutory footing – see **20.4.2**). Typically certain modifications to the Code will be required for a scheme (for example, as the scheme requires the involvement of the court, it may not be possible to adhere strictly to the timetable requirements set out in the City Code). The scope of the modifications should be agreed with the Panel in advance.

On 9 November 2005 the Panel Executive published the following Practice Statement to explain how it applies the City Code to a scheme of arrangement under s 425 of the CA 1985 in relation to both the definition of an offer period and note 1 to r 19.3 (holding statements).

THE TAKEOVER PANEL
PRACTICE STATEMENT NO. 14
SCHEMES OF ARRANGEMENT

The Executive has been reviewing the application of the Code to Schemes of Arrangement under Section 425 of the Companies Act 1985 ("Schemes") and wishes to explain how it applies the Code to Schemes in the following areas.

1. **Definition of "offer period"**

   An "offer period" is defined in the Code as follows:

   "Offer period means the period from the time when an announcement is made of a proposed or possible offer (with or without terms) until the first closing date or; if this is later, the date when the offer becomes or is declared unconditional as to acceptances or lapses...."

   In the case of a Scheme, the question arises as to when the offer period ends. There are a number of key events in Schemes. First, resolutions must be passed at the Court convened shareholders' meeting(s) to approve the Scheme proposals (the "Shareholders' Meetings"). Second, in order for a Scheme to become effective, the Scheme proposals must be sanctioned by the Court at a hearing (the "Court Hearing") which is usually convened within 3-4 weeks following the Shareholders' Meetings. Finally, the Court order sanctioning the Scheme is filed with the Registrar of Companies (the "Effective Date") at which point the Scheme will become binding on all shareholders.

   Whilst obtaining the shareholder approvals at the Shareholders' Meetings and the sanction of the Court at the Court Hearing are critical to the success of the Scheme, a Scheme will only become legally binding and effective on the Effective Date. Accordingly, the Executive's approach is normally to regard the offer period as ending on the Effective Date. Provisions in the Code which apply dining the "offer period" or "during the course of an offer" (or similar) will normally be interpreted as applying until the Effective Date.

2. **Note 1 on Rule 19.3**

   Note 1 on Rule 19.3 of the Code states:

   "While an offeror may need to consider its position in the light of new developments, and may make a statement to that effect, and while a potential competing offeror may make a statement that it is considering making an offer, it is not acceptable for such statements to remain unclarified for more than a limited time in the later stages of the offer period. Before any statements of this kind are made, the Panel must be consulted as to the period allowable for clarification. This does not detract in any way from the obligation to make timely announcements under Rule 2."

   In the case of a Scheme, the Executive will normally set the latest date for clarification on or around 10 calendar days prior to the date of the Shareholders' Meetings. In certain cases, however, the Executive may set a date which falls after the date of the Shareholders' Meetings but prior to the Court Hearing, in considering the appropriate latest date for clarification, the Executive will consider each case on its fiicts and will seek to balance the desirability for shareholders of the offeree company to be given sufficient time to understand the position of any potential competing offeror(s) before they vote on the Scheme proposals against the need for potential competing offeror(s) to have sufficient time to prepare their competing proposals.

The Executive should always be consulted at an early stage as to how the Code applies to Schemes, in particular in relation to timetable issues.

Practice Statements are issued by the Executive to provide informal guidance to companies involved in takeovers and practitioners as to how the Executive normally interprets and applies relevant provisions of the Code and the SARs in certain circumstances. Practice Statements do not form part of the Code or the SARs. Accordingly, they are not binding on the Executive or the Panel and are not a substitute for consulting the Executive to establish how the Code and the SARs apply in a particular case. All Practice Statements issued by the Executive are available on the Panel's website at www.thetakeoverpanel.org uk

9 November 2005

21.12.2.3 Advantages of a scheme

A scheme has the following advantages over a general offer:

(a) A scheme requires a smaller percentage of offeree shareholder support (see **21.12.2.1(a)**), in order to obtain 100% control of the offeree company, than a general offer (where the offeror must acquire not less than 90% in value of the shares to which the offer relates – see **22.7.2.1**).

(b) Once the requisite majority of shareholders has approved the scheme, all shareholders are bound by it (with a general offer the offeror must compulsorily acquire the remaining 10% under s 429 of the CA 1985 or Sch 2 to the Takeovers Regulations – see **22.7.2.1**).

(c) Usually a scheme is quicker than a general offer in reaching the stage where all offeree company shareholders are bound. In the case of a general offer, the compulsory acquisition procedure can increase the timetable considerably. (However, overall, a scheme tends to take longer to effect – see **21.12.2.4(c)**.)

(d) A scheme is not deemed to be an offer to the public for the purposes of s 85(1) of the FSMA 2000 (but nevertheless a prospectus will be required if the offeror shares will be admitted to trading and none of the exemptions to s 85(2) apply).

(e) A reduction scheme can offer stamp duty savings (but see **21.12.2.4(g)**).

21.12.2.4 Disadvantages of a scheme

(a) A scheme cannot be used with a hostile offer.

(b) It is more difficult to revise a scheme than a general offer, given the requirement for court approval.

(c) The requirement for court approval, filed at Companies House, means it can takes longer to effect the takeover than with a general offer (but see **21.12.2.3(c)**).

(d) There is more time for a competing bidder to intervene (unlike a general offer, a scheme cannot be declared unconditional on Day 21).

(e) Stakebuilding and irrevocable undertakings will not increase the offeror's chances of success (see **21.12.2.1(a)**).

(f) The offeree company controls the timing and implementation of the scheme (this may be a disadvantage from the offeror's perspective).

(g) A scheme involves greater costs (but see **21.2.2.3(e)**).

(h) A scheme does not bind offeree warrant holders or option holders.

21.13 Deal protection

If the offer is recommended, then the lawyer will be involved in drafting various documents to try to ensure that the takeover completes, and to protect their client's interest in the event that it does not. The documents are as follows:

(a) heads of agreement;

(b) exclusivity agreement;
(c) confidentiality agreement;
(d) standstill agreement; and
(e) break fee letter.

The exclusivity, confidentiality and standstill agreements are often incorporated into one agreement. Brief details of the documents are set out at **21.13.1** to **21.13.5** below.

21.13.1 Heads of agreement

This agreement is also referred to as heads of terms, a letter of intent or a memorandum of understanding. It is not legally binding, but aims to record the parties' agreement in relation to certain fundamental issues at an early stage in negotiations. Key issues which it addresses include:

(a) the parties;
(b) the shares which are to be acquired;
(c) consideration;
(d) the extent of the due diligence exercise;
(e) major terms and conditions;
(f) timing; and
(g) choice of law and jurisdiction.

21.13.2 Exclusivity agreement

This agreement is also referred to as a lock out agreement. Its aim is to prevent a party negotiating with a third party for a certain period. In *Walford v Miles* [1992] 2 WLR 174, it was held that while this type of agreement is enforceable, an agreement which seeks to force a party to negotiate (a 'lock in' agreement) would not be enforceable. This means the effect of an exclusivity is persuasive only; it will encourage (but not compel) a party to persevere with negotiations rather than start negotiations with another third party who may appear offering a better deal (as the agreement will prevent such negotiations within a certain time).

21.13.3 Confidentiality agreement

This agreement will set out the terms to govern the passing of confidential information from one party to another. It will provide what happens to the information if the deal falls through (usually that the information and any copies must be returned, but sometimes that it must be destroyed), and what will happen in the event of a breach of the agreement.

21.13.4 Standstill letter

A standstill agreement aims to prevent a recommended offeror from being able to launch a hostile offer. It will provide that the potential offeror will not buy any shares in the offeree for a specified period without the offeree's consent.

21.13.5 Break fee letter

Unlike the exclusivity, confidentiality and standstill arrangements referred to above, which are often recorded in a single agreement, the break fee arrangements will be entered into as a separate agreement (usually a letter executed by both parties). Also known as an inducement fee, a break fee is a sum paid by one party to another on the occurrence of a specified event leading to the deal falling through, such as the directors of the offeree company failing to recommend the offer, or the offeree company shareholders failing to pass any necessary resolutions. The lawyer must be aware of the law relating to directors' fiduciary duties, the financial assistance provisions of s 151 of the CA 1985 (see **Chapter 16**), r 21.2 of the City Code and LR 10.2.7R (see **19.4.7.5(d)**) when drafting a break fee arrangement. Details of any break fee must also be provided in the r 2.5 announcement of the offer (see **22.3.3.1(g)**).

Chapter 22

The Takeover Process

22.1	Introduction	313
22.2	Timetable	313
22.3	Announcing the offer	313
22.4	The offer	321
22.5	Accepting the offer	334
22.6	Success or failure?	337
22.7	Buying out minority shareholders	339
22.8	Future developments	345

22.1 Introduction

Chapter 20 considered the rules and regulations which can apply to a takeover. **Chapter 21** explained that a substantial part of the lawyer's work on a takeover is undertaken before the offer is announced, to ensure that, once announced, the offer will run smoothly. This chapter looks at what happens after that.

22.2 Timetable

Table 22.1 below sets out a typical timetable for a takeover offer. Note that the events which typically relate to hostile bids only are italicised. This chapter explains in more detail what happens at each stage, but it is useful to consider the timetable at the outset, as it provides an overview of the process.

The City Code sets out the timetable of the offer by reference to the date on which the offeror posts the offer document. There are three situations which might alter this timetable, namely:

(a) a rival offer is launched (note 4 to r 31.6 provides that, usually, the timetable of the original offer will default to that of the later offer);

(b) no competition authority decision has been reached by day 39 (the Panel will usually grant permission to freeze the timetable until the decision is announced); and/or

(c) if the Panel exercises any discretion given to it under the City Code to extend any time periods.

Note also that if the offer is referred to the Competition Commission, or if the European Commission initiates Phase II proceedings, r 12.2 of the City Code provides that the offer period will end (see **23.2.1**).

22.3 Announcing the offer

The lawyers will have worked extremely hard to plan the bid. The culmination of this work is when the offer is ready to announce. This is an exciting time, but again the lawyers need to make sure that the announcement is made pursuant to the provisions of the City Code.

22.3.1 Timing

Chapter 21 explained that a considerable amount of the work required to plan a takeover happens behind closed doors. How does an offeror know when to open those doors and announce the bid?

Table 22.1: Timetable for a takeover offer

Date	Event	Rule
Before the announcement	Due diligence Approach offeree board Draft documents Obtain any irrevocable undertakings Build stake in offeree company Possibly make r 2.4 announcement (if so, the offer period will begin)	2.2 to 2.8
D – 28	Announce the offer under r 2.5 (earliest date) (if no prior r 2.4 announcement, the offer period will begin)	2.2 to 2.8
D	**Post, display and announce offer document (and forms of acceptance)** Market purchases now count towards CA 1985, s 429 and Takeovers Regulations, Sch 2, para 1	30.1
D + 14	*Dispatch, display and announce first defence document if offer is hostile (latest date)*	30.2
D + 21	First closing date (earliest date)	31.1
By 8.00 am, the business day after closing date	Announce acceptance levels Announce any extension of the offer	17.1
D + 39 (or 2nd day after any competition decision is announced, if later)	*Offeree releases any material new information (latest date)*	31.9
D + 42 (assuming first closing date is D + 21)*	*Accepting shareholders can withdraw acceptances if offer not yet declared unconditional as to acceptances (earliest date)*	34
D + 46	*Improve offer (latest date)*	32.1
D + 56	(If offer to remain open for acceptance beyond D + 70) give 14 days' written notice to shareholders who have not accepted	31.2
By midnight, D + 60	Fulfil acceptance condition and declare 'unconditional as to acceptances' (latest date)	31.6
D + 74 (assuming offer declared unconditional on D + 60)	Offer can close (earliest date)	31.4
D + 81 (assuming offer declared unconditional on D + 60)	Fulfil other conditions (latest date)	31.7

Date	Event	Rule
14 days after offer becomes unconditional in all respects	Post consideration (latest date)	31.8

*This rule also applies to recommended offers (but is less likely to be an issue).

Rule 1 provides that, when the offeror is ready to announce the bid, it must first put forward the offer to the offeree board. Rule 2.2 then provides that where a serious source has notified the board of the offeree company of a firm intention to make an offer which is not subject to a pre-condition, this triggers the requirement for an announcement. The announcement must be made to an RIS (r 2.9). Subject to DR 2.5.1R (see **7.4.2.8**), an announcement may also be required pursuant to the general obligation of disclosure under DR 2.2.1R (see **7.4.1**). In practice, the announcement required by r 2.2 will satisfy both obligations.

In an ideal world, then, the offeror will notify the offeree company board and then the offer will be announced. In these circumstances, it is the offeree company's obligation to make the announcement (r 2.3). In a hostile bid (see **21.2.2**), typically the offeror will seek to keep the amount of time, between putting the offer to the board and releasing the press announcement, to a bare minimum, and will telephone the offeree company's chairman just minutes before releasing the press announcement. This ensures that the offeree company is as ill-prepared as possible to deal with the takeover offer (and the offeree company's lawyers will have to get up to speed with the details of the offer from a standing start).

The obligation to announce the offer under r 2.2 can also arise in other circumstances, namely:

(a) there is an acquisition which gives rise to a r 9 mandatory bid (see **21.8.11.3** above);

(b) if the offeror has approached the board (but has not notified the offeree company board of a firm intention to make the offer) and the offeree company is then the subject of rumour and speculation, or there is an 'untoward' movement in its share price (the Panel will interpret 'untoward');

(c) if the offeror has not even approached the board, but the offeree company is the subject of rumour and speculation, or there is an untoward movement in its share price, and there are reasonable grounds for concluding that it is the potential offeror's actions which have led to the situation;

(d) negotiations are about to be extended beyond the parties and their immediate advisers (see **21.3** above); or

(e) the offeree company is seeking a buyer for an interest or interests in 30% or more of its voting shares and there is either rumour and speculation, or an 'untoward' movement (as determined by the Panel) in the share price, or the number of potential purchasers approached is about to exceed a very restricted number.

You will note that rumour and speculation can lead to the need for the offer to be announced. This explains why secrecy is paramount in the preparation of any bid (see **21.3**).

Note 1 to r 2.2 provides that parties should consult the Panel if they are in doubt as to whether an announcement is required. It is common for the Panel to be consulted in relation to (d) above in particular, as parties may wish to seek irrevocable undertakings (see **21.10**) or non-binding indications of intention to accept (see **21.11**) without triggering an obligation to announce the offer.

The Panel has reprimanded publicly financial advisers who have decided that no announcement is necessary without first consulting the Panel (see, for example, Panel Statement 2004/9, criticising Nabarro Wells & Co, financial adviser to Transcomm plc, which became the subject of a bid by British Telecommunications plc). However, if it is obvious that an announcement is required, the parties should not use consultation as a delaying tactic (see Panel Statement 2003/15).

22.3.2 Responsibility

Who is responsible for making the announcement in the circumstances listed at (a) to (e) above? Rule 2.3 of the City Code provides that, if the announcement is required before the offeror has approached the offeree company, or a r 9 obligation has arisen (see (a) above), responsibility for making the announcement lies with the offeror. If the announcement is required after the offeror has approached the offeree company, then responsibility lies with the offeree company. However, Panel Statement 2003/15 provides that if the offeror's approach has been rejected before the announcement is required, usually responsibility for making the announcement will revert back to the offeror.

22.3.3 Method

Rule 2.2 requires that an announcement should be made. To what type of announcement does this refer? There are two options:

(a) the announcement of a firm intention to make an offer (r 2.5); and

(b) the announcement of a possible offer (r 2.4).

22.3.3.1 The announcement of a firm intention to make an offer

The ideal scenario is that the announcement triggered by r 2.2 will be of a firm intention to make an offer. This is often referred to as the 'Rule 2.5 announcement', or the 'press announcement'. The potential offeror can make this announcement only after the most careful and responsible consideration, and only if it has every reason to believe that it can, and will continue to be able to, implement the offer (r 2.5(a)). It must also be certain that it can fulfil any cash consideration, and has taken all reasonable measures to secure the implementation of any other type of consideration (General Principle 5); in other words, it must have decided what consideration it will offer, and its financing arrangements must be in place. If it has any doubts, it must make a r 2.4 announcement rather than a r 2.5 announcement (see **22.3.3.2** below).

The r 2.5 announcement is a key document. Typically, it is the first public document to contain details of the offer. It is vital, therefore, that it contains the right message. As well as complying with r 2.5, there are certain conventions as to the matters which the announcement will address.

Content

Rule 2.5 sets out the content requirements of the announcement. The requirements include:

(a) the terms of the offer;

(b) the identity of the offeror;

(c) details of any relevant securities (as defined by the City Code; see **15.7.4.3**) in the offeree company:
  (i) in which the offeror, or any concert party has an interest, or right to subscribe;
  (ii) in respect of which the offeror or any associate has procured an irrevocable commitment (see **21.10**);
  (iii) the offeror or any concert party has borrowed or lent;
(d) the conditions of the offer (including details of any circumstances where the offeror cannot invoke the conditions);
(e) details of any indemnity;
(f) a summary of r 8 (see **15.7.4.3**);
(g) details of any inducement fees; and
(h) if the offer is for cash, or includes an element of cash, confirmation by the offeror's financial adviser that the offeror's resources are sufficient to make the offer (known as the 'cash confirmation').

Publication

Rule 2.9 governs the publication of any r 2.5 announcement. The announcement must be typed and faxed or emailed to an RIS. If the announcement is submitted outside business hours, it must also be distributed to at least two national newspapers and two newswire services in the UK.

Rule 2.6 sets out what must be done following the publication under r 2.9. The offeree company must send a copy of the announcement (or a circular summarising the terms and conditions of the offer, together with a r 8 summary – see **15.7.4.3**) promptly to its shareholders and the Panel (r 2.6(b)(i)). In practice, the offeree company tends to send the announcement itself rather than a circular, so will arrange for a glossy version of it to be published for this purpose.

The offeror and offeree company must also make the announcement (or circular) available to their respective employee representatives (or, if there are none, to their employees) (r 2.6(b)(ii)). If the company has chosen to distribute a circular rather than the announcement itself, nevertheless the announcement must be made readily available to them (perhaps by posting it on the offeror or offeree company's website) (Note 1 to r 2.6).

If there has been no r 2.4 announcement, then the publication of the r 2.5 announcement will start the offer period, and the offeree company must make the disclosure required by r 2.10 (see **15.7.4.3**). (The offeror must also do this unless the offer is wholly for cash.)

Effect

Once the offeror has made a r 2.5 announcement, r 2.7 provides that it must proceed with the offer (unless the offer is stated to be subject to a pre-condition which has not been met, or is subject to a condition which could be invoked if the offer were made). In other words, once the r 2.5 announcement is made, usually there is no going back. The only way an offer can be withdrawn is with the consent of the Panel, which will be given only in exceptional circumstances.

22.3.3.2 The announcement of a possible offer

If the potential offeror must issue an announcement under r 2.2 but is not in a position to issue a r 2.5 announcement then, as a temporary measure, it, or the offeree company, may issue what is known as a 'possible offer announcement' or a 'holding announcement' under r 2.4.

Content

An example of a possible offer announcement is set out below. The announcement will contain limited information, such as a potential offeree company announcing that talks are in progress with a potential offeror (which does not have to be named), or a potential offeror announcing that it is considering making an offer for a potential offeree company (which, again, can remain anonymous). The announcement should also include a summary of the provisions of r 8 (see **15.7.4.3**) unless the Panel consents to waive this requirement.

> NOT FOR RELEASE, PUBLICATION OR DISTRIBUTION IN, INTO OR FROM AUSTRALIA, CANADA, JAPAN OR THE UNITED STATES
>
> May 27, 2004
>
> REVIVAL ACQUISITIONS LIMITED
> ("REVIVAL")
>
> ---
>
> POSSIBLE OFFER FOR MARKS AND
> SPENCER GROUP P.L.C. ("MARKS & SPENCER")
>
> Revival, a company owned by Philip Green and members of his family, confirms that Revival is considering a possible offer for Marks & Spencer. Revival intends to approach the board of Marks & Spencer in the next few days with its proposal and to seek a recommendation. Any proposal would involve a mixture of cash and shares in a new company which would seek a listing. There can be no assurance that any offer will be made. A further announcement will be made when appropriate.

Publication

A r 2.4 announcement must be published under r 2.9 in exactly the same way as a r 2.5 announcement (see **22.3.3.1**).

As the r 2.4 announcement will start the offer period (see **22.3.4**), the offeree company must also:

(a) send the announcement to its shareholders and the Panel under r 2.6(a); and

(b) make the disclosure required by r 2.10 (see **15.7.4.3**). (The offeror must also do this unless the offer is wholly for cash.)

Effect

A typical example of when a holding announcement is required is if there has been a leak which breaches the secrecy requirement under r 2.1, and which starts rumours that trigger the requirement for an announcement under r 2.2. As explained at **21.3** above, no lawyer would want this leak traced back to him. In such circumstances, the potential offeror not only has to make a r 2.4 announcement and therefore alert everyone, including the offeree, to the existence of the offer, but, as stated above, this is just a temporary measure.

Even though the leak may have occurred at a very early stage in planning the offer, once the potential offeror has made a r 2.4 announcement, the offeree can request the Panel, under r 2.4(b), to require the offeror to 'put up or shut up'. This means that the Panel can impose a time-limit within which the potential offeror must make either a r 2.5 announcement, or a statement under r 2.8 that it does not intend to make an offer. This can leave an under-prepared offeror with little choice but to make a r 2.8 statement. An example of a 'put up or shut up' notice is set out below.

2005/26

THE TAKEOVER PANEL

MANCHESTER UNITED PLC
("MANCHESTER UNITED")
THE MALCOLM I GLAZER FAMILY LIMITED PARTNERSHIP
("GLAZER")

Following recent representations made by the advisers to Manchester United, the Panel Executive has been considering the application of Rule 2.4(b) of the Code to the approach by Glazer to Manchester United. Following discussions with both parties' advisers, the Panel Executive has ruled that Glazer must, by 12.00 noon on Tuesday, 17 May, either announce a firm intention to make an offer for Manchester United under Rule 2.5 of the Code or announce that it does not intend to make an offer for Manchester United. No extension to this deadline will be granted, except with the consent of the Panel Executive. In the event that Glazer announces that it does not intend to make an offer for Manchester United, Glazer and any person acting in concert with it will, except with the consent of the Panel Executive, be bound by the restrictions contained in Rule 2.8 of the Code for six months from the date of such announcement.

Each of the parties has accepted this ruling.

22.3.3.3 Statement of intention not to make an offer

The effect of a r 2.8 statement is that the potential offeror (or any concert party) must 'down tools'. It will not be able to:

(a) make another offer for the offeree company;

(b) acquire any interest in shares in the offeree company which would trigger a r 9 mandatory bid (see **21.8.11.3** above);

(c) acquire any interest in, or procure an irrevocable undertaking (see **21.10**) in respect of, shares in the offeree company which, when aggregated with the shares of other concert parties, would carry 30% or more of the voting rights in the offeree company;

(d) make any statement which raises or confirms the possibility that an offer might be made for the offeree company; or

(e) take any steps to prepare a possible offer for the offeree company where knowledge of the possible offer might extend beyond the offeror and its immediate advisers,

for six months from the date of the r 2.8 statement, unless:

(i) it has the consent of the Panel;

(ii) there is a material change of circumstances; or

(iii) an event has occurred which the potential offeror specified in the r 2.8 statement as an event which would enable the statement to be set aside.

These requirements are severe (in fact, they are the same as those which apply under r 35.1 to a failed bid (see **22.6.1.1**), albeit for a shorter period).

Much can happen to the fortunes of a potential offeror and offeree company during this six-month period, and of course the potential offeror can no longer launch a surprise offer, so a r 2.8 statement can mean the end of any takeover offer plans. Now it may be clearer why so much care is taken to ensure that the r 2.1 secrecy obligation (see **21.3**) is not breached.

Rule 2.8 will apply to any statement to the effect that the company does not intend to make an offer. The lawyer should advise the board not to make such a statement, simply with a view to keeping its intentions secret, if in fact it does intend to make an offer (and, in particular, warn about the severe implications of r 2.8 before the board members give interviews to the media).

An example of a r 2.8 statement is set out below.

> NOT FOR RELEASE, PUBLICATION OR DISTRIBUTION IN, INTO OR FROM AUSTRALIA, CANADA, JAPAN OR THE UNITED STATES
>
> July 14, 2004
>
> REVIVAL ACQUISITIONS LIMITED ("REVIVAL")
>
> RE. WITHDRAWAL OF PROPOSED OFFER FOR
> MARKS AND SPENCER GROUP PLC ("M&S")
>
> Philip Green announces on behalf of Revival that it has decided not to proceed with an offer to acquire M&S.
>
> Despite the continuing support for Revival from M&S's largest and longstanding shareholder, Brandes Investment Partners, LLC*, representing 11.7 per cent. of the issued ordinary share capital, Schroder Investment Management Limited** representing 1.2 per cent. of the issued ordinary share capital and others*** representing, in aggregate, 21.1 per cent. of the issued ordinary share capital, Revival has concluded from today's M&S AGM statement and conversations with Paul Myners that Revival will not gain the co-operation of the Board of M&S to provide it access to the information necessary for Revival to make its offer, including the necessary meeting with the pension Trustees, by 6 August. Since it has never been Revival's intention to disrupt the business of M&S, Revival is making this announcement promptly and wishes to thank the many M&S employees and shareholders who have expressed their support.
>
> Philip Green believes that he has played an important part in bringing about a new direction for M&S and he wishes the employees and shareholders of M&S good fortune.
>
> For the purposes of Rule 2.8 of the City Code on Takeovers and Mergers, Revival reserves the right to make or participate in an offer within the next six months in the event that the Board of M&S agrees to recommend an offer or a third party announces a firm intention to make an offer for M&S.
>
> * On July 7, 2004, Revival announced that Brandes Investment Partners, LLC has provided an irrevocable undertaking representing approximately 11.7 per cent. of the issued ordinary share capital of M&S, subject to the conditions set out in that announcement.
>
> ** On July 8, 2004, Revival announced that it has received a non-binding letter of intention from Schroder Investment Management Limited representing approximately 1.2 per cent. of the issued ordinary share capital of M&S, subject to the conditions set out in that announcement.
>
> *** M&S shareholders who, in aggregate, currently own or have investment control over ordinary shares of M&S representing approximately 9.0 per cent. of the issued ordinary share capital of M&S, and holders of outstanding derivative contracts in respect of ordinary shares of M&S, representing approximately 12.1 per cent of the issued ordinary share capital of M&S (a combined total of 21.1 per cent.), have confirmed to Revival that they believe that the board of M&S should allow Revival access to its requested due diligence on the basis of the proposal set out by Revival in its announcement dated July 7, 2004.

22.3.4 The offer period

The offer period will begin:

(a) when the offeror makes either a r 2.5 announcement of a firm intention to make an offer (see **22.3.3.1**), or a r 2.4 announcement of a possible offer (see **22.3.3.2**); or

(b) when a company announces that shares carrying 30% or more of the voting rights in the company are for sale, or that the board is seeking potential offerors.

When an offer begins, the offeree company and, unless the offer is wholly for cash, the offeror, must make the disclosure required by r 2.10 (see **15.7.4.3**).

The offer period will end:

(a) on the first closing date (a minimum of 21 days from the date the offeror posts the offer document – see **22.5.2**); or

(b) if later, the date the offer becomes or is declared unconditional as to acceptances (see **22.5.3**) or lapses (see **22.4.7** and **22.5.7**).

The Disclosure Table on the Panel's website lists all the companies which are currently in an offer period.

22.4 The offer

22.4.1 The offer document

The offer document is the principal document that the lawyer must draft in relation to a takeover offer.

22.4.1.1 Nature

The offer document is addressed to the offeree shareholders. It makes the formal contractual offer to acquire their shares in the offeree. Does the document constitute a financial promotion under s 21 of the FSMA 2000 (see **Chapter 12**)? It should be outside the scope of s 21, as it will be issued by a financial adviser who is an authorised person (see **12.2**) (arguably, it would also benefit from the art 62 exemption – see **12.9.2.5**).

22.4.1.2 Timing

While the offer period can begin with either a r 2.4 or a r 2.5 announcement, the timetable will start to run with effect from the r 2.5 announcement. Rule 30.1(a) provides that the offeror has 28 days from the date of the r 2.5 announcement in which to post the offer document. In practice, however, it is unlikely that the offeror will want to leave 28 days between making the announcement and posting the offer document. This is because the offeror will want the offeree company shareholders to be reading *its* offer document, not that of any other offeror who announces a rival offer and posts an offer document during this 28-day period.

As the timetable at **Table 22.1** shows, the day the offer document is posted is referred to as 'D day', and other dates in the offer timetable are calculated from this day.

22.4.1.3 Publication

First, the document must be lodged with the Panel (r 19.7). This requirement was introduced on 20 May 2006; however, in Response Statement 2005/5 the Code

Committee confirmed that the pre-20 May 2006 practice, where, under the direction of a financial adviser, the document is sent to the Panel at the same time it is posted to shareholders, will continue to be acceptable.

The offer document becomes a public document. Rule 30.1 requires the offeror to:

(a) post the offer document to the offeree company shareholders (r 30.1(a));

(b) put the offer document on display, in accordance with r 26, on the date it posts the document to offeree company shareholders (r 30.1(a));

(c) announce to an RIS, in accordance with r 2.9, that it has displayed the document, and where (r 30.1(a)) ; and

(d) make the document available to its employee representatives, and if there are none, to its employees (the offeree company must also do this) (r 30.1(b)).

Rule 30.3 provides a general derogation in relation to sending documents to shareholders outside the EEA.

22.4.1.4 Content

Rule 24 (and, for a recommended offer, r 25) set out the detailed content requirements of the offer document. Typically, it will include the following:

(a) a letter from the Chairman of the offeror, which explains the rationale of the offer and urges the offeree shareholders to accept it;

(b) a letter from the Chairman of the offeree company (under r 30.2 of the City Code), which recommends the offer to the offeree shareholders (if the offer is recommended: if not, see **22.4.2** below);

(c) a formal letter from the offeror's financial advisers, who will usually make the offer on behalf of the offeror;

(d) a detailed appendix setting out the full terms and conditions of the offer;

(e) a detailed appendix setting out the information relating to the offeror which is required by r 24 of the City Code and, if the offer is recommended, the information relating to the offeree company which is required by r 25 of the City Code; and

(f) information about how the offeree company shareholders can accept the offer.

An example of the front page of an offer document is set out opposite.

22.4.2 The defence document

22.4.2.1 Nature

If the offer is recommended, the views of the board of the offeree company will usually be included in the offer document. However, if the offer is hostile, the offer document will have been prepared by the offeror only. Rule 25.1(a) requires the board of the offeree company to communicate with its shareholders by way of circular, which is often referred to as a 'defence document'.

Once the defence document has been circulated, the offeror will usually circulate a further document, to respond to the arguments raised in the defence document and draw the attention of the offeree company shareholders once more to the merits of the offer. The offeree may then circulate a further defence document to the offeree shareholders in response to the offeror's latest claims, and so on.

THIS DOCUMENT IS IMPORTANT AND REQUIRES YOUR IMMEDIATE ATTENTION. If you are in any doubt as to the action you should take, you are recommended to seek your own financial advice immediately from your stockbroker, bank manager, solicitor, accountant or other independent financial adviser authorised under the Financial Services and Markets Act 2000, if you are in the United Kingdom, or from another appropriately authorised independent financial adviser.

If you have sold or otherwise transferred all of your Safeway Shares, please forward this document, together with the accompanying documents, at once to the purchaser or transferee, or to the bank, stockbroker or other agent through whom the sale or transfer was effected for transmission to the purchaser or transferee. The distribution of this document in jurisdictions other than the UK may be restricted by law and therefore persons into whose possession this document comes should inform themselves about and observe such restrictions. Any failure to comply with these restrictions may constitute a violation of the securities laws of any such jurisdiction.

This document should be read in conjunction with the accompanying documents, including the Form of Acceptance and the Listing Particulars relating to Morrisons, which have been prepared in accordance with the Listing Rules made under section 74 of the Financial Services and Markets Act 2000. A copy of the Listing Particulars has been delivered to the Registrar of Companies in England and Wales for registration in accordance with section 83 of that Act. All information in the Listing Particulars is deemed to be incorporated herein.

Offer by
ABN AMRO Corporate Finance Limited
on behalf of
Wm Morrison Supermarkets PLC for Safeway plc

ABN AMRO Corporate Finance Limited is acting for Morrisons and no-one else in connection with the Offer and will not be responsible to any other person for providing the protections afforded to clients of ABN AMRO Corporate Finance Limited or for providing advice in relation to the Offer.

To accept the Offer, the Form of Acceptance should be completed, signed and returned, whether or not your Safeway Shares are in CREST, as soon as possible and, in any event, so as to be received by post or (during normal business hours only) by hand at Northern Registrars, Northern House, Woodsome Park, Fenay Bridge, Huddersfield, HD8 0LA no later than 3.00 p.m. on 21 February 2003. The procedure for acceptance of the Offer is set out in paragraph 14 of Part 1 of this document and in the accompanying Form of Acceptance.

The Offer is not being made, directly or indirectly, in or into, or by use of the mails, or any means or instrumentality (including, without limitation, telephonically or electronically) of interstate or foreign commerce of, or any facility of a national, state or other securities exchange of, the United States, Canada, Australia or Japan. Accordingly, copies of this document and any related documents are not being, and must not be, directly or indirectly, mailed or otherwise forwarded, distributed or sent in or into or from the United States, Canada, Australia or Japan and the Offer cannot be accepted by any such use, instrument or facility or from within the United States, Canada, Australia or Japan and persons receiving this document (including custodians, nominees and trustees) must not mail or otherwise forward, distribute or send it in or into or from the United States, Canada, Australia or Japan as doing so may render invalid any purported acceptance of the Offer. The availability of the Offer to persons who are not resident in the United Kingdom may be affected by the laws of the relevant jurisdictions. Persons who are not resident in the United Kingdom should inform themselves about and observe any applicable requirements. Further information for overseas shareholders is set out in paragraph 6 of Part B of Appendix I to this document. Any person (including, without limitation, any nominee, trustee or custodian) who would, or otherwise intends to, or who may have a contractual or legal obligation to, forward this document and/or any related document to any jurisdiction outside the United Kingdom should read that paragraph before taking any action.

The new Morrisons Shares have not been and will not be registered under the US Securities Act, or under the securities laws of any state, district or other jurisdiction of the United States; the relevant clearances have not been, nor will they be, obtained from the securities commission of any province or territory of Canada; no prospectus has been lodged with, or registered by the Australian Securities and Investments Commission or the Japanese Ministry of Finance; and the new Morrisons Shares have not been, nor will they be, registered under or offered in compliance with applicable securities laws of any state, province, territory or jurisdiction of the United States, Canada, Australia or Japan. Accordingly, the new Morrisons Shares may not (unless an exemption under relevant securities laws is applicable) be offered, sold, resold or delivered, directly or indirectly, in or into the United States, Canada, Australia or Japan, or any other jurisdiction if to do so would constitute a violation of the relevant laws of, or require registration thereof in such jurisdiction, or for the account or benefit of, any US, Canadian, Australian or Japanese person.

Reproduced by kind permission of ABN AMRO Corporate Finance Ltd.

22.4.2.2 Timing

Rule 30.2 provides that the offeree company board must advise its shareholders of its views on the offer as soon as practicable following publication of the offer document and normally within 14 days. For lawyers advising a company which is the subject of a surprise hostile offer, this can involve some swift drafting and several late nights.

22.4.2.3 Publication

The defence document is also a public document. Rule 30.2 requires the offeree company to:

(a) post the defence document to its shareholders (r 30.2(a)(i));

(b) put the defence document on display, in accordance with r 26, on the date it posts the document to offeree company shareholders (r 30.2(a));

(c) announce to an RIS, in accordance with r 2.9, that it has displayed the document, and where (r 30.2(a)); and

(d) make the document available to its employee representatives, and if there are none, to its employees (r 30.2(a)ii)).

As mentioned at **22.4.1.3** above, r 30.3 provides a general derogation in relation to sending documents to shareholders outside the EEA.

22.4.2.4 Content

The content of the defence document is prescribed by r 25.1. The information the offeree company must set out includes:

(a) the substance of the advice it has received from its r 3 advisers (see **21.3.1**);

(b) the board's views on:
 (i) the effects of the offer on the offeree company's interests (including, specifically, employment); and
 (ii) the offeror's strategic plans for the offeree company and their likely repercussions on employment and the locations of the offeree company's place of business; and

(c) an opinion from its employee representatives on the effects of the offer on employment (provided the representatives provide the opinion in good time) (r 30.2(b)).

The defence document will seek to make clear to the offeree company shareholders that the offeror's offer is poor (for example, it undervalues the offeree company, or the premium offered is too low) and will advise the offeree company shareholders to reject the offeror's offer. As acceptance of the offer involves offeree company shareholders relinquishing their offeree company shares to the offeror, the defence document tends to focus on the benefits to the shareholder of keeping their shares. However, it must be careful not to make a profit forecast unless it is willing to report on that forecast (see **22.4.5.1**). If the consideration for the offer is shares in the offeror (a securities exchange offer), the defence document may also attack the worth of the offeror, further fanning the flames of the hostile bid.

22.4.3 The forms of acceptance

The offeree company shareholder must complete a form of acceptance and return it to the offeror's registrars in order to accept the offer. These forms are of crucial importance, and the lawyer will make sure that they are as clear and straightforward as possible.

22.4.4 Other documentation

As you will now be aware, the lawyer cannot consider the takeover in isolation from the other rules relating to listed companies. While the main documents relating to the takeover itself are the r 2.5 announcement and the documents considered at **22.4.1** to **22.4.3** above, the following circumstances will also call for further documentation.

22.4.4.1 Class 1 transaction

The takeover is an acquisition of shares, and if the offeror is a listed company then the acquisition must be classified under the Listing Rules and the offeror must comply with the requirements which attach to that classification (see **Chapter 19**). It is likely that a large takeover will constitute a Class 1 transaction. This means that the offeror must make a Class 2 announcement, send a circular to its own shareholders (that is, the offeror shareholders) and obtain the consent of those shareholders to the takeover (by ordinary resolution).

22.4.4.2 Securities exchange offer

If the offeror is offering shares as consideration, then if that class of shares is listed (which is likely, as a listing gives shares an identifiable value), the consideration shares will also need to be listed. This means that the offeror must prepare a marketing document. Under the old listing regime, the document required was listing particulars and not a prospectus, as there was an exemption for an issue in connection with a takeover offer.

However, this is not the case under the new regime (remember that listing particulars are now required only for certain types of security which are not the focus of this book). Instead, under the new regime, the rule is that a prospectus will be required for a takeover unless the exemption in connection with takeovers applies. This exemption, referred to at **6.4.1.5(f)** and **6.4.2.4(c)** above, is that a prospectus is not required if the takeover involves a share-for-share exchange (that is, the consideration for the takeover is shares) and a document is available containing information regarded by the FSA as being 'equivalent to' a prospectus. Issue 10 of *List!* provides further information about this exemption. In order to decide whether a document is 'equivalent to' a prospectus, the FSA will fully vet the document, which must be submitted at least 10 days before approval is required (PR 3.1.14R and PR 3.1.15R).

There is a disadvantage to using an equivalent document; it will not benefit from the passporting rights referred to at **6.11** above. However, if an equivalent document is used, then there is no obligation to produce a supplementary prospectus, so it has the advantage that it will not raise the potential problem of withdrawal rights outlined at **22.5.5**.

The prospectus (or equivalent document) will be published as a separate document, but sent out to shareholders at the same time as the offer document. Pendragon plc used an equivalent document in its offer for Lookers plc in March 2006.

Finally, it is possible that the offeror will need the consent of its own shareholders to increase its authorised share capital and authorise the directors to allot shares under s 80 of the CA 1985. (Remember that no disapplication of s 89 is required if the issue is for non-cash consideration.)

22.4.4.3 Resulting extra documentation

As a result of either of the circumstances discussed at **22.4.4.1** and **22.4.4.2** above, the offeror might need to produce:

(a) a circular (which contains the Class 1 information, if appropriate, information relating to any required increase in share capital and/or the s 80 authority, and the notice of the EGM which convenes the meeting where the shareholders of the offeror can vote on these issues); and

(b) a prospectus, or 'equivalent document'.

There will also be various r 17.1 press announcements (for example, of the level of acceptances (see **22.5.3**), or notifying an extension to the bid) during the course of the offer.

22.4.5 Standard of information

The City Code sets high standards for any information provided to shareholders during an offer. As noted at **22.4.1.4**, the specific requirements regarding this information are contained in rr 24 and 25. However, the City Code also sets out the following general rules about the nature and quality of that information.

22.4.5.1 Rule 19.1: accuracy of information

Rule 19.1 provides that:

(a) any document or advertisement issued, or statement made, during the course of an offer must be prepared with the highest standard of care and accuracy; and

(b) the information given must be adequately and fairly presented.

Again, the lawyers will use the verification process to help to protect the board in this regard.

The notes to r 1 provide valuable drafting guidance to the lawyer. They advocate the use of unambiguous language, citing sources for any material facts stated (typically this is done in a 'sources and bases' section in the document), and warn against using quotations out of context.

Note 1 to r 19.1 highlights certain areas of particular sensitivity, including profit forecasts, on which comment should be avoided. A profit forecast is any statement which puts a floor under, or a ceiling on, the expected profits for a certain period (for example, 'don't accept the bid as we are going to be much more profitable next year in any event'). As is the case with a flotation (see **6.5.2.1**), any profit forecast made during the course of a takeover must be reported on (r 28). Typically, a forecast will not be made unless it has already been decided that the benefit of making a forecast outweighs the work necessary to report on that forecast. This may be the case, for example, if the offer falls late in the financial year, and the most recent published accounts appear a little dated. Even then, as recognised by Note 1, it should not be the subject of media comment.

The Panel considers that the financial adviser is responsible for ensuring that its client complies with this rule (see **21.5.1(g)**). This can lead to something of a strain in relationships between the financial adviser, who needs to advise caution in making media statements, and the financial public relations consultants (see **21.5.5**), who want to deliver powerful messages to the media.

Burson Censured by Panel
Jason Nisse

The panel on Takeovers and Mergers has censured Burson-Marsteller, the US-owned public relations group, for serious breaches of the Takeover Code in its unsuccessful defence of Dowty Group against a bid from TI Group earlier this year, writes Jason Nisse.

The panel's executive ruled that Burson committed a "serious breach of the code" when one of its directors, Hamish McFall, telephoned a number of Sunday newspapers and stockbrokers and implied that Dowty's profits for the year to 31 March next year would rise from £32.7m to £50m.

In fact, TI estimates that the profits could be as little as half that figure. Mr McFall's call to a specialist salesman at County NatWest was taped and the tape was passed to the panel.

The panel said that the calls constituted new financial information that should have been communicated to the investing public through a Stock Exchange announcement.

Burson declined to comment on the censure but it is believed that Mr McFall is continuing to work at the firm.

Lazard Brothers, the merchant bank working for Dowty, has also been criticised for failing to exercise full control over Burson. While it accepted the rap over the knuckles, it is understood that Lazard was happy with Burson's work and will use Burson again in takeover bids.

The censure mirrored an incident in April 1990 when there was a leak of the terms of a bid for the property group London & Edinburgh Trust by the Swedish pension fund SPP. Then, the panel said there had been a serious breach of the rules but, despite strong rumours in the City about the source of the leaks, it could not be proven where the information had come from. The panel said everybody concerned had denied responsibility for the leaks.

Source: *The Independent*, 14 August 1992

22.4.5.2 Rule 19.2: the responsibility statement

Rule 19.2 makes clear that it is the directors who must ensure that these standards are met. Each document issued to shareholders, or advertisement published in connection with an offer, must contain what is referred to as a 'responsibility statement' from the directors of the offeror and/or, where appropriate, the offeree. The information that must be included in the statement is provided by r 19.2. Typically, the statement is drafted as follows:

> The directors of [the company], whose names appear on page [ ], accept responsibility for the information contained in this [document/advertisement]. To the best of the knowledge and belief of the directors (who have taken all reasonable care to ensure that such is the case) the information contained in this document is in accordance with the facts and does not omit anything likely to affect the import of such information.

In a recommended bid, the offer document will include a responsibility statement from the directors of the offeror in relation to the information provided about the offer and about the offeror. However, it will also include a responsibility statement from the directors of the offeree company in respect of the information it includes about the offeree.

In a hostile offer, the directors of the offeree company will not usually have provided the offeror with any of the information which is included in the offer document. The offer document will include a responsibility statement from the directors of the offeror only. However, any defence documents circulated by the offeree company must include a responsibility statement from the directors of the offeree company (see **22.4.2** above).

The wording of the responsibility statement should be familiar. As explained at **6.5.2.1** above, Appendix 3 of the Prospectus Rules requires a similar responsibility statement in a prospectus. You will remember that the purpose of the flotation verification process is to make sure that the directors are in a position to make this statement. The position on a takeover is no different. The junior lawyer will be involved in the process of ensuring that each statement in the offer document is properly verified, and will produce a verification note. The verification process is discussed in more detail at **5.3.5** above.

22.4.5.3 Rule 19.3: misleading statements

Rule 19.3 provides that the parties to the offer and their advisers must take care not to issue statements which, while not factually incorrect, may mislead shareholders and the market, or which may create uncertainty. In particular, the offeror should not make a statement which hints that it may improve the offer without committing itself to doing so and specifying the improvement.

22.4.5.4 Rule 20: equality of information

Rule 20.1

Rule 20.1 develops General Principle 1 (see **20.5.5**). It provides that information about companies involved in an offer must be made equally available to all offeree company shareholders as nearly as possible at the same time and in the same manner.

Note 3 to r 20.1 provides guidance in relation to meetings the board may have with shareholders, analysts, brokers or other investment professionals prior to the announcement of the offer, and during the offer itself. It provides that the directors must not disclose, in the case of a meeting prior to the announcement of the offer, any material new information or significant new opinions that will not be in the r 2.5 announcement and, in the case of a meeting during the offer period, any material new information or significant new opinions at all. Again, a profit forecast is capable of falling within r 20.1.

Of course, the board is very keen to enthuse the audience at such meetings with just the type of statements that r 20.1 seeks to prevent. The financial adviser or corporate broker of the party convening any such meeting must be present at the meeting and has the happy task of providing written confirmation to the Panel, by midday the following day, that the restrictions were complied with. The lawyers tend not to attend these meetings: the risk to their hearts is too high.

If any material information or significant new opinion is released at the meeting, a circular must be sent to shareholders (in the final stages of an offer, an advertisement in a newspaper may be required). If the information or opinion cannot be substantiated, this must be made clear and it must be withdrawn formally. Not a strong public relations message!

Rule 20.2

Rule 20.2 seeks to level the playing field for any competing offeror. It provides that the offeree, on request, must provide the same information to each offeror or genuine potential offeror, no matter how unwelcome that offeror's offer is.

The problem which r 20.2 can cause to an offeree company is illustrated well by the takeover of Midland Bank plc in 1992. Midland had provided information to its preferred offeror, HSBC Holdings Ltd (HSBC) (a subsidiary of the Hong Kong and Shanghai Banking Corporation). Lloyds Bank plc, a high street rival, then stated that it was also 'considering' making an offer for Midland. A pre-condition of Lloyds' offer was the receipt by Lloyds of all the information that Midland had provided to HSBC. Midland objected, on the grounds that it was not fair to oblige it to give commercially sensitive information to one of its arch rivals. Lloyds argued that, without the information, it would not be able to progress its offer and so the shareholders of Midland would lose out on an offer from Lloyds. The Panel upheld

Lloyds' request. It saw no reason to modify or relax r 20.2. Lloyds was a genuine potential offeror, and it was in the best interests of Midland shareholders that Midland provide the information to Lloyds. It follows that an offeree company should exercise caution when revealing information, even to a preferred offeror.

Two practical points are worthy of note here. First, the potential offeror must specify the information it requires from the offeree company; it cannot simply ask the offeree company to provide everything which it gave to the preferred offeror. Secondly, r 20.2 is usually of use only once the rival bid is public. As many hostile bids are launched as surprise attacks, and all the preparation and due diligence is undertaken in secret, the usefulness of r 20.2 is limited.

22.4.5.5 Rule 23: sufficiency of information

Rule 23 relates to the documents which the offeror and the offeree company prepare during an offer. The rule embodies General Principle 2 of the City Code (see **20.5.5** above) and provides that the offeree shareholders must be given sufficient information and advice, in a timely manner, to enable them to reach a properly informed decision as to the merits or demerits of the offer, and that no relevant information should be withheld from those shareholders.

Note 1 to r 23 recognises that a takeover, particularly a hostile one, can take some time to complete. It provides that if there has been any material change in any information previously published during the offer period, then any subsequent documentation must either detail the change or provide an appropriate negative statement. Rule 27.1 sets out specific matters which must be updated, including irrevocable undertakings and letters of intent, interests and dealings in shares and changes to directors' service contracts.

22.4.5.6 Bid documentation rules

As detailed at **20.5.7.2**, the failure to comply with the bid documentation rules in Appendix 6 of the City Code is a criminal offence punishable by a fine.

22.4.6 Consideration

In certain circumstances the City Code will dictate the level and type of consideration which must be offered (see **21.8.11.4** above).

22.4.7 Conditions of the offer

The offeror will make the offer subject to certain conditions. The r 2.5 announcement and the offer document will set out the detailed terms of these conditions. If the conditions are not fulfilled, the offer will lapse, unless the offeror can waive the conditions.

There will always be a condition as to the number of offeree company shares which the offeror must acquire in order for the offer to succeed (the 'acceptance condition'; see **22.4.7.1** below), but usually there will be other conditions too. The City Code regulates the conditions which the offeror can impose. Rule 13 provides that the offer must not normally be subject to conditions which depend solely on subjective judgements by the directors of the offeror, or the fulfilment of which is in their hands.

The most common conditions which may be attached to an offer are set out at **22.4.7.1** to **22.4.7.7** below. Note, however, that if the offeror seeks to rely on the non-fulfilment of a condition as justification for lapsing the offer, and invoke that condition, it must consult the Panel (Panel Statement 1999/14). In particular, it must satisfy the Panel that the issue in question could not have been discovered through the due diligence exercise carried out before the offer was announced (if the offer was recommended) and that the issue is genuinely material to the offeror. The exception to this rule is if the offer will lapse because any of the conditions referred to at **22.4.7.1**, **22.4.7.4** or, in practice, **22.4.7.2** below are not fulfilled.

Usually, the offeror will reserve the right to waive conditions (other than those set out at **22.4.7.2** and **22.4.7.3** below, which, in practice, must be fulfilled), and the acceptance condition cannot be waived in its entirety; see **22.4.7.1**). This means that the offeror can choose to declare an offer unconditional despite certain conditions not being fulfilled, if it so chooses.

22.4.7.1 Acceptance

This is a key condition which must reflect r 10 of the City Code. Rule 10 provides that the offeror must have acquired, or agreed to acquire, shares carrying over 50% of the voting rights in the offeree company. Once the offeror has acquired such shares it can declare the offer 'unconditional as to acceptances'.

However, in practice, the offer condition is usually drafted so that it will be fulfilled only if the offeror acquires 90% of the shares to which the offer relates. This is to enable the offeror to acquire the remaining 10% of shares by invoking s 428 of the CA 1985 or Sch 2 to the Takeovers Regulations (in relation to offers to which the Regulations apply) (see **22.7** below). Typically the offeror will not want to be left with troublesome minority shareholders whom it is not entitled to buy out.

Usually the condition will specify that the offeror can waive the condition at a level of acceptances below 90% (but not 50% or below as this would breach the minimum acceptance requirement of r 10).

As explained at **22.5.5.1**, until the offer is declared unconditional as to acceptances, shareholders who have already accepted the offer can withdraw their acceptances (typically from Day 42 of the offer). However, once the offer is declared unconditional as to acceptances, such shareholders are bound by their acceptances, subject to the fulfilment of any other conditions to which the offer is subject.

22.4.7.2 Admission of consideration shares to listing and trading

If the offeror is issuing shares of a class which is already listed as consideration then, as explained at **17.4.3** above, in order to:

(a)   comply with the requirements of the Listing Rules; and

(b)   give value to the shares,

these shares must be admitted to listing on the Official List and to trading on the Main Market.

In this case a condition will be included which states that the offer will become wholly unconditional only once the consideration shares are effectively admitted to listing and to trading.

Note that, since 20 May 2006, a similar condition is also required if the offeror is issuing shares in order to raise cash consideration for the offer (see Note to rr 13.1 and 13.3).

22.4.7.3 Offeror shareholder approval

If the takeover is a Class 1 transaction then the Listing Rules require the transaction to be approved by the offeror shareholders (see **Chapter 19**). In addition, the offeror shareholders may need to authorise the increase of share capital and the issue of shares (if the offeror is offering its shares as consideration). Again, if the offeror is issuing shares to raise cash consideration, then, since 20 May 2006, it will need to include a condition regarding any required shareholder approval, relating to issues such as increasing the share capital, issuing the shares and/or disapplying pre-emption rights (Note to rr 13.1 and 13.3).

It is usual for the offer to be conditional upon the passing at an EGM of the offeror of all resolutions that are necessary to implement the offer.

22.4.7.4 Merger control clearance

Rule 12.1(c) of the City Code allows an offeror to make the offer conditional on a decision being made that there will be no reference to the Competition Commission (see **23.4.3**), or, in the case of a takeover which falls within the scope of the EC Merger Regulation, that the European Commission will clear the offer within Phase I (see **23.3**). (Rule 12.1 of the City Code also provides that it must be a *term* of the offer that it will lapse if the Competition Commission or the European Commission take certain action in relation to the offer – see **23.2.1**.) While the offeror can waive any condition relating to merger control, and proceed without clearance from the relevant UK or EC competition authority, it cannot waive the term imposed by r 12.1.

22.4.7.5 Authorisations

This condition states that all authorisations for carrying on the business of the offeree company and other offeree group companies are in full force and effect.

22.4.7.6 Material litigation

This condition provides that no material litigation or arbitration proceedings have been instituted or threatened against the offeree group.

22.4.7.7 Material adverse change

This condition (the 'MAC condition') states that there are no material adverse changes in the offeree company's financial or trading position, other than those which the offeree has already disclosed. In 2001, the Panel refused to allow an offeror, WPP, to invoke its MAC condition on the basis that a material adverse change had taken place in the prospects of the offeree company, Tempus, after the announcement of WPP's offer on 10 September 2001 and, in particular, following the terrorist attacks in the US on 11 September 2001. The Panel stated that a change in economic, industrial or political circumstances will not normally justify the withdrawal of an announced offer.

WPP gives up attempt to halt Tempus deal
RAYMOND SNODDY Media Editor

WPP, the advertising group, hoisted the white flag in its battle to renege on a £432 million takeover bid for Tempus Group, its rival, yesterday.

Sir Martin Sorrell, the WPP chairman, has decided not to appeal against a ruling by the Takeover Panel that the company should proceed with its 555p-a-share cash offer for Tempus.

Sir Martin had sought to cancel the deal by citing "a material adverse change" after the September 11 terrorist attacks caused a sharp downturn in demand for advertising services.

However, the Panel, whose judgment was made public yesterday, said that Sir Martin had "failed by a considerable margin" to make the case for the deal to be scuppered.

Tempus, which had earlier opposed the WPP takeover, subsequently advised its shareholders to accept the offer.

The deal has been dubbed the City's first ever "hostile sale".

The Panel ruled that the temporary effect on profitability of an event such as September 11 was not enough to justify frustration of a legal contract.

The Panel also noted that Sir Martin had accepted that there were strategic and financial benefits in the deal. In the days following the attacks WPP actually increased its Tempus shareholding, making it more difficult for any counter-offer from a third party.

WPP shares fell 18p to 647p yesterday, while Tempus rose 11½p to 535p.

Source: *The Times*, 7 November 2001

22.4.8 Frustrating action

If an offeree company receives an unwelcome takeover offer, the directors may be tempted to frustrate the offer by taking some action which will make the offeree company more difficult to acquire, or less attractive to the offeror. Rule 21 expands General Principle 3 of the City Code (see **20.5.5** above) by providing that directors of an offeree company cannot undertake frustrating action without the approval of the offeree company shareholders. Remember that an offer which may be unwelcome from the offeree company board's point of view may be very welcome from the offeree company shareholders' perspective.

A non-exhaustive list of frustrating actions is set out in r 21.1(b). It includes:

(a) the issue of, or granting of options over, unissued shares;

(b) the sale, disposal or acquisition of assets; and

(c) the entering into of contracts other than in the ordinary course of business (such as amending a director's service contract to improve his terms without justification).

22.4.9 Poison pills

A poison pill is a general term used to describe defensive measures a company may take even before a bid is imminent (when the City Code rules on frustrating action described at **22.4.8** do not apply). Examples of poison pills include:

(a) placing restrictions on the transfer of shares (to deter shareholders selling shares to a potential offeror). These are common in the US, but less common in the UK where traditionally shareholders, and in particular institutional shareholders, are hostile to defensive measures; and

(b) drafting change of control clauses into key agreements (for example, Marks and Spencer Group plc inserting a clause into its contracts with suppliers of all socks and underwear that such contracts would terminate if anyone made a takeover offer for Marks and Spencer Group plc, thus leaving an offeror potentially with a much less valuable offeree company). These are common in the UK, but in practice do not tend to pose too much of a deterrent to a hostile offeror (who may have its own contacts with whom to contract, or indeed have good relations with the party subject to the change of control clause in any event).

When considering whether to adopt a poison pill, the board must take care not to breach its fiduciary duty to the company. *Criterion Properties plc v Stratford Properties UK plc and Others* [2004] UKHL 28 provides some guidance on this issue. In that case, Criterion Properties plc ('Criterion') had entered into a joint venture agreement with Stratford Properties UK plc ('Oaktree') under which Oaktree had a put option, namely the option to require Criterion to purchase Oaktree's shares, in the event that there was a change of control of Criterion, or if two named directors left the Criterion board. The purchase price was so high that it guaranteed Oaktree a minimum return of 25% pa on the investment. Obviously, the effect of the change of control clause was to deter any potential offeror from making an offer for Criterion. Criterion applied to the court to set aside the agreement.

The House of Lords found that the case turned on whether the Criterion directors had authority to enter into the contract. If the directors had actual or apparent authority, the agreement would be valid. If they did not, the court discussed whether the directors had ostensible authority. The court noted that this issue raised a question of considerable public importance, namely whether the directors of a public company have the power to authorise the signing of a poison pill agreement intended to deter third parties from making offers to purchase the company's shares and, in particular, whether they had authority to do so when the deterrent consisted of divesting of some of the company's assets.

Unfortunately, the court of first instance and the Court of Appeal had not considered the issue of authority, and so the House of Lords could not resolve the issue further; however, the case contains some useful commentary on poison pills.

22.4.9.1 Breakthrough provisions

Article 11 of the Takeovers Directive (see **20.3**) sets out what it refers to as 'breakthrough provisions'. These provisions provide that, on a takeover, the offeror can override some poison pills in certain circumstances. Article 11 specifies the types of poison pill which can be overridden. It includes restrictions on transferring shares which are contained in the company's articles or contracts, and restrictions on voting rights.

However, the breakthrough provisions proved so controversial that art 12 of the Directive permits Member States to opt out of art 11. In the event that a Member State does opt out, however, the Directive provides that companies must be able to opt back in (and, if required subsequently, back out) of the breakthrough provisions if they so choose.

In the UK, the Government has opted out of art 11. It prefers to leave to shareholders the decision on whether to have enforceable poison pills. Regulations 20 to 24 of the Takeovers Regulations (see **20.4**) set out the procedures a UK company must follow to opt in (and, if required, then opt back out) to the breakthrough procedures.

In order to opt in, the company must pass a special resolution, and fulfil the following conditions:

(a) the company must have voting shares admitted to trading on a regulated market (see **20.3.1**) (that is, it must be a potential offeree company in a takeover to which the Directive applies (see **20.3**));

(b) the company's articles of association must not contain:
 (i) any of the restrictions on share transfer or voting rights which are listed in art 11 (or if they do, they must fall away in the same circumstances as they would under the breakthrough provisions); or
 (ii) any other provisions that would be incompatible with art 11 of the Directive; and

(c) no shares conferring special rights in the company can be held by a Government minister, his nominees or any company he directly or indirectly owns or controls.

The company must notify the Panel of any special resolution passed to opt in to (or subsequently opt out of) the breakthrough provisions, within 15 days of the passing of that resolution. Regulation 22 sets out the consequences of opting in, and in particular which poison pills will be invalid.

When Pt 28 of the Companies Bill is enacted, the Takeovers Regulations will be repealed and the new Companies Act 2006 will contain the breakthrough regulations required by the Directive. Note that, even then, the breakthrough provisions will continue to apply only to companies which have voting shares admitted to trading on a regulated market.

22.5 Accepting the offer

Once the offer documents and any defence documents have been posted, the fate of the offer will be determined by whether the offeree shareholders choose to accept it.

22.5.1 Method of acceptance

The offeree company shareholders accept the offer by completing the forms of acceptance (referred to at **22.4.3**) and returning them to the company's registrars, who will then count the votes (as explained at **21.5.6**).

22.5.2 First closing date

Most forms of acceptance will urge shareholders to vote by a specified time and date, known as the 'first closing date'. Rule 31.1 provides that the offer must be open for a minimum of 21 days from the date the offeror posts the offer document. The offeror will be keen to complete the takeover as soon as possible, and therefore the first closing date is usually the 21st day following the posting of the offer document, but it can be a longer period. Most offers are extended beyond the first closing date, but the offeror could use the acceptance condition to lapse the offer at this date if it no longer wished to proceed.

Institutional shareholders may delay casting their votes, to see if anything happens to change their decision to vote for or against the offer (such as a rival offeror announcing a better offer, or a dramatic change in market conditions).

22.5.3 Announcing the level of acceptances

Rule 17.1 provides that the offeror must announce the level of acceptances by 8.00 am on the day after the first closing date.

If the bid is recommended, the offeror will expect to be able to declare the offer unconditional as to acceptances on the first closing date. However, if the offer is hostile, the offeror is unlikely to have received the required level of acceptances (see **22.4.7.1** above), as shareholders may wait to see if the offeror will improve the offer, or whether another rival offer will be made.

The level of acceptances must also be announced, under r 17.1, after any further closing date and after any extension or revision of the offer (see **22.5.4**).

22.5.4 Extending and revising the offer

If the conditions of the offer, including the condition as to acceptances, have not been met by the first closing date, the offeror can withdraw the offer. Rule 31.3 provides that the offeror is not obliged to extend the offer. However, usually the offeror will extend the offer in the hope that it will eventually receive a sufficient level of acceptances. The offeror may also improve the terms of the offer. Typically the offeror will announce the extension or revision of the offer at the same time that it announces the level of acceptances.

If the offeror does decide to revise its offer, it must do as it did with the original offer (see **22.4.1.3**), namely:

(a) post a revised offer document to the offeree company shareholders. This must comply with the content requirements of r 24, and also with r 27, which provides that any documents sent to shareholders after the offer document must contain details of any material changes to the documents published previously during the offer period (or state that there are no such changes) (r 32.1(a));

(b) put the revised offer document on display, in accordance with r 26, on the date it posts the document to offeree company shareholders (r 32.1(a));

(c) announce to an RIS, in accordance with r 2.9, that it has displayed the document, and where (r 32.1(a)); and

(d) make the document available to its employee representatives, and if there are none, to its employees (the offeree company must also do this) (r 32.7(a)).

As mentioned at **22.4.1.3** above, r 30.3 provides a general derogation in relation to sending documents to shareholders outside the EEA.

Rule 32.1(b) provides that the revised offer must be open for at least 14 days following the posting of the revised document. The effect of this requirement, together with the final day rule, referred to at **22.5.7** below, is that the offer cannot be revised after the 46th day following the posting of the announcement of the original offer document.

Rule 32.3 provides that any shareholder who accepted the original offer is entitled to receive the revised consideration.

In the event of a revised offer, the offeree company must do as it did with the defence document (see **22.4.2.3**), namely:

(a) post a circular to its shareholders setting out its views on the revised offer, as required by r 25.1(a), drawn up in accordance with rr 25 and 27 (see **22.5.4(a)**) (r 32.6(a)). The offeree company must append to the circular an opinion from its employee representatives on the effects of the offer on employment (provided the representatives provide the opinion in good time) (r 32.6(b));

(b) put the circular on display, in accordance with r 26, on the date it posts the document to offeree company shareholders (r 32.6(a));

(c) announce to an RIS, in accordance with r 2.9, that it has displayed the circular, and where (r 32.6(a)); and

(d) make the circular available to its employee representatives, and if there are none, to its employees (r 32.7(b))).

Again, r 30.3 provides a general derogation in relation to sending documents to shareholders outside the EEA.

22.5.5 The right of withdrawal

22.5.5.1 Withdrawal rights under the City Code

Any shareholder who has accepted the offer can change his mind and withdraw that acceptance at any time after the date which is 21 days after the first closing date (so, usually, any time after the 42nd day following the announcement of the offer) until the date the offer has become, or is declared, unconditional as to acceptances.

This is why so much importance is attached to the offer becoming or being declared unconditional; once this has happened, shareholders who have accepted the offer are bound by this acceptance, and cannot withdraw.

22.5.5.2 Withdrawal rights under the FSMA 2000

We have just noted that, under the City Code, usually withdrawal rights cease to be available after an offer has become or has been declared unconditional. As explained at **6.9.4** above, however, the new s 87Q of the FSMA 2000 provides that investors have the right to withdraw their acceptances during the two days following publication of any supplementary prospectus (referred to as a 'statutory withdrawal period'). So what happens if a takeover is made by way of share-for-share exchange, and a supplementary prospectus is required? Can withdrawal rights arise under the FSMA 2000 after the offer has become or has been declared unconditional, meaning that the offeror's acceptance level could drop below 50%? Neither the FSMA 2000 nor the City Code are clear on this point. The Panel has addressed this issue in Panel Statement 2005/29. It states that it has received legal advice that the new FSMA 2000 provisions can be interpreted as meaning:

(a) that the period for withdrawal by an acceptor of an offer ends once the offer has become or has been declared wholly unconditional and the relevant securities have been unconditionally allotted (that is, wholly unconditional bids, where the unconditional allotments of securities have been made, could not be reopened through the exercise of withdrawal rights); and

(b) that the withdrawal rights under the FSMA 2000 will not arise if a share-for-share offer is made by way of an 'equivalent document' (see **22.4.4.2**) rather than a prospectus.

The FSA confirmed, in Issue 11 of *List!*, that it agrees with this view. Until the courts ultimately decide this matter, practically it is prudent for the offeror to make use of the Panel Statement and either:

(i) make the offer by way of an equivalent document rather than a prospectus (but see **22.4.4.2** for the disadvantages in this approach); or

(ii) take steps to avoid becoming or being declared unconditional as to acceptances when a statutory withdrawal period is running, or when there is a possibility that a supplementary prospectus may be required (possibly by organising matters so that the offer becomes wholly unconditional at the same time the offer becomes or is declared unconditional as to acceptances, which is already common practice); and/or

(iii) include an extra condition to the offer which it can invoke should the exercise of withdrawal rights under the FSMA 2000 result in acceptance levels dropping below 50% after the offer has become or been declared unconditional as to acceptances.

22.5.6 Day 39

Rule 31.9 provides that the offeree company should not, without the consent of the Panel, announce any material new information after the 39th day following the posting of the initial offer document. If any relevant competition authority has not given its decision by this time, the Panel will usually grant permission to extend the deadline until the second day after the decision is announced.

22.5.7 Day 60: the final day rule

For reasons of the offeree's stability (and the advisers' sanity), the takeover process is not allowed to continue indefinitely. Rule 31.6 provides that, except with the consent of the Panel, the offer will lapse if the offeror cannot declare the offer unconditional as to acceptances by midnight on the 60th day after the initial offer document was posted. The circumstances when the Panel will grant consent to an extension of this period are set out in r 31.6(a)(i) to (v).

22.5.8 Day 74: earliest date the offer can close

Rule 31.4 provides that, after the offer has become or been declared unconditional as to acceptances, it must still remain open for further acceptances for at least 14 days after the current closing date. As explained at **22.5.7**, the latest closing date will tend to be Day 60, and so, if this is the case, the earliest date the offer can close will be Day 74.

Rule 31.2 provides that if the offer remains open for acceptances beyond Day 70, the offeror must give at least 14 days' written notice to all offeree company shareholders who have not accepted the offer.

In practice, typically the offeror keeps the offer open until further notice, and then runs the offer in parallel to the compulsory acquisition procedure (see **22.7**).

22.5.9 Day 81: last date to fulfil other conditions

Rule 31.7 provides that, except with the consent of the Panel, the other conditions of the offer must be fulfilled or waived within 21 days of either the first closing date, or the date on which the offer becomes unconditional as to acceptances (whichever is the later), otherwise the offer will lapse.

The Panel's consent to the extension of this period will be granted only if the outstanding condition involves a material official authorisation or regulatory clearance relating to the offer, and it has been impossible to obtain an extension under r 31.6.

The effect of r 31.6 and r 31.7 is that the latest date on which the other conditions may be satisfied is the 81st day after the posting of the initial offer document. However, in practice most offers are declared wholly unconditional at the same time they are declared unconditional as to acceptances.

22.6 Success or failure?

22.6.1 The failed offer

22.6.1.1 The 12-month restriction

If the offeror withdraws the offer, or the offer lapses, r 35.1 of the City Code provides that, without the consent of the Panel, neither the offeror nor any concert parties (see **22.6.1.2**) can:

(a) make another offer for the offeree company;

(b) acquire any interest in shares in the offeree which would trigger a r 9 mandatory bid (see **21.8.11.3** above);

(c) acquire any interest in, or procure an irrevocable undertaking (see **21.10**) in respect of, shares in the offeree company which, when aggregated with the shares of other concert parties, would carry 30% or more of the voting rights in the offeree company;

(d) make any statement which raises or confirms the possibility that an offer might be made for the offeree company; or

(e) take any steps to prepare a possible offer for the offeree company where knowledge of the possible offer might extend beyond the offeror and its immediate advisers, for at least 12 months from the date the offer is withdrawn or lapses. The rationale for this rule is to promote certainty in the market and avoid companies becoming embroiled in an endless takeover battle (as reflected in General Principle 6). Note that the requirements to 'down tools' are the same as those that apply following a r 2.8 statement (see **22.3.3.3**), albeit for a longer period.

The note to r 35.1 of the City Code sets out the usual circumstances when the Panel will waive the 12-month restriction imposed by r 35.1 These include:

(a) if the offeror wants to announce a new offer which is recommended;

(b) if the offeror wants to announce a new offer to compete with another offer; or

(c) if the original offer lapsed in accordance with r 12.2 (see **23.2.1**) and the offeror wants to announce a new offer following competition clearance.

22.6.1.2 Acting in concert

The definition of 'acting in concert' under the City Code is different to that under ss 204 to 207 of the CA 1985 (considered at **15.6.6.3**). The City Code defines 'persons acting in concert' as persons:

> who, pursuant to an agreement or understanding (whether formal or informal), co-operate to obtain or consolidate control [see **20.3.1.3**] of a company or to frustrate the successful outcome of an offer for a company.

Affiliated persons (such as a majority shareholder; see Note 2 to the definition) are deemed to be acting in concert with each other.

Certain persons, such as directors and other companies in the same group, are presumed to be acting in concert unless the contrary is established.

22.6.1.3 Restrictions on dealings

If an offer has lapsed which was one of two or more competing offers, then, until the other competing offer(s) have also lapsed, or become wholly unconditional, r 35.4 prevents the failed offeror from acquiring any interest in shares of the offeree company on terms more favourable than under its lapsed offer.

22.6.2 The successful bid

Once the offer is declared wholly unconditional, the offeror can breathe a sigh of relief: the takeover has been successful. However, r 31.4 of the City Code provides that the offer must still remain open for acceptance for between 14 days and the date that is four months from the date the initial offer document was posted. This affords offeree company shareholders, who did not accept the offer before the offer was declared unconditional as to acceptances, an opportunity to accept the offer once the offeror has acquired control of the offeree.

Ideally, an offeror will want to acquire 100% of the offeree company's shares, to avoid being left to cope with unfriendly minority shareholders (see **22.7.1**). If the offeror has received acceptances in respect of at least 90% of the shares to which the offer relates, it can compel the other offeree company shareholders to sell their shares to the offeror using the compulsory acquisition procedure under ss 428 to 430 of the CA 1985 or Sch 2 to the Takeovers Regulations (in relation to offers to which the Regulations apply) (see **22.7** below). However, if the offeror cannot invoke the compulsory acquisition procedure, it must abide with the minority shareholders who rejected the offer. After six months following the closure of the original offer, however, the offeror may be able to buy the shares of this minority by offering them more favourable terms than those of the original offer.

22.7 Buying out minority shareholders

22.7.1 The problem with minority shareholders

The typical offeror will not want to become the majority shareholder of the offeree company alongside minority shareholders who did not accept the offer. Minority shareholders can be problematic for a variety of reasons, including their ability to disrupt EGMs and create bad publicity for the company. The presence of a minority can also prevent the company from carrying out its day to day business effectively (for example, the minority may be able to block special resolutions if they hold more than 25% of the company's shares, or prevent an EGM from being held on short notice if they hold more than 5%).

The minority shareholders, too, may be less than happy to find themselves holding a minority stake in a company which is controlled by the offeror. In particular, if the offeror decides to take the company private after the takeover, the minority may struggle to find a market for their shares in order to exit from the company.

For the reasons outlined above, once the majority of shareholders have accepted the offer, ss 428 to 430 of the CA 1985 give a statutory right:

(a) to the offeror, to buy out the minority shareholders, and so acquire 100% of the offeree company (referred to as a 'squeeze out' right); and

(b) to each minority shareholder who has refused the takeover offer, to require the offeror to purchase his shares (referred to as a 'sell out' right).

The Companies Act procedures referred to at (a) and (b) are in the process of change, however. First, as a result of the Company Law Review 2001, and secondly, in order to be consistent with the Takeovers Directive (see **20.3**). These changes are due to be processed using the Companies Bill. However, as referred to at **20.3.2** above, the Bill did not progress through Parliament in time for the implementation date for the Directive of 20 May 2006. The Directive was implemented in the UK instead using an interim measure, the Takeovers Regulations. The Takeovers Regulations, therefore, implement the squeeze out and sell out provisions of the Directive.

This has created a temporary dual regime for squeeze out and sell out; the provisions in the Regulations (Sch 2) apply only to those offers to which the Directive applies. As explained at **20.3.1** above, this excludes offers for AIM companies. The provisions in the CA 1985 (ss 425 to 430) will continue to apply for the offers to which the Directive does not apply until the Companies Bill comes into force, when the Regulations will fall away and there will be one, Directive-compliant regime for all takeover offers.

There is considerable overlap between ss 425 to 430 of the CA 1985 and Sch 2 to the Takeovers Regulations. However, where there are differences, they are highlighted below.

22.7.2 The right of the offeror to buy out minority shareholders ('squeeze out')

22.7.2.1 The conditions

Two conditions must be satisfied before the offeror can invoke the compulsory acquisition provisions:

(a) the takeover offer condition; and

(b) the 90% squeeze out threshold condition (this involves an additional test under the Takeovers Regulations; see below).

The takeover offer condition

There must be a 'takeover offer', which is defined by s 428(1) of the CA 1985 as an offer made for the entire issued share capital (or all the shares of any class or classes) of the offeree company (other than the offeree company shares which are already held by the offeror, or contracted to be acquired by it) on terms which are the same in relation to all the shares to which the offer relates.

Note that, under the CA 1985 procedure, it may be difficult for an offeror to comply with this requirement if it has shareholders in a jurisdiction in which it is difficult to make the offer (for example, the USA, which has draconian securities laws). The Court of Appeal's decision in *Winpar Holdings Ltd v Joseph Holt Group plc* [2001] 2 BCLC 604 offers some guidance on this issue.

Here, the Court held that the offeror, Joseph Holt Group plc, could acquire minority shareholdings even though the offer had not been communicated directly to certain overseas shareholders (including Winpar Holdings Ltd), but instead was advertised in the Gazette. However, the Court stated expressly that the case was *not* to be taken as sanctioning the practice of not posting the offer document to persons in countries with different securities laws.

However, in relation to the issue of overseas shareholders, the Takeovers Regulations reflect the decision in *Winpar Holdings Ltd*. The offer can constitute a 'takeover offer' for the purposes of the Takeovers Regulations even if the offer is not made to an overseas shareholder, provided:

(a) the offer is not made to the shareholder in order to avoid contravening the law of an overseas territory;

(b) the shareholder does not have a registered UK address; and

(c) the offer is either:
 (i) published in the Gazette; or
 (ii) available for inspection at, or can be obtained from, a place in an EEA State, or a website, and notice of this is published in the Gazette.

The 90% squeeze out threshold condition

The offeror must have acquired or contracted to acquire, by virtue of acceptances of the offer, not less than 90% in value of all the shares *to which the offer relates* (or, if the offer is for more than one class of share, not less than 90% in value of all the shares of the class in which the minority shareholder is interested). Note that any shares acquired by the offeror or its associates *before* the offer document was posted do not count towards the 90% threshold, but any shares acquired *after* the document was posted will count towards the threshold.

For example, if the offeror already owned 25% of the offeree company's shares before the offer document was posted, the offer relates to only 75% of the offeree company's share capital. The offeror must, therefore, secure acceptances in respect of 90% of this 75%.

Shares which are the subject of irrevocable undertakings (see **21.10**) as at the date of the offer are not treated as being held by the offeror, or contracted to be acquired by it (CA 1985, ss 428(1) and (5); Takeovers Regulations, Sch 2, para 1(10)), nor are shares which the offeror's 'associates' hold or have contracted to acquire as at the date of the offer (CA 1985, s 430E(1); Takeovers Regulations, Sch 2, para 8(1)).

Under the Takeovers Regulations, the offeror must have acquired, or unconditionally contracted to acquire, not only at least 90% of the shares to which the offer relates, but also 90% of the voting rights in the company to which the offer relates (Takeovers Regulations, Sch 2, para 2(2)(b)). In practice, however, this should not cause the procedure materially to differ from the CA 1985 procedure.

Section 430C(5) and para 6(6) of Sch 2 to the Takeovers Regulations provide that the offeror can apply to the court for an order which allows it to serve a squeeze out notice (see **22.7.2.2**) even though it has not acquired the 90% threshold, if it can prove that:

(a) after reasonable enquiry the offeror has been unable to trace one or more of the persons holding shares to which the offer relates;

(b) if account were taken of the shares of these missing persons, the 90% threshold would be reached; and

(c) the consideration offered is fair and reasonable.

However, the court will make such an order only if it considers it just and equitable to do so, having regard to the number of shareholders who have been traced but who have rejected the offer.

22.7.2.2 The squeeze out notice

Provided the offeror has acquired or agreed to acquire 90% of the shares to which the offer relates within four months of the date on which the offer is document was posted, then the offeror can give notice to those offeree company shareholders who did not accept the offer that it wishes to acquire their shares. It must serve this notice within two months of reaching the 90% squeeze out threshold (in the case of the CA 1985 procedure) and within three months of the last day on which the offer could be accepted (in the case of the Takeovers Regulations procedure).

The squeeze out notice entitles, and also obliges, the offeror to acquire the offeree company shareholder's shares on the same terms as those of the takeover offer. For example, if the offer gave shareholders a choice of paper or cash consideration, the same choice must be given to shareholders who did not accept the offer. However, if any non-cash consideration available under the original offer is no longer available (for example, because it was provided by a third party who is no longer under an obligation to provide it), the offeree must pay the shareholder the cash equivalent as at the date of the notice (CA 1985, s 430(4) and Takeovers Regulations, Sch 2, para 3(5)).

The notice must make clear:

(a) that the shareholder must make his choice known to the offeror, in writing, within six weeks of the notice; and

(b) the default consideration that the shareholder will receive if he does not make his choice known to the offeror.

The offeror must copy the first notice (they are usually distributed in the order they appear on the register of members) to the offeree company, together with a statutory declaration (Form 429, in the case of the CA 1985 procedure) that the conditions referred to at **22.7.2.1** above have been satisfied.

22.7.2.3 The acquisition

Six weeks after serving the notice the offeror must send to the offeree:

(a) a copy of all the squeeze out notices;
(b) a stock transfer form executed by a person the offeror nominates on behalf of the shareholder; and
(c) the consideration for the shares.

The offeree will then:

(a) register the offeror as the holder of the shares to which the s 429 notice relates; and
(b) hold the consideration on trust for the relevant shareholders.

Section 430C(5) of the CA 1985 provides what should happen on the rare occurrence that a shareholder cannot be traced.

22.7.2.4 Preventing the acquisition

Section 430C of the CA 1985 and para 6 of Sch 2 to the Takeovers Regulations provide that any shareholder who receives a s 429 notice can apply to the court, within six weeks of the date on which the notice was given, to apply for an order preventing the acquisition or allowing the acquisition only on different terms. However, the courts are unlikely to be willing to investigate the merits of an offer which has already been endorsed by at least 90% of shareholders, unless there is a compelling reason to do so.

22.7.3 The right of minority shareholders to be bought out ('sell out')

Section 430A of the CA 1985 and para 4 of Sch 2 to the Takeovers Regulations provide a mechanism whereby an offeree company shareholder who has refused the takeover offer may be able to 'sell out', that is, require the offeror to purchase his shares.

22.7.3.1 The conditions

Two conditions must be satisfied before an offeree company shareholder can force the offeror to take his shares:

(a) the takeover offer condition; and
(b) the 90% sell out threshold condition.

The takeover offer condition

This condition is the same as for squeeze out (see **22.7.2.1**).

The 90% sell out threshold condition

A shareholder can compel the offeror to buy his shares only when the offeror has obtained an interest in 90% in value of *all the shares in the offeree company* (or the class of shares to which the shares of the minority shareholder belong). Note that the 90% sell out threshold is different to the 90% squeeze out threshold (see **22.7.2.1**). For squeeze out purposes, only shares *to which the offer relates* are included. For sell out, *all shares* in the offeree are included. Shares held by the offeror before the offer document was posted will count, therefore, towards the 90% sell out threshold but not towards the 90% squeeze out threshold (as they would not be shares to which the offer relates). Irrevocable undertakings and shares held by any associate of the offeror also count towards the sell out threshold.

The effect of this difference is that the offeror may meet the 90% sell out threshold before it meets the 90% squeeze out threshold.

> **Example**
>
> Imagine that the offeror acquired a 25% stake in the offeree before it posted the offer document. For squeeze out, the offeror must acquire 90% of the remaining 75%, which will be triggered once the offeror has acquired an aggregate of 92.5% (90% x 75% + the existing 25%). For sell out, the offeror must acquire only 90%, and the 25% already acquired will count towards this.

Under the Takeovers Regulations, as with the 90% squeeze out threshold, the 90% sell out threshold involves a further test; the offeror must have obtained an interest not only in 90% in value of all the issued offeree company shares, but also 90% of the *voting rights* in the offeree company.

22.7.3.2 The sell out notice

The average shareholder of an offeree company is unlikely to be aware of his sell out rights. Therefore, within one month of reaching the 90% threshold, the offeror must notify those shareholders who have not accepted the offer of their sell out rights. If the sell out notice is served before the end of the offer period, it must state that the offer is still open for acceptance.

The offeror must specify the period within which the shareholder can take up his sell out rights. Under the CA 1985 procedure, this period must be at least three months from the date the offer closes. Under the Takeovers Regulations, it must be *within* three months from the last date on which the offer could be accepted or, if later, the date on which the offeror serves the sell out notice.

Of course, if the offeror has already served a squeeze out notice to acquire the minority shareholders' shares (which is usual), the offeror does not need to notify the shareholders of their sell out rights. For this reason, sell out notices are not common.

If the minority shareholder exercises his sell out rights, the offeror must acquire those shares on terms which are the same as the terms of the takeover offer, or on such other terms as may be agreed. If the offer included a choice of consideration, the position is similar to that under squeeze out: if the chosen consideration is not available, the shareholder will receive the cash equivalent. The court has an overriding jurisdiction, on the application of either the shareholder or the offeror, to determine the terms on which the shares will be acquired.

22.7.3.3 The notice from the shareholder

The shareholder must give the offeror written notice of his desire to sell out. If there is a choice of consideration under the offer, the shareholder must state his choice of consideration.

22.7.3.4 Timetable

Figure 22.1 below summarises the squeeze out and sell out timetable under both the CA 1985 and the Takeovers Regulations.

Figure 22.1

```
┌──────────┐ ┌──────────┐ ┌──────────┐ ┌──────────┐ ┌──────────┐ ┌──────────┐ ┌──────────┐
│Post offer│ │ Offeror  │ │Last date │ │ Send out │ │ Send out │ │Last date │ │Last date │
│ document │ │ acquires │ │for       │ │ sell out │ │squeeze   │ │to sell   │ │to        │
│          │ │ sell out │ │accepting │ │ notice[2]│ │out       │ │out       │ │complain  │
│          │ │threshold[1]│ │the offer│ │          │ │notice[2] │ │          │ │to court  │
└──────────┘ └──────────┘ └──────────┘ └──────────┘ └──────────┘ └──────────┘ └──────────┘
```

Period	Reference
1 month	(CA 1985, s 430A(3); TR, Sch 2, para 4(8))
2 months	(CA 1985, s 429(3))
3 months	(TR, Sch 2, para 1(5))
3 months (min)	(CA 1985, s 430A(4));
3 months (max)	(TR, Sch 2, para 4(7))[3]
6 weeks	(CA 1985, s 430C(1); TR, Sch 2, para 6(1))

Notes:

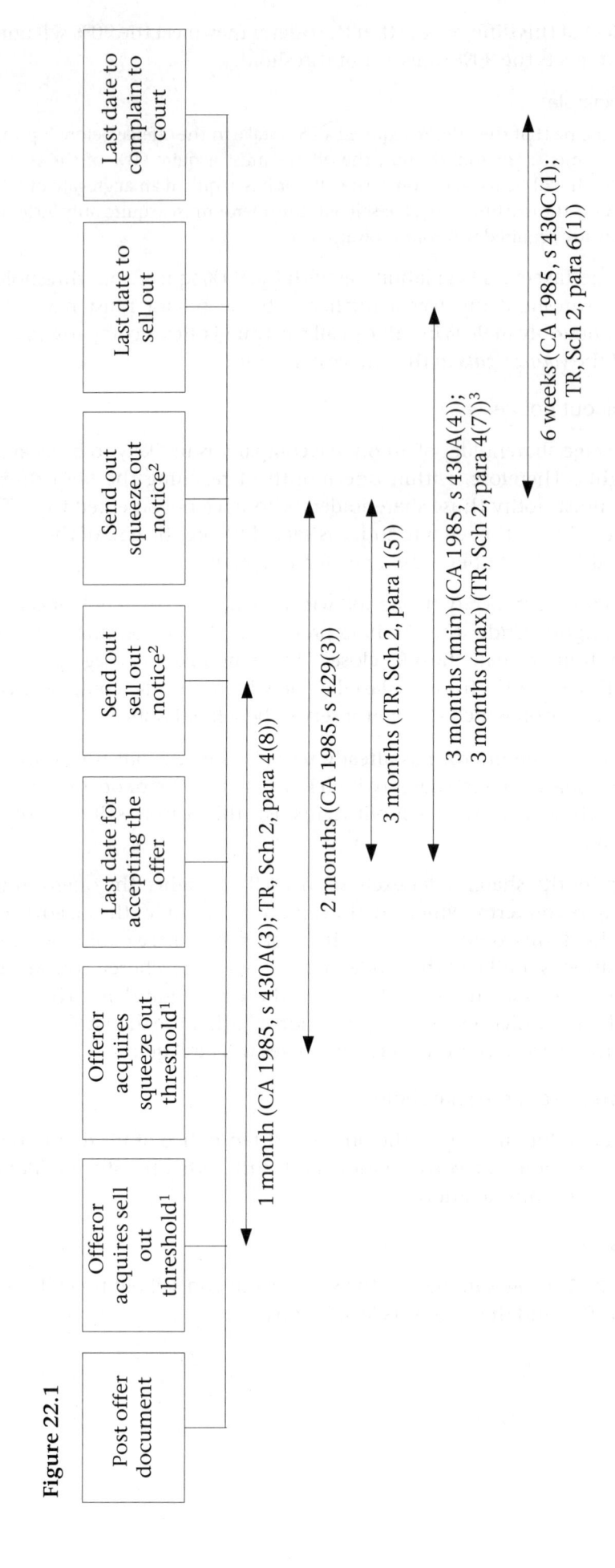

1. This may happen simultaneously, but sometimes the sell out threshold is acquired before the squeeze out threshold is acquired (see 22.7.3.1).
2. Offeror will try to send out squeeze out notice first, but sometimes this is not possible, on criteria.
3. Period begins with sending out of sell out notice, if later than last date for accepting.

22.8 Future developments

As explained at **20.8** above, when Pt 28 of the Companies Bill is enacted (which, at the time of writing, was expected to be soon after October 2006), the Takeovers Regulations will be repealed. This will have the effect of removing the dual regime for squeeze out and sell out. Instead, there will be one, Directive-complaint compulsory acquisition procedure for all transactions which fall within the definition of 'takeover offer' in cl 941 of the Bill. This procedure will follow, broadly, the procedure currently set out in Sch 2 to the Regulations.

Chapter 23

Takeovers: Merger Control

23.1	Introduction	347
23.2	Merger control provisions in the City Code	347
23.3	EC merger control	348
23.4	UK merger control	351

23.1 Introduction

As **20.3.1** above explains, it is difficult to define exactly what constitutes a merger and, from a legal perspective, the distinction between a takeover and a merger is not particularly important. It follows that the law relating to *merger* control can, in fact, apply to a *takeover*.

Why would the competition authorities be concerned with a takeover? Imagine that a car manufacturer, with a 40% market share, decides to make an offer for the entire issued share capital of one of its rivals, which also has a 40% market share. If the takeover is successful, the result will be a car manufacturer with a substantial share of the market. It will have considerable bargaining power and is likely to be able to source parts on very competitive terms. It is possible that other, smaller car manufacturers might be squeezed out of the market, and that others who wanted to break into the market would not be able to do so. The probable result of all of this is that the consumer who wants to buy a new car will have less choice and may have to pay more. This is why the competition authorities will keep a close eye on any takeover offer.

Practically, the corporate lawyer will enlist the help of his colleagues who specialise in competition law, who will then advise in relation to any merger control issues relevant to the takeover. However, this means that the corporate lawyer must be aware of the merger control rules to know when he should consult such colleagues; and, as always, the corporate lawyer will need to know enough about the process to follow discussions at meetings and to understand the impact it may have on the takeover offer. This chapter aims to introduce the corporate lawyer to the basics of merger control.

23.2 Merger control provisions in the City Code

23.2.1 Rule 12

23.2.1.1 Rule 12.1

Rule 12.1 of the City Code provides that it must be a term of the takeover offer that the offer will lapse if, before the first closing date, or the date the offer becomes or is declared unconditional as to acceptances (see **Chapter 22**), whichever is later:

(a) the offer is referred to the Competition Commission for investigation under the Enterprise Act 2002 (EA 2002) (see **23.4**); or

(b) the offer gives rise to a concentration with a Community dimension within the scope of the EC Merger Regulation (see **23.3**), and the European Commission either:

(i) commences Phase II proceedings under art 6(1)(c) of the EC Merger Regulation (see **23.3.6**), or

(ii) refers the matter back to the UK under art 9 of the EC Merger Regulation and there is then a reference to the Competition Commission (see **23.3.7**).

23.2.1.2 Rule 12.2

If the offer, or possible offer, is referred to the Competition Commission, or if the European Commission initiates Phase II proceedings, the offer period will end. A new offer period will begin when the 'competition reference period' ends. The competition reference period is defined in the City Code. It covers the period between the date a reference is made, or Phase II proceedings are initiated, and the date the authorities reach a decision on the matter.

23.2.2 Rule 35.1

The effect of r 35.1 of the City Code is that, if the offer has lapsed under r 12 (see **23.2.1**), the offeror cannot make another offer for the offeree for at least 12 months from the date of lapse, unless the Panel consents. The Panel will usually provide such consent if the offer lapsed under r 12 but subsequently received competition clearance.

23.3 EC merger control

On 1 May 2004 the Regulation on the control of concentrations between undertakings (EC Council Regulation 139/2004) (the 'EC Merger Regulation') came into force, replacing EC Council Regulation 4064/89.

The EC Merger Regulation will apply if the takeover constitutes a *concentration* with a *Community dimension*. If the takeover fulfils these criteria then, subject to limited exceptions (see **23.3.7** below), the Regulation will apply to the exclusion of any national competition law rules and the takeover will fall within the exclusive jurisdiction of the European Commission. This is intended to relieve the burden on the parties to the takeover, by reducing the number of regulatory authorities to which they are subject. For this reason the Regulation is often referred to as 'the one-stop shop'.

If the takeover does not fulfil these criteria, then it falls outside the scope of the EC Merger Regulation, but it may still be caught by domestic merger control rules (see **23.4**).

23.3.1 Concentration

Article 3 of the EC Merger Regulation provides that a concentration can arise on:

(a) the merger of two or more independent undertakings;

(b) the acquisition of direct or indirect control of the whole or part of an undertaking or undertakings; or

(c) some joint ventures.

This definition reflects the fact that the EC Merger Regulation is drafted to catch more than simply takeovers. Remember that a takeover involves the acquisition of an interest, or interests, in shares which carry 30% or more of the voting rights of a company, regardless of whether the interest gives actual control. It is category (b), then, which may bring a takeover within the EC Merger Regulation. Note, however, that (b) can also can also catch acquisitions which do not constitute a takeover, for example the acquisition of assets.

'Control' in the context of the EC Merger Regulation is wider than the definition of 'control' in the City Code (see **20.3.1.3**). In this context, 'control' means more than just voting control. It includes, for example, where one party can exercise 'decisive influence' (art 3). A 25% holding may constitute control for the purposes of the EC Merger Regulation.

23.3.2 Community dimension

Article 1 provides that a concentration will have a Community dimension if, subject to the two-thirds rule (see **23.3.3** below), it fulfils certain turnover criteria. There are two alternative sets of criteria, namely:

(a) the aggregate *worldwide* turnover of *all* parties exceeds €5,000m (c. £3,000m); and

(b) the aggregate *Community-wide* turnover of *at least two* of the parties exceeds €250m (c. £150m);

or

(a) the aggregate *worldwide* turnover of *all* parties exceeds €2,500m (c. £1,500m);

(b) the aggregate *Community-wide* turnover of *at least two* of the parties exceeds €100m (c. £60m); and

(c) in at least three Member States:

    (i) the aggregate *national* turnover of *all* the parties exceeds €100m (c. £60m), and

    (ii) the aggregate *national* turnover of *at least two* of the parties exceeds €25m (c. £15m).

Even if the takeover does not have a Community dimension, art 4, para 5 of the EC Merger Regulation provides that, if the takeover is capable of being reviewed under the national competition laws of at least three Member States, the parties can request the European Commission to take jurisdiction over the offer instead of the national authorities.

23.3.3 The two-thirds rule

A concentration will not have a Community dimension if each of the parties achieves more than two-thirds of its Community-wide turnover within the same Member State. This means, practically, that if the main impact of the takeover is within one Member State, it will not have a Community dimension. It could, of course, still be caught by the national competition rules of that Member State.

Practically, when calculating whether a takeover falls within the jurisdiction of the Commission, it is helpful to check whether the two-thirds rule applies *before* applying the 'Community dimension' test referred to at **23.3.2** above. If the two-thirds rule applies then there is no need to apply the 'Community dimension' test; the Commission will not have jurisdiction.

23.3.4 Notification

If the takeover constitutes a concentration with a Community dimension then the EC Merger Regulation provides that the parties must notify the European Commission before completion. The takeover cannot complete until the European Commission clears it. The notification should answer the

Commission's questionnaire, Form CO, which requires considerable information about the parties and the transaction. Form CO is annexed to Regulation 802/2004/EC, which implemented the EC Merger Regulation.

23.3.5 Phase I

Article 10 provides that the Commission has 25 working days from the date of notification to decide that it:

(a) does not have jurisdiction because the offer does not fall within the scope of the EC Merger Regulation;

(b) will clear the offer (because it does not create or strengthen a dominant position in any relevant Community market);

(c) will allow the offer to proceed, subject to conditions (for example, the parties agreeing to dispose of part of the business);

(d) will investigate the offer further (because it has serious doubts whether it creates or strengthens a dominant position in any relevant Community market); or

(e) will refer the offer back to a Member State under art 9 (because the offer threatens to affect significantly competition in a distinct market within that Member State; see **23.3.7**).

This period of 25 days is referred to as Phase I. Phase I can be extended to 35 working days in certain circumstances, such as where remedies are offered, or where a Member State makes a request for an art 9 reference (see **23.3.7** below).

If the Commission decides (d) above, and commences a Phase II investigation, or decides (e) above, and refers the offer back to the OFT and there is then a subsequent reference to the Competition Commission, the takeover offer will lapse under r 12.1 of the City Code (see **23.2.1.1(b)**).

23.3.6 Phase II

If, at the end of Phase I, the Commission decides to investigate the offer further (option (d) above), that period of investigation is referred to as Phase II. As explained at **23.2.1**, if the European Commission initiates Phase II proceedings, the offer period will end. Phase II can last up to 90 working days. It can be extended by 20 working days at the request of the parties or the Commission (if the parties so consent). Phase II will automatically be extended by 15 working days where the parties offer remedies after the 54th day of the Phase II investigation.

At the end of Phase II, the Commission can:

(a) clear the takeover; or

(b) allow the takeover to proceed subject to certain conditions; or

(c) block the takeover.

23.3.7 Exceptions

As **23.3** explains, the EC Merger Regulation is intended to be a 'one-stop shop' and applies to the exclusion of any national competition laws. However, a Member State can intervene to request repatriation of a case if it can demonstrate to the Commission that a reference back to the national authorities is necessary:

(a) to protect legitimate interests (such as national security) (art 21); or

(b) because the takeover threatens to affect significantly competition in a distinct market within that Member State (art 9). For example, in 1996, under the original EC Merger Regulation, the European Commission granted the UK's request for an art 9 reference with regard to the offer by a German pharmaceuticals company for Lloyds Chemists.

Commission's knock-back recalls the bad old days

THE European Court of First Instance's decision to overturn the Commission's approval for the merger between Bertelsmann and Sony was a reminder of the criticism which used to dog internal competition policy procedures before they were overhauled in 2004.

This reached a peak four years ago when the Luxembourg-based court ruled that the Commission had been wrong when blocking three proposed mergers. In June 2002 the judges said that the Commission had made "a series of incorrect findings" when opposing a tie-up between Airtours and First Choice.

In October the Commission was severely rapped over the knuckles twice in four days. The court said its thumbs down to a merger between Schneider and Legrand was based on "several obvious errors, omissions and contradictions", while its decision to block a marriage between packaging companies Tetra Laval and Sidel overestimated the anti-competitive effects of the merger.

Highly embarrassed by the criticism, Mario Monti, then the Competition Commissioner, made it a priority to review internal procedures for assessing proposed mergers. As a reaction to the court's criticism of its level of economic analysis, the reforms provided for the creation of the new post of chief competition economist. It also introduced guidelines for assessing mergers between competing firms.

The reforms took effect from May 1, 2004, several months after the two international media companies had informed the Commission on January 9 that they planned to merge their global recorded music activities. As a result, their case was dealt with under the old rules and procedures.

Since the reforms were introduced, the Commission has not lost a single merger decision before the Luxembourg court. And, just last week, the judges rejected a complaint from easyJet and said the Commission had been correct two years ago in deciding that the merger between Air France and KLM was compatible with EU rules.

Source: *The Times*, 14 July 2006

23.4 UK merger control

The EA 2002 governs merger control in the UK. The merger control provisions of the EA 2002 will apply to a takeover if:

(a) it is a *relevant merger situation*; and

(b) it results, or may be expected to result, in a *substantial lessening of competition*.

23.4.1 Relevant merger situation

A takeover will constitute a 'relevant merger situation' if:

(a) it is not caught by the EC Merger Regulation (see **23.3** above);

(b) two or more enterprises cease to be distinct;

(c) the time limit for a reference to the Competition Commission has not yet expired; and

(d) either:

　(i) the turnover test, or

　(ii) the share of supply test,

　is fulfilled.

Let us now consider each criterion in turn.

23.4.1.1 Not caught by the EC Merger Regulation

As stated at **23.3** above, if the takeover constitutes a *concentration* with a *Community dimension* then, subject to limited exceptions (see **23.3.7** above), the Regulation will apply to the exclusion of any national competition law rules. It is only if the takeover falls outside the EC Merger Regulation that the provisions of the EA 2002 may apply.

23.4.1.2 Two or more enterprises cease to be distinct

Enterprise

Section 129(1) of the EA 2002 provides that an 'enterprise' is the activities, or part of the activities, of a business. 'Business' in this context includes an undertaking carried on for gain or reward, or in the course of which goods or services are supplied otherwise than free of charge.

At least one of the enterprises must be carried on in the UK (or by, or under the control of, a body corporate which is incorporated in the UK).

Ceasing to be distinct

Enterprises cease to be distinct if either:

(a) they are brought under common ownership or control; or
(b) one of the enterprises ceases to be carried on at all pursuant to some arrangement entered into to prevent competition between the enterprises.

In the case of a takeover, it is (a) above which is relevant. An offeror will acquire 'control' for these purposes if:

(a) it can materially influence the policy of the offeree ('influential control');
(b) it can control the policy of the offeree ('de facto control'); or
(c) it has a controlling interest (that is, more than 50% of the voting rights) in the offeree ('legal control').

23.4.1.3 The time limit for a reference has not expired

Section 24 of the EA 2002 provides that the takeover must either:

(a) not have completed; or
(b) have completed less than four months ago (unless the takeover completed without a public announcement, and the OFT was not notified, in which case the four-month period will start from the time the takeover comes to the attention of the OFT).

23.4.1.4 The turnover test and the share of supply test

To qualify for investigation the takeover must satisfy at least one of the following tests:

Turnover test

This test (EA 2002, s 28(1)) will be fulfilled if the value of the *UK* turnover of the *offeree* exceeds £70m.

Share of supply test

This test (EA 2002, s 23) will be fulfilled if:

(a) after the takeover, the offeror will supply, or be supplied with, at least 25% of a defined class of goods or services which are supplied in the UK (or a substantial part of it (see below)); or
(b) if this was already the case before the takeover, then after the takeover the offeror acquires an even greater share of the market.

Example

If X plc, which controls 20% of the market for the supply of cars, makes a bid for Y plc, another car manufacturer with a market share of 10%, this would fulfil the market share test, because after the takeover X plc would own at least 25% of the UK car market. Even if X plc owned 25% of the car market before the takeover, the takeover of Y plc would still qualify for a reference as it would increase further X plc's market share.

Note that the example above assumes that the car market is a distinct market. In practice it can be difficult for lawyers to predict what is a distinct market. Ultimately, the OFT has the discretion to determine what the criteria are for determining the market. For example, it may consider the number of units sold, the value of goods sold, or the number of employees engaged in the manufacture or supply of the goods.

In a case (decided under the Fair Trading Act 1973, the predecessor of the EA 2002) involving bus companies in the north of England, the House of Lords held that a region which amounted to 1.65% of the area of the UK and which contained 3.2% of the population was a substantial part of the UK for the purposes of the EA 2002 (*South Yorkshire Transport Ltd and Another v Monopolies and Mergers Commission and Another* [1993] 1 All ER 289).

23.4.2 A substantial lessening of competition

The EA 2002 does not define this term, which is referred to in practice as an 'SLC'. However, the explanatory notes to the EA 2002 state the following:

> Similar language is used in the legislation controlling mergers in a number of other major jurisdictions including the US, Canada, Australia and New Zealand. The concept is an economic one, best understood by reference to the question of whether a merger will increase or facilitate the exercise of market power (whether unilateral or through co-ordinated behaviour), leading to reduced output, higher prices, less innovation or lower quality of choice. A number of matters may be potentially relevant to the assessment of whether a merger will result in a substantial lessening of competition. These matters include, but are not limited to:
> - market shares and concentration
> - extent of effective competition before and after the merger
> - efficiency and financial performance of firms in the market
> - barriers to entry and expansion in the relevant market
> - availability of substitute products and the scope for supply – or demand – substitution
> - extent of change and innovation in a market
> - whether in the absence of the merger one of the firms would fail and, if so, whether its failure would cause the assets of that firm to exit the market, and
> - the conduct of customers or of suppliers to those in the market.

In fact, the OFT ('Mergers: Substantive Assessment' (OFT 516), May 2003) and the Competition Commission ('Merger References – Competition Commission Guidelines') produce their own guidance for determining whether or not there has been an SLC.

HMV cleared by watchdog to bid for Ottakar's

The competition watchdog gave the green light yesterday for the bookseller Waterstone's to swallow its smaller, independent rival Ottakar's.

The provisional verdict of a three-month investigation by the Competition Commission - that a takeover by HMV, the owner of Waterstone's, will not reduce competition by much - is likely to dismay authors, if not the City.

When HMV's £96.8m bid was accepted by Ottakar's in September, a flurry of publishers and high-profile writers claimed the deal would narrow the choice of titles available on the high street.

The commission disagreed, finding an amalgamation of the two would not create any "substantial lessening of competition", even in towns with a Waterstone's and an Ottakar's.

Diana Guy, who led the inquiry, said in a statement: "There is growing competition from supermarkets and internet retailers in terms of both price and range, so the merged company would have little ability to raise prices either on bestsellers or other titles."

The commission also agreed with HMV that such a deal would see Waterstone's heavier distribution clout push a wider range of books into Ottakar's shops.

HMV's offer of 440p per Ottakar's share lapsed in December, when the proposal was referred to the commission by the Office of Fair Trading. The high street music group had trumped a management buyout attempt, led by the managing director James Heneage, pitched at 400p a share.

HMV, advised by the Swiss investment bank UBS, is expected to keep its powder dry until the commission publishes its final findings on 22 May. Then it is likely to return with another offer, significantly lower than before, since Ottaker's trading has deteriorated significantly since HMV first made its interest known. Nick Bubb, an analyst at the investment bank Evolution Group, thought HMV need not pay more than 300p a share to secure an agreed takeover with Ottakar's board.

Other experts, including Richard Ratner at Seymour Pierce, told clients HMV would not need to bid more than 400p a share unless a rival predator, such as WH Smith, emerged.

He, like HMV, applauded the commission's decision, congratulating the watchdog for rejecting "hypocritical" arguments that a combined group would choke the availability of less popular books. "The publishers have been shedding crocodile tears for the authors and the public," he said. "At the same time, they are supplying Amazon and the supermarkets at lower prices than the specialist booksellers are getting."

The prospect of a second bid from HMV spurred Ottakar's shares 25.75p to 350.75p, valuing it at £71.8m. HMV shares eased 0.25p to 173.75p.

HMV has the been the subject of takeover interest from the private equity group Permira. Talks broke down over price.

Source: *The Independent*, 31 March 31 2006

23.4.3 The competition authorities

The EA 2002 is administered by the following authorities:

23.4.3.1 The Office of Fair Trading ('OFT')

The OFT is the government department which conducts the initial merger control investigation. If the OFT decides that:

(a) the takeover constitutes a relevant merger situation (see **23.4.1** above); and

(b) the takeover has resulted, or may be expected to result, in an SLC within any UK market(s) for goods or services (see **23.4.2** above),

then s 33(1) of the EA 2002 provides that it must refer the case to the Competition Commission (see **23.4.3.2** below). In *OFT v IBA Health Limited* [2004] EWCA Civ 142, concerning the takeover by iSoft plc of Torex plc, the Court of Appeal clarified the meaning of 'or may be expected to result'.

The Court ruled that the relevant test is whether the OFT itself believes that a takeover may be expected to result in an SLC. The OFT does not have to predict what the Competition Commission might decide. The OFT's belief must be more than a mere suspicion, and must be reasonable and objectively justified. If the OFT believes the probability of the takeover resulting in an SLC is over 50%, it should refer. If it believes the probability is less than 50%, but more than fanciful, the OFT has discretion as to whether to refer.

As stated at **23.2.1** above, if the OFT does refer to the Competition Commission a takeover which is subject to the City Code, the takeover must lapse.

23.4.3.2 The Competition Commission

The Competition Commission is a statutory body which is independent of the Government. It must investigate takeovers which the OFT refers to it. In doing so, it must decide:

(a) whether the takeover has resulted, or will result, in an anti-competitive outcome. Note that this involves deciding whether it is more likely than not that the takeover has resulted, or will result, in a substantial lessening of competition. The OFT, in contrast, only had to reasonably believe that there had been, or might be, an SLC; and

(b) (if there is, or will be, an anti-competitive outcome) what remedies are appropriate.

The Competition Commission has the power to require attendance of witnesses and production of documents. It must take into account any representations made to it by those with a substantial interest in the subject matter of the reference.

Within 24 weeks from the date of the reference, the Competition Commission must consider the reference and make its decisions. In exceptional circumstances the 24-week period can be extended by up to a further eight weeks. It will then publish a report on its assessment of the takeover, the remedies it recommends and the reasons for its decisions. The report will be made available on the Competition Commission's website.

A guidance note, 'Merger References – Competition Commission Guidelines', which sets out how the Competition Commission will assess cases, is also available on its website.

23.4.3.3 The Secretary of State for Trade and Industry

The Secretary of State's power to intervene in merger control decisions is limited to mergers involving particular public interest issues. In such cases, the Secretary of State, rather than the OFT, can decide, first, whether to refer the merger to the Competition Commission and, secondly, whether to follow the Competition Commission's decision.

23.4.4 Notification

23.4.4.1 Clearance

Unlike the EC merger control process, outlined at **23.3.4** above, under the EA 2002 there is no obligation on the parties to notify a merger or proposed merger to the OFT. However, most parties to a takeover choose to notify the OFT in advance in order to seek formal confirmation that it will not be referred to the Competition Commission. This is referred to as a 'clearance'. The takeover process is expensive in terms of both time and money, and the parties will want to be certain that they are not going to make such an investment only for the Competition Commission to block the takeover at a later stage in the process.

There are two methods by which the parties to a takeover can seek clearance:

(a) *Written submission.* The offeror (possibly jointly with the offeree) submits a memorandum, together with supporting documentation, to the OFT, explaining why a Competition Commission reference is not required and why clearance should be given.

(b) *Pre-notification by Merger Notice.* This method is for pre-notification only, ie, it can only be used for a takeover which has been announced but not yet completed. The parties file a Merger Notice which answers questions about the takeover and which markets it may affect.

23.4.4.2 Confidential guidance

As an alternative to seeking clearance, for many years the offeror or offeree was able to seek confidential guidance from the OFT in relation to a proposed takeover which had not been announced. This had the advantage of confidentiality, which is clearly important in relation to a takeover. However, it also had a disadvantage, namely that once the takeover became public, the OFT could then ascertain the views of other interested parties, and, if any material new fact emerged, or indeed there was a material change in circumstances, then the OFT could decide to refer the takeover to the Competition Commission, despite its confidential guidance to the contrary.

The provision of confidential guidance placed considerable pressure on the resources of the OFT. In 2005 the OFT announced that it would no longer provide confidential guidance, and would concentrate instead on dealing with transactions in the public domain.

The OFT intends to consult publicly on this issue, in time to publish new guidance in March 2007. In the interim, it will not provide any confidential guidance. However, on 12 April 2006 the OFT announced that it will consider applications for informal advice for confidential transactions as an interim arrangement, but only where there is a good faith intention to proceed, and where the OFT's duty to refer to the Competition Commission is a genuine issue. Details of this interim arrangement are available from the OFT website.

23.4.5 Undertakings

If the OFT concludes that, having considered the two issues referred to at **23.4.3.1** above, it is under an obligation to make a reference to the Competition Commission, the parties may be able to provide certain undertakings with the effect that the takeover will not result in an SLC and so no reference is necessary. A good example of the use of undertakings was in the bid by Morrison for Safeway, which was cleared when Morrison provided an undertaking (referred to as a 'divestment undertaking') that it would sell 53 Safeway stores (see the article opposite).

Note that the provision of undertakings can have an impact on the takeover timetable (see **Table 22.1** above), so any party seeking to provide such undertakings must keep the Panel informed and seek any necessary extensions to the timetable.

Safeway ruling gives Morrison pole position

By SUSANNA VOYLE, Retail Correspondent

SIR KEN Morrison was last night in pole position to buy Safeway and turn his regional supermarket chain into a national group after a government ruling barred larger rivals from bidding and tied the hands of financial buyers.

Patricia Hewitt, trade and industry secretary, yesterday said she had accepted the findings of the Competition Commission which blocked any bid for Safeway by the big three supermarkets – Tesco, Asda/Wal-Mart and J. Sainsbury.

Wm Morrison Supermarkets. however, was cleared to bid as long as it agrees to sell 53 Safeway stores.

The ruling will he seen as a triumph for Sir Ken, who has emerged triumphant after a tough, costly and protracted auction. He built-up Morrison from market stalls run by his father in Bradford in the 1940s.

Competition experts said the wording of the ruling – which stressed the need to maintain four strong national groups and prevent the big three from getting bigger – blocked any attempt by financial bidders to buy Safeway and break it up.

Shares in Safeway fell heavily, closing down 20½p at 276p, fractionally below the now-lapsed 277½p-a-share offer made by Morrison in January.

Philip Green, the only financial bidder left in the running, said he was studying the commission's findings. "We have got to read the report over the weekend," he said.

However, people close to Mr Green admitted that the findings limited his room for manoeuvre. "For a financial buyer, selling stores to the big three supermarket groups is the main tool in your kitbag," said one

Analysts said any financial bidder would have to buy Safeway to run it – but would be unlikely to bid as much as Morrison, which will achieve cost savings from merging the businesses.

The commission's report said any bid by the three biggest supermarket operators would reduce competition and could lead to higher prices for consumers. It also expressed concern about the effects on suppliers.

Tesco, Asda/Wal-Mart and Sainsbury said that they were disappointed but accepted the findings and would study the 500-page report to see how many stores they might pick up.

Asda has all but ruled out the possibility of seeking a judicial review.

The commission has set down strict rules about the disposal of the 53 stores. Ironically, it appears that Tesco, Britain's biggest retailer, stands to get the most. It qualifies to buy 21, Sainsbury 20 and Asda just 12.

Tesco was the only supermarket group to see its shares rise yesterday – up 6p at 241p – as investors took the view that its dominance of the market had been set in stone for years to come.

Shares in Morrison fell 8¼p to 211¾p – meaning a retabled bid at the same level would value Safeway at £2.95bn.

Source: *Financial Times*, 27 September 2003.

23.4.6 The lawyer's role

The competition lawyer's role will include the following:

(a) giving preliminary advice on the likelihood of the takeover being referred to the Competition Commission;

(b) co-ordinating other advisers who may be needed to formulate arguments in favour of the offeror, such as economists and, perhaps, political consultants;

(c) preparing submissions on behalf of the offeror, and representing the offeror at hearings before the Competition Commission; and

(d) negotiating undertakings to ensure the takeover falls outside the scope of the EA 2002.

23.4.7 EC v UK merger regimes

The relationship between the two merger control regimes is illustrated in the case of the takeover of Midland by HSBC (see **22.4.5.4**). After HSBC made its initial offer for Midland, Lloyds announced that it would make a rival offer subject to certain pre-conditions. One of the pre-conditions was that the merger authorities would treat the rival bids alike.

The HSBC offer amounted to a concentration with a Community dimension, and so fell within the scope of the EC Merger Regulation's one-stop shop. However, the

European Commission cleared the takeover, as HSBC and Midland competed in only a few sectors and, even after the takeover, intense competition in those sectors would remain.

The proposed Lloyds offer, however, did not fall within the scope of the EC Merger Regulation. Instead, it became apparent that it would be referred under the UK merger control regime. Lloyds therefore withdrew its offer, and the takeover by HSBC was successful.

Part V
AIM

Part V
AIM

Chapter 24
AIM

24.1	Background to this chapter	361
24.2	An introduction to AIM	361
24.3	Why AIM?	362
24.4	Eligibility criteria	362
24.5	The marketing document	363
24.6	Continuing obligations	365
24.7	Corporate governance	367
24.8	Future developments	367

24.1 Background to this chapter

The focus of Parts I to IV of this book is the company which has its shares admitted to listing on the Official List and admitted to trading on the Main Market. However, in recent years much of the flotation activity in the UK has been on AIM. As a result, it would be impossible to practice corporate law in today's climate without at least a basic understanding of AIM, how it compares to the Main Market, and the perceived advantages and disadvantages of an admission to AIM. This chapter seeks to help provide that basic understanding.

24.2 An introduction to AIM

In 1995 the Stock Exchange established the Alternative Investment Market as its international market for smaller and growing companies. The Stock Exchange states that its objective 'was to offer smaller and companies – from any country and any industry sector – the chance to raise capital on a market with a pragmatic and appropriate approach to regulation. With this in mind, AIM was designed to be a highly flexible public market offering many unique attributes both for companies and investors'.

AIM has proved a great success. In fact, it is the most successful growth market in the world. Since its launch in 1995, over 2,100 companies have joined the market (now known simply as 'AIM'), raising more than £30 billion between them. As at August 2006, 1,567 companies were trading on AIM, with a total market capitalisation in excess of £70 billion. The market's appeal is not limited to the UK. During 2005 and 2006, 183 overseas companies joined AIM; some 270 overseas companies were trading on AIM as at June 2006. Typically it is the smaller companies who list on AIM, particularly natural resources, technology and fast-growing companies. Some AIM companies are household names, such as Domino's Pizza, Majestic Wine and Coffee Republic.

AIM is regulated by the Stock Exchange. The Listing Rules do not apply to AIM companies (see **3.5.2**). Instead, AIM companies are governed by a set of rules helpfully titled the 'AIM Rules'. The AIM Rules are drafted with smaller companies in mind; they do not contain much legal or technical jargon, and this allows them to be applied flexibly and comprehensively. The AIM Rules are available from the AIM section of the Stock Exchange website.

24.3 Why AIM?

The advantages of listing, set out at **1.7** above, apply equally to AIM as they do the Main Market. As, typically, it is the smaller, emerging companies who use AIM, the accessible market, easy access to capital and acquisition opportunities and employee incentives AIM offers are a particular draw.

So why list on AIM rather than the Main Market? In addition to the benefits referred to above, the following aspects of AIM can render it more attractive than the Main Market, particularly for smaller companies:

(a) AIM is easier to access:
  (i) it has reduced eligibility requirements (see **24.4**); and
  (ii) the role of the 'nomad' (see **24.4.1**) means the admission process is more straightforward.
(b) AIM has a more relaxed regulatory regime. In particular:
  (i) there are reduced disclosure requirements;
  (ii) shareholder approval is required only for a reverse takeover (see **24.6.2.3**) and a disposal resulting in a fundamental change of business (see **24.6.2.4**). (However the company may still require shareholder approval for ancillary matters relating to other transactions, such as a disapplication of s 89 pre-emption rights);
  (iii) the brevity of the AIM Rules means that the day-to-day regulatory work required for an AIM company costs less than that for a Main Market company; and
  (iv) the requirement for a prospectus is confined to circumstances where there is a public offer; s 85(2) does not apply to AIM companies (see **24.5.1**).
(c) AIM offers tax advantages for investors which the Main Market does not.

24.4 Eligibility criteria

The minimum requirements for admission to AIM are different from those of the Main Market (set out at **4.3.1.1** above). For example, unlike the Main Market, there are no requirements in respect of market capitalisation, the number of shares in public hands, or a three-year trading record.

In order to seek admission to AIM, a company must comply with the following minimum requirements:

(a) *Incorporation.* The company must be legally established under the laws of its place of incorporation and be able to offer shares to the public. (For UK companies this means being a public company.)
(b) *Transferability.* Shares admitted to AIM must be freely transferable.
(c) *Whole class to be listed.* All issued shares of the same class must be admitted.
(d) *Electronic settlement.* All shares admitted must be eligible for electronic settlement.
(e) *Accounts.* The company (if it is incorporated in an EEA country) must have published accounts which conform with International Accounting Standards ('IAS').
(f) *Nominated adviser.* A nominated adviser (known as a 'nomad') and broker must be appointed and retained at all times (see **24.4.1**).

In the event that the company's main activity is a business that has been generating revenue and/or been independent for less than two years prior to its admission to AIM, it is subject to a condition that all directors (and their families) and employees who hold an interest in the company and certain substantial shareholders must agree not to dispose of their interests for at least one year following admission to AIM (AIM Rules, r 7).

24.4.1 The nomad

One of the most significant differences between the Main Market and AIM is the role of the nomad. The Stock Exchange attributes the success of AIM largely to the role of the nomad, whose role is to guide a company first through the admission process and then through its life as a publicly quoted company. Rule 34 of the AIM Rules requires every AIM company to retain a nomad at all times. The Stock Exchange will suspend trading in the securities of any AIM company which ceases to have a nomad.

The nomad owes its responsibilities, set out in Rule 39 of the AIM Rules, solely to the Stock Exchange. The nomad must:

(a) ensure that the company:
   (i) is suitable for admission to AIM; and
   (ii) complies with the AIM Rules;
(b) review on a regular basis the company's actual trading performance and financial condition against any profit forecast, estimate or projection which is in the public domain (including in the admission document or prospectus – see **24.5**); and
(c) most importantly, confirm to the Stock Exchange that any admission document or prospectus (see **24.5**) complies with the requirements of Sch 6 to the AIM Rules.

A list of nomads is available on the AIM section of the Stock Exchange website.

24.4.2 The broker

An AIM company must retain a broker at all times (AIM Rules, r 35). If there is no registered market maker (see **2.5.2**), the broker must use its best endeavours to find a matching business. Any member firm of the Stock Exchange can act as broker, subject to any required authorisation by any other regulator. A list of member firms is available on the AIM section of the Stock Exchange website, together with a separate list of brokers which AIM companies have appointed.

24.5 The marketing document

When a company applies for admission to AIM, or is raising further equity finance on AIM then, subject to exemptions (see **24.5.1.1**), the company must produce a prospectus or admission document.

24.5.1 Prospectus or admission document?

Chapter 6 sets out in detail when a company is required to publish a prospectus pursuant to the Prospectus Rules and s 85 of the FSMA 2000. As stated at **3.5.1** above, the Prospectus Rules apply to AIM companies as well as to Main Market companies. A prospectus is required when a company either:

(a) offers transferable securities to the public in the UK (s 85(1)); or

(b) requests admission of transferable securities to trading on a regulated market situated or operating in the UK (s 85(2)).

AIM is a Stock Exchange regulated market. This is not a 'regulated market' for the purposes of s 85(2), so s 85(2) does not apply to an AIM company, or a company seeking admission to AIM. Nevertheless, if an AIM company, or a company seeking admission to AIM, is offering transferable securities to the public in the UK then, subject to any applicable exemptions, a prospectus is required under s 85(1).

As a company seeks admission to AIM because of its more flexible and pragmatic regulation, typically AIM companies will seek to structure any public offer to fall within one of the exemptions set out in s 85(5) and s 86 of the FSMA 2000.

If a prospectus is not required, the company must instead produce an admission document, which must comply with a more relaxed version of the Prospectus Rules (see **24.5.3**). An admission document does not require approval by the FSA.

24.5.1.1 Exemptions to the requirement to produce a prospectus

The exemptions to s 85(1) are set out at **6.4.1.5** above. The most common exemptions relied upon by AIM companies are those set out at **6.4.1.5(a)** (offers to qualified investors), **6.4.1.5(b)** (offers to fewer than 100 persons in each EEA State who are not qualified investors), **6.4.1.5(c)** (offers involving significant investment by each investor), **6.4.1.5(d)** (small offers) and **6.4.1.5(f)** (offers in conjunction with takeovers by way of share for share exchange).

If any of the FSMA 2000 exemptions to s 85(1) apply, a prospectus will not be required (remember that s 85(2) is not relevant in relation to AIM). In practice, any sizeable rights issue or open offer to raise further finance will tend to be to more than 100 persons per EEA State (as is the case with the Main Market), and therefore in these circumstances it will be necessary to draft a prospectus and have it approved by the FSA.

24.5.2 Responsibility

The directors take overall responsibility for a prospectus or admission document (although a third party may take responsibility for a specific part of the document). The directors are responsible for ensuring compliance with the AIM Rules.

24.5.3 Content requirements

24.5.3.1 Prospectus

The content requirements of a prospectus are as set out in the Prospectus Directive (see **6.5**).

24.5.3.2 Admission document

The Stock Exchange has carved out certain requirements of the Prospectus Rules in relation to the content requirements of an admission document. The carve-outs reflect the nature of AIM and the companies admitted to it.

The content requirements for what lawyers refer to as 'an AIM-PD: compliant admission document' are set out in Sch 2 to the AIM Rules (which includes Annexes I–III of the Prospectus Rules, as amended by the AIM Rules).

24.6 Continuing obligations

24.6.1 The general obligation of disclosure

As stated at **3.5.3**, the Disclosure Rules do not apply to AIM companies. The AIM Rules set out continuing obligations of AIM companies. The primary obligation is a general duty of disclosure, set out in r 11. This provides that every AIM company must announce, without delay, any new developments which:

(a) are not public knowledge; and

(b) concern a change in its financial condition, its sphere of activity, performance of its business, or its expectation of its performance; and

(c) if made public, would be likely to cause a substantial movement in the price of its securities.

The company must make the announcement through an RIS. Rule 10 of the AIM Rules requires that the company must take reasonable care to ensure that any information it notifies is not misleading, false or deceptive, and does not omit anything likely to affect the import of such information.

24.6.2 Specific disclosure obligations

In addition to the general obligation to disclose price sensitive information, there are specific obligations of disclosure in relation to the following:

(a) substantial transactions (AIM Rules, r 12 – see **24.6.2.1** below);

(b) related party transactions (AIM Rules, r 13 – see **24.6.2.2** below);

(c) reverse takeovers (AIM Rules, r 14 – see **24.6.2.3** below);

(d) any disposal resulting in a fundamental change of business (AIM Rules, r 15 – see **24.6.2.4** below);

(e) dealings by directors (AIM Rules, r 17);

(f) changes in directors, significant shareholders, nomad or broker (AIM Rules, r 17);

(g) any material change in the company's actual trading performance or financial condition and between any profit forecast or estimate included in the company's admission document, or which is otherwise in the public domain (AIM Rules, r 17); and

(h) other matters set out in r 17 of the AIM Rules, including any change to the accounting reference date, registered office address or legal name.

24.6.2.1 Substantial transactions

As set out at **24.6.2(a)**, an AIM company must disclose details of any substantial transactions. A transaction is substantial if it exceeds 10% of any class test contained in Sch 3 to the AIM Rules (which are similar to the class tests set out in Chapters 10 and 11 of the Listing Rules; see **19.4**).

Schedule 3 sets out a comparison between the size of the transaction and the company itself in respect of the following:

(a) gross assets;

(b) profits;

(c) turnover;

(d) consideration to market capitalisation; and

(e) gross capital (in acquisitions of a company or business).

If a transaction is revenue in nature and occurring in the ordinary course of the business of the company, or if it has undertaken to raise finance that does not involve a change in the fixed assets of the company, it will not constitute a substantial transaction.

If the transaction exceeds 10% of any of the Sch 3 class tests, and so constitutes a substantial transaction, an announcement must be made pursuant to Sch 3, which must include the prescribed information set out in Sch 4. However, there is no requirement for shareholder approval, or for a circular (unless required under another AIM rule). Directors of AIM companies often cite this as a reason for choosing AIM over the Main Market.

24.6.2.2 Related party transaction

If the transaction is with a related party (as defined by the AIM Rules) and exceeds 5% in any of the Sch 3 class tests referred to at **24.6.2.1** above, an announcement containing prescribed information as set out in Sch 4 to the AIM Rules is required. The announcement must include a statement that the directors (excluding any director involved directly in the transaction) having consulted with the company's nomad, consider that the terms of the transaction are fair and reasonable.

Where the class test exceeds 0.25%, the company must include details of any related party transaction in the company's annual audited accounts (see **24.6.3**).

24.6.2.3 Reverse takeover

A transaction (or transactions) over a 12-month period which either:

(a) exceeds 100% of any of the class tests sets out in Sch 3 to the AIM Rules (see **24.6.2.1**); or

(b) results in a fundamental change to the AIM company's business, board or voting control (or, in the case of an investing company (as defined by the AIM Rules), departs substantially from the investing strategy set out in its prospectus or admission document),

constitutes a reverse takeover under r 14 of the AIM Rules.

The company must:

(a) obtain shareholder approval (by ordinary resolution) for any reverse takeover (and any agreement relating to a reverse takeover must be conditional upon such approval); and

(b) prepare a prospectus or admission document, which must describe the circumstances and details of the transaction and convene the shareholders' general meeting to approve the transaction.

Trading in the company's securities will be cancelled. The enlarged entity must seek admission in the same manner as any other AIM company which is seeking admission for the first time.

24.6.2.4 Disposal resulting in a fundamental change of business

Any disposal which, when aggregated with any other disposal or disposals over the previous 12 months, exceeds 75% in any of the class tests set out in Sch 3 to the AIM Rules (see **24.6.2.1** above), is a disposal which results in a fundamental change of business ('DFCB') (AIM Rules, r 15).

A DFCB must be conditional on shareholder approval (by ordinary resolution). A circular containing the information specified in Sch 4 to the AIM Rules (and r 13 insofar as the disposal is to a related party) and a notice of EGM will also be required. Where the proposed disposal will divest the company of all, or substantially all, of its trading business activities, the circular must state the company's investing strategy going forward.

The Company must notify an RIS of the DFCB without delay, disclosing the information specified by Sch 4 to the AIM Rules. If the transaction involves a related party, the information required by r 13 of the AIM Rules must also be disclosed.

The company must make the acquisition (or acquisitions) constituting a reverse takeover under r 14 of the AIM Rules within 12 months of receiving the consent of its shareholders.

24.6.3 Financial information

The AIM Rules supplement the financial obligations in the CA 1985 with more specific obligations.

The AIM Rules require companies incorporated in an EEA country to publish annual accounts in accordance with International Accounting Standards ('IAS'). The company must send the accounts to shareholders within six months of the end of the financial year to which they relate (AIM Rules, r 19). The accounts must disclose any transaction with a related party (see **24.6.2.2**), whether or not previously disclosed under the AIM Rules, where any of the class tests in Sch 3 to the AIM Rules exceed 0.25%, and specify the identity of the related party and the consideration for the transaction.

The AIM Rules also require listed companies to prepare interim reports in respect of the first six months of the company's financial period. The company must publish the interim reports within three months of the end of this half-year period and must notify an RIS that they have been published (AIM Rules, r 18).

In addition, although not mandatory, it is best practice for an AIM company to include a statement in its annual report which discloses the extent to which it has complied with the principles set out in the Combined Code (see **24.7**).

24.6.4 Share dealing code

Rule 21 of the AIM Rules prohibits dealings by directors and other key employees in the company's securities in certain circumstances, such as when they are in possession of unpublished price sensitive information, or during specified periods. Generally, companies admitted to AIM will adopt a share dealing code which complies with this Rule.

24.7 Corporate governance

The Combined Code does not apply to AIM companies, although they are encouraged to comply with it. In July 2005, the Quoted Company Alliance ('QCA') published corporate governance guidelines for AIM companies. The guidelines are available to order from the QCA website.

24.8 Future developments

On 2 October 2006 the Stock Exchange issued a consultation on proposed changes to the AIM Rules, including the codification of the role and responsibilities of the nomad (via an additional rulebook) and the introduction of supplemental disclosure requirements for AIM companies. The consultation documents are available on the AIM section of the Stock Exchange website. The consultation period is due to close on 1 December 2006.

Appendices

Appendix 1	THE ADMISSION AND DISCLOSURE STANDARDS	371
Appendix 2	RESOLUTIONS	377
Appendix 3	FORMS	379
Appendix 4	THE COMBINED CODE ON CORPORATE GOVERNANCE	383
Appendix 5	THE ABI GUIDELINES	399
Appendix 6	STATEMENT OF PRINCIPLES OF THE PRE-EMPTION GROUP	401
Appendix 7	WEBSITES	405
Appendix 8	THE TAKEOVERS REGULATIONS	407

Appendix 1

The Admission and Disclosure Standards

July 2005

1. Admission

Conditions

1.1 An application for **admission to trading** of any **class** of **securities** must:
 (a) relate only to **securities** which are **listed** or proposed to be **listed** or equivalent; and
 (b) relate to all **securities** of that **class**, issued or proposed to be issued; or
 (c) if **securities** of that **class** are already traded on the **Exchange's** markets for **listed securities**, relate to all further **securities** of that **class**, issued or proposed to be issued.

1.2 When further **securities** are allotted of the same **class** as **securities** already traded, application for trading of such further **securities** must be made at the same time as the application for **listing**.

1.3 An **issuer** must be in compliance with the requirements of:
 (a) any **securities** regulator by which it is regulated; and
 (b) any stock exchange on which it has **securities** traded.

1.4 The **Exchange** may refuse an application for the **admission to trading** of **securities** if it considers that:
 (a) the **applicant's** situation is such that **admission** of the **securities** may be detrimental to the orderly operation of the **Exchange's** markets or to the reputation of the markets as a whole; or
 (b) the **applicant** does not or will not comply with the **Standards** or with any special condition imposed upon the **applicant** by the **Exchange**.

Settlement

1.5 To be admitted to trading, securities must be eligible for electronic settlement. The Exchange also requires that the securities are admitted for settlement in either CREST or Euroclear. Other central securities depositaries will be considered on a case by case basis. Issuers should note that in order to be eligible for **SETS** or **SETSmm**, the securities must be accepted by **LCH.Clearnet** for clearing purposes.

Attribute Groups

1.6 An **issuer** may also seek **admission** to one of the **Attribute Groups**. The process and criteria for such applications are set out in the relevant **Attribute Group's Eligibility Criteria**.

Communication

1.7 An **issuer** must identify a contact who will be responsible for communications between the **Exchange** and the **issuer**. The contact should be fully conversant with the **issuer's** responsibilities under these **Standards** and will be either a director or senior employee of the **issuer** in a position to act as the **Exchange's** point of contact. At the **issuer's** discretion, a nominated representative from another organisation may also be selected to act as the primary day-to-day contact point with the **Exchange** on regulatory matters. Details of the **issuer's** contact and any nominated representative must be provided to the **Exchange** at the time of the application for **admission to trading** and the **Exchange** must be notified in writing of any changes thereafter.

372 Public Companies and Equity Finance

Admission process

1.8 An **issuer** proposing to make any issue of **securities** that will be the subject of an application for **admission to trading** must agree the timetable for the **admission to trading** of those **securities** in advance with the **Exchange**. The **issuer's** contact or nominated representative (see paragraph 1.6) must contact the **Exchange** no later than the date on which draft documentation is first submitted to its **EEA competent authority**.

2. Application

2.1 Admission of **securities** becomes effective only when the decision of the **Exchange** to admit the **securities** to trading has been announced by the **Exchange** through its website (www.londonstockexchange.com). (Should the Exchange's website be unavailable, an RNS announcement will be submitted. Should RNS suffer an outage; a notice will be made available at the Exchange's ground floor reception.)

2.2 Except where otherwise agreed by the **Exchange**, applications for **admission to trading** are considered on business days between the hours of 09:00 and 17:30.

2.3 The **Exchange** will not, except in exceptional circumstances, admit **securities** to trading until each of the documents and items listed below have been lodged with the **Exchange** (marked for the attention of **Issuer Implementation**) in so far as they are relevant. All documents submitted to the **Exchange** must be written in English.

2.4 An invoice for the admission fee will be raised on admission. The admission fee is calculated in accordance with the **Exchange's** scale of fees for the time being in force. Payment of the admission fee must be received no later than 30 days after the date of this invoice.

Documents

Before admission

2.5 For **new applicants** who are listing shares, Form 1 must be submitted to the **Exchange** (marked for the attention of **Issuer Implementation**) by no later than 12:00 at least ten business days prior to the day on which the **issuer** is requesting that the **Exchange** consider the application for **admission to trading**.

The submission of Form 1 shall be provisional. Formal application will only be deemed to be made when a Prospectus relating to the securities to be admitted to trading has been approved.

2.6 Except as set out in paragraphs 2.5 above or 2.9 below, or as otherwise agreed by the **Exchange**, the following documents must be submitted to the **Exchange** (marked for the attention of **Issuer Implementation**) by no later than 12:00 at least two business days prior to the day on which the **issuer** is requesting that the **Exchange** consider the application for **admission to trading**:

(a) an application for **admission to trading** in the appropriate form issued by the **Exchange** (see Form 1) signed by a duly authorised officer of the **issuer**;

(b) an electronic copy of any **prospectus, listing particulars,** circular, announcement or other document relating to the issue, together with copies of any notice of meeting referred to in such documents (email: issuerimplementation@londonstockexchange.com); and

(c) an electronic copy of the board resolution allotting the **securities** or authorising the issue. Where a copy of the board resolution is not available for lodging at this time, written confirmation (email to issuerimplementation@londonstockexchange.com) from the **issuer's** contact or its nominated representative that the **securities** have been allotted must be received by the **Exchange** no later than 07:30 on the day that admission is expected to become effective.

After admission

2.7 Where relevant, a statement of the number of **securities** which were in fact issued, and where different from the number which were the subject of the application, the aggregate number of **securities** of that **class** in issue, must be lodged with the

Exchange (marked for the attention of **Issuer Implementation**) as soon as it becomes available.

Block admission

2.8   Where an **issuer** issues **securities** on a regular basis (including pursuant to an employees' share scheme, a regular savings scheme or a dividend re-investment plan, and following the exercise of warrants or of conversion rights attaching to a **class** of convertible **securities**) an **issuer** may make an application for a specified number of **securities** which may be issued in a particular case ('a block admission').

Issuance programmes

2.9   Where specialist **securities** are issued under an issuance programme, an applicant must submit a subsequent application for admission to trading in the case of an increase in the maximum number of securities which may be in issue and listed at any one time under an issuance programme.

If the **Exchange** approves the application, it will admit to trading all **securities** which may be issued under the programme within 12 months after the publication of the **prospectus** or **listing particulars**, subject to the **Exchange** receiving:

(a)   advice of the final terms of each issue;
(b)   electronic copies of any supplementary **prospectus** or **listing particulars**; and
(c)   confirmation that the **securities** in question have been issued.

2.10   The final terms of each issue which is intended to be **admitted to trading** must be submitted in writing to the **Exchange** as soon as possible after they have been agreed and in any event no later than 14:00 on the day before **admission** is required to become effective. The final terms may be submitted by the **issuer** or its nominated representative.

3. Continuing obligations

General

3.1   **Issuers** must comply with all of the rules for listing as produced by their **EEA competent authority**, and the provisions set out in the **Standards**, including any modification to the application of the **Standards** which has been notified to an **issuer**, in order for its **securities** to be **admitted to trading** and to remain on the **Exchange's markets**.

3.2   The **Exchange** may make additions to, dispense with or modify the application of the **Standards** (either unconditionally or subject to conditions) in such cases and by reference to such circumstances as it considers appropriate.

3.3   **Issuers** and their nominated representatives must provide to the **Exchange** any information or explanation that the **Exchange** may reasonably require for the purpose of verifying whether the **Standards** are being or have been complied with or which relates to the integrity or orderly operation of the **Exchange's markets for listed securities**.

Timetables

This section relates to proposed timetables for all corporate actions for **Exchange** traded **securities** (e.g. dividends, open offers, rights issues, bonus issues, schemes of arrangement, early redemptions).

General

3.4   Except in respect of **specialist securities**, an **issuer** must inform the **Stock Situation Analysis Team** (telephone +44 (0)20 7797 1920) in advance of any announcement of the timetable for any proposed action affecting the rights of existing holders of its **listed securities** traded on our markets.

3.5   The **Exchange** may request amendments to the timetable, if considered necessary for the purpose of maintaining orderly markets.

3.6   Any proposed amendments to a timetable, including amendment to the publication details of an announcement, must be immediately notified to the **Exchange**.

3.7 Except in the case of a dividend timetable notification, the reference to 'in advance' in rule 3.4 means that the **Exchange** should receive the proposed timetable by no later than 09:00 on the day before the proposed announcement.

Dividends (including interest payments for debt securities)

3.8 A dividend timetable which follows the guidelines set by the Dividend Procedure Timetable, published on the **Exchange's** web-site at www.londonstockexchange.com, need not be notified to the **Exchange** in advance, provided the announcement of the dividend includes:
- the net amount;
- the record and payment dates; and
- the availability of any scrip or DRIP options.

3.9 The term 'dividend' includes all interest payments for **debt securities**. An announcement is not required for interest payments but the **Exchange** must receive notification of any payment no later than seven business days prior to the record date. This notification must include:
- the appropriate net or gross amount;
- the record and payment dates; and
- any conversion period details.

3.10 Where fixed payment details are available the **issuer** may use one timetable to inform the **Exchange** of all future payments, providing any subsequent amendments are notified to the **Exchange** immediately.

Open offers

3.11 The timetable for an open offer must ensure that valid claims through the market can be promptly satisfied and must comply with the following:
- there must be a period of at least 15 business days from the date of posting of the application forms to shareholders (or from the date on which the existing **securities** were made 'ex' if that is earlier) until the close of the offer. The business days must exclude the 'ex' date but may include the application closing date where the time for closing is no earlier than 15:00. Where the 'ex' date is earlier than the date of posting, application forms must be posted no less than 10 business days before the close of the offer; and
- where possible, the open offer record date should be the business day before the expected 'ex' date. A record date preceding the 'ex' date by more than 6 days will only be approved in exceptional circumstances.

Settlement

3.12 The Exchange requires that the securities are admitted for settlement in either CREST or Euroclear. Other central securities depositaries will be considered on a case by case basis. Issuers should note that to be eligible for **SETS** or **SETSmm**, the securities must be accepted by **LCH.Clearnet** for clearing purposes.

Fees

3.13 An **issuer** must pay the annual fee for **admission to trading** calculated in accordance with the **Exchange's** scale of fees for the time being in force as soon as such payment becomes due.

Suspension

3.14 The **Exchange** will suspend the **admission** to and trading of any **securities** on its markets if the **listing** of such **securities** is suspended.

3.15 The **Exchange** may suspend trading of such **securities** with effect from such time as it may determine, and in such circumstances as it thinks fit where the ability of the **Exchange** to ensure the orderly operation of its markets for **listed securities** is, or may be, temporarily jeopardised.

3.16 Any request by an **issuer** to suspend trading of its **securities** must be confirmed to the **Exchange** in writing by the **issuer** or its nominated representative.

3.17 Where trading has been suspended, the **Exchange** may impose such conditions as it considers appropriate prior to resumption of trading.

3.18 An **issuer** must continue to comply with the **Standards**, even when **admission** of its **securities** to trading is suspended, unless the **Exchange** otherwise agrees.

Cancellation

3.19 The **Exchange** may cancel the right of any **securities** to be traded.

3.20 An **issuer** that wishes the **Exchange** to cancel the right of any of its **securities** to be traded must advise the **Exchange** in writing, not later than 20 business days before the date it intends trading in its **securities** to be discontinued. If agreed, the **Exchange** will announce the intention to cancel individual securities through the Reference Data Service and the intention to cancel companies through **RNS**.

Sanctions

3.21 Where the **Exchange** considers that an **issuer** has contravened the **Standards** and considers it appropriate to impose any sanction as set out in paragraph 3.22 it will follow the procedure set out in the **Disciplinary and Appeals Handbook**.

3.22 If an **issuer** has contravened the **Standards** one of the following actions may result:
 (a) censure of the **issuer** and, in addition, publication of such censure; or
 (b) cancellation of the right of the **issuer** to have its **securities**, or any **class** of its **securities**, traded on the **Exchange's** markets.

3.23 An **issuer** may appeal against a decision of the **Exchange** in relation to the application and interpretation of the **Standards**. The procedures for such appeals are set out in the **Disciplinary and Appeals Handbook**.

Appendix 2
Resolutions

1. Ordinary resolution to increase the company's authorised share capital

That the authorised share capital of the company be increased from £[ ] to £[ ] by the creation of [*number*] [*type*] shares of £ [*nominal value*] each ranking pari passu in all respects with the existing [*type*] shares of £ [*nominal value*] each in the capital of the company.

Appendix 3
Forms

G   COMPANIES FORM No. 123
**Notice of increase
in nominal capital**

123

CHWP000

Please do not write in this margin

Pursuant to section 123 of the Companies Act 1985

Please complete legibly, preferably in black type, or bold block lettering

To the Registrar of Companies
(Address overleaf)

For official use

Company number

Name of company

* insert full name of company

*

gives notice in accordance with section 123 of the above Act that by resolution of the company

dated _____ the nominal capital of the company has been

increased by £ _____ beyond the registered capital of £ _____.

† the copy must be printed or in some other form approved by the registrar

A copy of the resolution authorising the increase is attached. †

The conditions (eg. voting rights, dividend rights, winding-up rights etc.) subject to which the new shares have been or are to be issued are as follows :

Please tick here if continued overleaf ☐

‡ Insert Director, Secretary, Administrator, Administrative Receiver or Receiver (Scotland) as appropriate

Signed   Designation ‡   Date

Presentor's name address and reference (if any) :

For official Use
General Section

Post room

Notes

The address for companies registered in England and Wales or Wales is :-

The Registrar of Companies
Companies House
Crown Way
Cardiff
CF4 3UZ

or, for companies registered in Scotland :-

The Registrar of Companies
Companies House
37 Castle Terrace
Edinburgh
EH1 2EB

DX 235 Edinburgh
or LP - 4 Edinburgh 2

Forms 381

Companies House
— for the record —

Please complete in typescript, or in bold black capitals.
CHWP000

88(2)
Return of Allotment of Shares

Company Number

Company name in full

Shares allotted (including bonus shares):

Date or period during which shares were allotted
(If shares were allotted on one date enter that date in the "from" box)

From — Day Month Year
To — Day Month Year

Class of shares *(ordinary or preference etc)*

Number allotted

Nominal value of each share

Amount (if any) paid or due on each share *(including any share premium)*

List the names and addresses of the allottees and the number of shares allotted to each overleaf

If the allotted shares are fully or partly paid up otherwise than in cash please state:

% that each share is to be treated as paid up

Consideration for which the shares were allotted
(This information must be supported by the duly stamped contract or by the duly stamped particulars on Form 88(3) if the contract is not in writing)

When you have completed and signed the form send it to the Registrar of Companies at:

Companies House receipt date barcode

This form has been provided free of charge by Companies House.

Companies House, Crown Way, Cardiff CF14 3UZ   DX 33050 Cardiff
For companies registered in England and Wales

Companies House, 37 Castle Terrace, Edinburgh EH1 2EB
For companies registered in Scotland   DX 235 Edinburgh
or LP - 4 Edinburgh 2

Form revised 10/03

382 Public Companies and Equity Finance

Names and addresses of the allottees *(List joint share allotments consecutively)*

Shareholder details	Shares and share class allotted
Name Address UK Postcode ⌴ ⌴ ⌴ ⌴ ⌴ ⌴ ⌴	Class of shares allotted Number allotted
Name Address UK Postcode ⌴ ⌴ ⌴ ⌴ ⌴ ⌴ ⌴	Class of shares allotted Number allotted
Name Address UK Postcode ⌴ ⌴ ⌴ ⌴ ⌴ ⌴ ⌴	Class of shares allotted Number allotted
Name Address UK Postcode ⌴ ⌴ ⌴ ⌴ ⌴ ⌴ ⌴	Class of shares allotted Number allotted
Name Address UK Postcode ⌴ ⌴ ⌴ ⌴ ⌴ ⌴ ⌴	Class of shares allotted Number allotted

Please enter the number of continuation sheets (if any) attached to this form

Signed _____ **Date** _____

A director / secretary / administrator / administrative receiver / receiver manager / receiver   *Please delete as appropriate*

You do not have to give any contact information in the box opposite but if you do, it will help Companies House to contact you if there is a query on the form. The contact information that you give will be visible to searchers of the public record.

Tel

DX number   DX exchange

Appendix 4
The Combined Code on Corporate Governance
June 2006

PREAMBLE

1. This Code supersedes and replaces the Combined Code issued in 2003. It follows a review by the Financial Reporting Council of the implementation of the Code in 2005 and subsequent consultation on possible amendments to the Code.

2. The Financial Services Authority, as the UK Listing Authority, is obliged by statute to carry out a separate consultation before listed companies can be formally required under the Listing Rules to disclose how they have applied this new version of the Combined Code. This consultation is expected to begin in September 2006 and, subject to views received, the Listing Rules would be expected to apply to the new version of the Combined Code with effect from some time in the second quarter of 2007.

3. In the meantime, in view of the limited nature of the changes and the strong support that they have received, the FRC would encourage companies and investors to apply the revised Code voluntarily for reporting years beginning on or after 1 November 2006.

4. The Code contains main and supporting principles and provisions. The Listing Rules require listed companies to make a disclosure statement in two parts in relation to the Code. In the first part of the statement, the company has to report on how it applies the principles in the Code. This should cover both main and supporting principles. The form and content of this part of the statement are not prescribed, the intention being that companies should have a free hand to explain their governance policies in the light of the principles, including any special circumstances applying to them which have led to a particular approach. In the second part of the statement the company has either to confirm that it complies with the Code's provisions or — where it does not — to provide an explanation. This 'comply or explain' approach has been in operation for over ten years and the flexibility it offers has been widely welcomed both by company boards and by investors. It is for shareholders and others to evaluate the company's statement.

5. While it is expected that listed companies will comply with the Code's provisions most of the time, it is recognised that departure from the provisions of the Code may be justified in particular circumstances. Every company must review each provision carefully and give a considered explanation if it departs from the Code provisions.

6. Smaller listed companies, in particular those new to listing, may judge that some of the provisions are disproportionate or less relevant in their case. Some of the provisions do not apply to companies below the FTSE 350. Such companies may nonetheless consider that it would be appropriate to adopt the approach in the Code and they are encouraged to consider this. Investment companies typically have a different board structure, which may affect the relevance of particular provisions.

7. Whilst recognising that directors are appointed by shareholders who are the owners of companies, it is important that those concerned with the evaluation of governance should do so with common sense in order to promote partnership and trust, based on mutual understanding. They should pay due regard to companies' individual circumstances and bear in mind in particular the size and complexity of the company and the nature of the risks and challenges it faces. Whilst shareholders have every right to challenge companies' explanations if they are unconvincing, they should not be evaluated in a mechanistic way and departures from the Code should not be automatically treated as breaches. Institutional shareholders and their agents should be careful to respond to the statements from companies in a manner that supports the 'comply or explain' principle. As the principles in Section 2 make clear, institutional shareholders should carefully consider explanations given for departure from the Code and make reasoned judgements in each case. They should put their views to the company and be prepared to enter a dialogue if

they do not accept the company's position. Institutional shareholders should be prepared to put such views in writing where appropriate.

8. Nothing in this Code should be taken to override the general requirements of law to treat shareholders equally in access to information.

SECTION 1 COMPANIES

A. DIRECTORS

A.1 The Board

Main Principle

Every company should be headed by an effective board, which is collectively responsible for the success of the company.

Supporting Principles

The board's role is to provide entrepreneurial leadership of the company within a framework of prudent and effective controls which enables risk to be assessed and managed. The board should set the company's strategic aims, ensure that the necessary financial and human resources are in place for the company to meet its objectives and review management performance. The board should set the company's values and standards and ensure that its obligations to its shareholders and others are understood and met.

All directors must take decisions objectively in the interests of the company.

As part of their role as members of a unitary board, non-executive directors should constructively challenge and help develop proposals on strategy. Non-executive directors should scrutinise the performance of management in meeting agreed goals and objectives and monitor the reporting of performance. They should satisfy themselves on the integrity of financial information and that financial controls and systems of risk management are robust and defensible. They are responsible for determining appropriate levels of remuneration of executive directors and have a prime role in appointing, and where necessary removing, executive directors, and in succession planning.

Code Provisions

A.1.1 The board should meet sufficiently regularly to discharge its duties effectively. There should be a formal schedule of matters specifically reserved for its decision. The annual report should include a statement of how the board operates, including a high level statement of which types of decisions are to be taken by the board and which are to be delegated to management.

A.1.2 The annual report should identify the chairman, the deputy chairman (where there is one), the chief executive, the senior independent director and the chairmen and members of the nomination, audit and remuneration committees. It should also set out the number of meetings of the board and those committees and individual attendance by directors.

A.1.3 The chairman should hold meetings with the non-executive directors without the executives present. Led by the senior independent director, the non-executive directors should meet without the chairman present at least annually to appraise the chairman's performance (as described in A.6.1) and on such other occasions as are deemed appropriate.

A.1.4 Where directors have concerns which cannot be resolved about the running of the company or a proposed action, they should ensure that their concerns are recorded in the board minutes. On resignation, a non-executive director should provide a written statement to the chairman, for circulation to the board, if they have any such concerns.

A.1.5 The company should arrange appropriate insurance cover in respect of legal action against its directors.

A.2 Chairman and chief executive

Main Principle

There should be a clear division of responsibilities at the head of the company between the running of the board and the executive responsibility for the running of the company's business. No one individual should have unfettered powers of decision.

Supporting Principle

The chairman is responsible for leadership of the board, ensuring its effectiveness on all aspects of its role and setting its agenda. The chairman is also responsible for ensuring that the directors receive accurate, timely and clear information. The chairman should ensure effective communication with shareholders. The chairman should also facilitate the effective contribution of non-executive directors in particular and ensure constructive relations between executive and non-executive directors.

Code Provisions

A.2.1 The roles of chairman and chief executive should not be exercised by the same individual. The division of responsibilities between the chairman and chief executive should be clearly established, set out in writing and agreed by the board.

A.2.2[1] The chairman should on appointment meet the independence criteria set out in A.3.1 below. A chief executive should not go on to be chairman of the same company. If exceptionally a board decides that a chief executive should become chairman, the board should consult major shareholders in advance and should set out its reasons to shareholders at the time of the appointment and in the next annual report.

A.3 Board balance and independence

Main Principle

The board should include a balance of executive and non-executive directors (and in particular independent non-executive directors) such that no individual or small group of individuals can dominate the board's decision taking.

Supporting Principles

The board should not be so large as to be unwieldy. The board should be of sufficient size that the balance of skills and experience is appropriate for the requirements of the business and that changes to the board's composition can be managed without undue disruption.

To ensure that power and information are not concentrated in one or two individuals, there should be a strong presence on the board of both executive and non-executive directors.

The value of ensuring that committee membership is refreshed and that undue reliance is not placed on particular individuals should be taken into account in deciding chairmanship and membership of committees.

No one other than the committee chairman and members is entitled to be present at a meeting of the nomination, audit or remuneration committee, but others may attend at the invitation of the committee.

Code provisions

A.3.1 The board should identify in the annual report each non-executive director it considers to be independent[2]. The board should determine whether the director is independent in character and judgement and whether there are relationships or

---

1 Compliance or otherwise with this provision need only be reported for the year in which the appointment is made.
2 A.2.2 states that the chairman should, on appointment, meet the independence criteria set out in this provision, but thereafter the test of independence is not appropriate in relation to the chairman.

circumstances which are likely to affect, or could appear to affect, the director's judgement. The board should state its reasons if it determines that a director is independent notwithstanding the existence of relationships or circumstances which may appear relevant to its determination, including if the director:

- has been an employee of the company or group within the last five years;
- has, or has had within the last three years, a material business relationship with the company either directly, or as a partner, shareholder, director or senior employee of a body that has such a relationship with the company;
- has received or receives additional remuneration from the company apart from a director's fee, participates in the company's share option or a performance-related pay scheme, or is a member of the company's pension scheme;
- has close family ties with any of the company's advisers, directors or senior employees;
- holds cross-directorships or has significant links with other directors through involvement in other companies or bodies;
- represents a significant shareholder; or
- has served on the board for more than nine years from the date of their first election.

A.3.2 Except for smaller companies[3], at least half the board, excluding the chairman, should comprise non-executive directors determined by the board to be independent. A smaller company should have at least two independent non-executive directors.

A.3.3 The board should appoint one of the independent non-executive directors to be the senior independent director. The senior independent director should be available to shareholders if they have concerns which contact through the normal channels of chairman, chief executive or finance director has failed to resolve or for which such contact is inappropriate.

A.4 Appointments to the Board

Main Principle

There should be a formal, rigorous and transparent procedure for the appointment of new directors to the board.

Supporting Principles

Appointments to the board should be made on merit and against objective criteria. Care should be taken to ensure that appointees have enough time available to devote to the job. This is particularly important in the case of chairmanships.

The board should satisfy itself that plans are in place for orderly succession for appointments to the board and to senior management, so as to maintain an appropriate balance of skills and experience within the company and on the board.

Code Provisions

A.4.1 There should be a nomination committee which should lead the process for board appointments and make recommendations to the board. A majority of members of the nomination committee should be independent non-executive directors. The chairman or an independent non-executive director should chair the committee, but the chairman should not chair the nomination committee when it is dealing with the appointment of a successor to the chairmanship. The nomination committee should make available[4] its terms of reference, explaining its role and the authority delegated to it by the board.

A.4.2 The nomination committee should evaluate the balance of skills, knowledge and experience on the board and, in the light of this evaluation, prepare a description of the role and capabilities required for a particular appointment.

A.4.3 For the appointment of a chairman, the nomination committee should prepare a job specification, including an assessment of the time commitment expected, recognising

---

3 A smaller company is one that is below the FTSE 350 throughout the year immediately prior to the reporting year.
4 The requirement to make the information available would be met by including the information on a website that is maintained by or on behalf of the company.

the need for availability in the event of crises. A chairman's other significant commitments should be disclosed to the board before appointment and included in the annual report. Changes to such commitments should be reported to the board as they arise, and included in the next annual report. No individual should be appointed to a second chairmanship of a FTSE 100 company[5].

A.4.4 The terms and conditions of appointment of non-executive directors should be made available for inspection[6]. The letter of appointment should set out the expected time commitment. Non-executive directors should undertake that they will have sufficient time to meet what is expected of them. Their other significant commitments should be disclosed to the board before appointment, with a broad indication of the time involved and the board should be informed of subsequent changes.

A.4.5 The board should not agree to a full time executive director taking on more than one non-executive directorship in a FTSE 100 company nor the chairmanship of such a company.

A.4.6 A separate section of the annual report should describe the work of the nomination committee, including the process it has used in relation to board appointments. An explanation should be given if neither an external search consultancy nor open advertising has been used in the appointment of a chairman or a non-executive director.

A.5 Information and professional development

Main Principle

The board should be supplied in a timely manner with information in a form and of a quality appropriate to enable it to discharge its duties. All directors should receive induction on joining the board and should regularly update and refresh their skills and knowledge.

Supporting Principles

The chairman is responsible for ensuring that the directors receive accurate, timely and clear information. Management has an obligation to provide such information but directors should seek clarification or amplification where necessary.

The chairman should ensure that the directors continually update their skills and the knowledge and familiarity with the company required to fulfil their role both on the board and on board committees. The company should provide the necessary resources for developing and updating its directors' knowledge and capabilities.

Under the direction of the chairman, the company secretary's responsibilities include ensuring good information flows within the board and its committees and between senior management and non-executive directors, as well as facilitating induction and assisting with professional development as required.

The company secretary should be responsible for advising the board through the chairman on all governance matters.

Code Provisions

A.5.1 The chairman should ensure that new directors receive a full, formal and tailored induction on joining the board. As part of this, the company should offer to major shareholders the opportunity to meet a new non-executive director.

A.5.2 The board should ensure that directors, especially non-executive directors, have access to independent professional advice at the company's expense where they judge it necessary to discharge their responsibilities as directors. Committees should be provided with sufficient resources to undertake their duties.

A.5.3 All directors should have access to the advice and services of the company secretary, who is responsible to the board for ensuring that board procedures are complied with. Both

---

[5] Compliance or otherwise with this provision need only be reported for the year in which the appointment is made.
[6] The terms and conditions of appointment of non-executive directors should be made available for inspection by any person at the company's registered office during normal business hours and at the AGM (for 15 minutes prior to the meeting and during the meeting).

the appointment and removal of the company secretary should be a matter for the board as a whole.

A.6 Performance evaluation

Main Principle

The board should undertake a formal and rigorous annual evaluation of its own performance and that of its committees and individual directors.

Supporting Principle

Individual evaluation should aim to show whether each director continues to contribute effectively and to demonstrate commitment to the role (including commitment of time for board and committee meetings and any other duties). The chairman should act on the results of the performance evaluation by recognising the strengths and addressing the weaknesses of the board and, where appropriate, proposing new members be appointed to the board or seeking the resignation of directors.

Code Provision

A.6.1 The board should state in the annual report how performance evaluation of the board, its committees and its individual directors has been conducted. The non-executive directors, led by the senior independent director, should be responsible for performance evaluation of the chairman, taking into account the views of executive directors.

A.7 Re-election

Main Principle

All directors should be submitted for re-election at regular intervals, subject to continued satisfactory performance. The board should ensure planned and progressive refreshing of the board.

Code Provisions

A.7.1 All directors should be subject to election by shareholders at the first annual general meeting after their appointment, and to re-election thereafter at intervals of no more than three years. The names of directors submitted for election or re-election should be accompanied by sufficient biographical details and any other relevant information to enable shareholders to take an informed decision on their election.

A.7.2 Non-executive directors should be appointed for specified terms subject to re-election and to Companies Acts provisions relating to the removal of a director. The board should set out to shareholders in the papers accompanying a resolution to elect a non-executive director why they believe an individual should be elected. The chairman should confirm to shareholders when proposing re-election that, following formal performance evaluation, the individual's performance continues to be effective and to demonstrate commitment to the role. Any term beyond six years (e.g. two three-year terms) for a non-executive director should be subject to particularly rigorous review, and should take into account the need for progressive refreshing of the board. Non-executive directors may serve longer than nine years (e.g. three three-year terms), subject to annual re-election. Serving more than nine years could be relevant to the determination of a non-executive director's independence (as set out in provision A.3.1).

B. REMUNERATION

B.1 The Level and Make-up of Remuneration

Main Principles

Levels of remuneration should be sufficient to attract, retain and motivate directors of the quality required to run the company successfully, but a company should avoid

paying more than is necessary for this purpose. **A significant proportion of executive directors' remuneration should be structured so as to link rewards to corporate and individual performance.**

Supporting Principle

The remuneration committee should judge where to position their company relative to other companies. But they should use such comparisons with caution, in view of the risk of an upward ratchet of remuneration levels with no corresponding improvement in performance. They should also be sensitive to pay and employment conditions elsewhere in the group, especially when determining annual salary increases.

Code Provisions

Remuneration policy

B.1.1 The performance-related elements of remuneration should form a significant proportion of the total remuneration package of executive directors and should be designed to align their interests with those of shareholders and to give these directors keen incentives to perform at the highest levels. In designing schemes of performance-related remuneration, the remuneration committee should follow the provisions in Schedule A to this Code.

B.1.2 Executive share options should not be offered at a discount save as permitted by the relevant provisions of the Listing Rules.

B.1.3 Levels of remuneration for non-executive directors should reflect the time commitment and responsibilities of the role. Remuneration for non-executive directors should not include share options. If, exceptionally, options are granted, shareholder approval should be sought in advance and any shares acquired by exercise of the options should be held until at least one year after the non-executive director leaves the board. . Holding of share options could be relevant to the determination of a non-executive director's independence (as set out in provision A.3.1).

B.1.4 Where a company releases an executive director to serve as a non-executive director elsewhere, the remuneration report[7] should include a statement as to whether or not the director will retain such earnings and, if so, what the remuneration is.

Service Contracts and Compensation

B.1.5 The remuneration committee should carefully consider what compensation commitments (including pension contributions and all other elements) their directors' terms of appointment would entail in the event of early termination. The aim should be to avoid rewarding poor performance. They should take a robust line on reducing compensation to reflect departing directors' obligations to mitigate loss.

B.1.6 Notice or contract periods should be set at one year or less. If it is necessary to offer longer notice or contract periods to new directors recruited from outside, such periods should reduce to one year or less after the initial period.

B.2 Procedure

Main Principle

There should be a formal and transparent procedure for developing policy on executive remuneration and for fixing the remuneration packages of individual directors. No director should be involved in deciding his or her own remuneration.

Supporting Principles

The remuneration committee should consult the chairman and/or chief executive about their proposals relating to the remuneration of other executive directors. The remuneration committee should also be responsible for appointing any consultants in respect of executive director remuneration. Where executive directors or senior management are

---

7 As required under the Directors Remuneration Report Regulations 2002.

involved in advising or supporting the remuneration committee, care should be taken to recognise and avoid conflicts of interest.

The chairman of the board should ensure that the company maintains contact as required with its principal shareholders about remuneration in the same way as for other matters.

Code Provisions

B.2.1 The board should establish a remuneration committee of at least three, or in the case of smaller companies[8] two, independent non-executive directors. In addition the company chairman may also be a member of, but not chair, the committee if he or she was considered independent on appointment as chairman. The remuneration committee should make available[9] its terms of reference, explaining its role and the authority delegated to it by the board. Where remuneration consultants are appointed, a statement should be made available[10] of whether they have any other connection with the company.

B.2.2 The remuneration committee should have delegated responsibility for setting remuneration for all executive directors and the chairman, including pension rights and any compensation payments. The committee should also recommend and monitor the level and structure of remuneration for senior management. The definition of 'senior management' for this purpose should be determined by the board but should normally include the first layer of management below board level.

B.2.3 The board itself or, where required by the Articles of Association, the shareholders should determine the remuneration of the non-executive directors within the limits set in the Articles of Association. Where permitted by the Articles, the board may however delegate this responsibility to a committee, which might include the chief executive.

B.2.4 Shareholders should be invited specifically to approve all new long-term incentive schemes (as defined in the Listing Rules) and significant changes to existing schemes, save in the circumstances permitted by the Listing Rules.

C. ACCOUNTABILITY AND AUDIT

C.1 Financial Reporting

Main Principle

The board should present a balanced and understandable assessment of the company's position and prospects.

Supporting Principle

The board's responsibility to present a balanced and understandable assessment extends to interim and other price-sensitive public reports and reports to regulators as well as to information required to be presented by statutory requirements.

Code Provisions

C.1.1 The directors should explain in the annual report their responsibility for preparing the accounts and there should be a statement by the auditors about their reporting responsibilities.

C.1.2 The directors should report that the business is a going concern, with supporting assumptions or qualifications as necessary.

---

8 See footnote 3
9 See footnote 4
10 See footnote 4

C.2 Internal Control[11]

Main Principle

The board should maintain a sound system of internal control to safeguard shareholders' investment and the company's assets.

Code Provision

C.2.1 The board should, at least annually, conduct a review of the effectiveness of the group's system of internal controls and should report to shareholders that they have done so. The review should cover all material controls, including financial, operational and compliance controls and risk management systems.

C.3 Audit Committee and Auditors[12]

Main Principle

The board should establish formal and transparent arrangements for considering how they should apply the financial reporting and internal control principles and for maintaining an appropriate relationship with the company's auditors.

Code provisions

C.3.1 The board should establish an audit committee of at least three, or in the case of smaller companies[13] two, members, who should all be independent non-executive directors. The board should satisfy itself that at least one member of the audit committee has recent and relevant financial experience.

C.3.2 The main role and responsibilities of the audit committee should be set out in written terms of reference and should include:

- to monitor the integrity of the financial statements of the company, and any formal announcements relating to the company's financial performance, reviewing significant financial reporting judgements contained in them;
- to review the company's internal financial controls and, unless expressly addressed by a separate board risk committee composed of independent directors, or by the board itself, to review the company's internal control and risk management systems;
- to monitor and review the effectiveness of the company's internal audit function;
- to make recommendations to the board, for it to put to the shareholders for their approval in general meeting, in relation to the appointment, re-appointment and removal of the external auditor and to approve the remuneration and terms of engagement of the external auditor;
- to review and monitor the external auditor's independence and objectivity and the effectiveness of the audit process, taking into consideration relevant UK professional and regulatory requirements;
- to develop and implement policy on the engagement of the external auditor to supply non-audit services, taking into account relevant ethical guidance regarding the provision of non-audit services by the external audit firm; and to report to the board, identifying any matters in respect of which it considers that action or improvement is needed and making recommendations as to the steps to be taken.

C.3.3 The terms of reference of the audit committee, including its role and the authority delegated to it by the board, should be made available[14]. A separate section of the annual report should describe the work of the committee in discharging those responsibilities.

C.3.4 The audit committee should review arrangements by which staff of the company may, in confidence, raise concerns about possible improprieties in matters of financial reporting or other matters. The audit committee's objective should be to ensure that

---

11 The Turnbull guidance suggests means of applying this part of the Code. Copies are available at www.frc.org.ukl corporate/internalcontrol.cfm
12 The Smith guidance suggests means of applying this part of the Code. Copies are available at www.frc.org.uk/corporate/combinedcode.cfm
13 See footnote 3
14 See footnote 4

arrangements are in place for the proportionate and independent investigation of such matters and for appropriate follow-up action.

C.3.5 The audit committee should monitor and review the effectiveness of the internal audit activities. Where there is no internal audit function, the audit committee should consider annually whether there is a need for an internal audit function and make a recommendation to the board, and the reasons for the absence of such a function should be explained in the relevant section of the annual report.

C.3.6 The audit committee should have primary responsibility for making a recommendation on the appointment, reappointment and removal of the external auditors. If the board does not accept the audit committee's recommendation, it should include in the annual report, and in any papers recommending appointment or re-appointment, a statement from the audit committee explaining the recommendation and should set out reasons why the board has taken a different position.

C.3.7 The annual report should explain to shareholders how, if the auditor provides non-audit services, auditor objectivity and independence is safeguarded.

D. RELATIONS WITH SHAREHOLDERS

D.1 Dialogue with Institutional Shareholders

Main Principle

There should be a dialogue with shareholders based on the mutual understanding of objectives. The board as a whole has responsibility for ensuring that a satisfactory dialogue with shareholders takes place[15].

Supporting Principles

Whilst recognising that most shareholder contact is with the chief executive and finance director, the chairman (and the senior independent director and other directors as appropriate) should maintain sufficient contact with major shareholders to understand their issues and concerns.

The board should keep in touch with shareholder opinion in whatever ways are most practical and efficient.

Code Provisions

D.1.1 The chairman should ensure that the views of shareholders are communicated to the board as a whole. The chairman should discuss governance and strategy with major shareholders. Non-executive directors should be offered the opportunity to attend meetings with major shareholders and should expect to attend them if requested by major shareholders. The senior independent director should attend sufficient meetings with a range of major shareholders to listen to their views in order to help develop a balanced understanding of the issues and concerns of major shareholders.

D.1.2 The board should state in the annual report the steps they have taken to ensure that the members of the board, and in particular the non-executive directors, develop an understanding of the views of major shareholders about their company, for example through direct face-to-face contact, analysts' or brokers' briefings and surveys of shareholder opinion.

D.2 Constructive Use of the AGM

Main Principle

The board should use the AGM to communicate with investors and to encourage their participation.

---

[15] Nothing in these principles or provisions should be taken to override the general requirements of law to treat shareholders equally in access to information.

Code Provisions

D.2.1 At any general meeting, the company should propose a separate resolution on each substantially separate issue, and should in particular propose a resolution at the AGM relating to the report and accounts. For each resolution, proxy appointment forms should provide shareholders with the option to direct their proxy to vote either for or against the resolution or to withhold their vote. The proxy form and any announcement of the results of a vote should make it clear that a 'vote withheld' is not a vote in law and will not be counted in the calculation of the proportion of the votes for and against the resolution.

D.2.2 The company should ensure that all valid proxy appointments received for general meetings are properly recorded and counted. For each resolution, after a vote has been taken, except where taken on a poll, the company should ensure that the following information is given at the meeting and made available as soon as reasonably practicable on a website which is maintained by or on behalf of the company:

- the number of shares in respect of which proxy appointments have been validly made;
- the number of votes for the resolution;
- the number of votes against the resolution; and
- the number of shares in respect of which the vote was directed to be withheld.

D.2.3 The chairman should arrange for the chairmen of the audit, remuneration and nomination committees to be available to answer questions at the AGM and for all directors to attend.

D.2.4 The company should arrange for the Notice of the AGM and related papers to be sent to shareholders at least 20 working days before the meeting.

SECTION 2 INSTITUTIONAL SHAREHOLDERS

E. INSTITUTIONAL SHAREHOLDERS[16]

E.1 Dialogue with companies

Main Principle

Institutional shareholders should enter into a dialogue with companies based on the mutual understanding of objectives.

Supporting Principles

Institutional shareholders should apply the principles set out in the Institutional Shareholders' Committee's "The Responsibilities of Institutional Shareholders and Agents — Statement of Principles"[17], which should be reflected in fund manager contracts.

E.2 Evaluation of Governance Disclosures

Main Principle

When evaluating companies' governance arrangements, particularly those relating to board structure and composition, institutional shareholders should give due weight to all relevant factors drawn to their attention.

---

[16] Agents such as investment managers, or voting services, are frequently appointed by institutional shareholders to act on their behalf and these principles should accordingly be read as applying where appropriate to the agents of institutional shareholders.

[17] Available at www.investmentuk.org/news/research/2005/topic/corporate_governance/isc0905.pdf

Supporting Principle

Institutional shareholders should consider carefully explanations given for departure from this Code and make reasoned judgements in each case. They should give an explanation to the company, in writing where appropriate, and be prepared to enter a dialogue if they do not accept the company's position. They should avoid a box-ticking approach to assessing a company's corporate governance. They should bear in mind in particular the size and complexity of the company and the nature of the risks and challenges it faces.

E.3 Shareholder Voting

Main Principle

Institutional shareholders have a responsibility to make considered use of their votes.

Supporting Principles

Institutional shareholders should take steps to ensure their voting intentions are being translated into practice.

Institutional shareholders should, on request, make available to their clients information on the proportion of resolutions on which votes were cast and non-discretionary proxies lodged.

Major shareholders should attend AGMs where appropriate and practicable. Companies and registrars should facilitate this.

Schedule A: Provisions on the design of performance related remuneration

1. The remuneration committee should consider whether the directors should be eligible for annual bonuses. If so, performance conditions should be relevant, stretching and designed to enhance shareholder value. Upper limits should be set and disclosed. There may be a case for part payment in shares to be held for a significant period.

2. The remuneration committee should consider whether the directors should be eligible for benefits under long-term incentive schemes. Traditional share option schemes should be weighed against other kinds of long-term incentive scheme. In normal circumstances, shares granted or other forms of deferred remuneration should not vest, and options should not be exercisable, in less than three years. Directors should be encouraged to hold their shares for a further period after vesting or exercise, subject to the need to finance any costs of acquisition and associated tax liabilities.

3. Any new long-term incentive schemes which are proposed should be approved by shareholders and should preferably replace any existing schemes or at least form part of a well considered overall plan, incorporating existing schemes. The total rewards potentially available should not be excessive.

4. Payouts or grants under all incentive schemes, including new grants under existing share option schemes, should be subject to challenging performance criteria reflecting the company's objectives. Consideration should be given to criteria which reflect the company's performance relative to a group of comparator companies in some key variables such as total shareholder return.

5. Grants under executive share option and other long-term incentive schemes should normally be phased rather than awarded in one large block.

6. In general, only basic salary should be pensionable.

7. The remuneration committee should consider the pension consequences and associated costs to the company of basic salary increases and any other changes in pensionable remuneration, especially for directors close to retirement.

Schedule B: Guidance on liability of non-executive directors: care, skill and diligence

1. Although non-executive directors and executive directors have as board members the same legal duties and objectives, the time devoted to the company's affairs is likely to be significantly less for a non-executive director than for an executive director and the detailed knowledge and experience of a company's affairs that could reasonably be expected of a non-executive director will generally be less than for an executive director. These matters may be relevant in assessing the knowledge, skill and experience which may reasonably be expected of a non-executive director and therefore the care, skill and diligence that a non-executive director may be expected to exercise.

2. In this context, the following elements of the Code may also be particularly relevant.

(i) In order to enable directors to fulfil their duties, the Code states that:
 - The letter of appointment of the director should set out the expected time commitment (Code provision A.4.4) and
 - The board should be supplied in a timely manner with information in a form and of a quality appropriate to enable it to discharge its duties. The chairman is responsible for ensuring that the directors are provided by management with accurate, timely and clear information. (Code principle A.5).

(ii) Non-executive directors should themselves:
 - Undertake appropriate induction and regularly update and refresh their skills, knowledge and familiarity with the company (Code principle A.5 and provision A.5.1).
 - Seek appropriate clarification or amplification of information and, where necessary, take and follow appropriate professional advice. (Code principle A.5 and provision A.5.2).
 - Where they have concerns about the running of the company or a proposed action, ensure that these are addressed by the board and, to the extent that they are not resolved, ensure that they are recorded in the board minutes (Code provision A.1.4).
 - Give a statement to the board if they have such unresolved concerns on resignation (Code provision A.1.4).

3. It is up to each non-executive director to reach a view as to what is necessary in particular circumstances to comply with the duty of care, skill and diligence they owe as a director to the company. In considering whether or not a person is in breach of that duty, a court would take into account all relevant circumstances. These may include having regard to the above where relevant to the issue of liability of a non-executive director.

Schedule C: Disclosure of corporate governance arrangements

Paragraph 9.8.6 of the Listing Rules states that in the case of a listed company incorporated in the United Kingdom, the following items must be included in its annual report and accounts:

- a statement of how the listed company has applied the principles set out in Section 1 of the Combined Code, in a manner that would enable shareholders to evaluate how the principles have been applied[18]
- a statement as to whether the listed company has
  - complied throughout the accounting period with all relevant provisions set out in Section 1 of the Combined Code; or

---

18 As noted in the Preamble, the form and content of this part of the statement are not prescribed, the intention being that companies should have a free hand to explain their governance policies in the light of the principles, including any special circumstances applying to them which have led to a particular approach.

- not complied throughout the accounting period with all relevant provisions set out in Section 1 of the Combined Code and if so, setting out:
  (i) those provisions, if any, it has not complied with;
  (ii) in the case of provisions whose requirements are of a continuing nature, the period within which, if any, it did not comply with some or all of those provisions; and
  (iii) the company's reasons for non-compliance.

In addition the Code includes specific requirements for disclosure which are set out below:

The annual report should record:

- a statement of how the board operates, including a high level statement of which types of decisions are to be taken by the board and which are to be delegated to management (A.1.1);
- the names of the chairman, the deputy chairman (where there is one), the chief executive, the senior independent director and the chairmen and members of the nomination, audit and remuneration committees (A.1.2);
- the number of meetings of the board and those committees and individual attendance by directors (A.1.2);
- the names of the non-executive directors whom the board determines to be independent, with reasons where necessary (A.3.1);
- the other significant commitments of the chairman and any changes to them during the year (A.4.3);
- how performance evaluation of the board, its committees and its directors has been conducted (A.6.1);
- the steps the board has taken to ensure that members of the board, and in particular the non-executive directors, develop an understanding of the views of major shareholders about their company (D.1.2).

The report should also include:

- a separate section describing the work of the nomination committee, including the process it has used in relation to board appointments and an explanation if neither external search consultancy nor open advertising has been used in the appointment of a chairman or a non-executive director (A.4.6);
- a description of the work of the remuneration committee as required under the Directors' Remuneration Report Regulations 2002, and including, where an executive director serves as a non-executive director elsewhere, whether or not the director will retain such earnings and, if so, what the remuneration is (B.1.4);
- an explanation from the directors of their responsibility for preparing the accounts and a statement by the auditors about their reporting responsibilities (C.1.1);
- a statement from the directors that the business is a going concern, with supporting assumptions or qualifications as necessary (C.1.2);
- a report that the board has conducted a review of the effectiveness of the group's system of internal controls (C.2.1);
- a separate section describing the work of the audit committee in discharging its responsibilities (C.3.3);
- where there is no internal audit function, the reasons for the absence of such a function (C.3.5);
- where the board does not accept the audit committee's recommendation on the appointment, reappointment or removal of an external auditor, a statement from the audit committee explaining the recommendation and the reasons why the board has taken a different position (C.3.6); and
- an explanation of how, if the auditor provides non-audit services, auditor objectivity and independence is safeguarded (C.3.7).

The following information should be made available (which may be met by placing the information on a website that is maintained by or on behalf of the company):

- the terms of reference of the nomination, remuneration and audit committees, explaining their role and the authority delegated to them by the board (A.4.1, B.2.1 and C.3.3);

- the terms and conditions of appointment of non-executive directors (A.4.4) (see footnote 6 on page 8); and
- where remuneration consultants are appointed, a statement of whether they have any other connection with the company (B.2.1).

The board should set out to shareholders in the pagers accompanying a resolution to elect or re-elect directors:

- sufficient biographical details to enable shareholders to take an informed decision on their election or re-election (A.7.1);
- why they believe an individual should be elected to a non-executive role (A.7.2); and
- on re-election of a non-executive director, confirmation from the chairman that, following formal performance evaluation, the individual's performance continues to be effective and to demonstrate commitment to the role, including commitment of time for board and committee meetings and any other duties (A.7.2).

The board should set out to shareholders in the papers recommending appointment or reappointment of an external auditor:

- if the board does not accept the audit committee's recommendation, a statement from the audit committee explaining the recommendation and from the board setting out reasons why they have taken a different position (C.3.6).

Appendix 5
The ABI Guidelines

The ABI Guidelines are available on the website of the Institutional Voting Information Service.

Note: The references to the Pre-Emption Group guidelines are now historic (see **14.6.16**), but these ABI Guidelines nevertheless remain current.

1. THE ABI GUIDELINES

A. Directors' powers to allot share capital and disappply shareholders' pre-emption right

The attached example resolutions are intended to assist companies and their advisers in understanding the limitations which ABI member Offices have indicated they would expect to see placed on the directors' authority to allot share capital under Section 80 of the Companies Act 1985 and the general authority to disapply shareholders' pre-emption rights under Section 95.

Resolution 1 (Section 80 General Power to Allot)

The figure inserted at 'A' should be the lesser of

(i) the unissued Ordinary share capital or
(ii) a sum equal to one-third of the issued Ordinary share capital.

To the one-third figure can be added amounts for which the company requires further additional powers under Section 80. For example, further powers may be required to allot shares in respect of deferred consideration or options. If the resolution contains a figure greater than one-third of the issued Ordinary share capital (by reference to the total issued Ordinary share capital shown in the last Annual Report and Accounts or date used in compliance with disclosure under the Listing Rules) it is important to explain clearly in the supporting documents the basis on which the figure is calculated, including the nature of any amounts which have been specifically added to the basic one-third figure. It is emphasised that this recommended level is not an absolute limit on the amount of share capital the directors may allot: it will merely require the board to return to shareholders if the company proposes significantly to increase the amount of issued share capital.

Resolution 2 (Section 95 General Power to Disapply Pre-emption Rights)

The figure inserted at 'B' should not be more than 5% of the issued Ordinary share capital of the company. If the resolution contains a figure greater than five per cent of the issued Ordinary share capital (by reference to the total issued Ordinary share capital shown in the last Annual Report and Accounts or date used in compliance with disclosure under the Listing Rules), it is important to explain clearly in the supporting documents the basis on which the figure is calculated. The Pre-Emption Group guidelines deal with the practical application of this particular resolution in some detail and are available from the Primary Markets Division of the Stock Exchange

Ordinary Resolution

1 THAT the board be and it is hereby generally and unconditionally authorised to exercise all powers of the company to allot relevant securities (within the meaning of Section 80 of the Companies Act 1985) up to an aggregate nominal amount of £...A... provided that this authority shall expire on ....*...... save that the company may before such expiry make an offer or agreement which would or might require relevant securities to be allotted after such expiry and the board may allot relevant

securities in pursuance of such an offer or agreement as if the authority conferred hereby had not expired. * a period up to 5 years is acceptable

Special Resolution

2   THAT subject to the passing of the previous resolution the board be and it is hereby empowered pursuant to Section 95 of the Companies Act 1985 to allot equity securities (within the meaning of Section 94 of the said Act) for cash pursuant to the authority conferred by the previous resolution as if sub-section (1) of Section 89 of the said Act did not apply to any such allotment provided that this power shall be limited
   (i)   to the allotment of equity securities in connection with a rights issue in favour of Ordinary shareholders where the equity securities respectively attributable to the interests of all Ordinary shareholders are proportionate (as nearly as may be) to the respective numbers of Ordinary shares held by them and,
   (ii) to the allotment (otherwise than pursuant to sub-paragraph (i) above) of equity securities up to an aggregate nominal value of £...B...

and shall expire {on the date of the next annual general meeting of the company after the passing of this resolution, or, following a change to the Listing Rules in 1997, a period of up to five years from the passing of the resolution is acceptable} save that the company may before such expiry make an offer or agreement which would or might require equity securities to be allotted after such expiry and the board may allot equity securities in pursuance of such an offer or agreement as if the power conferred hereby had not expired.

B. Shareholders' pre-emption rights and vendor placings

The Investment Committee's guidelines on shareholders' pre-emption rights, issued on 29 April 1987, were superseded by the Stock Exchange Pre-emption Group guidelines issued on 21 October 1987 *except* in respect of the last paragraph which refers to vendor placings in the following terms:

> 'It is also considered that in the related matter of vendor placings shareholders are entitled to expect a right of claw-back for any issues of significant size which are offered at more than a very modest discount to market price. Members of ABI will therefore expect that issues involving more than 10% of issued equity share capital or a discount greater than 5% will be placed on a basis which leaves existing shareholders with a right to claw-back their pro rata share of the issue if they so wish.'

Appendix 6
Statement of Principles of the Pre-Emption Group

OVERARCHING PRINCIPLES

1. Pre-emption rights are a cornerstone of UK company law and provide shareholders with protection against inappropriate dilution of their investments. They are enshrined in law by the 2nd Company Law Directive and the Companies Act 1985, which provides that they may be disapplied only by a special resolution of shareholders at a general meeting of the company.
2. Whilst not undermining the importance of pre-emption rights, a degree of flexibility is appropriate in circumstances where new equity issuance on a non-pre-emptive basis would be in the interests of companies and their owners.
3. The principles set out in this paper aim to provide clarity on the circumstances in which flexibility might be appropriate and the factors to be taken into account when considering the case for disapplying pre-emption rights and making use of an agreed authority for a non-pre-emptive share issue.
4. Companies, institutional investors and voting advisory services all have an important role to play in ensuring the effective and flexible application of this guidance:
    - Companies have a responsibility to signal an intention to seek a non-pre-emptive issue at the earliest opportunity and to establish a dialogue with the company's shareholders. They should keep shareholders informed of issues related to an application to disapply their pre-emption rights.
    - Shareholders have a responsibility to engage with companies to help them understand the specific factors that might inform their view on a non-pre-emptive issue by the company. They should review the case made by companies on its merits and decide on each case individually using the usual investment criteria. Where a shareholder does intend to vote against a resolution to disapply pre-emption rights, the Institutional Shareholders' Committee Statement of Principles[1] on the responsibilities of shareholders makes dear that it is best practice to explain in advance the reasons for the decision.
    - While companies should in any case consult their main shareholders, advisory services should be prepared to receive representations from companies. In such circumstances the advisory services should explain any recommendations made in light of the reasons provided. This should involve setting out the pros and cons of the proposal so that the ultimate decision maker can take an informed view.

APPLICATION OF THE PRINCIPLES

5. The principles set out here relate to issues of equity securities for cash other than on a pre-emptive basis pro rata to existing shareholders by all UK companies which are primary listed on the Main Market of the London Stock Exchange. Companies quoted on AIM are encouraged to apply these guidelines but investors recognise that greater flexibility is likely to be justified in the case of such companies.
6. These principles are supported by the ABI, NAPF and IMA as representatives of owners and investment managers. These associations hope that the guidance they contain will be helpful to companies in approaching requests for disapplication and in gauging the likely reaction of shareholders to proposals they may wish to make.

ROUTINE DISAPPLICATIONS

7. In a significant number of situations a request for disapplication is likely to be considered non-controversial by shareholders. While this does not reduce the importance of effective dialogue and timely notification, routine requests are less

---

[1] 'The Responsibilities of Institutional Shareholders and Agents – Statement of Principles'; Institutional Shareholders' Committee; September 2005 [available at: http://www.investmentuk.org/news/research/2005/topic/corporate_governance/iscl005.pdf]

likely to need in-depth discussion and shareholders will be more inclined in principle to support them.

8. Requests are more likely to be routine in nature when the company is seeking authority to issue non-pre-emptively no more than 5% of ordinary share capital in any one year.

9. This principle applies whatever the structure of the proposed issue. For example, an issue of shares which contains both a pre-emptive and non-pre-emptive element ("combination issues") would normally be considered routine provided that the non-pre-emptive element met the criteria specified for routine applications within these guidelines. This would include issues that comprised a placing of shares with a partial clawback by existing shareholders.

10. In the absence of (a) suitable advance consultation and explanation or (b) the matter having been specifically highlighted at the time at which the request for disapplication was made, companies should not issue more than 7.5% of the company's ordinary share capital for cash other than to existing shareholders in any rolling three year period.

11. Where a request is made for the disapplication of pre-emption rights in respect of a specific issue of shares, the price at which the shares are proposed to be issued will also be relevant. Shareholders' approach to the pricing of non-pre-emptive issues is set out in paragraphs 18 and 19 below. Companies should note that a discount of greater than 5% is not likely to be regarded as routine.

12. Treasury shares issued for cash will be counted within the guideline levels set out in paragraph 8, but not those in paragraph 10.

13. **These principles are intended to ease the granting of authority below those figures, not to rule out approvals above them. Requests which, if granted, would exceed these levels should be considered by shareholders on a case by case basis.** In these instances it is particularly important that there is early and effective dialogue, and that the company is able to communicate to shareholders the information they need in order to reach an informed decision. The considerations set out in the following section are critical to making a decision.

CRITICAL CONSIDERATIONS RELATING TO NON-ROUTINE REQUESTS FOR DISAPPLICATION

14. It is neither possible nor desirable to define all the circumstances in which shareholders might be willing to agree to disapply pre-emption rights above the level set out in paragraphs 8 and 10 above. Nevertheless, there are some general considerations that are likely to be relevant in the majority of cases; these are set out below. Companies should ensure they are in a position to communicate such information to shareholders to help them make an informed decision.

15. The critical considerations are likely to include:
    - **the strength of the business case:** In order to make a reasoned assessment shareholders need to receive a dear explanation of the purpose to which the capital raised will be put and the benefits to be gained – for example in terms of product development or the opportunity cost of not raising new finance to exploit new commercial opportunities – and how the financing or proposed future financing fits in with the life-cycle and financial needs of the company.
    - **the size and stage of development of the company and the sector within which it operates.** Different companies have different financing needs. For example, shareholders might be expected to be more sympathetic to a request from a small company with high growth potential than one from a larger, more established company.
    - **the stewardship and governance of the company.** If the company has a track record of generating shareholder value, clear planning and good communications, this may give shareholders additional confidence in its judgement.
    - **financing options.** A wide variety of financing options are now available to companies. Companies should explain why a non-pre-emptive issue of shares is the most appropriate means of raising capital, and why other financing methods have been rejected.
    - **the level of dilution of value and control for existing shareholders.**

- **the proposed process following approval:** Companies should make dear the process they would follow if approval for a non-pre-emptive issue were to be granted, for example how dialogue with shareholders would be carried out in the period leading up to the announcement of an issue.
- **contingency plans:** Company managers should explain what contingency plans they have in place in case the request is not granted, and the implications of such a decision.

TIMING OF REQUESTS FOR DISAPPLICATION

16. Companies should signal the possibility of their intention to seek a non-pre-emptive issue at the earliest opportunity. For example if, at the time of the initial public offering, a company is aware that it is likely to have a need relatively quickly for additional cash, it should alert potential investors to this in the prospectus. In other cases it might be appropriate for the company to signal a potential request in its annual report. In some cases it may be appropriate for companies to consult a small number of major shareholders before making any announcement. Companies and shareholders should be mindful of the possible legal and regulatory issues in doing this.

17. Authority to disapply pre-emption rights following a 'routine' request would normally be granted by shareholders' approval of an appropriate resolution at an AGM. As discussed above, shareholders will not generally agree to a non-routine disapplication request without a sufficiently strong business case for this course of action. Thus, non-routine requests would be made at an AGM only when the company is in a position to justify this approach by providing relevant information such as that set out in paragraph 15; otherwise a specially convened EGM would be needed.

OTHER CONSIDERATIONS RELATING TO NON PRE-EMPTIVE ISSUES

18. Companies should aim to ensure that they are raising capital on the best possible terms, particularly where the proposed issue is in the context of a transaction likely to enhance the share price. Any discount at which equity is issued for cash other than to existing shareholders will be of major concern. Companies should, in any event, seek to restrict the discount to a maximum of 5% of the middle of the best bid and offer prices for the company's shares immediately prior to the announcement of an issue or proposed issue.

19. Where an issue is priced on a date after the announcement date, the level of discount should be assessed at the time of pricing rather than the time of announcement. Companies should also have regard to any adverse impact on the share price of the earlier announcement, which may create the potential for a significant loss or transfer of value, in deciding whether to proceed with an issue in such circumstances.

20. The principles and critical considerations set out above apply to requests for the disapplication of pre-emption rights. Once a request to disapply pre-emption rights has been approved, shareholders expect companies to discharge and account for this authority appropriately. It is recommended that the subsequent annual report should include relevant information such as the actual level of discount achieved, the amount raised and how it was used and the percentage amount of shares issued on a non-pre-emptive basis over the last year and three years.

ROLE OF THE PRE-EMPTION GROUP

21. The Pre-Emption Group will monitor the development of practice in relation to disapplying pre-emption rights. It expects that this Statement of Principles will inform the way in which all interested parties participate in this process. It will monitor and report annually on the application of these principles. The Pre-Emption Group will not express a view on or otherwise intervene in specific cases.

DEFINITIONS

Clawback

Clawback as it is referred to in paragraph 9 is the right of existing shareholders to subscribe for a share of an issue at the pre-agreed price. This differs from a full rights entitlement since it is non-renounceable and therefore does not permit the shareholder to sell this entitlement to another investor.

Discounts

In general terms, the "discount" (paragraphs 18 and 19) is defined as the aggregate of (a) the amount by which the offering price differs from the market price, and (b) expenses directly relevant to the making of the issue. In the case of issues of a new class of deferred equity in the form of convertibles, warrants or other deferred equity, the amount of the opening market price above the issue price and any difference at point of pricing of the instrument to underlying fair value will be regarded as part of the discount.

Market Movements

Where the pricing takes place at a time later than that of the announcement of the proposed issue (paragraph 19), it is recognised that the achievable price of the placing may vary in accordance with general market conditions. For the purposes of these guidelines the measurement of discount therefore relates to the time and date of the pricing rather than the time and date of the announcement of the issue.

Appendix 7
Websites

The following websites are referred to in this book:

Competition Commission	www.competition-commission.org.uk
CREST	www.crestco.co.uk
DTI	www.dti.gov.uk
European Commission	www.ec.europa.eu/index_en.htm
Financial Reporting Council	www.frc.org.uk
Hermes	www.hermes.co.uk
Institute of Chartered Secretaries and Administrators	www.icsa.org.uk
Institutional Voting Information Service	www.ivis.co.uk
London Stock Exchange	www.londonstockexchange.com
OFT	www.oft.gov.uk
Pre-Emption Group	www.pre-emptiongroup.org.uk
Quoted Companies Alliance	www.qcanet.co.uk
Standard Life shareholder website	http://prospectus.standardlife.com/shareoffer
Takeover Panel	www.thetakeoverpanel.org.uk
UK Parliament	www.parliament.uk

The following websites may also be of interest:

ABI	www.abi.org.uk
CBI	www.cbi.org.uk
Companies House	www.companieshouse.gov.uk
EFTA	www.efta.int
European Union	www.europa.eu
Institute of Chartered Accountants in England and Wales	www.icaew.co.uk
Institute of Directors	www.iod.com
NAPF	www.napf.co.uk
NASDAQ	www.nasdaq.com
New York Stock Exchange	www.nyse.com
PIRC	www.pirc.co.uk

Appendix 8

The Takeovers Directive (Interim Implementation) Regulations 2006

PART 1

General

1. **Citation and Commencement**

These Regulations may be cited as the Takeovers Directive (Interim Implementation) Regulations 2006 and shall come into force on 20th May 2006.

2. **Interpretation**
(1) In these Regulations—

'Code' means the City Code on Takeovers and Mergers and the Rules of Procedure of the Panel's Hearings Committee as they stand immediately before the day these Regulations are made and are expressed to have effect on 20th May 2006;

'EEA State' means a state which is a Contracting Party to the Agreement on the European Economic Area signed at Oporto on 2nd May 1992 (as it has effect from time to time);

'Panel' means the Panel on Takeovers and Mergers;

'regulated market' has the meaning given by Article 1(13) of Directive 93/22/EEC on investment services in the securities field;

'takeover bid' has the same meaning as in the Takeovers Directive;

'Takeovers Directive' means Directive 2004/25/EC of the European Parliament and of the Council on Takeover Bids;

'voting rights' means rights to vote at general meetings of the company in question, including rights that arise only in certain circumstances;

'voting shares' means shares carrying voting rights.

(2) In these Regulations 'rules' means rules in the Code insofar as necessary to implement Articles 3.1, 4.2, 5, 6.1 to 6.3, 7 to 9 and 13 of the Takeovers Directive or arising out of or related to obligations in those Articles, including rules which—
   (a) confer on the Panel the power to—
      (i) give a direction to a person to secure compliance with a rule; or
      (ii) order a person to pay compensation if he is in breach of a rule; or
      (iii) impose sanctions on a person who has acted in breach of a rule or failed to comply with a direction;
   (b) make provision for a decision of the Panel to be reviewed by a committee of the Panel and for a decision of that committee to be appealed to an independent tribunal;
   (c) make provision for fees or charges to be payable to the Panel for the purpose of meeting its expenses;
   (d) make provision subject to exceptions or exemptions;
   (e) authorise the Panel to dispense with or modify the application of rules in particular cases and by reference to any circumstances;
   (f) provide for the Panel to make rulings on the interpretation, application or effect of rules;
   (g) provide for rulings in sub-paragraph (f) to have binding effect.
(3) For the purposes of regulations 8 and 24—
   (a) 'officer' includes director, manager or secretary;
   (b) an officer is 'in default' if he authorises or permits, participates in, or fails to take all reasonable steps to prevent, a contravention.
(4) Except as provided in paragraph (5), in these Regulations 'court', in relation to a company, means—
   (a) in Great Britain, the court having jurisdiction to wind up the company; and
   (b) in Northern Ireland, the High Court.

(5) For the purposes of regulations 11, 17 and 22 'court' means the High Court or, in Scotland, the Court of Session.

PART 2
The Takeover Panel

CHAPTER 1
The Panel and its rules

3. The rules
The rules shall have effect.

4. The Panel
(1) For the purposes of these Regulations, a reference to the functions of the Panel is a reference to functions provided for in this Part.
(2) The Panel shall supervise takeover bids for the purposes of the rules.
(3) The Panel may do anything that it considers necessary or expedient for the purposes of, or in connection with, its functions.
(4) The Panel may make arrangements for any of its functions to be discharged by—
 (a) a committee or sub-committee of the Panel; or
 (b) an officer or member of staff of the Panel, or a person acting as such.

5. Publication of the Code
(1) The Code must be made available to the public, with or without payment, in whatever way the Panel thinks appropriate.
(2) A person is not to be taken to have contravened a rule if he shows that at the time of the alleged contravention the Code had not been made available as required by paragraph (1).
(3) The production of a document purporting to be a printed copy of the Code endorsed with a certificate signed by an officer of the Panel authorised by it for that purpose and stating—
 (a) that it is a true copy of the Code, and
 (b) that on a specified date the Code was made available to the public as required by paragraph (1),
is evidence (or in Scotland sufficient evidence) of the facts contained in the certificate.
(4) A certificate purporting to be signed as mentioned in paragraph (3) is to be treated as having been properly signed unless the contrary is shown.
(5) A person who wishes in any legal proceedings to rely on the Code may require the Panel to endorse a copy of the Code with a certificate of the kind mentioned in paragraph (3).

CHAPTER 2
Information

6. Power to require documents and information
(1) The Panel may by notice in writing require a person—
 (a) to produce any documents that are specified or described in the notice;
 (b) to provide, in the form and manner specified in the notice, such information as may be specified or described in the notice.
(2) A requirement under paragraph (1) must be complied with—
 (a) at a place specified in the notice; and
 (b) before the end of such reasonable period as may be so specified.
(3) This regulation applies only to documents and information reasonably required in connection with the exercise by the Panel of its functions.
(4) The Panel may require—
 (a) any document produced to be authenticated, or
 (b) any information provided (whether in a document or otherwise) to be verified, in such manner as it may reasonably require.
(5) The Panel may authorise a person to exercise any of its powers under this regulation.
(6) A person exercising a power by virtue of paragraph (5) must, if required to do so, produce evidence of his authority to exercise the power.

(7) The production of a document in pursuance of this regulation does not affect any lien that a person has on the document.
(8) The Panel may take copies of or extracts from a document produced in pursuance of this regulation.
(9) A reference in this regulation to the production of a document includes a reference to the production of—
  (a) a hard copy of information recorded otherwise than in hard copy form; or
  (b) information in a form from which a hard copy can be readily obtained.
(10) A person is not required by this regulation to disclose documents or information in respect of which a claim to legal professional privilege (in Scotland, to confidentiality of communications) could be maintained in legal proceedings.

7. **Restrictions on disclosure**
(1) This regulation applies to information (in whatever form)—
  (a) relating to the private affairs of an individual, or
  (b) relating to any particular business,
  that is provided to the Panel in connection with the exercise of its functions.
(2) No such information may, during the lifetime of the individual or so long as the business continues to be carried on, be disclosed without the consent of that individual or (as the case may be) the person for the time being carrying on that business.
(3) Paragraph (2) does not apply to any disclosure of information that—
  (a) is made for the purpose of facilitating the carrying out by the Panel of any of its functions;
  (b) is made to a person specified in Part 1 of Schedule 1;
  (c) is of a description specified in Part 2 of that Schedule; or
  (d) is made in accordance with Part 3 of that Schedule.
(4) Paragraph (2) does not apply to—
  (a) the disclosure by an authority within paragraph (5) of information disclosed to it by the Panel in reliance on paragraph (3);
  (b) the disclosure of such information by anyone who has obtained it directly or indirectly from an authority within paragraph (5).
(5) The authorities within this paragraph are—
  (a) the Financial Services Authority;
  (b) an authority designated as a supervisory authority for the purposes of Article 4.1 of the Takeovers Directive;
  (c) any other person or body that exercises functions of a public nature, under legislation in an EEA State other than the United Kingdom, that are similar to the Panel's functions or those of the Financial Services Authority.
(6) This regulation does not prohibit the disclosure of information if the information is or has been available to the public from any other source.
(7) Nothing in this regulation authorises the making of a disclosure in contravention of the Data Protection Act 1998.

8. **Offence of disclosure in contravention of regulation 7**
(1) A person who discloses information in contravention of regulation 7 is guilty of an offence, unless—
  (a) he did not know, and had no reason to suspect, that the information had been provided as mentioned in regulation 7(1); or
  (b) he took all reasonable steps and exercised all due diligence to avoid the commission of the offence.
(2) A person guilty of an offence under this regulation is liable—
  (a) on conviction on indictment, to imprisonment for a term not exceeding two years or a fine (or both);
  (b) on summary conviction, to imprisonment for a term not exceeding three months, or to a fine not exceeding the statutory maximum (or both).
(3) Where a company or other body corporate commits an offence under this regulation, an offence is also committed by every officer of the company or other body corporate who is in default.
(4) Proceedings for an offence under this regulation are not to be brought—

(a) in England and Wales except by or with the consent of the Secretary of State or the Director of Public Prosecutions;

(b) in Northern Ireland except by or with the consent of the Department of Enterprise, Trade and Investment or the Director of Public Prosecutions for Northern Ireland.

CHAPTER 3
Co-operation

9. Duty of co-operation

(1) The Panel must take such steps as it considers appropriate to co-operate with—

(a) the Financial Services Authority;

(b) an authority designated as a supervisory authority for the purposes of Article 4.1 of the Takeovers Directive;

(c) any other person or body that exercises functions of a public nature, under legislation in any country or territory outside the United Kingdom, that appear to the Panel to be similar to its own functions or those of the Financial Services Authority.

(2) The Financial Services Authority must take such steps as it considers appropriate to cooperate with—

(a) the Panel;

(b) an authority designated as a supervisory authority for the purposes of Article 4.1 of the Takeovers Directive;

(c) any other person or body that exercises functions of a public nature, under legislation in any country or territory outside the United Kingdom, that appear to the Financial Services Authority to be similar to those of the Panel.

(3) Co-operation may include the sharing of information that the Panel or the Financial Services Authority, as the case may be, is not prevented from disclosing.

CHAPTER 4
Contravention of rules etc.

10. Failure to comply with rules about bid documentation

(1) This regulation applies where there is a takeover bid to which the offer document rules apply.

(2) Where an offer document published in respect of the bid does not comply with offer document rules, an offence is committed by—

(a) the person making the bid; and

(b) where the person making the bid is a body of persons, any director, officer or member of that body who caused the document to be published.

(3) A person commits an offence under paragraph (2) only if—

(a) he knew that the offer document did not comply, or was reckless as to whether it complied; and

(b) he failed to take all reasonable steps to secure that it did comply.

(4) Where a response document published in respect of the bid does not comply with response document rules, an offence is committed by any director or other officer of the company for which the bid is made, who—

(a) knew that the response document did not comply, or was reckless as to whether it complied; and

(b) failed to take all reasonable steps to secure that it did comply.

(5) Where an offence is committed under subsection (2)(b) or (4) by a company or other body corporate ('the relevant body')—

(a) subsection (2)(b) has effect as if the reference to a director, officer or member of the person making the bid included a reference to a director, officer or member of the relevant body;

(b) subsection (4) has effect as if the reference to a director or other officer of the company referred to in subsection (1) included a reference to the director, officer or member of the relevant body.

(6) A person guilty of an offence under this regulation is liable—

(a) on conviction on indictment, to a fine;

(b) on summary conviction, to a fine not exceeding the statutory maximum.

(7) Proceedings for an offence under this regulation are not to be brought—

        (a) in England and Wales except by or with the consent of the Secretary of State or the Director of Public Prosecutions;
        (b) in Northern Ireland except by or with the consent of the Department of Enterprise, Trade and Investment or the Director of Public Prosecutions for Northern Ireland.
    (8) Nothing in this regulation affects any power of the Panel in relation to the enforcement of its rules.

11. Enforcement by the court
    (1) If, on the application of the Panel, the court is satisfied—
        (a) that there is a reasonable likelihood that a person will contravene a rule-based requirement, or
        (b) that a person has contravened a rule-based requirement or a disclosure requirement,
        the court may make any order it thinks fit to secure compliance with the requirement.
    (2) Except as provided by paragraph (1), no person—
        (a) has a right to seek an injunction, or
        (b) in Scotland, has title or interest to seek an interdict or an order for specific performance,
        to prevent a person from contravening (or continuing to contravene) a rule-based requirement or a disclosure requirement.

12. No action for breach of statutory duty etc.
    (1) Contravention of a rule-based requirement or a disclosure requirement does not give rise to any right of action for breach of statutory duty.
    (2) Contravention of a rule-based requirement does not make any transaction void or unenforceable or affect the validity of any other thing.

13. Interpretation of Chapter 4
In this Chapter—
   'contravene' includes fail to comply;
   'contravention' includes failure to comply;
   'disclosure requirement' means a requirement imposed under regulation 6;
   'offer document' means a document required to be published by Rules 30.1 and 32.1 of the Code;
   'offer document rules' means rules set out in Rules 24 and 27 of the Code to the extent that they are referred to in section 10(e) of the Introduction to the Code;
   'officer' includes director, manager or secretary;
   'response document' means a document required to be published by Rules 30.2 and 32.6(a) of the Code;
   'response document rules' means rules set out in Rules 25 and 27 of the Code to the extent that they are referred to in section 10(e) of the Introduction to the Code;
   'rule-based requirement' means a requirement imposed by or under rules.

CHAPTER 5
Miscellaneous and supplementary

14. Recovery of fees or charges
A fee or charge payable by any person by virtue of the rules is a debt due from that person to the Panel, and is recoverable accordingly.

15. Panel as party to proceedings
In the exercise of its functions the Panel is capable (despite being an unincorporated body) of—

    (a) bringing proceedings under this Part in its own name;
    (b) bringing or defending any other proceedings in its own name.

16. Exemption from liability in damages
    (1) Neither the Panel, nor any person within paragraph (2), is to be liable in damages for anything done (or omitted to be done) in, or in connection with, the discharge or purported discharge of the Panel's functions.
    (2) A person is within this paragraph if—

(a) he is (or is acting as) a member, officer or member of staff of the Panel; or
(b) he is a person authorised under regulation 6(5).
(3) Paragraph (1) does not apply—
(a) if the act or omission is shown to have been in bad faith; or
(b) so as to prevent an award of damages in respect of the act or omission on the ground that it was unlawful as a result of section 6(1) of the Human Rights Act 1998 (acts of public authorities incompatible with Convention rights).

17. Privilege against self-incrimination
(1) A statement made by a person in response to—
(a) a requirement under regulation 6(1), or
(b) an order made by the court under regulation 11 to secure compliance with such a requirement,

may not be used against him in criminal proceedings in which he is charged with an offence to which this paragraph applies.

(2) Paragraph (1) applies to any offence other than an offence under one of the following provisions (which concern false statements made otherwise than on oath)—
(a) section 5 of the Perjury Act 1911;
(b) section 44(2) of the Criminal Law (Consolidation) (Scotland) Act 1995;
(c) Article 10 of the Perjury (Northern Ireland) Order 1979.

18. Amendments and modifications to Financial Services and Markets Act 2000
(1) Section 348 of the Financial Services and Markets Act 2000 does not apply to—
(a) the disclosure by an authority to which paragraph (2) applies of confidential information disclosed to it by the Financial Services Authority in reliance on subsection (1) of that section;
(b) the disclosure of such information by a person obtaining it directly or indirectly from an authority to which paragraph (2) applies.

'Confidential information' has the meaning given by section 348(2) of that Act.

(2) This paragraph applies to—
(a) the Panel;
(b) an authority designated as a supervisory authority for the purposes of Article 4.1 of the Takeovers Directive;
(c) any other person or body that exercises functions of a public nature, under legislation in an EEA State other than the United Kingdom, that are similar to the Financial Services Authority's functions or those of the Panel.

(3) The Financial Services and Markets Act 2000 is amended as follows.
(4) In section 143 (power to make rules endorsing the City Code on Takeovers and Mergers etc.), after subsection (1) insert—

'(1A) The Authority may not make endorsing rules in respect of provisions of that Code that are given effect by regulation 3 of the Takeovers Directive (Interim Implementation) Regulations 2006.'

(5) At the end of section 349 (exceptions from section 348) insert—

'(8) Section 348 has effect subject to regulation 18(1) of the Takeovers Directive (Interim Implementation) Regulations 2006.'

PART 3
Impediments to Takeovers

CHAPTER 1
Interpretation

19. Interpretation of Part
(1) In this Part—
'company' means—
(a) a company within the meaning of section 735 of the Companies Act 1985;
(b) an unregistered company within the meaning of section 718 of that Act;
(c) a company within the meaning of Article 3 of the Companies (Northern Ireland) Order 1986; or
(d) an unregistered company within the meaning of Article 667 of that Order;

'daily default fine' has the meaning in section 730(4) of the Companies Act 1985 (or in the case of Northern Ireland, Article 678(4) of the Companies (Northern Ireland) Order 1986;

'offeror' has the same meaning as in the Takeovers Directive;

'offer period', in relation to a takeover bid, means the time allowed for acceptance of the bid by—
- (a) rules in the Code giving effect to Article 7(1) of the Takeovers Directive; or
- (b) where the rules giving effect to that Article which apply to the bid are those of an EEA State other than the United Kingdom, those rules;

'opted-in company' means a company in relation to which—
- (a) an opting-in resolution has effect; and
- (b) the conditions in regulation 20(2) and (4) continue to be met;

'opting-in resolution' has the meaning given by regulation 20(1);

'opting-out resolution' has the meaning given by regulation 20(5);

'registrar' has the meaning in section 744 of the Companies Act 1985 (or in the case of Northern Ireland in Article 653(2) of the Companies (Northern Ireland) Order 1986).

(2) For the purposes of this Part—
- (a) securities of a company are treated as shares in the company if they are convertible into or entitle the holder to subscribe for such shares;
- (b) debentures issued by a company are treated as shares in the company if they carry voting rights.

CHAPTER 2
Opting in and opting out

20. Opting in and opting out

(1) A company may by special resolution (an 'opting-in resolution') opt in for the purposes of this Part if the following three conditions are met in relation to the company.

(2) The first condition is that the company has voting shares admitted to trading on a regulated market.

(3) The second condition is that—
- (a) the company's articles of association—
  - (i) do not contain any such restrictions as are mentioned in Article 11 of the Takeovers Directive; or
  - (ii) if they do contain any such restrictions, provide for the restrictions not to apply at a time when, or in circumstances in which, they would be disapplied by that Article; and
- (b) those articles do not contain any other provision which would be incompatible with that Article.

(4) The third condition is that—
- (a) no shares conferring special rights in the company are held by—
  - (i) a minister,
  - (ii) a nominee of, or any other person acting on behalf of, a minister, or
  - (iii) a company directly or indirectly controlled by a minister, and
- (b) no such rights are exercisable by or on behalf of a minister under any enactment.

(5) A company may revoke an opting-in resolution by a further special resolution (an 'optingout resolution').

(6) For the purposes of paragraph (3), a reference in Article 11 of the Takeovers Directive to Article 7(1) or 9 of that Directive is to be read as referring to rules in the Code giving effect to the relevant Article.

(7) In paragraph (4) 'minister' means—
- (a) the holder of an office in Her Majesty's Government in the United Kingdom,
- (b) the Scottish Ministers,
- (c) a Minister within the meaning given by section 7(3) of the Northern Ireland Act 1998,

and for the purposes of that paragraph 'minister' also includes the Treasury, the Board of Trade, the Defence Council and the National Assembly for Wales.

21. **Further provisions about opting-in and opting-out resolutions**
(1) An opting-in resolution or an opting-out resolution must specify the date from which it is to have effect (the 'effective date').
(2) The effective date of an opting-in resolution may not be earlier than the date on which the resolution is passed.
(3) The second and third conditions in regulation 20 must be met at the time when an opting-in resolution is passed, but the first one does not need to be met until the effective date.
(4) An opting-in resolution passed before the time when voting shares of the company are admitted to trading on a regulated market complies with the requirement in paragraph (1) if, instead of specifying a particular date, it provides for the resolution to have effect from that time.
(5) The effective date of an opting-out resolution may not be earlier than the first anniversary of the date on which a copy of the opting-in resolution was forwarded to the registrar.
(6) Where a company has passed an opting-in resolution, any alteration of its articles of association that would prevent the second condition in regulation 20 from being met is of no effect until the effective date of an opting-out resolution passed by the company.

CHAPTER 3
Consequences of opting in

22. **Effect on contractual restrictions**
(1) The following provisions have effect where a takeover bid is made for an opted-in company.
(2) An agreement to which this regulation applies is invalid in so far as it places any restriction—
   (a) on the transfer to the offeror, or at his direction to another person, of shares in the company during the offer period;
   (b) on the transfer to any person of shares in the company at a time during the offer period when the offeror holds shares amounting to not less than 75% in value of all the voting shares in the company;
   (c) on rights to vote at a general meeting of the company that decides whether to take any action which might result in the frustration of the bid;
   (d) on rights to vote at a general meeting of the company that—
      (i) is the first such meeting to be held after the end of the offer period; and
      (ii) is held at a time when the offeror holds shares amounting to not less than 75% in value of all the voting shares in the company.
(3) This regulation applies to an agreement—
   (a) entered into between a person holding shares in the company and another such person on or after 21st April 2004, or
   (b) entered into at any time between such a person and the company,
and it applies to such an agreement even if the law applicable to the agreement (apart from this paragraph) is not the law of a part of the United Kingdom.
(4) The reference in paragraph (2)(c) to rights to vote at a general meeting of the company that decides whether to take any action which might result in the frustration of the bid includes a reference to rights to vote on a written resolution concerned with that question.
(5) For the purposes of paragraph (2)(c), action which might result in the frustration of a bid is any action of that kind specified by rules in the Code giving effect to Article 9 of the Takeovers Directive.
(6) If a person suffers loss as a result of any act or omission that would (but for this regulation) be a breach of an agreement to which this regulation applies, he is entitled to compensation, of such amount as the court considers just and equitable, from any person who would (but for this paragraph) be liable to him for committing or inducing the breach.
(7) A reference in this regulation to voting shares in the company does not include—
   (a) debentures; or
   (b) shares carrying rights to vote that, under the company's articles of association, arise only where specified pecuniary advantages are not provided.

In sub-paragraph (b) 'rights to vote' means rights to vote at general meetings of the company.

23. Power of offeror to require general meeting to be called

(1) Where a takeover bid is made for an opted-in company, section 368 of the Companies Act 1985 (extraordinary general meeting on members' requisition) and section 378 of that Act (extraordinary and special resolutions) have effect as follows.

(2) Section 368 has effect as if a member's requisition included a requisition of a person who—
   (a) is the offeror in relation to the takeover bid; and
   (b) holds at the date of the deposit of the requisition shares amounting to not less than 75% in value of all the voting shares in the company.

(3) In relation to a general meeting of the company that—
   (a) is the first such meeting to be held after the end of the offer period, and
   (b) is held at a time when the offeror holds shares amounting to not less than 75% in value of all the voting shares in the company,

section 378(2) (meaning of 'special resolution') has effect as if '14 days' notice' were substituted for '21 days' notice'.

(4) A reference in this regulation to voting shares in the company does not include—
   (a) debentures; or
   (b) shares carrying rights to vote that, under the company's articles of association, arise only where specified pecuniary advantages are not provided.

In sub-paragraph (b) 'rights to vote' means rights to vote at general meetings of the company.

(5) In its application to Northern Ireland, references in this regulation to sections 368 and 378 of the Companies Act 1985 are to be read, respectively, as references to Articles 376 and 386 of the Companies (Northern Ireland) Order 1986.

CHAPTER 4
Supplementary

24. Communication of decisions

(1) A company that has passed an opting-in resolution or an opting-out resolution must notify—
   (a) the Panel; and
   (b) where the company—
      (i) has voting shares admitted to trading on a regulated market in an EEA State other than the United Kingdom, or
      (ii) has requested such admission,
      the authority designated by that State as the supervisory authority for the purposes of Article 4.1 of the Takeovers Directive.

(2) Notification must be given within 15 days after the resolution is passed and, if any admission or request such as is mentioned in paragraph (1)(b) occurs at a later time, within 15 days after that time.

(3) If a company fails to comply with this regulation, an offence is committed by—
   (a) the company; and
   (b) every officer of it who is in default.

(4) A person guilty of an offence under this regulation is liable on summary conviction to a fine not exceeding level 3 on the standard scale and, for continued contravention, to a daily default fine not exceeding £100.

PART 4
Directors' Report etc.

25. Matters to be dealt with in directors' report

(1) In this Part 'directors' report' means the report prepared under section 234 of the Companies Act 1985 (or in the case of Northern Ireland, Article 242 of the Companies (Northern Ireland) Order 1986).

(2) This Part applies to a directors' report for a financial year beginning on or after 20th May 2006, if the company had securities carrying voting rights admitted to trading on a regulated market at the end of that year.

26.
(1) In addition to the matters required by section 234ZZA of the Companies Act 1985 (or in the case of Northern Ireland, Article 242ZZA of the Companies (Northern Ireland) Order 1986 to be contained in the directors' report, that report shall contain detailed information, by reference to the end of that year, on the following matters—
    (a) the structure of the company's capital, including in particular—
        (i) the rights and obligations attaching to the shares or, as the case may be, to each class of shares in the company; and
        (ii) where there are two or more such classes, the percentage of the total share capital represented by each class;
    (b) any restrictions on the transfer of securities in the company, including in particular—
        (i) limitations on the holding of securities; and
        (ii) requirements to obtain the approval of the company, or of other holders of securities in the company, for a transfer of securities;
    (c) in the case of each person with a significant direct or indirect holding of securities in the company, such details as are known to the company of—
        (i) the identity of the person;
        (ii) the size of the holding; and
        (iii) the nature of the holding;
    (d) in the case of each person who holds securities carrying special rights with regard to control of the company—
        (i) the identity of the person; and
        (ii) the nature of the rights;
    (e) where—
        (i) the company has an employees' share scheme, and
        (ii) shares to which the scheme relates have rights with regard to control of the company that are not exercisable directly by the employees,
    how those rights are exercisable;
    (f) any restrictions on voting rights, including in particular—
        (i) limitations on voting rights of holders of a given percentage or number of votes;
        (ii) deadlines for exercising voting rights; and
        (iii) arrangements by which, with the company's co-operation, financial rights carried by securities are held by a person other than the holder of the securities;
    (g) any agreements between holders of securities that are known to the company and may result in restrictions on the transfer of securities or on voting rights;
    (h) any rules that the company has about—
        (i) appointment and replacement of directors; or
        (ii) amendment of the company's articles of association;
    (i) the powers of the company's directors, including in particular any powers in relation to the issuing or buying back by the company of its shares;
    (j) any significant agreements to which the company is a party that take effect, alter or terminate upon a change of control of the company following a takeover bid, and the effects of any such agreements;
    (k) any agreements between the company and its directors or employees providing for compensation for loss of office or employment (whether through resignation, purported redundancy or otherwise) that occurs because of a takeover bid.
(2) For the purposes of paragraph (1)(a) a company's capital includes any securities in the company that are not admitted to trading on a regulated market.
(3) For the purposes of paragraph (1)(c) a person has an indirect holding of securities if—
    (a) they are held on his behalf; or
    (b) he is able to secure that rights carried by the securities are exercised in accordance with his wishes.
(4) Paragraph (1)(j) does not apply to an agreement if—
    (a) disclosure of the agreement would be seriously prejudicial to the company; and
    (b) the company is not under any other obligation to disclose it.

(5) The directors' report shall also contain any necessary explanatory material with regard to information that is required to be included in the report by paragraph (1).

(6) In this regulation 'securities' means shares or debentures.

27. Summary financial statement

If, in accordance with section 251 of the Companies Act 1985 (or as the case may be Article 259 of the Companies (Northern Ireland) Order 1986), a company sends to an entitled person a summary financial statement instead of a copy of its directors' report the company shall—

(a) include in the statement the explanatory material required to be included in the directors' report by regulation 26(5); or

(b) send that material to the entitled person at the same time as it sends the statement.

For the purposes of paragraph (b), section 251(2A) to (2E) (or as the case may be Article 259(2A) to (2E)) applies in relation to the material referred to in that paragraph as it applies in relation to a summary financial statement.

28. Expressions in the Companies Act 1985

Except as otherwise provided expressions that are defined for the purposes of Part 7 of the Companies Act 1985 (or in the case of Northern Ireland, Part 8 of the Companies (Northern Ireland) Order 1986) have the same meaning in this Part.

PART 5
Squeeze-out and sell-out

29. Takeover offers

This Part applies to any takeover offer where the date of the offer as defined in paragraph 11 of Schedule 2 is on or after 20 May 2006.

30.

Where a takeover offer is made for a company that has securities carrying voting rights admitted to trading on a regulated market, Part 13A of the Companies Act 1985 (or in the case of Northern Ireland, Part 14A of the Companies (Northern Ireland) Order 1986) shall not apply and Schedule 2 to these Regulations shall apply.

31.

In this Part 'company' means—

(a) a company within the meaning of section 735 of the Companies Act 1985;

(b) an unregistered company within the meaning of section 718 of that Act;

(c) a company within the meaning of Article 3 of the Companies (Northern Ireland) Order 1986; or

(d) an unregistered company within the meaning of Article 667 of that Order.

32.

Except as otherwise provided expressions that are defined for the purposes of Part 13A of the Companies Act 1985 (or in the case of Northern Ireland, Part 14A of the Companies (Northern Ireland) Order 1986) have the same meaning in this Part.

SCHEDULE 1   Regulation 7

SPECIFIED PERSONS, DESCRIPTIONS OF DISCLOSURES ETC. FOR THE PURPOSES OF REGULATION 7

PART 1
SPECIFIED PERSONS

1. The Secretary of State.

2. The Department of Enterprise, Trade and Investment for Northern Ireland.

3. The Treasury.

4. The Bank of England.

5. The Financial Services Authority.

6. The Commissioners for Her Majesty's Revenue and Customs.

7. The Lord Advocate.

8. The Director of Public Prosecutions.

9. The Director of Public Prosecutions for Northern Ireland.

10. A constable.

11. A procurator fiscal.

12. The Scottish Ministers.

PART 2
SPECIFIED DESCRIPTIONS OF DISCLOSURES

13. A disclosure for the purpose of enabling or assisting a person authorised under section 245C of the Companies Act 1985 (persons authorised to apply to court) to exercise his functions.

14. A disclosure for the purpose of enabling or assisting an inspector appointed under Part 14 of the Companies Act 1985 (investigation of companies and their affairs, etc.) to exercise his functions.

15. A disclosure for the purpose of enabling or assisting a person authorised under section 447 of the Companies Act 1985 (power to require production of documents) or section 84 of the Companies Act 1989 (exercise of powers by officer etc.) to exercise his functions.

16. A disclosure for the purpose of enabling or assisting a person appointed under section 167 of the Financial Services and Markets Act 2000 (general investigations) to conduct an investigation to exercise his functions.

17. A disclosure for the purpose of enabling or assisting a person appointed under section 168 of the Financial Services and Markets Act 2000 (investigations in particular cases) to conduct an investigation to exercise his functions.

18. A disclosure for the purpose of enabling or assisting a person appointed under section 169(1)(b) of the Financial Services and Markets Act 2000 (investigation in support of overseas regulator) to conduct an investigation to exercise his functions.

19. A disclosure for the purpose of enabling or assisting the body corporate responsible for administering the scheme referred to in section 225 of the Financial Services and Markets Act 2000 (the ombudsman scheme) to exercise its functions.

20. A disclosure for the purpose of enabling or assisting a person appointed under paragraph 4 (the panel of ombudsmen) or 5 (the Chief Ombudsman) of Schedule 17 to the Financial Services and Markets Act 2000 to exercise his functions.

21. A disclosure for the purpose of enabling or assisting a person appointed under regulations made under section 262(1) and (2)(k) of the Financial Services and Markets Act 2000 (investigations into open-ended investment companies) to conduct an investigation to exercise his functions.

22. A disclosure for the purpose of enabling or assisting a person appointed under section 284 of the Financial Services and Markets Act 2000 (investigations into affairs of certain collective investment schemes) to conduct an investigation to exercise his functions.

23. A disclosure for the purpose of enabling or assisting the investigator appointed under paragraph 7 of Schedule 1 to the Financial Services and Markets Act 2000 (arrangements for investigation of complaints) to exercise his functions.

24. A disclosure for the purpose of enabling or assisting a person appointed by the Treasury to hold an inquiry into matters relating to financial services (including an inquiry under section 15 of the Financial Services and Markets Act 2000) to exercise his functions.

25. A disclosure for the purpose of enabling or assisting the Secretary of State or the Treasury to exercise any of their functions under any of the following—
(a) the Companies Acts;
(b) Part 5 of the Criminal Justice Act 1993 (insider dealing);
(c) the Insolvency Act 1986;
(d) the Company Directors Disqualification Act 1986;
(e) Part 2 of the Companies Act 1989 (eligibility for appointment as company auditor);
(f) Part 3 (investigations and powers to obtain information) or 7 (financial markets and insolvency) of the Companies Act 1989;

(g)   the Financial Services and Markets Act 2000.

26. A disclosure for the purpose of enabling or assisting the Scottish Ministers to exercise their functions under the enactments relating to insolvency.

27. A disclosure for the purpose of enabling or assisting the Department of Enterprise, Trade and Investment for Northern Ireland to exercise any powers conferred on it by the enactments relating to companies or insolvency.

28. A disclosure for the purpose of enabling or assisting a person appointed or authorised by the Department of Enterprise, Trade and Investment for Northern Ireland under the enactments relating to companies or insolvency to exercise his functions.

29. A disclosure for the purpose of enabling or assisting the Pensions Regulator to exercise the functions conferred on it by or by virtue of any of the following—
(a)   the Pension Schemes Act 1993;
(b)   the Pensions Act 1995;
(c)   the Welfare Reform and Pensions Act 1999;
(d)   the Pensions Act 2004;
(e)   any enactment in force in Northern Ireland corresponding to any of those enactments.

30. A disclosure for the purpose of enabling or assisting the Board of the Pension Protection Fund to exercise the functions conferred on it by or by virtue of Part 2 of the Pensions Act 2004 or any enactment in force in Northern Ireland corresponding to that Part.

31. A disclosure for the purpose of enabling or assisting—
(a)   the Bank of England,
(b)   the European Central Bank, or
(c)   the central bank of any country or territory outside the United Kingdom,
to exercise its functions.

32. A disclosure for the purpose of enabling or assisting the Commissioners for Her Majesty's Revenue and Customs to exercise their functions.

33. A disclosure for the purpose of enabling or assisting organs of the Society of Lloyd's (being organs constituted by or under the Lloyd's Act 1982) to exercise their functions under or by virtue of the Lloyd's Acts 1871 to 1982.

34. A disclosure for the purpose of enabling or assisting the Office of Fair Trading to exercise its functions under any of the following—
(a)   the Fair Trading Act 1973;
(b)   the Consumer Credit Act 1974;
(c)   the Estate Agents Act 1979;
(d)   the Competition Act 1980;
(e)   the Competition Act 1998;
(f)   the Financial Services and Markets Act 2000;
(g)   the Enterprise Act 2002;
(h)   the Control of Misleading Advertisements Regulations 1988;
(i)   the Unfair Terms in Consumer Contracts Regulations 1999.

35. A disclosure for the purpose of enabling or assisting the Competition Commission to exercise its functions under any of the following—
(a)   the Fair Trading Act 1973;
(b)   the Competition Act 1980;
(c)   the Competition Act 1998;
(d)   the Enterprise Act 2002.

36. A disclosure with a view to the institution of, or otherwise for the purposes of, proceedings before the Competition Appeal Tribunal.

37. A disclosure for the purpose of enabling or assisting an enforcer under Part 8 of the Enterprise Act 2002 (enforcement of consumer legislation) to exercise its functions under that Part.

38. A disclosure for the purpose of enabling or assisting the Charity Commissioners (or in the case of Northern Ireland, the Department for Social Development) to exercise their functions.

39. A disclosure for the purpose of enabling or assisting the Attorney General to exercise his functions in connection with charities.

40. A disclosure for the purpose of enabling or assisting the National Lottery Commission to exercise its functions under sections 5 to 10 (licensing) and 15 (power of Secretary of State to require information) of the National Lottery etc. Act 1993.

41. A disclosure by the National Lottery Commission to the National Audit Office for the purpose of enabling or assisting the Comptroller and Auditor General to carry out an examination under Part 2 of the National Audit Act 1983 into the economy, effectiveness and efficiency with which the National Lottery Commission has used its resources in discharging its functions under sections 5 to 10 of the National Lottery etc. Act 1993.

42. A disclosure for the purpose of enabling or assisting a qualifying body under the Unfair Terms in Consumer Contracts Regulations 1999 to exercise its functions under those Regulations.

43. A disclosure for the purpose of enabling or assisting an enforcement authority under the Consumer Protection (Distance Selling) Regulations 2000 to exercise its functions under those Regulations.

44. A disclosure for the purpose of enabling or assisting an enforcement authority under the Financial Services (Distance Marketing) Regulations 2004 to exercise its functions under those Regulations.

45. A disclosure for the purpose of enabling or assisting a local weights and measures authority in England and Wales to exercise its functions under section 230(2) of the Enterprise Act 2002 (notice of intention to prosecute, etc.).

46. A disclosure for the purpose of enabling or assisting the Financial Services Authority to exercise its functions under any of the following—
(a) the legislation relating to friendly societies or to industrial and provident societies;
(b) the Building Societies Act 1986;
(c) Part 7 of the Companies Act 1989 (financial markets and insolvency);
(d) the Financial Services and Markets Act 2000.

47. A disclosure for the purpose of enabling or assisting the competent authority for the purposes of Part 6 of the Financial Services and Markets Act 2000 (official listing) to exercise its functions under that Part.

48. A disclosure for the purpose of enabling or assisting a body corporate established in accordance with section 212(1) of the Financial Services and Markets Act 2000 (compensation scheme manager) to exercise its functions.

49. A disclosure for the purpose of enabling or assisting a recognised investment exchange or a recognised clearing house to exercise its functions as such.
'Recognised investment exchange' and 'recognised clearing house' have the same meaning as in section 285 of the Financial Services and Markets Act 2000.

50. A disclosure for the purpose of enabling or assisting a person approved under the Uncertificated Securities Regulations 2001 as an operator of a relevant system (within the meaning of those Regulations) to exercise his functions.

51. A disclosure for the purpose of enabling or assisting a body designated under section 326(1) of the Financial Services and Markets Act 2000 (designated professional bodies) to exercise its functions in its capacity as a body designated under that section.

52. A disclosure with a view to the institution of, or otherwise for the purposes of, civil proceedings arising under or by virtue of the Financial Services and Markets Act 2000.

53. A disclosure for the purpose of enabling or assisting a body designated by order under section 46 of the Companies Act 1989 (delegation of functions of Secretary of State) to exercise its functions under Part 2 of that Act (eligibility for appointment as company auditor).

54. A disclosure for the purpose of enabling or assisting a recognised supervisory or qualifying body, within the meaning of Part 2 of the Companies Act 1989.

55. A disclosure for the purpose of enabling or assisting an official receiver (including the Accountant in Bankruptcy in Scotland and the Official Assignee in Northern Ireland) to exercise is functions under the enactments relating to insolvency.

56. A disclosure for the purpose of enabling or assisting the Insolvency Practitioners Tribunal to exercise its functions under the Insolvency Act 1986.

57. A disclosure for the purpose of enabling or assisting a body that is for the time being a recognised professional body for the purposes of section 391 of the Insolvency Act 1986 (recognised professional bodies) to exercise its functions as such.

58. A disclosure for the purpose of enabling or assisting an overseas regulatory authority to exercise its regulatory functions.

> 'Overseas regulatory authority' and 'regulatory functions' have the same meaning as in section 82 of the Companies Act 1989.

59. A disclosure for the purpose of enabling or assisting the Regulator of Community Interest Companies to exercise functions under the Companies (Audit, Investigations and Community Enterprise) Act 2004.

60. A disclosure with a view to the institution of, or otherwise for the purposes of, criminal proceedings.

61. A disclosure for the purpose of enabling or assisting a person authorised by the Secretary of State under Part 2, 3 or 4 of the Proceeds of Crime Act 2002 to exercise his functions.

62. A disclosure with a view to the institution of, or otherwise for the purposes of, proceedings on an application under section 6, 7 or 8 of the Company Directors Disqualification Act 1986 (disqualification for unfitness).

63. A disclosure with a view to the institution of, or otherwise for the purposes of, proceedings before the Financial Services and Markets Tribunal.

64. A disclosure for the purposes of proceedings before the Financial Services Tribunal by virtue of the Financial Services and Markets Act 2000 (Transitional Provisions) (Partly Completed Procedures) Order 2001.

65. A disclosure for the purposes of proceedings before the Pensions Regulator Tribunal.

66. A disclosure for the purpose of enabling or assisting a body appointed under section 14 of the Companies (Audit, Investigations and Community Enterprise) Act 2004 (supervision of periodic accounts and reports of issuers of listed securities) to exercise functions mentioned in subsection (2) of that section.

67. A disclosure with a view to the institution of, or otherwise for the purposes of, disciplinary proceedings relating to the performance by a solicitor, barrister, advocate, foreign lawyer, auditor, accountant, valuer or actuary of his professional duties.

> 'Foreign lawyer' has the meaning given by section 89(9) of the Courts and Legal Services Act 1990.

68. A disclosure with a view to the institution of, or otherwise for the purposes of, disciplinary proceedings relating to the performance by a public servant of his duties.

> 'Public servant' means an officer or employee of the Crown.

69. A disclosure for the purpose of the provision of a summary or collection of information framed in such a way as not to enable the identity of any person to whom the information relates to be ascertained.

70. A disclosure in pursuance of any Community obligation.

PART 3
OVERSEAS REGULATORY BODIES

71. A disclosure is made in accordance with this Part of this Schedule if—
(a) it is made to a person or body within paragraph 72; and
(b) it is made for the purpose of enabling or assisting that person or body to exercise the functions mentioned in that paragraph.

72. The persons or bodies that are within this paragraph are those exercising functions of a public nature, under legislation in any country or territory outside the United Kingdom, that appear to the Panel to be similar to its own functions or those of the Financial Services Authority.

73. In determining whether to disclose information to a person or body in accordance with this Part of this Schedule, the Panel must have regard to the following considerations—

(a) whether the use that the person or body is likely to make of the information is sufficiently important to justify making the disclosure;

(b) whether the person or body has adequate arrangements to prevent the information from being used or further disclosed otherwise than for the purposes of carrying out the functions mentioned in paragraph 72 or any other purposes substantially similar to those for which information disclosed to the Panel could be used or further disclosed.

SCHEDULE 2 Regulation 30
SQUEEZE-OUT AND SELL-OUT

1. Meaning of takeover offer

(1) In this Schedule 'a takeover offer' means an offer to acquire all the shares, or all the shares of any class or classes, in a company (other than shares which at the date of the offer are already held by the offeror), being an offer on terms which are the same in relation to all the shares to which the offer relates or, where those shares include shares of different classes, in relation to all the shares of each class.

(2) In sub-paragraph (1) 'shares' means shares (other than relevant treasury shares) which have been allotted on the date of the offer, but a takeover offer may include among the shares to which it relates—

(a) all or any shares that are allotted after the date of the offer but before a specified date;

(b) all or any relevant treasury shares that cease to be held as treasury shares before a specified date;

(c) all or any other relevant treasury shares.

(3) In this paragraph—

'relevant treasury shares' means shares which—

(a) are held by the company as treasury shares on the date of the offer; or

(b) become shares held by the company as treasury shares after that date but before a specified date;

'specified date' means a date specified in or determined in accordance with the terms of the offer.

(4) The terms offered in relation to any shares shall for the purposes of this paragraph be treated as being the same in relation to all the shares or, as the case may be, all the shares of a class to which the offer relates notwithstanding—

(a) any difference permitted by sub-paragraph (5); or

(b) any variation permitted by sub-paragraph (6).

(5) A difference is permitted by this sub-paragraph where—

(a) shares carry an entitlement to a particular dividend which other shares of the same class, by reason of being allotted later, do not carry; and

(b) the difference is the value of consideration offered for the shares allotted earlier as against that offered for those allotted later, and merely reflects the difference in entitlement to the dividend.

(6) A variation is permitted by this sub-paragraph where—

(a) the law of a country or territory outside the United Kingdom precludes an offer of consideration in the form or any of the forms specified in the terms in question or precludes it except after compliance by the offeror with conditions with which he is unable to comply or which he regards as unduly onerous; and

(b) the variation is such that the persons to whom an offer of consideration in that form is precluded are able to receive consideration otherwise than in that form but of substantially equivalent value.

(7) Where there are holders of shares in a company to whom an offer to acquire shares in the company is not communicated, that does not prevent the offer from being a takeover offer for the purposes of this Schedule if—

(a) those shareholders have no registered address in the United Kingdom;
(b) the offer was not communicated to those shareholders in order not to contravene the law of a country or territory outside the United Kingdom; and
(c) either—
   (i) the offer is published in the Gazette; or
   (ii) the offer can be inspected, or a copy of it obtained, at a place in an EEA State or on a website, and a notice is published in the Gazette specifying the address of that place or website.

(8) Where an offer is made to acquire shares in a company and there are persons for whom, by reason of the law of a country or territory outside the United Kingdom, it is impossible to accept the offer, or more difficult to do so, that does not prevent the offer from being a takeover offer for the purposes of this Schedule.

(9) It is not to be inferred—
(a) that an offer which is not communicated to every holder of shares in the company cannot be a takeover offer for the purposes of this Schedule unless the requirements of subparagraphs (7)(a) to (c) are met; or
(b) that an offer which is impossible, or more difficult, for certain persons to accept cannot be a takeover offer for those purposes unless the reason for the impossibility or difficulty is the one mentioned in sub-paragraph (8).

(10) The reference in sub-paragraph (1) to shares already held by the offeror includes a reference to shares which he has contracted to acquire (whether unconditionally or subject to conditions being met) but that shall not be construed as including shares which are the subject of a contract binding the holder to accept the offer when it is made, being a contract entered into by the holder either for no consideration and under seal or for no consideration other than a promise by the offeror to make the offer.

(11) In the application of sub-paragraph (10) to Scotland, the words 'and under seal' shall be omitted.

(12) Where the terms of an offer make provision for their revision and for acceptances on the previous terms to be treated as acceptances on the revised terms, the revision shall not be regarded for the purposes of this Schedule as the making of a fresh offer and references in paragraph 11(1) to the offer shall accordingly be construed as references to the original offer.

2. Right of offeror to buy out minority shareholders

(1) Sub-paragraph (2) applies in a case where a takeover offer does not relate to shares of different classes.

(2) If the offeror has, by virtue of acceptances of the offer, acquired or unconditionally contracted to acquire—
(a) not less than nine-tenths in value of the shares to which the offer relates, and
(b) in a case where the shares to which the offer relates are voting shares, not less than nine-tenths of the voting rights carried by those shares,

he may give notice to the holder of any shares to which the offer relates which the offeror has not acquired or unconditionally contracted to acquire that he desires to acquire those shares.

(3) Sub-paragraph (4) applies in a case where a takeover offer relates to shares of different classes.

(4) If the offeror has, by virtue of acceptances of the offer, acquired or unconditionally contracted to acquire—
(a) not less than nine-tenths in value of the shares of any class to which the offer relates, and
(b) in a case where the shares of that class are voting shares, not less than nine-tenths of the voting rights carried by those shares,

he may give notice to the holder of any shares of that class to which the offer relates which the offeror has not acquired or unconditionally contracted to acquire that he desires to acquire those shares.

(5) No notice shall be given under sub-paragraph (2) or (4) after the end of the period of three months beginning with the day after the last day on which the offer can be accepted.

(6) Sub-paragraph (7) applies where—

(a) the requirements for the giving of a notice under sub-paragraph (2) or (4) are satisfied; and
(b) there are shares in the company which the offeror has contracted to acquire subject to conditions being met, and in relation to which the contract has not become unconditional.

(7) The offeror's entitlement to give a notice under sub-paragraph (2) or (4) shall be determined as if—
(a) the shares to which the offer relates included shares falling within sub-paragraph (6)(b); and
(b) in relation to shares falling within that paragraph, the words 'by virtue of acceptances of the offer' in sub-paragraph (2) or (4) were omitted.

(8) Any notice under this paragraph shall be given in the manner prescribed by regulation 4 of the Companies (Forms) Regulations 1985 ('the 1985 Regulations') for a notice given for the purposes of section 429(4) of the Companies Act 1985 (or in the case of Northern Ireland by regulation 4 of the Companies (Forms) Regulations (Northern Ireland) 1986 ('the 1986 Regulations') for a notice given for the purposes of Article 422(4) of the Companies (Northern Ireland) Order 1986); and when the offeror gives the first notice in relation to an offer he shall send a copy of it to the company together with a statutory declaration by him in the form prescribed by regulation 5(2) of the 1985 Regulations (or in the case of Northern Ireland by regulation 5(2) of the 1986 Regulations), stating that the conditions for the giving of the notice are satisfied.

(9) Where the offeror is a company (whether or not a company within the meaning of the Companies Act 1985 or, in the case of Northern Ireland, the Companies (Northern Ireland) Order 1986) the statutory declaration shall be signed by a director.

(10) Any person who fails to send a copy of a notice or a statutory declaration as required by sub-paragraph (8) or makes such a declaration for the purposes of that sub-paragraph knowing it to be false or without having reasonable grounds for believing it to be true commits an offence.

(11) A person who commits an offence under sub-paragraph (10), but would have committed an offence under section 429(6) of the Companies Act 1985 (or as the case may be, Article 422(6) of the Companies (Northern Ireland) Order 1986) had that section (or Article) not been disapplied by regulation 30, is liable on conviction to the penalties in that section (or Article).

(12) In all other cases a person who commits an offence under sub-paragraph (10) is liable—
(a) on conviction on indictment, to imprisonment for a term not exceeding two years or a fine or both;
(b) on summary conviction, to imprisonment for a term not exceeding three months or to a fine not exceeding the statutory maximum or both;
(c) for continued contravention, to a daily default fine not exceeding £100.

(13) If any person is charged with an offence for failing to send a copy of a notice as required by sub-paragraph (8) it is a defence for him to prove that he took reasonable steps for securing compliance with that sub-paragraph.

(14) Sub-paragraph (15) applies where a takeover offer is made and, during the period beginning with the date of the offer and ending when the offer can no longer be accepted, the offeror acquires or unconditionally contracts to acquire any of the shares to which the offer relates but otherwise than by virtue of acceptances of the offer.

(15) If—
(a) the value of the consideration for which the shares are acquired or contracted to be acquired ('the acquisition consideration') does not at that time exceed the value of the consideration specified in the terms of the offer; or
(b) those terms are subsequently revised so that when the revision is announced the value of the acquisition consideration, at the time mentioned in paragraph (a), no longer exceeds the value of the consideration specified in those terms,
the offeror shall be treated for the purposes of this paragraph as having acquired or contracted to acquire those shares by virtue of acceptances of the offer; but in any other case those shares shall be treated as excluded from those to which the offer relates.

3. **Effect of notice under paragraph 2**
(1) The following provisions shall, subject to paragraph 6, have effect where a notice is given in respect of any shares under paragraph 2.
(2) The offeror shall be entitled and bound to acquire those shares on the terms of the offer.
(3) Where the terms of an offer are such as to give the holder of any shares a choice of consideration the notice shall give particulars of the choice and state—
   (a) that the holder of the shares may within six weeks from the date of the notice indicate his choice by a written communication sent to the offeror at an address specified in the notice, and
   (b) which consideration specified in the offer is to be taken as applying in default of his indicating a choice as aforesaid,
   and the terms of the offer mentioned in sub-paragraph (2) shall be determined accordingly.
(4) Sub-paragraph (3) applies whether or not any time-limit or other conditions applicable to the choice under the terms of the offer can still be complied with.
(5) If the consideration offered to or (as the case may be) chosen by the holder of the shares—
   (a) is not cash and the offeror is no longer able to provide it, or
   (b) was to have been provided by a third party who is no longer bound or able to provide it,
   the consideration shall be taken to consist of an amount of cash payable by the offeror which at the date of the notice is equivalent to the consideration offered or (as the case may be) chosen.
(6) At the end of six weeks from the date of the notice the offeror shall forthwith—
   (a) send a copy of the notice to the company; and
   (b) pay or transfer to the company the consideration for the shares to which the notice relates.
(7) If the shares to which the notice relates are registered the copy of the notice sent to the company under sub-paragraph (6)(a) shall be accompanied by an instrument of transfer executed on behalf of the shareholder by a person appointed by the offeror; and on receipt of that instrument the company shall register the offeror as the holder of those shares.
(8) If the shares to which the notice relates are transferable by the delivery of warrants or other instruments the copy of the notice sent to the company under sub-paragraph (6)(a) shall be accompanied by a statement to that effect; and the company shall on receipt of the statement issue the offeror with warrants or other instruments in respect of the shares and those already in issue in respect of the shares shall become void.
(9) Where the consideration referred to in paragraph (b) of sub-paragraph (6) consists of shares or securities to be allotted by the offeror the reference in that paragraph to the transfer of the consideration shall be construed as a reference to the allotment of the shares or securities to the company.
(10) Any sum received by a company under paragraph (b) of sub-paragraph (6) and any other consideration received under that paragraph shall be held by the company on trust for the person entitled to the shares in respect of which the sum or other consideration was received.
(11) Any sum received by a company under paragraph (b) of sub-paragraph (6), and any dividend or other sum accruing from any other consideration received by a company under that paragraph, shall be paid into a separate bank account, being an account the balance on which bears interest at an appropriate rate and can be withdrawn by such notice (if any) as is appropriate.
(12) Where after reasonable enquiry made at such intervals as are reasonable the person entitled to any consideration held on trust by virtue of sub-paragraph (10) cannot be found and twelve years have elapsed since the consideration was received or the company is wound up the consideration (together with any interest, dividend or other benefit that has accrued from it) shall be paid into court.
(13) In relation to a company registered in Scotland, sub-paragraphs (14) and (15) shall apply in place of sub-paragraph (12).
(14) Where after reasonable enquiry made at such intervals as are reasonable the person entitled to any consideration held on trust by virtue of sub-paragraph (10) cannot be

found and twelve years have elapsed since the consideration was received or the company is wound up—
(a) the trust shall terminate;
(b) the company or, as the case may be, the liquidator shall sell any consideration other than cash and any benefit other than cash that has accrued from the consideration; and
(c) a sum representing—
(i) the consideration so far as it is cash,
(ii) the proceeds of any sale under paragraph (b), and
(iii) any interest, dividend or other benefit that has accrued from the consideration,
shall be deposited in the name of the Accountant of Court in a bank account such as is referred to in sub-paragraph (11) and the receipt for the deposit shall be transmitted to the Accountant of Court.
(15) Section 58 of the Bankruptcy (Scotland) Act 1985 (so far as consistent with the Companies Act 1985) shall apply with any necessary modifications to sums deposited under subparagraph (14) as that sub-paragraph applies to sums deposited under section 57(1)(a) of the Bankruptcy (Scotland) Act 1985.
(16) The expenses of any such enquiry as is mentioned in sub-paragraph (12) or (14) may be defrayed out of the money or other property held on trust for the person or persons to whom the enquiry relates.

4. Right of minority shareholder to be bought out by offeror
(1) Sub-paragraphs (2) and (3) apply in a case where a takeover offer relates to all the shares in a company.
For this purpose a takeover offer relates to all the shares in a company if it is an offer to acquire all the shares in the company within the meaning of paragraph 1.
(2) The holder of any voting shares to which the offer relates who has not accepted the offer may require the offeror to acquire those shares if, at any time before the end of the period within which the offer can be accepted—
(a) the offeror has by virtue of acceptances of the offer acquired or unconditionally contracted to acquire some (but not all) of the shares to which the offer relates; and
(b) those shares, with or without any other shares in the company which he has acquired or contracted to acquire (whether unconditionally or subject to conditions being met)—
(i) amount to not less than nine-tenths in value of all the voting shares in the company (or would do so but for paragraph 10(1)); and
(ii) carry not less than nine-tenths of the voting rights in the company (or would do so but for paragraph 10(1)).
(3) The holder of any non-voting shares to which the offer relates who has not accepted the offer may require the offeror to acquire those shares if, at any time before the end of the period within which the offer can be accepted—
(a) the offeror has by virtue of acceptances of the offer acquired or unconditionally contracted to acquire some (but not all) of the shares to which the offer relates; and
(b) those shares, with or without any other shares in the company which he has acquired or contracted to acquire (whether unconditionally or subject to conditions being met), amount to not less than nine-tenths in value of all the shares in the company (or would do so but for paragraph 10(1)).
(4) If a takeover offer relates to shares of any class or classes and at any time before the end of the period within which the offer can be accepted—
(a) the offeror has by virtue of acceptances of the offer acquired or unconditionally contracted to acquire some (but not all) of the shares of any class to which the offer relates, and
(b) those shares, with or without any other shares of that class which he has acquired or contracted to acquire (whether unconditionally or subject to conditions being met)—
(i) amount to not less than nine-tenths in value of all the shares of that class, and

(ii) in a case where the shares of that class are voting shares, carry not less than nine-tenths of the voting rights carried by the shares of that class,

the holder of any shares of that class to which the offer relates who has not accepted the offer may require the offeror to acquire those shares.

(5) For the purposes of sub-paragraphs (2), (3) and (4), in calculating nine-tenths of the value of all the shares in the company, or all the shares of any class or classes of shares of the company, any shares held by the company as treasury shares shall be treated as having been acquired by the offeror.

(6) Rights conferred on the holder of shares by sub-paragraph (2), (3) or (4) are exercisable by a written communication addressed to the offeror.

(7) Rights conferred on the holder of shares by sub-paragraph (2), (3) or (4) are not exercisable after the end of the period of three months from—
   (a) the end of the period within which the offer can be accepted; or
   (b) if later, the date of the notice that must be given under sub-paragraph (8).

(8) Within one month of the time specified in sub-paragraph (2), (3) or (4), as the case may be, the offeror shall give any shareholder who has not accepted the offer notice in the manner prescribed by regulation 4 of the Companies (Forms) Regulations 1985 for the purposes of section 430A(3) of the Companies Act 1985, (or in the case of Northern Ireland by regulation 4 of the Companies (Forms) Regulations (Northern Ireland) 1986 for the purposes of Article 423A(3) of the Companies (Northern Ireland) Order 1986), of—
   (a) the rights that are exercisable by the shareholder under that sub-paragraph, and
   (b) the period within which the rights are exercisable,

and if the notice is given before the end of the period within which the offer can be accepted, it shall state that the offer is still open for acceptance.

(9) Sub-paragraph (10) applies where—
   (a) a shareholder exercises rights conferred on him by sub-paragraph (2), (3) or (4);
   (b) at the time when he does so, there are shares in the company which the offeror has contracted to acquire subject to conditions being met, and in relation to which the contract has not become unconditional; and
   (c) the requirement imposed by paragraph (b) of sub-paragraph (2), (3) or (4) (as the case may be) would not be satisfied if those shares were not taken into account.

(10) The shareholder shall be treated for the purposes of paragraph 5 as not having exercised his rights under this paragraph unless the requirement imposed by paragraph (b) of sub-paragraph (2), (3) or (4) (as the case may be) would be satisfied if—
   (a) the reference in paragraph (b) of that sub-paragraph to other shares in the company which the offeror has contracted to acquire unconditionally or subject to conditions being met were a reference to such shares which he has unconditionally contracted to acquire; and
   (b) the reference in that sub-paragraph to the period within which the offer can be accepted were a reference to the period referred to in sub-paragraph (7).

(11) Sub-paragraph (8) does not apply if the offeror has given the shareholder a notice in respect of the shares in question under paragraph 2.

(12) If the offeror fails to comply with sub-paragraph (8) he and, if the offeror is a company, every officer of the company who is in default or to whose neglect the failure is attributable, commits an offence.

(13) A person who commits an offence under sub-paragraph (12), but would have committed an offence under section 430A(6) of the Companies Act 1985 (or as the case may be, Article 423A(6) of the Companies (Northern Ireland) Order 1986) had that section (or Article) not been disapplied by regulation 30, is liable on conviction to the penalties in that section (or Article).

(14) In all other cases a person who commits an offence under sub-paragraph (12) is liable—
   (a) on conviction on indictment, to a fine;
   (b) on summary conviction, to a fine not exceeding the statutory maximum;
   (c) for continued contravention, to a daily default fine not exceeding £100.

(15) If an offeror other than a company is charged with an offence for failing to comply with sub-paragraph (8) it is a defence for him to prove that he took all reasonable steps for securing compliance with that sub-paragraph.

5. Effect of requirement under paragraph 4

(1) The following provisions shall, subject to paragraph 6, have effect where a shareholder exercises his rights in respect of any shares under paragraph 4.

(2) The offeror shall be entitled and bound to acquire those shares on the terms of the offer or on such other terms as may be agreed.

(3) Where the terms of an offer are such as to give the holder of shares a choice of consideration the holder of the shares may indicate his choice when requiring the offeror to acquire them and the notice given to the holder under paragraph 4(8)—

(a) shall give particulars of the choice and of the rights conferred by this sub-paragraph, and

(b) may state which consideration specified in the offer is to be taken as applying in default of his indicating a choice,

and the terms of the offer mentioned in sub-paragraph (2) shall be determined accordingly.

(4) Sub-paragraph (3) applies whether or not any time-limit or other conditions applicable to the choice under the terms of the offer can still be complied with.

(5) If the consideration offered to or (as the case may be) chosen by the holder of the shares—

(a) is not cash and the offeror is no longer able to provide it, or

(b) was to have been provided by a third party who is no longer bound or able to provide it,

the consideration shall be taken to consist of an amount of cash payable by the offeror which at the date when the holder of the shares requires the offeror to acquire them is equivalent to the consideration offered or (as the case may be) chosen.

6. Applications to the court

(1) Where a notice is given under paragraph 2 to the holder of any shares the court may, on an application made by him within six weeks from the date on which the notice was given—

(a) order that the offeror shall not be entitled and bound to acquire the shares; or

(b) specify terms of acquisition different from those of the offer.

(2) If an application to the court under sub-paragraph (1) is pending at the end of the period mentioned in sub-paragraph (6) of paragraph 3 that sub-paragraph shall not have effect until the application has been disposed of.

(3) Where the holder of any shares exercises his rights under paragraph 4 the court may, on an application made by him or the offeror, order that the terms on which the offeror is entitled and bound to acquire the shares shall be such as the court thinks fit.

(4) On an application under sub-paragraph (1) or (3)—

(a) the court shall not require consideration of a higher value than that specified in the terms of the offer ('the offer value') to be given for the shares to which the application relates unless the holder of the shares shows that the offer value would be unfair;

(b) the court shall not require consideration of a lower value than the offer value to be given for the shares.

(5) No order for costs or expenses shall be made against a shareholder making an application under sub-paragraph (1) or (3) unless the court considers—

(a) that the application was unnecessary, improper or vexatious; or

(b) that there has been unreasonable delay in making the application or unreasonable conduct on his part in conducting the proceedings on the application.

(6) Where a takeover offer has not been accepted to the extent necessary for entitling the offeror to give notices under sub-paragraph (2) or (4) of paragraph 2 the court may, on the application of the offeror, make an order authorising him to give notices under that sub-paragraph if satisfied—

(a) that the offeror has after reasonable enquiry been unable to trace one or more of the persons holding shares to which the offer relates,

(b) that the requirements of that sub-paragraph would have been met if the person, or all the persons, mentioned in paragraph (a) had accepted the offer, and

(c) that the consideration offered is fair and reasonable,

but the court shall not make an order under this sub-paragraph unless it considers that it is just and equitable to do so having regard, in particular, to the number of shareholders who have been traced but who have not accepted the offer.

7. Joint offers

(1) A takeover offer may be made by two or more persons jointly and in that event this Schedule has effect with the following modifications.

(2) The conditions for the exercise of the rights conferred by paragraph 2 shall be satisfied by the joint offerors acquiring or unconditionally contracting to acquire the necessary shares jointly (as respects acquisitions by virtue of acceptances of the offer) and either jointly or separately (in other cases).

(3) The conditions for the exercise of the rights conferred by paragraph 4 shall be satisfied—

(a) as respects acquisitions by virtue of acceptances of the offer, by the joint offerors acquiring or unconditionally contracting to acquire the necessary shares jointly;

(b) in other cases, by the joint offerors acquiring or contracting (whether conditionally or subject to conditions being met) to acquire the necessary shares either jointly or separately.

(4) Subject to the following provisions, the rights and obligations of the offeror under paragraphs 2 to 5 shall be respectively joint rights and joint and several obligations of the joint offerors.

(5) It shall be a sufficient compliance with any provision of paragraphs 2 to 6 requiring or authorising a notice or other document to be given or sent by or to the joint offerors that it is given or sent by or to any of them; but the statutory declaration required by paragraph 2(8) shall be made by all of them and, in the case of a joint offeror being a company, signed by a director of that company.

(6) In paragraphs 1, 3(9) and 8 references to the offeror shall be construed as references to the joint offerors or any of them.

(7) In paragraph 3(7) and (8) references to the offeror shall be construed as references to the joint offerors or such of them as they may determine.

(8) In paragraphs 3(5)(a) and 5(5)(a) references to the offeror being no longer able to provide the relevant consideration shall be construed as references to none of the joint offerors being able to do so.

(9) In paragraph 6 references to the offeror shall be construed as references to the joint offerors except that any application under sub-paragraph (3) or (6) may be made by any of them and the reference in sub-paragraph (6)(a) to the offeror having been unable to trace one or more of the persons holding shares shall be construed as a reference to none of the offerors having been able to do so.

8. Associates

(1) The requirement in paragraph 1(1) that a takeover offer must extend to all the shares, or all the shares of any class or classes, in a company shall be regarded as satisfied notwithstanding that the offer does not extend to shares which associates of the offeror hold or have contracted to acquire; but, subject to sub-paragraph (3), shares which any such associate holds or has contracted to acquire, whether at the date of the offer or subsequently, shall be disregarded for the purposes of any reference in this Schedule to the shares to which a takeover offer relates.

(2) In sub-paragraph (1) 'contracted' means contracted unconditionally or subject to conditions being met.

(3) Where during the period mentioned in paragraph 2(14) any associate of the offeror acquires or unconditionally contracts to acquire any of the shares to which the offer relates, then, if the condition specified in paragraph 2(15)(a) or (b) is satisfied as respects those shares they shall be treated for the purposes of that paragraph as shares to which the offer relates.

(4) A reference in paragraph 2(6) or paragraph 4(2)(b), (3)(b), (4)(b), (9) or (10) to shares which the offeror has acquired or contracted to acquire shall include a reference to shares which any associate of his has acquired or contracted to acquire.

(5) In this paragraph 'associate', in relation to an offeror, means—
   (a) a nominee of the offeror;
   (b) a holding company, subsidiary or fellow subsidiary of the offeror or a nominee of such a holding company, subsidiary or fellow subsidiary;
   (c) a body corporate in which the offeror is substantially interested; or
   (d) any person who is, or is a nominee of, a party to an agreement with the offeror for the acquisition of, or of an interest in, the shares which are the subject of the takeover offer, being an agreement which includes provisions imposing obligations or restrictions such as are mentioned in section 204(2)(a) of the Companies Act 1985 or as the case may be Article 212(2)(a) of the Companies (Northern Ireland) Order 1986.

(6) For the purposes of sub-paragraph (5)(b) a company is a fellow subsidiary of another body corporate if both are subsidiaries of the same body corporate but neither is a subsidiary of the other.

(7) For the purposes of sub-paragraph (5)(c) an offeror has a substantial interest in a body corporate if—
   (a) that body or its directors are accustomed to act in accordance with his directions or instructions; or
   (b) he is entitled to exercise or control the exercise of one-third or more of the voting power at general meetings of that body.

(8) Subsections (5) and (6) of section 204 of the Companies Act 1985 or as the case may be paragraphs (5) and (6) of Article 212 of the Companies (Northern Ireland) Order 1986 shall apply to sub-paragraph (5)(d) above as they apply to that section and Article and subsections (3) and (4) of section 203 of the Companies Act 1985 or as the case may be paragraphs (3) and (4) of Article 211 of the Companies (Northern Ireland) Order 1986 shall apply for the purposes of subparagraph (7) above as they apply for the purposes of subsection (2)(b) of that section and paragraph (2)(b) of that Article.

(9) Where the offeror is an individual his associates shall also include his spouse or civil partner and any minor child or step-child of his.

9. Convertible securities

(1) For the purposes of this Schedule securities of a company shall be treated as shares in the company if they are convertible into or entitle the holder to subscribe for such shares; and references to the holder of shares or a shareholder shall be construed accordingly.

(2) Sub-paragraph (1) shall not be construed as requiring any securities to be treated—
   (a) as shares of the same class as those into which they are convertible or for which the holder is entitled to subscribe; or
   (b) as shares of the same class as other securities by reason only that the shares into which they are convertible or for which the holder is entitled to subscribe are of the same class.

10. Debentures carrying voting rights

(1) For the purposes of this Schedule debentures issued by a company to which subparagraph (2) applies shall be treated as shares in the company if they carry voting rights.

(2) This sub-paragraph applies to a company that has voting shares, or debentures carrying voting rights, which are admitted to trading on a regulated market.

(3) In this Schedule, in relation to debentures treated as shares by virtue of sub-paragraph (1)—
   (a) references to the holder of shares or a shareholder shall be construed accordingly;
   (b) references to shares being allotted shall be construed as references to debentures being issued.

11. Interpretation

(1) In this Schedule—
'the company' means the company whose shares are the subject of the offer;
'date of the offer' means—
   (a) the date of publication; or

(b) where any notices of the offer are given before the date of publication, the date when notices of the offer (or the first such notices) are given;

'non-voting shares' means shares that are not voting shares;

'the offeror' means, subject to paragraph 7, the person making a takeover offer.

(2) For the purposes of this Schedule a person contracts unconditionally to acquire shares if his entitlement under the contract to acquire them is not (or is no longer) subject to conditions or if all conditions to which it was subject have been met.

A reference to a contract becoming unconditional is to be construed accordingly.

Glossary

ABI Guidelines	See **14.5.7**
accounting reference date	The date on which the financial year of a company ends
Admission and Disclosure Standards	Rules made by the Stock Exchange in relation to admission to trading and disclosure of information (see **2.9**)
AGM	An Annual General Meeting of shareholders and directors held pursuant to s 306 of the CA 1985
AIM	The Alternative Investment Market of the London Stock Exchange: a global market for smaller and growing companies
AIM Rules	Rules published by the Stock Exchange
analyst	Person employed by an investment bank or stockbroking firm to study a company or sector's performance
analyst's report	Report produced by an analyst, rating a company's share as a buy, sell or hold. Often the report will coincide with the release of the company's results, and can influence the decision of investors as to whether to buy or sell shares in that company
audit committee	A committee of the board of directors, concerned with matters relating to the company's accounts and auditing (see **8.3.5.3**)
Authorisation Manual	A manual published by the FSA, which forms part of the FSA Handbook of Rules and Guidance, and which gives guidance about authorisation under the FSMA 2000
bonus issue	See capitalisation of reserves
bookbuilding	See **4.4.2.1**
Cadbury Report	The 1992 report of the Committee on the Financial Aspects of Corporate Governance under the chairmanship of Sir Adrian Cadbury (see **8.3.2.1**)
call option	See options
capitalisation of reserves	An issue of securities, credited as fully paid, out of the issuer's reserves, to existing shareholders in proportion to their existing shareholdings (also known as a 'bonus' or 'scrip' issue) (see **13.5.5**)
certificate of approval	See **6.11**
Code of Market Conduct	A code produced by the FSA, pursuant to s 119 of the FSMA 2000, to assist on the question whether particular behaviour is market abuse (see **10.1.2**). Forms part of the FSA Handbook of Rules and Guidance
Conduct of Business Sourcebook	An FSA sourcebook which forms part of the FSA Handbook
Combined Code	The Combined Code on Corporate Governance (Financial Reporting Council, July 2003) (see **8.3**)
Companies Bill	Formerly the Company Law Reform Bill, the Bill which replaces and restates the majority of existing companies legislation, and which was passed in the House of Lords on 23 May 2006

continuing obligations	Obligations set out in the Prospectus Rules, the Listing Rules and the Disclosure Rules to which a company becomes subject when its securities are admitted to the Official List (see **Chapter 7**)
Continuing Obligations Guide	The UKLA's guide to the continuing obligations regime (set out at Appendix 3 of the UKLA Guidance Manual)
contract for differences	See **21.8.11.5**
CREST	The electronic settlement system for uncertificated securities trading (see **2.5.3.1**)
CRESTCo Limited	The operator of CREST
dematerialisation	The process of replacing paper share certificates and stock transfer forms with an electronic system (see **2.10.2**)
derivative	A financial instrument whose value depends on the performance of an underlying asset or security. Examples include futures, options and swaps (see **21.8.11.5**)
Disclosure Rules	Rules published by the FSA relating to the disclosure of inside information and transactions by PDMRs and their connected persons
EEA	European Economic Area, a trading area comprising the Member States and the EFTA States
EFTA States	Iceland, Liechtenstein and Norway
EFTA	European Free Trade Association: a free trade area established in 1960. Its current members are the three EFTA States and Switzerland
equity shares	As defined in the CA 1985 and the Listing Rules, shares comprised in a company's equity share capital, that is, the issued share capital excluding any part of that capital which, neither as respects dividends nor as respects capital, carries any right to participate beyond a specified amount in a distribution
European Union (EU)	An economic and political union of European Member States created on 1 November 1993 by the Treaty on European Union (the 'Maastricht Treaty')
Financial Reporting Council	An independent regulator which has responsibility for accounting standards in the UK and promotes high standards of corporate governance
financial year	The period for which a company must prepare statutory accounts pursuant to the CA 1985
FSA Handbook of Rules and Guidance	A handbook published by the FSA, and updated monthly, of the rules and guidance issued by the FSA under the FSMA 2000, including the Authorisation Manual and the Code of Market Conduct
FTSE 100	A Stock Exchange index of the largest (by market capitalisation) 100 companies admitted to trading on the Stock Exchange
gearing	The ratio of a company's debt to its equity (see **18.9.1**)
Greenbury Report	The 1995 report of the Committee on Directors' Remuneration under the chairmanship of Sir Richard Greenbury (see **8.3.2.1**)
Hampel Report	The 1998 report of the Committee on Corporate Governance under the chairmanship of Sir Ronald Hampel (see **8.3.2.1**)
Higgs Review	The 2003 review of the role and effectiveness of non-executive directors made by Derek Higgs
International Accounting Standards	Accounting standards adopted for use in the EU in accordance with art 3 of the IAS Regulation (EC) No 1606/2001

IPCs	Investment Protection Committees (representative bodies of major institutional investors)
IPO	Initial public offering, also known as flotation. This refers to the company's first offer of shares in a public market
ISC	Institutional Shareholders' Committee, a committee which represents the interests of the main institutional investors
leverage	The opportunity to create profit by financing a business through debt which is entitled to only a finite return (see **18.2.2**)
liquidity	The ease with which a security can be traded on a market
listing particulars	A selling document published, in terms acceptable to the FSA, as a condition of admission of certain specialist securities to listing (see **Chapter 6**)
Listing Rules	Rules published by the FSA, relating to the admission of securities to listing on the Official List and the continuing obligations of listed companies
lock-up	See **21.10**
long form articles	See **1.9.3.1**
member firms	See **2.5.1**
Main Market	The Stock Exchange's principal market for listed securities
market capitalisation	See **13.3.6**
market-makers	A member of the Stock Exchange offering the market a two-way price (ie, buying and selling) in particular securities (see **2.5.2**)
Member States	The 25 Member States of the European Union, namely Austria, Belgium, Cyprus, Czech Republic, Denmark, Estonia, Finland, France, Germany, Greece, Hungary, Ireland, Italy, Latvia, Lithuania, Luxembourg, Malta, the Netherlands, Poland, Portugal, Slovak Republic, Slovenia, Spain, Sweden and the UK
mini-prospectus	See **6.9.2**
Model Code	A code regulating dealings by directors and certain others in the shares of their own companies. Listed companies must comply with this code or some other no less exacting in its terms (see **7.6**)
NASDAQ	National Association of Securities Dealers Automated Quotation, a stock market based in the US
new regime	The listed company regime under the Prospectus Rules, the Listing Rules and the Disclosure Rules
nomad	The nominated adviser of an AIM Company (see **24.4.1**)
OFEX	A secondary market for the trading of unlisted securities in the UK, off exchange
offer period	See **22.3.4**
Official List	The list of securities which have been admitted to listing, maintained by the FSA under s 74(1) of the FSMA 2000 (see **3.3**)
Old Listing Rules	The Listing Rules in force before 1 July 2005 (which have now been replaced by the Prospectus Rules, the Listing Rules and the Disclosure Rules)
old regime	The listed company regime under the Old Listing Rules
options	The right to buy (a 'call option') or sell (a 'put option') securities at a fixed price within a particular time-frame (see **15.6.3.2**)

PAL	Provisional allotment letter, which is a negotiable document issued by a company which notifies the recipient that securities have been allotted to him on a provisional basis (see **17.7.3.1**)
Perimeter Guidance Manual	A regulatory guide introduced on 1 July 2005, which does not form part of the FSA Handbook
Part 6 rules	The Disclosure Rules, the Listing Rules and the Prospectus Rules
PDMR	See **7.4.1**
person discharging managerial responsibility	See **7.4.1**
poison pills	See **22.4.9**
Practice Statements	Informal guidance issued by the Panel Executive (see **20.5.6.1**)
Pre-emption Guidelines	See **14.6.16**
price-sensitive information	See **7.4.2.3**
Primary Information Provider	See **7.4.2.2**
private equity house	See venture capital company
Professional Securities Market	The Stock Exchange's new market for listing debt, convertibles and depositary receipts
profit forecast	See **22.4.5.1**
prospectus	A selling document, published in terms acceptable to the FSA. See **Chapter 6**
Prospectus Rules	Rules published by the FSA setting out the form, content and approval requirements for a prospectus
put option	See options
QCA	The Quoted Companies Alliance (formerly known as CISCO), an alliance established to protect the interests of the smaller quoted company (that is, outside the FTSE 350)
QCA Guidelines	The corporate governance guidelines for AIM published in July 2005 by the Quoted Companies Alliance (see **24.7**)
Regulatory Information Service	See **7.4.2.1**
remuneration committee	A committee of the board of directors with responsibility primarily for determining or recommending the remuneration of the executive directors (see **8.3.5.2**)
responsibility statement	See **6.5.2.1** and **22.4.5.2**
rights issue	An issue to existing holders of securities of rights to subscribe or purchase further securities pro rata their existing holdings made by means of the issue of a PAL or other negotiable document (see **17.7**)
rump	Those shares not taken up by the shareholders on a rights issue which it is sought to place in the market (see **17.7.5**)

SARs	The Rules Governing Substantial Acquisitions of Shares, being rules administered by the Panel which regulate the speed and secrecy with which a person can build a stake in a listed company
scrip issue	See capitalisation of reserves
SEAQ	The Stock Exchange Automated Quotations System, a computer screen system enabling Stock Exchange members to advertise share prices (see **2.5.2**)
Secondary Information Provider	See **7.4.2.2**
settlement	See **2.5.3**
SETS	The Stock Exchange Electronic Trading System, an order-driven electronic trading system for FT-SE 100 securities (see **2.5.2**)
short form articles	See **1.9.3.1**
Smith Report	The report of an independent group, chaired by Sir Robert Smith, to clarify the role and responsibility of audit committees (see **8.3.2.2**)
Societas Europaea	A European public limited liability company, which must be registered in a Member State with a share capital of at least €120,000. The legal framework for this new form of company is set out in the European Public Limited-Liability Company Regulations 2004 (SI 2004/2326)
sponsor	A person approved by the FSA to sponsor an application for listing of securities and to assist the issuer in fulfilling its continuing obligations
stamp duty reserve tax	A tax introduced by the Finance Act 1986 to cover paperless share transactions (which fall outside the ambit of stamp duty)
stick	Those shares not taken up by shareholders on a rights issue, nor subsequently placed in the market, and which, therefore, fall to the underwriters or sub-underwriters (see **17.7.5**)
Stock Exchange	The London Stock Exchange plc
sub-underwriter	A person to whom the underwriters have laid off some or all of the underwriting risk on a marketing of securities
Turnbull Report	Guidance, published by the Institute of Chartered Accountants of England and Wales, for directors of listed companies regarding internal controls (see **8.3.2.1**)
UKLA	The FSA acting in its capacity as the competent authority for the purposes of Pt VI of the FSMA 2000
UKLA Guidance Manual	A manual which used to be published by the UKLA, incorporating guidance in respect of the powers and procedures contained in FSMA 2000, including the PSI Guide and the Continuing Obligations Guide. As of 1 July 2005, the UKLA has included more guidance alongside the Listing Rules and so no longer publishes a separate Guidance Manual
underwriter	In insurance terms, a person who takes on an insurance risk; in terms of the marketing of securities, a person who agrees to take up shares not purchased or subscribed for
venture capital company	A company which specialises in investing, typically, in unlisted, high risk businesses. The venture capital company helps to develop the business, often with a view to listing, with the aim of achieving significant return on its investment

Bibliography

The Prospectus Rules, the Listing Rules and the Disclosure Rules (Financial Services Authority)

The Takeover Code (The Panel on Takeovers and Mergers)

Practical Law Company (online articles)

Brett, *How to Read the Financial Pages* (Century, 1995)

Tolley's *Company Law Service* (online)

Butterworth's *Corporate Law Direct* (online)

Butterworth's *Company Law Handbook*

Index

ABI Guidelines 243
    authority to allot 179
    issue of shares 171, 174, 179-80, 222
    text 399-400
abuse of market *see* **market abuse**
accountants 291-2
    reporting accountant 28-9
accounting date
    disclosure of change 94
accounts 5, 154
acquisition issue
    advantages 242
    definition 240
    disadvantages 242
    documentation 242
    prospectus 242
    sale and purchase agreement 242
    share-for-share exchange 240
    structure 241
    see also **vendor consideration placing**
acquisitions and disposals
    by agents 198
    circular 268-70
        Class 1 transactions 269-70
        content 269
        lodgement with FSA 268
        non-routine 268
        related party 270
        routine 268
        sponsor's role 269-70
        verification 270
    Class 1 transactions 259-60
        circular 269-70
        circular waiver 259
        percentage ratios 259
        shareholder approval waiver 259
        specific transactions 260
        sponsor's role 259-60
        takeover offer 325
    Class 2 transactions 258-9
    Class 3 transactions 258
    classification of transactions 255-62
        Class 1 259-60, 269-70, 325
        class tests 256-7
        percentage ratios 256, 258, 259, 260-1
        reverse takeover 260-2
    consideration 253, 254
    continuing obligations 254
    contractual protection 253-4
    disclosure of interests in shares 198, 254
    due diligence 253
    finance 253
    financial promotion 255
    financial regulation 255
    insider dealing 254-5
    listed companies 7-8
    Listing Rules 255-6

acquisitions and disposals – *continued*
    market abuse 254-5
    market manipulation 254-5
    misleading statements 254-5
    Model Code 255
    regulated activities 255
    related party transactions 262-8
        articles of association 268
        associate 263, 264-5
        CA 1985 267-8
        Chapter 11 requirements 265-6
        circular 270
        definition 263
        director 263-4
        exceptions 266-7
        joint venture partner 263, 264
        memorandum of association 268
        related parties 263-4
        relaxation of rules 267
        shadow director 263-4
        sponsor's role 267
        substantial shareholder 263
    reverse takeover 260-2
        sponsor's role 262
    timetable 270-1
    see also **takeovers**
acting in concert
    agreement 199
    disclosure of interests in shares 199-200
    failed offer 338
    irrevocable undertakings 306
    takeovers 338
Admission and Disclosure Standards 19
    continuing obligations 104
    sanctions for breach 105
    text 371-5
admission to listing
    primary issue *see* **flotation**
    secondary issue of shares 223-4
admission to trading
    Listing Rules continuing obligation 91
    regulatory requirements 34
    secondary issue of shares 223-4
    see also **Stock Exchange**
advertisements
    listing application and 53
advisers to flotation
    appointment 27-31
    broker 28
    company 28
    directors 28
    financial adviser 28
    financial public relations consultants 30-1
    lawyers 29-30
    printers 31
    receiving bank 30

442 Public Companies and Equity Finance

advisers to flotation – *continued*
   registrars 30
   reporting accountants 28-9
   sponsor 28, 31
   underwriters 30
advisers to takeover
   accountants 291-2
   financial advisers 290-1
   financial public relations consultants 292
   lawyers 291
   printers 292
   receiving bankers 292
   registrars 292
   stockbrokers 291
agents
   acquisitions and disposals by 198
Alternative Investment Market (AIM) 3, 15, 16
   accounts 362
   admission document 363-4
      content requirements 364
      responsibility for 364
   AIM Rules 361
   broker 363
   continuing obligations
      financial information 367
      share dealing code 367
      see also disclosure
   corporate governance 367
   disclosure
      disposals 366-7
      fundamental change in business 366-7
      general obligation 365
      related party transactions 366
      reverse takeover 366
      special obligations 365-6
      substantial transactions 365-6
   electronic settlement 362
   eligibility criteria 362-3
   future developments 367-8
   incorporation 362
   investors 18
   marketing document 363-4
   member firms 16
   nominated adviser (nomad) 362, 363
   prospectus 363-4
      content requirements 364
      exemptions 364
      responsibility for 364
   reasons for 362
   regulation by Stock Exchange 361
   settlement 17-18
   trading 16-18
   transferability 362
annual information update 102-3
annual report 112
   financial promotion exemption 154
articles of association 10
   debt to equity ratio 248
   raising equity finance 248
   related party transactions 268
   variation of class rights 167-8
associate 263, 264-5

audit committee 117-18
auditors
   in prospectus 67
authorised share capital 10, 160
   checking filings 173-4
   increasing 174
      forms 379-82
   issue of shares 172-5
   Listing Rules 175
   locating filings at Companies House 173

bibliography 439
bidder 290
board of directors 40
   accountability 117-18
   audit 117-18
   chairman 114-15
   changes to 94
   Chief Executive 114-15
   Combined Code 113-14
   disclosure of members 94
bonus shares 166
   pre-emption rights 183
bookbuilding 37
break fee letter 310-11
broker 28

Cadbury Report 108
capital
   debt finance 246
   equity finance 246
   shares *see* **share capital**
capital growth
   debt finance 246
   equity finance 246
capital redemption reserve 166
censure 77, 104, 105
certificate of incorporation 10
   re-registration of company 12-13
circulars 100-2
   acquisitions and disposals
      Class 1 269-70
      content 269
      lodgement with FSA 268
      non-routine 268
      related party 270
      routine 268
      sponsor's role 269-70
      verification 270
   equity finance 227
   FSA approval 101-2
   general content requirement 101
   non-routine nature 268
   routine nature 268
   when required 101
City Code 284
   application of 208, 277-8
   consideration 329
   control 278
   Dealing Disclosure Forms 209
   disclosure of dealings 209
   disclosure of interests in shares 194, 208-11

City Code – *continued*
    issued shares 208-9
    obligation 208-9
    enforcement 281-3
        by court 282
        by FSA 282
        by Panel 281-2, 284
        compensation rulings 281
        compliance rulings 281
        disciplinary powers 282-3
        monitoring powers 281
    general principles 279-80
    information provision 326-9
    merger control 347-8
    nature of 208, 279
    in practice 280-1
    Practice Statements 281
    purpose 278-9
    secrecy requirement 288-9
    stakebuilding 297-303
    to whom applicable 278
Class 1 transactions
    acquisitions and disposals 259-60
    circulars 101, 269-70
    communication with shareholders 101, 269-70
    takeovers 325
Class 2 transactions
    acquisitions and disposals 258-9
Class 3 transactions
    acquisitions and disposals 258
classification of transactions
    acquisitions and disposals 255-62
    Class 1 101, 259-60, 269-70, 325
    Class 2 258-9
    Class 3 258
    class tests 256-7
    percentage ratios 256, 258, 259, 260-1
    reverse takeover 260-2
clearance (merger control) 356
    as condition of takeover 331, 347
    notification 355-6
    pre-notification by Merger Notice 356
    written submission 355
close period, dealings during 97, 99
Code of Market Conduct 129-30, 132
Combined Code on Corporate Governance
    annual report 112
    background 107, 108, 110
    compliance 108, 112-13
    directors' remuneration 112
    disclosure statement 112
    institutional investors 112, 113-16
    institutional shareholders 112, 119-20
    listed companies 111-12
    nature 107
    structure 110-11
    text 383-97
comfort letters 29
communication with shareholders
    circulars *see* **circulars**
    Class 1 transactions 101, 269-70

communication with shareholders – *continued*
    continuing obligation 100-2
    prescribed information 101
companies
    listed *see* **listed company**
    public *see* **public company**
    quoted 4
Companies Bill 13-14
    issue of shares 192
    shares 170
Companies House
    checking filings 173-4
    disapplication of pre-emption rights 187
    ensuring filings up to date 173-4
    increasing share capital notification 173-4, 379-82
    issue of shares
        filing details 191
        resolution 178
    locating filings 173
competition *see* **merger control**
Competition Commission 347, 351, 353, 354, 355
    see also **UK merger control**
completion meetings
    board meeting 47-8
    EGM 47
concert parties
    agreement 199
    disclosure of interests in shares 199-200
    failed offer 338
    irrevocable undertakings 306
    takeovers 338
confidentiality agreement 310
connected persons 96, 97-8
consideration
    acquisitions and disposals 253, 254
    cash 182, 295, 300-1
    issue of shares 190
        at discount 191
        non-cash 191
    non-cash 191
    paper 302
    stakebuilding 299-302
    takeovers 283, 295, 299-302, 329, 330
continuing obligations
    acquisitions and disposals 254
    Admission and Disclosure Standards 104
        sanctions for breach 105
    admission to trading 91, 104
    AIM
        disclosure 365-7
        financial information 367
        share dealing code 367
    changes to board 94
    communication with shareholders *see* **communication with shareholders**
    dealings *see* **dealings by director**
    Disclosure Rules 84-90
        breach of general obligation 89
        fulfilling the obligation 85-9
        general obligation 84-5

444 Public Companies and Equity Finance

continuing obligations – *continued*
   information gathering 89
   insider lists 90
   misleading information 90
   notification to RIS 90
   persons discharging managerial
     responsibilities 90, 204-6
   sanctions for breach 104
   see also **disclosure**
  equal treatment 91-2
  listed company 9, 83-105
  Listing Rules 90-5
   documents requiring prior approval 92
   financial information 95
   notifications 93-5
   requirements with obligations 91
   sanctions for breach 104
   shareholders 91-2
   transactions 93
  Model Code 95-100
   applicability 96-8
   clearance to deal 98-100
   prohibited dealings 98
   purpose of code 96
   sanctions for breach 100
  pre-emption rights 92
  Primary Information Provider 85
  Prospectus Rules 102-3
   sanctions for breach 104
  reasons for 83-4
  Regulatory Information Service 85, 90
  shares in public hands 91
  Stock Exchange 104
convertible preference shares 176-7, 183
convertible securities
  pre-emption rights 233
convertible shares 166
corporate governance
  AIM 367
  annual corporate governance statement
   121
  associated guidance 111
  Cadbury Report 108
  Combined Code *see* **Combined Code on
   Corporate Governance**
  compliance requirement 40
  disclosure requirements 40
  future 120-1
  Greenbury Report 108
  Hampel Report 108
  Higgs Report 108, 114
   good practice suggestions 111, 116-17
  listed company 40
  meaning 107
  shareholders' rights 121
  Smith Guidance on Audit Committees
   111
  Smith Report 108
  Turnbull Guidance 111
  Turnbull Report 108
  UK framework 107
corporate lawyers
  CREST and 17-18

creditors 153
CREST
  corporate lawyers and 17-18
  member 17
  nominee shareholder 17
  personal member 17
  sponsored member 17
CRESTCo Ltd 17
criminal offences
  disclosure breaches 89
  prospectus 76-7

Dealing Disclosure Forms 209
dealings, disclosure of 209
dealings by director
  clearance
   person able to give 98
   procedure 98-9
   refusal 99-100
  close period 97, 99
  connected persons 96, 97-8
  exceptional circumstances 100
  inside information 97, 99
  insider dealing *see* **insider dealing**
  market abuse provisions 95, 97
   see also **market abuse**
  Model Code 95-100
  price-sensitive information 97
  prohibited 98
  related party transactions 101
  share option prohibition 96
  short-term considerations 96, 99-100
debt finance
  capital 246
  capital growth 246
  equity finance compared 245-9
  gearing 248
  income 245-6
  investors 247
  leverage 246
  rights of lender 247
  takeover consideration 295
  taxation 246
dematerialisation 20
derivatives
  takeovers 302
Deutsche Börse 3, 19
directors 5
  board 40, 94, 113-14
  Chairman 114-15
  changes to board 94
  Chief Executive 114-15
  Combined Code 112, 113-16
  continuing obligations 94
  corporate governance *see* **Combined
   Code on Corporate Governance**;
   corporate governance
  dealings
   clearance, refusal 99-100
   connected persons 96, 97-8
   during close period 97, 99
   exceptional circumstances 100
   inside information 97, 99

directors – *continued*
   insider dealing *see* **insider dealing**
   market abuse provisions 95, 97
   Model Code 95-100
     price-sensitive information 97
     prohibited 98
     related party transactions 101
     share option prohibition 96
     short-term considerations 96, 99-100
   disclosure of interests in shares 194-5
   flotation 28
   issue of shares 190
   non-executive 113-14, 115-16
   related party transactions 101, 263-4
   remuneration 112, 116-17
     Regulations 2002 118-19
     report 119
     shareholder approval 119
   shareholders and 118
   see also **board of directors**
disclosure
   accounting date change 94
   acquisitions and disposals and 254
   adverse consequences for company 87-8
   AIM 365-7
   amendments to constitution 91
   annual information update 102-3
   board members 94
   breach of general obligation 89
   capital structure 93
   civil offences 89
   Combined Code 112
   contact details 91
   continuing obligation 9, 84-90, 254, 365-7
   copies of documents 93
   criminal offences 89
   dealings 209
   delaying 87
   Disclosure Rules 84-90
   dispensation 88
   financial information 95
   fulfilling the obligation 85-9
   future developments 105
   general obligation 84-5
   information gathering 89
   inside information 99, 142
     financial instrument 86, 99
     not generally available 85, 86
     precise nature 85, 86
     significant effect on price 86-7
   insider lists 90
   interests in shares *see* **disclosure of interests in shares**
   Listing Rules 90-5
   lock-up arrangements 94
   major interests in shares 93
   misleading information 90
   name change 94
   persons discharging managerial responsibilities 90, 204-6
   price-sensitive information 86-7
   Primary Information Provider 85

disclosure – *continued*
   Prospectus Rules 102-3
   publishing information 89
   reasonable investor test 86
   Regulatory Information Service 85, 90
     when not open 94-5
   share capital 93
   shareholder resolutions 94
   shares in public hands 91
   as soon as possible 88-9, 93
   stakebuilding 297
   to advisers 87
   to negotiators 87
   Transparency Directive 14, 105
   'without delay' 88-9
disclosure of interests in shares
   acquisitions and disposals and 254
   agents 198
   attributed interests 198
   beneficial ownership 193-4, 195
     company investigation 201-2
     DTI investigation 203
   CA 1985 194-203
   City Code 194, 208-11
   concert parties 199-200
   content of notification 197-8
   criminal penalties 200
   Dealing Disclosure Forms 209
   directors 194-5
   Disclosure Rules 194, 203-6
   knowledge requirement 195, 198-200
   Listing Rules 194, 206-7, 211
   mandatory disclosures 196-7
   nominee shareholders 193
   non-notifiable interest 196
   non-statutory requirements *see* City Code; Listing Rules; Substantial Acquisition Rules
   notifiable interest 196
   percentage level 196-7
   pre-conditions 195
   register of members 193-4
   register of share interests 203
   restrictions on shares 200-1
   sanctions for breach 200-1
   shareholders 193-4, 195-203
   Substantial Acquisition Rules 194, 208
   when obligation arises 196
Disclosure Rules 8-9, 21, 25
   compliance of Listing Rules with 91
   continuing obligations 84-90
     sanctions for breach 104
   interests in shares 194, 203-6
   sanctions for breach 25-6
   see also **disclosure**
discount
   issue of shares at 191
disposals *see* **acquisitions and disposals**
distortion of market 133
   abusive squeeze 132
   price positioning 132, 133
dividends
   cumulative right to 164

dividends – *continued*
    preferential 163-4
    on winding up 164
documentation
    equity finance
        circulars 227
        PAL 229, 236
        placing agreement 227, 240, 243
        press announcement 226, 236, 239, 240, 242, 243
        prospectus 224-6, 236, 239, 240, 242, 243
        RIS notification 226
        sale and purchase agreement 227, 242, 243
        underwriting agreement 227, 231, 236, 239, 240, 243
    flotation
        '10 day' documents 52
        '48 hour' documents 52
        advertisements 53
        drafting 46-7
        list of documents 43-4, 46-7
        listing particulars *see* **listing particulars**
        lodged after admission day 53
        lodged on day of application hearing 52
        printers 31
        prospectus *see* **prospectus**
        responsibility for accuracy 30
        submission to FSA 51-3
        submission to Stock Exchange 53-4
        verification 49-51
    Stock Exchange
        application for admission to trading 53
        fee payable on application hearing 54
        information lodged on admission day 54
        submission to 53-4
        'two day' documents 53
DTI *see* **Secretary of State for Trade and Industry**
due diligence
    acquisitions and disposals 253
    business 48
    financial 48
    flotation 48-9
    hostile offer 294
    legal 48-9
    meaning 292
    process 293-4
    publicly available information 294-5
    purpose 293
    recommended offer 293
    requirement for 292
    takeovers 292-5
    verification 49-51

employee insiders 97
employee offering 38
employee share schemes 154
    approved company share option plan 170

employee share schemes – *continued*
    approved savings-related share option plan 169
    enterprise management incentives 170
    pre-emption rights 183
    share incentive plan 170
employees
    in prospectus 69
enterprise management incentives 170
equal treatment of shareholders 91-2
equity finance
    acquisition issue *see* **acquisition issue**
    articles of association 248
    capital 246
    capital growth 246
    circulars 227
    debt finance compared 166-7, 245-9
    flotation *see* **flotation**
    gearing 248
    income 245
    investors 247
    issue of shares 222-3
    meaning 221-2
    need for 222
    open offer *see* **open offer**
    PAL 229, 236
    placing *see* **placing**
    placing agreement 227, 240, 243
    press announcement 226, 236, 239, 240, 242, 243
    prospectus 224-6, 236, 239, 240, 242, 243
    rights and 247
    rights issue *see* **rights issue**
    RIS notification 226
    sale and purchase agreement 227, 242, 243
    shares *see* **shares**
    takeover consideration 295
    taxation 246
    underwriting agreement 227, 231, 236, 239, 240, 243
    underwriting rights issue 230-1
    vendor consideration placing *see* **vendor consideration placing**
European merger control 347, 348-51
    Community dimension 349
    concentration 348-9
    exceptions 350-1
    notification before completion 349-50
    one-stop shop 350
    period of investigation 350
    Phase I 350
    Phase II 350
    turnover criteria 349
    two-thirds rule 349
    UK regime and 357-8
European Union Action Plans
    company law and corporate governance 219
    financial services 120
exclusivity agreement
    takeovers 310

finance
    see also debt finance; equity finance
financial advisers
    to flotation 28
    to takeover 290-1
financial assistance 6
    'commonsense' exceptions 217
    criminal sanctions 219
    definition 215
    employee exception 218
    example 215-16
    exceptions to prohibition
        'commonsense' 217
        employees 218
        money lending 218
        purpose 216-17
    future developments 219
    given after acquisition 214-15
    given before or at same time as acquisition 214
    issue of shares 191
    money lending exception 218
    purpose exception 216-17
        Brady v Brady 217
        larger purpose 217
        principal purpose 217
    rationale for prohibition 213-14
    sanctions 219
    void and unenforceable acquisitions 219
    whitewash 6, 218
financial information
    annual report and accounts 95
    disclosure of 95
    interim reports 95
    preliminary statement 95
    takeovers 326-9
financial promotion
    acquisitions and disposals 255
    annual report and accounts 154
    application for listing exemption 154
    certified high net worth individuals 154-5
    communication 151-2
    consequences of breach 148
    course of business 151
    creditors 153
    employee share schemes 154
    engaging in investment activity 152
    exemptions 152-5
    flowchart 149
    FSMA 2000 147-55
    group companies 154
    high net worth companies 154-5
    inducement 152
    invitation 152
    meaning 148
    non real time communications 153
    'person' 151
    professional investors 154-5
    prospectus 154
    purpose of restriction 151
    real time communications 153
    regulatory framework 123
    relevance in practice 148-9

financial promotion – *continued*
    sale of body corporate 154
    shareholders 153
    solicited communications 153
    sophisticated investors 154-5
    territorial scope 152
    unsolicited communications 153
financial public relations consultants
    advisers to flotation 30-1
    advisers to takeover 292
financial services
    appointed representative 125
    authorised person 124, 125, 148
    Code of Market Conduct 129-30, 132
    exempt person 124, 125
    financial crime reduction 123
    financial promotion regulatory framework 123
    FSMA 2000 123-7
    general prohibition 123, 124-5
    market abuse *see* **market abuse**
    market confidence 123
    market manipulation 123, 127
    misleading statements 123, 125-7
    promotion *see* **financial promotion**
    protection of consumers 123
    public awareness 123
    regulated activities 123, 124-5
    relevant agreement 126
    relevant investment 126
    safe harbours 135
Financial Services Action Plan (EU) 120
Financial Services Authority 18
    takeovers 282, 284
    as UKLA 22
fines
    breach of continuing obligations 104
    liability for prospectus 77
flotation
    admission day 56-7
    admissions hearing 55-6
    advertisement 53
    advisers
        appointment 27-31
        see also individual advisers eg broker
    application procedure 34, 55
        letters of acceptance 57
    broker 28
    capital of issuer 67
    commercial requirements 34-5
    company 28
    completion board meeting 47-8
    completion EGM 47
    conditions for listing 31-4
    directors 28
    disclosures 40
    documentation
        '10 day' documents 52
        '48 hour' documents 52
        advertisements 53
        drafting 46-7
        letters of acceptance 57
        list of documents 43-4, 46-7

flotation – *continued*
  listing particulars *see* **listing particulars**
  lodged after admission day 53
  lodged on day of application hearing 54
  printers 31
  prospectus *see* **prospectus**
  responsibility for accuracy 30
  submission to FSA 51-3
  submission to Stock Exchange 53-4
 due diligence 48-9
  business 48
  financial 48
  legal 48-9
  verification 49-51
 financial advisers 28
 financial promotion exemption 154
 financial public relations consultants 30-1
 fully subscribed 30, 55
 impact day 45, 54
 intermediaries offer 35, 36, 38, 64
 issuer of shares 67
 key dates
  admission day 56-7
  after admission day 57
  impact day 54
  impact day to admission day 54-6
 lawyers 29-30
 lawyers' perspective 43-54
 letters of acceptance 57
 material contracts 70
 meetings
  completion board meeting 47-8
  completion EGM 46-7
  drafting meetings 46
  verification 47
 negative statement 69
 offer for sale and/or for subscription 13, 30, 35-6, 38, 64
 offering, types of
  bookbuilding 37
  employee 38
  fixed price 37
  friends and family 38
  institutional 37
  retail 38
 Official List announcement 56
 over-subscribed 55
 placing 13, 35, 36, 38, 64
 preparation 27-41
 printers 31
 process 43, 44-6
 prospectus *see* **prospectus**
 readiness to float 31-5
 receiving bank 55
 registrars 30
 regulatory requirements 31-4
 reporting accountants 28-9
 restructuring prior to 39-41
 role of Stock Exchange 19
 simple admission 35, 36-7, 38, 64
 sponsor 28, 31

flotation – *continued*
 timetable 43, 44-6
 undersubscribed 30, 55
 underwriters 30
 verification 49-51
 verification meeting 47
friends and family offering 38

gearing 248
glossary 433-7
Greenbury Report 108
group companies
 financial promotion exemption 154

Hampel Report 108
heads of agreement
 takeovers 310
Higgs Report 108, 114
 good practice suggestions 111, 116-17

impact day 45, 54
income
 debt finance 245-6
 equity finance 245
incorporation
 public company 10
inside information
 dealings by director 97
 insider dealing 139-40
 meaning 85-6
 not made public 140
insider dealing 95, 97, 98, 99
 acquisitions and disposals 254-5
 dealing offence 141, 142, 143
 defences
  general 143
  special 143-5
 disclosing offence 142
 encouraging another to deal 141, 142, 143
 inside information 139-40
 inside source 140
 insider 139
 irrevocable undertakings 305
 market abuse 131
 market information 144
 market-makers 143
 offence 139-40
 price stabilisation 145
 price-sensitive information 140
 professional intermediaries 141
 regulated markets 141
 sanctions 143
 scope of offence 145
 securities 141
 stakebuilding 296
 territorial scope 142
insider lists 90
institutional investors 18, 112, 113-16
institutional offering
 bookbuilding 37
 fixed price 37
institutional shareholders 112

interests in shares
  takeovers 302-3
interim reports 95
intermediaries offer 35, 36, 38, 64
investment advertisement 53
investors
  AIM 18
  debt finance 247
  equity finance 247
  institutional 18, 112, 113-16
  members of public 18
  sophisticated 154-5
  Stock Exchange 18
issue of shares
  ABI Guidelines 171, 174, 179-80, 222, 399-400
  allotted shares 171-2
  authorised share capital 172-5
    Listing Rules 175
  authority to allot 172
    ABI Guidelines 179, 399-400
    convertible loan stock 176
    convertible preference shares 176-7
    existing authority 177
    expiry date 178
    Listing Rules 179
    obtaining new authority 177-8
    options 176
    relevant securities 175-7
    resolution 177-8, 377
    sanctions for breach 180
  CA 1985 223
  class rights 191
  Companies Bill 192
  Companies House 191
  consideration
    at discount 191
    non-cash 191
  directors' duties 190
  discount 191
  equity securities 182
  financial assistance prohibition 190
  issued shares 171-2
  Listing Rules 223
  Pre-Emption Group Statement of Principles 171, 174, 401-4
  Pre-Emption Guidelines 222
  pre-emption rights *see* **pre-emption rights**
  Prospectus Rules 191
  raising equity finance 222-4
  relevant securities 175-7
    maximum amount 178
  resolution 177-8, 377
  rights issue 185
  secondary 223-4
  transfer compared 171

joint venture partner
  related party transactions 263, 264

landMARK 15

lawyers
  advisers to flotation 29-30
  advisers to takeover 291
  company's 29-30
  sponsors' 30
leverage 246
listed company 3-4
  access to capital 7
  accessible market 7
  acquisition opportunities 7
  acquisitions *see* **acquisitions and disposals**
  advantages 7-8
  continuing obligations *see* **continuing obligations**
  corporate governance 40
  costs of listing 10
  disadvantages 8-10
  disposals *see* **acquisitions and disposals**
  efficiency 8
  employee incentives 8
  external forces 9
  listing for first time *see* **flotation**
  market conditions 9
  prestige 8
  profile 8
  public compared 4
  regulatory regime 8-9
  rules *see* **Listing Rules**
  shareholders 9
  statutory provisions 9
listing
  admission to *see* **flotation**
  authority *see* **UK Listing Authority**
  costs 10
  time taken 10
listing particulars
  financial promotion 154
  prospectus or 59-60
  purpose 59
Listing Rules 8-9, 21, 24-5
  acquisitions and disposals 255-6
  authorised share capital 175
  continuing obligations 90-5
    admission to trading 91
    compliance with Disclosure Rules 91
    compliance with Model Code 91
    documents requiring prior approval 92
    equal treatment of shareholders 91-2
    financial information 95
    notifications 93-5
    requirements with obligations 91
    sanctions for breach 104
    shareholders 91-2
    transactions 93
  disclosure of interests in shares 194-5, 206-7, 211
  issue of shares
    authorised share capital 175
    authority to allot 179
    pre-emption rights 185-6, 187-8
    raising equity finance 223
    sanctions for breach 190

Listing Rules – *continued*
  listing principles 24-5
  pre-emption rights 233-4
  sanctions for breach 25-6, 104, 190
  stakebuilding 297
  see also **Model Code**
lock-up arrangements
  disclosure 94
London Stock Exchange *see* **Stock Exchange**

management
  private company 5
  in prospectus 68
  public company 5
market abuse 123
  abusive squeeze 132
  acquisitions and disposals 254-5
  civil offence 129
  Code of Market Conduct 129-30, 132
  dealings by director 95, 97
  defences 136-7
  Directive 130
    changes to existing regime 130
  dissemination of information 132
  distortion 133
  false or misleading impression 132, 133
  improper disclosure 131
  insider dealing 131
  irrevocable undertakings 305
  main offence 130-3
  manipulating transactions 132
  meaning 130
  'Measuring Market Cleanliness' (FSA) 138
  misuse of information 131-2
  new regime 130
  prescribed market 131
  price positioning 132, 133
  qualifying investment 130, 131
  regular market user test 133
  related investments 131
  relevant information 132
  requiring or encouraging 133, 135, 137
  safe harbours 135
  sanctions 135
  secondary offence 133, 135
  stakebuilding 297
Market Abuse Directive 130
  safe harbours 135
market capitalisation 161
market information
  insider dealing 144
market manipulation
  acquisitions and disposals 254-5
  criminal offence 127
  defence 127
  financial services 123, 127
  prospectus 77
  sanctions 127
market-makers 143
'Measuring Market Cleanliness' (FSA) 138

meetings
  attendance at 163, 165
  completion meetings 47
  notice of 161, 163, 165
  verification meeting 47
memorandum of association 10
  related party transactions 268
  variation of class rights 168
merger control 283
  City Code provisions 347-8
  clearance as condition of takeover 331, 347
  European merger control 347
    Community dimension 349
    concentration 348-9
    exceptions 350-1
    notification before completion 349-50
    one-stop shop 350
    period of investigation 350
    Phase I 350
    Phase II 350
    turnover criteria 349
    two-thirds rule 349
    UK regime and 357-8
  UK merger control 351-8
    ceasing to be distinct 352
    clearance 331, 347, 355-6
    competition authorities 354-5
    Competition Commission 347, 351, 353, 354, 355
    confidential guidance 356
    EC regime and 357-8
    enterprises 352
    lawyer's role 357
    notification 355-6
    Office of Fair Trading 354, 356
    relevant merger situation 351
    Secretary of State for Trade and Industry 355
    share of supply test 352-3
    substantial lessening of competition 353-4
    time limit for reference 352
    turnover test 352-3
    undertakings 356
  see also **takeovers**
minority shareholding 284
  90 threshold 340-1
  acquisition 342
  buying out 339-45
  conditions 339-41
  notices 341, 343
  preventing the acquisition 342
  problem with 339
  right to be bought out 342-4
  right to buy out 339-42
  squeeze out 339-42
  timetable 343-4
misleading statements
  acquisitions and disposals 254-5
  criminal offence 125
  example 126-7
  financial services 123, 125-7

misleading statements – *continued*
  information provision in takeovers 328
  prospectus 77
  reckless 126
  relevant agreement 126
  relevant investment 126
  sanctions 127

Model Code
  acquisitions and disposals 255
  applicability 96-8
  clearance to deal 98-100
  compliance of Listing Rules with 91
  connected persons 96, 97-8
  continuing obligations 95-100
  dealings 95-100
  employee insiders 97
  persons discharging managerial
    responsibilities 97
  prohibited dealings 98
  purpose 96
  sanctions for breach 100

Modernising Company Law and Enhancing Corporate Governance in the UK (consultation document) 120

money lending
  financial assistance exception 218

name of company
  disclosure of change 94
NASDAQ 3
New York Stock Exchange 3
nominee shareholders 193
non-executive directors 113-14, 115-16
notice of meetings 161, 163, 165

offer for sale and/or for subscription 13, 35-6, 38, 64
  receiving bank 30
offeree 277-8, 290
offeror 277, 290
Office of Fair Trading 354, 356
Official List 22
open offer
  advantages 239
  disadvantages 239
  documentation 239
  equity finance 227, 237-9
  meaning 237
  price 237-8
  prospectus 239
  structure 238
  timing 238-9
  underwriting agreement 239
options 176
  share option plans 169, 170
  takeovers 302
ordinary shares
  capital rights 163
  income rights 162-3

Panel on Takeovers and Mergers
  Committees
    Code 274

Panel on Takeovers and Mergers – *continued*
    hearings 274
    nomination 274
  composition 273-4
  nature of 275
  Panel Executive 274
passporting of prospectus 79-80
pathfinder (red herring) prospectus 78-9, 149, 150
percentage ratios 256, 258, 259, 260-1
persons discharging managerial responsibilities
  Disclosure Rules 90, 204-6
  Model Code 97
placing 13, 35, 36, 38, 64
  advantages 240
  agreement 227
  definition 239
  disadvantages 240
  documentation 240
  equity finance 227, 239-40
  placing agreement 227, 240
  price 240
  secondary issue 227
  underwriting agreement 240
  see also **vendor consideration placing**
placing agreement 227, 240, 243
Pre-Emption Group 188-90, 233
Pre-Emption Group Statement of Principles 188-90
  issue of shares 171, 174, 223
  text 401-4
Pre-Emption Guidelines 188, 191
pre-emption rights
  bonus/subscriber shares 183
  for cash 182
  continuing obligations 92
  convertible loan stock 182-3
  convertible preference shares 183
  convertible securities 233
  disapplication 186-7
    Companies House 187
    duration 187
    example 187
    general 187
    Listing Rules 187-8
    non-routine 189
    procedure 190
    routine 189
    special 186-7
  employee share scheme shares 183
  equity securities 182
  examples 184-5
  fractional entitlements 232-3
  issue of shares 180-90
  legislation 181-2
  Listing Rules 185-6, 233-4
  meaning 181
  obstruction 181
  overseas shareholders 233
  Pre-Emption Group Statement of
    Principles 188-90, 401-4

pre-emption rights – *continued*
   Pre-Emption Guidelines 188, 191
   problems 186
   rationale 181
   relevant shares 182-3
   rights issue 231-4
   sanctions for breach 190
   triggers 183, 186
preference shares
   capital rights 165
   convertible 176-7, 183
   cumulative right to dividend 164
   income rights 163-5
   meetings 165
   participating 164-5
   preferential dividend 163-4
premium 160
press announcement
   equity finance 226, 236, 239, 240, 242, 243
prestige
   listed company 8
   public company 4
price stabilisation
   insider dealing defence 145
price-sensitive information
   dealings by director 97
   disclosure 86-7
   insider dealing 140
Primary Information Provider 85
printers
   advisers to flotation 31
   advisers to takeover 292
private company
   public compared 5-7
   re-registration as public company 11-13
promotion *see* **financial promotion**
prospectus
   acquisition issue 242
   administrative, management and supervisory bodies 68
   admission to trading 62-3
   application for securities for listing 60-2
   auditors 67
   board practices 69
   business overview 68
   capital of issuers 67
   capital resources 68
   content 64
      checking 73
      general requirements 65
      special requirements 65-73
   derogations 72-3
   employees 69
   equity finance 224-6, 236, 239, 240, 242, 243
   financial information 67, 69
   financial promotion exemption 154
   flotation 54-5
   format 66-72
   full 78
   incorporation by reference 72
   issuer of shares 67

prospectus – *continued*
   liability for 74-5
      civil liability 75-6
      in contract 76
      criminal liability 76-7
      fines 77
      FSMA 2000 75-7
      public censure 77
      Theft Act 1968 77
      in tort 76
   listing particulars or 59-60
   management of company 68
   market manipulation 77
   material contracts 70
   mini 78
   misleading statements 77
   offer 61
   offering securities to public 60-2
   open offer 239
   operating and financial review 68
   organisational structure 68
   passporting 79-80
   pathfinder (red herring) 78-9, 149, 150
   persons responsible for 67, 70, 73-4
   profit forecasts 68
   property, plant and equipment 68
   public inspection 54
   publishing 54-5
   purpose 59
   R & D 68
   registration document 67-70
   related party transactions 69
   remuneration and benefits 69
   responsibility for
      persons responsible 67, 70, 73-4
      statement 74
   risk factors 67
   securities note 70-2
   senior management 68
   shareholders 69
   submission to FSA 51-3
   summary 66-7
   supplementary 79
   to public 61
   trend information 68
   in UK 61
   validity 79
   vendor consideration placing 243
   verification 49-51, 77-8
Prospectus Directive 21, 23-4
   implementation 23, 24
Prospectus Rules 8-9, 21, 23
   annual information update 102-3
   content of prospectus 64-73
   continuing obligations 102-3
      sanctions for breach 104
   issue of shares 191
   sanctions for breach 25-6
provisional allotment letter (PAL)
   rights issues 229, 236
public censure
   breach of continuing obligations 104, 105

public censure – *continued*
   liability for prospectus 77
public company
   advantages 4
   articles of association 10
   authorised share capital 10
   certificate of incorporation 10, 12-13
   disadvantages 4-5
   incorporation 10
   listed compared 4
   meaning 3
   memorandum of association 10
   prestige 4
   private compared 5-7
   re-registration of private company as 11-13
   registration 10-11
   trading certificate 11
'Purple Book' 21

quoted company 4
   see also **listed company**

raising capital
   see also **debt finance; equity finance**
re-registration of company
   application 12
   certificate of incorporation 12-13
   identification of company 13
   private as public 11-13
   resolution 11
   share capital 12
reasonable investor test 86
receiving bank
   advisers to flotation 30
   advisers to takeover 292
recognised investment exchange 18
'red herring' document 78-9, 149, 150
redeemable shares
   creation 165
   redemption 165-6
register of directors' interests 194-5
register of members 193-4
register of share interests 203
registrars
   advisers to takeover 292
   flotation 30
registration of company
   private company re-registration as public 11-13
   public company 10-11
   resolution 11
regulated market 62
Regulatory Information Service 85, 90, 226
   changes in directors 94
   details of directors 94
   when not open 94-5
related party transactions 101
   acquisitions and disposals 262-8
   articles of association 268
   associate 263, 264
   CA 1985 267-8

related party transactions – *continued*
   Chapter 11 requirements 265-6
   circular 270
   definition 263
   director 263-4
   exceptions 266-7
   joint venture partner 263, 264
   memorandum of association 268
   in prospectus 69
   related parties 263-4
   relaxation of rules 267
   shadow director 263-4
   sponsor's role 267
   substantial shareholder 263
relevant securities
   authority to allot 175-7
   convertible loan stock 176
   convertible preference shares 176-7, 183
   options 176
remuneration of directors
   Combined Code 112
   Regulations 2002 118-19
   remuneration report 119
   shareholder approval 119
reporting accountants
   comfort letters 29
   flotation 28-9
   long form report 29
   working capital report 29
resolutions
   increasing authorised capital 174, 377
   issue of shares 177-8, 377
      Companies House 178
   re-registration of private company as public 11
   variation of class rights 167-8
restructuring
   before flotation 39-41
   board 40
   capital structure 40
   company constitution 40
   group structure 39
retail offering 38
reverse takeover 260-2
   sponsor's role 262
rights issue 185, 227
   advantages 236
   appropriateness 236
   convertible securities 233
   deep-discount 228
   disadvantages 236
   documentation
      PAL 229, 236
      underwriting agreement 236
   fractional entitlements 232-3
   IPCs 234
   meaning 228
   nil paid dealings 230
   offer period 233
   overseas shareholders 233
   pre-emption rights 231-4
   price 228
   prospectus 236

rights issue – *continued*
   provisional allotment letter (PAL) 229, 236
   renouncing right 229
   renouncing some rights 230
   taking up right to subscribe 230
   taking up some rights 230
   timetable 234-5
   timing 230
   underwriting 230-1
   underwriting agreement 231, 236

safe harbours 135
sale and purchase agreement 227
   acquisition issue 242
   vendor consideration placing 243
scheme of arrangement, takeovers 306-9
   advantages 309
   City Code 307-9
   court approval 307
   disadvantages 309
   explanatory statement 307
   meaning 306-7
   members' meeting 307
scrip/scrip issues 166
SEAQ International system 16
SEAQ system 16
SEATS Plus 16
secretary 6
Secretary of State for Trade and Industry
   beneficial ownership investigation 203
   merger control role 355
SETS 16
settlement 17-18
   CREST 17-18
shadow director 263-4
share capital 6-7
   authorised 10, 160
     checking filings 173-4
     increasing 174, 377, 379-82
     issue of shares 172-5
     Listing Rules 175
   increasing 174, 377
     forms 379-82
     percentage level and 197
   issued 160
   market capitalisation 161
   market value 160
   nominal value 159-60
   par value 159-60
   premium 160
   re-registration of private company as public 11-13
share incentive plan 170
share option plans
   approved company 170
   approved savings-related 169
share-for-share exchange *see* **acquisition issue**
shareholders
   communication with 100-2
   communication with *see* **communication with shareholders**

shareholders – *continued*
   dividends *see* **dividends**
   equal treatment 91-2
   financial promotion exemption 153
   institutional 112
   listed company 9
   meetings and 161
   minority shareholdings 284, 339-45
   nominee 193
   numbers 7
   overseas 233
   pre-emption rights 92
   prescribed information to 92
   in prospectus 69
   register of members 193-4
   relations with directors 118
   risk factors 67, 70-1
   substantial 263
   voting rights 161
shares
   allotted 171-2
   applications for 55
     letters of acceptance 57
     opening dealing 57
   beneficial ownership 193-4, 195
     company investigation 201-2
     DTI investigation 203
   bonus 166, 183
   capital growth 162
   capital rights 161-2, 163
   class rights 161-2
     in articles 167-8
     issue of shares and 191
     memorandum of association 168
     registration of rights 168
     variation of class rights 167-8
     see also variation of class rights
   classes *see individual types eg* ordinary
   Companies Bill 170
   convertible 166, 176-7, 183
   debt finance compared 166-7
   employees *see* **employee share schemes**
   fully paid 161
   income rights 161, 162-3
   interest in *see* **disclosure of interests in shares**
   issue *see* **issue of shares**
   issued 171-2
   limited liability 161
   meaning of 159
   meetings and 163, 165
   nil paid 161, 230
   ordinary 162-3
   part paid 161
   pre-emption rights *see* **pre-emption rights**
   preference 163-5
     convertible 176-7, 183
   premium 160
   redeemable 165-6
   register of share interests 203
   registration of rights 168
   rights attached *see* class rights

shares – *continued*
  scrip/scrip issues 166
  subscriber 166, 183
  transfer 171
  use of 161-2
  variation of class rights
    articles of association 167-8
    memorandum of association 168
    special resolution 167-8
  voting rights 161
simple admission 64
Smith Report 108
  guidance on audit committees 111
sponsor
  flotation 28, 31
  lawyers of 30
  role 259-60, 262, 267, 269-70
squeeze out
  acquisition 342
  conditions 339-41
  irrevocable undertakings 305
  notice 341
  right of offeror 339-42
stakebuilding
  acquiring 30or more 297-8
  advantages 295-6
  City Code 297-303
  consideration 299-302
  control of company 297-8
  disadvantages 296
  disclosure requirements 297
  insider dealing 296
  irrevocable undertakings 305
  Listing Rules 297
  mandatory offer 298-9
  market abuse 297
  meaning 295
  prohibited dealings 297
  purpose 295
  rules and regulations 296
  Substantial Acquisition Rules 297
  thresholds 303-4
  see also **takeovers**
standstill letter 310
'the stick' 231
Stock Exchange
  Admission and Disclosure Standards 19, 104, 105, 371-5
  admission to trading 34
  AIM *see* **Alternative Investment Market (AIM)**
  continuing obligations *see* **continuing obligations**
  dealing 57
  documents 53-4
  flotation role 19
  future developments 19-20
  investors 18
  landMARK 15
  Main Market 3, 15
  member firms 16
  Official List announcement 56
  regulation 18-19

Stock Exchange – *continued*
  secondary issue of shares 223-4
  settlement 17-18
  submission of documents
    application for admission to listing 53
    fee payable on application hearing 54
    information lodged on admission day 54
    'two day' documents 53
  as takeover target 19
  takeovers 284
  techMARK 15
  trading 16-18
  UKLA and 22
Stock Exchange Automated Quotations (SEAQ) system 16
Stock Exchange Electronic Trading Service (SETS) 16
stockbrokers
  advisers to takeover 291
strike-off 7
sub-underwriters 30
subscriber shares 166
  pre-emption rights 183
subscribers 166
Substantial Acquisition Rules 208
  disclosure of interests in shares 194
  stakebuilding 297
  takeovers 283
supplementary listing particulars 79
supplementary prospectus 79

tail-swallowing 230
takeovers
  acceptance form 324-5
  acceptance of offer 330
    announcement of level 334
    day 39 336
    day 74 337
    day 81 337
    earliest closure date 337
    extending the offer 334-5
    final day rule 336-7
    first closing date 334
    last date to fulfil conditions 337
    method 334
    revising the offer 334-5
    withdrawal 335-6
  acquisition of shares 283
  acting in concert 306
  advisers
    accountants 291-2
    financial advisers 290-1
    financial public relations consultants 292
    lawyers 291
    printers 292
    receiving bankers 292
    registrars 292
    stockbrokers 291
  analysis 289-90
  announcement of level of acceptance 334
  announcement of offer 313-21

456   Public Companies and Equity Finance

takeovers – *continued*
    content 316-17, 318
    firm intention to make offer 316-17
    intention not to make offer 319-20
    method 316-20
    offer period 321
    possible offer 317-19
    publication 317, 318
    responsibility for making 316
    timing 314-16
bidder 290
break fee letter 310-11
breakthrough provisions 333-4
City Code 284
  application of 277-8
  control 278
  enforcement 281-3
  general principles 279-80
  information provision 326-9
  merger control 347-8
  nature of 279
  in practice 280-1
  Practice Statements 281
  purpose 278-9
  secrecy 288-9
  stakebuilding 297-303
  to whom applicable 278
code names 290
conditions
  acceptance 330
  authorisations 331
  breakthrough provisions 333-4
  frustrating actions 332
  last day to fulfil 337
  material adverse change 331
  material litigation 331
  merger control clearance 331, 347
  offeror shareholder approval 330-1
  poison pills 332-4
confidentiality agreement 310
consideration 283
  admission of shares to listing and trading 330
  cash 295, 300-1
  City Code 329
  debt finance 295
  equity finance 295
  minimum 299-300
  option to take shares or cash 295
  paper 295, 302
  stakebuilding 299-302
control 278
deal protection 309-11
defence document 322-4
  content 324
  nature 322
  publication 324
  timing 324
derivatives 302
documentation 325-6
due diligence
  directors' reports 294-5
  hostile offer 294

takeovers – *continued*
  meaning 292
  process 293-4
  publicly available information 294-5
  purpose 293
  recommended offer 293
  requirement for 292
example 289-90
exclusivity agreement 310
failed offer
  12-month restriction 337-8
  acting in concert 338
final day rule 336-7
Financial Services Authority 284
financing the offer 295
  see also consideration
frustrating actions 332
future developments 284-5, 345
general offer 306
heads of agreement 310
hostile offer 288
  due diligence 294
information provision
  accuracy 326-7
  City Code 326-9
  equality 328-9
  misleading statements 328
  responsibility statement 327-8
  sufficiency 329
insider dealing 305
intention to accept 306
interests in shares 302-3
irrevocable undertakings 304-6
  acting in concert 306
  financial promotion 305
  insider dealing 305
  market abuse 305
  squeeze out provisions 305
  stakebuilding 305
market abuse 305
material adverse change 331
merger control *see* **merger control**
minority shareholding
  conditions 339-41, 342-3
  squeeze out 339-42
  timetable 343-4
minority shareholdings 284
  90threshold 340-1, 342-3
  acquisition 342
  buying out 339-45
  notices 341, 343
  preventing the acquisition 342
  problem with 339
  right to be bought out 342-4
  right to buy out 339-42
nature of panel 275
non-binding indications 306
offer
  acceptance 330, 334-7
  acceptance form 324-5
  announcement *see* announcement of offer
  Class 1 transaction 325

takeovers – *continued*
    conditions 329-31
    defence document 322-4, 325-6
    document *see* **offer document**
    extending 334-5
    failed 337-8
    information *see* information provision
    poisoned pill tactics 332-4
    revising 334-5
    securities exchange 325-6
    successful 338-9
  offer document
    content 322
    nature of 321
    publication 321-2
    timing 321
  offer period 321
  offeree 277-8, 290
  offeror 277, 290
  options 302
  Panel Committees
    Code 274
    hearings 274
    nomination 274
  Panel Executive 274
  Panel on Takeovers and Mergers 273-5
  parties 290
  poisoned pill tactics 332-4
  preparation 287-311
  protection of deal 309-11
  recommended offer 287-8
    due diligence 293
  regulatory bodies 284
  reverse takeover 260-2
  scheme of arrangement 306-9
    advantages 309
    City Code 307-9
    court approval 307
    disadvantages 309
    explanatory statement 307
    meaning 306-7
    members' meeting 307
  secrecy, need for 288-9
  securities exchange offer 325-6
  shareholder approval 330-1
  squeeze out
    acquisition 342
    conditions 339-41
    irrevocable undertakings 305
    notice 341
    right of offeror 339-42
  squeeze out provisions 305
  stakebuilding
    acquiring 30 or more 297-8
    advantages 295-6
    City Code 297-303
    consideration 299-302
    control of company 297-8
    disadvantages 296
    disclosure requirements 297
    insider dealing 296
    irrevocable undertakings 305
    Listing Rules 297

takeovers – *continued*
    mandatory offer 298-9
    market abuse 297
    meaning 295
    prohibited dealings 297
    purpose 295
    rules and regulations 296
    Substantial Acquisition Rules 297
    thresholds 303-4
  standstill letter 310
  statement of intention not to make offer 319-20
  Stock Exchange 284
  Substantial Acquisition Rules 283
  successful bid 338-9
  Takeover Panel 284
  target 290
  timetable 313, 314-16
  UK Listing authority 284
  withdrawal of acceptance 335-6
Takeovers Directive
  application 275
  implementation 275-6
  offers 275
  regulated market 275
Takeovers Regulations 284
  application 276
  Companies Bill and 276
  dual regime 276
  text 407-31
target 290
taxation
  debt finance 246
  equity finance 246
techMARK 15
trading
  dematerialisation 20
trading, admission to
  regulatory requirements 34
  see also **Stock Exchange**
trading certificate 11
Transparency Directive 14, 105, 212
Turnbull Guidance 111
Turnbull Report 108

UK Listing Authority
  continuing obligations *see* **continuing obligations**
  FSA as 22
  Official List announcement 56
  'Purple Book' 21
  responsibilities of 22
  Stock Exchange and 22-3
  takeovers 284
UK Listing Authority Guidance Manual 21, 25
UK merger control 351-8
  ceasing to be distinct 352
  clearance 355-6
  competition authorities 354-5
  Competition Commission 347, 351, 353, 354, 355
  confidential guidance 356

UK merger control – *continued*
  EC regime and 357-8
  enterprises 352
  lawyer's role 357
  notification 355-6
  Office of Fair Trading 354, 356
  relevant merger situation 351
  Secretary of State for Trade and Industry 355
  share of supply test 352-3
  substantial lessening of competition 353-4
  time limit for reference 352
  turnover test 352-3
  undertakings 356
underwriters
  flotation 30
  rights issue 230-1
  secondary issue of shares 227
underwriting agreement
  open offer 239
  placing 240
  rights issue 231, 236
  vendor consideration placing 243

vendor consideration placing 227, 242-3
  advantages 243
  disadvantages 243
  documentation 243
  placing agreement 243
  price 242
  prospectus 243
  sale and purchase agreement 243
  underwriting agreement 243
verification
  acquisitions and disposals 270
  flotation 47, 49-51
  note 49
  prospectus 77
  questionnaire 50
verification meeting 47
voting rights 161

websites 405
whitewash 6, 218
winding up
  dividend on 164